Harry Brelsford

# SAMS
# Teach Yourself
# Microsoft®
# Small Business
# Server 4.5

## in 21 Days

SAMS

*A Division of Macmillan Computer Publishing*
*201 West 103rd St., Indianapolis, Indiana, 46290*

# Sams Teach Yourself Microsoft® Small Business Server 4.5 in 21 Days

## Copyright © 1999 by Sams

International Standard Book Number: 0-672-31513-0

Library of Congress Catalog Card Number: 98-87944

Printed in the United States of America

First Printing: June 1999

01    00                4    3    2

## Trademarks

## Warning and Disclaimer

**EXECUTIVE EDITOR**
Jeff Koch

**DEVELOPMENT EDITOR**
Hugh Vandivier

**MANAGING EDITOR**
Brice Gosnell

**PROJECT EDITOR**
Sara Bosin

**COPY EDITOR**
Michael Dietsch

**INDEXER**
Eric Schroeder

**PROOFREADER**
Billy Fields

**TECHNICAL EDITOR**
Tim Catura-Houser

**SOFTWARE DEVELOPMENT SPECIALIST**
Craig Atkins

**INTERIOR DESIGN**
Gary Adair

**COVER DESIGN**
Aren Howell

**COPY WRITER**
Eric Borgert

**LAYOUT TECHNICIANS**
Brandon Allen
Stacey Richwine-DeRome
Timothy Osborn
Staci Somers

# Contents at a Glance

# Table of Contents

# Contents

# Foreword

I should first point out that I am biased about Microsoft Small Business Server (SBS). I have devoted most of my waking hours (and several dream hours) on this product since its public release in 1997. I think it is a great value and combination of products for many small businesses. It has limitations, though, and this book will help you to identify what they are and whether they apply to your scenario.

As Harry emphasizes, just because you might be an NT guru or even an MCSE, SBS can be a humbling experience. The first two days of the book define the SBS product, the market, and the end users. I don't exactly know how to say this, but Harry does a great job not only of defining the market as a business with 50 computers or fewer, but also pointing out its state of mind and expectations. You should simply cut-and-paste much of this information into your own company's mission statement if you intend to deal with SBS for income.

Harry has done a great job of accumulating many of the tips, tricks, and gotchas we SBSers have encountered since its release and putting them together in this book. He not only covers what is supposed to happen, but he also shows what *really* happens in the real world. Many of the items he mentions—items that I, as a self-proclaimed SBS guru, take for granted—will be invaluable to the *newbies* (first time SBSers).

Harry Brelsford has real-world experience that he applies to all the tasks encountered when planning, implementing, maintaining, and growing an SBS site, compared to writings from the marketing department at Microsoft.

Many of the details are here for first-timers, whereas the experienced SBSer can discover Power User Tips, Cautions, and advanced information.

When SBS was first introduced, Microsoft promoted it as a do-it-yourself magic wand in an hour or less. The 21-day approach is much more feasible and realistic. I wish that everyone would read this book *before* starting your SBS marriage, but many of you will buy it after the fact as a fire extinguisher to solve problems you have encountered.

You can spend much time fighting an SBS problem, or you can avoid the problem by reading this book. The time saved will very easily offset this book's price.

**Note**

Grey Lancaster MVP SBS (grey@smallbizserver.com)

Grey Lancaster, founder and president of Solutions, is a successful, self-determined, and independent consultant with ten years of experience in small-business computing solutions. He has primarily devoted the past two years to the development and implementation of Microsoft BackOffice Small Business Server Suite.

# About the Author

**Harry Brelsford**, MCT, MCSE, CNE, CLSE, CNP, MBA

A 15-year veteran of the business technology community, Harry Brelsford is the network consulting manager for CN Consulting, a subsidiary of Clark Nuber PS in Seattle, Washington. A holder of numerous network vendor certifications, Harry is an instructor in Seattle Pacific University's AATP MCSE online certification program (www.spu.edu/dcs). Harry has published over 100 articles in numerous magazines including *Washington CEO*, *Alaska Business Monthly*, and *Architectural and Engineering Digest*. Harry is a contributing editor for *Microsoft Certified Professional Magazine* (www.mcpmag.com) where he pens the regular column "Professionally Speaking." He is a founding member of the BackOffice Professionals Association (BOPA), based in Redmond, Washington. Harry can be reached at harryb@nwlink.com and www.cnuber.com/cn.

# Dedication

*Again, Kristen my wife, you have made the words contained herein flow with ease. And to Barb, mother of Kristen, a giver of energy to our family.*

# Acknowledgments

It takes a village. The first acknowledgement goes to my SBS clients, for it is they who provided the SBS experience that I share with you in this book. The group at Macmillan Computer Publishing is an important second, for they professionally reworked my work when needed. I praise those editors along the way who've shaped me into the writer I am today: Linda Briggs, Dian Schaffhauser, Kevin Dwyer, and Judy Griffin. And all the usual suspects: my parents, Harry and Diane Brelsford; my siblings, Gregg, Jim, Taylor, and Ginna; my in-laws, Ron, Barb, Karen, and Lauren; and mentors et al.

# Tell Us What You Think!

As the reader of this book, *you* are our most important critic and commentator. We value your opinion and want to know what we're doing right, what we could do better, what areas you'd like to see us publish in, and any other words of wisdom you're willing to pass our way.

As a Publisher for Sams, I welcome your comments. You can fax, email, or write me directly to let me know what you did or didn't like about this book—as well as what we can do to make our books stronger.

*Please note that I cannot help you with technical problems related to the topic of this book, and that due to the high volume of mail I receive, I might not be able to reply to every message.*

When you write, please be sure to include this book's title and author as well as your name and phone or fax number. I will carefully review your comments and share them with the author and editors who worked on the book.

Fax:     317.581.4770
E-mail:  opsys@mcp.com
Mail:    Dean Miller
         Sams
         201 West 103rd Street
         Indianapolis, IN 46290 USA

# Introduction

Welcome to Microsoft Small Business Server 4.5 (SBS). As a fellow SBSer, I've written this book to prepare you for SBS 4.5, the latest BackOffice networking solution from Microsoft. This book achieves several goals within these pages. First, you are introduced to SBS 4.5 and its many powerful features. Second, this book is one of the few bona fide SBS 4.5 learning resources available. You will create an SBS 4.5 network for an imaginary company, Springer Spaniels Unlimited, over the 21 days. Third, after performing the tasks for Springer Spaniels Unlimited, you will have mastered SBS 4.5, and you'll be prepared to implement SBS 4.5 in your own organization. Fourth, I write to two SBS 4.5 audiences: newcomers and gurus. That's because the SBS community is divided as such. I'll talk more on that in the next section. Finally, this book is fun. Just when you're fatigued from a morning of SBS 4.5 activity, turn the page and see what guest speaker or lunch recipe awaits you!

## How This Book Is Organized

But first, a few words about how this book is organized. With you in mind, the book uses the "day" metaphor of morning (AM), lunch, and afternoon (PM) sessions. It also focuses on SBS 4.5 setup, management, and configuration issues from Days 1–17. Starting with Day 18, I present advanced issues.

### AM The Morning (AM) Session

If you are new to computers, networks, and SBS, the morning section is especially oriented toward you. In fact, if you were to first read this book by only "attending" the morning sessions, you would know everything you would need to know: You would know the basics of SBS. In fact, many of you in the small business world who have other job responsibilities—be it paralegal, medical assistant, secretary, business owner, or just plain old manager—can benefit from reading or attending the morning sessions so that you can run a simple SBS network and get on with your other jobs.

### Lunch Time

I've tailored the lunch break in each chapter in several ways. First, more often than not, a compelling guest speaker presents a column on SBS. In many cases, I've recruited people just like yourselves, small-business people running SBS networks, to share their stories. Other times, I have an expert speak to you about some facet of SBS that should be of interest to you. Occasionally, I provide a real recipe for you to use in actually cooking your lunch (yes, we SBSers need to eat, too!). Finally, the lunch break typically provides a necessary and convenient demarcation line between the morning session with its focus on basics and the afternoon sessions that have an advanced focus.

## PM  The Afternoon (PM) Session

The afternoon session is indeed my forum for presenting advanced topics. Here you will find the hidden SBS treasures that I've dug up from the real world. If you're looking for SBS secrets, answers, troubleshooting tips, and the like, the afternoon session is for you. If you are a beginner, you might consider reading the afternoon sections after you've installed SBS and it has been running for a few months. At that time, the more advanced topics will be of interest. Those who might benefit immediately from the afternoon session include business computer consultants, experience network administrators, power users (experienced personal computer users), and Microsoft Certified Professionals (including MCPs and MCSEs).

## Task-Oriented: Setting Up a Fictional Networking Solution

To get the most out of this book, it is important to understand that this book is task-oriented. Over the course of 21 days, you will implement a successful SBS-based networking solution for a fictional company, Springer Spaniels Unlimited. I highly recommend that you complete each day—ergo, complete the entire book—and really learn SBS (strengths and all) prior to implementing SBS live in your own organization. SBS demands study for you to be successful. This book is your tool for providing that study.

# What's Included on the CD-ROM

You'll notice a CD-ROM attached to the back of this book. Along with some sample documents from our faux company, Springer Spaniels Unlimited, here's what you'll find on the CD.

## Primary Software

- Ping Plotter v2.03 Software from Nessoft
- Diskeeper 4.0 Trialware from Executive Software
- Undelete Server v1.2 for Win NT 4 from Executive Software
- SPQuery v3.0 Demo from MTE Software
- SPClean Utilities from MTE Software
- Y2K Hotfixes from MTE Software

## Productivity Utilities

- Source Check 2000 from GPP Software
- Acrobat Reader from Adobe Systems Incorporated
- WinZip v7.0 from Nco Mak

## Browsers

- Internet Explorer 5
- Netscape Communicator 4.5

# Conventions Used in This Book

**Note**

Notes are used to draw your attention to interesting or important SBS 4.5 points. Notes increase your understanding of SBS 4.5.

**Tip**

Tips are discrete tidbits of information that help you perform your best in real-world scenarios. Typically, tips are shortcuts or hard-won secrets that allow you to work easier or faster.

**Power Tool Tip**

Power Tools are advanced points directed to SBS gurus. Power Tools discussion items are typically beyond the scope of the basic Springer Spaniels Unlimited.

**Caution**

Cautions provide information about detrimental performance issues or dangerous errors. Pay careful attention to these.

For the sake of convenience, I say "right-click the mouse" throughout this book, which assumes that you, the reader, are right-handed. My apologies to you lefties.

Any time I want you to type an entry into a dialog box, the type will appear in **boldface type**. That's your signal to type exactly what's in bold.

# Feedback

This book was, of course, the result from my interaction with my existing SBS customers in the Pacific Northwest. It is my sincere desire to have that same level of interaction with you, the reader of this book. By communicating, it's my belief that I can provide more germane discussion in future releases of this book, to your direct benefit. Kindly e-mail your observations to me at `harryb@nwlink.com`, and I'll reply within several business days. Please, in advance, pardon my delay in responding to you. The life of a SBSer is a busy one!

# WEEK 1

# Getting Started With Small Business Server (SBS)

1

2

3

4

5

6

7

DAY **1**

# Welcome to Small Business Server 4.5

Welcome to Microsoft BackOffice Small Business Server 4.5, better known as *SBS*. SBS is nothing short of a major paradigm shift in Microsoft's view of network computing. This evolution, the SBS revolution, addresses a long-neglected area of client/server or personal computer–based computing: the small-business market. SBS clearly represents Microsoft's commitment to the small-business market, which as you will see later today, represents the largest computing market when measured by sheer number of businesses. Finally, with a single Microsoft networking product, it is possible to rightsize a small-business networking solution, and all on one reasonably priced and powerful personal computer known as a *server*.

Before SBS, trying to implement BackOffice—Microsoft's networking solution, which I'll call *Big BackOffice* in this book—at a small-business site was a frustrating exercise in budget creep and was placing too big of an engine in a small car!

And apparently enough of you agree that SBS fills a niche that needed filling: serving the business computing needs of the small business. You have made SBS one of the hottest selling Microsoft offerings of the late 1990s. Perhaps you've discovered that a properly set up SBS network can improve the way you run your business, help lower your computing costs, and perhaps most importantly, make it easier for you, the SBS administrator, and your users to use and enjoy computers.

## AM Defining SBS

Exactly what is SBS? Actually, there is more than one answer to that question. For many business people, this is a perfectly legitimate answer.

SBS provides cheap, reliable, and easy-to-manage business networking solutions. The business crowd wants to work with business applications, send and receive e-mail, print, and make sure the data is backed up. SBS scores high marks in these respects. And what a huge crowd this is. Of all the SBS installations that I've completed, this is by far the largest segment of SBSers.

For others, SBS is a cost-effective way of bundling Big BackOffice applications and the Windows NT Server operating system. Here, the emphasis in on bang-for-buck and the full exploitation of SBS components, such as Microsoft Exchange and SQL Server. These people, the SBS feature creatures, are interested in Table 1.1, which is divided, as much as possible, into the server-side (the powerful personal computer that typically resides in a closet) and the client-side (user workstations) components.

Also note that each component is discussed further in this book, so don't worry if you don't understand each one right now. You will be able to later. Each server component is defined in great detail at the start of its own day. For example, the Windows NT Server operating system is defined on Day 3, "Installing Small Business Server." The client components are defined at the start of Day 4, "Setting Up the Workstation Client."

**TABLE 1.1**  SBS COMPONENTS

| Component | Description | Server or Client Component |
|---|---|---|
| Windows NT Server 4.0 with Service Pack 4 | Microsoft's 32-bit network operating system. An operating system controls the basic functions of a computer including security, storage, printing management, and so on. | Server |

| Component | Description | Server or Client Component |
|---|---|---|
| Option Pack | This is an add-on that includes Internet Information Server 4.0 (discussed later today), Transaction Server 2.0, Index Server 2.0, Script Debugger. | Server |
| Microsoft Exchange Server 5.5 with Service Pack 2.0 | E-mail application. | Server |
| Microsoft SQL Server 7.0 | Database application. | Server |
| Microsoft Proxy Server 2.0 | Internet security and firewall gateway application with the capability to store or cache frequently accessed Web pages. | Server |
| Microsoft Internet Information Server 4.0 | Internet/Intranet development and management application. | Server |
| Microsoft Fax Service 4.5 | Fax pooling and management application. | Server |
| Microsoft Modem Sharing Service 4.5 | Modem pooling and management application. | Server |
| Microsoft Index Server 2.0 | Search engine application. | Server |
| Microsoft Active Server Pages Server 1.0b | Internet development environment for *.asp files. | Server |
| Additional Goodies | HP JetAdmin tools, and so on on SBS CD-ROM. Also note that Microsoft Exchange Client 5.0 and Schedule 7.0 are installed on the SBS machine, but are rarely used (Microsoft Outlook is preferred). | Server |

*continues*

**TABLE 1.1**    CONTINUED

| Component | Description | Server or Client Component |
|-----------|-------------|----------------------------|
| SBS Console | GUI-based management console that uses powerful yet friendly administrative wizards. | Server |
| Server-based Wizards | SBS Server Setup Wizard, Internet Connection Wizard, device and peripheral management. | Server |
| To-Do List | Step-by-Step To-Do list. | Server |
| Online Guide | Robust online help manual for SBS administrators. | Server |
| Default Intranet Page | Provides extensive SBS information for administrators/users. | Client /Server |
| Internet Explorer 5.0 | Internet browser for navigating both the Internet and intranets. Installed on both the SBS server machine and SBS clients. | Client /Server |
| Setup Computer Wizard | Step one creates and registers machines on the SBS server machine. Step two, via the client installation disk, configures and attaches a network-ready workstation to the SBS network. | Client /Server |
| Client Installation Disk | A disk that is formatted and created on the SBS server machine. At the client workstation, the setup phase configures the client (TCP/IP protocol, NetBIOS name, user name assigned to machine, and so on). Affectionately known as the "magic disk." | Client /Server |

| Component | Description | Server or Client Component |
|---|---|---|
| Microsoft Outlook 2000 | Client-based e-mail, scheduling and contact management application. | Client |
| Microsoft FrontPage 2000 | Web site creation application. | Client |
| SBS Fax client | Faxing functionality and capabilities. | Client |
| SBS Modem Pool client | Modem pooling functions (port redirector). | Client |
| SBS Proxy Client | Client-side Microsoft Proxy Server functions (WinSock Proxy redirector). | Client |
| SBS Client | Basic SBS workstation client application (assist in modifying client configuration). | Client |
| Office 2000 | This is an optional purchase with SBS and includes: Word 2000, Excel 2000, Access 2000, PowerPoint 2000, and Publisher 2000. | |

The third group of SBSers view SBS as a state of mind or at least a different view of Windows NT computing. These are the people who get it; they know that SBS is different from regular Windows NT Server and Big BackOffice. Their view can best be summarized by Figure 1.1, the SBS Console.

The SBS Console is a feature that makes SBS a very different product from Big BackOffice. And when you get it with SBS, you'll understand why it is so different. That theme, *getting it*, is an early one that I'll often repeat as I draw out the difference between SBS and Big BackOffice.

Another view on defining SBS is looking at it from a business perspective: that is, how does SBS support the mission of the businesses to be efficient and successful? The SBS wheel in Figure 1.2 address this point of view.

**FIGURE 1.1**

*The SBS Console.*

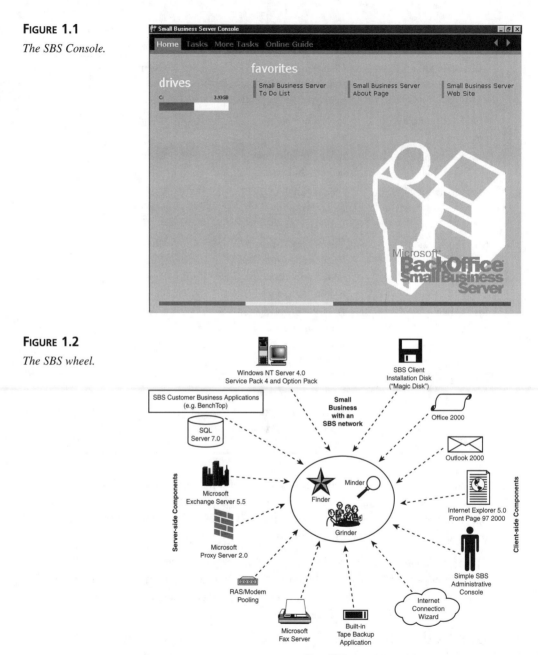

**FIGURE 1.2**

*The SBS wheel.*

1

The right side of the wheel predominately speaks toward server-side components such as Windows NT Server 4.0, SQL Server, and the like. The lower portion of the wheel speaks to the management function via the SBS Console. The left side of the wheel speaks to the client-side applications, such as Microsoft Outlook and Office 2000.

With respect to how SBS supports business operations, let me take a moment to speak about the three major functions of a small business: finder, minder, and grinder.

## Finder

A finder is a rainmaker: the person who markets and gets the business. In many firms, it is the owner, CEO, or president type. In other firms, it is a salesperson. Whoever has this important responsibility can directly benefit from SBS in many ways. I'll discuss two of those. First, there is the new area of electronic commerce. Electronic commerce includes everything from basic e-mail to elaborate Web pages that provide direct updates to your accounting system. A salesman in the late 1990s, at a minimum, can benefit from using Internet e-mail. This feature is supported by SBS with the Microsoft Exchange Server.

A finder can also benefit from SBS applications such as Microsoft Outlook. Outlook provides contact management and scheduling capabilities in addition to serving as an e-mail client. Outlook is discussed on Day 8, "Implementing Outlook." You will learn basic Outlook functionality with an emphasis on e-mail use and how to create a company-wide contact list that is low maintenance yet allows everyone to have an updated list of contacts, such as important clients and vendors.

And then there is the CEO of the landscaping company in Issaquah, Washington who wanted to use SBS to increase his company's sales. His idea was to fax a "spring cleaning" notice to his past landscaping clients. SBS does this very well with its desktop faxing and fax server support. Broadcast faxing is a breeze, and as an added bonus, this CEO found that he could fax directly to the names listed in the company-wide Outlook contact list.

## Minder

There's one law of business that I've never seen successfully broken. For every finder, there is at least one minder. *Minders* serve as office managers, administrators, COOs, and all-around nags. Bless 'em because we need them. SBS was designed with minders in mind (please don't *mind* the pun!). Typically, when I've deployed SBS from a minder's perspective, it has been to implement a piece of industry-specific business software. One of my examples is Xtek, a Redmond, Washington–based service firm that calibrates medical instruments. Norm serves as president and Mike is the minder. You will see in Figure 1.2 that I listed business applications on the server side. One such application is BenchTop, a very powerful service management software application implemented on the SBS system at

Xtek. BenchTop, which uses SBS's SQL Server for its engine, is very much a minder tool. This application brings control to the workflow and allows Mike to compile performance metrics specific to his industry. Mike unknowingly benefits from SBS because SQL Server is included as part of the SBS bundle. All Mike knows is that BenchTop makes his job easier and he is more productive.

Another example of a minder tool in SBS is, in my opinion, Microsoft Proxy Server. This is basically a firewall that not only protects the SBS network from the evil comings and goings of the Internet but also allows the minder in all of us to control and monitor access to the Internet. On Day 5, "Managing the Small Business Server Management Console," I show some built-in reports that show Internet usage, sites visited, and traffic by hour. You would be surprised how many firms place equal emphasis on controlling employee Internet usage as they do on their firewall to prevent intrusion. I guess you could call it *minding* the store.

And because minders are typically the ones who get stuck running SBS networks, the SBS Console, shown in Figure 1.1, is a fast friend. Instead of having to learn a variety of Windows NT Server tools that are "under the hood" (that is, not part of the SBS Console), SBS minders administer their networks with the push-button simplicity of the SBS Console. More on the SBS Console on Day 5.

## Grinder

Grinders are the worker bees. These are the people who are typically task oriented and look at the SBS infrastructure as a support system that makes them more productive. Grinders benefit from SBS in two distinct ways.

First, applications such as BenchTop that run on top of SBS's SQL Server allow the repair staff to enter important job and task information. This helps track the flow of goods in the system and effectively lowers cost by allowing better control. Another business application that uses SQL Server is Great Plains Dynamics. I've had tremendous success installing this on SBS machines and I can attest that the worker bees—typically accounting clerks and bookkeepers—have been able to complete their work in an efficient and reliable manner. Most importantly, in both cases with BenchTop and Great Plains, the grinders trust that SBS allows them to better do their work. Such has been the case.

Second, basic communication applications such as Outlook e-mail, contacts, and scheduling have allowed grinders to improve the quality of their work. Many times SBS is being introduced into environments that have no prior network or e-mail service. SBS often fundamentally changes how people do their work and, in its own way, reengineers workflow. The improvement in communications is but one example. Throughout this book many more business workflow improvements are presented.

# SBS Philosophy 101

1

It is difficult to overlook the sheer numbers of small businesses that could benefit from a tailor-made BackOffice-type networking solution. Such was the idea behind SBS, a viewpoint that seems, on the surface, to fly right in the face of Microsoft's overt push into the enterprise with both the existing release of Windows NT Server 4.0 and the forthcoming release of Windows 2000 Server. But the numbers speak for themselves. Although you can easily say that there are only 1,000 companies in the Fortune 1000 list, conversely you might be surprised to know that there are over 22 million small businesses in the United States, according to the U.S. Small Business Administration. It's a stretch, but can't you see the marketing wheels at Microsoft turning and dreaming of an SBS installation at every small business? You betcha.

Understanding that small businesses are fundamentally different from larger enterprises, SBS sells itself when positioned as a tool to help small business run better, with less effort, and, ultimately, more easily. You could say that SBS is nothing more than a return to the original LAN paradigm that both Apple Computer and Novell rode in the 1980s. This LAN paradigm, with a few modifications to accommodate SBS, is anchored by these key tenets:

- Sharing—The major justification for implementing SBS in the small business is the ability to share information. Sharing information, such as cost accounting data at the construction company, allows staff to work together with less redundancy (multiple entries are eliminated). Owners get better information about their operations. Staff works together as a team.

- Security—Like the enterprise, small businesses demand that reasonable levels of security be provided to protect sensitive information from competition and from loss or casualty. SBS provides regular Windows NT Security plus the security afforded by Microsoft Proxy Server.

- Cost Effectiveness—Relatively speaking, SBS is cheap. The 25-user version of SBS can be purchased on the street for around $2,250 (the 50-user version is, of course, more). Add a $5,000 server machine and $1,500 workstations plus a few other necessities (approximately $1,000 for hubs, modems, cable, and so on) and you're up and running.

**Note**

Amortized, for accounting purposes, over the typical five-year holding period seen in many small businesses (versus the more aggressive three-year holding period typically seen at the enterprise-level), SBS is really cost effective. After the basic installation and allowance for training (say, $500 per user), an SBS network typically costs $1,000 per user per year.

- Efficiency—After an initial period of negative productivity while installing SBS and when everyone is learning SBS and its powers, company-wide productivity increases to a level exceeding pre-SBS days. One example of this is the use of broadcast e-mails and faxes instead of making telephone calls.

- Better Work, New Work—This includes fewer mistakes because of better communications (for example, e-mail with staff, vendors, and customers; better scheduling with Outlook's calendar; and so on.) and new work, such as winning new contracts because your work is of higher quality (proposals with accurate financial information derived from staff, and so on). In fact, as an SBS site starts using more and more SBS features, I've seen these small businesses dramatically increase their business. For example, a landscaping company client used SBS's faxing capabilities to fax "Spring planting announcements" to its clients resulting in increased sales. Small businesses, enlightened by the powers of SBS, have also been known to enter into new business areas, feeling confident that they have the network infrastructure to back up promises. For example, the small construction company I worked with, confident that SBS-based e-mail and remote communications solutions wouldn't fail them, took on work in other cities.

- Bottom Line—How does SBS sum up? Properly implemented, SBS can help small businesses to enjoy higher quality work and get more work finished with the same resources:

    Land—Office space is used more efficiently as older office machines, file cabinets, and the like are eliminated.

    Labor—Existing staff works more efficiently, allowing owners to squeeze more productivity out of existing staff. Fear not that SBS will result in staff downsizing. I've worked with a variety of SBS sites and have never seen a layoff or firing related to SBS. In fact, the opposite tends to occur. Small businesses get excited very quickly at SBS when they understand it and see it working. In short order, additional (and unplanned) work requests roll in. For example, several of my small-business clients that barely knew what the Internet was prior to the SBS installation call back and ask for WWW home page development assistance. I typically refer an intern from the local college to these clients, allowing them to save on Web page development costs and allowing a starving college kid the chance to earn some money. And guess what! More often than not the college intern becomes a full-time employee, actually increasing headcount at the client site as a result of the SBS implementation.

Capital—Not to understate the initial capital investment in getting an SBS network up and running, but, after that outlay is made, there is a general consensus that SBS delivers a positive return on investment (ROI) by generally increasing the firm's productivity and mitigating additional large capital outlays for the foreseeable future. One example of this is the reduced wear and tear on photocopiers. One of my clients, who has aggressively exploited SBS features, now stores documents electronically and faxes directly to vendors. By doing so, this customer found it could forego the purchase of a new, expensive photocopier.

Microsoft extends this paradigm specifically for SBS by adding these design goals.

- Ease of Use/Simplicity—The idea was to make everything easy, easy, easy. And when compared to the old command-line interface of NetWare 3.x (which a surprisingly high number of small businesses are still running, having foregone the opportunity to upgrade to NetWare 4.x, 5.x), you could say that SBS is easier to manage and use. For example, Dawn at an athletic club I've assisted took many years (appropriately so) to master NetWare. When Dawn was confronted with the decision to upgrade to the newly released NetWare 5.0, I loaned her a training machine that had SBS installed. One week later, Dawn was confident and had even confirmed that her narrow market vertical applications would run on SBS. Not surprisingly, Dawn and her firm became another SBS success story.

  But *easy* is in the eye of the beholder. Whereas Dawn was coming from a more complex networking environment, allowing her to enjoy the ease of SBS when compared to NetWare, SBS has sometimes fallen short for small businesses that have never been networked. These firms, accustomed to working manually with file cabinets, fax machines, and basic word processing, are often disappointed with SBS initially when they (a) can't believe installing a network is so difficult and (b) don't understand why servers don't work perfectly all the time (for example, blue-screen crashes). So take Microsoft's SBS ease of use argument with a grain of salt.

  However, if it is usability that you are measuring, clearly SBS wins when compared to other NOSs such as NetWare. With its Windows 98–type interface, SBS encourages even users unaccustomed to managing a network server to feel comfortable using the Start button, menus, mouse, and so on. Score one for SBS for high usability.

- Making Decisions for the Customer—In the context of having an automated setup and implementation process ("just add water"), SBS (in Microsoft's view) reduces the research, engineering, and guesswork that goes into making the networking decision. Microsoft correctly asserts that users do not have to decide whether the SBS machine should be a primary domain controller (it should because it controls the operations of the network) and whether to install the Dynamic Host Configuration Protocol server (DHCP). DHCP is automatically installed so that you don't need to worry about which network addresses the workstation's need (remember that all workstations on a network need an address to send and receive data). If you don't understand what DHCP is, it is discussed in the afternoon session on Day 9, "Connecting to the Internet."

- Designing for Success—This point speaks toward the SBS Console that I've previously discussed. The idea is that SBS administrators should enjoy a "simple stupid" networking management experience and not really have to plan what they intend to do. Adding a user is a click away via the Manage Users button in the Task sheet of the SBS Console (see Figure 1.1). Simple.

**Power Tool Tip**

Here again, I must interject a few clarifying comments regarding the pro-Microsoft comments. For new users and NetWare administrators coming over to SBS (such as Dawn), I've found the SBS Console is great and really aids the SBS learning process. So on that count, Microsoft is correct with its ease of use, automatic decision making, and successful design assertions. But for good old Windows NT Server gurus with headstrong ways of doing things, the SBS Console is more of an enemy. Through pain and agony, these Windows NT Server gurus begrudgingly use the SBS Console (but not the first, second, or third time they attempt to perform a task—that would have been too easy!). I'll say it now and most assuredly say it again: do everything from the SBS Console (and its wizards).

## Task 1.1: Test for Understanding

▼ TASK

Now that you've read several perspectives on defining SBS, test your understanding of defining SBS by reading, in detail, the retail box that SBS shipped in. There you will find that Microsoft has attempted, in a few pictures and under 300 words, to define SBS. Do you now get it? Do you better understand what Microsoft is trying to say, having read the previous section? If not, consider rereading the section or visiting Microsoft's general Web site for SBS at www.microsoft.com/backofficesmallbiz which is shown in Figure 1.3.

Note that this and many other SBS resources will be reviewed throughout the book. Appendix A, "SBS Resources," also provides a cumulative and exhaustive listing of SBS

▲ resources.

**FIGURE 1.3**

*Microsoft's Small Business Server Web page*

# Deciding Whether SBS Is for You

Early in your decision-making process to either install a new network or upgrade the existing network at your business, you need to decide whether SBS is for you. SBS has several practical limitations that you should be aware of.

## Concurrent User Limit

Only 50 users can be logged on at one time with SBS. Microsoft imposed this 50-user limit as the break point between SBS and Big BackOffice. Typically businesses that are growing rapidly and have over 40 users today need to consider Big BackOffice instead of SBS as the correct networking solution. Note that on Day 21, "Upgrading to Big BackOffice," the easy upgrade path to Big BackOffice is discussed. Also note that more than 50 users can be entered on SBS as users, but only 50 may be logged on at any time. This preceding discussion assumes that you have the 50-user version of SBS installed.

There is another side to the concurrent-user-limit discussion. Suppose that you have a five-user license for SBS. That would mean the sixth user is locked out and is unable to work on the SBS network. In order for the sixth user to log on, you would need to purchase a five-license disk and install these additional licenses.

## SQL Server Database Limits

The individual database (table and log file) size is limited to 10GB in SBS Server. Although that limit might appear to be a hindrance, in reality it isn't a problem for the small business. Remember that data stored in a SQL Server database is typically stored in a raw text format, so 10GB is an awful lot of data. This limitation was a concern for Xtek with its BenchTop application. But after six months of use, Norm (the president) was pleasantly surprised to see that he had used only 50MB of database space. Norm was further relieved to learn that individual SBS components can be upgraded to their big brothers. That is, the lean SQL Server included with SBS can be upgraded with ease to the full SQL Server version, thus allowing an easy way to overcome the restrictions imposed by SBS on 10GB individual databases.

## Exchange Optimization

In order for Microsoft Exchange Server to fit on the same server as Windows NT Server and the SBS components, its footprint was made much smaller. Thus, SBS's Microsoft Exchange Server is optimized for a smaller environment than its big brother (the full Microsoft Exchange Server). One example of this trimming is that, by default, Exchange Server uses only 8MB of RAM in SBS. If you've ever worked with the full version of Microsoft Exchange Server, you know that this is very little RAM. It's one of the reasons that Exchange Server in SBS runs noticeably slower than when implemented in enterprises running Big BackOffice.

## System Partition Limit

SBS 4.5 has increased the system partition limit from a measly 2GB to 4GB, and such an increase is very much appreciated by us practicing SBSers. It is within the 4GB that you will install the operating system and many of the SBS components (although you can install components such as SQL Server, Exchange, Proxy on other partitions in SBS 4.5, which is something you couldn't do in SBS 4.0). But all praise aside, be advised that the 4GB system partition limit exists and respond accordingly. This 4GB partition limit exists because this partition is first formatted as FAT (which has a true 4GB limit) and then converted to NTFS later in the SBS installation process. And now you know the rest of the story, as famed radio announcer Paul Harvey likes to say on his daily radio show.

## Single Domain, No Workgroups

SBS is limited to a single domain (an administrative unit to manage servers and users in a Windows NT Server–based environment). This limitation is a hindrance if your organization is really part of a larger enterprise that has other Windows NT Servers and typically uses "trust relationships" to interact with other domains. Don't forget this SBS rule: SBS trusts no one!

Another reason for multiple domains, even in a small organization, relates to adherence to the security model surrounding Microsoft Proxy Server and live Internet connections. In medium and large organizations, Microsoft Proxy Server is typically installed on a server that is housed in a separate domain, far away from corporate databases and the like. Such is not the case with SBS, where you are limited to one domain. I further discuss this important topic on Day 11, "Internet Security: Proxy Server."

**NEW TERM**  Workgroups are not allowed in the SBS networking model because SBS must act as something called a *primary domain controller* (*PDC*). A PDC is the central security authority for the network. It is responsible for logging you on, auditing usage if so configured, and whatnot. Workgroups do not use such a robust security model, and interestingly, many small businesses that are upgrading to SBS have been using peer-to-peer networks built on the workgroup model. This change from workgroups to domains is often startling to the small business and requires extra care and planning. Why? For one, domains are by their nature are a much more centralized management approach; workgroups are decentralized. So people who were comfortable with the workgroup sharing model are often put off by the heavy-handed centralized management domain view. Be careful here.

## Costs

Another SBS consideration is cost. The standalone version of Windows NT Server is dramatically less expensive (by over 50%) than a comparably licensed version of SBS. I've lost SBS consulting opportunities in the past because customers decided that all they really needed the network for was to store common accounting files and print. One such case was a small construction company. E-mail, Internet connectivity, faxing, and other SBS features weren't part of the picture. Enough said. Out with SBS and in with regular Windows NT Server. I guess the $800 saved by this construction company by not purchasing SBS was used to make a monthly lease payment on the owner's $130,000 Mercedes sedan. It's a matter of priorities. For them, SBS wasn't a priority.

Not honoring these limitations might cause you to make a bad decision concerning your firm's computer network. The key point is to make sure that SBS is the right fit for your organization.

# Business Reasons for SBS

Ultimately, it's a dollars-and-cents decision. How does SBS contribute to the bottom line? Does SBS have a favorable ROI?

It has been my experience in working with SBS and small businesses that the business software application typically drives the SBS decision (although there are exceptions that

I'll mention in a moment). Although certainly not as lucrative as owning tons of Microsoft stock options, if only I received $10 for each time I've taken a call from someone on a Novell NetWare network saying their (pick from the following) accounting, design, CAD, CAM, retail, legal, medical, or time/billing software vendor will no longer support its NetWare version… These independent software vendors (ISV) typically migrate their applications to Windows NT Server, leaving their older NetWare installations orphaned. That translates into the small business taking a look at Windows NT Server to meet its ongoing computing needs. And if I can get a small business with fewer than 25 concurrent users to consider Windows NT Server, I can most likely rightsize them right into SBS. So call it an SBS law: business applications are clearly driving most of the migrations to SBS!

Other business reasons for migrating to SBS include cost-effectiveness. Microsoft has mastered the art of bundling software applications and selling these bundles at a price point far below the combined costs of purchasing these software applications on an individual basis. You saw this over the past several years with Microsoft Office. SBS is no exception. For over $1,000 (less if you are upgrading, which is discussed during the afternoon of Day 2, "Planning for Small Business Server"), you can have a five-user network with SBS's modified BackOffice suite.

I once sold SBS and my consulting services to a land development firm that was considering a new network for its four users. This firm had decided that its old NetWare 3.x server was ready for replacement. Initially, armed with a warehouse catalog showing the upgrade price for Windows NT Server at $400, this firm wanted and *only* wanted regular Windows NT Server. But after sitting down and further discussing its needs, the firm decided that purchasing a third-party modem pooling and faxing solution to supplement regular Windows NT Server would exceed the SBS upgrading cost (approximately $900) for five users. At the end of this meeting, needless to say, SBS sold itself with its built-in modem pooling and fax server capabilities.

Now that "exception" for selecting SBS that I promised. First on this list is politics. Here I look no further than the Athletic Club. This Seattle-based club has many members who are employees or vendors of Microsoft. Rumor has it that the big Bill (Bill Gates) himself is a member. Here, the management team concluded that having a NetWare network was a political negative that it didn't want to advertise. Exit NetWare and enter SBS. Whatever works.

Finally, more and more SBS purchases are being swayed by the increasing catalog of SBS-specific applications that are entering the market. First and foremost in this category are SBS tools. Software vendors such as Seagate and Computer Associates have released SBS suites of their backup products (Backup Exec and ARCserve, respectively). These

SBS-enabled software applications use the SBS Console, making the applications easier to operate than their big Windows NT Server–specific brothers. Note that I discuss these two backup applications during Day 6, "Daily and Weekly SBS Administration (The Dirty Dozen)."

# Lunch

So it's time for lunch. Today's guest speaker is Steve Brown, an SBS product manager with Microsoft. His topic is especially meaningful as it helps bridge the morning basics session with the more advanced afternoon session. In particular, his message is directed toward Microsoft Certified Professionals who might like to provide SBS consulting services. Take it away, Steve.

## Big Opportunities with Small Business Server
*by Steve Brown*
*Microsoft Corporation*

Microsoft Certified Professionals serving small- and medium-sized customers know that there's big demand for technology solutions in the small-business sector. To help small businesses, and to help Microsoft Certified Solution Providers expand their business opportunities, Microsoft offers BackOffice Small Business Server.

Small Business Server is an ideal product if you're an MCP already certified on Microsoft Windows NT Server, Microsoft Exchange Server, or Microsoft SQL Server because it leverages your existing product knowledge. At the same time, it's also a great choice if you're an MCP just getting certified on Windows NT Server, because it gives you a way to get your feet wet in the waters of BackOffice.

Small Business Server is designed for your small business customers who have 25 or fewer PCs. It includes the following:

- File and print services (Windows NT Server)
- A database server (SQL Server)
- Email and scheduling (Exchange and Outlook)
- Secure Internet and communications services (Internet Information Server, Proxy Server, FrontPage, Internet Explorer) and remote access
- Modem pooling
- Fax capabilities (Fax Server, and Modem Sharing Server)

If you're an MCP, Small Business Server represents an opportunity for you to demonstrate your technical knowledge and create innovative solutions by unlocking the power of the products contained in Small Business Server. You'll also be able to take advantage of the hundreds of third-party applications designed specifically for Small Business Server.

You'll find that installing Small Business Server is easy, as most of the setup process is automated. At the same time, you can install and manage all components individually if you wish. This flexibility allows you to focus your skills on higher margin services. It also allows you to handle a greater volume of business, which further increases your profitability.

Best of all, Small Business Server provides a foundation that will continue to serve you and your customers as their needs grow, so you can keep adding the new technologies and services they require over time while maintaining your position as their technology partner.

Want to learn more? The latest information on Small Business Server, including details on one-day ATEC training courses, is available on-line at www.microsoft.com/backofficesmallbiz. Be sure to check out our Direct Access Web site, specially designed for Microsoft resellers, at www.microsoft.com/directaccess. It includes tools to help you be more successful, including our self-assessment tool to help you gauge your knowledge of Small Business Server and to identify the training you'll need, if any, to begin to put this powerful software to work for you and your customers.

**Note** | This guest column is reprinted with permission of Microsoft Certified Professional Magazine, at www.mcpmag.com.

## PM Microsoft SBS Design Goals

There is no argument that Microsoft's primary SBS design goals were to serve the small-business market. That said, something that I've learned and heard from others is that serving the small-business customer is dramatically different from serving the enterprise. Because of this observation, allow me to spend a few pages presenting these differences and defining the small-business market. Such discussions are bound to make you more successful in your SBS implementations. If you are a small-business person seeking to set up and use SBS, discover whether you don't see a little of yourself in these forthcoming section (although I make many comments that pertain specify to SBS consultants).

# Defining the SBS Market: The Small-Business Model

Now that I've installed several dozen SBS networks, I can wax poetically as an SBS elder statesman about the small-business firm. Small businesses are, of course, very different from the enterprise. Three areas separate the small business from the enterprise:

- Attitude
- Affluence
- Expertise

## Attitude

Small businesses are rightly more focused on delivering goods and services than being concerned about the technology being implemented. In fact, many small-business people have a hostile attitude toward computers, viewing them as a drain on time and financial resources. Remember, these are the firms that complain long and loud when you purchase an unplanned network adapter card for $80!

Such hostile attitudes can be overt, such as criticizing your effort, or hidden, like not sending staff (including the owner) to basic computer training. Don't forget that the real measure of success of the SBS network one year hence will be a function of training. Are the users using the SBS network? Have they taken advantage of many of the SBS features such as robust Internet connectivity, faxing, and the SQL Server database application? If not, the significant investment of time and money in implementing the SBS network will be viewed unfavorably.

And even when you find and help a technology-friendly small business, you can't help but see that the owner and manager really should leave the SBS networking to you, the SBS consultant. Their energies are best allocated toward running their business, not running an SBS network.

I have one client, the aforementioned Norm, who is the owner of a small medical instrument repair facility. Norm is from the technical field, having worked for years in numerous technical roles in the firm he started. Several years ago, Norm hired a renowned management consultant who mentored Norm into being a president and CEO. One of the critical success factors in Norm's transformation from butcher, baker, and candlestick maker to president and CEO was his shift from doing the work to managing the work. It's arguably as difficult a shift as any small-business founder will ever have to make, and

Norm is no exception. The point is this: When I arrived as Norm's SBS consultant, I inherited a large case of boundary definition and expectation management. Norm wanted to participate in the SBS administration, troubleshooting, and whatnot. But better senses prevailed, and Norm reluctantly did the things that presidents and CEOs do: get the business.

Many times the negative attitude that is demonstrated by small businesses towards technology, such as SBS, is based on fear. We all get defensive when confronted with the unknown, and small-business people fear that SBS might make them look stupid. As an SBS consultant, you need to wear their moccasins for a moment.

**Tip**

A fear-based negative attitude toward SBS by the small-business person is really, I've found, a cry for more information. In the absence of sufficient information about SBS, small-business people make up their own. And, as you will see in the next section, SBS already suffers a definition problem, so you hardly need anyone in your life manufacturing incorrect information about what SBS does and does not do.

What's my recommendation? Overcommunicate with the small-business person about SBS. Once they're educated, expectations are kept in line, and you can chalk up another SBS victory. In fact, I've taken to communicating to my clients in writing, either via e-mail, fax, or mailed letter every time I perform SBS-related work at their site. What's cool about this method is that, months later when both you and the SBS customer have forgotten something technically related, you can easily go back to your files and look up the facts (and here again, prevent SBS misinformation).

**Tip**

Be sure to keep your own attitude in check. I can directly trace my SBS failures more times than not to having brought an enterprise "know-it-all" arrogance to the small-business person. Needless to say, it didn't go over well. The small-business person in many cases has a perceived negative notion about arrogant computer people. Don't validate that perception. Remember that you're typically serving as both a technical consultant and a business consultant. At the small-business level, you wear multiple hats. It's hard to do, and few MCSE-types really do it well. But a few random acts of kindness go a long way with the SBS clientele (even though your enterprise experience frowns on such openness).

What's my solution to this alleged attitude problem from the SBS consultant side? I now have more communicators on my consulting staff than I did in the past. Yes, there is still a role for tech heads who are appreciated for their expertise, but I've enjoyed great success with the SBS product line by taking liberal arts majors, training them on SBS, and having them score wins with my SBS clients. So, leave that big league Windows NT Server attitude outside the door when working with SBS!

## Affluence

One of the earliest lessons learned with SBS was that the small business isn't the enterprise, and although that should have been obvious, remember that the small business truly watches dollars closer than the enterprise ever will. Remember my example at the top of this section regarding $80 network adapter cards. The enterprise-level Windows NT Server site probably has a half-dozen SBS cards stacked in the server room ready for use. An enterprise-level Windows NT administrator wouldn't think twice about getting another network adapter card from the pile. But that cavalier attitude pales against the dollar-conscious small business that disapproves so greatly of unnecessary SBS-related expenditures that I've witnessed:

- A small firm struggles with the built-in SBS tape backup instead of purchasing a $500 third-party tape backup solution that provides greater services and piece of mind.

- A small firm struggles with an older network adapter card for hours instead of buying a new card for $80 or less.

- A small firm didn't hook up an HP laser printer directly to the network (via the built-in HP JetDirect card) because it didn't want to run to the store to purchase another strand of CAT 5 cable. (Instead, this high-priced printer was attached to the SBS server via a parallel cable, which of course had significantly lower performance than a direct network connection.)

## Expertise

One of the great consulting opportunities today in the world of Windows NT Server is SBS. I've found, when performing SBS engagements, that I'm a large fish in a small pond. That's opposite of the typical enterprise-level Windows NT Server engagement at the Boeings of the world where, even as a know-it-all, you're really nothing more than a cog in a huge networking machine. So I guess you could say that rank has its privileges. Working with small businesses and helping them implement SBS can be tremendously rewarding.

The expertise coin has another side, however. As the SBS guru, you will be relied on in more ways, often unexpected, than you might be at the enterprise level. Here is what I mean: When working with Windows NT Server at the enterprise level, you likely benefit from having someone on-staff who can walk through a series of steps to solve a problem (often while you're speaking via telephone from a different location). But at the small-business level with SBS, this is often not the case. Here you are interacting directly with paralegals, bookkeepers, cashiers, clerks, and owners—not necessarily in that order! Not only do these people often lack the technical aptitude to assist your SBS troubleshooting efforts, but they usually become intimidated and nervous when working with you, the SBS guru.

So at one level there is a bona fide expertise gap when you work with SBS sites, and on another level, your commitment to SBS sites will be certainly no less than the commitment you make to regular Windows NT Server sites. Ask a friend of mine, who, approaching the front of the waiting line in Washington's San Juan Islands ferry, was paged by a small-business site. Apparently, this SBS site was unable to connect to the Internet. Without in-house technical competency, the SBS site doomed my friend to drive back to the city and assist it. Bummer! Somewhere here is a lesson for the Windows NT Server guru who wants to master SBS.

# Who Are the SBS Customers?

To understand who the SBS customers are, it is necessary to understand the small-business community. As previously stated, there are over 22 million small businesses in the United States alone. As stated by the U.S. Small Business Administration (SBA), these businesses account for

- 39% of the gross national product
- Creation of two out of every three new jobs
- Creation of more than half of the nation's technological innovation

Given that basic premise, a lot is known about the small business from a technology perspective. According to IDC/Link, a highly respected East Coast (U.S.) research firm, of the small businesses that fit the profile for SBS:

- 74.6% of these small businesses currently have one or more PC.
- 29.9% of these small business have their PCs networked.
- Over 40.9% of these small businesses will have their PCs networked by the year 2001, which represents a 37% increase from 1998. In fact, I find this figure to be low if my parent company's portfolio of 800 active small-business clients is any measure. The IDC study most likely understates this rate because small businesses are feeling extreme competitive pressures to both modernize (to upgrade out of Year 2000–related PC BIOS incompatibilities) and be attached to the Internet for e-mail and have a WWW presence. When these numbers are revisited several years hence, I suspect you'll see that over 50% of the eligible small businesses became networked during this timeframe. I'd bet the house mortgage on it!

## Size Alone Doesn't Matter

One of the great fallacies that I've learned with SBS customers is the idea that business size alone matters. Such is not the case. Small businesses with fewer than 25 users typically have more than that in terms of head count or *fulltime equivalents* (*FTEs*). For example, the landscaping company that I've mentioned previously has 20 SBS users (well within SBS's 50-user limit) but over 100 employees. Many of these employees work in the field and don't fall under the traditional definition of user.

**Tip**

> SBS allows you to add as many users, up to the theoretical 40,000-user limit for a Windows NT Server 4.0 domain, as you see fit. However, only up to 50, or the logon user limit specified by your SBS licenses, can be logged on at any given time. Thus, at the landscaping company, I've probably added 40 users to SBS (which has a 25-user license at this site), but at any given moment, only 15 or so users are actually logged on to the SBS network. Why the additional users on the system? Many employees with an interest in computers use one of the three computers set up in the employee work staging area when the work shifts start and end. These employees like to check e-mail, write reports, update the Outlook calendar, and so forth.

So as you look at a small business and its fitness for implementing SBS, always consider the actual number of users when sizing up the organization. Employee headcount, sure to be a larger number, could be very misleading.

## Business Planning

More often than not, in the early planning stages of an SBS implementation, you will find yourself providing as much business-planning advice as you do technical SBS implementation advice. SBS planning is discussed on Day 2. Case in point is the lumber supply firm I once worked with where the founder was in the process of transferring ownership of the business to his well-qualified son for care and feeding. Implementing the technology at times played second fiddle to resolving delicate succession-planning issues. Other examples abound, including the property management firm that understood the need to implement SBS in its old space prior to its office move so that users could grow accustomed to the network and then introduce advanced SBS functionality (such as an Internet connection) later.

And you might really help the firm complete its actual business plan. Often the SBS planning documents result in the firm asking Who has what functional responsibilities? What clients and markets are being served? Can SBS help increase sales? (Yes, it can with a WWW page, broadcast faxing, and e-mails.)

## Cultural and Organizational Reengineering

If you think the paradigm shift I'm promoting today is hard going from regular Windows NT to SBS, think about how your SBS customer must feel when introducing a network into the organization. Communications go from traditional vertical lines on the organizational chart to horizontal democratic flows. (More than one small-business owner has grumped that introducing e-mail via SBS has increased organization dissension.) For many small firms, introducing SBS radically alters the work flow, and sometimes, especially in family-owned and -operated businesses, such radical reengineering efforts can ruffle the feathers of those at the top!

## Keeping Up with the Joneses

In all seriousness, small businesses are demanding enterprise-level network functions at a fraction of the price. Small businesses find themselves with an increasing need for business technology to

- Provide better customer service
- Level the playing field with larger organizations
- Take advantage of the Internet

SBS delivers with its implementation of proven BackOffice applications (modified for SBS) on top of Windows NT Server 4.0.

**Note**

In fact, SBS provides many features beyond that of Big BackOffice. For example, the fax server and the outbound mode pooling capabilities of SBS are not to be found in Big BackOffice (a key distinction you will want to keep clear in your own mind). Conversely, many of the enterprise-level applications found in Big BackOffice are appropriately absent in SBS, such as SNA Server.

That's not to say you can't implement modem pooling or fax server functionality in Big BackOffice; it just doesn't occur natively. I can recommend SAPS as one third-party modem pooling/fax server solution that integrates well with Big BackOffice. However, the third-party SAPS solution comes at a price (starting at $500) that SBS customers take for granted.

**Tip**

In fact, this price differential from not having to purchase additional third-party solutions, which I call riding the SBS yield curve, has allowed me to successfully market SBS to reluctant small businesses. After they are educated that buying Big BackOffice or going with regular Windows NT Server would require an additional cash outlay for modem pooling and fax server functionality (sometimes approaching or exceeding the total cost of SBS!), they quickly reconsider and often select SBS.

> **Tip**
>
> One trick I've played for small businesses on the SBS cusp (that is, approaching the 50 user limit) is to start the customer on SBS and then, using the Windows NT Server Upgrade for BackOffice Small Business Server application later, implement Big BackOffice to meet their growing needs (more users, more database size, and so on). The cool thing about this approach is that their newly minted big BackOffice installation brought forward the additional SBS modem pooling and fax server applications not otherwise natively available in Big BackOffice.
>
> Note that this trick, although functional, still imposes the four port limit of fax and modem pooling.

## Competitive Advantage

This issue speaks towards playing both a good offense and a good defense. Consider it the universal challenge for all businesses.

### Offense

Several of my progressive and proactive SBS customers have specifically sought out and implemented SBS for the advantages it brings to their business. For example, one client, a mail order solicitation firm that sells property tax reduction services to households, needed a robust networking solution such as Windows NT Server with a workhorse database engine such as SQL Server. At first thought, you might suggest Big BackOffice. Wrong answer. This firm has two employees, and those two employees specifically wanted the easy-to-use SBS Console so that they could manage the network after the initial SBS installation and see less of you-know-who (me, the hourly SBS consultant). This is a case of SBS allowing a small business the opportunity to expand its marketing reach dramatically. Needless to say, countless other examples exist.

### Defense

Not to generalize, but the old, family-run businesses that I've introduced SBS to tend to implement SBS for defensive reasons. This is a completely legitimate decision-making framework for selecting SBS. These firms' defensive SBS strategy is analogous to the fax machine wave that hit the business community starting in the late 1970s. At first, only larger companies had faxes. Soon, as costs dropped, nearly every business had a fax machine. In fact, if you didn't have a fax number on your business card after the mid-1980s, you received a puzzled look from your clients. Nothing in that era was more embarrassing than having your receptionist recite to a caller that "We don't have a fax machine." Fast-forward a decade or so. Today it's e-mail and a Web page. Lacking both, you're clearly behind the times and not a very attractive firm to do business with.

These old-thinking firms are actually some of the best SBS candidates, if for no other reason than prices have dropped so low on hardware (historically speaking), that you can leapfrog these customers right into the latest and greatest technology! Case in point, by being pulled into the SBS era, these Neanderthal firms have avoided suffering through the NetWare 2.x era (ouch!), and so on. This defensive strategy, usually unintended by these old-line small-business proprietors, kills a few birds with one stone. They can proudly tout their own InterNIC-registered domain name at their next fraternal lodge meeting and brag about how much money they saved as a late adopter of personal computer and networking technology!

## Technical Considerations

Finally, as part of the goal to define and segment the SBS customer population, consider the following. Microsoft officially states that there are three candidate firms for SBS:

- The soon-to-be-newly networked
- Peer-to-peer upgraders
- Novell NetWare Converters

### Soon-to-Be-Newly Networked

These are the last frontiers in networking left today. Networking consultants, acting as explorers, seek out this type of SBS customer with a vengeance. Why? Because we can put our stamp on their successful network, and it's likely this type of client hasn't yet had a negative networking experience (or negative experience with their network consultant). Great SBS customers if you can find them.

### Peer-To-Peer Upgraders

Another great SBS customer group because two factors are driving the upgrade decision: pain and gain.

**Pain**   Having started on a peer-to-peer network, these SBS customers want to upgrade because the performance and reliability of the peer-to-peer network no longer cuts it. Either print jobs take forever, or they recently lost data because the decentralized nature of a peer-to-peer environment doesn't lend itself to proper backup procedures.

**Gain**   Revenues are up, earnings are exceeding expectations, you're growing like wildfire. Let's get a new SBS network. Enough said.

### Novell NetWare Converters

This is perhaps one of the touchiest and most-difficult SBS customer groups to work with for several reasons.

1

**Anti-Microsoft Sentiments**   The big red crowd (existing NetWare users) are in an interesting bind in the late 1990s. Having made the correct decision in the 1980s and most of the 1990s, this groups is now faced with the prospect of converting to the often-perceived evil empire's network operating system.

In reality, many NetWare customers have taken a politically correct if-you-can't-beat-'em-join-'em attitude, but there are lingering "better red than dead" sites out there. Just be respectful of this customer group.

**But NetWare Did It This Way**   This trap requires you to show the former-NetWare, new-SBS customer how old NetWare features are implemented in SBS. Often, the client isn't interested in the facts but rather wants to vent some anti-Microsoft anger. Go ahead and let them; it's healthy.

**Power Tool Tip**

> When you get caught in one of these donnybrooks, consider the following to win over the reluctant Red Heads. Quickly drop under the hood and show off Performance Monitor. Then compare that to the MONITOR.NLM monitoring tool on their NetWare server. Because Performance Monitor is much more robust than NetWare's Monitor, you will have made your point.

**My New Software Runs Only on NT**   I've saved the real reason small businesses are converting from NetWare to SBS for last. With the dramatic increase in popularity in the Windows NT Server operating system and the relative decline in NetWare's popularity, developers have flocked to the Microsoft development camp. In fact, the Professional Developers Conference in Denver (October 1998) had over 8,000 attendees! With that interest in Windows NT Server, it's not surprising that many independent software vendors (ISV) have not only ported their applications over to Windows NT Serer, but they no longer support NetWare.

A case in point is a product that my firm resells: Great Plains Dynamics. Great Plains has effectively stopped future development work on its older NetWare/Btrieve-based accounting applications and shifted those resources to the Windows NT Server/SQL Server product line. That shift has been responsible for over one-third of my firm's SBS installs as customers have been forced to convert from NetWare to SBS to keep up with Great Plains latest accounting applications. (For example, its accounting/e-commerce module only runs on a server having Windows NT Server/SQL Server, which of course SBS does!)

I guess you could say that the ISV community has been very good to me, as it has to many in the SBS consulting trade!

# SBS Architecture

SBS is essentially a trimmed-to-fit version of Big BackOffice with additional SBS-specific client-side applications. SBS can be viewed as a complex circle, as shown in Figure 1.4.

FIGURE 1.4

*SBS architecture.*

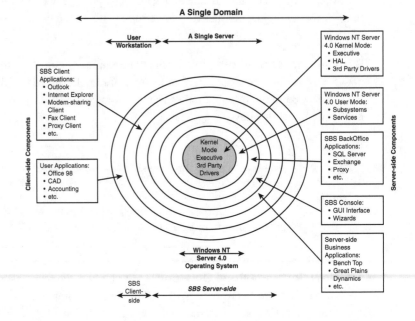

Let's discuss the SBS architecture model from the outer rings and work inward. I'll start with discussing a single domain and end at the Windows NT Server operating system kernel. Note as you read the next few pages, it is to your benefit to refer back to Table 1.1 that not only lists the SBS components but makes a distinction between server-side and client-side components.

## A Single Domain

SBS operates in a single-domain environment. As mentioned earlier, the SBS architectural model does not provide for multiple domains or trust relationships. A domain, often known as a *security domain*, is an administrative or logical grouping of computers that participate in a common security model. This security domain model manages the user accounts and security. Such security includes providing logon authentication for valid user accounts.

## A Single Server

Only one computer on an SBS network can act as the primary domain controller (PDC). This is a truism that holds for all Windows NT Server domains. Out of the box, the SBS architectural model is to have one server, with the SBS machine acting as a PDC, per network. It is possible to have additional servers on the SBS network acting either as backup domain controllers (BDC) or a member server.

A BDC houses a backup copy of the PDC's security accounts manager (SAM) and directory databases. A BDC can verify a user's logon, but, in my experience, it is extremely rare to have a BDC on an SBS network. That's because a BDC is typically placed on either a larger LAN or across slow WAN links on an enterprise-level network (two qualifications that typically aren't met with SBS).

Less rare on an SBS network is a member server. Member servers, known as *application servers*, typically run one or two specific business applications that can't run satisfactorily on the SBS PDC. One example of this is an animal service organization where I installed an SBS network. After installing the SBS machine as the PDC, I discovered that the fundraising software would run best on its own server. This software, known as Raisers Edge, has its own SQL engine separate from SBS-included Microsoft SQL Server. Raisers Edge's SQL engine proved itself to be quite a resource hog, necessitating the need for a standalone application server on this SBS network.

Because the BackOffice components included with SBS can't be installed on separate member servers (unlike Big BackOffice where several of the applications each have its own member server), it is critical that you purchase a machine with sufficient horsepower to optimally run SBS. I discuss hardware specifications during the afternoon of Day 2.

**Note**

Be advised that any additional servers on an SBS network may not be installed with the SBS product. Only one SBS server is allowed per network. The other servers, if serving as a Windows NT Server domain BDCs or member servers, must run regular Windows NT Server. Note that it is possible to have non–Windows NT Server application servers. I've worked on SBS networks where a NetWare server acted as an file/printer/application server on an SBS network (and did fine running a large Computer Associates business accounting application). The wilderness advocacy organization kept the Sun UNIX-based servers as application servers so that the GIS specialists could continue using their high-end GIS/mapping software.

## End User Workstations

As you know by now, assuming you have the full licensing allowed for SBS (50 clients), up to 50 user workstations can be concurrently logged on to the SBS network at any time. SBS natively provides full support for three operating systems: Windows NT Workstation 4.0, Windows 98, and Windows 95. By *native support* I mean that the SBS client setup routine is fully supported as well as client-side proxy, fax, and modem server–related clients.

> **Note**    Windows NT workstations operating systems prior to the 4.0 release aren't natively SBS client supported.

SBS provides limited support for other clients including older versions (pre-4.0) of Windows NT Workstation, Windows For Workgroups, Windows 3.x, Macintosh, UNIX workstations, and LAN Manager Clients 2.2c. SBS does not offer support for OS/2 clients. Workstation support is discussed in the morning session of Day 4.

## User Applications

This area typically includes Office 2000, a suite of applications including Microsoft Word for word processing, Microsoft Excel for spreadsheets, and Microsoft PowerPoint for presentations. Other user applications include narrow vertical-market software such as WESTMATE by Westlaw if you are an attorney, Timeslips if you're a professional who bills for your time, or QuickBooks if you are the bookkeeper in small company. You get the picture.

## SBS Client Components

This includes many of the things listed as client components in Table 1.1. This includes not only common applications, such as Microsoft Outlook 2000 (discussed on Day 8), but also SBS-specific components such as the modem-sharing redirector (discussed during Day 13, "Dial-In/Dial-Out"). In order for you to have a fully compliant SBS network, the assumption is that the SBS client components have been installed on the user's workstations.

Be advised that after the initial setup of SBS, the majority of your time will be spent dealing with users, client workstations, end-user applications, and the like. This isn't much different than any small network, but clearly Figure 1.4 isn't drawn to scale with respect to the time commitment you will ultimately make to end user workstations, user applications, and SBS client components.

## Server-Based Business Applications

Next in the SBS architecture in Figure 1.4 is server-based business applications such as BenchTop and Great Plains Dynamics, two applications that use SBS's SQL Server as their engine. To reiterate, it is this layer of the SBS architectural model that is so important. Powerful business applications, typically server-based, will drive the purchase decision to implement an SBS-based solution. Every industry has its own narrow vertical-market application that the small business seeks to implement. It is critical to assess that the SBS architecture will faithfully support such an application.

## SBS Console

The SBS Console was shown earlier today in Figure 1.1 and represents the server-based graphical user interface (GUI) from which the vast majority of your SBS management duties are performed. When an SBS Console option is selected, an easy-to-use wizard is typically launched. This wizard often completes complex tasks without the user's knowledge. I discuss the SBS Console in detail on Day 5, but to whet your appetite, you will be interested to know that some human architectural considerations went into designing the SBS Console. Clearly, the emphasis is on usability, but did you know that the first screen, Tasks, is meant to represent the most common tasks you perform in SBS? The second screen, More Tasks, is meant to represent SBS-related tasks that are performed less frequently.

### Task 1.2: Find the Pope in the Pizza

Do you remember, from the early years of NBC's late-night comedy *Saturday Night Live*, the humorous skit called "Find the Pope in the Pizza"? Here is my own version, SBS-style. Your challenge is to find the button on the More Tasks sheet that should really be on the Tasks sheet, given that its function is performed more frequently, not less.

The answer? Manage Computers. I and other SBSers use this button second only to the Manage Users button. Call it an *oops*, but under the SBS architectural guideline of having the most-popular buttons on page one, Tasks, clearly the Manage Computers button has been misplaced.

Interestingly, many vendors are writing to the SBS Console, placing their own button on the SBS Console from which you can run and manage their applications. Seagate's Backup Exec and Computer Associates' ARCserve were two of the earliest ISVs to do this in SBS. Undoubtedly more ISVs will follow. On the afternoon of Day 20, "Advanced Server Management," I'll discuss how to modify and customize the SBS Console.

## SBS BackOffice Applications

SBS includes several traditional BackOffice applications, such as Microsoft Exchange Server, SQL Server, and several others that are listed in Table 1.1. As previously mentioned, several of these applications have been trimmed when compared to their Big BackOffice brothers. Each of these applications is discussed in this book, many in the context of their own days. Days 16, "Using Microsoft Exchange," and 17, "SQL Server," are but two examples of what awaits on the pages contained within.

## Windows NT Server 4.0

As you might recall, Windows NT Server can be cleanly divided between user mode and kernel mode. Figure 1.4 reflects this division.

### User Mode

This is where services and applications run in protected memory (Ring 3) environmental space. To make a long story short, that means an individual application or service can not explicitly crash the operating system.

### Kernel Mode

This contains the Windows NT Server executable, hardware abstraction layer (HAL), and third-party device drivers. More advanced discussion regarding User and Kernel mode can be found in Microsoft's Official Curriculum (MOC) MCSE course 922: "Supporting Microsoft Windows NT 4.0 Core Technologies." Further discussion here is beyond the scope of this book.

# The Future of SBS

There are two angles to this discussion. First is the SBS product itself. Microsoft, and more importantly, the marketplace, have given every indication that SBS is here to stay. Release 4.5 of SBS will undoubtedly be followed by future SBS upgrades, each one providing more functionality and stability. In fact, Microsoft is already hard at work on SBS 5.0, which will incorporate many components that didn't make it into the SBS 4.5 release, including Windows 2000 Server.

The second dimension is what your future with SBS is. Ideally, if you have a growing business, SBS is merely a stepping stone to implementing Big BackOffice, and this path is certainly in alignment with Microsoft's view. If you can use SBS as an incubator to help you expand your business, Microsoft will be more than happy to upgrade you to Big BackOffice at a future date!

# Summary

This lesson fulfills several roles. The morning session introduces you to SBS with a brief introduction of each component and describes SBS's capability to deliver a single-server comprehensive networking solution that is relatively simple for the small business to implement and maintain. A key tenet to SBS, business application support, is emphasized. The lunch hour shares insights on the consulting opportunities for certified professionals that SBS brings. The afternoon session defines the small-business market for SBS and provides an in-depth look at SBS's underlying architecture. The future of SBS is discussed in closing.

The day also provides you, in passing, with an overview of where this book is headed and how it is organized. Several topics are briefly described in Day 1 and cross-referenced to future days where the topic area or feature is covered in more depth.

You are now ready to proceed to Day 2. And before you know it, three weeks will have passed, making you a competent SBS professional!

# DAY **2**

# Planning for Small Business Server

 ## AM Planning Basics

Welcome to Day 2! You now leave the high-level discussion of Day 1 behind and proceed with your increasingly hands-on approach.

## Springer Spaniels Unlimited

First off, let's take a moment to meet Springer Spaniels Unlimited, the company for which you'll implement a complete and successful SBS-based networking solution over the remainder of the 21 days. There are some very important reasons to work with an imaginary company the first pass through this book. It has been my experience with SBS (and life in general) that you know much more after you've done something once. It's another way of saying that hindsight is 20/20.

Such is the case with SBS. Typically, you set up SBS based on some assumptions that are made early in the planning process. Such assumptions might include the domain name you create and so on. But fast-forward several weeks. More than once, an SBS administrator has commented to me that, now that she knows what SBS really is, she would have set it up differently. Those observations about getting it right are analogous to creating the chart of accounts when installing accounting software. You make some early decisions that you have to live with the rest of your life.

Now back to Springer Spaniels Unlimited. By using this company for the remainder of the book, you have the chance to learn SBS, warts and all, before installing it for real. These methods also allow you to avoid the scenario mentioned previously, wherein weeks after your "real" SBS install, you might lament that you would have done a few things differently if you had the chance to do it over again. With Springer Spaniels Unlimited, I'm providing you that chance at a very low cost.

By completing the activities in the remaining chapters, you will learn what works for you and what doesn't. When you go to install SBS for real, again with live company data, you will have your feet on much more solid ground. That will result in a successful SBS install for you and your organization.

Springer Spaniels Unlimited, for these purposes, is a small company with 10 users and 30 employees. Please note that not every employee uses a computer (many clean kennels and so forth). The company breeds, raises, and shows prize-winning springer spaniels. It has five departments in addition to the executive offices, as shown in Figure 2.1.

**FIGURE 2.1**

*Springer Spaniels Unlimited organizational chart.*

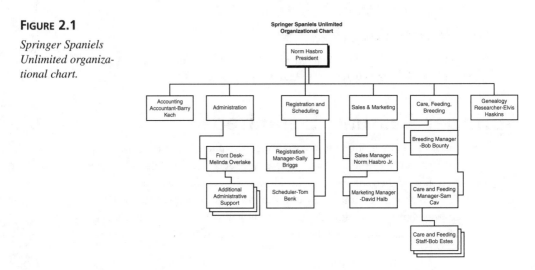

As you will see, Springer Spaniels Unlimited benefits from SBS in many ways, including its robust built-in Internet connectivity. How? Because canine breeders everywhere are worried about genetic variety in breeding (that is, they want to avoid inbreeding), the Internet is used to find suitable breeding partners. Springer Spaniels Unlimited also benefits from other easy-to-use SBS features, such as the SBS Console that was introduced on Day 1, "Welcome to Small Business Server," and detailed on Day 5, "Managing the Small Business Server Management Console." In successive days, I will present more details of Springer Spaniels Unlimited as needed. Periodically, you will enter Springer Spaniels Unlimited information into SBS to complete the exercises.

| Tip | Now is a great time to start your own *needs analysis* for your SBS project. A needs analysis typically involves looking at the ebbs and flows of business activity in your firm, often for the first time. Start by creating your own organization chart similar to Figure 2.1. From that, you might discover that your company and SBS users are organized in ways that might not have been apparent. In fact, early in the SBS planning process, I have found that many people use the SBS computer project as an opportunity to reorganize their businesses. |

# SBS Project Management

You should never undertake an SBS project without sufficient planning. In fact, I typically spend a day or more with an SBS client doing nothing more than planning for the new SBS network. I can't emphasize enough how important planning is with an SBS implementation. These up-front hours are certainly some of the best you spend.

An SBS project can be divided into five phases. These phases, which will be described in detail, follow:

1. Planning Phase—It is here the logical and physical design of the SBS network occurs. Early expectation management occurs here to avoid future disappointments.

2. Server Installation Phase—The SBS server is installed.

3. Workstation Installation Phase—The workstations are installed and configured.

4. Follow-up Phase—Over the course of several weeks, new SBS features are introduced. This mirrors the design of this book from Day 8, "Implementing Outlook," and forward. General troubleshooting, user support, and network optimization occur during this phase.

5. Celebration Phase—Projects create stress, and an SBS installation is no different. Phase 5 is an opportunity to not only release some tension but also solicit feedback from SBS network stakeholders.

## Planning Phase

For anyone considering SBS, the earliest planning exercises involve identifying and communicating why you want to implement SBS in your organization. That can be accomplished by answering the following questions. You will note that appropriate responses from Springer Spaniels Unlimited have been entered.

### Early Planning Questions

Q  List the three reasons you plan to use SBS.

A  (1) Ultimately to install our accounting system, Great Plains Dynamics, using Microsoft SQL Server 7.0 (which is included with SBS). (2) To have a secure and robust Internet connection for communications (e-mail) and Web-based research purposes. (3) To lower our information system costs by performing much of the ongoing administration ourselves via the friendly SBS Console.

Q  What is the time frame for implementing SBS?

A  We intend to set up, install, troubleshoot, and train everyone on the network over a 10-week period starting in 20 days when the new computer equipment arrives (and when you finish reading this book!).

Q  What roadblocks or problems can you identify today that might make the SBS project more difficult to complete?

A  First and foremost would be staff turnover. If our accountant leaves, not only would we have lost the individual we've identified as the SBS administrator, but we will have also lost our Great Plains Dynamics talent. To combat this potential problem, we plan to have the receptionist assist with the SBS setup and administration so she can act as a backup SBS administrator in an emergency. A second possible problem is the bank financing for our computer equipment purchase. We anticipate that the lending process will take only two weeks and the equipment will arrive roughly two weeks later. Being a critical path item, any delay in bank financing would delay the start of the SBS installation.

Q  How have you arranged for training for the new SBS network.

A  The SBS consultant will train those responsible for network administration. The SBS administrators will show the users how to log on, print, and save information. These users will also attend three half-day training sessions on the following topics: Microsoft Windows 98, Office 97, and Outlook.

### Task 2.1: Answering Early Questions

As a convenience, these questions are presented as a table in Appendix C, "SBS Project Kit." Now is a great time to answer those questions for your own SBS project.

## ▼ Existing Network Layout

Early on in the planning process, it is incumbent on SBS consultants and small-business owners alike to know exactly what they have when it comes to computer hardware and software. This baseline measurement allows you to determine what must be ordered, replaced, repaired, and so on. This information is typically gathered by inventorying the network and presenting your findings in a spreadsheet table or a network diagram. My preference has been to use a network diagram because its graphical benefits facilitate ease of understanding.

These network diagrams are typically drawn by hand, or with a network diagramming software application such as Visio, resulting in a schematic or drawing of your existing network. More information on Visio is available at www.visio.com. Visio can be purchased for under $500. Such a drawing might look similar to the drawing created for Springer Spaniels Unlimited in Figure 2.2.

**FIGURE 2.2**

*Existing network for Springer Spaniels Unlimited.*

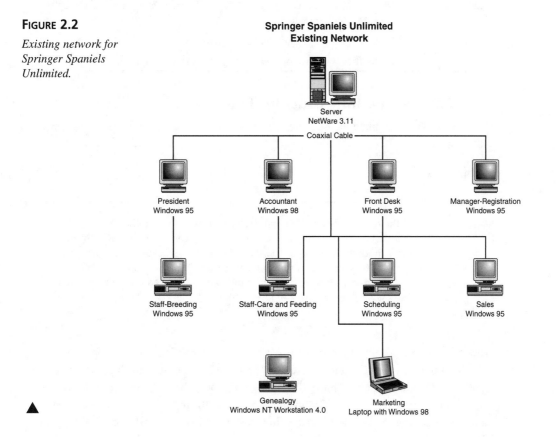

Springer Spaniels Unlimited
Existing Network

Server
NetWare 3.11

Coaxial Cable

President
Windows 95

Accountant
Windows 98

Front Desk
Windows 95

Manager-Registration
Windows 95

Staff-Breeding
Windows 95

Staff-Care and Feeding
Windows 95

Scheduling
Windows 95

Sales
Windows 95

Genealogy
Windows NT Workstation 4.0

Marketing
Laptop with Windows 98

## Task 2.2: Creating Your Existing Network Layout

In fact, if you are ready, now is a good time to create your own network diagram. Using a drawing program (even Paint via the Accessories program group in Windows 9x or SBS) or drawing by hand, sketch your existing network.

### Check Existing Infrastructure

Assuming a network diagram has been created, you need to gather a little more information for SBS planning purposes. Take a tour of your existing physical site and make notes regarding the following items: cabling, hubs, and wall jacks. Table 2.1 shows the existing infrastructure information for Springer Spaniels Unlimited.

**TABLE 2.1**   EXISTING INFRASTRUCTURE

| Item | Condition/Notes |
|------|-----------------|
| Cabling | Need to implement Category 5 10BASE-T type cabling at site. Existing coaxial cabling will not work. |
| Hubs | Will purchase and install dual-speed hubs. |
| Wall jacks | Each office will have one wall jack plus extra wall jacks in hallway. |

## Task 2.3: Existing Infrastructure Table

It is now time to complete the existing infrastructure form in Appendix C for your SBS network.

### Cabling

**Note**

In the case of Springer Spaniels Unlimited, you will note in Figure 2.1 that the existing cabling media is coaxial, which is considered inferior to the more modern Category 5, 10BASE-T, Ethernet-type cabling (or perhaps the new Cat 6 cable that was recently announced). Because Springer Spaniels Unlimited intends to replace the cabling, it is so noted on the proposed network layout (see Figure 2.4) later in the day.

**Hubs**   A hub is a central gathering point for network cabling. Many people today who are using the Category 5 cabling described previously are opting for high-speed hubs to replace older, slower hubs. Thus, when designing your SBS network, consider the faster (and more expensive) 100Mbps hubs over the 10Mbps hubs. With an eye on the future and getting the best long-term value from your SBS network, you will be glad that you did.

**Note**   Some older machines on a network, such as older laptops that use a parallel port–based network adapter, might not be able to run at 100Mbps (the new, higher network speed). If such is the case, you might need to purchase a dual-speed hub that supports both the older 10Mbps and the newer 100Mbps speeds. In fact, you will note in Table 2.2 that dual-speed hubs will be purchased and installed.

**2**

**Wall Jacks**   It is common when planning an SBS project to discover that your site has an inadequate number of wall jacks present. This typically occurs for two reasons. The first is that additional networked workstations will be added as part of the SBS implementation. This is very common. More often than not, when a new network is installed, so are additional workstations. These additional workstations typically are purchased for new hires, suggesting company growth is a driving factor in implementing a new SBS network. Or, the additional workstations might be from existing employees who were reluctant players now stepping up to the table to join the networked world.

Here is what I mean. At a property management firm I serve, the commissioned-based real estate agents must contribute financially to join the SBS network. That is, they have to buy a node on the network. Prior to introducing SBS, the old network was based on a NetWare server, something that didn't thrill many of the agents. Thus, several agents went without network connectivity in the past. Enter SBS, and these do-withouts became more excited about networking, especially SBS's Internet connectivity. Thus, existing stand-alone computers were added to the network when the SBS network was up and running.

Another cause for ordering additional wall jacks is the pervasive use of network-connected printers. A popular setup is the Hewlett Packard (HP) laser printers connected directly to the network with a JetDirect card. These network printers are typically connected directly to the network using one of the wall jacks. Many firms use the SBS network project as an opportunity to upgrade their existing printers or add more printers, so it is very common when planning an SBS network to order additional network wall jacks.

**Note**   Attaching printers to the network in no way affects your user count with respect to SBS licensing. Some of you from the old NetWare days might recall that network devices, such as printers and Shiva LanRover modems, could and would consume one or more of your network logon licenses. Such is not the case with SBS. You can have as many network printers as you'd like. Your user limit in SBS is ultimately determined by counting how many machines are actually logged on to the SBS network at any one time.

Given that you probably need to order wall jacks for your SBS network, be sure to overengineer the number of wall jacks ordered. I like to order up to 25% more wall jacks than I anticipate needing. These extra wall jacks are typically placed in the conference room when training occurs or temporary employees work. In my book, you can never have enough wall jacks. Plus it is cheaper to install them once rather than have the cabling specialist make return visits.

## List of SBS Stakeholders

Another important SBS planning item is to create your list of SBS stakeholders. Stakeholders include yourself, any consultants, service providers, and so on who have a role on the SBS project. And because everyone today has multiple telephone numbers (work, work-private, work fax, home, cellular, pager, and so on), I highly recommend that you add each stakeholder's telephone numbers and e-mail addresses to your SBS stakeholders list.

**TABLE 2.2**   SBS STAKEHOLDERS

| Name | Role | Contact Information |
| --- | --- | --- |
| (example) David Jaeger | SBS Consultant | SBS Surgeons, Inc. 123 Main Street Redmond, WA 98000 W: 425-555-1212 Fax: 425-123-1234 Home: 206-222-2222 Cellular: 206-333-3333 Pager: 206-123-0987 Ski Condo: 503-200-1999 davidj@sbsrus.com |
| Jane Union | Cabling Specialist | Union Cabling Box 3333 Union, ST 98111 W: 222-333-4455 Cellular: 222-444-3344 Pager: 222-123-4567 union@cablespec.com |
| Bob Estes | Manager, Springer Spaniels Unlimited (In-house project manager) | Springer Spaniels Unlimited 3456 The Pass Road Iski, WA 98111 W: 206-123-1234 Fax: 206-123-1235 Home: 206-111-1234 |

| Name | Role | Contact Information |
|------|------|--------------------|
| | | bob@springers.nwnexussbs.com |
| | | Note: Bob Estes is a dogtrainer who will use the server machine as his "workstation". |
| Roni Vipaul | Lender, SBS project financing | Small Business Bank<br>123 Small Business Blvd.<br>Small Town, WA 99882<br>W: 425-111-8888<br>Fax: 425-SBB-LEND |
| Ted Tedson | Sales Associate, Software and Hardware | National Overnight Warehouse<br>PO Box 8855<br>Acorn, WA 98234<br>1-800-111-0000 ext. 334<br>ted@sales.now.com |

**Note**

The users contained in Table 2.2 will be the first names entered into Microsoft Outlook on Day 8.

## Task 2.4: SBS Stakeholders List

It is now time to complete the SBS stakeholders list in Appendix C for your SBS project.

## User List

Next, create a user list for your SBS network. The key point here is to spell each user's name correctly on the network and have an initial password to use. Each user's name at Springer Spaniels Unlimited (ten users) is shown next. These names will be entered into the SBS network on Day 4, "Setting Up the Workstation Client." You will also find this information in Appendix E, "Springer Spaniels User Information," when you are ready to enter the information into SBS.

| | |
|---|---|
| First: | Norm |
| Last: | Hasbro |
| User Name: | NormH |
| Password: | Purple3 |
| Job Title: | President |
| Department: | Executive |
| Computer Name: | PRESIDENT |

▼       First:                          Barry
        Last:                           Kech
        User Name:                      BarryK
        Password:                       2redRed
        Job Title:                      Accountant
        Department:                     Accounting
        Computer Name:                  ACCT01

        First:                          Melinda
        Last:                           Overlake
        User Name:                      MelindaO
        Password:                       Blue33
        Job Title:                      Front Desk Reception
        Department:                     Administration
        Computer Name:                  FRONT01

        First:                          Sally
        Last:                           Briggs
        User Name:                      SallyB
        Password:                       Golden1
        Job Title:                      Manager, Registration
        Department:                     Registration and Scheduling
        Computer Name:                  MANREG01

        First:                          Bob
        Last:                           Bounty
        User Name:                      BobB
        Password:                       BROWNish4
        Job Title:                      Breeding Manager
        Department:                     Care, Feeding, Breeding
▼       Computer Name:                  BREED01

▼    First:                    Sam
     Last:                     Cav
     User Name:                SamC
     Password:                 Silver999
     Job Title:                Care and Feeding Manager
     Department:               Care, Feeding, Breeding
     Computer Name:            CAREFEED01

     First:                    Tom
     Last:                     Benk
     User Name:                TomB
     Password:                 White101
     Job Title:                Scheduler
     Department:               Registration and Scheduling
     Computer Name:            SCHEDULE01

     First:                    Norm
     Last:                     Hasbro Jr.
     User Name:                NormJR
     Password:                 Yellow55
     Job Title:                Sales Manager
     Department:               Sales and Marketing
     Computer Name:            SALES01

     First:                    David
     Last:                     Halb
     User Name:                DaveH
     Password:                 greeN25
     Job Title:                Marketing Manager
     Department:               Marketing
▼    Computer Name:            MARKET01

▼

| First: | Elvis |
|---|---|
| Last: | Haskins |
| User Name: | Elvis |
| Password: | Platinium1 |
| Job Title: | Researcher |
| Department: | Genealogy |
| Computer Name: | GENE01 |

| First: | Bob |
|---|---|
| Last: | Estes |
| User Name: | BobE |
| Password: | dogcatcher1 |
| Job Title: | Dog Trainer |
| Department: | Care, Feeding, and Breeding |

▲ Computer Name: SPRINGERS01 (note: Bob is using the SBS Server machine as his "limited use" workstation)

## Task 2.5: SBS User List

It is now time to complete the user list in Appendix C for your SBS project.

## Security

Not surprisingly, small organizations have many of the same computer network security needs as larger enterprises. The owner of a small business typically has confidential information that should not be widely distributed.

Security is a recurring theme in this book as different SBS components are discussed, such as Microsoft SQL Server and Proxy Server. But for your initial SBS planning purposes, the first security issue to address is membership in the Administrators group. Administrators are the functional equivalent of Admins and Supervisors in NetWare or the superuser account in a UNIX environment. Thus, it behooves you to select carefully who should have "full control" as an administrator over your SBS network. Typically, this membership group is limited to the organization's leader (owner, CEO, President), the day-to-day SBS administrator, and perhaps the SBS consultant you've retained.

## Project Schedule

The next step is to create an SBS project schedule. Because of the nature of SBS projects—working with small organizations—it is not necessary to use Microsoft Project to create complex Gantt/Pert/CPM charts. These high-end project-scheduling applications are better left for putting pipelines across Alaska.

However, I do recommend that you create a simple calendar-based schedule for your SBS project. Microsoft Outlook has a calendar that works fine. The project schedule for Springer Spaniels Unlimited is shown in Figure 2.3.

**FIGURE 2.3**

*SBS project schedule for Springer Spaniels Unlimited.*

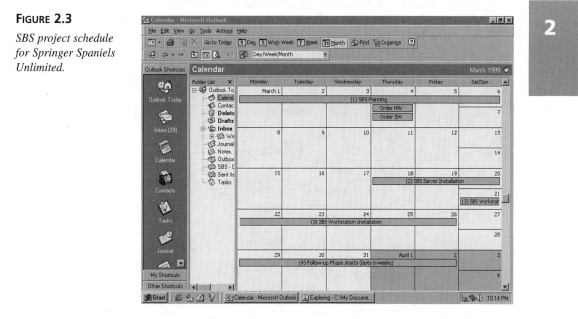

## Task 2.6: SBS Project Schedule

Go ahead and use Microsoft Outlook on your computer, if possible, to create a draft of a SBS project schedule for your SBS network installation. Note that if you don't have Microsoft Outlook installed, you can create a project schedule by hand using any calendar.

> **Tip**
>
> For more complex scheduling, consider using other scheduling programs. These range from Calendar Creator (The Learning Company) which creates more detailed calendars than Microsoft Outlook to Microsoft Project. Microsoft Project can be used for complex projects that track durations, resources, and predecessor/successor relationships.

## Hardware, Software, and Services List and Budget

You must now create the hardware, software, and services lists for your SBS network. Regarding hardware, a new server and new hub are being purchased. With respect to software, SBS and additional software are being purchased. Several types of services will be required, including additional telephone lines for the new Internet connection and new wiring (because a new star topology based on the Ethernet standard has been selected). A *star topology* occurs when each workstation and the server is connected to the hub in a "spoke and hub" configuration similar to a bicycle tire. In computerese, such a topology is known as a *star*.

You will also see that, by adding an additional column in Table 2.3 for costs, the list not only serves as your purchase specifications but also your budget. Note that I describe hardware, software, services, and budgets in much more detail this afternoon.

**TABLE 2.3**  HARDWARE, SOFTWARE, AND SERVICES LIST FOR SPRINGER SPANIELS UNLIMITED

| Item | Description | Cost |
| --- | --- | --- |
| Hardware | Server, tape backup unit, hub, laser printer (network-ready), UPS backup battery, modems | $8,500 |
| Software | SBS, Add'l Software (third-party Tape Backup, AntiVirus, pcAnywhere) | $2,500 |
| Services | SBS Consultant, wiring with wall jacks, telephone line hookup, Internet service | $12,500 |

## ▼ TASK  Task 2.7: SBS Hardware, Software, and Services List

It is now time to complete the SBS Hardware, Software, and Services List included in Appendix C.

## Proposed Network Layout

The next step is to create a drawing of the proposed network. The proposed network for Springer Spaniels Unlimited, shown in Figure 2.4, graphically depicts many of the items discussed previously in the section "Hardware, Software, and Services List and Budget." Also shown is how the old NetWare server will be "recycled." Here, the old NetWare server will be reformatted as a Windows 98 workstation to act as the dial-in computer with Symantec's pcAnywhere (I discuss remote access options on Day 13, "Dial-In/Dial-Out").

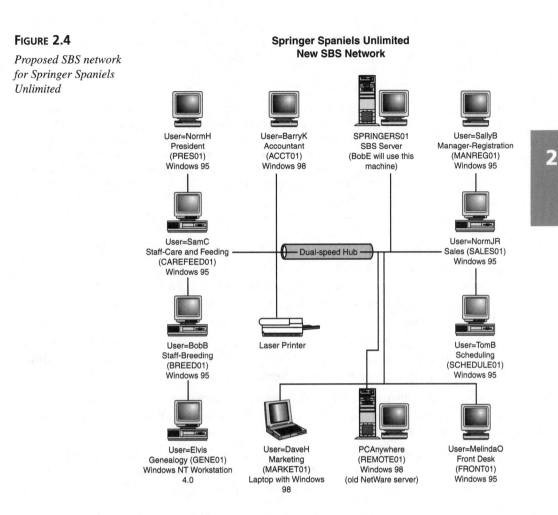

**FIGURE 2.4**

*Proposed SBS network for Springer Spaniels Unlimited*

**Springer Spaniels Unlimited**
**New SBS Network**

User=NormH
President
(PRES01)
Windows 95

User=BarryK
Accountant
(ACCT01)
Windows 98

SPRINGERS01
SBS Server
(BobE will use this
machine)

User=SallyB
Manager-Registration
(MANREG01)
Windows 95

User=SamC
Staff-Care and Feeding
(CAREFEED01)
Windows 95

Dual-speed Hub

User=NormJR
Sales (SALES01)
Windows 95

User=BobB
Staff-Breeding
(BREED01)
Windows 95

Laser Printer

User=TomB
Scheduling
(SCHEDULE01)
Windows 95

User=Elvis
Genealogy (GENE01)
Windows NT Workstation
4.0

User=DaveH
Marketing
(MARKET01)
Laptop with Windows
98

PCAnywhere
(REMOTE01)
Windows 98
(old NetWare server)

User=MelindaO
Front Desk
(FRONT01)
Windows 95

## Task 2.8: Proposed Network Layout

It is now time to create the proposed SBS network at your site. Use a drawing program if possible, but you can draft this by hand as well.

## Final Planning Activities

Three items remain as part of the SBS planning process: ordering, walkthrough, and documentation.

**Ordering**   A "critical path" item in your SBS project is the need to order your hardware, software, and services. Why? Under even the best of conditions, it can take ten or more business days to receive your new server machine. Services such as scheduling your SBS consultant and ordering additional telephone lines can take even longer (especially when the telephone company is involved).

> **Tip**
>
> If you use an SBS consultant, consider having her attend the calls placed when you are ordering. Typically I sit in a conference room with my SBS customer on "order day." The vendors are placed on the speakerphone, allowing for all parties to speak up and clarify anything. I've found that, by clarifying purchase specifications on order day, I save the client significantly more than my hourly consulting fee charges. Consider it another win for my SBS customer.

**Walkthrough**   Now that you are near the end of the planning phase, I highly recommend that you walk the floors of the site that will house the new SBS network again. By taking a fresh look at the site where the SBS network will be installed, you might notice a few things you initially missed. Items that have caught my eye on this final walkthrough include

- Server placement—Where will the actual server reside? Is it near power outlets? Have you coordinated the extra telephone lines, some of which are used by SBS, to terminate at or near the SBS server machine?
- Workstation accessibility—Can you easily reach each workstation on the network? Is there enough room between the desks and walls to allow the cabling specialist to install wall jacks?
- Building access—Do your service providers have access codes and keys to perform after-hours work on the SBS project? Believe me, you can count on some unexpected late-evening visits from members of the SBS team!

**Documentation and Loose Ends!**   It is essential that you take a few moments to gather the letters, e-mails, bids, drawings, yellow sticky notes, and the like and organize these in an SBS project notebook. The SBS project documentation serves several purposes.

First, if you should leave the organization, you properly share your SBS knowledge with your SBS successors via the SBS project notebook. In effect, people who follow you don't have to start from the beginning. You, of course, would appreciate the same courtesy.

Second, because of the demands a small organization places on its staff, it's unlikely that you will remember the finer points of your SBS installation several months hence. Thus the value of an SBS project notebook.

Loose ends run the whole spectrum of SBS computing. You name it, and perhaps I've seen it. Some doozies in this category include

- Do you have enough telephone cabling to hook up the modems?
- Are the telephone cables long enough?
- Do you need a fan to help keep the server cool (because the work area is too warm)?

Another loose end while planning your SBS network is training. One of the keys to success with an SBS network is to overtrain your users! It's a theme worth repeating (I do several times in this book!). Training can take several forms, all of which are discussed on Day 6, "Daily and Weekly SBS Administration (The Dirty Dozen)."

**Note**

> Note the SBS project planning phase is typically 10 to 15 hours of consulting work. If you are undertaking your SBS project without a consultant, budget for one to two days of planning time.

## Server Installation Phase

The big day arrives. Sitting in your workspace are large boxes on a pallet, representing the new server, monitor, and additional networking accessories (hub, modems, UPS, and so on.).

The server installation phase is more completely detailed on Day 3, "Installing Small Business Server," and includes

- Unpacking and physically building the server.
- Physically installing the network accessories such as the UPS, modems, and hub.
- Reseating the existing adapter cards that might have come loose during shipping.
- Installing SBS.
- Installing server-based applications such as virus detection utilities, third-party tape backup applications, and so on.
- Performing several post-server installation tasks, such as creating the emergency repair disk (ERD), sharing folders, mapping drives, installing printers, verifying security, and adding SBS licenses.
- Configuring BackOffice applications. Typically Microsoft SQL Server must be configured for use. By itself, Microsoft SQL Server isn't especially useful. It is also common to configure Microsoft Exchange above and beyond its basic configuration to accommodate public folders and direct Internet connections (Exchange for e-mail, and so on.).
- Installing applications such as Great Plains Dynamics (accounting software).

It is important to have a server installation worksheet similar to Table 2.4.

**TABLE 2.4**    SERVER INSTALLATION WORKSHEET FOR SPRINGER SPANIELS UNLIMITED

| Item | Description | Completed |
| --- | --- | --- |
| Server Name | SPRINGERS01 | |
| Domain Name | SPRINGERS | |
| Initial SBS Registration Name | Bob Estes | |
| Organization | Springer Spaniels Unlimited | |
| CD-ROM | SBS (use from your CDs) | |
| Installation Codes | Office 2000 (use from your CDs) | |
| Area Code | 206 | |
| Dial Outside Number | 0 | |
| Tone Dialing | Yes | |
| Address | 3456 The Pass Road | |
| City | Iski | |
| State/Province | WA | |
| Zip | 98111 | |
| Country | United States of America | |
| Business Telephone | 206-123-1234 | |
| Business Fax | 206-123-1235 | |
| Initial Administrator Password | password | |
| Hard disk partitions | SBS operating system partition is 2GB. Data partition is 8GB. Both are formatted NTFS. | |
| Time Zone | Pacific | |
| User Accounts | Administrator (password = husky99). | |
| Printers | Install new HP 5M printer on network with HP5 share name. | |
| Registry | Modify Registry for opportunistic locking settings as per Great Plains Dynamics worksheet. | |
| Folders | Create additions folders on Data partition: | |
| | Accounting (this is where Great Plains Dynamics will be installed and the storage area for the accounting data) | |
| | Old (this is where old data migrated from the NetWare server will reside until verified and either deleted or moved to Company Folders) | |

| Item | Description | Completed |
|------|-------------|-----------|
| | Applications (this is where third-party applications such as virus utilities, and so on will be installed) | |
| | Backup (this folder will contain on-the-fly backups of company data between tape backups, such as internal SQL Server database backups) | |
| Shares | Create ACCT on the Accounting folder. Everyone allowed change rights. Full control rights to NormH, BarryK. | |
| Misc. | SBS components (Exchange, SQL Server, and so on.) to be installed on C:\ by default. Will approve all licensing questions with "Yes". Will accept default SQL Server configurations (Character Set = ISO, Sort Order/Case Sensitivity = Dictionary, Case Insensitive, Unicode = default). (note additional items here) | |

Regarding partitions, SBS requires that the partition containing the operating system (typically the C: drive) be formatted as NTFS to operate correctly. NTFS (NT file system) is the Windows NT Server partition scheme that allows advanced security and file management. The other partition selection is FAT (file allocation table), the type used primarily in the MS-DOS days of old. FAT partitions are less protected and considered less robust. The Microsoft Web site at www.microsoft.com provides extensive information on NTFS and FAT. Further discussion here would be beyond the scope of this book.

## Task 2.9: Server Installation Worksheet

Began to familiarize yourself with the Server Installation Worksheet in Appendix C. If you are ready, go ahead and complete this worksheet. Note this worksheet will be revisited on Day 3.

# Workstation Installation Phase

The workstation installation phase is really the work that occurs on Day 4. That said, there are a few key steps in the workstation installation stage worth listing:

- Complete the SBS workstation installation sheet. This will be performed on Day 4.
- Physically unpack and construct workstations.
- Reseat the existing adapter cards that might have come loose during shipping.
- Complete installation of client operating system if necessary.
- Create and SBS client installation disk for each workstation.

- Install SBS client components on each workstation.
- Perform basic SBS client component tests, answer limited user questions, and so on.
- Enable and demonstrate network file sharing from client PCs.
- Enable and demonstrate network printing from client PCs.
- Enable and demonstrate basic *internal* e-mail via Outlook and Microsoft Exchange.
- Set a date to return to fully configure Outlook (calendar, contact list).
- Propose a date for network usage (logon, printing, saving) and Outlook training.

The middle steps involve testing the setup. Those are key steps in the success of attaching and using an SBS workstation. Too often, I've observed homegrown SBS networks where the connectivity wasn't fully tested. In effect, the SBS network never did completely work. Unfortunately, those SBS networks that forego workstation testing usually discover such things later rather than sooner.

And it shouldn't be lost on you that training is mentioned as the last step of the workstation installation phase. Again, training is important.

## Follow-up Phase

As far as this book is concerned, the follow-up phase encompasses Days 5 to 21, for it is the follow up phase where additional SBS functions (such as faxing) and applications such as SQL Server are introduced. There are important reasons for staging the introduction of many SBS features as separate, discrete tasks contained within a phase separate from server and workstation setup.

It has been my experience with organizations implementing SBS that the mere introduction of a computer network is enough to start with. The users need to become familiar with the basic Windows networking environment that is the foundation of SBS and so on. In fact, for many users, being able to log on, save a file, and print are features enough to start out with.

Even network-experienced and computer-savvy organizations cannot absorb too many features too early. For example, e-mail is a great early candidate to introduce on the SBS network, but it has been my experience that even the best users aren't ready to tackle SQL Server and its strengths too early.

Lastly, there is the Christmas-morning emotional response. Given a pile of wrapped toys, a child will eagerly attack, opening each and every gift until, several hours later, the child is overstimulated and sobbing in a corner. Such is the case with many SBS sites. Users want to do everything right now, on the first day the network is available, but by the end of the day, the same users are bewildered, frustrated, and worst of all, have negative feelings toward the new SBS network. You, the SBS administrator, don't want and can't tolerate such an early defeat. Be smart. Stage the rollout of SBS features over time. More on this discussion on Days 5 through 21.

## Celebration Phase

Call it an opportunity to get a free lunch, but one of the most successful things I've accomplished as an SBS consultant is to have an end-of-project pizza lunch for all SBS users. Understand that there really is a method to this madness. Not only can I solicit user feedback that might not readily reveal itself during day-to-day SBS network use, but I can offer the opportunity to provide additional meaningful services that my SBS customer might not have initially considered. Four additional services have proven popular:

- Public folders—Many users, when they become addicted to e-mail, want additional help implementing public folders (shared resources) in Microsoft Exchange.

- Microsoft Outlook customization—When users start to use the contact list in Microsoft Outlook, the follow-up requests to create custom forms can be expected.

- SQL Server tables—The really hard-core SBS sites know that SQL Server can handle their most demanding database challenges, but few of these SBS sites actually know how to execute SQL queries and so on.

- Web page development—Last and certainly not least, the discussion over the pizza lunch inevitably turns to Web pages and electronic commerce.

# SBS Expectation Management and Perception

Avoiding disappointments is perhaps job one as an SBS administrator and certainly an SBS consultant. Recall that on Day 1, I set the framework for understanding what SBS actually is. Disappointment can be avoided early, for example, by understanding that you will need to purchase a third-party virus scanning application because SBS is devoid of such a critical goodie.

## Scope of Work

If you are using a consultant, a scope of work should be defined, largely based on much of the planning work accomplished previously. In my firm, the scope of work is typically delivered as a detailed proposal that describes how the work will be accomplished. Likewise, the engagement letter, which refers to the proposal for scope items, is a contract between my consulting firm and the client. An engagement letter typically covers items such as terms and conditions of payment, how disputes will be resolved, and so on.

**Power Tool Tip**

Here is an additional thought for SBS consultants about the scope of work and engagement letters. Many SBS consultants ask how you get paid for your planning efforts if you haven't yet created a scope of work or gotten the client to sign the engagement letter.

Here you should contract with the client for 10 to 20 hours of your consulting time to assist with planning. Perhaps this consulting time could be evidenced with an engagement letter separate from the SBS project engagement letter you intend to present later. It has been my experience that if the customer is not interested in paying you for 10 to 20 hours of your planning time, that customer isn't very serious about having a successful SBS installation. Also, if the SBS customer is cautious about the planning phase, explain that the scope of work you create with 10 to 20 hours of planning time can be easily converted into a request for proposals (RFP) that could be distributed to other consulting firms and resellers.

The thought here is that you can get 10 to 20 hours into your SBS project with this customer, and either one (or both) of you decide that you don't care to work together anymore. This approach provides an out for all involved.

The scope of work would likely contain the following items:

- A detailed proposal
- A schedule
- A budget
- A project task list or checklist

### Task 2.10: SBS Proposals

Much of this information has already been presented previously as part of the SBS project planning exercise. It is also presented again as part of Appendix C for your benefit. Take a moment to review the contents of Appendix C and see whether these documents might benefit you.

## Overcommunicate

Another theme to this book is that of overcommunicating before, during, and after your SBS project. It is very easy to do. You can do it in person via periodic SBS network meetings, pizza lunches, and the like. You might consider sending out an SBS project update e-mail, such as presented in Figure 2.5.

**FIGURE 2.5**

*SBS newsletter via e-mail.*

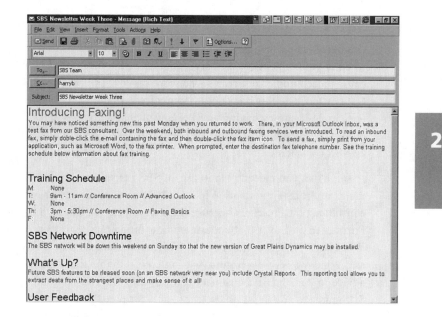

2

# Selecting SBS Service Providers

Another planning issue is that of selecting the service providers for products and services for your SBS network. There are several types of SBS service providers:

- SBS consultants
- Hardware and software resellers
- Wiring and cabling contractors
- Telcos
- Internet service providers (ISP)

First, a comment regarding service providers. In general, the very best way to retain the services of another is via referral of a mutually respected third party. This third party is typically a friend at another organization that has used a service provider that he is pleased or displeased with. Acquiring or avoiding one's service via this avenue is greatly recommended. In fact, as an SBS consultant, one of my key motivators to perform at the highest level is the prospect of getting referrals from my existing SBS client base!

You should try to avoid retaining a service provider based on an advertisement in the media, telephone book, and so on. Under these circumstances, it is very difficult to ascertain the quality of one's work, communications style, and so on.

## SBS Consultants

Of course one of the earliest and most important decisions that you will make relates to whether you will engage the services of an SBS consultant. I wrote this book so that you could indeed implement an SBS network on your own with both study and practice (the two key tenets to this book). But many of you might want to extend the SBS best practices in this book by having an SBS consultant on your team for all or part of the SBS project. Furthermore, many of you are reading this book with the thought of becoming an SBS consultant.

Assume that you indeed plan to use an SBS consultant. You need to consider a few things up front. First, many Windows NT Server gurus have bestowed the title of SBS consultant on themselves because the shoe appears to fit. Such is not the case for reasons I presented on Day 1 that underscore how different SBS is from Big BackOffice and Windows NT Server. This point is further communicated by today's lunch speaker who, as a Windows NT Server guru, was bitten bad by his first SBS installation. What's my advice to you, the SBS customer? Avoid being the early training grounds for tomorrow's SBS guru.

However, SBS gurus are in relatively short supply right now, so what should you do if all you have to select from are SBS newbies? At a minimum, negotiate a training rate that is significantly less (perhaps 50%) than the consultant's normal fees. That recognizes that your SBS installation will indeed be a learning exercise that at least you can afford. I also recommend that, armed with this book, you work side-by-side with the SBS consultant to make it right!

Those consultants who are SBS gurus tend to be nichers. Like a medical specialist, true, SBS gurus basically live and breathe SBS all day long. You'll potentially pay extra for this level of expertise (perhaps a 50% premium), but it's typically considered to be well worth it.

## Hardware and Software Resellers

To be brutally honest, I've found the very best hardware and software buys, when purchasing for SBS networks, on the Internet and via 800 numbers. A few vendors that I've used via this approach include the following.

### Hardware

- Dell (1-800-WWW-DELL)
- Compaq (www.compaq.com)
- Micron (www.micron.com)

### Software

- PCZone (www.zones.com)
- Data Warehouse (1-800-328-2261)

I've advised clients to be cautious about using resellers to perform the installation work because these organizations, often storefront retail establishments, typically lack SBS-specific expertise.

**Power Tool Tip**

> Hardware and software resellers can be a good source of free consulting as long as you keep in mind you get what you pay for. For example, if you call Dell to order your server, the sales consultant who takes your call at Dell can serve as a reality check regarding the number of processors, amount of RAM, and hard disk storage to order. That second opinion is of value and can be obtained for free. You will also note with interest that the SBS Online Guide, found via the SBS Console, also addresses hardware scaling issues. Look under "Getting Started" in Chapter 2, "Preparing to Install and Run Small Business Server."

## Wiring and Cabling Contractors

Here again, getting a reference is a great way to locate a competent wiring and cabling service provider. You might check with the property management firm that manages your office space. They most likely use one or two such firms when building out office space.

**Tip**

> Be sure to have the wiring and cabling contractor test and certify his work (network cabling, wall jacks, and so on). Faulty network cabling can wreak havoc on an SBS network, and you should have some type of recourse against the contractor. A cabling and wiring certification provides the documentation you need to seek relief.
>
> One of my SBS jobs, at a mortgage brokerage, suffered from faulty wiring. After trying to troubleshoot the software, server, other hardware, and so on, it was finally discovered the wiring was the culprit. So beware. Bad cabling happens.

## Telcos

Here my options are limited for giving advice. You might not have the ability to select from multiple telephone companies (telcos) that can provide you with the additional lines needs for your Internet connection, faxing, and remote access. Increasingly though, many areas now have local telco competition, so choice is increasingly becoming available.

> **Tip**
>
> Whenever working with a telco on any matter related to your SBS network, be sure to allow plenty of lead-time for the delivery of the services that you are requesting. Due to a booming demand for telephone lines, backlogs in filling service orders can be measured in weeks in many locations. And the recent US West strike didn't help SBSers in Colorado, Washington, and other Rocky Mountain states.

## Internet Service Providers

Aside from a referral that you deem trustworthy, there is a great source already built in to SBS for picking an ISP: the SBS-aware ISPs listed via the Internet Connection Wizard (ICW) process. The ICW is displayed and discussed on Day 5, "Managing the Small Business Server Management Console," and discussed at length on Day 9, "Connecting to the Internet."

# Lunch

Today's lunch speaker is Tim Catura-Houser, a certified BackOffice guru who earned his SBS medals the hard way. This compelling speech about his first SBS installation, truly a lesson learned, has meaning for both SBS customers and SBS consultants. SBS customers can heed the underlying moral that an NT guru isn't automatically an SBS guru. SBS consultants can read into the speech that SBS victories, at least initially, are hard-won affairs. Here's Tim!

## A Spine-Tingling Tale of SBS Horror
*by Tim Catura-Houser, MCSE, MCT*

## The Dream

Help two companies meld their computing into one glorious, integrated whole.

## The Nightmare

Users newly addicted to e-mail, too little experience with Small Business Server installations, and an annual shopping trip to Fry's that might have to be postponed.

# The Lesson

SBS really only works when you follow all the rules. Sometimes, though, even that isn't enough.

Sometimes, regardless of how well you do and how—ahem—talented you are, projects just don't work. In order to make myself feel better, I like to refer to this type of learning experience as arrows in the back. In this tale, I play the role of General Custer.

## The Scene of the Crime

The location: downtown Seattle, where 18 employees push paper in a lovely high-rise. The office contains two separate, similar businesses that share a common receptionist. I'd been handling small digital challenges for one of these firms for 10 years. Over time, the computers at both firms had grown into more powerful machines with larger hard drives. Still nothing big though. The second firm had Category 5 cable installed by the building maintenance folks. I'd added some Cat 5 connectors, popped in generic 16-bit ISA network interface cards, set up a common storage area on one worker's computer, and called it a workgroup. Life was good.

Then one day Firm 2 added a Hewlett-Packard 5 color laser printer. Soon, they wanted the new printer on the network so that everyone could use it. They asked me whether I could network their 12 workers, like they'd seen over at Firm 1. Sure! Same plan, except now it was Windows 95. Over a weekend, I dropped in the NICs and punched the cable. At that point if anyone was yelling, "Incoming!" I didn't hear it.

## I Wish the Butler Had Done It

The challenge wasn't a simple network error. It was the printer drivers! In a shortsighted attempt to save Firm 2 some money, I told them, "Your network is up and tested. Just have everyone click on Add Printer to access the color laser." Yep, you're right. It was stupid of me to turn that task over to users.

Chaos resulted. Some users inserted their Windows 95 CD-ROM when the computer asked for a driver. Others used the HP-supplied disks. Suddenly, a team working on a 400-page report weighed in with different colors and fonts.

You're thinking, "So what's the nightmare? Just go back and install the same driver for all." Great idea, but whose "color" wins? I killed that small feud by:

1. Downloading the latest HP drivers everywhere

2. Announcing that these were the latest drivers (true) and that they should make printing faster (not really)

3. Announcing that this would give everyone the same colors (true).

Everyone was happy (for a short while).

Suddenly, Firms 1 and 2 (for reasons I won't go into) decided they wanted to be on the same network and share printers. But both firms had security concerns: they didn't want the other company looking at their data. I realized that Windows 95 wasn't going to cut it anymore.

But I had a brilliant solution. Why not put NT Workstation on the front desk, make it the central repository for data, and lock down the subdirectories by user permissions? The data would be safe from the other side, and whoever was working the front desk had access to data based on login name and password. The offices never seemed to have all able bodies working at once, so the Workstation user limit of 10 connections wouldn't be an issue. I popped NT Workstation on over a weekend and said, "Give it a try."

## Small Business Server Rears Its Head

So, a few days and one DELPART.EXE later, we were back to Windows 95, and I had learned that subtle differences, such as the order of icons on an Office toolbar, are a huge issue with end users. Believe it or not, that became the reason for pulling out NT. What next? Well, I'd been mucking with a new Microsoft product called BackOffice Small Business Server for about six months. I knew it was due in about three months, so I suggested they wait. They agreed. Little did I know that I'd just recommended my own death warrant.

For one, I knew that the minimum specifications of SBS are, to put it simply, wrong. Sure, SBS will run on far fewer computers than I would ever dream of using for several BackOffice products. I also knew from watching the workflow that, except for printing, Firm 2 was light on server usage, but heavy on the client side.

So, I suggested one of the weaker Pentiums as an SBS server only, replacing it with a newer Pentium for the user. A real server at last! It was only a low-cost Intel work-alike with 166M of memory, a couple of 2G IDE drives, and 96M of RAM. Not a killer box, but for the workload and SBS, it looked fine. I threw an IDE CD-ROM on the second channel IDE controller, along with a pair of NICs (one for the wire set of each company), and we were good to go.

Just one more thing, however. Two new employees had just joined Firm 2 in a new area of the building. I left instructions for maintenance to drop wire back to the hub of Firm 2. What did they do instead? They saw the new server and put the wire there.

Suddenly, we had three LANs: Firm 1 and its hub, Firm 2 and that hub, and Firm 2 with the new cable pulls. At a larger site, you'd just redo the cable, but this was a small firm paying hundreds of dollars per cable job. I was punching the connectors, but running the cable had to be done by building personnel to meet fire code requirements.

Having three ISA-based NICs was going to generate more interrupts than I wanted to throw at a single Pentium clone, so I went to Plan B. I put an eight-port hub in at the server so that the two new connections could plug into the hub and brought a connection from the two original hubs to the new third hub. I figured that traffic was light enough that a one-hop cascade on the hubs wouldn't slow things down too much. True. However, it also didn't work. The hubs from the first two LANs were too old to know how to cascade!

Time for Plan C: change the original hubs. We cascaded the hubs and had traffic down to one Intel Pro 100+ PCI NIC. Someday, some tech will thank me for putting this in. You see, I later found out that when you use the SBS client license bump-up disk, the MAC address gets written to the disk. This is the Microsoft solution to keep SBS legal since each NIC has a unique serial number consists of a manufacture code number and serial number. In theory, no two NICs in the world have the same ID in the Media Access Control layer. Therefore, most operating systems use the MAC to determine which computer is which. The problem with that was, if I'd gone with a 10Mbit card in the server, and the client later wanted to go to Fast Ethernet, the MAC would change. Since this would mean a different MAC, the client license disk would refuse to bump up a legal server. Of course, you could always spend $195 on a product support call to Microsoft to get a one-time use password. I dodged that arrow without even knowing it.

So in went SBS. I moved the data files, set passwords and permissions, wrestled the HP color laser drivers into Windows 95, and got ready to say Miller time! That blissful feeling lasted about as long as a bottle of beer stays cold.

## Deeper Into the Abyss with Exchange

The next step on my fatal path involved the wizard to select a new ISP for SBS. I launched the wizard, filled in a few questions about the client, and hit go. Mere moments later, I was very, very thankful that I'd chosen to work evenings and weekends because the Blue Screen of Death had appeared on the monitor.

The NT kernel had been messed up somehow and immediately threw up the intimate details of its protest. I wondered (for a very brief time) if it wasn't just a fluke. It wasn't. Something in the Active Server Pages really didn't like my very cool, very inexpensive, very easy-to-set-up Cyclades multiport serial board. (Check out this product at www.cyclades.com.)

After the initial panic wore off, I moved the DigiCom 33.6 external modem to COM2. From previous arrows in my back, I knew to put a mouse on COM1 and leave it there. For some reason, SBS didn't like COM1 to be changed once it was set.

With baited breath, I tried again. It worked! For a moment, I was a truly happy person.

At this time, there were only two ISP offerings, one for $100 a month and the other for $50. I said to myself, "Self, could you justify telling them they're going to spend $1,200 dollars a year for e-mail?" I went for the $50 pop. The wizard gleefully guided me through the sign-up process. I could almost taste a cold dark stout waiting for me.

There was just one glitch between me and it: the mail wasn't working. I was alone, and it was late, which gave me the freedom to try one of my favorite repair attempts. I proclaimed, as loudly as possible, a voodoo chant mostly comprising four-letter words about the lineage of Exchange. Surprisingly, this didn't work either. By now it was getting close to midnight, so I called it a day.

Early the next morning, I pored through both the instructor Microsoft Official Curriculum (I had, after all, a dream of becoming a certified instructor) and third-party books, wondering, first, how I could have messed up so badly and second, how a wizard-based setup could have led me astray.

By early afternoon, I had no choice but to call the ISP, since nothing looked wrong with Exchange. After six hours of making the support rounds, I was told to speak with the first person I had called that morning.

My conclusion: If the ISP doesn't have ETRN support, either blow off the ISP or blow off Exchange.

## Never Say Die

I was born with a stubborn streak. I told Firm 2 to cancel that credit card charge and step up to the $100 a month option. This time, the finger-pointing circle took over eight hours to travel.

By now, the Christmas holidays were approaching. I was getting ready to head to Silicon Valley for my annual adventure of spending piles of money at the big Fry's sale the day after Christmas. But I wasn't at Fry's yet, and the natives were getting restless. I heard the calls for communications. If I didn't provide it soon, I saw that they'd start using smoke signals, with me as the blanket!

I was getting desperate. I hit some of the best-hidden, high-tech watering holes in Seattle and started buying rounds for anybody willing to attempt to help me fix the e-mail hell I was in. It took great quantities of beer and a few Benjamin Franklins, but shortly I had a qualified person lined up. We agreed to meet at 9 the next morning. My man owned a hosting site.

We started on time. We skipped lunch. Still no results. By 4 p.m., it was looking bleak. The man said, "Rip out Exchange." I protested. He said, "Do you want to go to Fry's?" By 4:14 Exchange was history.

He put in a little 32-bit service called Ftgate. He threw in the NIC's IP address (the default for the server on SBS is 10.0.0.2) and remotely logged into his hosting site. We set up user names for both companies. Ftgate bounced any internal mail right back to the correct internal user. Mail with a different address went out the modem.

By 5 p.m. users at both companies could send and receive mail to each other and to the outside world, using anything from Internet Mail and News to Outlook. We danced down 37 floors and I bought him a Salmon Stout. I also slipped him a stack of papers, all with green pictures of Ben on them.

All that was left was to set up shared faxing and a few other trinkets. I made it to San Jose, poorer but happier. Returning to Seattle, I set up shared faxes. The only thing the Cyclades board didn't like was the .ASP pages for a wizard setup. Both companies were sharing the expense of a $20 account for mail. I placed and set up Proxy Server faster than a trip up and down in the elevator. Everyone had Internet access and, because of Proxy Server, it looked very fast. Once again, life was good. Famous last words.

## The Feathers Hit the Fan

On Monday morning, I made a courtesy visit. Everything was A-OK. I left the client and received an urgent page. It was the phone number of the office I'd just visited. Someone couldn't log in. I returned to the 37th floor. Nobody could log in.

I popped the event viewer and found error codes for WINS and DHCP. The bottom line: SERVER.SYS was hung up in a pending state. I rebooted. Same result. The workers were a little panicky; they had that large report to work on, and the deadline was looming.

I could log in locally. I started grabbing files with WINFILE.EXE because Explorer wouldn't launch. E-mail was still working. I fussed and muddled. I was stumped. I went home and read up. No answers. I called a few buddies at Microsoft. No clear answers. In desperation, I started a PSS call, and thereby put the gun to my head.

The person I got was very sharp. Quickly, the conversation escalated to a "babblesoup" of techno-jargon. He was confused and didn't have anything showing up on his end. Of course, I had already searched TechNet, to no avail. No clear direction from the pleas for help on the dozens of listservs that I haunt regularly either. PSS suggested trying a repair with "vanilla" NT setup disks. The next morning I tried just that. The "repair" killed the e-mail that the clients had depended so much on. A few hours later, I received a voice mail from PSS: "You really don't want to do what I suggested last night. If you did, it's reinstall time. Sorry." Gee, thanks.

I reran SBS. Because a large unattended install file does all the work, SBS discovered that there wasn't enough space on the first drive; after all, SBS was already there. So, it went to the second drive: the one I had earmarked for archive files and Proxy Server. Two hours later, it was done, yet again. I knew enough from SBS experiments at home always to use the wizard when populating SBS with users. I had to be logged in with Administrator privileges, because the re-creation of SBS also re-created new security identifiers. The SIDs attached to the data files were for the broken SBS install. I took possession of the data, copied it, and reassigned rights according to users and folders. I also got the folks at Ftgate to recreate the mail.

Life for the client was almost back to normal. I went in frequently to check on things.

Then the client called me in for a meeting. I took a seat, and they said, "First, here's your retainer check. Second, we want you to know we really appreciate your responsiveness. Third, we know you really want to go teach. We think that's a grand idea. Thanks so much. Drop by sometime when you're downtown."

## The Makings of a Career Change

What would have I done differently? Well, raised my rates. Since Firm 2 was run by someone I grew up with, I named a ridiculously low retainer. Further, it was my first professional SBS installation. I stopped counting the hours per month against the retainer when I realized I could have made more saying, "Would you like fries with that?" Also, I would never again accept a job where two companies need to work together. Getting desires and spending limits to mesh between them could require an act of God.

## Postscript

Firm 2 got a company to evaluate its situation. They were charged $7,000 for this evaluation, which was really a proposal for a department-class server, with all Fast Ethernet, for a total number of users you could count on your fingers. They accepted the proposal, which is in the tens of thousands of dollars. Firm 1 elected not to be part of this. I've since found VPOP3 as a better solution than Ftgate for a small site, and it has Exchange support built in. Microsoft refunded my fees for the support call.

For the most part, I'm now either teaching BackOffice products or preparing battle-scarred engineers for the Certified Technical Trainer tests. My aging process has slowed considerably now that I'm no longer consulting.

**Note**

> Tim Catura-Houser is an MCSE, MCT, and CTT. He also has certifications from different hardware vendors. Since writing this article in mid-1998, Tim has gone on to master SBS and is a frequently sought after SBS consultant and writer on SBS issues. His hobbies are gardening and leading the Seattle chapter of the Network Professionals Association. Reach him at tcat@usa.net.
>
> (Reprinted with permission of Microsoft Certified Professional Magazine, www.mcpmag.com.)

## PM Advanced Planning Issues

This afternoon presents more details on software and hardware issues surrounding your SBS project. I offer a few comments with respect to SBS budgeting and the purchasing process.

# Software

SBS ships in a variety of user-license, upgrade, and preinstallation configurations. I'll review each here and provide only the estimated retail pricing. As you know, street prices are substantially lower. Also be advised that you should consult your software reseller for the very latest prices. No book could hope to stay current with pricing when even the monthly and weekly trade magazines are challenged to do so.

## SBS 5-User, 25-User, and 50-User Version—Full Product

As of press time, SBS 4.5 will be sold off-the-shelf to the first-time buyer in 5-user, 25-user, and 50-user configurations. The estimated retail price for the 5-user version of SBS 4.5 is $1,499. The predicted retail price for the 25-user version of SBS 4.5 is $2,500. For the 50-user version of SBS, it is anticipated the retail price will be slightly below $5,000. Nothing special here.

But suppose you have a 10-user network, such as Springer Spaniels Unlimited does. Then you would need to purchase an additional five-user client access license (CAL) pack to install over your initial five-user SBS network.

**Tip**

> There is a substantial discount for purchasing the 25-user version of SBS, making it advisable to consider if you have over 15 users on your planned SBS network and you plan to grow! To see for yourself, go to the Web site for one of the software resellers mentioned before lunch. There you will see that the total purchase price of the 25-user version is substantially cheaper than purchasing the 5-user version of SBS than purchasing CALs to bump up your SBS license count. The crossover point between purchasing CALs versus purchasing the 25-user version of SBS occurs after 15 users. Call it a quantity discount!

## Five-User Client Access Licenses (CAL)

Additional SBS licenses are sold in five packs (CAL). You cannot purchase individual SBS licenses for any lot other than five. So, Springer Spaniels Unlimited would need to purchase a five-user CAL in addition to its initial five-user SBS version to reach a total of 10 users. But because Springer Spaniels Unlimited is actually migrating from an existing NetWare network, it qualifies for the upgrade pricing for the first five users, discussed next. A client add pack containing five CALs has an estimated retail price of $309.

## SBS Competitive Upgrade: Five Users

Suppose, like Springer Spaniels Unlimited, you have a NetWare network that you are converting to SBS. You would qualify for upgrade pricing on the first five users on your SBS network. Additional CALs would have to be purchased at full price ($309 per five pack) for any users over the initial five. At press time, there is no 25-user or 50-user SBS competitive upgrade offering. The SBS upgrade offering for five users has an estimated retail price of $929. As you can see, it represents a $570 discount from purchasing the full retail version of SBS (five users). That is significant, but again, this great upgrade pricing applies only to your first five users (again, you must then purchase CALs at the standard price).

**Tip**

> To be honest, the upgrade pricing scheme in a 25-user scenario works out to nearly the same price (within $100 on the street) when compared to purchasing the full retail version of SBS (25-user) version. In other words, with the larger user numbers, given the fact you have to buy so many CALs at the regular price, there is little difference from purchasing the 25-user retail version of SBS. You should work closely with your software reseller and look at all the SBS purchase options. What appears cheaper at first glance might indeed not be the best purchase option for you. Do your homework.

## SBS 4.0/4.0a-to-4.5 Upgrade Version

New to SBS 4.5 is an upgrade version for older versions of SBS, including versions 4.0 and 4.0a. This special upgrade version does not include Office 2000. Upgrading from older version of SBS to SBS 4.5 is discussed in Appendix D, "Advanced SBS Setup Analysis," of this book. Luckily, you can upgrade from SBS 4.0 directly to SBS 4.5 without having to perform an interim upgrade to SBS 4.0a first.

**Note**
There is no difference in the regular or upgrade versions of SBS. Each contains the same features and functions. Also, the upgrade version of SBS does not check for an existing installation of a qualifying competitive upgrade. You might recall that this type of check is typically performed when upgrading desktop operating systems or common applications such as word processing programs.

There are several ways to qualify for SBS upgrade pricing. If you have an existing network that is running on the following operating systems, you will qualify for this competitive upgrade:

- Novell NetWare
- Novell intraNetWare
- Novell intraNetWare for Small Business
- IBM LAN Server
- DEC PATHWORKS
- Microsoft LAN Manager
- Artisoft LANtastic
- SCO: Xenix, UNIX, OpenServer, UnixWare
- Sun: Solaris, Solaris X86, SunOS
- Hewlett-Packard: HP-UX
- IBM: AIX
- Digital: Ultrix, OSF/1, UNIX
- SGI: Irix

**Note** You are encouraged to check with Microsoft at www.microsoft.com/ smallbusinessserver for updates to this list. It is anticipated other popular operating systems such as Linux will be added to this list of qualifying competitive upgrades.

## OEM Preinstalled SBS

Another SBS purchasing option includes purchasing your server machine from an original equipment manufacturer (OEM) with SBS preinstalled. For example, if you purchase a server from Dell, you might have SBS preinstalled (at the full retail price of the SBS software).

**Note** Having the hardware manufacturer install SBS is not the same as having SBS completely installed. A preinstall basically copies the necessary files over to the server's hard disk (which saves a good 45 to 60 minutes), but you must still answer several questions to complete the SBS installation. These questions relate to organization name, domain name, time zone, and so on.

Many of my SBS customers have considered the preinstall option with the thought that they wouldn't need to do anything to complete the SBS installation or hire an SBS consultant. Such is clearly not always the case.

I have evaluated this scenario several times, and it depends on your specific situation as to whether this option makes sense. The key point to having hardware manufacturers install SBS is that they charge full retail price. Here is a story about why you might decline the SBS preinstallation option.

Recall several paragraphs ago that you determined the difference between the 5-user version of SBS when comparing retail pricing to upgrade pricing was nearly $600. I had an SBS customer with 10 users, converting from an existing NetWare network, who hoped to see less of me, the SBS consultant, by having Dell install SBS. In the purchase analysis for this client, two things became apparent. First, the nearly $600 difference between the preinstalled SBS version and the upgrade version this client qualified for made the Dell preinstallation option unattractive. Second, I identified that the client would only save one of my billable hours by electing to have Dell install SBS, so the $600 pricing differential that was identified didn't justify one hour savings of consultant's time (my SBS bill rates varies between $125 to $155 per hour). In this case, before I looked closer at the SBS purchase options for this client, there was a risk of being pennywise and pound foolish!

## SBS and Office 2000 Professional Suite

SBS can be purchased bundled with Office 2000 Professional Suite. This saves SBS customers both money and time if they need Office 2000 Professional Suite. You might be interested in knowing that the Office 2000 Professional Suite contains

- Word 2000
- Excel 2000
- Access 2000
- PowerPoint 2000
- Publisher 2000
- Microsoft Small Business Tools (financial analysis templates, and so on)

In my experience, organizations on older networks that are upgrading to SBS typically take advantage of the Office 2000 bundle (previously Office 97 in SBS 4.0). That is because these are the same types of organizations that typically use older word processing, spreadsheet, and presentation applications. However, organizations that install SBS on a brand new network typically can't take advantage of this offer in a meaningful way for one simple reason: Major manufacturers bundle Office 2000 as part of the workstation purchase. Here again, it depends on your particular situation as to whether the SBS plus Office 2000 bundling option makes sense for you. Plan carefully and accordingly.

## SBS Freshness

When ordering SBS over the Internet or through a national warehouse via a 1-800 number, be sure to avoid the following problem that afflicted one of my clients. As planned, this client called a leading national warehouse via a 1-800 number to order SBS. A few days later, SBS arrived. When installed, the customer and I discovered that it was SBS version 4.0, not 4.0a. This occurred even though 4.0a had been shipping for several months. Further investigative work revealed that the reseller apparently was filling orders with old stock, not the latest SBS release. That realization was a major disappointment. Beware of resellers who aren't shipping you the freshest product. And although this story applies specifically to SBS 4.0/4.0a, you can bet that additional releases of SBDS are forthcoming (SBS 4.5a, SBS 5.0), making this issue germane.

## Other Licensing Issues

It is possible, as discussed on Day 1, to upgrade individual SBS components to similar Big BackOffice applications. For example, you can upgrade to the full version of SQL Server 7.0 to get around the table and log size restriction. Such a decision involves additional licensing issues. I discuss these specific licensing matters on the appropriate days later in the book. For example, issues surrounding SQL Server upgrades are discussed on Day 21, "Upgrading to Big BackOffice."

**Note** And don't forget something discussed earlier in this book. The SBS license count applies to machines that are actually logged on to the SBS network. So, a 50-user SBS network might actually support a company with 100 employees. However, in this scenario, only 50 machines could be logged onto the SBS network simultaneously.

## Other Software

It is not uncommon to purchase other software to run on the server machine running SBS. I have found that SBS customers typically purchase:

- Third-party tape backup applications
- Virus detection applications
- Remote access applications, such as pcAnywhere
- Accounting applications
- Other business applications

Each of these application areas is discussed on future days. The key point is that SBS is rarely purchased and installed in a software vacuum. There is typically a support cast of other software applications, running on the SBS machine, to provide an organization with a complete computing solution.

# Hardware

With respect to hardware, you name it, and it has probably been run on an SBS network. Why? Because smaller organizations often have lots of legacy equipment that they want to continue using on their SBS network. And small businesses aren't known for over-spending. But there is another side to this story. With the Year 2000 (Y2K) problem making many older personal computers obsolete because the built-in BIOSes aren't Y2K compliant, many SBS customers order brand-new workstations that are both Y2K compliant and very powerful. Such SBS sites are a true pleasure to work with. Unfortunately, I can't extend the same heartfelt warmth toward those sites recycling their legacy machines (a strategy that is hard on SBS consultants!).

Microsoft has a set of recommended hardware specifications for the server and client workstations on an SBS network. These specifications appear in the following sections.

## Server

- Intel and compatible systems—Pentium 120 MHz or higher processor (Pentium 200 MHz or higher recommended)
- 64MB of RAM
- One 3.5-inch high-density disk drive
- 2GB of hard disk space (3GB if Office 2000 is installed)
- CD-ROM drive
- Super VGA or other video graphics adapter (800 × 600 × 65K colors)
- Network adapter card (see www.microsoft.com/smallbusinessserver for the latest network adapters that are supported)
- Fax/Modem card
- Microsoft Mouse or compatible pointing device
- Optional: Uninterruptable Power Supply (UPS), tape backup, multiport board (for modem sharing)

## Workstation

- Microsoft Windows 95, 98, or Microsoft Windows NT Workstation version 4.0
- PC with a Pentium 90 or higher processor
- 32MB of RAM
- One 3.5-inch high-density disk drive
- Up to 250MB of hard disk space, depending on the applications chosen to install (if installing full Office 2000, have 600MB of hard disk space available)
- VGA, Super VGA, or other video graphics adapter (800×600 × 65K colors)
- Network adapter card
- Optional: Microsoft Mouse or compatible pointing device

## SBS Server Machine Roles

The actual SBS server must be a primary domain controller (PDC). As a PDC, the SBS server machine maintains the original copy of the account database, known as the security accounts manager. This machine also performs the basic logon authentication activities for the network. Note that an SBS server machine can only act as a PDC and there can be only one PDC per network.

You might be interested to know that other "regular" (or non-SBS) Windows NT Servers can be added to the SBS network. These machines can participate as a backup domain controller (BDC) or member server. A BDC is similar to a PDC, but it stores a copy of the accounts database while assisting in basic logon authentication duties. A member server is typically used for special functions such as running a specific application (for example, an Oracle database).

## Real-World Hardware Issues

Allow me to speak for a moment to several real-world hardware matters, many with respect to Microsoft's recommended server and client configurations.

### Server

Microsoft's recommended hardware configuration is sufficient except for one item: RAM. I've installed SBS on only one system with 64MB of RAM, and needless to say, it was a poor performer among servers. I insist on a minimum of 128MB RAM for SBS server machines. The hard disk storage requirements, after the first 2GD, are entirely up to you. Because SBS is typically used in business settings, it is common to see 10GB or more of hard disk space available for data.

### Name Brands Versus Clones

At the server-level, I tend to recommend name brand machines such as Dell, Compaq, and Micron at the $5,000 price point. Servers at that level provide over 128MB RAM, a small RAID array (under 10GB), or mirrored drives and an Intel chip in the P300 range on a dual processor motherboard. You can typically get a tape backup unit at this price level. As with any pricing estimate, understand that prices *might* have dropped dramatically since I wrote this.

These comments, of course, lead to the broader discussion of name brand servers versus clones. Perhaps I have too many purple hearts from too many network wounds, but with any SBS customer that I take on as a client, I strongly push for using name brand equipment. The times that I haven't succeeded in that arrangement, I've gotten into trouble. Such trouble has taken many forms including unsatisfied warranty claims with the clone maker.

One case was a tape backup unit on a clone server at a property management firm that the clone maker wouldn't replace. Across town, with the same tape backup issues (same type of backup unit, errors, and so on.), Dell had a technician out the same week providing a new backup device. What a difference the name brand warranty made in this case.

Another consideration relates to the tools provided by name brand server manufacturers. Compaq provides SmartStart and Insight Manager as part of its CD-ROM bundle. Likewise, Dell provides Server Assistant. Although these tools are oriented toward the one-time set up of the server and monitoring at the enterprise level, such tools are appreciated additions at SBS sites.

What's the final decision between name brand servers and clones? The choice is yours, but my vote is now with name brand servers.

## Workstations

Regarding workstations, rarely do I install SBS workstation components on anything less than a recent Pentium class personal computer (say P200 or above) with at least 48MB of RAM. With workstation prices cheaper than ever, it is common to see Pentium 300Mhz-based workstations with 64MB RAM at the desktop. Now that's the kind of performance level that makes SBS look good.

### Don't Be an SBS Cheapskate!

**Tip**

> Don't poorboy (that is, chintz on) that SBS hardware purchase. I've seen people scrimp several ways with SBS-related hardware, none of it acceptable. Here are three examples.

First, people have attempted to recycle older monitors from retired workstations so that they didn't have to purchase a new monitor with the new server (a cost savings of perhaps $150). The problem is that older monitors can't provide the screen resolution you need to work with the SBS Console. In fact, improperly configured, the SBS Console might not show up on the screen or only part of it might appear on the screen, forcing you to scroll uncomfortably to reach distant SBS Console selection buttons.

Second, I've observed small business that wanted to use the SBS server machine as a workstation for one of its users. At a land development company, the president ran Microsoft Word, Outlook, and CompuServe right on the SBS server machine. The performance was unacceptable. Several months later, the president purchased a workstation, allowing the SBS server machine to do what it does best: act as a dedicated server.

Finally, there is the case of the green machine. Here, a paving contractor decided to save a few bucks by using a workstation as an SBS server, and although it can be done, the results are sometimes really strange. In this case, the BIOS-level energy saving function couldn't be turned off, so each night, when the server had several hours of inactivity, it went to sleep. Well, Windows NT Server, the underlying network operating system in SBS, didn't like that one bit, forcing the general manager at the paving company to reboot every morning. I finally solved this problem by creating artificial server activity every 15 minutes. To do this, I downloaded a program that executes the TCP/IP ping command on schedule. This tool, Ping Plotter, is available from www.winfiles.com as shareware. Richard Ness at Nessoft (www.nessoft.com) developed it. As seen in Figure 2.6, Ping Plotter can be set to generate ping activity on a fixed schedule. Such activity prevents green machine workstations, being used as SBS server machines, from sleeping.

**FIGURE 2.6**

*Ping Plotter can be used to generate SBS system activity.*

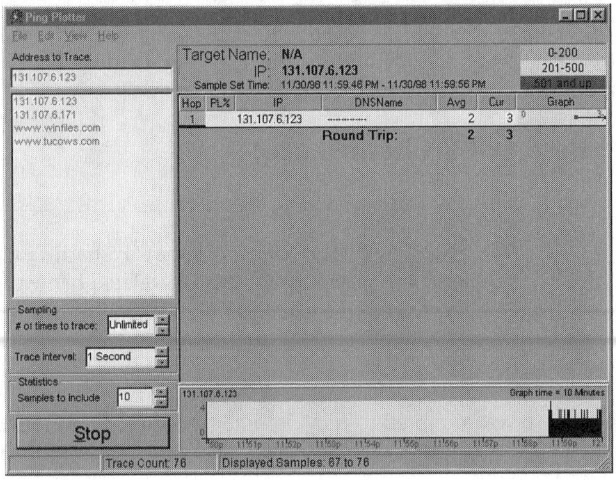

Better yet, buy a really honest server to run SBS on and avoid many of the problems described previously.

## Hardware Necessities

It goes without saying that you should purchase the tape backup unit listed as "optional" in Microsoft's server requirements to back up your valuable data. Other necessities include an uninterruptable power supply (UPS) to protect your system and properly shut it down in a power outage. UPS devices from American Power Corporation (APC) ship with a free copy of PowerChute, a UPS monitoring application that is far superior to the UPS applet found in Control Panel in SBS.

> **Tip**
>
> Another item to consider is a Zip- or Jaz-type drive with removable cartridges. I've used these in one specific case with great success in an SBS scenario. That case is SQL Server. SQL Server allows you to run, via the daily maintenance wizard, an on-the-fly device and table backup separate from the SBS-based tape backup you typically perform at night. This internal backup to SQL Server typically runs at midday, so you get a fresh backup between tape runs. I like to drop these internal SQL Server backups down on a Zip or Jaz drive or CD-ROM burner so that the tape drive is not disturbed. It's something to consider if you are working with SQL Server on your SBS network. And as an aside, if you ever hear a grinding sound with a Zip or Jaz drive, beware.

## Hardware Compatibility List

One of the final hardware issues to be discussed is also one of the most important. SBS is especially finicky about the hardware you select for use on the server machine. Hardware devices that have been tested are listed at www.microsoft.com/smallbusinessserver. This list should be honored under all circumstances. More importantly, if you don't select hardware from the HCL, it is likely you won't receive official Microsoft support when you have problems.

### Network Adapter Cards

I've narrowed my choices for the network adapter cards on the SBS HCL down to two brands (Intel and 3COM), and even then I have a clear favorite.

> **Tip**
>
> That favorite is the 3Com 3C509B Etherlink III Parallel Tasking Adapter (ISA). It always works with SBS. Unfortunately, it's hard to find anymore. Many resellers have stopped carrying this ISA-based gem in favor of the newer PCI network adapters. But you might know that Windows NT Server, the underlying network operating system for SBS, doesn't have native PCI support. Thus, this ISA card remains my favorite!
>
> The 3C905-TX PCI works depending on the release number of the network adapter card. It has been my experience that the 3C905-TX is correctly detected by SBS yet the 3C905B-TX isn't. Note the *B* in the second model listed (it a revision to the original 3C905 network adapter card).
>
> I've had mixed results with the Intel EtherExpress PRO/100B PCI LAN Adapter. On many machines, it has been autodetected flawlessly. On other machines, it has shown up as the Intel 82557-based Ethernet Adapter, which is incorrect. Interestingly, this phantom Intel network adapter isn't even listed on the HCL.

The bottom line regarding SBS network adapters is that I've tried to stay with the major brands to avoid autodetection problems during setup of the SBS server machine.

**Power Tool Tip**

> If your NIC fails to autodetect, install the supplied phantom NIC, called the MS LoopBack Adapter.
>
> After the initial install has been completed, you can go to the Network control panel and select the Adapters tab. At this point you can add an adapter with the Add button. Use the Have Disk button to install the drivers for NT4. After protocols have been installed for your new adapter, say No to the reboot. At this point, remove the MS LoopBack Adapter, accepting the warning that this adapter will no longer function. Reboot after this change. Assuming the NIC and supplied drivers are functional, SBS now supports the undetected NIC.

### Modems

The SBS HCL lists several modems that are considered acceptable. My SBS experience has shown that only the US Robotics Sportster 33600 External works perfectly day in and day out and is always autodetected during the SBS setup phase. Even the internal version of this prized modem wouldn't always correctly autodetect when setting up SBS. I remain puzzled, but at least I do know what works.

# SBS Budgeting

To wrap up Day 2, don't forget to keep an eye on the farm, that is the SBS budget. I've seen many good SBS project fail not for technical reasons but because business basics, such as creating and adhering to a budget, were ignored.

**Tip**

> When budgeting for your network, be sure to consider the following budget tip. If you're eyeing a more powerful server than you planned on purchasing and are concerned about its cost, perhaps the more-powerful one isn't as expensive as it first appears. For example, let's say a server with more processors, RAM, and storage would cost you an additional $1,500. Now, assuming you recover your costs or depreciate the server over three years, that incremental amount ($1,500) adds up to an extra $500 per year, or roughly $1.50 per day. So ask yourself this: for an extra $1.50 per day, shouldn't you purchase the server you really want? In all likelihood, you will probably enjoy more than $1.50 per day in increased network performance, as measured by your staff's ability to get more work accomplished. Think about it!

**TASK**

## Task 2.11: SBS Budget Sheet

You will find an SBS budget spreadsheet that I've used in Appendix C. If you're ready, go ahead and create a detailed budget, by phase, for your SBS project.

# Summary

I've now completed two days of SBS definition, needs analysis, and planning, and you know what? That is exactly the amount of time I budget for working with SBS customers when performing the same tasks.

2

# DAY 3

# Installing Small Business Server

## AM Time To Install

Today is a big day, the day that you actually install SBS! On the one hand, you could say that installing SBS is nothing more than inserting three setup floppy disks and two SBS CD-ROMs, and performing four reboots. But such an over-simplification of the SBS installation task is incorrect. Already, you have invested two days defining what SBS is, performing a needs analysis, and planning. And don't forget the physical setup of the network awaits as a preinstallation task before you can actually start swapping SBS setup floppies and CD-ROMs.

I assume that you are using a new server machine for SBS. If you are using an old server machine that will be redeployed as an SBS server, many of these steps, such as unpacking the server, do not apply. In the case of Springer Spaniels Unlimited, the firm has purchased the following hardware and software, shown in Table 3.1. The following table is used to verify that everything ordered was indeed received.

**TABLE 3.1**  SPRINGER SPANIELS UNLIMITED HARDWARE AND SOFTWARE

| Item | Description |
|------|-------------|
| Server | Dell PowerEdge 2300, Pentium 350 microprocessor, 128MB RAM, 10GB HD  RAID, 15" VGA Monitor, internal tape backup device, internal CD-ROM drive |
| Modem | US Robotics Sportster 33.6 |
| Network Adapter Card | 3Com 3C509 |
| Printer | HP Color LaserJet 5M with HP JetDirect Card |
| Other Hardware | External Jaz drive, APC UPS with PowerChute |
| Software | Microsoft BackOffice Small Business Server (SBS) version 4.5 5-user version, 5-user SBS client access license (CAL) bump pack, Seagate Backup Exec Small Business Server Suite (tape backup program), Cheyenne AntiVirus Inoculan 4 for Windows NT |
| Miscellaneous | Modem cable, extra CAT5 patch cables, telephone cable, power strip/power tree |

**Note**

> All of this required hardware adheres to the SBS hardware compatibility list (HCL) discussed on Day 2, "Planning for Small Business Server," and present- ed in Appendix B, "HCL." You can find updates to the HCL at  HYPERLINK http:// www.microsoft.com/smallbusinessserver. You are encour- aged to monitor this site regularly and look for changes to either the HCL or System Requirements.

### Task 3.1: Verify Hardware and Software

Now is a great time to verify the received hardware and software against the original orders. This task is typically overlooked, but it is all-important if you need to return something to the manufacturer (for instance, you didn't receive the hardware in good order). Or, as SBS consultants, when we seek to bill our SBS customers, it is important to document that the hardware purchased was indeed received. (Such attention to detail early on this day helps greatly when you, the SBS consultant, want to get paid.)

# Preinstallation Tasks

You need to perform several tasks before the actual setup process commences.

# Unpack and Connect

Assuming that your infrastructure, such as cabling, is in place and the server you have ordered has arrived, it's time to unpack the server and its components from the shipping boxes. If you haven't built a computer before from boxes, it's quite simple. Many name brand servers have color-coded guides so that you know which port the keyboard and mouse attach to. If you are still unsure of yourself, don't hesitate to hire a computer consultant to help you attach and build the computer. In fact, consider hiring a competent high school or college student who is both computer literate and is seeking a few extra dollars. Again, putting together the computer from boxes is quite simple.

After physically building the server, make sure the following items are properly attached to the server box:

- A monitor or screen (be sure to attach the monitor to a power source)
- A keyboard
- A mouse
- A power cable
- External modems (if applicable; your modem might be an internal version)
- An external tape backup device (if applicable)
- Other external devices that connect directly to the server (printers, Zip- or Jaz-type drives, scanners, and so on)
- A network cable (attach the network cable to both the network adapter card port and the wall jack; this connects your server to the network)
- UPS (you can connect the power cables to the UPS, but do not connect the serial cable from the UPS to the serial port on the server yet; see my note on this matter, later in this chapter)

**Caution**

Performing this action affects

- The hardware configuration—You are unpacking the manufacturer's hardware from its shipping boxes and putting the computer together.
- The health of your server and components—Any time you attach components together and introduce electricity, a certain degree of risk exists that an improperly grounded or connected component could be damaged when the power is turned on. Be sure to verify that the computer components are properly connected and plugged in.

Consider reading a book on basic computer hardware definitions and configuration. The following books are suggested:

- *Networking Essentials, Second Edition* from Microsoft Press's MCSE self-study series (ISBN 1-57231-527-X)
- *Peter Norton's Complete Guide to PC Upgrades, Second Edition* from Sams (ISBN 0-672-31483-5)

**Note**

If you have a UPS (discussed on Day 2), do not attach it to the server at this time. UPS devices are attached to the SBS machine via COM ports (the same type of port used by modems). However, SBS integrates each COM port as part of the installation of the mode-related services, so an attached UPS can cause the SBS machine to become confused during the installation of SBS. Bottom line: after SBS is installation of SBS. Bottom line: after SBS is installed, you will hook up the UPS.

**Tip**

Take a moment to open the SBS machine and reseat all of the adapter cards. It has been my experience that a new server shipped across the country from places such as Austin, Texas, can arrive with loose cards, cables, and even memory chips!. Such befallen cards have wreaked havoc with some of my early SBS installs when the internal network adapter card couldn't be detected during setup because it had become partially dislodged from its slot. Another experience I have had when working with new computers is that the ribbon cable located inside the machine (used to connect internal devices to cards or the motherboard) can come loose. If you need to reattach a ribbon cable, remember the rule of thumb regarding which way the cable attaches is the side of the ribbon cable with the red line points to the power supply.

## Check the Network

First, has the cabling been properly attached to the hub? Perhaps this was a task that you assigned to the cabling specialist who installed the cabling at your site. If it hasn't been done, do that now.

### Task 3.2: Green Light Test

To verify the fitness of your network, you must perform the green light test. After everything has been plugged in properly to the network, including the network hub, do the following:

1. Turn on the network hub.

2. Briefly turn on the server computer.

3. Observe whether a port light on the hub turns on (typically illuminates as the color green).

4. Observe whether the network adapter card connection light on the back of the server illuminates (typically green).

5. If you see green lights at both the hub and network adapter connection, you're green lighting!

> **Caution**
>
> Performing this action affects
>
> • Your SBS installation—It is essential that your server and network pass the green light test. Failure to pass this test results in a failed SBS installation because it is a requirement that the SBS server machine be attached to an active hub.
>
> • Your future capability to fully use SBS—If SBS does not install correctly (including being properly attached to an active hub), certain features such as the SBS Console might not work correctly.

> See my advanced topics discussion this afternoon on the SSUP1 error. This error results when SBS is installed without being attached to an active hub.

## Perform Server Quick Tests

So you've connected the computer together and to the network at this point. Now is the time to turn on the computer for a few moments to see whether the BIOS information is correctly displayed on the screen. This quick-and-dirty test is important for several reasons:

• Video card test—If you see no information displayed on the computer monitor, it is possible that the video card has failed. Such was the case during an SBS class I once taught. Not only was the computer unusable for the SBS class, but valuable time was wasted trying to determine exactly what the problem was. At first and second blush, it wasn't entirely clear that the video card had failed; it is the type of problem that can disguise itself.

- Component attachment test—Did you know that if a ribbon cable between the computer motherboard and floppy drive is incorrectly attached, the computer might fail to start, leaving you with only the sound of a failed start up: three quick beeps? This is but an example of how incorrectly configured internal components in your server can prevent you from having success with your computer. These are exactly the type of issues that you want to catch immediately, before you try to install SBS.

- Hidden partition server tools—Starting up the computer also allows us to determine whether the computer manufacturer's server tools were correctly installed on a hidden partition on the hard disk. When manufacturers ship their servers to you, they might or might not install their server tools (Compaq's SmartStart, Dell's Server Assistant, and so on). Typically the paperwork received with the server remains unclear on this point. The best way to test that is to look for language at the top of the screen during the server's power on startup (a.k.a. POST) phase. In the case of Compaq, such language instructs you to hit the F10 key to launch SmartStart.

**Caution**

If the manufacturer's server tool hasn't been installed to a hidden partition on the server, it is essential that you do this now. Failure to do this now would mean that you would forever be prevented from installing these wonderful and helpful tools designed to configure and manage your server. That's because after the operating system and SBS are installed, you cannot go back and install the manufacturer's server tools on a hidden partition.

To install the manufacturer's server tools on your system, be sure to follow the setup instructions for the specific tool. In the case of Compaq's SmartStart, it is very simple. Because a Compaq server is designed, by default, to boot from the CD-ROM drive, you simply place the SmartStart CD-ROM in the CD-ROM drive and restart the computer. On startup, you are (with no further fuss) presented with the SmartStart installation screen. Several minutes and one reboot later, SmartStart is installed on your system. Again, tools such as SmartStart provide the capability to configure your server properly, create driver disks, monitor your server's health, and so on.

- BIOS operating correctly—There is simply no better test to make sure the computer's all-important BIOS is functional than to turn on the machine and observe that the BIOS information (copyright, date, storage device configuration, and so on) is displayed on the screen. Common BIOS names are American Megatrends and Phoenix.

## Task 3.3: BIOS Updates

Take a moment to write down the BIOS vendor, version information, and manufacturing date on a pad of paper for your files. Next, go to the Internet site for that BIOS manufacturer and research whether a BIOS upgrade has been released.

 **Tip**

> It is very common for BIOS manufacturers to release upgrades shortly after the original BIOS has been shipped to market. These upgrades typically consist of bug fixes and the like.

Download the BIOS upgrade and prepare to install or flash the BIOS upgrade.

**Caution**

> Be extremely careful about applying a BIOS upgrade to your server. If you've applied the incorrect BIOS version to your server, the server can be rendered inoperable or become unreliable.

> See the BIOS discussion on upgrades, installation, and flashing at your BIOS manufacturer's home page.
>
> Consider hiring a qualified technician or consultant to research and implement a BIOS upgrade for your server.

- Operating system status—By performing the quick power up test, you can determine whether any operating system has been installed on the computer. It is common for clone makers to both format and SYS (apply basic MS-DOS files) the primary drive (C: drive) of the server. If no operating system has been installed, you will see a character-based error message that indicates the operating system is missing.

> **Note**
>
> If you purchased a name brand server and elected to have SBS preinstalled as discussed on Day 2, you will notice the SBS setup process launches after the initial POST phase terminates.

Yet another test exists that should be performed on your system. This test is the Windows NT Server hardware detection compatibility application (NTHQ) that, as much as possible, determines whether your computer is compatible with Windows NT Server. You will recall from Day 1, "Welcome to Small Business Server," that Windows NT Server, in a modified form, is the underlying network operating system for SBS. Thus, it is essential that you ascertain whether the system is Windows NT Server–compatible.

> **Tip**
>
> Although an important and necessary step, running the Windows NT Server NTHQ application isn't the final word on compatibility. It is meant to serve only as a guide or early warning system. I've installed many systems that, at first appearance, weren't 100% Windows NT Server–compliant. This tool is an aid for you but not the final word.

You'll find the NTHQ application on SBS CD-ROM Disc 1 in the \support\hqtool directory. Run the MAKEDISK.BAT application to create a NTHQ utility disk.

I've used other software tools to assess the fitness of a computer for business use. The \support director on SBS CD-ROM Disc 1 contains other assessment tools. One is a tool, shown in Figure 3.1, that checks ATAPI DMA settings (look in the \support\utils\i386 directory).

**FIGURE 3.1**

*ATAPI DMA settings.*

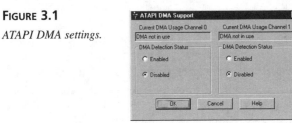

One tool, MSD, is very easy to acquire. Simply copy it from one of your machines running true MS-DOS 5.0 or greater and place it on a MS-DOS system-formatted floppy disk. Boot from the floppy disk and type **MSD** at the command prompt for the floppy drive (typically A:). I've also used CheckIt, a relatively low cost computer assessment application from Touchstone Software. For more information, visit www.checkit.com.

## Backup Your Data

With Springer Spaniels Unlimited, you will recall that you are installing SBS on a brand new Dell server. The company's data initially remains on the old NetWare server until this afternoon, when it will be transferred over the wire or across the network to the new SBS server. That said, the data backup precautions are nothing out of the ordinary: last night's backup should be verified.

Assuming you are like many small businesses and hope to reuse your existing server for SBS, you are confronted with major data backup issues. That is, how do you transfer data, via a single machine, from your previous operating system (say NetWare) to SBS. This is an advanced topic that I address this afternoon in the section "Advanced SBS Setup Issues."

## Review Release Notes

Take my advice and print the README.DOC file contained on SBS CD-ROM Disc 1 in the root directory (for example, D:README.DOC). Not only are some of the preinstallation topics discussed, but many of your questions regarding SBS and its limitations will be answered.

### Task 3.4: Read the README!

Take the Release Notes you printed (README.DOC) and go get a cup of coffee for 20 minutes. Use that opportunity to review these notes. Be sure to take a highlighter pen, because you will inevitably mark interesting and important passages.

## SBS Installation Overview

Allow me to take a moment to outline the SBS installation process for you. This setup blueprint is important to understand because, if your setup fails at midpoint, you can quickly assess at what stage your setup failed. That failure assessment is extremely beneficial in troubleshooting any setup problems you might be having. Your understanding of the setup process will also help you communicate with your SBS consultant or Microsoft support.

**Note** These setup steps assume that you have purchased SBS as a stand-alone software package. These are not the same steps undertaken by the preinstalled (or OEM) version of SBS. The SBS preinstallation approach is discussed this afternoon.

## Task 3.5: SBS Setup for Springer Spaniels Unlimited

Starting here, you set up the SBS server computer for Springer Spaniels Unlimited. You'll complete this before lunch. More advanced SBS setup topics are covered after lunch.

The SBS installation process can be divided into six discrete steps (shown in Figure 3.2).

**FIGURE 3.2**

*SBS installation overview.*

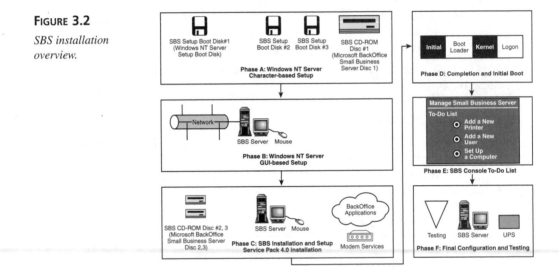

## Phase A: Windows NT Server Character-Based Setup

This phase consists of inserting the three SBS setup floppy disks and the first SBS CD-ROM (Microsoft BackOffice Small Business Server Disc 1) when requested. You must answer questions regarding the standard hardware and software components that were detected (Standard PC, Microsoft Serial Mouse, and so on). Create and format a hard disk partition between 2GB and 4GB in size. Extensive file copying occurs at this stage from each of the floppies and CD-ROM Disc 1. The computer reboots twice.

This phase is represented by SBS setup tasks 1 through 12 below.

## Phase B: Windows NT Server GUI-Based Setup

After the second reboot, you are presented with a Windows-like graphical user interface (GUI) to complete the installation of Windows NT Server. Provide a user name for registration purposes and an organization name. Either accept the automatically created computer and domain name (created from your organization), or provide your own computer and domain name.

▼

▼ Observe the networking components being installed and tell Windows NT Server to start the networking services. Select the correct time zone for the SBS computer. The correct computer monitor settings are tested and, after additional Windows NT Server files are copied over, the SBS computer reboots.

This phase is represented by SBS setup tasks 13 through 17 below.

## Phase C: SBS Installation and Setup

The computer automatically restarts, selects the BackOffice Small Business Server boot option, and performs an autologon. The Microsoft Small Business Server Setup Welcome dialog box appears, and you answer setup questions regarding

- Software licensing
- SBS CD-Key entry
- Installed modems
- Installed hardware
- Company information
- Administrator's password
- Office 2000 CD-Key
- Telephone settings
- SQL Server settings
- General SBS installation paths

After you provide this information, all of the SBS components and applications (Internet Explorer, SQL Server, Exchange Server, and the like) are installed. During this phase, you insert at least SBS CDs #2 and #3. If you are installing Microsoft Office 2000, insert the two Office 2000 CDs. At the end of this phase, you need to click Finish in a dialog box indicating the SBS setup process has completed. The SBS computer asks you to approve a reboot.

This phase is represented by SBS setup tasks 18 through 36 below.

**Note**

Regarding the SBS installation process, actual installation time varies greatly. It can take anywhere from 30 minutes to over two hours depending on the speed of your CD-ROM drive, hard disk, and CPU microprocessor and the installation selections that you made (Complete or Custom). The amount of RAM also affects setup times.

▼

## ▼ Phase D: Completion and Initial Boot (Boot Phase Details)

This phase represents the first official logon to the underlying Windows NT Server operating system. The boot stages within this phase are beyond the scope of the AM session, but are discussed in advanced texts such as the *Windows NT Server Resource Kit* (Microsoft Press). Log on with the administrator user account and password.

### Phase E: SBS Console / To-Do List

When you first log on to the SBS computer after completing the installation, you are presented with a To Do List of tasks to complete. These are

1. Add a New Printer. This is where you would add a new printer to the SBS computer and make it available to the network.

2. Add a New User. This is where you would add a new user to the SBS network.

3. Set Up a Computer. This is where you would set up a computer on the network.

4. Sign Up with an Internet Service Provider (ISP). This is where you would select an ISP that supports modem-based connections from an SBS computer.

5. Add User Licenses. This is a very important step where you add the additional client access licenses (CALs) to the system.

6. Create an Emergency Repair Disk. This disk, known as the ERD, contains critical system configuration information, so it is important that you create this disk and store it in a safe place.

Microsoft created the To Do List with the idea that you would complete each step in order, but experience has shown that this order isn't necessarily practical or desirable. Understand that nothing prevents you from either following the To Do List step-by-step or using a modified To Do List approach.

In the case of Springer Spaniels Unlimited, use a modified To Do List approach. Before lunch, as part of the initial SBS setup process, you will add a printer, add the additional user licenses, and create the emergency repair disk (ERD). On Day 4, "Setting Up the Workstation Client," you will return to the To Do List and add new users and set up new computers. You will also create another ERD to reflect the new system configuration. On Day 9, "Connecting to the Internet," you will return to the To Do List and connect to an Internet service provider.

**Note**

You can return to the To Do List at any time, not just the first time that you log on to the SBS computer.

## ▼ Phase F: Final Configuration and Testing

This phase resolves loose ends. This includes attaching and making operational the uninterruptable power supply (UPS) that I specified on Day 2. You also check the event log to ensure that the SBS installation went well (from a Windows NT Server event log or problem-monitoring point of view). You also perform some basic SBS system tests so

▲  that you know you're ready to proceed to Day 4, with confidence.

# Ready, Set, Go

Make sure you're familiar and armed with the numerous SBS setup sheets from Day 2. If this is your first pass through the book, these sheets, reflecting setup information for Springers Spaniels Unlimited, have been completed for you. If this is your second pass through the book, and you're installing SBS for real, gather the setup sheets from Appendix C, "SBS Project Kit," that you have completed. Much of the information on the setup sheets will be called for in the next section. You are now ready to install SBS.

**3**

---

**Note**

The first step assumes that you have the three boot floppy disks needed by SBS's setup process. If you don't, here are the steps for creating the three setup disks. To create boot disks:

1. Insert Disc 1 into the CD-ROM drive.

2. On the Start menu, point to Programs, and then click Command Prompt.

3. In Command Prompt, change the drive to your CD-ROM drive letter. If your CD-ROM drive is E:, type **E:** and press the Enter key.

4. Type **cd i386**.

5. Type **winnt32 /ox**.

6. After the third boot disk is created, copy winnt.sif from d:\support directory (replace d: with the correct drive letter for your CD-ROM) to boot disk 2.

If you do not copy winnt.sif to boot disk 2, SBS will not install properly.

If you want to run the emergency repair process, you need three boot disks without winnt.sif on boot disk 2, which suggests you should make a copy of Disk 2 adhering to this condition.

# SBS Setup

1. Insert the Windows NT Server Setup Boot Disk in floppy drive A: and turn on your computer.

2. When you see the following screen, insert SBS Setup Disk #2 (a.k.a. Windows NT Server Setup Disk #2) and press the Enter key.

```
Please insert the disk labeled
Microsoft BackOffice Small
Business Server 4.5  Diskette #2
into Drive A:
* Press ENTER when ready.

ENTER=Continue    F3=Exit
```

3. A Windows NT Server Setup screen appears after several minutes which communicates the following:

```
Setup automatically detects floppy disk controllers
and standard ESDI/IDE hard disks without user intervention.
However, on some computers, detection of certain
other mass storage devices, such as
SCSI adapters and CD-ROM drives, can cause
the computer to become unresponsive or to malfunction.

For this reason, you can bypass Setup's mass storage device
detection and manually select SCSI adapters, CD-ROM drives,
and special disk controllers (such as drive arrays) for
installation.

*     To continue, press ENTER.  Setup will attempt to
detect mass storage devices in your computer.
*     To skip mass storage device detection, press S.
Setup will allow you to manually select SCSI

F3=Exit    ENTER=Continue    S=Skip Detection
```

Here you select Enter to continue the setup if you have a equipment that is supported by SBS's HCL. If you know that you need to specify a device driver, such as a RAID array controller, select S to skip detection.

**Power Tool Tip**

> If you have an IDE hard disk (a.k.a. large IDE hard disk), you need to select S and insert a disk containing the latest atapi.sys (contained on the Service Pack 4 CD-ROM). The old atapi.sys driver, supplied as of Service Pack 3, doesn't support IDE hard disks over 8GB, and Service Pack 4 isn't installed on your SBS Server machine until after Windows NT Server with Service Pack 3 has been installed. See Microsoft TechNet article ID: Q197667 titled "Installing Windows NT Server on a Large IDE Hard Disk" at www.microsoft.com/support on your TechNet CD-ROM.

In the case of Springer Spaniels Unlimited, select Enter to continue.

4. When you see the following screen, insert SBS Setup Disk #3 (a.k.a. Windows NT Server Setup Disk #3) and press the Enter key.

```
Please insert the disk labeled
Microsoft BackOffice Small
Business Server 4.5 Diskette #3
into Drive A:
*  Please ENTER when Ready

F3=Exit    ENTER=Continue
```

5. You see the following screen:

```
Setup has recognized the following mass storage devices
in your computer:
IDE CD-ROM (ATAPI 1.2)/PCI IDE Controller

*    To specify additional SCSI adapters, CD-ROM drives, or
special disk controllers for use with Windows NT,
including those for which you have a device support
disk, from a mass storage manufacturer, press S.
*    If you do not have any device support disks from a
mass storage device manufacturer, or do not want to
specify additional mass storage devices for use with
Windows NT, press ENTER.

S=Specify Additional Device    ENTER=Continue    F3=Exit
```

In the case of Springer Spaniels Unlimited, press Enter.

**Power Tool Tip**

Regarding the large IDE hard disk issue, you cannot specify the revised atapi.sys driver by pressing **S** at this point because, as you just saw, the existing IDE driver doesn't support large IDE hard disks (IDE CD-ROM (ATAPI 1.2)/PCI IDE Controller) and cannot be deleted.

6. When you see the following screen, insert the SBS CD-ROM Disc 1 (a.k.a. Microsoft BackOffice Small Business Server Disc 1). Press Enter.

```
Please insert the compact disc labeled
Microsoft BackOffice Small Business Server Disc 1
into your CD-ROM drive.
*  Press ENTER when ready.

F3=Exit    ENTER=Continue
```

7. When you see the following screen, press Enter if you want to make no changes; otherwise, make the necessary changes, and press Enter. This screen reflects what hardware the Windows NT Server setup program detected on your system.

```
Setup has determined that your computer contains the
following hardware and software components.

Computer:  Standard PC
Display:  Auto Detect
Keyboard:  XT, AT, or Enhanced Keyboard (83-104 keys)
Keyboard Layout:  US
Pointing Device:  Microsoft Serial Mouse

No Changes:  The above list matches my computer.

If you want to change any item in the list, press the UP or DOWN
ARROW key to move the highlight to the item you want
to change.  Then press ENTER to see alternatives for that item.

When all the items in the list are correct, move the
highlight to "The above list matches my computer"
and press ENTER.

ENTER=Select   F3=Exit
```

8. Assuming you have a new hard disk, you see the following screen. The actual
   space value (MB) varies depending on how large your hard disk is. In this case, the
   hard disk is 4GB.

```
The list below shows existing partitions and spaces
available for creating new partitions.

Use UP and DOWN ARROW keys to move the highlight
to an item in the list.
* To install Windows NT on the highlighted partition
or unpartitioned space, press ENTER.
* To create a partition in the unpartitioned space, press C.
* To delete the highlighted partition, press D.

 _ _ _ _ _ _ _ _ _ _ _ _ _ _ _ _ _ _ _ _ _ _ _ _ _ _
|                                                      |
| 4119 MB Disk 0 at Id 0 on bus 0 on atapi             |
|    Unpartitioned space                    4118 MB    |
|                                                      |
|                                                      |
|                                                      |
|                                                      |
|                                                      |
|                                                      |
|                                                      |
 _ _ _ _ _ _ _ _ _ _ _ _ _ _ _ _ _ _ _ _ _ _ _ _ _ _

ENTER=Install   C=Create Partition   F1=Help  F3=Exit
```

9. You need to create a partition for Windows NT Server and SBS to install on. Select
   **C** on your keyboard to create this partition. This partition ranges in size from 2GB

(the smallest system partition size SBS supports) to 4GB (the largest system partition size that SBS supports). In the case of Springer Spaniels Unlimited, enter 4000 (for 4GB) on the following screen (which is displayed after you select C.

```
You have asked Setup to create a new partition on
4119 MB Disk 0 at Id 0 on bus 0 on atapi.

*To create the new partition, enter a size below and press ENTER.
*To return to the previous screen without creating the partition,
press ESC.

The minimum size for the new partition is    8 megabytes (MB).
The maximum size for the new partition is 4118 megabytes (MB).
Create partition of size (in MB):  4000
```

Press Enter to return to the screen similar to that shown above in step 8 above.

10. Press Enter when you see the screen below to install Windows NT Server and (in several steps) SBS on the newly created 4GB system partition.

```
The list below shows existing partitions and spaces available
for creating new partitions.

Use UP and DOWN ARROW keys to move the highlight to an
item in the list.
*To install Windows NT on the highlighted partition or
unpartitioned space, press ENTER.
* To create a partition in the unpartitioned space, press C.
* To delete the highlighted partition, press D.
```

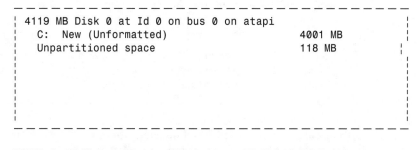

```
 _ _ _ _ _ _ _ _ _ _ _ _ _ _ _ _ _ _ _ _ _ _ _ _ _ _ _ _ _
¦ 4119 MB Disk 0 at Id 0 on bus 0 on atapi                ¦
¦   C:  New (Unformatted)                  4001 MB        ¦
¦     Unpartitioned space                  118 MB         ¦
¦                                                         ¦
¦                                                         ¦
¦                                                         ¦
¦                                                         ¦
¦                                                         ¦
¦                                                         ¦
 _ _ _ _ _ _ _ _ _ _ _ _ _ _ _ _ _ _ _ _ _ _ _ _ _ _ _ _ _
```

```
ENTER=Install   C=Create Partition   F1=Help  F3=Exit
```

11. The following screen asks you to format the C: drive (or system partition). It is essential that you select the NTFS formatting option because SBS installs only on an NTFS partition. Press Enter after selecting NTFS.

```
The partition you have chosen is newly created and thus unformatted.
Setup will now format the partition.
```

```
Select a file system for the partition from the list below.
Use the UP and DOWN ARROW keys to move the highlight
to the file system you want and then press ENTER.

If you want to select a different partition for Windows NT,
 press ESC.

  Format the partition using the FAT file system.
  Format the partition using the NTFS file system.
```

> Note that you will receive an error message at this point if you have tried
> to create and format a partition greater than 4GB in size. If you receive such
> an error message, you must go back and create a partition that is smaller
> than 4GB before continuing.

Setup now formats the hard disk partition you have just created. Initially, the partition is formatted as FAT and then converted to NTFS later when the machine reboots. This formatting process takes several minutes. Feel free to get a cup of coffee to pass the time.

12. You must now remove SBS Setup Disk #3 from your floppy drive A: even though nothing requests that you do so. After several minutes of file copying from SBS CD-ROM Disc 1, the computer automatically reboots itself. If SBS setup Disk #3 is still in drive A:, the machine will not boot properly.

    Remove SBS setup Disk #3 now from floppy drive A:.

> After the initial partition formatting has been completed, numerous
> Windows NT Server–related files (.inf, .exe, .dll, .wav, .sys, .fon, .hlp) are
> copied over to the newly FAT formatted partition.

13. The SBS machine reboots after several minutes. After the NTFS partition is completely formatted and another reboot occurs, the GUI-based Windows NT Server phase commences.

14. You are next presented with the Name and Organization dialog box. Recall from Day 2, Table 2.4, that the information you need to enter is readily available. That information is

```
Name:  Bob Estes
Organization:  Springer Spaniels Unlimited
Computer Name:  SPRINGERS01
Domain:  SPRINGERS
```

After entering this information, click Next.

**Caution**
Never use all numeric digits for your Computer Name with SBS 4.5. Doing so is problematic and causes numerous problems on your SBS network. Also avoid using hyphens in your Computer Name if you plan to use SQL Server 7.0. Needless to say, SQL Server 7.0 doesn't like hyphens in computer names.

15. Click Next when presented with the dialog box advising you the Setup is now ready to guide you through the setup of Windows NT Networking.

**Note**
If your network adapter card is not automatically detected, the MS Loopback adapter is installed by default. Unlike in regular Windows NT Server, you are not offered the opportunity to select a network adapter card from a list or provide a network adapter card driver on a disk.

The MS Loopback adapter is installed to allow completion of the Windows NT Server networking services and functionality. After SBS is installed, you need to properly install your network adapter card via the Network applet in the Control Panel.

I have also found that SBS misdetects network adapters, such as I discussed on Day 2 with the Intel network adapter cards. When such is the case, you need to install the correct network adapter card drivers via the Network applet in Control Panel after SBS has been completely installed.

Finally, this applies to systems that have two or more network adapter cards. Only one network adapter card is installed during setup. SBS installs the first network adapter card it finds. And even if both NIC cards are identical, only the first network adapter card is installed. You install the second network adapter card (manually).

16. Select your time zone when presented with the Date and Time Properties dialog box, as shown in Figure 3.3.

**FIGURE 3.3**

*Select your time zone.*

Check the time displayed at the lower-right corner of your monitor. If necessary, select the Date and Time tab sheet as shown in Figure 3.4.

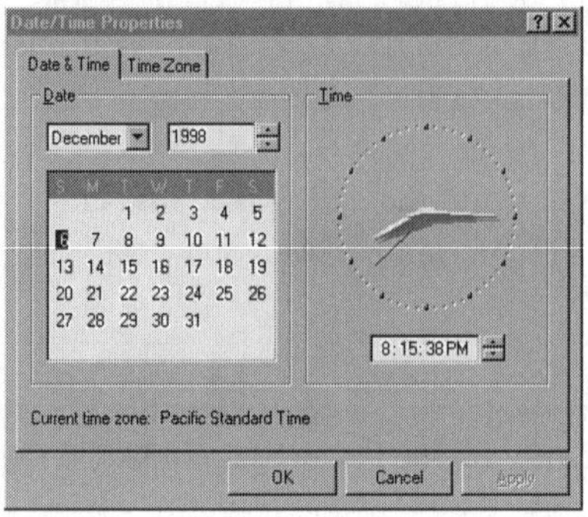

**FIGURE 3.4**

*Adjust your time and date.*

After selecting your time zone and correcting the date and time, click Close.

For Springer Spaniels Unlimited, select Pacific Time. You can enter whatever day and time you desire.

17. After additional computer files are copied and initial security settings are invoked, the SBS computer reboots and displays the following information on its boot screen.

```
OS Loader V4.00

Please select the operating system to start:

    BackOffice Small Business Server
    BackOffice Small Business Server (VGA Mode)

Use Up Arrow or Down Arrow to move the highlight to your choice.
Press Enter to choose.
```

The first selection, BackOffice Small Business Server, is selected if no key on your keyboard is touched within the 30-second default menu selection time frame. If you want to expedite the process, hit Enter while the BackOffice Small Business Server menu option is selected.

You do not need to log on manually at this point because an autologon occurs.

18. You are greeted by the Small Business Server 4.5 Setup Wizard. The Welcome notice shown in Figure 3.5 tells you that Service Pack 4 will now be installed. Click Next.

**FIGURE 3.5**

*Welcome.*

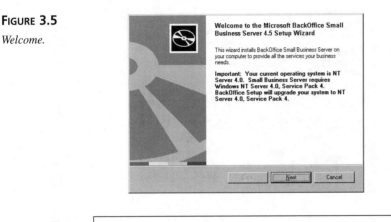

**Power Tool Tip**

Now is the time to drop under the hood and run Disk Administrator (found in the Administrative Tools (Common) program group) to create, format, and assign drive letters to your additional, unused hard disk space. By doing that now, when you're presented with the screens that allow you to redirect where specific applications are installed and data is stored, you will have additional hard disk space ready and be able and willing to go to work. That is, on the "Your Small Business Server Installation" and "Folders for Small Business Server Data" dialog boxes shown in several pages, you can select drive D: or higher.

Note that this is an undocumented trick.

19. You are presented with the Software License Agreement. If you select the I Agree button, the setup routine continues. If you select the I Disagree button, the setup routine terminates.

    Read the software license agreement, select I Agree, and click Next.

20. The Identification screen now appears. You are shown the Name (Bob Estes) and Organization (Springer Spaniels Unlimited) fields. This is your last chance to change the Name and Organization fields. You also need to enter the 10-digit CD Key that is found on the yellow sticker on the back of your SBS CD case. Click Next.

21. You now see the Installed Modems screen as seen in Figure 3.6. This is your opportunity to agree or disagree with the results of the modem detection that occurred. In fact, the legend displays an *X* and an informational symbol (!) to better assist you with determining the current status of your modem.

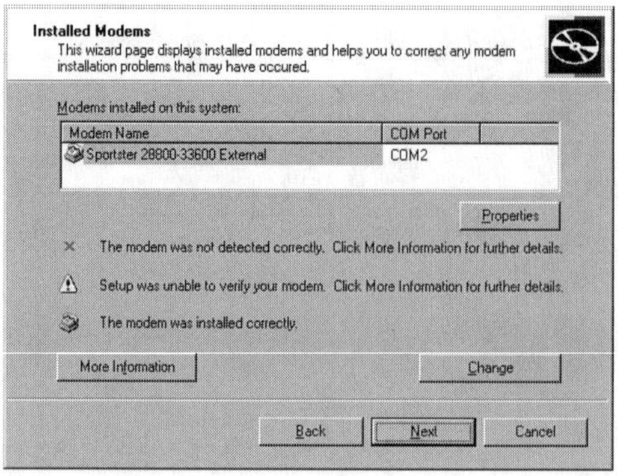

**FIGURE 3.6**

*Installed Modems.*

**Note**

The Installed Modems screen is one of the best fixes in SBS 4.5 compared to earlier SBS versions. This screen allows you to provide a modem manufacturer's drivers disk and prevent the ill-fated "standard modem" installation of the SBS 4.0/4.0a days.

Assuming the modem information is accurate, click Next.

22. The Hardware Confirmation screen appears. Critical hardware devices such as network adapters are displayed. This is seen in Figure 3.7.

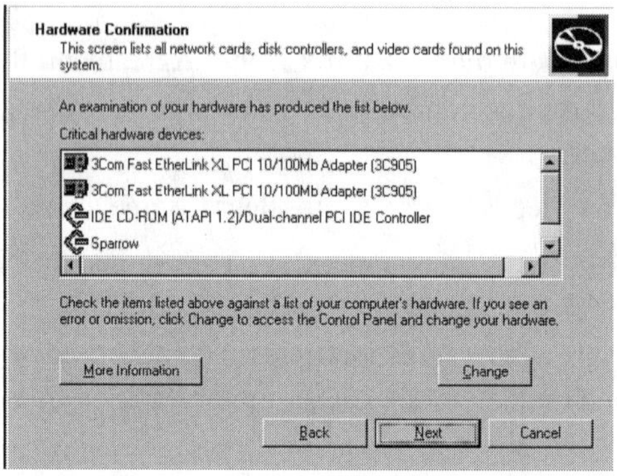

**FIGURE 3.7**

*Hardware Confirmation.*

**Note**

Even though two network adapter cards are displayed in Figure 3.7, only one is actually installed as part of the SBS setup.

If the hardware information is accurate, click Next.

Service Pack 4.0 is automatically installed and the machine reboots.

23. After you're automatically logged on, the Small Business Server 4.5 Setup wizard informs you that Service Pack 4.0 was successfully installed and that your server applications will now be installed. This is shown in Figure 3.8. Click Next.

**FIGURE 3.8**

*Service Pack 4.0 installation completed.*

24. The Company Information dialog box, shown in Figure 3.9, is displayed. Fill in the Company Address, City, State/Province, and Zip/Postal Code fields. For Springer Spaniels Unlimited, obtain this information from Table 2.4 on Day 2.

**FIGURE 3.9**

*Company Information.*

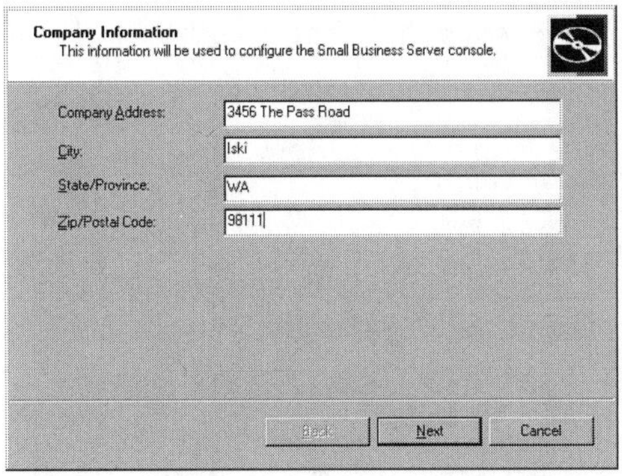

25. The Administrator Account Password screen appears. Enter the Administrator's password. In the case of Springer Spaniels Unlimited, this is password. Click Next.

26. If you have purchased the SBS version that included Microsoft Office 2000, you are presented with the Microsoft Office 2000 Identification screen as shown in Figure 3.10.

**FIGURE 3.10**

*Microsoft Office 2000
CD Key.*

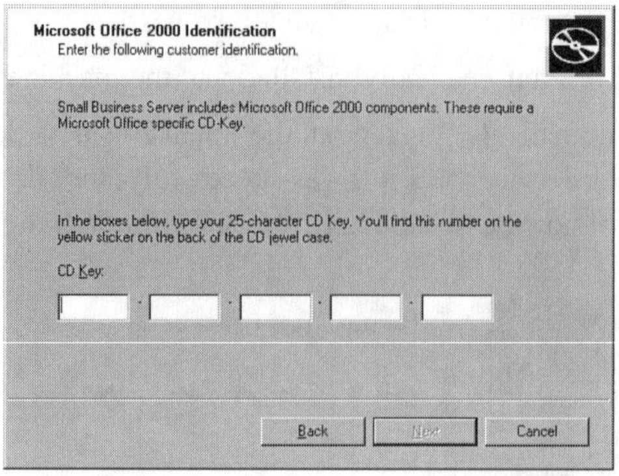

> **Note**
>
> I've left the fields blank because the contents are displayed on the screen. You need to enter your own CD Key numbers found on the case of your Office 2000 CD box. Click Next.

27. You now select between a Complete or Custom Installation on the Installation Options screen. Select Complete as the installation type for Springer Spaniels Unlimited and click Next.

28. The Telephone Properties dialog box appears. Complete the country, area code, fax number, outside line, and tone/pulse options as shown in Figure 3.11 and documented in your server setup sheet for Springer Spaniels Unlimited (Table 2.4 from Day 2).

**FIGURE 3.11**

*Telephone Properties.*

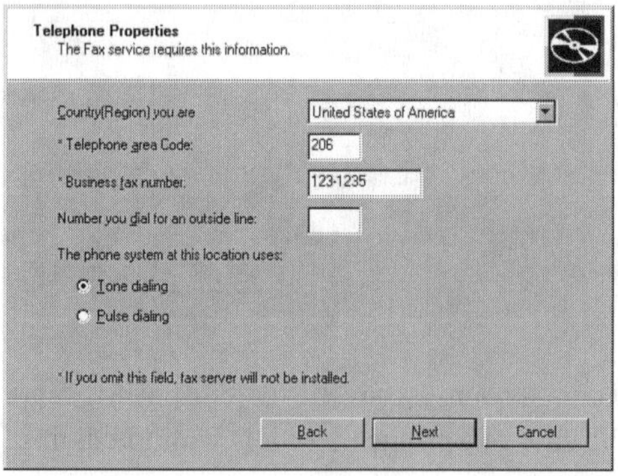

**Tip**

Complete as many fields as possible on all SBS setup dialog boxes when you set up your own SBS machine. Much of this information, known as *metainformation*, is used in other places within SBS for the life of the system.

29. The SQL Database Configuration screen appears, as seen in Figure 3.12. For Springer Spaniels Unlimited, accept the default Character Set, Sort Order, and Unicode Collation settings. Click Next.

**FIGURE 3.12**

*SQL Database Configuration.*

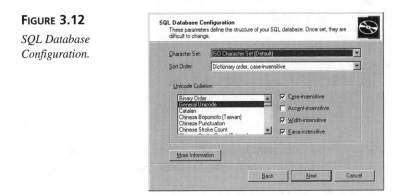

30. The next screen, Your Small Business Server Installation, allows you to redirect the installation path for numerous SBS components. This is a major improvement in the installation process from previous versions of SBS and is shown in Figure 3.13.

**FIGURE 3.13**

*Installation Paths.*

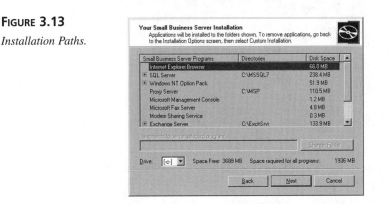

For Springer Spaniels Unlimited, accept the default settings and click Next.

31. The Folder for Small Business Server Data is now displayed as seen in Figure 3.14. In the case of Springer Spaniels Unlimited, accept the defaults and click Next.

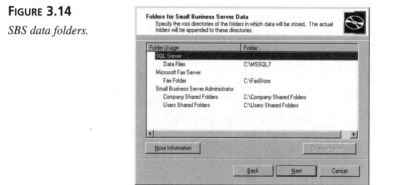

32. The Small Business Server Component Installation screen appears as seen in Figure 3.15. This installation process starts automatically; you don't need to click Next.

The following SBS components are installed in the order shown:

1. Internet Explorer browser

2. Microsoft Management Console

3. SQL Server

4. Windows NT Option Pack

5. Proxy Server

6. Microsoft Fax Server

7. Modem Sharing Service

8. Exchange Server

9. Small Business Server Administrator

10. Client applications

 **Note**
> After Internet Explorer is installed, the SBS server machine reboots. The SBS component installation continues upon restart.

33. When requested, insert Microsoft BackOffice Small Business Server 4.5 CD #2 and click OK. Be sure to not confuse this request with a later request for the Office 2000 CD #2. This request is, as stated, for SBS's CD #2.

34. When requested, insert the Microsoft BackOffice Small Business Server 4.5 CD #3 and click OK. The installation continues with Exchange Server.

35. (Optional) When requested, insert the Microsoft Office 2000 Professional Disc #1 and click OK.

36. (Optional) When requested, insert the Microsoft Office 2000 Professional Disc #2 and click OK.

    Near the end, you see a dialog box titled Windows NT Service Pack Setup that communicates that the Service Pack Setup is updating system files. A progress bar shows you how much of the task has been completed.

**Note**
> It's very common to reapply a service pack after installing BackOffice components. That's exactly what is occurring here.

37. You are ultimately presented with the Completing the Microsoft BackOffice Small Business Server 4.5 Setup Wizard dialog box. Click Finish. Click Yes when asked to restart the SBS computer.

Congratulations! You have now completed the base installation of your SBS Server. Now, more configuration items await you.

| Note | After restarting, SBS performs some background housekeeping duties. You see a dialog box that communicates that data access is being configured. Don't be alarmed. These are one-time configuration events. |

## Time Flies!

The basic SBS setup process from Phase A to the end of Phase D should take anywhere from 90 to 180 minutes, depending on the speed of your computer. Dual-processor computers are much faster than single processor computers and complete this SBS installation process in under 90 minutes. I've heard rumors that one SBS 4.5 server machine was installed in just over 30 minutes with four processors and a 40×-speed CD-ROM drive. That's flying!

## Initial Boot

SBS is completely installed, so the next reboot, caused by step 25 above, results in an autologon. You aren't asked for your username (administrator) or password (password) yet. The technical stages of the boot and logon process are reviewed after lunch in an advanced section, but for now, enjoy the free ride; you get to log on with your user name and password soon.

## SBS Console/To Do List

After successfully logging on for the first time, the To Do List shown in Figure 3.16 automatically appears.

As mentioned earlier in this chapter, right now you completed only three tasks on behalf of Springer Spaniels Unlimited. Other tasks, such as Add a New User, Set Up a Computer, and Sign Up with an Internet Service Provider, are completed on future days.

### Add a New Printer

This, of course, is very simple (like many tasks in SBS). For Springer Spaniels Unlimited, assume that an HP 5M Color LaserJet is attached directly to the SBS computer via the LPT1 port:

1. From SBS Console's To Do List (seen in Figure 3.16 above), select Add a Printer. The Add Printer Wizard launches.

2. Select the My Computer radio button on the Add Printer Wizard, as shown in Figure 3.17. Click Next.

**FIGURE 3.16**

*SBS Console To Do List.*

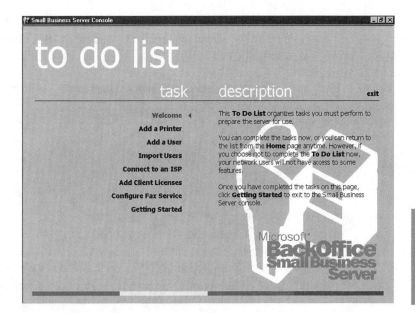

**FIGURE 3.17**

*My Computer selection.*

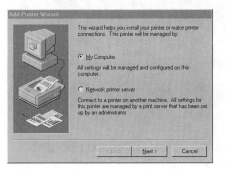

3. Select the LPT1 check box, as shown in Figure 3.18. Click Next.

**FIGURE 3.18**

*LPT1 port.*

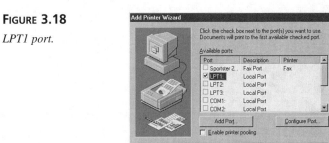

4. Select the HP Color LaserJet 5M printer, as shown in Figure 3.19. You do this by selecting HP in the Manufacturers list box and then HP Color LaserJet 5M in the Printers list box. Click Next.

**FIGURE 3.19**

*Selecting the HP Color LaserJet 5M printer.*

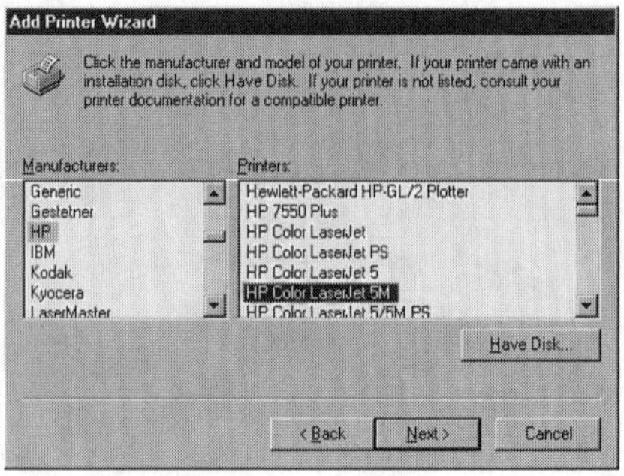

5. Accept the default printer name. Select Yes for whether Windows programs should use this as the default printer, as shown in Figure 3.20. Click Next.

**FIGURE 3.20**

*Printer Name.*

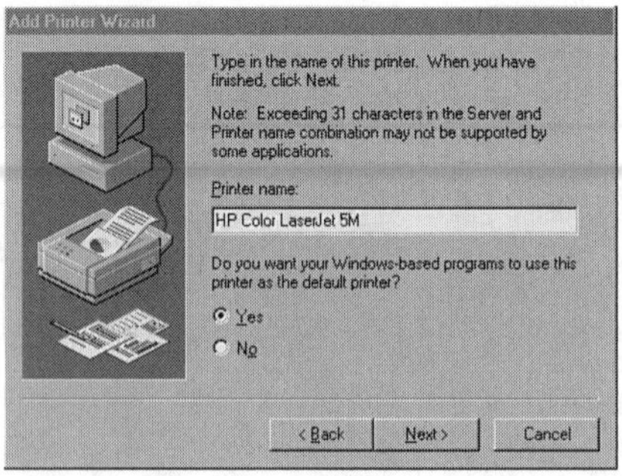

6. Type the share name **HP5MCOLOR** in the Share Name field, as shown in Figure 3.21. Click Next.

**FIGURE 3.21**

*Share Name.*

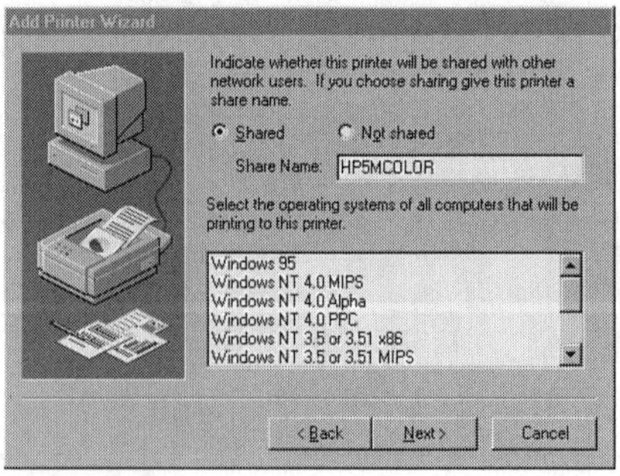

**Tip**

> I recommend that you select the other operating systems that be use this shared printer from the list shown on the bottom half of Figure 3.21. If you do so, what occurs is that the drivers for say, Windows 98, are installed on the SBS server. Later, when you are installing workstations on the SBS network (Day 4), the printer drivers for the workstation are automatically installed. This saves you from having to carry the printer driver disk to each workstation to complete the printer installation. Great trick!

7. Select Yes when asked whether you would like to print a test page as seen in Figure 3.22.

**FIGURE 3.22**

*Print a test page.*

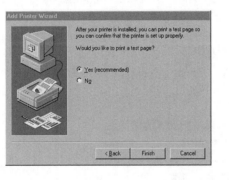

**Tip**

> Printing this test page is actually your first test to see whether your SBS computer is working. You'll perform other tests shortly before lunch.

8. Insert SBS Setup CD-ROM Disc 1 when requested, as shown in Figure 3.23. Disc 1 contains the printer drivers, even though the dialog box doesn't explicitly ask for CD-ROM Disc 1. Also note that the dialog box makes an assumption where the about the Disc 1 drive letter where the \i386 directory is located. Correct this driver letter as necessary.

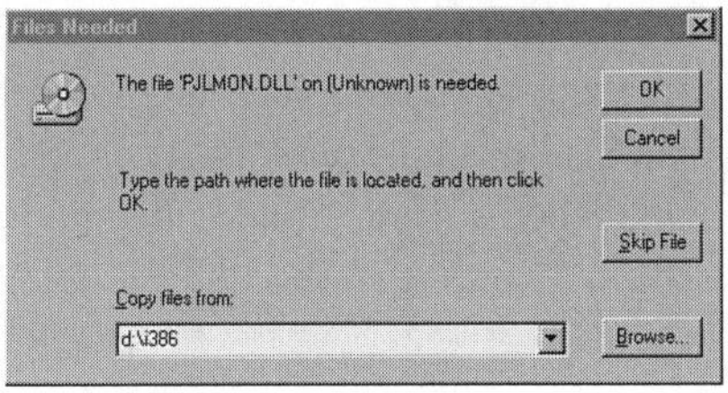

**FIGURE 3.23**

*Files Needed. Insert SBS Setup CD-ROM Disc 1.*

9. Answer Yes if the test page correctly printed. (You probably don't have this type of printer connected to LPT1, but you'll pretend that you did and it worked properly)

Of course, when you install your printer on your SBS computer for real, you should answer truthfully, either Yes or No, as to whether the printer test page printed.

**Note**

It is not and wasn't a problem to install the above printer for Springer Spaniels Unlimited even if your computer system has no such printer. SBS isn't smart enough to check LPT1 and confirm the printer setup.

This afternoon I discuss advanced SBS printer configuration issues including the use of HP JetDirect cards.

## Add Client Licenses

Selecting this option, Add Client Licenses, from the SBS Console To Do List displays the Help screen shown in Figure 3.24.

**FIGURE 3.24**

*Add Client Licenses help screen.*

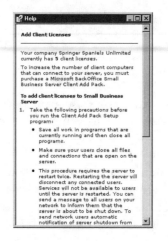

The process for adding user licenses is very simple. Put the license disk in the your floppy drive A: and click the *here* hypertext field at step 3 at the bottom of the Add User License help screen. After a moment of copying licensing information, you are asked to remove the license disk and the SBS machine reboots. After additional licensing configuration activity, the SBS machine reboots again. You log on and your license upgrade is complete.

**Note**

You need to perform the above activity for as many license disks as you have, and, because it can take up to 10 minutes for an SBS machine to reboot, be sure to factor that time consumption in as you plan to add more licenses. In short, the process is simple, but it takes longer than you might think.

You might have to call Microsoft Product Support (PSS) if you've already used your license disk once before. The license disk makes an entry that it has been used previously by recording the network adapter card address (MAC address) on the disk. If you call PSS, they will give you a new code to unlock the license disk for another use. You might not encounter this problem at all, but just be advised.

## Create an Emergency Repair Disk

This is one of the most important steps in the SBS setup routine. The Emergency Repair Disk (ERD) contains very important system information (user accounts, system settings, and configurations) that can recover your system in an emergency. You should update ERD periodically after significant changes have been made to your SBS network.

For the purposes of Springer Spaniels Unlimited, you create an ERD right now and again at the end of Day 4:

1. From the SBS Console, select More Tasks, then Manage Disks, and then Create an Emergency Repair Disk.

2. Read the Create an Emergency Repair Disk help menu. Select option #1 on this help menu to start the ERD creation process, as shown in Figure 3.25.

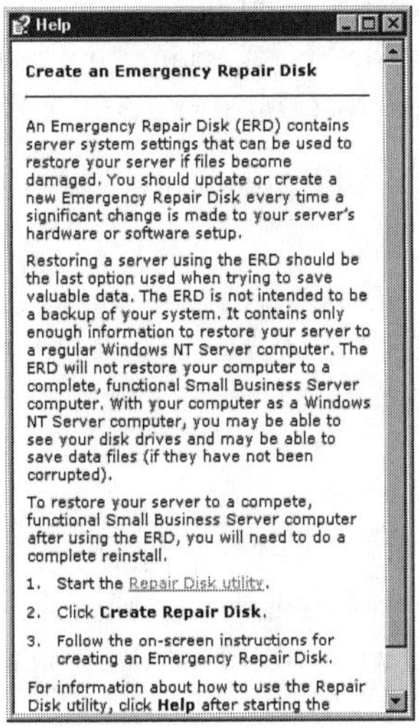

**FIGURE 3.25**

*The Create an Emergency Repair Disk help menu.*

> **Help**
>
> **Create an Emergency Repair Disk**
>
> An Emergency Repair Disk (ERD) contains server system settings that can be used to restore your server if files become damaged. You should update or create a new Emergency Repair Disk every time a significant change is made to your server's hardware or software setup.
>
> Restoring a server using the ERD should be the last option used when trying to save valuable data. The ERD is not intended to be a backup of your system. It contains only enough information to restore your server to a regular Windows NT Server computer. The ERD will not restore your computer to a complete, functional Small Business Server computer. With your computer as a Windows NT Server computer, you may be able to see your disk drives and may be able to save data files (if they have not been corrupted).
>
> To restore your server to a compete, functional Small Business Server computer after using the ERD, you will need to do a complete reinstall.
>
> 1. Start the Repair Disk utility.
> 2. Click **Create Repair Disk**.
> 3. Follow the on-screen instructions for creating an Emergency Repair Disk.
>
> For information about how to use the Repair Disk utility, click **Help** after starting the

**3**

3. Select the Create Repair Disk button on the Repair Disk Utility application dialog box, as shown in Figure 3.26.

**FIGURE 3.26**

*Repair Disk Utility.*

4. Label an Emergency Repair Disk, insert a floppy disk into drive A:, and select OK at the Repair Disk Utility dialog box that warns you that all data will be erased on this floppy disk.

   First, the disk is formatted, and then important system information will be copied. Be sure to store this floppy disk in a secure area, such as the company's locked safe.

5. Approve the dialog box that reminds you to store the ERD in a safe location.

6. Click Exit from the Repair Disk Utility application.

# Final Configuration and Testing

You're almost finished, and lunch is near.

## UPS

Attach the APC UPS device that was purchased for Springer Spaniels Unlimited. (Don't worry if you don't have this item at your site, but I highly recommend you purchase a UPS for your SBS network.) After the UPS is physically attached, via a serial cable from the back of the UPS to a COM port on the SBS machine, you then install PowerChute, a power management software application that ships with APC UPS devices.

Assuming you installed PowerChute, its UPS monitoring screen appears, as seen in Figure 3.27.

When your site loses power, the UPS (via PowerChute) starts a gradual and safe shutdown of your SBS computer. This type of shutdown is critical for protecting important company data such as accounting information, e-mail, and so on.

## Event Log

I also enjoy checking the system event log under Event View to see how clean my SBS setup and installation was. This is where the rubber meets the road. You will also want to check the application event log to see how the SBS BackOffice applications are functioning.

To view the event logs:

1. Select the Start button at the lower-left of your SBS monitor.

2. Select Programs, Administrative Tools (Common), Event Viewer.

3. By default, the system log is displayed in Event Viewer, as shown in Figure 3.28.

**FIGURE 3.27**

*PowerChute UPS monitoring application.*

**FIGURE 3.28**

*System log in Event Viewer.*

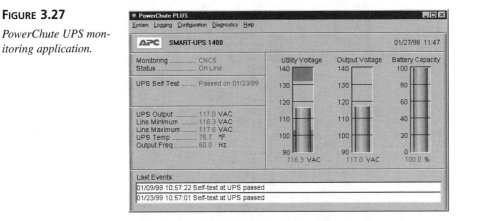

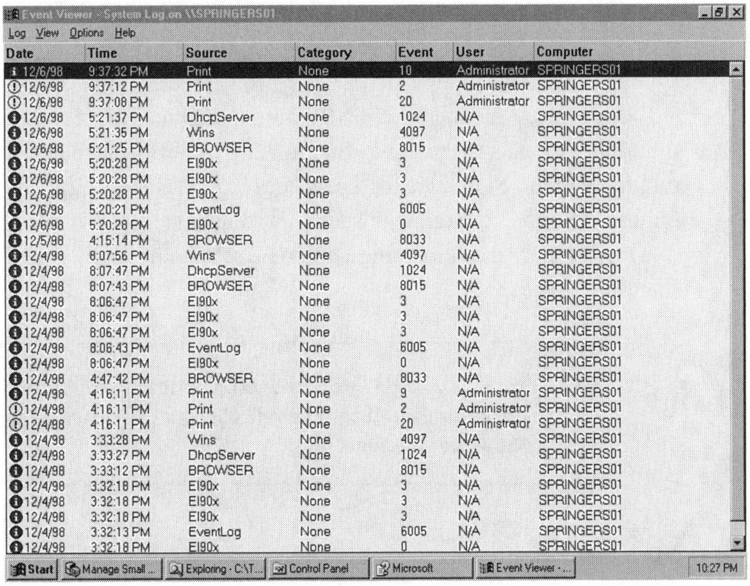

4. Click the Log menu in the upper-left of Event Viewer and select the Application menu option. The application log is displayed similar to that shown in Figure 3.29.

**FIGURE 3.29**

*Application log in Event Viewer.*

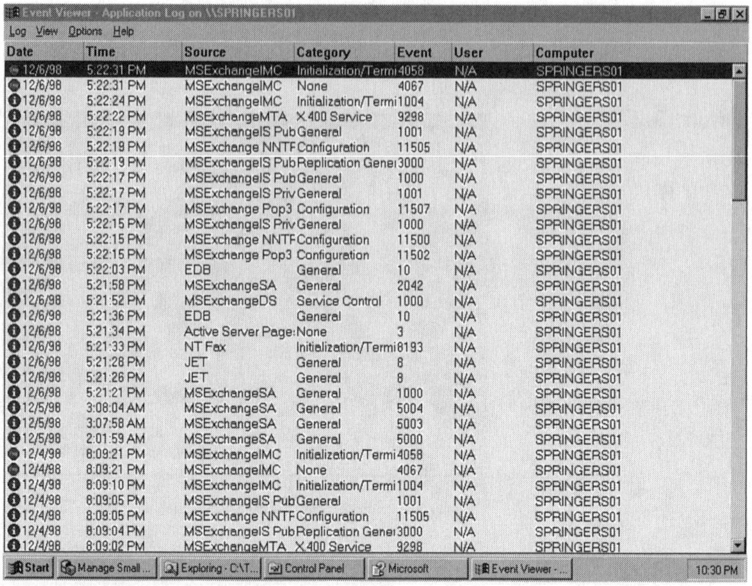

Event Viewer - Application Log on \\SPRINGERS01

Log View Options Help

| Date | Time | Source | Category | Event | User | Computer |
|---|---|---|---|---|---|---|
| 12/6/98 | 5:22:31 PM | MSExchangeIMC | Initialization/Termi | 4058 | N/A | SPRINGERS01 |
| 12/6/98 | 5:22:31 PM | MSExchangeIMC | None | 4067 | N/A | SPRINGERS01 |
| 12/6/98 | 5:22:24 PM | MSExchangeIMC | Initialization/Termi | 1004 | N/A | SPRINGERS01 |
| 12/6/98 | 5:22:22 PM | MSExchangeMTA | X.400 Service | 9298 | N/A | SPRINGERS01 |
| 12/6/98 | 5:22:19 PM | MSExchangeIS Pub | General | 1001 | N/A | SPRINGERS01 |
| 12/6/98 | 5:22:19 PM | MSExchange NNTF | Configuration | 11505 | N/A | SPRINGERS01 |
| 12/6/98 | 5:22:19 PM | MSExchangeIS Pub | Replication Gene | 3000 | N/A | SPRINGERS01 |
| 12/6/98 | 5:22:17 PM | MSExchangeIS Pub | General | 1000 | N/A | SPRINGERS01 |
| 12/6/98 | 5:22:17 PM | MSExchangeIS Priv | General | 1001 | N/A | SPRINGERS01 |
| 12/6/98 | 5:22:17 PM | MSExchange Pop3 | Configuration | 11507 | N/A | SPRINGERS01 |
| 12/6/98 | 5:22:15 PM | MSExchangeIS Priv | General | 1000 | N/A | SPRINGERS01 |
| 12/6/98 | 5:22:15 PM | MSExchange NNTF | Configuration | 11500 | N/A | SPRINGERS01 |
| 12/6/98 | 5:22:15 PM | MSExchange Pop3 | Configuration | 11502 | N/A | SPRINGERS01 |
| 12/6/98 | 5:22:03 PM | EDB | General | 10 | N/A | SPRINGERS01 |
| 12/6/98 | 5:21:58 PM | MSExchangeSA | General | 2042 | N/A | SPRINGERS01 |
| 12/6/98 | 5:21:52 PM | MSExchangeDS | Service Control | 1000 | N/A | SPRINGERS01 |
| 12/6/98 | 5:21:36 PM | EDB | General | 10 | N/A | SPRINGERS01 |
| 12/6/98 | 5:21:34 PM | Active Server Page: | None | 3 | N/A | SPRINGERS01 |
| 12/6/98 | 5:21:33 PM | NT Fax | Initialization/Termi | 8193 | N/A | SPRINGERS01 |
| 12/6/98 | 5:21:28 PM | JET | General | 8 | N/A | SPRINGERS01 |
| 12/6/98 | 5:21:26 PM | JET | General | 8 | N/A | SPRINGERS01 |
| 12/6/98 | 5:21:21 PM | MSExchangeSA | General | 1000 | N/A | SPRINGERS01 |
| 12/5/98 | 3:08:04 AM | MSExchangeSA | General | 5004 | N/A | SPRINGERS01 |
| 12/5/98 | 3:07:58 AM | MSExchangeSA | General | 5003 | N/A | SPRINGERS01 |
| 12/5/98 | 2:01:59 AM | MSExchangeSA | General | 5000 | N/A | SPRINGERS01 |
| 12/4/98 | 8:09:21 PM | MSExchangeIMC | Initialization/Termi | 4058 | N/A | SPRINGERS01 |
| 12/4/98 | 8:09:21 PM | MSExchangeIMC | None | 4067 | N/A | SPRINGERS01 |
| 12/4/98 | 8:09:10 PM | MSExchangeIMC | Initialization/Termi | 1004 | N/A | SPRINGERS01 |
| 12/4/98 | 8:09:05 PM | MSExchangeIS Pub | General | 1001 | N/A | SPRINGERS01 |
| 12/4/98 | 8:09:05 PM | MSExchange NNTF | Configuration | 11505 | N/A | SPRINGERS01 |
| 12/4/98 | 8:09:04 PM | MSExchangeIS Pub | Replication Gene | 3000 | N/A | SPRINGERS01 |
| 12/4/98 | 8:09:02 PM | MSExchangeMTA | X.400 Service | 9298 | N/A | SPRINGERS01 |

Start | Manage Small ... | Exploring - C:\T... | Control Panel | Microsoft | Event Viewer - ... | 10:30 PM

If you can read these logs, don't worry. In general, you're only really worried about the red Stop signs. An experienced SBS consultant can interpret these logs for you. According to the system log in Figure 3.28, the SBS machine is healthy, booting and running with no Stop signs in the system log! The Stop signs in the application log in Figure 3.29 refer to Exchange's attempt to use Internet e-mail. You'll configure that feature on Days 8, "Implementing Outlook," 9, "Connecting to the Internet," and 16, "Using Microsoft Exchange."

**Tip**

> You will also be interested to know that in the system log, when an entry is made for Event Log (Event 6005), that represents a reboot or a restart of the SBS server machine.

## SBS Tests

You can now perform some basic tests to see whether your SBS server machine is functioning properly. You'll perform two such tests, but there are many. First, you'll test the networking capability of SBS with the simple ping test. You'll finish with an SBS application test.

ping

The ping command allows you to quickly test the TCP/IP protocol (a communication) on your SBS network. When you *ping*, you establish that a low-level connection exists between two computers on a network. It is a very useful test for basic connectivity.

1. Click the Start button at the lower left of your SBS monitor.
2. Select Programs, Command Prompt.
3. At the command prompt (c:>), type **ping 10.0.0.2** (this command pings or "calls" the network adapter card with the 10.0.0.2 address located in your SBS server machine).
4. You should see the successful reply activity shown in Figure 3.30.

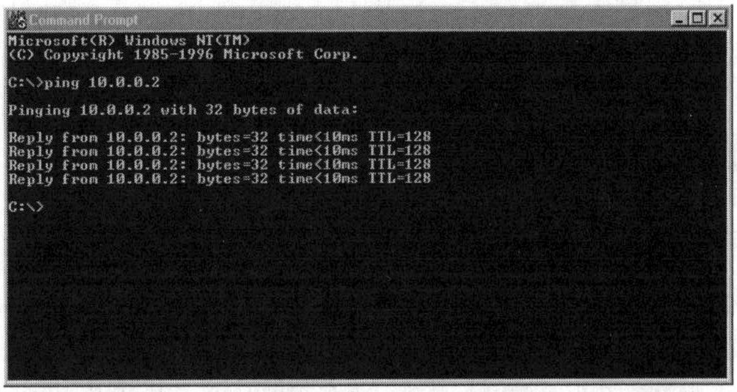

**FIGURE 3.30**

*A successful ping test.*

## Application Test

Now you want to know whether one of the SBS applications runs correctly. In this case, you are going to run Index Server Manager, a powerful indexing tool:

1. Click the Start button at the lower-left of your SBS monitor.
2. Select Programs, Windows NT 4.0 Option Pack, Microsoft Index Server, Index Server Manager.
3. The Index Server Manager application launches as seen in Figure 3.31.

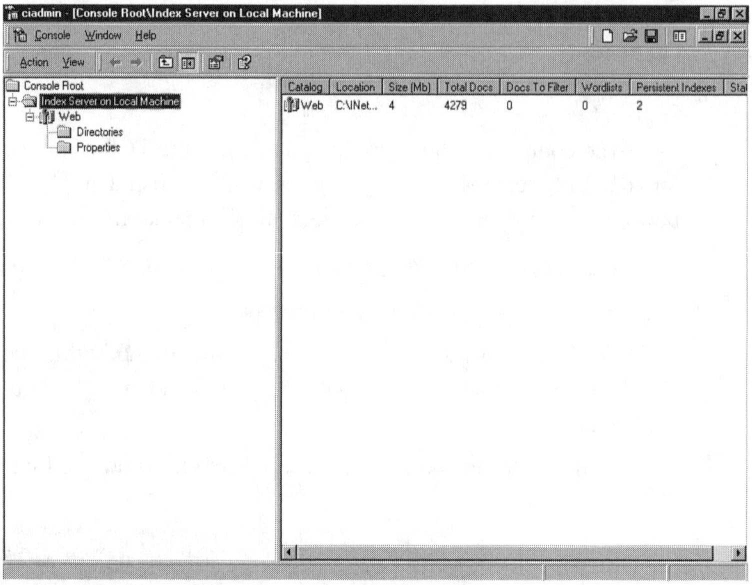

**FIGURE 3.31**

*Index Server Manager.*

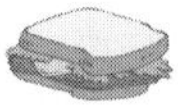

![Index Server Manager screenshot]

## Lunch

Time for lunch. Today it's turkey soup!

### Turkey Soup

The recipe is an old family favorite for using up holiday turkey meat. It's tasty and rejuvenating to the soul of any SBSer. As configured, this will make 6 to 7 cups of soup.

1/4 to 1/2 cup of minced onion

1 cup sliced celery

1 cup sliced carrots

1/4 cup snipped parsley

3 T. regular rice (uncooked)

6 to 7 cups water

Cook slowly for 1 to 2 hours.

Add 2 cups cubed turkey meat.

Cook additional 10 to 20 minutes.

Salt and pepper to taste. Enjoy!

# PM Advanced Setup Issues

Welcome back from lunch. This afternoon I share with you a variety of advanced setup issues.

## Single Machine SBS Upgrades and Critical Data Backup

Assume that you are converting from a small Novell NetWare network to SBS. Also assume that, to save money, you plan to reformat the hard drive on your existing NetWare server and install SBS. Thus, your first challenge is to make darn sure that you've completely protected the businesses data located on the existing NetWare server prior to reformatting its hard disk. If not, let's say that there aren't enough hours in the day to re-create the data you've lost!

The challenge here is that the tape created on a NetWare server using an NLM-based tape backup application isn't readable by the SBS's native tape backup application. In fact, relying on such a strategy results in the following error message regarding a foreign tape when you try to access the tape under SBS.

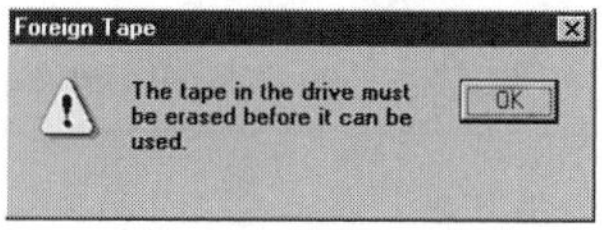

**FIGURE 3.32**

*This is the error message that SBS returns when you try to access and restore data from a storage tape created in a Novell NetWare environment.*

So what can you do? I've performed the following workaround to transfer this data from NetWare to SBS server-based environments (see Figure 3.33). What makes this work around so SBS-specific is that you can play this trick in a smaller environment, the kind of environment that SBS caters to. Obviously, this trick wouldn't be possible in larger enterprise environments that the full version of Windows NT Server caters to.

First, copy the NetWare-based data to a second server or even one or two client workstations. As you know, today's workstations have huge hard drives that are often larger than those found on older servers in smaller companies. In my case, I pursued both strategies. I literally copied the firm's data from its existing NetWare server (2.5GB of data on a NetWare partition) to a loaner NetWare 4.11 server that I brought from home. I also copied the same data to a subdirectory of a robust workstation. After I completed my

SBS installation, I (of course) copied the data back to the newly created SBS server from the client workstation. By using the data copy stored on the workstation, I saved a lot of time by not dropping under the hood on SBS and performing a somewhat nasty NT-ism or installing Gateway Services For NetWare (GSNW) to retrieve the data from my loaner NetWare 4.11 server.

**FIGURE 3.33**

*To avoid the error message in 3.32, consider copying the data on the existing NetWare server that you are converting to (a) a workstation or (b) a spare server with enough hard disk space, as shown in Figure 3.34.*

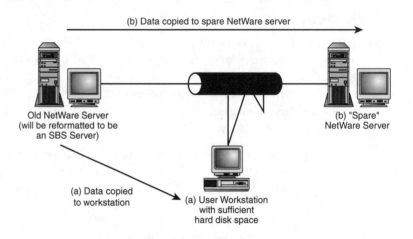

**FIGURE 3.34**

*After the old NetWare server is reformatted and SBS is installed, the data is copied up from (a) the workstation or (b) the spare server.*

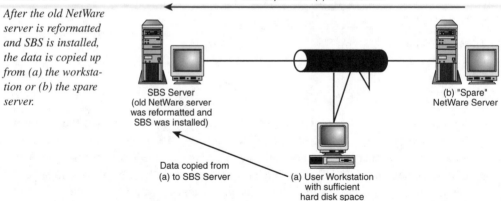

By the way, the Migration Tool for NetWare is worthless when performing a conversion from NetWare to SBS server on a single server. That's because this tool is used in a two-server scenario. This has been a point of confusion for SBS purchasers who want to reuse their existing NetWare server. I discuss this Migration Tool in a moment where it is used, appropriately, in a two-server scenario.

> I've done the same thing with an SBS installation converting from a Linux server to a new SBS server. In this case, you weren't interested in wasting the time to perfect the ICE.TEN terminal emulation connection between the Linux box and the SBS server. Thus, you copied the data from the Linux box to a workstation and back to the new SBS server.

# Advanced SBS Setup Issues

After you've installed SBS dozens of times, you'll likely recognize many of the following advanced SBS setup issues. It's also likely you'll see a thing or two not mentioned here. If so, be sure to share your wisdom with some of the SBS newsgroups and mailing lists listed in Appendix A, "SBS Resources."

## OEM Setup Scenario

As mentioned on Day 2, there are different SBS purchase and installation scenarios. One of these options was the preinstallation or OEM installation option. There, a hardware manufacturer partially installs SBS on your computer, saving you some installation time (less than one hour). For the record, the OEM installation option essentially takes the process through "Phase A: Windows NT Server Character-Based Setup" (Tasks 2.1 through 2.10) and starts with "Phase B: Windows NT Server GUI-Based Setup" (SBS setup task 2.11).

## Avoid This Mistake

Many of you have received the two-user demo version of SBS for testing and learning purposes. You can acquire this two-user demo either via a marketing mailer included in the CD-ROMs or via the official Microsoft courses. . Beware! This is a very dangerous release. Here's why. One day, when performing an installation at a land development company, I was advised that their SBS software product had been backordered at the software reseller.

I immediately thought no problem. As an MCT, I was carrying the SBS course #1049 notebook with me that had the two-user demo version used in the classroom. So I installed this version to complete the SBS installation on the appointed setup day. (You have to remember that the land developer staff had made special accommodations for the conversion that day.)

A few days later, when the real SBS product arrived at the customer site, I returned to install the real SBS version over the two-user demo version, fully expecting the Windows NT Server Registry and SAM values and SBS licensing to migrate seamlessly. Of course, such wasn't the case. Not only did the Registry value and the like not migrate, but I was still stuck with only two user licenses available. Long story short, I had to install the real SBS from the ground up: That is, I FDISKed the server's hard disk. Several hours later, the SBS network was running in fine shape and, although I was embarrassed, I learned an early and valuable lesson to share with you.

## License Enforcement

This SBS licensing story draws out differences between Windows NT Server and SBS. As you might know, you can turn off the License Logging Service via Services in Control Panel in Windows NT Server to prevent per-seat and per-server errors from writing out to the system log, as shown in Figure 3.35. It's an old NT guru trick.

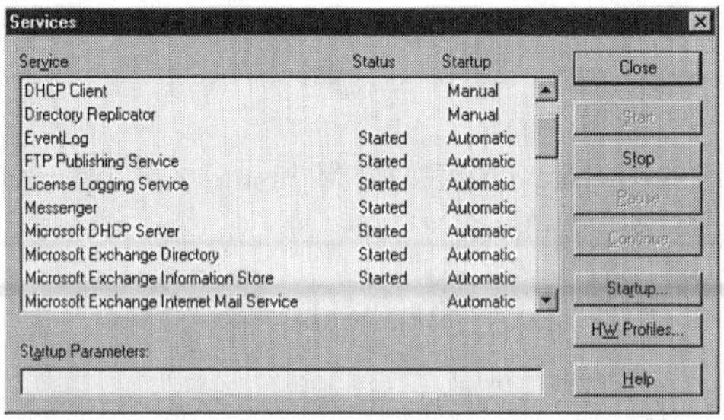

**FIGURE 3.35**

*License Logging Service.*

But the same trick has no effect on SBS. Witness the site wherein I followed behind an acclaimed Redmond-trained NT guru who tried such a feat with SBS, hoping to spare his client the expense of having to purchase additional SBS CALs. He thought that, by turning off the License Logging Service in SBS, you could purchase only the five-user version of SBS and have up to 25 users logged on to the SBS network at the same time.

Well, of course, that didn't work. Turning off the License Logging Service has no effect on your SBS CAL count maintained by the SBS network or the 25-user limit. In short, there are no shortcuts here to avoid purchasing the number of SBS CALs that you need!

## HP JetDirect Printers

Perhaps the most popular printer option on an SBS network is that of the network-installed printer. This is where the printer is cabled directly into the network. It plugs into a network wall jack just like a networked workstation. One of the most popular options for attaching network printers has been the HP JetDirect card. Recognizing this, Microsoft added the JetAdmin program, HP's printer management application, to SBS CD-ROM Disc 1. You can find it in the \Jetadmin directory on this disc.

To install an HP JetDirect networked printer on your SBS network, you must first install the JetAdmin application. Here's why. In Figure 3.37, you will notice that I've discovered that there is no printer port for the HP JetDirect device. Here is how you can discover that:

1. Click the Start button on the lower-left of your SBS monitor.

2. Select Settings, Printers.

3. Select the Add Printer Wizard.

4. Select My Computer (the HP JetDirect-connected printer will actually be managed, in this case, by the SBS server machine).

5. When the Available Ports are displayed, select the Add Port button.

6. Observe in Figure 3.36 that there is no HP JetDirect port support in SBS's native state.

FIGURE 3.36

*Printer Ports.*

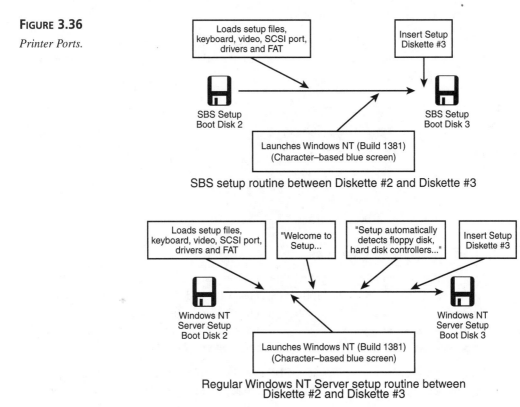

SBS setup routine between Diskette #2 and Diskette #3

Regular Windows NT Server setup routine between
Diskette #2 and Diskette #3

For the HP JetDirect port support to appear, you must first install the HP JetAdmin tool. You can do this from either the SBS setup CDs or the CD that shipped with your HP Jet Admin card. Follow these steps to install the HP JetAdmin tool from SBS Setup CD #1:

1. Insert the SBS Setup CD-ROM Disc 1 in your CD-ROM drive.

2. Launch the jetsetup.exe program from the \Jetadmin\i386 directory on Disc 1.

3. Click Next at the HP JetAdmin Welcome screen.

4. Select the JetAdmin components to install on the Install Components screen and click Next. The default is to install all JetAdmin components.

5. Accept or change the HP JetAdmin Utilities program folder name. Click Next.

6. Click Next at the Start Copying Files dialog box. The files will copy and JetAdmin will be installed. This process takes less than two minutes.

7. Answer Yes or No when asked to view the JetAdmin README file.

8. Click Finish in the Setup Complete dialog box.

9. Click Yes in the Restart Windows dialog box. You must restart Windows (SBS) for the HP JetDirect port to appear.

After rebooting, if you check the Printer Ports dialog box, you will see the HP JetDirect Port listed, as in Figure 3.37. You can now install a printer connected to the network via an HP JetDirect card.

**FIGURE 3.37**

*HP JetDirect Port.*

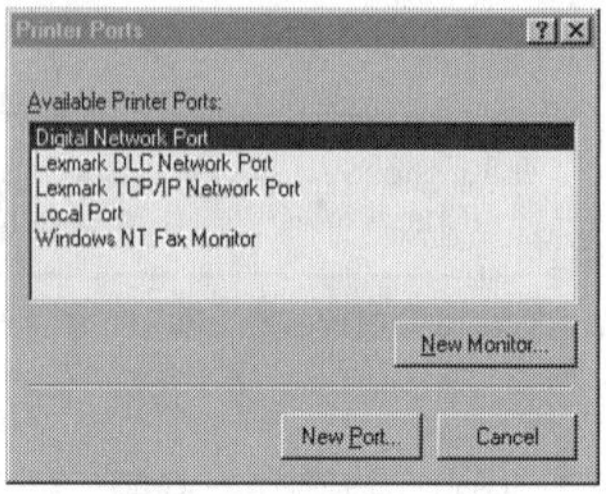

## Unsupported Devices

Every SBS installation has a right way and a wrong way to do it. There is the easy way and the hard way. There is the "follow the rules way" and the "break the rules" way. Surprisingly, you're likely to try, suffer, cheer, celebrate, and curse all approaches during your tenure as an SBS guru. So far, I've demonstrated only the correct way to install SBS. Now, let's break the rules and understand why you would do so.

Without question, one of the greatest SBS installation challenges today is that of managing your library of current drivers from third-party vendors. By that I mean when you install and maintain SBS, you have the latest drivers from the vendors of the components attached to your system. This is extremely important because operating systems are built and released at a point in time. Although the periodic release of service packs allows the operating system to refresh its library of drivers, in no way can an operating system hope to ship with the latest and most current drivers from all of the third-party vendors. It's a common and daunting challenge that confronts system engineers everywhere.

What's the bottom line? If you have unusual or new drivers, you need to specify **S** when installing SBS in the early setup stages when you are asked to specify additional controller and adapter cards. And when you communicate that you want to specify drivers, you often have to specify the drivers for existing controller and adapter cards because setup's autodetection has not been stopped. That is, once you press **S**, you'll likely have to specify all controller and adapter cards, not just the unsupported one you were trying to add.

# NetWare Data Migration for a Second Server

Many of my SBS conversions have, as I've previously mentioned, been from existing NetWare networks. This type of conversion presented its own issues.

## Migration Tool for NetWare

You will want to use the Migration Tool for NetWare to transfer your data files from your existing NetWare server to your new SBS server. It's a very powerful tool with priceless trail migration capabilities that allow you to observe any data migration errors prior to copying over your real data. Wonderful!

You will not want to transfer your user and group accounts from your NetWare server to SBS with the tool for three important reasons:

- The transferred users appear in the User Manager for Domains tool via the underlying Windows NT Server operating system, but these users do not appear in the user list on the SBS Console, rendering the SBS user management features worthless. That's a crime.

- The transferred users do not appear as Microsoft Exchange mailboxes. You can perform a complex import feature inside of the Microsoft Exchange Administrator to correct this but what a pain for so few users!

- Such a small number of users suggests you're better off to rekey the user accounts into SBS via the Add User capabilities of the SBS Console. If you had 2,500 users in a real enterprise Windows NT Server environment, it might make sense to use the Migration Tool for NetWare, but for 25 or fewer users, no way!

To install the Migration Tool for NetWare, you must first install the NWLink IPX/SPX Compatible Protocol from the Protocol tab sheet from the Network applet in Control Panel. Under the Services tab sheet in the Network applet, you will want to install the Gateway (and Client) Services for NetWare. You will then reboot the machine.

On reboot at the SBS server computer, you log on to your NetWare server in addition to SBS and launch the Migration tool for NetWare from the Administrative Tools (Common) program group. You then select which directories and files from which volumes you want to perform a NetWare to SBS migration. This is shown as Figure 3.38.

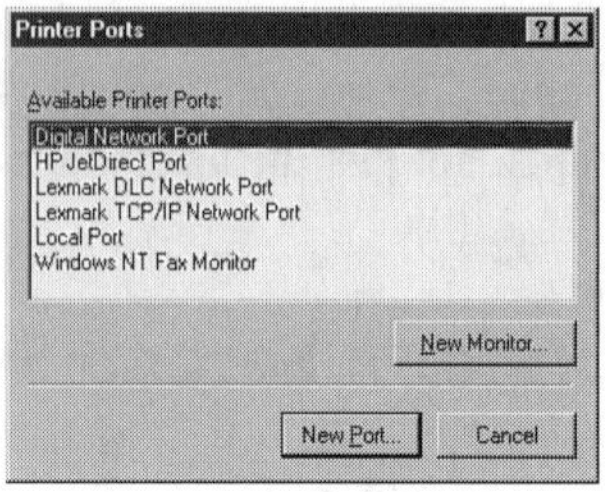

**FIGURE 3.38**

*Migration Tool for NetWare.*

Microsoft has posted a great white paper concerning NetWare migrations in SBS-networked environments. The paper, titled NetWare Migration Guide, is available at www.microsoft.com/smallbusinessserver. Several of my best SBS customers have been able to install and use the Migration Tool for NetWare based on this resource without any assistance from yours truly.

# Upgrading to SBS

Believe it or not, there are customers running regular Windows NT Server 4.0 and Big BackOffice who want to upgrade to SBS. Typically they do this to take advantage of features such as modem pooling and fax service that aren't available natively. I've seen other clients make this change to take advantage of the SBS Console for ease-of-use purposes.

Whatever the reasons, a couple of issues surround this upgrade. One I've already mentioned in Day 2: The operating subdirectory name under SBS is \winnt.sbs (not \winnt as in regular Windows NT Server). This naming difference can be problematic.

Another problem is the surprise that SBS doesn't inherit any Registry or SAM settings from regular Windows NT Server. That means when you upgrade from regular Windows NT Server to SBS, you must add all your users and machines names again. You must also reinstall your applications. I discuss this and other upgrading-related issues on Day 21, "Upgrading to Big BackOffice."

# Troubleshooting Setup Errors

In your career as an SBS professional, you will possibly have occasion to troubleshoot setup errors. One such error I encountered early on at an SBS installation at a biotechnology company was the dreaded SSUP1 error shortly after setup.

This error prevented me from launching the SBS Console, a key part of SBS. Because this was very early in the life of SBS, there were no support documents on the Web or Microsoft TechNet (Microsoft's monthly support CD-ROM library) that addressed this issue.

I ultimately discovered what the problem was. The SBS server machine during setup hadn't been properly connected to an active hub (remember the green light test early in the chapter!). After I connected the SBS server machine directly to the active hub, the SSUP1 error went away, and I was able to use the SBS Console.

Many months later, Microsoft released TechNet article Q178270 that addresses this issue, but in a slightly different way. Microsoft claims the error message is related to a bad network adapter, IP address or subnet mask value, not an unplugged SBS server computer.

# Summary

As you reach the end of the SBS server machine setup and installation discussion, remember to go forward keeping a healthy perspective. Often I witness SBS professionals spending hours troubleshooting some setup or installation-related problem. In many cases, that is not a good use of time. Remember that it often takes less than three hours to do a complete SBS server machine reinstall. Just a thought!

# DAY 4

# Setting Up the Workstation Client

## AM The Client Side

Congratulations! You are more than half the way to a completed, functional, and optimally performing SBS network. One major set of tasks remains: setting up the workstations. This task area shouldn't be marginalized. Whereas you most likely performed the SBS server machine setup out of sight (and hearing range) from your end users, you don't have that same luxury with the workstation setup phase today. Your role will be very public, and so will the users' feedback. So, take the extra time needed to get it right.

# Workstation Installation Plan

The following half-dozen tasks are necessary to be completed prior to performing the SBS hands-on workstation configuration tasks such as adding users and setting up the workstations. These tasks include the following:

- Setting up a staging area
- Building the new workstations
- Completing the installation of the workstation operating system
- Testing the workstation's network connectivity
- Procuring floppy disks to use as the client setup disk
- Completing the workstation installation worksheet

First, be sure to find a place to set up the workstations if you purchase new workstations for your SBS network. This workstation staging area is typically a conference room. If you are converting from an existing network or the users already have the their workstations in place, you probably won't need a workstation setup area.

**Note**

If you indeed use a workstation staging area, it is very helpful to have a network hub (connected to the SBS network) in the center of your work area. That way, as you build each workstation, you can complete the workstation setup tasks in an assembly line–like fashion. It's very efficient.

Second, if you have new workstations, physically build the workstation by unpacking all the components from the shipping boxes (monitor, computer, keyboard). Be sure to reseat each adapter card inside the new workstation in case it came loose during shipping. After connecting all the workstation components, turn on the power and verify that the workstation is functional. I recommend that you check the workstation BIOS settings similar to how the server BIOS was observed on Day 3, "Installing Small Business Server." (You typically press the Delete key during the power on phase to see the BIOS settings.)

**Tip**

Be sure to confirm that the workstations you specified and ordered on Day 2, "Planning for Small Business Server," are the same as the workstations now in your possession. And does each workstation have a network adapter card as I specified?

Whether the workstation is new or not, take a moment to confirm that your workstation meets the minimum system requirements specified by Microsoft for participating on an SBS network. Recall that I discussed these minimum system requirements on the afternoon of Day 2. In particular, make sure that you have enough hard disk space to accommodate the SBS client applications you intend to install in a few moments. The most popular SBS workstation setup error that I've witnessed is a shortage of hard disk space on the client workstation. Unfortunately, you typically aren't advised of such space shortage problems until well into the SBS client workstation setup process. I agree with you that it would be nice if the SBS workstation setup routine performed an early workstation space calculation routine.

Third, new workstations typically have no operating system completely installed. Depending on the workstation manufacturer, the workstation might have a partial installation of Windows 98. Such is the case when you purchase from name-brand manufacturers such as Dell, Compaq, Micron, Gateway, and the like. With true clone workstations, such as the PC that your Uncle Charlie built, it might or might not have any operating system (here it varies on a case-by-case basis). Regardless, it is essential that each workstation have a functional operating system such as Windows 98. Now is the time to make sure that each of your workstations indeed has an operating system installed. In fact, the SBS client applications and networking functionality cannot be installed on a workstation until a supported workstation operating system is installed. Recall from Day 2 that Springer Spaniels Unlimited has a mixture of three popular operating systems: Windows 98, Windows 95, and Windows NT Workstation 4.0.

**4**

**Note**

SBS fully supports the following workstation operating systems:

- Windows 98
- Windows 95
- Windows NT Workstation with Service Pack #3

Full support includes use of the modem sharing client, fax client, and WinSock Proxy client (related to the firewall protection).

SBS has limited support for other popular workstation operating systems:

- Microsoft Windows for Workgroups
- Windows NT Workstation version 3.x
- Windows 3.x
- MS-DOS
- UNIX clients
- Macintosh

I discuss advanced issues related to these operating systems this afternoon.

Operating systems that are not supported by SBS in any way, shape, or form include OS/2, CP/M, Apple DOS, and Apple ProDOS. If you have such a workstation, do yourself a favor and strongly consider purchasing an Intel-based workstation running one of the supported operating systems so that you can participate on the SBS network.

Fourth, perform a workstation-level green light test: plug a network cable (that is, CAT5 10BASE-T cable) into the workstation's network adapter card jack. Make sure the other end of the network cable is connected to an active hub connection (for example, the hub in your workstation staging area). Much like the testing you performed on the server on Day 3, make sure the both the hub and workstation network adapter card jack have a green or active light.

If you use existing workstations on an existing network, you can also perform this test with little effort. Simply turn on the existing workstation and see whether the network adapter card jack is green or active. Then trot over to the network hub and confirm the same.

Fifth, be sure to procure enough floppy disks to create a client installation disk (a.k.a. magic disk) for each workstation you intend to add to the SBS network. The magic disk is discussed more in a moment.

Sixth, be sure to revisit the SBS network user and machine information created on Day 2 (see the "User List" section following Table 2.2) and complete the Workstation Installation Worksheet for each user. The Workstation Installation Worksheet has been completed for Norm Hasbro, president of Springer Spaniels Unlimited (see Table 4.1). The entries for the remaining Springer Spaniels Unlimited users are provided in Appendix E, "Springer Spaniel User Information."

**Tip**

> Remember that it is far better with SBS to populate each field, even with N/A (Not Applicable or Not Available). That way, you know at a later date that you didn't overlook any user and computer setup configuration field. Also, SBS uses user and computer setup configuration information in other areas of the SBS network, making it important to complete each and every user and computer setup configuration field.

**TABLE 4.1**  SBS WORKSTATION SETUP SHEET

| Setup Field | Input/Value/Description | Where Used |
| --- | --- | --- |
| User's Full Name (First, Last) | Norm Hasbro | Add a User |
| User's Account Name (20-character limit) | NormH | Add a New User |
| Description for User | Founder and President | Add a New User |
| Password | Purple3 | Add a New User |
| Allowed to change password (Y/N)? | N | Add a New User |
| Title (Job Title) | President | Add a New User |
| Company | Springer Spaniels Unlimited | Add a New User |
| Department | Executive | Add a New User |
| Office | Main | Add a New User |
| Assistant | N/A | Add a New User |
| Phone | 206-123-1234 | Add a New User |
| Address | 3456 The Pass Road | Add a New User |
| City | Iski | Add a New User |
| State | WA | Add a New User |
| ZIP Code | 98111 | Add a New User |
| Country | USA | Add a New User |
| Business telephone | 206-123-1234 | Add a New User |
| Business 2 telephone | N/A | Add a New User |
| Fax telephone | 206-123-1235 | Add a New User |
| Assistant telephone | N/A | Add a New User |
| Home telephone | 206-111-1235 | Add a New User |
| Home 2 telephone | N/A | Add a New User |
| Mobile telephone | 206-999-1236 | Add a New User |
| Pager telephone | N/A | Add a New User |
| E-Mail Distribution List (the default entry is the same name as the SBS network Domain name: for example, SPRINGERS) | SPRINGERS | Add a New User |

4

*continues*

**TABLE 4.1**   CONTINUED

| Setup Field | Input/Value/Description | Where Used |
|---|---|---|
| Shared Folders: (R)ead, (E)dit, (D)elete Permissions | *company FaxStore NormH* | Add a New User |
| Shared Folders: (R)ead Permission | *Administrator users BarryK MelindaO SallyB BobB SamC TomB NormJR DaveH Elvis* | Add a New User |
| Shared Printer | *HP5MCOLOR* | Add a New User |
| Shared Fax Printer | *Fax* | Add a New User |
| Access the Internet? (Y/N) | *Y* | Add a New User |
| Use a modem to access the server computer? (Y/N) | *Y* | Add a New User |
| Administrative Privileges (Y/N) | *N* | Add a New User |
| Workstation NetBIOS (Set Up Computer name Wizard) | *PRESIDENT* | Set Up A Computer |
| Operating System: Windows 95, Windows 98, or Windows NT 4.0 Workstation | *Windows 95* | Set Up A Computer |
| SBS Programs to Install None, Complete or Microsoft Fax Client, Microsoft Internet Explorer, Microsoft Modem Sharing Client, Microsoft Outlook E-mail Client, Microsoft Proxy Client, Microsoft Office 97 (optional) | *Complete* | Set Up A Computer |
| Verify available work-station hard disk space based on SBS Programs to install listed immediately above (for example, 98 MB required) | *Yes* | Set Up A Computer |

| Setup Field | Input/Value/Description | Where Used |
|---|---|---|
| Network Protocols | *TCP/IP* | Misc. |
| IP Address (Static or Dynamic) | *Dynamic* | Misc. |
| Mapped Drives | *S: SPRINGERS01\NORMH* *T: SPRINGERS01\USERS* *U: SPRINGERS01\COMPANY* *V: SPRINGERS01\ACCOUNTING* *W: SPRINGERS01\OLD* *X: SPRINGERS01\APPLICATIONS* | Misc. |
| Workstation Shares (shares on workstation) | *N/A* | Misc. |
| Additional Applications to install (for example, Great Plains Dynamics accounting): | *Great Plains Dynamics client* *FRX Report Writer* | Misc. |
| Special configuration issues | *Double-check security* *This is the president's PC.* | Misc. |
| Comments | *Complete this one last after all other workstations.* | Misc. |
| Tested Logon (Y/N) | *N* | Misc. |
| Repairs /Reconfiguration Needed | | Misc. |

**Tip**

Remember that the workstation name is typically based on job title or function. Thus, the workstation names associated with the users at Springer Spaniels Unlimited are closely related to the user's job title.

**Note**

The access to the Internet and access to the server via modem are commonly selected, but you should always consider the reasons for doing so.

**Tip**

You typically want to reply No to giving any user account administrator privileges. Even the SBS project manager for Springer Spaniels Unlimited, Bob Estes, will only have normal user rights assigned to his username (that is, the administrative privileges selection will be No). When any administrative functions need to be performed on the SBS network, the best practice is to log on as the Administrator to perform that action. And don't forget to log out and log on again as a normal user after performing your required administrative-level duties.

# SBS Workstation Setup Process

The SBS workstation setup approach is a four-step process, and compared to the SBS server machine installation, it is relatively simple. Another interesting point is that, whereas you perform the SBS server machine setup only once, you perform the SBS workstation setup several times, once for each workstation. I've found that such repetition breeds familiarity; your comfort-level with increase with this process.

Of the four steps, the first two (running the User Account Wizard and running the Set Up Computer Wizard) are performed on the SBS server machine via the To Do List (part of the SBS Console). The last two steps are performed on the SBS workstation. Run the Setup program on the magic disk and install the client applications. This process is shown in Figure 4.1.

**FIGURE 4.1**

*SBS Workstation setup process.*

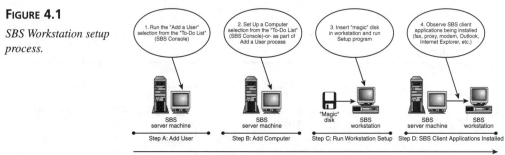

**Note**

As promised on Day 3, you now revisit the To Do List in the next several steps. Recall that on Day 3, you completed several of the To Do List items and promised to complete the Add a New User and Set Up a Computer items on Day 4, "Setting Up the Workstation Client." That time has now arrived.

## Task 4.1: Add User

In Task 4.1, you first add user NormH (refer to Table 4.1) to the SPRINGERS SBS network. Task 4.1 is broken into two parts. In steps 1 through 12 you enter basic user information. In steps 13 through 18 you enter user resource settings such as rights to access the Internet, use a printer, and so on.

1. Make sure you are logged on to the SBS server machine as an administrator. In the case of Springer Spaniels Unlimited, the correct username is Administrator, and the correct password is password (note the lowercase form).

2. Launch the SBS Console by clicking the Start button on the lower-left corner of your display monitor. Select the SBS Console menu option.

3. Launch the To Do List by selecting Small Business Server To Do List found on the Home sheet underneath Favorites.

4. Select Add a User. The User Account Wizard launches. Click Next.

5. Complete the User Account Information screen, as shown in Figure 4.2, based on the information for NormH contained in Table 4.1. Click Next.

**FIGURE 4.2**

*User Account Information.*

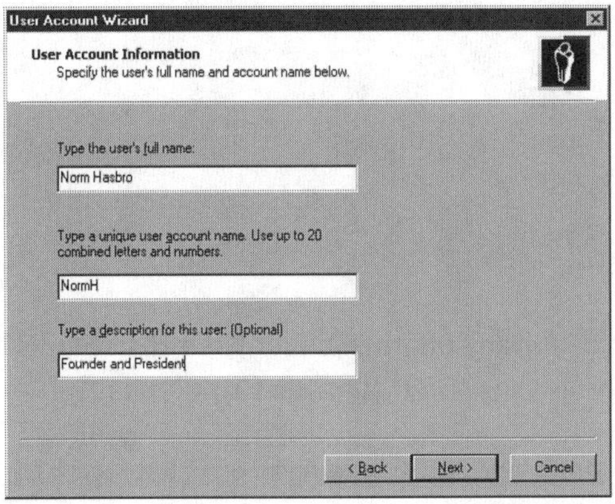

6. On the Create a Password for NormH screen, select the I Want to Specify the Password for NormH radio button (see Figure 4.3). Click Next.

7. On the Password Information for NormH screen, type the password for NormH (from Table 4.1, this password is Purple3). See Figure 4.4. Also, NormH is not allowed to change his password, so select the NormH Is Not Allowed to Change the Password radio button. Click Next.

▼ **FIGURE 4.3**

*Create a Password for
NormH.*

**FIGURE 4.4**

*Password Information
for NormH.*

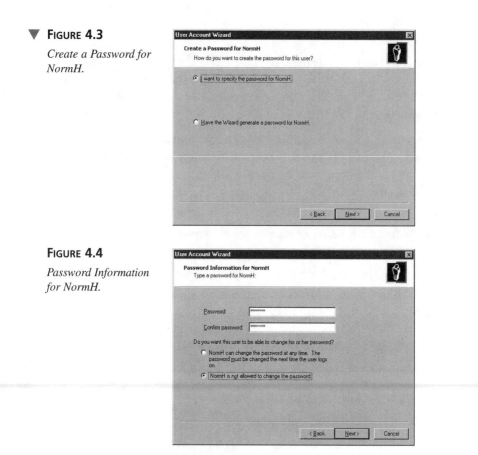

8. Complete the Company Information for NormH screen with the information from
Table 4.1. This is shown in Figure 4.5. Click Next.

**FIGURE 4.5**

*Company Information
for NormH.*

▼

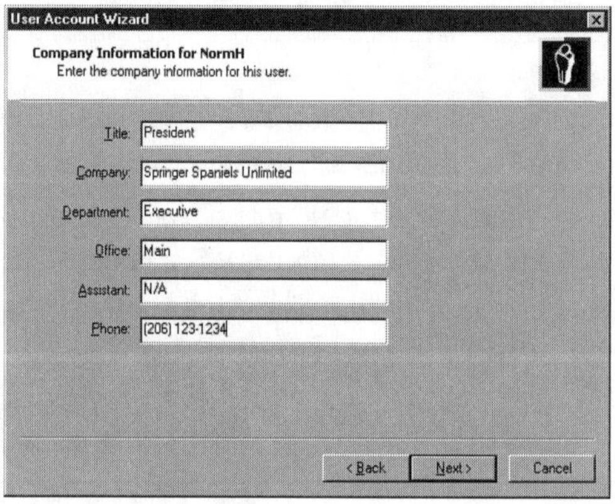

▼  9. Complete the Address Information for NormH screen as shown in Figure 4.6. You
can find this information in Table 4.1, if it already isn't present. (These fields
should be filled based on the information that you entered on Day 3 during the
SBS server machine setup.) Click Next.

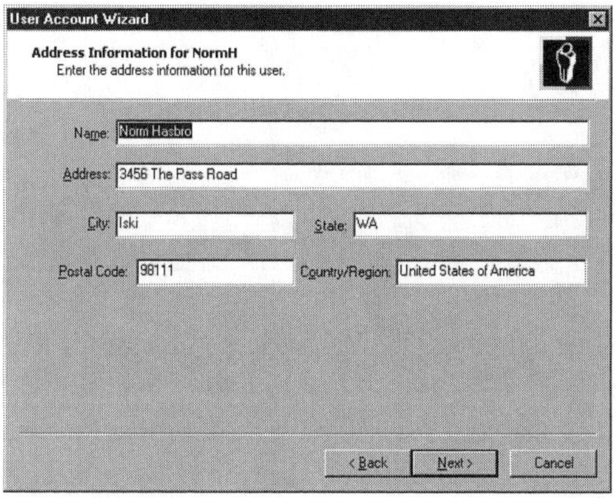

**FIGURE 4.6**

*Address Information
for NormH.*

10. Complete the Communication Information for NormH screen based on the information contained in Table 4.1 (see Figure 4.7). Note the Business and Fax fields
should already be filled in for you based on information you entered in on Day 3
during the SBS server machine setup. Click Next.

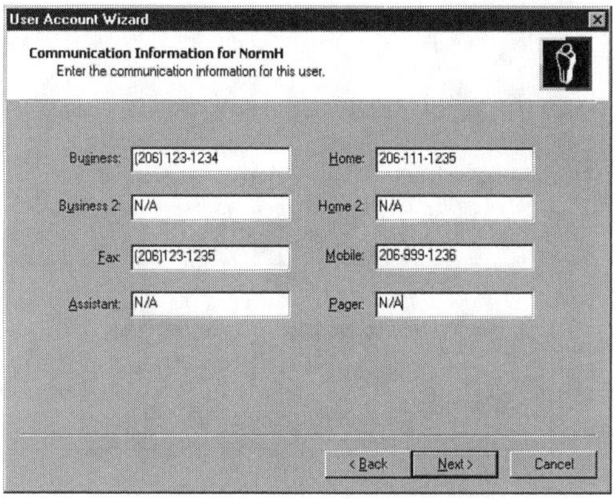

**FIGURE 4.7**

*Communication
Information for
NormH.*

11. Approve the default e-mail distribution list selection (Springers) on the Select the
E-Mail Distribution Lists for NormH screen (see Figure 4.8). Note this e-mail distribution list was automatically created for you during the SBS Server setup
▼      process and is based on the SBS network domain name. Click Next.

4

▼ **Figure 4.8**

*E-mail Distribution
List selection.*

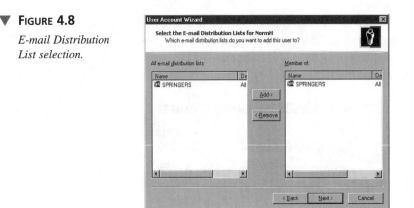

12. Click the Finish button on the Create User Account for NormH screen. This completes the first part of Task 4.1 wherein you have entered basic user information (see Figure 4.9). You will then be presented with a "success" dialog box (shown in Figure 4.10) indicating the account for NormH was successfully created.

**Figure 4.9**

*Finish creating
NormH.*

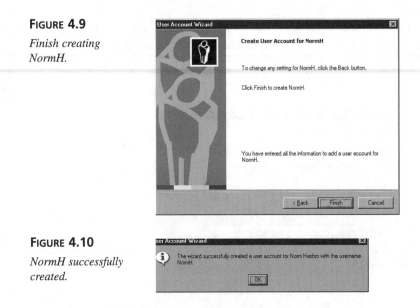

**Figure 4.10**

*NormH successfully
created.*

13. You are returned to the User Access Wizard. The second step, Give access to network resources, is selected. Click Next.

▼    14. The User Resource Wizard automatically launches in what will be a series of sev-
        eral screens that allow you to select the security settings for NormH. The first
        screen (see Figure 4.11), Select the Shared Folders for NormH, is displayed, allow-
        ing you to accept or reject the default file settings. Click Next.

**FIGURE 4.11**

*Select the Shared
Folders for NormH.*

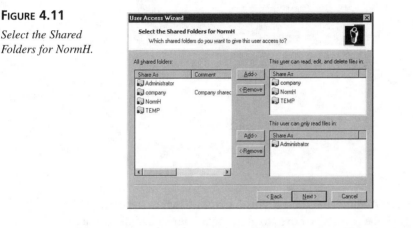

> **Note**
>
> The selection closely matches the shared folders settings presented in Table
> 4.1 for NormH with a few exceptions. These exceptions are the missing addi-
> tional users listed where NormH will have read permissions (BarryK through
> Elvis). Because NormH is the first user listed, these other user's shared folders
> don't exist. However, as the other users are added to the system, SBS auto-
> matically creates these default read permissions for NormH.

4

    15. The Select the Shared Printers for NormH screen appears (see Figure 4.12) and
        automatically selects the HP5MCOLOR printer for you. Click Next.

**FIGURE 4.12**

*Select the Shared
Printers for NormH.*

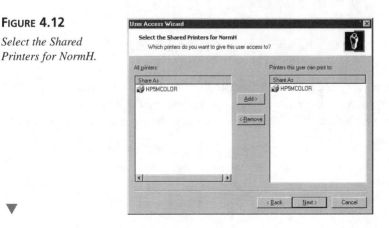

▼

▼ 16. The Select the Shared Fax Printers for NormH screen appears, allowing you to confirm the default selection (Fax). This is shown in Figure 4.13. Click Next.

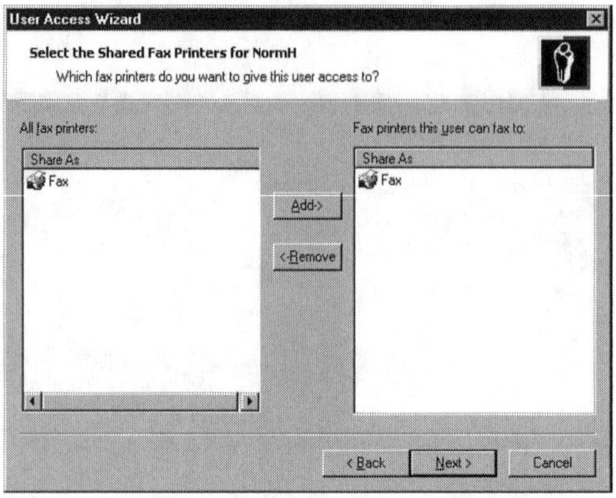

FIGURE **4.13**

*Select the Shared Fax Printers for NormH.*

17. The Select Additional Access Rights for NormH screen appears. As noted on Table 4.1, check the two check boxes to allow both Internet and dial-up access (see Figure 4.14). Click Next.

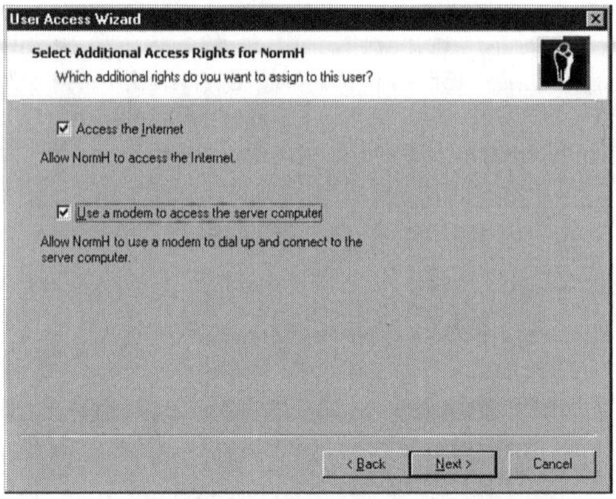

FIGURE **4.14**

*Select Additional Access Rights for NormH.*

18. You are now presented with the Administrative Privileges screen (see Figure 4.15). Remember that SBS best practices suggest that you should not allow any normal user to have administrator-level rights. Thus, select the No radio button for NormH.

▼ Click Next.

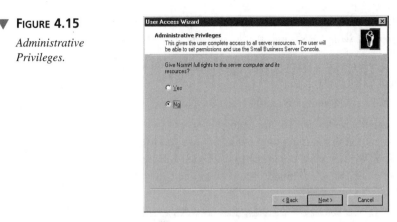

19. Click the Finish button on the Completing the User Access Wizard screen (see
    Figure 4.16).

You have now updated the permission for files, folders, printers, fax, Internet access, and
modems for this user. You will be presented with a dialog box that communicates that
you have successfully set up the resources for NormH to use.

FIGURE 4.16

*Update Resource
Permissions for
NormH.*

## Task 4.2: Add Workstation

After successfully completing all of Task 4.1 (creating the user and user resource settings), you are offered the chance to add a workstation (a.k.a. computer) for this user to
the network. During the setup of your SBS network, this is a common step to perform.
After your network is up and running, this add-workstation step is often handled differently to account for new hires in your organization. I discuss this second scenario this

▼ afternoon. In Task 4.2, you name the workstation and tell SBS what operating system the workstation is using and what SBS applications to install on the workstation.

1. Return to the User Access Wizard and selection three, Set Up a User's Computer, is highlighted. Click Next.

2. You see the Set Up Computer Wizard screen for NormH.

3. You are presented with the Set Up the Computer screen (see Figure 4.17). In the case of NormH, select the first radio button, which allows you to set up a Windows 95, Windows 98, or Windows NT computer to use Small Business Server. Recall from Table 4.1 that NormH has a Windows 95 workstation. Click Next.

**FIGURE 4.17**

*Set Up the Computer.*

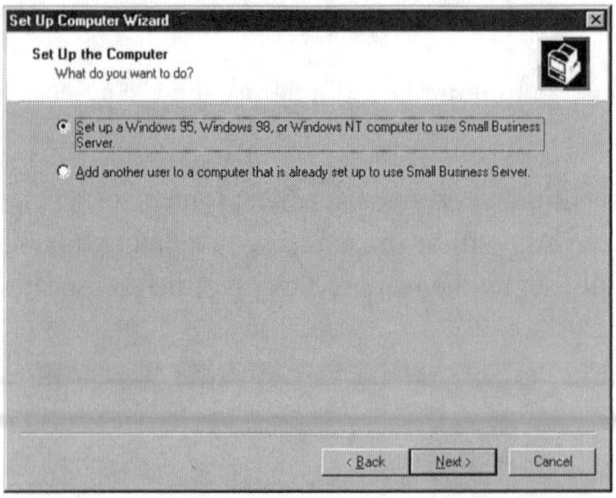

4. The Specify the Computer Name screen appears. In the case of NormH, note in Table 4.1 that his workstation name is PRESIDENT. Enter that name (see Figure 4.18) and click Next.

**FIGURE 4.18**

*Specify a Computer Name.*

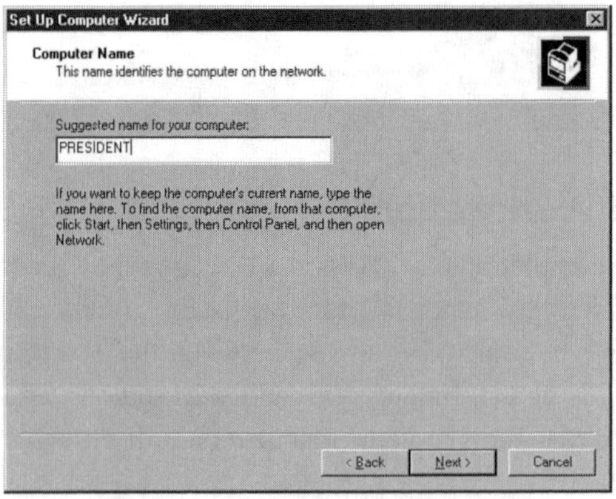

▼

**Tip**

SBS attempts to autoname the workstation by taking the username (for example, NormH) and appending underscore (_) and 01. Thus, the autonamed machine for NormH would be NormH_01. However, this isn't recommended for reasons I previously shared (user turnover makes autonamed workstations seem somewhat silly). I recommend (again) that workstations be named after a job title or function or a geographic location.

5. Select the operating system on the Operating System screen that the workstation is running. The choices are Windows 95/98 or Windows NT Workstation 4.0. In the case of NormH, select the Microsoft Windows 95/98 button (see Figure 4.19). Click Next.

**FIGURE 4.19**

*Select the operating system for NormH.*

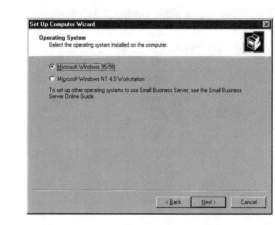

6. The Applications screen appears. NormH is to have all programs installed, so make sure the Install the Programs Checked in the List Below radio button is selected and that all programs (Fax, Internet Explorer, Modem Sharing, Outlook, Proxy) are selected as shown in Figure 4.20. Click Next.

7. The Setup Disk screen appears. The setup disk is also known as the magic disk and is similar to regular Windows NT Server's Network Client Setup Disk. You should both label a 3.5" floppy disk (NormH SBS Setup Disk) and insert it into the SBS server machine. Click Next. The disk is formatted (see Figure 4.21) and the SBS workstation setup files are copied (see Figure 4.22).

8. You will then be presented with the Completing the Set Up Computer Wizard screen. This screen presents specific workstation setup instructions, as seen in Figure 4.23. Click Finish.

▼ FIGURE **4.20**

*Select the Programs to Install.*

FIGURE **4.21**

*Setup disk is formatted.*

FIGURE **4.22**

*Setup files copied to disk.*

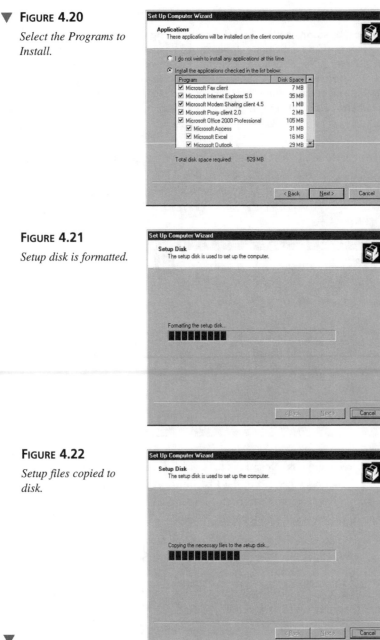

▼

▼ FIGURE 4.23

*Completing the Set Up
Computer Wizard.*

▲       You have now completed the server side of the SBS workstation setup process.

## Task 4.3: Run Workstation Setup

▼TASK

In Task 4.3, you go to the workstation that you want to add to the SBS network and turn it on. After successfully booting into the workstation operating system (for example, Windows 95), you start the SBS workstation setup tasks. In Task 4.3, the setup program installs and configures the workstation-side network components (networking protocol, networking client, and machine name), sets up the specified user (NormH), and reboots the client computer. You then log on to the client computer, and the desktop shortcuts to the Company and Users shares are created.

1. Insert the SBS workstation setup disk (magic disk) into the floppy drive of your computer. Run the Setup command from the disk. This is typically a:\setup.exe and can be executed from the Run dialog box of Windows 95, Windows 98, or Windows NT Workstation 4.0. The Run command is accessed via the Start button from your desktop.

**Note**

If you have previously configured a dial-up adapter on your workstation, you will receive an SBS workstation setup-related error message that communicates the following:

We detected Dial-Up Adapter installed on your system.

In order to configure this computer Dial-Up Adapter will be disabled.  Please consult the online guide.

▼

▼

> Continue Setup?
>
> Yes    No
>
> You must select Yes for setup to continue. Selecting No terminates the setup process.

2. The client setup screen appears (see Figure 4.24), allowing you to confirm the user's full name, logon name, and computer name. After reading this screen, click Begin.

FIGURE **4.24**

*SBS Client Setup.*

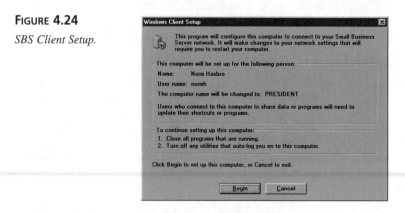

3. The SBS client networking components are installed, as shown in Figure 4.25.

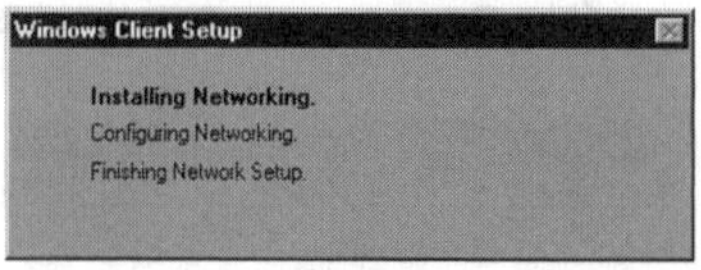

FIGURE **4.25**

*Installing workstation networking components.*

**Note**

The client setup program assumes that you have your Windows 98, Windows 95, or Windows NT Workstation 4.0 source files (a.k.a. CAB files) on your workstation's hard disk. The client setup program needs access to these source files in order to install the networking components. If these source files are not located on your workstation's hard disk, you are promoted for the location of these files (typically you insert the CD-ROM for your workstation operating system). If necessary, direct the client setup program to your source files and continue.

▼

▼    4. The user information is set up (user logon name and computer name), and the
        workstation asks you to approve a restart. Select Yes. This is the end of Task 4.3.

**Note**

> Be sure you remove the SBS magic disk from the floppy drive of the work-
> station you're working on before you reboot. If you fail to do this, the
> workstation will report a missing command file or operating system because
> the floppy disk, when left inadvertently in Drive A:, isn't bootable.

▲

## Task 4.4: SBS Client Applications Installed

Finally, you get a well-deserved rest after two days of SBS network setup activities.
Here, the applications you specified in Task 4.2, step 6 are automatically installed on
your workstation, so kick back and enjoy. At the end of the SBS client application installation process, you need to reboot your workstation and log on to the SBS network as the
user you are setting up.

1. When prompted via the network logon dialog box, log on as NormH with the password Purple3.

2. If prompted to Retain Your Individual Settings in the Future via a Windows
   Networking dialog box, select Yes.

3. If prompted, confirm your password (for example, Purple3) in the Set Windows
   Password dialog box. This sets the local password file to be the same as the network password file in Windows 95 and Windows 98. Don't forget that passwords
   are case-sensitive.

   A Small Business Workstation Setup dialog box (Creating User Profile) notifies
   you that a profile is being created at c:\windows\profiles\normh\applications.

   Next, Internet Explorer 5.0 is automatically installed. Afterwards, your workstation
   reboots. A Windows Setup dialog box appears notifying you that the computer is
   Updating System Settings.

4. Log on to the workstation as NormH. You are taken to the workstation's desktop.
   Notice that the Company and Users shared folders appears as a shortcut on your
   desktop. The Client Installation Wizard screen also appears (see Figure 4.26). Click
   Next.

5. At this point, the SBS client applications are automatically installed, as seen in
   Figure 4.27.

**4**

**▼ TASK**

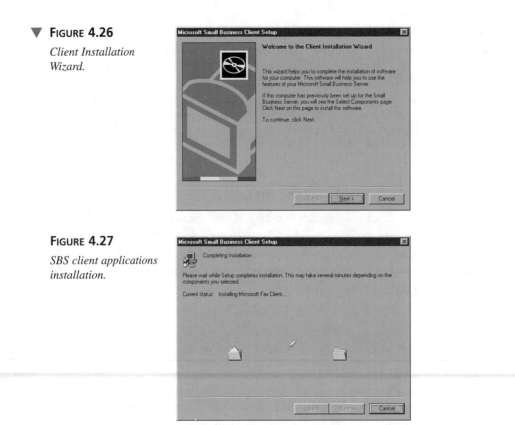

▼ FIGURE 4.26

*Client Installation
Wizard.*

FIGURE 4.27

*SBS client applications
installation.*

6. After the SBS client applications are installed, the machine will automatically reboot. You have completed the workstation setup.

You will now want to prove to yourself that the SBS client applications have correctly installed. To do so, follow these steps:

1. Log on as NormH.

2. Select Control Panel (Start, Settings).

3. In Control Panel, double-click the WSP Client applet.

4. The Microsoft WinSock Proxy Client dialog box appears. You should configure it similar to Figure 4.28, which shows Internet-related traffic is being redirected to SPRINGERS01.

▼ 5. Close the Microsoft WinSock Proxy Client dialog box and Control Panel.

**Figure 4.28**

*Proof of SBS setup.*

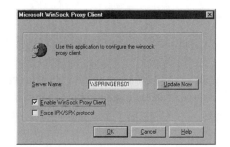

Congratulations! You have now set up the SBS server, a user, and a workstation over the past two days. You now have a functional SBS network. It is a milestone to be proud of!

## Task 4.5: Add Remaining Users and Workstations

Now is a great time to add the remaining Springer Spaniels Unlimited users and workstations to the SBS network. You need to complete this task because these users are necessary for tasks on future days. The complete list of Springer Spaniels Unlimited users to be added is found in Appendix E.

# ERD Update

Before going to lunch, take a moment to update the Emergency Repair Disk (ERD). Because you've added a lot of information to the SBS network (users, machines, and so on), it is important to capture these updated settings on the ERD (just in case!).

To update the ERD, select the Create an Emergency Repair Disk option from the To Do List (via the SBS Console). This is similar to the same ERD steps you performed on Day 3.

# Lunch

Today we have a guest speaker, Jon Eastlake. Jon is the vice president of finance for Delta Society, a nonprofit organization dedicated to training animals for service to disabled humans. Delta Society is best known for its work with service dogs. In mid-1997, Delta Society implemented an SBS network to replace its aging NetWare network. Here is Jon's story about how he lowered his fees.

# Working Smart With SBS Consulting Fees

*by Jon Eastlake*
*Delta Society*

As a nonprofit organization, we're vigilant about finding ways to minimize our administrative costs. From the perspective of installing and maintaining SBS, that can be done in a couple of ways via assisting or working with SBS consultants with the SBS build. First, faced with the prospect of consultants costing $80 an hour and more, I worked with our consultants to identify repetitive tasks that I could assist with after a modest amount of training. A good example of one of those tasks is running the SBS workstation setup disk on user workstations. After an introduction of what the task entailed and watching it work, I was largely able to perform it from there. I called a few times to resolve questions, but principally I did it without assistance, saving approximately 10 hours of consulting time. A byproduct of setting up user workstations is that a person learns the idiosyncrasies of various workstations, which can be of immense help when it comes to assisting users.

Second, I found that the more I participated in any part of the SBS installation process, the better I have been able to troubleshoot user problems. We no longer have a dedicated information technology person, I do not consider myself a techie, and calling a consultant over the phone to diagnose the cause of a user problem can waste time and be expensive. From my participation in the installation of SBS, I have been better able to determine the source of network and user problems. Accordingly, I can usually respond in the most efficient and cost-effective manner possible.

What's the result? Delta Society was able to implement the installation of our SBS network under budget and on time, and we have been able to minimize the continuing use of our consultants. Please understand, though, that situations definitely occur where only the consultants can fix a problem. The key is controlling their utilization.

The primary point of this is that SBS is touted as a low-cost solution for smaller organizations. That's exactly the type of solution Delta Society sought. We ensured our success by assisting in the process where possible (for example, running the SBS installation disk on user workstations) but not mistaking what we were able to do and what should be performed by professionals. It is important not to be penny wise and pound foolish.

# ☽PM Advanced Workstation Setup Topics

Welcome to the afternoon session, where we discuss advanced topics. The morning session had you implement a workstation on your SBS network. The underlying assumption was that nothing special or unusual would present any unique workstation challenges (and such is usually the case). However, I want to spend several pages sharing different workstation setup scenarios with you, based on my experience with SBS out in the real world, not my test laboratory.

# SBS Versus Regular Windows NT Server

The SBS workstation setup phase has been especially perplexing to seasoned Windows NT Server gurus who typically view workstation setups as a quick secondary click on Network Neighborhood, the installation of the TCP/IP protocol and Microsoft networking client, and a reboot. In fact, I'll never forget overhearing a Windows NT Server wizard telling a gullible small business client that the magic disk would screw up everything. Boy, was he wrong.

The magic disk process is very different from setting up a workstation on a regular Windows NT Server network. Over the past several pages, that much has become clear, but let me take one more stab at making the distinction. The closest process in regular Windows NT Server that even comes close to the magic disk is the client configuration disks you can create under the Network Client Administrator found under the Administrative Tools (Common) program group in Windows NT Server 4.0. If you select the Make Network Installation Startup Disk option in Network Client Administrator, as seen in Figure 4.29, you can create an installation startup disk. This process works for the following operating systems:

- Windows NT Server and Workstation
- Windows 95
- Windows for Workgroups version 3.11
- Microsoft Network Client for MS-DOS version 3.0

Much like the magic disk in SBS, the Windows NT Server 4.0–created installation startup disk automatically boots the client computer, connects to the server containing the installation files (via a UNC pathname), and commences the installation process. However, it does not install any applications for you such as the SBS magic disk facilitates. To accomplish any application installation tasks on a regular Windows NT Server 4.0 network, I suggest you consider using Microsoft System Management Server (SMS) packages (an application installation approach in SMS).

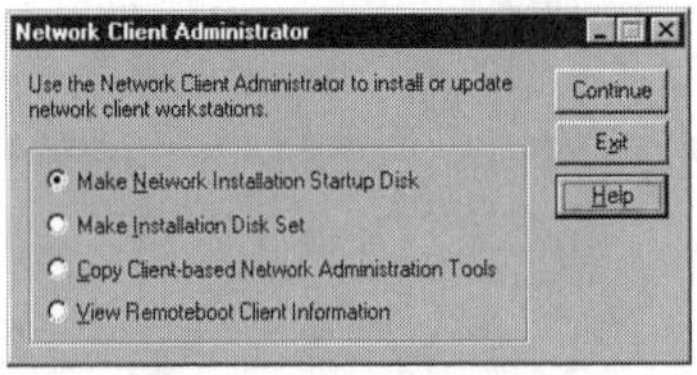

FIGURE 4.29

*Network Client Administrator.*

But the SBS magic disk is much more robust than the installation startup disk created by Windows NT Server. This is demonstrated best by looking at the Netparam.ini file contained on the SBS magic disk. (The Windows NT Server–created installation startup disk doesn't contain nearly this much information.)

Listing 4.1 shows the Netparam.ini file for NormH.

LISTING 4.1    THE NETPARAM.INI FILE FOR NORMH

```
;
; This file is revised by the Setup Computer Wizard and
written to the; startup floppy disk. It is subsequently
used by the SAM Integrated Client
; Setup process.
;
[NetParams]
;
; The FloppyDate entry specifies the date on which
the startup floppy disk
; was created. This string will be displayed for
informational purposes during
; the ICS process.
FloppyDate=Thursday, December 31, 1998  12:10:45


;
; The UserFullName entry specifies the user's
full name as entered by Admin
; when the user account was created. This string will
be displayed for; informational purposes
during the ICS process.
UserFullName=Norm Hasbro
```

```
;
; The NetCard entry will either be blank to indicate that the
; ICS process should autodetect the Network Interface Card, or will
; specify a network card that is supported, can be autoconfigured,
; but may not be autodetectable.
;
NetCard=


;
; The network protocol will always be TCP/IP
;
Protocol=TCPIP


;
; The redirection is predetermined.
;
Redir=BASIC


;
; Domain must be specified if Redir=FULL.
;
Domain=SPRINGERS


;
; The computer name is generated by the Setup Computer Wizard.
;
ComputerName=PRESIDENT


;
; The user name may either be chosen from a
; listbox in the Setup Computer
; Wizard or specified as a command line parameter.
;
; The entries in that listbox are found by
; enumerating the users in the domain.
;
; The username MUST be pre-existing !
;
User=NormH


;
; A password may be specified as a command line parameter.
;
Password=


;
; Server specifies the name of the SAM server, i.e. the computer on which
```

*continues*

**LISTING 4.1**   CONTINUED

```
; the Setup Computer Wizard runs, and to which the client computer will
; connect on initial startup.
;
Server=SPRINGERS01


;
; Share specifies the name of the share on the SAM
;server relative to which
; any files created or modified by the Setup Computer Wizard for any
; username/machine name combination will be stored.
;
;
Share=Clients


;
; The FormatDisk entry specifies whether the client
; computer hard disk is to
; be formatted as part of the ICS operation. A NULL or '0'
; entry means no.
;
FormatDisk=0


;
; The OSName entry supplies the string to be displayed in
; the ICS process to
; inform the user which operating system will be installed.
;
OSName=Microsoft Windows 95


;
; The SetupCmd entry specifies the command line, relative
; to \\Server\Share,
; for the procedure that initiates the operating system setup.
; A placeholder for a response file may be included in the command line
; expression: "MS\Win95\Setup.exe /IS %RespFile%"
; DO NOT SPECIFY THE RESPONSE FILE PATH INSTEAD OF THIS PLACEHOLDER.
;
SetupCmd=\Setup\Win95\startcli.exe


;
; The RespFile entry specifies the path, relative to \\Server\Share,
; of the the response file for unattended operating system setup.
;
RespFile=Response\PRESID~1\PRESID~1.TXT
```

# Windows For Workgroups

Microsoft claims that SBS supports Windows for Workgroups (WFW). In fact, the alleged support includes logon, file, and printer network-level support as you would expect. But you must use the 16-bit versions of the following applications with SBS when working with workstations running WFW:

- Microsoft Internet Explorer (IE)
- Microsoft Exchange client
- Microsoft Schedule +
- Modem sharing client
- Proxy client

Officially, there is no support for Microsoft Outlook or the Fax client program (neither of these are available in 16-bit versions).

The WFW setup process on an SBS network is manual, not automatic. First, you must install the TCP/IP networking protocol on the WFW computer. Second, you must configure the network settings, such as SBS domain name (for example, SPRINGERS). Third, after you reboot and log on to the SBS network, you must configure your drive mappings and printer resources. You then install the SBS client applications including IE, Microsoft Exchange client, Microsoft Schedule +, modem sharing client, and proxy client software. These steps are detailed in the SBS *Start Here* manual that ships with the SBS software. (It is also located in a file named shappd.doc on SBS CD-ROM Disc 2 in the \STARTHRE directory.)

So far, so good, if it all works. The bad news is that for all the discussion concerning WFW support on SBS networks, I've had very little luck with WFW. There are several culprits regarding WFW on an SBS network, starting with a misbehaving TCP/IP protocol trying to get a dynamic IP address and ending with the modem-sharing client never working. Bottom line? I have in 100% of the cases upgraded WFW workstations to at least Windows 95 in order to make them functional workstations on an SBS network. So I leave you with the advice from the field: WFW and SBS don't mix. Sorry.

# Other Workstation Operating Systems

Why would you ever be concerned about supporting UNIX-related, Macintosh, or NetWare clients on an SBS network? Because, in the real world, you will have to, as have I. Needless to say, there have been a few lessons learned along the way. I'll tell one war story from the UNIX, Macintosh, and NetWare camps.

## UNIX Scenarios

Many industries have historically rallied around solutions that were UNIX-based for a huge number of reasons. An example is the fundraising field in the nonprofit sector, which is exactly where I gained my experience. Here, the disease research organization needed to maintain access to its existing UNIX server in order to continue using its Raiser Edge fundraising software. We easily accomplished this by installing the ICE.TEN terminal emulation package, which allowed me to establish a character-based session from the SBS clients to the UNIX server. ICE.TEN runs on the client workstations with no involvement from the SBS server. The one lesson learned was that I had to carefully change the IP addressing from the default 10.0.0.X scheme to the IP addressing scheme already in use by the existing UNIX network (128.0.0.X). After that adjustment was made, the UNIX and SBS networks coexisted very well together.

The above example involved Intel-based PCs (with Windows 95) to access the UNIX server, but what if you are running a UNIX workstation trying to access an SBS server machine? Here, the situation is no different from regular Windows NT Server. You need to implement a network file system (NFS) client/server solution such as NetManage's Chameleon or WRQ's Reflection applications. This scenario limits you to basic logon, file, and printer services. You in no way, shape, or form participate as an SBS client.

## Macintosh Clients

This was certainly one of my more interesting SBS gigs. Here, the investment analysis firm was upgrading from its older Macintosh network to a brand-new SBS network. For reasons known only to the managing partners of the client firm, I was asked to allow a few Macintoshes to exist past the network conversion date. That meant these Macintosh workstations needed to access the SBS server for a limited period of time for e-mail, file sharing, printing, and logon/logoff purposes. No problem. Hey, I once set up a Macintosh/Windows NT Server network for the world's largest Macintosh temporary agency.

In fact, it wasn't a problem. Here is how you support Macintosh clients on an SBS network. There are three sides to this puzzle including the SBS server machine, the Macintosh workstation, and the applications.

On the server side, you need to confirm that you indeed installed SBS on an NTFS partition. (That should be an automatic affirmative, because NTFS is the default file system for SBS server machine.)

You then need to install Services for Macintosh via the Service tab sheet found on the Network property sheet. You might recall that the Network property sheet appears when you launch the Network applet in the Control Panel in Windows NT Server 4.0. Services for Macintosh automatically installs the AppleTalk Protocol, File Server for Macintosh, and Print Server for Macintosh.

On the Macintosh client side, you will need to install the Microsoft user authentication module (UAM). This process is well-documented in the Windows NT Server 4.0 Resource Kit. It is essential that you use Macintosh OS version 7.5 or higher to take advantage of the UAMs robust logon security. On the application side, you might be interested to know that Microsoft Exchange has a robust Macintosh e-mail client, found with the full Microsoft Exchange product (not the version contained in SBS).

## SBS and NetWare Clients

Many small businesses migrate from NetWare networks to SBS. That fact is well-established. But many times, things don't go quite as scheduled, and for a period of time, both the SBS network and NetWare network are up and running. I have seen this primarily in the context of accounting system conversions. Whereas the SBS network might be functional as planned, often, the accounting system isn't ready for conversion. So you have a situation where users are logging on to the NetWare network to run the accounting application (for example, Great Plains Dynamics) and logging on to the SBS network for e-mail, Internet access, printing, and so on.

Based on this need, how well do SBS and NetWare networks coexist? I've found that the two environments get along remarkably well. But there are several steps on both the SBS server and the SBS client workstation that must be performed to work with a NetWare network. If you want the SBS server to communicate with the NetWare server, you need to install the Nwlink IPX/SPX protocol and the Gateway Servers for NetWare (GSNW) services on the SBS server machine. (This process is well-documented in the Windows NT Server 4.0 Resource Kit.)

If you want the client workstation to log on to both the SBS network and the NetWare network, you need to do the following: For the SBS network, no further changes are necessary, assuming you performed the steps this morning. For the NetWare network, you need to install the IPX/SPX-compatible Protocol and the Client for NetWare Networks on your Windows 98 or Windows 95 machine. Upon rebooting your workstation, log on to both the SBS network and the NetWare network.

**Tip**

Make your username and password the same on both the SBS and NetWare networks for simplicity. Also, I highly recommend that the Primary Network Logon be the Client for Microsoft Networks so that the SBS network is the first network to provide your logon authentication and drive mappings.

4

# Devitt's Skinny Machine

As discussed on Day 1, "Welcome to Small Business Server," and reiterated by our guest speaker at lunch today, small businesses are always up for saving a buck or two. Such cost-saving behavior takes many forms, include Devitt's skinny machine. Devitt, a Seattle lawyer, is an expert in the legal field. He has little interest in mastering computers, and that lack of interest was manifested in his workstation configuration. Devitt hadn't upgraded for many years, resulting in his continued use of an older Compaq 486 workstation running Windows for Workgroups with 12MB RAM and 10MB free hard disk space (on a 125MB hard disk to begin with). When I arrived on the scene to implement SBS at the law firm, I knew Devitt's machine would present some interesting challenges.

By hook and by crook, I was able to upgrade Devitt's machine to Windows 95, which, as you recall from the section "Windows for Workgroups," removed several SBS-related workstation issues. This was accomplished by removing old versions of Lotus 123, WordPerfect, and an unusually large amount of .tmp (temporary) files. But I still didn't have close to the minimum amount of disk space required for the full SBS client applications.

Here I had to go under the hood on the SBS workstation setup process. First, I created a skinny magic disk for Devitt's workstation with only the Microsoft Fax client, Microsoft Modem Sharing client, and Microsoft Proxy client installed. That only consumed 10MB, leaving about 10MB free. Next, I installed IE and Microsoft Outlook manually from these application's respective standalone CD-ROMS. When installing these applications, I selected the custom installation options and not only deselected unnecessary IE and Outlook features (such as holiday clip art), but I also installed these applications to Devitt's user directory on the network. This, of course, dramatically reduced the application footprint on the workstation's hard disk, but not as much as you might think. Microsoft Outlook isn't without a footprint when a network installation of this application is installed. No matter what you do, Outlook insists on installing some components on the workstation's local hard disk. And because I manually installed IE and Outlook, I had to manually configure these applications to work with the SBS network. For IE, I had to modify the connection properties to use SBS's proxy server. For Outlook, I had to create a profile that attached to Devitt's Exchange-based mailbox.

When all was said and done, Devitt literally had 2MB of free space on his local hard disk, but he didn't care. Heck, he was participating on the SBS network, Devitt-style!

# Alternative Workstation Installations

There are two ways to implement the necessary SBS components without using the client installation or magic disk. The first involves a scenario using Windows NT Workstation. The second approach is much more manual, whereby you explicitly run the setup for each SBS program.

As promised, here is how you can add a Windows NT Workstation to an SBS network without the magic disk:

1. Make sure you are logged on to the SBS server machine as an Administrator or equivalent.

2. Select Server Manager from the Administrative Tools (Common) program group (found via Programs in the Start menu, Programs).

3. From the Computer menu in Server Manager, select Add to Domain menu option.

4. Add the computer name and select it as a Windows NT Workstation (for example, MANAGEMENT2). Close the Add Computer To Domain dialog box (see Figure 4.30).

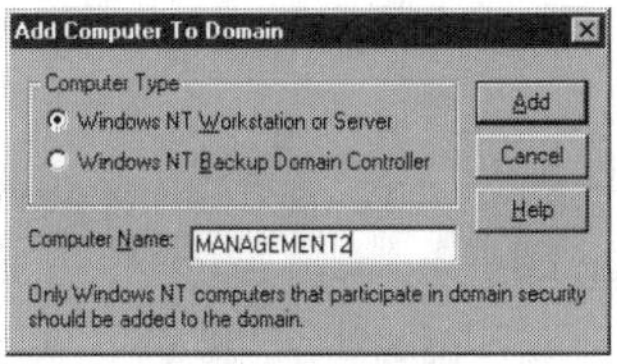

**FIGURE 4.30**

*Adding a computer name in Server Manager.*

5. From the SBS Console, select Manage Computers from the More Tasks tab.

6. Select Add a User to Use an Existing Computer option on the Manage Computers sheet.

7. Select the user to add to this computer from the list of users you are presented. Click Next.

8. Select the computer that you want to add the user to (for example, MANAGE-MENT2). Click Next.

9. Select the operating system of the workstation (for example, Windows NT 4.0). I realize this is somewhat redundant, but it is a required step for this process. Click Next.

10. Select the SBS client programs to install (fax, modem, proxy clients, IT, Outlook). Click Next.

11. On the Create the Setup Files dialog box, click Next. The Set Up computer wizard creates the setup files but does not ask you to insert a disk. This is a key point to this entire alternative approach.

12. Click the Finish button after reading the Completing the Set Up Computer Wizard dialog box.

13. Now, go to the workstation that you named in step 4. You want to set up and log on as the username that you selected in step 7. Make sure that you've configured the Windows NT Workstation, via the Network applet in Control Panel, to use the same computer name you indicated it would (for example, MANAGEMENT2).

14. Upon successful logon authentication, observe that the SBS client programs you selected in step 10 are installed. After the SBS client programs have been installed, you need to reboot the workstation.

I have seen this approach used on SBS networks that had Windows NT Workstation clients and the SBS consultant (me!) wanted to save valuable time by not formatting and creating a disk for each Windows NT Workstation computer. On one job, I found that I saved myself and my client one hour by avoiding the magic disk creation process.

I've used another nontraditional workstation setup approach that is also magic diskless: I manually install the SBS client applications. I've used this approach several times when, for reasons I've never been able to explain, the darn magic disk simply didn't work on a workstation. Simply stated, the textbook approach using the magic disk results in SBS connectivity and client application installation errors. Usually on a Sunday at 11:00 p.m. with the staff arriving in about nine hours.

To perform this, I assume that you're on a Windows 95 workstation with basic logon connectivity with the SBS Server (for example, SPRINGERS01). That is, you've installed the TCP/IP protocol and have logged on to the SBS network.

1. On the SBS server machine, verify that the client's share points to the \SmallBusiness\Clients directory.

2. At the workstation, log on to the SBS network.

3. From the workstation, map a drive to the client's share on the SBS server machine.

4. To install the SBS client applications, run the appropriate setup file as shown in Table 4.2.

**TABLE 4.2**   SBS CLIENT APPLICATION SETUP FILES

| SBS Client Application | Setup File (share name\directory\setup file) |
| --- | --- |
| Microsoft Fax client | \clients\ms\FAX\WIN95\Setup.exe |
| Microsoft Internet Explorer | \clients\ms\Ie\I386\Ie4setup.exe |
| Microsoft Modem Sharing client | \clients\ms\Modemshr\Win95\Setup.exe |
| Microsoft Outlook client | \clients\ms\Outlook\I386\Setup.exe |
| Microsoft Proxy client | \clients\ms\proxy\Setup.exe |

If you are on another type of workstation, the basic methodology remains the same, but the location of the SBS client application setup files would be slightly different. For example, if you were using a Windows NT Workstation 4.0 machine with this methodology, the SBS client application setup files are typically stored in a \I386 directory instead of a \WIN95 directory, but it varies on an application by application basis.

**Tip**

> If you manually install the SBS client applications using the method presented above, you need to manually configure the applications to participate on the SBS network. That is because the applications don't benefit from some of the SBS macro code that automatically performs such configurations for you. One example of this would be the connection type used by IE. You will need to configure IE to use the SBS-based Proxy Server (typically the NetBIOS name of the SBS server machine, for example, SPRINGERS01).

4

# Any User, Any Time!

One of my clients has a policy that any user may use any machine at any time. This policy has been put in place so that organization productivity isn't impeded by a failed workstation at someone's desk. This policy has several ramifications. First, I've noticed that each user keeps a workstation that is clean as a whistle. No unacceptable Internet-based photos here, given that anyone may use anyone else's machine on short notice. The second is that the users no longer have an excuse for why they can't work. Third, organization productivity has indeed risen, I guess based on the first two reasons, all amounting to this, the workstations are a business tool viewed much like a photocopier or fax machine.

To implement this policy, there are several steps. The first concerns adding each user to each machine. This is accomplished via the Allow a User to Use an Existing Computer option on the Manage Computers sheet via the SBS Console. I outlined this process in the "Alternative Workstation Installations" section (steps 5 through 12). So, if you have ten users and ten PCs and want to implement an any user/any time policy, you would have to make 90 entries via the Allow a User to Use an Existing Computer option. The formula for determining this is

(C X U) - U*1

where

C = the number of workstation computers

U = the number of users

The advantage to this approach is that you're creating a roving profile for each user on each machine. The drawback is that, depending on the SBS client applications you intend to install, you might find that 10 copies of Microsoft Outlook are being installed on each machine!

To prevent this last problem of multiple application copies (for example, Outlook) being installed on each workstation (and using too much local hard disk space), I've used an under-the-hood approach that has worked well. The two key components that must be customized for each user at each PC are the drive mappings and the Outlook profile. The fax, modem sharing, proxy clients, and IE do not need user-specific customization. Thus, I've implemented the any user/any time approach by going to each workstation and creating a new Outlook profile for each user who might use that workstation. I've also mapped the users' drives via their logon scripts, not locally. I discuss logon script drive mappings in much greater detail on Day 6, "Daily and Weekly SBS Administration (The Dirty Dozen)."

**Note**

The any user/any time approaches discussed above allow each user to enjoy secure and confidential e-mail and file storage on the SBS network. That is because the e-mail is managed via a Microsoft Exchange mailbox that uses network logon security. The stored files on the network also use network logon security. Thus, the CEO of a small company can have another employee use her machine without lingering concerns that her private e-mails will be exposed. (That's as long as she hasn't copied selected e-mails to a personal folder on the workstation's C:\ drive. Such a folder could theoretically be imported into the mailbox of another user for viewing.)

# Troubleshooting SBS Workstation Setups

A few rules of the road help you drive when troubleshooting workstation problems. These range from official Microsoft support proclamations to streetwise knowledge.

In general, the SBS workstation setup routine is a finicky process. You should not only adhere to the formal magic disk setup process, but you should also use common sense. Consider the following:

- Don't overwrite existing, newer applications with older, SBS client applications. For example, with SBS it is a mistake to install an older version of IE or Microsoft Outlook, via the magic disk, over newer versions you might have on your hard disk. If you have IE 4.0 on your hard disk, do not install IE 3.02 via the SBS magic disk setup (in SBS 4.0). It would cause numerous application-level problems when you attempted to run IE. If you have newer applications installed on your hard disk that you don't want to overwrite, I recommend you configure the newer applications manually. On Day 9, "Connecting to the Internet," I show you how to manually configure IE. On Day 8, "Implementing Outlook," I show you how to manually configure Microsoft Outlook.

  Be careful when using light versions of popular applications. For example, Outlook Express, a lightweight e-mail client with IE, never did work under SBS 4.0 or 4.0a. Believe me, I tried to make it work on workstations with too little local hard disk space. In fact, one of the workstations I tried to install Outlook Express on was Devitt's (you will recall Devitt's story above).

- Workstation operating system versions. Throughout the history of SBS, my experience has been that the SBS releases (4.0, 4.0a, 4.5) can't keep up with the more frequent workstation operating system releases and upgrades. Your challenge as an SBS administrator, consultant, and user will be to keep your SBS version in synch with your workstation operating system. For example, if you use SBS 4.0 or 4.0a with Windows 98, you will of course notice that all the SBS Console references to workstation operating systems didn't include Windows 98. (These references only included Windows 95 or Windows NT Workstation 4.0.)

  Under SBS 4.0 or 4.0a, if you run the magic disk on a Windows 98 workstation, upon reboot you receive an unusual character-based startup error on the Windows 98 workstation that the vserver.vxd resource couldn't be loaded. I solved this error message, without any detriment to the Windows 98 workstation, by using the REGEDIT tool to search for and remove all Windows 98 Registry calls to vserver.vxd. After these references were removed and I rebooted, the workstation functioned normally on the SBS network.

4

The point is this. With workstation operation systems growing and changing literally all the time, your SBS network possibly won't natively support the latest workstation operating system. Here you must use vision and common sense to make the marriage of your SBS network and your workstation happen. Here is what I recommend. First, monitor the SBS-related newsgroup and support articles at www.microsoft.com. Second, consider subscribing the Microsoft TechNet, a monthly CD-ROM library subscription server (approximately $300 annually, can be purchased from your favorite reseller). Third, interact with other SBS sites via local computer user groups.

- Can't read the magic disk. Perhaps your workstation can't read the formatting method used by SBS (called distribution media format). Simply copy the setup.exe and netparam.txt files from the SBS magic disk to another already-formatted disk. Then continue with the SBS workstation setup as usual.

Errors occur when attempting to run the magic disk at the workstation. Here I recommend you start over. Delete the user and computer from the SBS network (via the SBS Console) and then re-create the user and computer again. You might also view the c:\Startcli.log file on the workstation, which is displayed below for NormH, for setup play-by-play or error information:

```
Adding '\\SPRINGERS01\CLIENTS\SETUP\WIN95\STARTCLI.EXE
 /s:SPRINGERS01 /u:NormH /l:c:\startcli.log /i /c' to RunOnce
SetupInstallFileEx returned 1, FileWasInUse = 21037941
\\SPRINGERS01\CLIENTS\SETUP\WIN95\STARTCLI.EXE
/s:SPRINGERS01 /u:NormH /l:c:\startcli.log /i /c
SHGetSpecialFolderLocation 0x00000007 returned 0x00000000
SHGetPathFromIDList  returned 1 C:\WIN95\Start
Menu\Programs\StartUp
Creating C:\WIN95\Start Menu\Programs\StartUp\Small
Business Workstation Setup.lnk Path \\SPRINGERS01\CLIENTS\SETUP\
WIN95\STARTCLI.EXE Args /f
SHGetSpecialFolderLocation 0x00000000 returned 0x00000000
SHGetPathFromIDList  returned 1 C:\WIN95\Desktop
Creating C:\WIN95\Desktop\NormH.lnk Path
\\SPRINGERS01\NormH Args (NULL)
SHGetSpecialFolderLocation 0x00000000 returned 0x00000000
SHGetPathFromIDList  returned 1 C:\WIN95\Desktop
Creating C:\WIN95\Desktop\Company.lnk Path
\\SPRINGERS01\Company Args (NULL)
SHGetSpecialFolderLocation 0x00000000 returned 0x00000000
SHGetPathFromIDList  returned 1 C:\WIN95\Desktop
Desktop link Microsoft Internet Explorer 3.01 Setup.lnk not found
```

- SBS setup information isn't uploaded to the SBS server machine. Here you've run the magic disk on the workstation, but then the SBS setup process fails. First, make sure that the workstation configuration information was properly created in the c:\smallbusiness\clients\response\(workstation name) directory. The workstation name is the same as the NetBIOS name you assigned to the workstation during the workstation setup process this morning. For example, if you followed the example this morning, you would have a directory called PRESIDENT. As an example, Figure 4.31 shows the contents of the PRESIDENT directory.

**FIGURE 4.31**

*Machine configuration directory.*

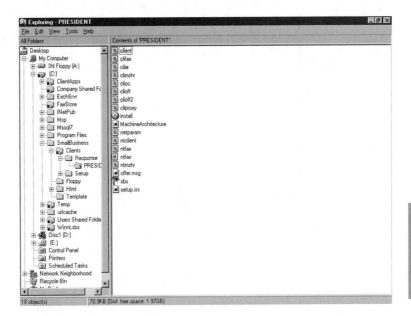

You will note the machine configuration directory contains numerous setup files (.inf) plus the Microsoft Exchange profile file (.prf).

**Note**

You might also want to verify that the administrator account has the full control for both the response directory mentioned immediately above plus the logon script directory (C:\winnt.sbs\system32\repl\Import\scripts\smallbusiness). In the logon script directory, verify that the user has a logon script file (for example, NormH.bat), which can be run when the user successfully performs a workstation logon to the SBS network. On Day 6, in the drive mapping discussion, I display the logon script for NormH.

- Similar to the point above, the SBS client applications aren't installed on the workstation. First, delete and re-create the user and workstation at the SBS console. Second, use my manual SBS client application workaround detailed earlier (see the "Alternative Workstation Installations" section, earlier today). Third, make sure the workstation has enough room for the SBS client application to be installed. If such free space doesn't exist, consider doing a skinny SBS client application installation (see the section "Devitt's Skinny Machine" earlier).

**Note**

> The SBS workstation setup process can be used to install other applications on the local workstation such as Microsoft Office and the application of your choice. I discuss this capability on Day 6 when I discuss installing applications.

- Any user/any time doesn't work on a Windows NT Workstation machine. Here, the SBS client applications were installed while user A was logged on and user B can neither see nor run the same SBS client applications. The solution here is to make sure the user that first installed the applications via the magic disk had administrator-level permissions on the local machine. If this wasn't done, perform the SBS client application setup, via the magic disk again, while logged on as a user with local administrator privileges.

- Others. Over the course of the remaining days, you will learn, on a feature-by-feature and application-by-application basis, how SBS client applications might or might not function as expected. For example, on Day 13, "Dial-In/Dial-Out," I'll show you how to troubleshoot modem pooling from both the server and workstation sides.

## Task 4.6: Uninstalling SBS Clients

**TASK**

In SBS 4.0a, there is not an automatic workstation client uninstall routine. There are four steps for removing the SBS 4.0a workstation client installation:

1. Remove the following Registry keys on your local machine after making a backup of your local Registry:

   ```
   HKEY_LOCAL_MACHINE\SOFTWARE\Microsoft\Small Business
   HKEY_LOCAL_MACHINE\SOFTWARE\Microsoft\Windows\
   CurrentVersion\Uninstall/Small Business
   ```

2. Remove the following files from the local hard disk:

   ```
   Startcli.exe
   Samc14.dll
   Ocmanage.dll
   Ocsam.dll
   ```

▼

▼ 3. Reset IE's default home page to a location other than the Small Business Server Web site.

4. Use the Add/Remove Software applet in Control Panel to remove the SBS applica-
▲ tions of your choice (modem client, Outlook, IE, fax client, proxy client).

# Summary

Whew! You've made it through four demanding days and your reward is a functional and operational SBS network. I started today by offering you congratulations and I end on the same note. Tomorrow both beginning and advanced SBSers will attend the entire day to discover and master the SBS Console.

4

# DAY 5

# Managing the Small Business Server Management Console

As part of your journey toward mastering SBS today, you'll tour the SBS Console. Many SBS Console screens are task-oriented; others are display- or report-oriented. You need both to properly manage your SBS network.

Today I want to educate you about SBS Console. Today prepares you for using SBS Console as you complete the dozen tasks on Day 6, "Daily and Weekly SBS Administration (The Dirty Dozen)," and the monthly and annual tasks on Day 7, "Monthly and Annual SBS Duties." This is one of the few days in which both beginners and advanced users should attend both the morning and afternoon sessions: The day doesn't necessarily divide itself between beginning and advanced sessions.

**Note**

> My advice for learning the SBS Console is to both read this chapter and play with the SBS Console. Because the recommended path with this book is first to set up an imaginary company Springer Spaniels Unlimited, you really can't do any harm to your system. The benefit of playing with the SBS console is that, after you've completed this book and then installed SBS for your real company, you will have learned the SBS Console inside and out.
>
> Why play with the SBS Console? In my experience, few SBS administrators actually take a few hours out of their busy days to click each link in the SBS Console. These few hours make a world of difference when it comes to improving how you use your SBS network at your small business.

## Task 5.1: Surfing the SBS Console

Before we begin looking at virtually every feature of the SBS Console, take a moment while you're having the first cup of coffee this morning to launch the SBS Console from the Start menu (lower-left corner of your desktop) and surf around the screens. Such creative play breeds familiarity and increases your comfort as we proceed.

**Note**

> With Version 4.0 or 4.0A, it is essential that you set your screen's desktop area to 800×600 pixels under Display Properties (accessed via Control Panel) and 256 colors so that the SBS Console is properly displayed. Failure to do so results in only part of the SBS Console being displayed, which is unpleasant, because you will need to physically move the console around the screen in order to see it. Neither the  color scheme nor screen resolution matters with V.4.5.

If you're a Microsoft Certification candidate, you might recall that one of the challenges on the Desktop Operating System exams was that there were several ways to answer the questions. For example, in Windows 95, there are seven ways to Egypt to run an application. The SBS Console has some similarities there. You will quickly see that SBS Console has a habit of repeating itself. That is, many screens that are accessed as a subscreen from one option are present as a standalone Task or More Tasks option themselves. When such repetition occurs, I will alert you to that point and cross-reference the repetition.

From the afternoon of Day 1, "Welcome to Small Business Server," recall the discussion about the design goals of the SBS Console: The Tasks sheet contains the most frequent tasks you will perform on an SBS network. The More Tasks sheet contains the less frequent tasks, based on Microsoft's design goals.

▼

> **Tip**
>
> Do not try to launch the SBS Console in the first few minutes after you log on to the SBS server machine. If you try to do that (from the Start menu), you might receive an error message from Internet Explorer 5.0 that the page could not be found. Don't fear. This occurs because the World Wide Web service starts later than other SBS services and it is a predecessor service for the SBS console. Just wait a few minutes and try to launch the SBS Console again. You'll be delighted to see it now starts without incident.

## AM Exploring the Home and Tasks Sheets

When you launch the SBS console, the first screen you see is the Home sheet. The other sheets (Tasks, More Tasks, and Online Guide) each have their own stories. Regarding the Tasks sheet, Microsoft believed that it should list the most popular tasks you perform. Okay, in every SBS site, it might not work that way. Still, I'll give the SBS design team an *A* for effort. In the meantime, you'll learn about each link on all the SBS Console sheets today.

## The Home Sheet

I'll start with the Home sheet displayed in Figure 5.1.

**FIGURE 5.1**

*SBS Console - Home sheet.*

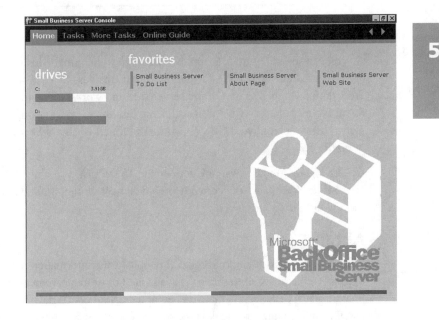

5

**Power Tool Tip**

On Day 20, "Advanced Server Management," I'll discuss how you can customize the SBS Console to add your own selections and information. You'll likely want to add these customized selections to the Home sheet, because it has the most room to accommodate such additions.

The Home sheet is where everything begins. Consider it the Garden of Eden for SBS. This addition to SBS 4.5 wasn't present in SBS 4.0/SBS 4.0a. It is also another example that shows that Microsoft was listening to your feedback from the SBS 4.0/4.0a release. With this starting page, you can see basic system information such as the free space status of the hard disks on your SBS server machine. Part of the idea was to offer a sheet that could, in the future, take on more of an executive information system (EIS) look. If you're not familiar with EISes, these are colorful screens that report critical business information in clever ways, such as traffic light metaphors (green = good, yellow = caution, and red = danger). Microsoft has taken the first step towards this mindset by not only supplying the home sheet but also reporting hard disk space information on it.

**Tip**

If you place the cursor over the hard disk graphic (say C: drive), a drop-down information box from the cursor displays the volume name and file system (FAT, NTFS, CDFS). This is a very nice touch!

## To Do List

As you can see in Figure 5.1, you can easily go to the Small Business Server To Do List that was used during Days 3, "Installing Small Business Server," and 4, "Setting Up the Workstation Client," as part of the server-side and workstation-side setup. Recall that the Small Business Server To Do List offers no less than seven start-up tasks for you to complete when you build your SBS network. The Small Business Server To Do List is shown in Figure 5.2.

By moving your mouse over any item on the To Do List, you will note that the Description on the right side changes to correctly provide a well-written if not warm description of the specific task. It's a nice touch.

## About Page

What a welcome addition to SBS 4.5! Previously, the information reported on the About page was either difficult to find or unavailable. For example, remember how hard it was to find the actual SBS version that you had in the SBS 4.0/4.0a days? You had to deeply dig into the Online Guide and look at the release notes. (Ouch!) No more—with the About sheet, it is displayed front and center (actually, slightly to the right!) as seen in Figure 5.3.

**FIGURE 5.2**

*Small Business Server To Do List.*

**FIGURE 5.3**

*About page.*

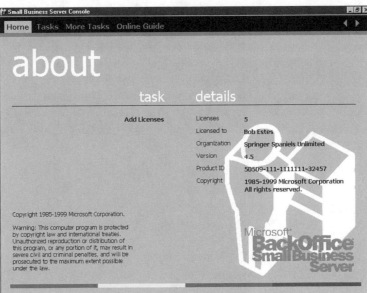

5

## Web Site

The Small Business Server Web Site selection launches Internet Explorer 5.0 and initiates a connection to Microsoft's SBS Web site at www.microsoft.com/backofficesmallbiz so that you can obtain the latest news pertaining to Small Business Server.

### Task 5.2: Coffee Break

If you're like me, you're probably ready to refill your coffee. Go ahead and do so. While you're sipping that second cup of java, go ahead and connect to the Internet and navigate to www.microsoft.com/backofficesmallbiz. Doing that now effectively reinforces the discussion we're currently having. Call it *active learning* or just another way to enjoy your coffee break. Whatever!

▲

> **Note**
>
> When working with the SBS Console, remember that you only need to single-click any option. You do not need to double-click. Such is the case because the SBS Console is really, under the hood, a Web page, so it doesn't behave like a traditional dialog box or menu. Its options are HTML-based like a Web page.

## The Tasks Sheet

Welcome back from your coffee break. Between that last cup of coffee and lunch, we'll explore the seven links shown in the Tasks sheet in Figure 5.4.

**FIGURE 5.4**

*Tasks.*

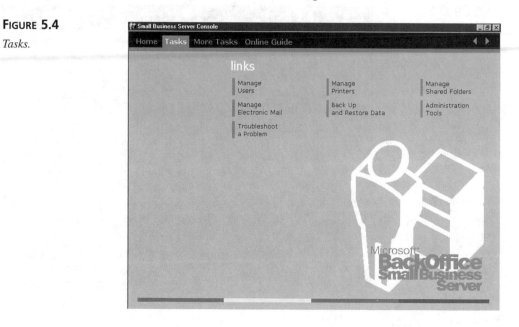

## Manage Users

This is where SBS primarily performs user management. Select the Manage Users link from the SBS Console to add new users, change user accounts and passwords, and manage user permissions. Don't underestimate that last point. Many SBS sites have asked for return visits to perfect how user permissions are implemented at their sites. In my experience, virtually all small-business owners need to protect their privacy (that is, certain files such as personal accounting information) from staff. It is a reasonable request. The Manage Users page is shown in Figure 5.5.

**FIGURE 5.5**

*Manage Users.*

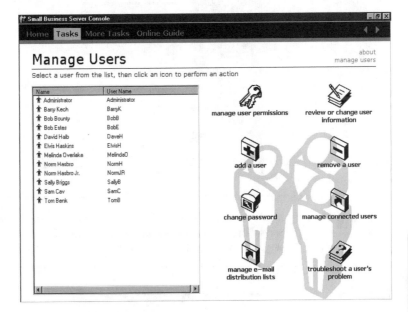

## Task 5.3: Adding Users

Notice in Figure 5.5 that all the users for Springer Spaniels Unlimited have been added to the SBS network. You can find the information you need to add each user in Appendix E, "Springer Spaniel User Information." If you didn't have the opportunity to add each user on Day 4, please do so now.

The Manage Users screen presents registered users on the left pane. On the right pane, eight additional links allow you perform a variety of tasks. While the Manage Users page is the primary way to manage users on our SBS network, I discuss alternative ways to manage users on Day 6.

5

## Manage User Permissions

This tool manages a user's ability to access files such as documents, folders (also known as subdirectories), printers, and fax devices. As mentioned on Day 1, when you select an SBS Console option, typically a sophisticated wizard runs. Such is the case when you select the Manage User Permissions link and the User Access Wizard appears (shown in Figure 5.6).

**FIGURE 5.6**

*User Access Wizard.*

**Note**    If you haven't selected an SBS user account in the left pane, the Manage Server error message displayed in Figure 5.7 appears when you attempt to select the Manage User Permissions link.

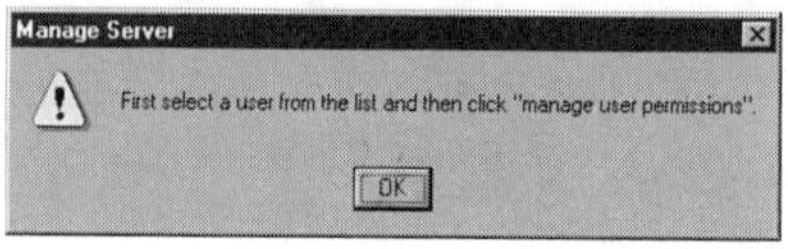

**FIGURE 5.7**

*Error message when no SBS user is selected to manage.*

The User Resource Wizard presents successive screens that allow you to manage the user's ability to

- Use shared folders
- Use printers
- Use fax printers (a.k.a. fax devices)
- Access the Internet
- Access the SBS network via modem dial-in
- Act as an administrator

Each of these screens will be shown and discussed on Day 6 as part of the daily dozen tasks lecture.

## Add a User

This link is, of course, where you add new users. When a user account is created, so is its associated Microsoft Exchange e-mail account (a.k.a. mailbox). You will recall this wizard (seen in Figure 5.8) from Day 4 when you added the users for Springer Spaniels Unlimited.

**FIGURE 5.8**

*User Account Wizard.*

Something I mentioned on Day 2 during SBS planning is worth repeating. Whenever you add a new user, I recommend that each field be populated so that you have rich metainformation about each user on your system. *Metainformation* is information that is used in more than one place. For example, one of the fields allows you to add department information. You should do this as you never know later how that information, captured early in the system life cycle, can return to benefit you.

> **Note**
>
> You can't manage groups from the SBS Console. I discuss groups (as in groups of users) on Day 6.

## Change Password for a User

This is a popular option for SBS administrators, for here you can change a password for security reasons, such as when one user discovers other users' passwords. This is also where you can create a new password if the user has forgotten a password. The Change Password Wizard is shown in Figure 5.9.

Here you can also disable an account by assigning a password that is unknown to the user. When the user attempts to log on, the attempt does, of course, fail. This effectively

disables the account. It is the only way to disable a user's account unless you want to go
under the hood and work the User Manager for Domains. Remember, though, that going
under the hood is exactly what we're trying to avoid with SBS!

**Figure 5.9**

*Change Password
Wizard.*

You can also grant the user the ability to change the new password at the user's next
logon. This lets you effectively reset the password and then have users select a password
known only to them at their next logon. Security issues are further discussed in the afternoon of Day 7.

## Manage E-mail Distribution Lists

This option (shown in Figure 5.10) is useful because it allows you to create, modify, or
remove an e-mail distribution list. Depending on how your company is set up, this can be
a real timesaver.

> **Note**
>
> This wizard affects internal e-mail accounts only. These are the SBS user
> accounts that you create via the User Account Wizard; and because an SBS
> network has a relatively small number of users, e-mail distribution lists are
> less prevalent on an SBS network than they are in a large enterprise.
> Typically, you have the default e-mail user group created during SBS setup
> (for example, Springers) that includes everyone and perhaps one or two
> additional groups (managers, owners). However, in some sites a little creativ-
> ity in user grouping can make distribution of information very efficient.
>
> This wizard does not create e-mail distribution lists that include external e-
> mail addresses. That need—and its been a great one in my SBS experience—
> is handled via Microsoft Outlook and its interaction with Microsoft Exchange
> Server. I discuss external e-mail distribution lists on Days 8, "Implementing
> Outlook," and 16, "Using Microsoft Exchange."

**FIGURE 5.10**

*Manage E-mail distribution lists.*

I will discuss the Manage E-Mail Distribution Lists options after lunch. This screen, an advanced topic, is presented as its own link on the More Tasks screen in the SBS Console.

## Review or Change User Information

First, select a user for whom you want to change information. Then single-click the Review or Change User Information option in Manage Users. You are then presented the user's current settings via the same User Account Wizard shown in Figure 5.8. When might you really use this? Perhaps one of your users has recently gotten married and, following old-fashioned traditions, changed her last name to that of her new husband. Equally likely, perhaps someone has gotten divorced on your staff and wants to change her name back to her maiden name.

## Remove a User

This option removes a user account and associated e-mail account (mailbox) from the SBS network. The Delete User Account option is a subset of the User Account Wizard and is shown in Figure 5.11.

5

Figure **5.11**

*Delete User Account.*

> **Caution**
>
> Be very careful with this wizard because it deletes the account after you click the Finish button. There is no confirmation that allows you to cancel or undo the operation. This lack of confirmation is unusual and makes the Delete User operation somewhat risky, especially if you aren't paying close attention! Another little gotcha about this wizard presents itself in the nature of NT security. When you remove a user, you cannot put the same person back. Sure, this sounds weird and, on the surface, makes no sense. What is happening is that NT bases its security on a number sequence that cannot be re-created. You might be able to restore Joe Doe by name; however, the security number for that user would be fresh and different. I strongly advise that you use Disable Account instead.

## Manage Connected Users

This option, shown in Figure 5.12, allows you to observe, manage, and disconnect users that are connected to your SBS network. It gives you the power bestowed on all network gods, kings, and queens.

This is a very popular option, because it answers the common question of Who is logged on? Regrettably, this tool can be unreliable on its grumpy days. It often doesn't report users who are logged on and often reports users who have logged off some time ago (something I call *ghosting*). I discuss this matter in-depth on Day 6 in the morning session.

**Disconnect a User**   This command terminates a user's session on the SBS network and is useful when a user has remained logged on and you want to reboot or restart the SBS machine. Here, you can pick on just one user.

FIGURE 5.12

*Manage Connected Users.*

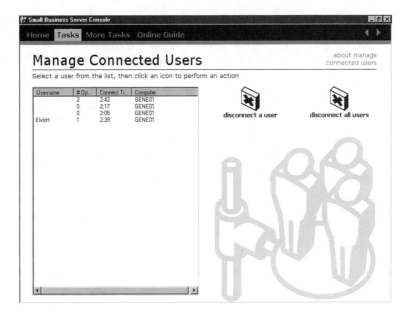

**Disconnect All Users**    Similar to the above command, this allows you to disconnect all users quickly. Again, this is useful when you want to reboot a server such as your SBS machine and you do not want any open connections or open files across the network. It's also useful if you have it out for all users!

The Return to Manage Shared Folders and Return to Manage Users options allow you to navigate within the SBS Console.

### Troubleshoot a User's Problem

This is an online reference using decision-tree logic that allows you to troubleshoot user and SBS network problems. Troubleshooting is further discussed on Day 20. Although it's helpful, believe you me it's no substitute for good old experience and chutzpah!

## Manage Printers

From this SBS console screen, as shown in Figure 5.13, you can manage your printers. However, be advised that this form provides printer management from SBS's perspective. By that, I mean to manage an HP JetDirect card, you need to use the JetAdmin application (which was discussed on Day 3). I discuss other printer issues on Day 6.

5

**FIGURE 5.13**

*Manage Printers.*

Only printers that have been shared for use on the SBS networks appear in the left pane, Share As. If a printer that you have installed doesn't appear, make sure you have shared it correctly. Sharing a printer is discussed on Day 3. It is also possible that you have a printer attached to the server locally (LPT-ports) that you do not care to share. If such is the case, this type of printer does not appear in the left pane of Manage Printers. You need to use the Printers applet via Control Panel to manage your unshared, local printer.

## Control User Access to Printers

This menu option allows you to manage printer security and displays the Printer Access Wizard I've controlled SBS user access to a printer under only one circumstance. A property management firm dedicated a printer to check writing (using Timberline accounting software) with special magnetic toner, and the restrictions placed on HP LaserJet II weren't so much from an untrusting security mindset as from an effort to preserve the magnetic toner.

## Add a Printer

This option allows you to add a new printer to your SBS network. It is the same wizard as the Add Printer Wizard found in the Printers applet in the Control Panel and is discussed in detail on Day 3.

## Change Printer Properties

This option displays a Help dialog box that allows you to display the property sheet for a selected printer. The Properties dialog box for a printer is discussed extensively on Day 6.

## Troubleshoot Printers

Selecting the Troubleshoot Printers option from the Manage Printers sheet displays help screens. This decision tree–type troubleshooting help sheet allows you, in noncomputer talk, to try to resolve your printer problems. It's not a bad start, and my vote is for Microsoft to continue developing such online help systems. Who knows? Perhaps by SBS 5.0, the online help systems will be surprisingly powerful (maybe putting us SBS consultants out of work).

## Show All Printers

This launches the Printers applet that is also found in the Control Panel. You will recall using the Printers applet on Day 3 when you set up the HP5MCOLOR printer.

## Remove a Printer

This option allows you to remove a shared printer from the SBS network. This is the preferred method of removing a printer. When this option is selected, you are presented with the confirmation dialog box that you must approve for the deletion to occur.

## Manage Printer Jobs

This option allows you to delete, pause, or otherwise view jobs sent to the printer. In order for it to function, you must pick a printer from the Manage Printers sheet (Figure 5.13).

Wanna witness a political struggle firsthand on your SBS network? Be advised that SBS network users are often frustrated that they cannot delete other users' print jobs that are displayed at their workstation (often these users want to delete other's print jobs to complete their own printing faster). To delete a print job, you must select, at the SBS machine, the print job and click the Cancel a Print Job option. Likewise, to hold or pause a print job, click the Pause a Print Job option. To resume or restart a print job that was paused, click the Resume a Print Job option.

# Manage Shared Folders

This option displays a list of all shared folders on your SBS machine and several folder management options (shown in Figure 5.14). Because you are striving to employ the

5

SBS Console as your primary SBS network management tool, you spend time here when managing folders (or at least start here before using other tools such as Windows NT Explorer. (I'll discuss folder settings on Day 6 as well.)

**FIGURE 5.14**

*Manage Shared Folders.*

## Control User Access to Shared Folders

This allows you to change user permissions so they may or may not have access to a folder. These settings are made on a folder-by-folder basis. When this option is selected, the Shared Folder Access Wizard is displayed in Figure 5.15.

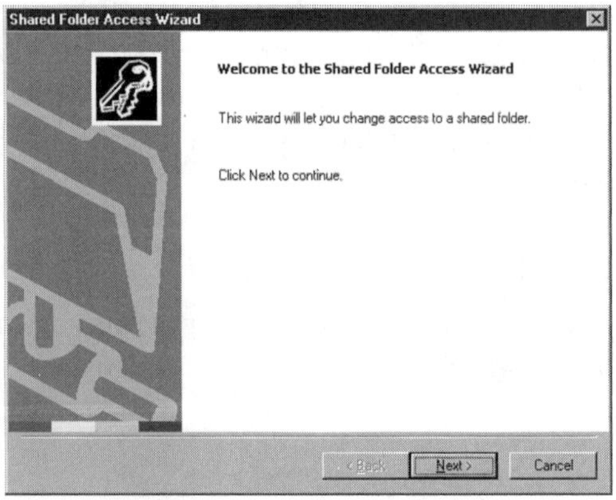

**FIGURE 5.15**

*Shared Folder Access Wizard.*

This important topic is discussed in much more detail on Day 6 where I discuss how SBS implements at the folder level security that is too liberal by default. At that time, you will also learn the differences between share-level and NTFS-based folder/file-level security options. To further pique your interest, you'll see how NTFS security works (more than you ever cared to know).

## Move a Folder

You can move a folder to a different location via the Move Folder Wizard. You might need to move a folder when you've added additional hard disk storage to your computer or simply want to better organize your storage.

> **Note**
>
> When a folder is moved, it retains its original security settings. When a folder is copied (via Windows NT Explorer), the folder permissions change to reflect those already in place at the destination site. The move occurs on the same hard disk partition. Be sure to file this little tidbit away just in case you ever plan to take the demand MCSE exams from Microsoft for Windows NT Server (where the same rules apply).

## Create or Share a Folder

This tool allows you to select a folder on the SBS machine that you would like to share for others to use. When this link is selected, the Share a Folder Wizard launches and guides you through the entire folder-creation or -sharing process. It's both handy and bulletproof, which is nice if you're new to network management.

> **Note**
>
> This Share a Folder Wizard is typically used under SBS rather than the Sharing option found via the secondary menu in Windows NT Explorer or the Shared Directories menu option in Server Manager (both traditional Windows NT Server ways to share folders).Just in case you're concerned that I'm starting to sound like a broken record, you're correct. Chant the mantra: *Do everything from the SBS Console.*

## Unshare a Folder

As the name implies, the Unshare a Folder option allows you to remove a shared folder from the SBS network. Although the folder still exists on the SBS machine, other SBS users can no longer use it or see it.

## Organize Your File Folders

This option launches the online help guide for organizing your files on the computer.

I've bumped into two considerations with SBS sites regarding file organization. First, you typically store your data files on a hard disk or hard disk partition separate from the system partition housing SBS. That is because the SBS system partition has a 2GB limit that is too small for storing lots of company data. Second, I encourage small businesses to make extensive use of folders that are organized like their existing paper-based file cabinets. That way, SBS users aren't confused by the new SBS computer network.

## Manage Folder Size

This option (shown in Figure 5.16) allows you to view the size of a shared folder at a glance and either invoke or terminate compression.

**FIGURE 5.16**

*Manage Folder Size.*

**Note**

Manage Folder Size does not allow you to place storage restrictions on your shared folders by users. This frequently requested feature, wherein you could restrict a user to 10MB of space, for example, won't be available until a future release of SBS. This is expected in the latter half of 2000 with the rumored SBS 5.0 product (which I'll discuss briefly at the end of Day 20).

The two options on the Manage Folder Size page allow you to compress or uncompress a folder. Compression allows more information to fit in a limited amount of space. It is typically used when you run out of space on your hard disk. Compression is managed by the Compress a Folder and Uncompress a Folder menu options and should be used under the guidance of your SBS consultant or guru. Using compression results in a loss of SBS machine performance because the file must be rapidly decompressed before use.

**Power Tool Tip**

This is another way to compress a folder, using the WinZip compression application found on the CD-ROM that accompanies this book. It's truly a workaround that allows you to efficiently archive older files and folders. Here's the drill. Via WinZip, simply create a .zip file of the files and folders you don't plan to use for some time. Then place the .zip file in the original folder. At that point, double-click the .zip file and perform a test extraction to the \TEMP directory. If everything goes well, feel free to delete the original files and folders, knowing your new .zip file contains the same contents.

## Manage Open Files

This option (shown in Figure 5.17) displays which user is using what files within a specific shared folder. It is a more important option than you might initially think. I failed this part of the SBS 4.5 usability test that I took at Microsoft's Redmond campus in the Spring of 1999. Confronted with a story problem wherein I was to make sure a specific file wasn't being used by a user, I took the overkill approach and simply disconnected the user from the SBS network via the Manager Users screen, but that wasn't what the question asked. Rather, the user was to remain connected to the network and only the file was to be closed. Oh well, don't you make the same mistake. To use this option, follow these steps:

1. Select the shared folder of interest in the left pane of Manage Shared Folders.

2. Select Manage Open Files.

3. Observe the activity in the left pane that shows user name and open files (displayed by path or location).

In my experience, the Manage Open Files screen file is slow to refresh and show actual files that are open within a folder. Sometimes the shared files do not appear until the SBS user has performed some type of file save.

You will notice that the Manage Open Files page has two options: close file and close all files. These options allow you to close files that are displayed in the left pane of Manage Open Files.

5

**Figure 5.17**

*Manage Open Files.*

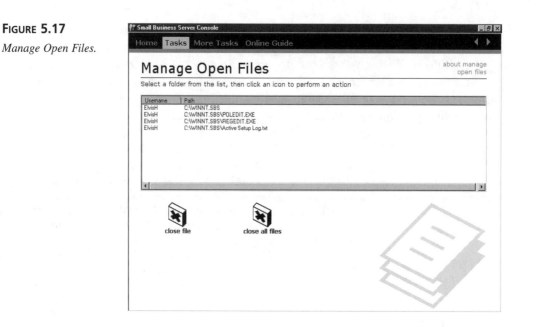

## Manage Connected Users

This is the same command as described in the "Manage Users" section. Again, there's nothing new to report.

## Manage Electronic Mail

This Task option (shown in Figure 5.18) is one of the best in the SBS Console. At a glance, you can determine the status of your Microsoft Exchange Server's user and Internet connections.

Two items shown on the left pane of the Manage E-mail screen are especially useful. The Outgoing E-mail and Incoming E-mail features allow you to see on one screen leading indicators about the health of your Internet e-mail connection. Believe me, as an SBS consultant, most of my SBS maintenance calls relate to Internet e-mail not working, and these calls always seem to come when I'm halfway up The Pass to take the family skiing.

This is the first screen for troubleshooting that problem: Internet e-mail malfunctions. More importantly, I don't have to direct an SBS customer to drill deep down into Microsoft Exchange Server Administrator's Internet Mail Service (ISM) dialog box (yuck!) when they can use the Manage E-Mail SBS Console options.

Several options on the Manage E-mail screen are discussed elsewhere in this chapter. The Manage E-mail Distribution Lists option is discussed after lunch. Manage Users was discussed and shown earlier today (see Figure 5.5).

FIGURE 5.18

*Manage E-mail.*

## Send and Receive Now

This is a very useful way to force e-mail delivery. Sometimes, when your Microsoft Exchange Server–based Internet e-mail appears to be acting up, you can force a dial-up connection to your Internet Service Provider (ISP) rather than wait for the next scheduled connection. You then use the Send and Receive Now option to force e-mail activity. This is very useful in troubleshooting and getting the user off your back with respect to Internet e-mail.

## Troubleshoot E-mail

The option displays the Troubleshooting E-mail help screen to assist your efforts in fixing an e-mail problem. Like other help screens, this is organized in a drill-down decision tree format. Hey, if it helps lower your SBS consulting fees by letting you do more of the work, so be it.

**Note**

Talk about a bummer! Microsoft deleted four very useful e-mail reports from the Manage E-Mail page in SBS 4.5. These reports, which were included in SBS 4.0/4.0a included (Exchange) Server Summary, Top N Message Receiver Report, Top N Message Sender Report, and Daily Message Traffic. These reports were great when you wanted to justify to the small-business owner what an overwhelming success the SBS network is, especially the Internet connection and e-mail. Arrghh!

5

## Back Up or Restore Data

This Tasks option (shown in Figure 5.19) allows you to perform data backup and restorations using Windows NT Server's native tape backup program (ntbackup.exe).

FIGURE **5.19**

*Back Up or Restore
Data.*

Each of the seven options displayed is described in Table 5.1. Selecting any of these options displays a help sheet that instructs you on how to use the option.

I discuss how to back up and restore data extensively on Day 6, including the use of third-party backup applications designed specifically for SBS.

**TABLE 5.1**   BACK UP OR RESTORE DATA OPTIONS

| Option | Description |
| --- | --- |
| Back Up Files to Tape | This help sheet discusses creating a backup copy of your server's hard disks (folders and files) on tape. |
| Restore Files from a Backup tape | This help sheet describes how to restore files from tape. Often files are replaced due to loss, corruption, or mistakes made to the existing files. |
| Back up E-mail Messages to Tape | This help sheet discusses how to use the Microsoft Exchange Backup screen, which is part of the Windows NT Server native tape backup program. It describes how to make a backup copy of your company's e-mail files on tape. |
| Restore E-mail Messages from a Backup Tape | Use this option to recover e-mail messages that have been lost or destroyed. |

| Option | Description |
|--------|-------------|
| Set Up Your Tape Drive | This help sheet describes how to implement the proper tape device drivers so you can correctly prepare your tape backup device for making backups. |
| Manage Backups | This help sheet introduces you to the importance of backing up your SBS system and having a backup plan. Information is provided on scheduling regular backups and creating a backup policy for your business. |
| Troubleshoot Backup | This help sheet provides a drill-down decision tree methodology for troubleshooting common backup problems. |

## Administration Tools

This is a wonderful addition to SBS 4.5 that wasn't present in past versions of SBS. Also known as the value-added provider (VAP) tools, the Administration Tools page, shown in Figure 5.20, is designed with the SBS Consultant in mind.

**FIGURE 5.20**

*Administration Tools.*

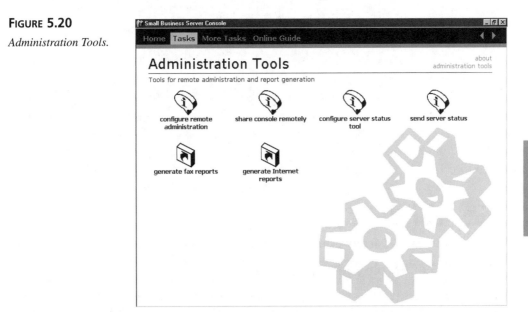

The top four options are discussed at length in the afternoon of Day 20. These options pertain to setting up remote access and system health reporting for SBS consultants to use. The two lower options are discussed this afternoon. I'll discuss Generate Fax Reports, which shows inbound and outbound faxing activity, with the Manage Faxes page. I'll discuss the Generate Internet Reports feature, which shows Internet-related activity such as Web sites visited, with the Manage Internet Access page.

## Troubleshoot a Problem

This Tasks menu option consolidates the different troubleshooting wizards presented on other pages. All these wizards use a drill-down decision tree methodology to assist you in efficiently solving SBS-related problems. By *efficient*, I mean that the methodology being used is tried and true to prevent you from going down dead-end roads, repeating the same solution set over and over again (a.k.a. chasing your tail), and the like. These troubleshooting wizards, listed in Figure 5.21, are worthwhile.

**FIGURE 5.21**

*Troubleshooting Guide.*

## Lunch

Today for lunch I'm serving up a Task for you to complete.

### Task 5.4: Employee Switcheroo

The answer is provided at the end of the lunch hour. I want you not only to explore the SBS Console but also to answer the following. Suppose Sally Briggs leaves the employ of Springer Spaniels Unlimited and is replaced by Diane Seditorial. How would you, using what we learned this morning, effectively delete Sally Briggs and add Diane Seditorial without actually adding or deleting any user account? Hint: You want to make Diane's security and system settings exactly the same as Sally's.

Answer: Simply modify Sally's account to reflect Diane's name and user information on the Manager Users page with the Review or Change User Information.

#  **PM** More Tasks and Online Guide

Welcome back from the lunch hour. This morning we completed half of the pages (Home, Task) listed at the top of the SBS Console. This afternoon we'll complete our exploration of the other two pages: More Tasks and Online Guide.

## The More Tasks Sheet

The More Tasks page (shown in Figure 5.22) has the same number of links (seven) as the Tasks page, but the alleged difference is that the More Tasks page focuses on tasks that you perform less frequently. Let's get started with the Manage E-mail Distribution Lists page.

**FIGURE 5.22**

*More Tasks.*

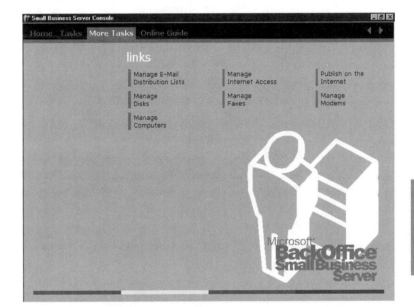

### Manage E-mail Distribution Lists

This SBS Console option allows you to manage your internal e-mail lists. As previously stated, the value of this option varies at smaller sites, which typically using SBS because the user count is relatively low. At the enterprise-level, you would use internal e-mail groups more extensively.

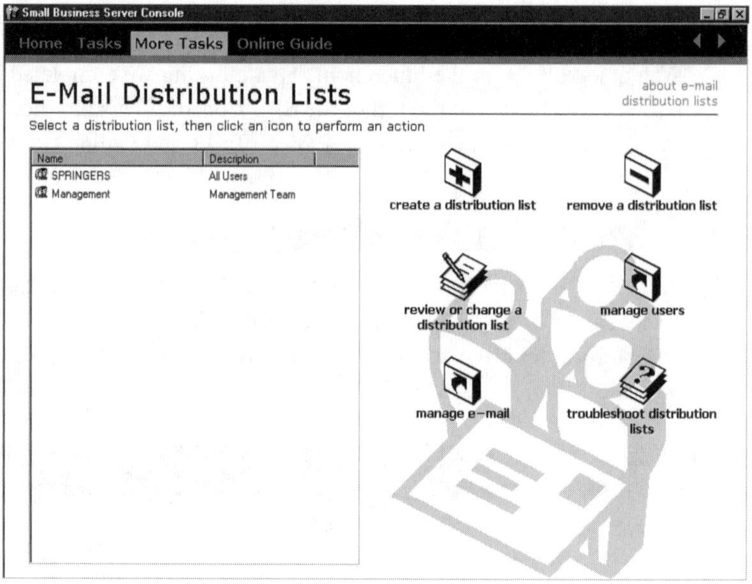

FIGURE 5.23

*Manage E-mail Distribution Lists.*

The E-Mail Distribution Lists page has six options, each of which are discussed in Table 5.2.

**TABLE 5.2** E-MAIL DISTRIBUTION LISTS OPTIONS

| Link | Description |
| --- | --- |
| Create a Distribution List | This allows you to select SBS users for a new distribution list. This link launches the E-mail Distribution List Wizard. |
| Remove a Distribution List | This option permanently removes an e-mail distribution list. |
| Review or Change a Distribution List | This option allows you to modify the members of a distribution list. |
| Manage Users | This option is the same as the Manage Users option from the Tasks page of the SBS Console (see Figure 5.5). |
| Manage E-mail | This option allows you to manage your e-mail server and troubleshoot e-mail problems. It is the same Manage E-mail sheet selected from the Tasks sheet |
| Troubleshoot Distribution Lists | This option presents another drill-down help sheet using decision tree logic to assist your e-mail distribution list troubleshooting. |

## Manage Disks

This is a very friendly view of another traditional Windows NT Server tool (Disk Administrator, discussed in the afternoon of Day 6). At a glance, as shown in Figure 5.24, you are able to determine how much free space you have on the disks attached to your SBS machine. You are also offered six options related to disk management.

FIGURE 5.24

*Manage Disks.*

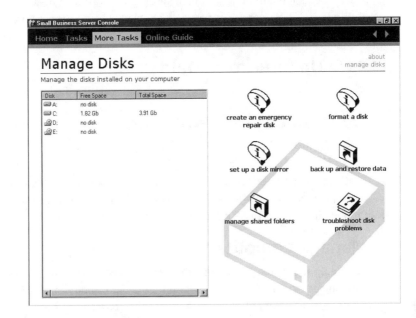

### Create an Emergency Repair Disk

This was previously discussed on Day 3, as part of the To Do List. However, it is worth noting that you should periodically use this option to create a new Emergency Repair Disk (ERD) so that you have a current copy of your system settings (user logon names and other settings) in case the same files on your SBS machine become damaged.

### Set Up a Disk Mirror

This is a help sheet that instructs you on how to create a disk mirror set for better online backup or redundancy. This option assumes that you have a second hard disk that is the same size as or larger than the original hard disk that you want to mirror. Disk mirroring is discussed in more detail on Day 20.

5

## Manage Shared Folders

This option presents the same screen displayed in via the link with the same name on the Tasks page.

## Format a Disk

This presents the Format a Disk help sheet. This help sheet instructs you to use traditional Windows NT Server–type tools like My Computer to format disks. You do not format disks from within the SBS Console.

# Back Up or Restore Data

This option presents the same screen displayed from the Task sheet link of a like name.

# Troubleshoot Disk Problems

This presents the Troubleshooting Disks help sheet. All of the Help sheets I'm mentioning as part of this chapter are available via the Troubleshoot a Problem link on the Tasks page. That's important to remember in case you're ever looking for one of the Help sheets but can't quite remember which link it is buried underneath; just go to the Troubleshoot a Problem link on the Tasks page.

# Manage Computers

You might recall from Day 1 that this was the answer to Task 1.2. The answer was that the Manage Computers link, shown in Figure 5.25, should have been placed on the Tasks list because of its popularity. You will use this option a lot. Believe me.

From the Manage Computers page, you can perform several SBS-specific tasks from Manage Computers that aren't available in Big BackOffice.

## Set Up a Computer

This is the same Set Up Computer Wizard (SCW) that was present on the To Do list on Day 3. This option allows you to set up a computer on an SBS network.

## Allow a User to Use an Existing Computer

This adds the user to your SBS-enabled workstation. This link also starts the SCW to complete its task. Unfortunately, it isn't a roving profile in the traditional Windows NT Server sense (using policies and profiles) nor does it set up the e-mail profile that is used by Outlook 2000. So that begs the question: What does this link really do? I asked the same question of a Microsoft SBS product manager in early 1999 in Redmond. What I found was the Allow a User to Use an Existing Computer link creates the desktop folder shortcuts that map to the user's server storage area. Any applications that you would like to install on the machine can also be selected from the SCW. To be brutally honest, this option over-promises and under-delivers.

**FIGURE 5.25**

*Manage Computers.*

On future days I discuss how to map individual drive mappings (Day 6) and create Outlook e-mail profiles (Day 8). I wish I could discuss those two topics here as part of the Allow a User to Use an Existing Computer, but I can't because those requests aren't satisfied here.

## Troubleshoot Computers

This option displays the Troubleshooting Computer Setup help sheet. You'll find no surprises here as this basically looks and feels like any other help sheet.

## Remove a Computer from Your Network

This option allows you to remove an existing SBS client workstation from an SBS network. When you select a computer to remove in the left pane of Manage Computers and you select this option, you are presented with the confirmation dialog box that requires your affirmation ("Yes") to remove the computer from the SBS network.

## Add Software to a Computer

Out of the box without any modifications, this link allows you to add SBS-specific client software (Microsoft Internet Explorer, Proxy Server client, and Fax client), over the network and via the SBS Client Set Up Wizard, to an SBS-compliant workstation. This option starts with the same screen as Figure 5.48. This is a powerful option that you should use when you want to install SBS client software at a future date after the initial workstation installation on the network. I've used this to install only one or two SBS client software components at a later date, after having set up the workstation.

5

**Note** | On Day 20 in the afternoon session, I show you, in a step-by-step manner, how you can modify the SCW to install third-party applications in addition to SBS-specific client applications.

## Manage Internet Access

This page, shown in Figure 5.26, is ideal for managing your SBS Internet connection. There is an underlying assumption that you implemented your Internet connection via the Sign Up with an Internet Service Provider option (a.k.a. Internet Connection Wizard) on the To Do List when you set up your SBS network. You will recall I discussed this on Day 3. I further discuss setting up your Internet connection on Day 9, "Connecting to the Internet." In the meantime, consider what you want to do for policies regarding e-mail, Internet access, and other related topics.

**FIGURE 5.26**

*Manage Internet Access.*

This page has six options to select from. I'll discuss each now.

## Control User Access to the Internet

This is a favorite option, shown in Figure 5.27, with small-business managers and owners who prefer that their employees do the company's work during business hours, not surf the Internet. Selecting this option displays the Internet Access Wizard as shown in Figure 5.52. This is the first step toward managing your Internet abuses, but stand by, because there are other steps as well.

**FIGURE 5.27**

*Internet Access Wizard.*

## Configure Internet Hardware

Selecting this option simply launches the Internet Connection Wizard and allows you to configure your Internet-related hardware. This is discussed at length on Day 9.

## Generate Internet Reports

This is the small-business owner/manager link. Here, those who care (such as owners) can monitor top sites visited and activity by hour. This is a great set of reports that is unavailable with Big BackOffice. When you select this option, you are taken to the Online Guide's Internet Access Reports (shown in Figure 5.28) where you can select from four Internet access reports: Top 10 Sites, Top 10 Users, Activity by Hour of the Day, and Cache to Non-Cache. All mumbo jumbo aside, the first two reports allow owners to catch staffers who are, shall we say, surfing for porn.

**Top 10 Sites Hit**   Shown in Figure 5.28, this report list and graphs the top 10 sites visited based on hit count. This graph also shows each site's percentage in the total number of hits.

This report not only allows you to observe what sites are most popular for business reasons but also displays nonbusiness or unacceptable sites. For example, see the hits for www.californiablondes.com, www.adultcheck.com, interxxx.com, and www.nympho.com. Most business owners and managers would find these sites to be unacceptable places to visit, at least during working hours. An owner is more likely to approve of CNN's news site at www.cnn.com or Microsoft's site at www.microsoft.com instead.

**Top 10 Users**   This report shows the heaviest users of the Internet at your location. It too is considered a useful report for the business owner and manager. Clearly, as shown in Figure 5.30, Elvis is a very active Internet surfer.

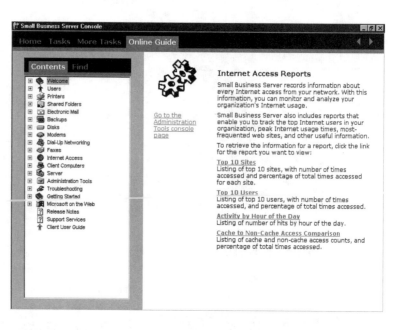

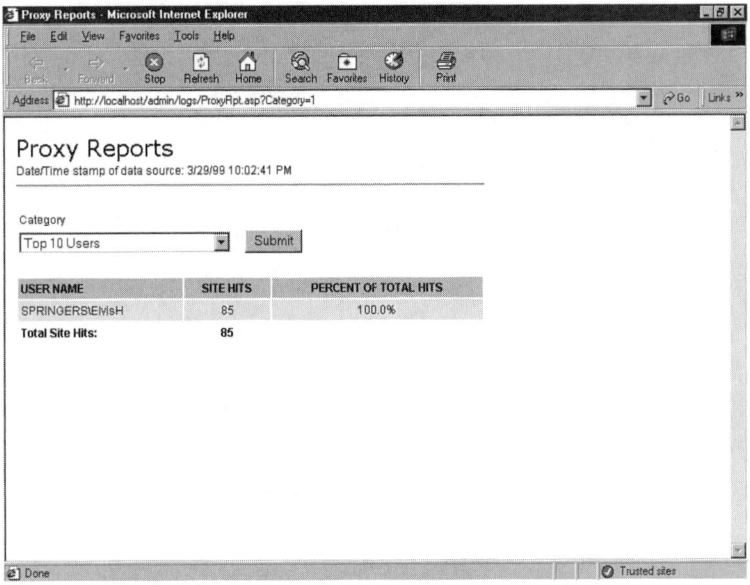

FIGURE **5.30**

*Top 10 Users.*

**Activity by Hour of the Day**    This report (shown in Figure 5.31) reports Internet activity as measured by hits per hour. This is useful in discovering whether excessive surfing is occurring over the lunch hour, or worse yet, during true working hours (assuming lunch is free time).

**Cache to Non-Cache Hits Comparison**    This advanced report (shown in Figure 5.32) shows the percentage of total hits that were freshly retrieved from the Internet and those that were retrieved from a stored copy (cache) on the hard disk of the SBS machine. Caching Web pages on the SBS server can dramatically improve Web browser performance as copies of the Web pages are retrieved from the cache at LAN speed, not Internet connection speed. On a periodic basis, the cached Web pages are updated to stay fresh. These settings are made in the Proxy Server Manager (via the Microsoft Management Console), discussed on Day 11, "Using Proxy Server."

## Small Business Server Web Site

This is the same link as found on the SBS Console that takes you to Microsoft's SBS home page. Clicking this link completes the trip for you by dialing your ISP and connecting to www.microsoft.com/backofficesmallbiz, as shown in Figure 5.33.

5

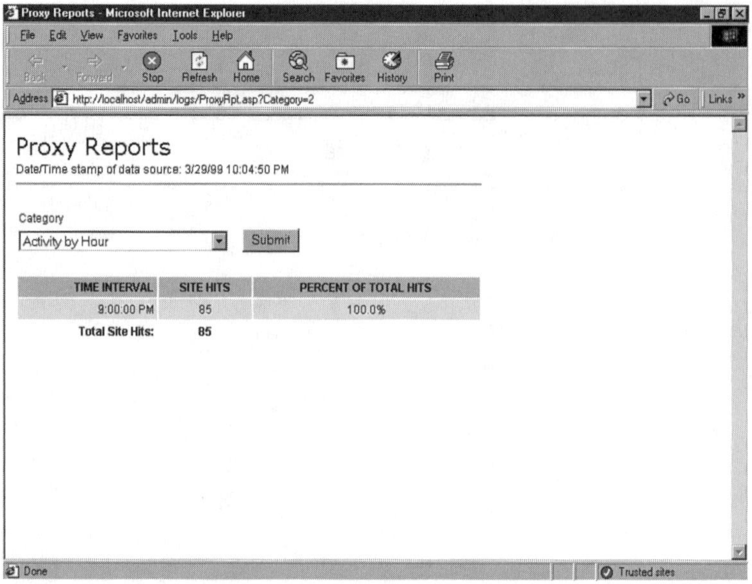

FIGURE **5.31**

*Activity by Hour.*

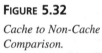

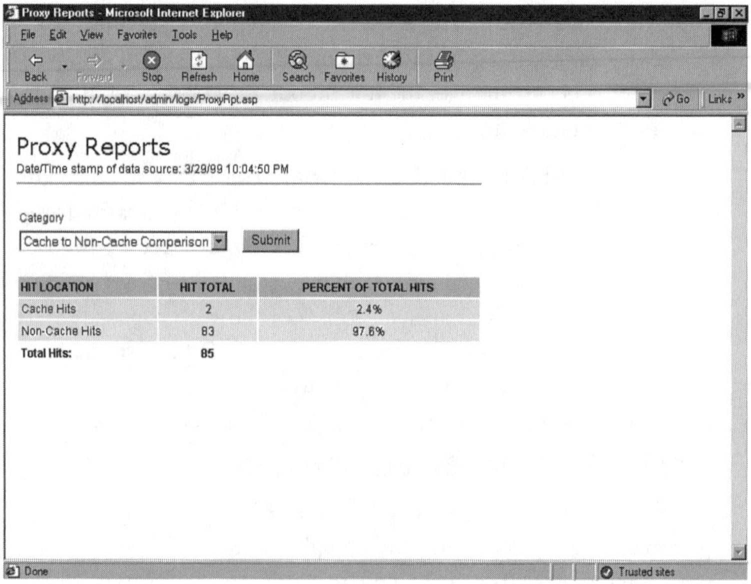

FIGURE **5.32**

*Cache to Non-Cache
Comparison.*

**FIGURE 5.33**

*Microsoft's SBS home page.*

## Connect to the Internet

This is the same link as the Connect to an ISP link from the SBS To Do List. When selected, the Small Business Server Internet Connection Wizard (ICW) launches, as seen in Figure 5.34. The ICW in SBS 4.5 is greatly improved over the ICW in SBS 4.0/4.0a. You will work with this link on Day 9. Stand by.

**FIGURE 5.34**

*Internet Connection Wizard.*

5

### Change Internet Settings

This is a new link in SBS 4.5 that wasn't present in SBS 4.0/4.0a. Via the ICW, which is launched when you select this link, you can change your ISP account password, Web site information, and Internet Domain Name.

### Publish on the Internet

This is the same link as found on the Publish on the Internet page, shown in Figure 5.38.

### Troubleshoot Internet Access

This option displays the Troubleshooting Internet access help sheet. Like other help sheets, it uses a drilldown decision tree methodology. I'll bet this is starting to sound very familiar to you by now.

## Manage Faxes

This sheet, displayed in Figure 5.35, provides you with eight options for better managing the SBS faxing process. The faxing process is discussed in detail on Day 14, "Faxing." The eight Manage Faxes options are discussed in Table 5.3.

**FIGURE 5.35**

*Manage Faxes.*

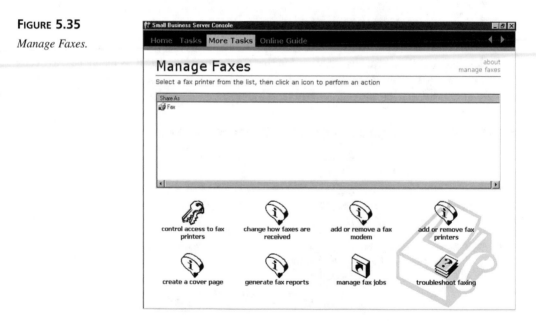

**TABLE 5.3**   MANAGE FAXES LINKS

| Link | Description |
| --- | --- |
| Control User Access to Fax Printers | This allows you to modify user access to fax printers (a.k.a. fax devices). When this option is selected, you are presented with the Printer Access Wizard, because the fax device is really treated as a fax printer. That is, the metaphor is that you print to the fax machine. |
| Change How Faxes Are Received | This option provides a help sheet for modifying how your SBS network handles incoming faxes. This topic is discussed at length on Day 14. |
| Add or Remove a Fax Modem | This is a help sheet that advises you on how to add or remove a fax modem. A fax modem was added to the SBS network on Day 3 and this topic is discussed at length on Day 14. |
| Add or Remove Fax Printers | This option provides a help sheet for adding or removing a fax printer from your SBS network. This topic is discussed at length on Day 14. |
| Create a Cover Page | This option presents a help sheet that instructs you on next steps for creating and managing fax cover pages. |
| Generate Fax Reports | As seen in Figure 5.36, four fax-related reports are offered: Received Faxes Report, Sent Faxes Report, Received Faxes - Top Numbers, and Sent Faxes - Top Numbers. In Figure 5.37, you will see the Sent Faxes Report displayed. |
| Manage Fax Jobs | Here you can pause, cancel, or restart a fax job. |
| Troubleshoot Faxing | This option displays a help sheet that uses a drill-down and decision-tree methodology. |

5

# Publish on the Internet

This is a very powerful tool for managing both your intranet and Internet Web sites. This page offers four options, as you can see in Figure 5.38.

## Update Your Web Site

This option launches the Web Publishing Wizard that, correctly configured, allows you to transfer your Web files to the server that is hosting your Web site. This process uses file transfer protocol (FTP).

**FIGURE 5.36**

*Fax Reports.*

**FIGURE 5.37**

*Sent Faxes Report.*

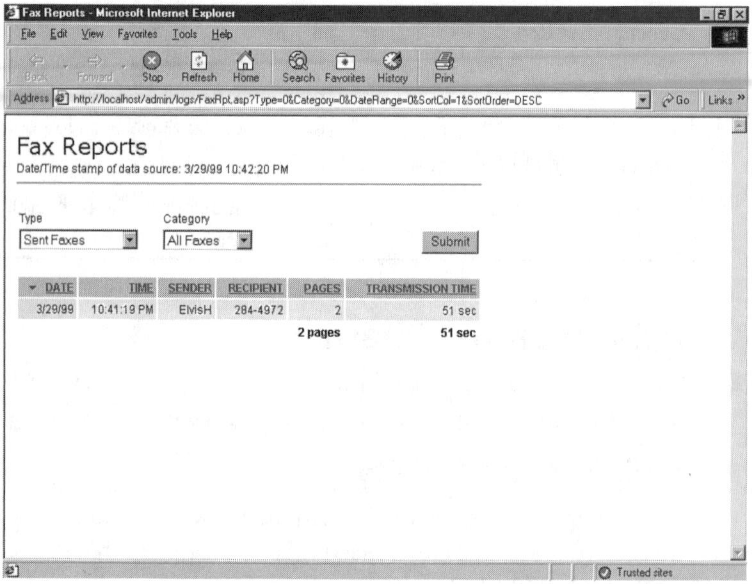

**FIGURE 5.38**

*Publish on the Internet.*

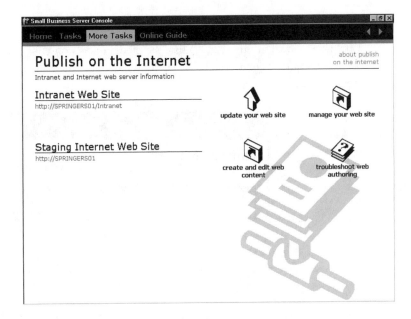

## Manage Your Web Site

This option provides information from the Online Guide for managing your Web site. It is a robust section of the Online Guide that I recommend you read.

## Create and Edit Web Content

This Help sheet, found in the Online Guide, offers tips for creating and editing information on your Web pages.

## Troubleshooting Web Publishing

This Help sheet offers two troubleshooting scenarios for you to use:

- Can't Create an ActiveX Component.
- Can't Publish to the Web Site Using the Web Publishing Wizard.

Sadly, what's missing in SBS 4.5 from the Publish to the Internet page, that was included in SBS 4.0/4.0a, is a rich set of reports ranging from the number of hits your Web site enjoyed daily, hourly, and by downloaded file to listing the most accessed directories. Rest in peace, oh missing Web site management reports.

5

## Manage Modems

This page (shown in Figure 5.39) lists the modem pools on your SBS network in the left pane. Five options are available for learning more about managing your modem or modem pool.

FIGURE 5.39

*Manage Modems.*

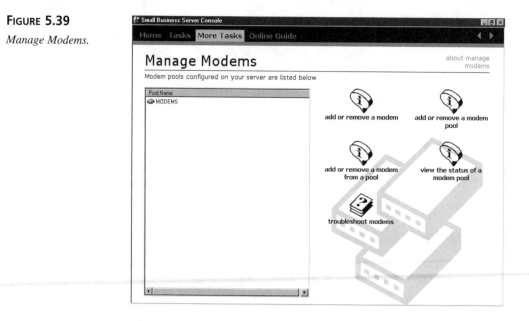

Each of the five options displays a help sheet that provides additional pertinent information. The options appear in Table 5.4.

**TABLE 5.4**   MANAGE MODEMS LINKS

| Link | Description |
| --- | --- |
| Add or Remove a Modem | Simply stated, this is how you add or remove a modem from the SBS computer. |
| Add or Remove a Modem from a Pool | This link is typically used after the fact or after the SBS server has been set up. This is where you would add or remove a modem from a modem pool on your SBS network. This is how a modem advertises itself on the SBS network. |
| Troubleshoot Modems | This option provides tips and tricks on how to troubleshoot modem problems. |
| Add or Remove a Modem Pool | This provides information on adding or removing a modem pool from your SBS network. To be honest, it's rarely done. |
| View the Status of a Modem Pool | This option shows the number of users connected and modem pool activity (status). |

> **Note**
>
> Modems and modem polls are discussed at length on Day 13, "Dial-In/Dial-Out."

# Relationship to Windows NT Server and Big BackOffice

The SBS Console and SBS itself necessarily interact with the underlying Windows NT Server operating system. Yet, within Windows NT Server and Big BackOffice there is no tool as powerful and friendly as SBS Console. And that's one of the things that makes SBS Console so special and worthwhile. It is also one of the reasons for the SBS Law: Always attempt to accomplish any task first from the SBS Console.

The only tool that even approaches the SBS Console from Windows NT Server and Big BackOffice is the Administrative Wizards application shown in Figure 5.40.

**FIGURE 5.40**

*Windows NT Server's Administrative Wizards.*

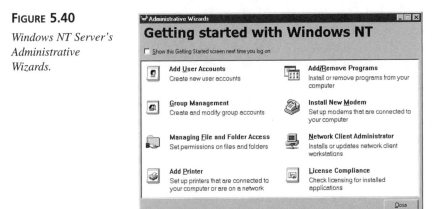

# Summary

You have now been exposed to the heart and soul of SBS: the SBS Console. It is this foundation that, combined with the server and client setup experience gained from Days 3 and 4, now allows you to master the daily dozen tasks of an SBS Administrator in Day 6. By the way, because it's the end of Day 5, that means it's Friday afternoon (assuming you started this book on Monday morning). So, if you finished early, enjoy a few extra hours off this Friday afternoon. Saturday morning is Day 6 and it starts bright and early.

# DAY **6**

# Daily and Weekly SBS Administration (The Dirty Dozen)

Welcome to Day 6. Today both beginners and advanced SBSers should attend the full day. But within each of the 12 topics, I'll attempt to segregate the beginning from the advanced areas. Typically, each topic starts with the beginning issues and proceeds to the advanced. Enjoy and understand that today doesn't break conveniently into an AM (Basics) and PM (Advanced) format. And fear not, I haven't forgotten lunch (I'd be crazy to do that).

This chapter is an assortment of tasks and duties you are likely to perform on a daily or weekly basis, depending on several factors. These factors include your skill level as an SBS administrator or consultant, the activity on your SBS network, the computer knowledge of your users, and the quality of your network from wiring to server brand. I hope that, based on the first four days of this book, you've correctly set up a robust SBS network that won't take over your life and that enables you to perform other work. (I understand that small businesses ask much of us and we often have several jobs, not just SBS guru.)

## ☀ AM SBS Dirty Dozen

Yesterday you learned the finer points about the SBS Console so that you could better
understand the SBS network that you created. Today, I'm sharing the top 12 things that
confront us SBSers during the day-to-day activities of running our SBS networks. Again,
you might not perform all twelve tasks each day, but hardly a week goes by where each
item isn't address in some way. To help you understand how the SBS Dirty Dozen stacks
up with respect to frequency, the SBS Dirty Dozen is listed in Table 6.1 with the approx-
imate frequency you can expect to address each item.

**TABLE 6.1**  THE SBS DIRTY DOZEN

| Task | Frequency |
| --- | --- |
| Tape Backup and Restore | Daily |
| Sharing Files and Folders | Weekly |
| Mapping Drives | Weekly |
| Adding and Managing Users, Groups, Computers | Daily/Weekly |
| UPS Power Levels | Daily |
| Logon/Logoff Status | Daily |
| End-user Support | Daily |
| Check System Health | Daily |
| Run Virus Detection | Daily |
| Installing/Removing Applications | Weekly |
| Reporting | Daily |
| Working Smarter Each Day | Daily |

Appendix C presents this table as a checklist for your benefit and use. With no further
ado, explore the SBS Dirty Dozen, starting with perhaps the most important task of all,
the daily tape backup and restore.

# Tape Backup and Restore

First things first: to back up your important data in SBS you have basically two options.
The first option is to use the native backup utility (Backup), accessed via the Back Up
and Restore Data button on the Task sheet of the SBS Console. The second option is to
use a more sophisticated third-party backup program such as Seagate's Backup Exec
application to perform your data backups.

## SBS's Backup Application

This backup and restore program is relatively easy to use.

### Backing Up Your Data

Simply complete the following steps to back up your data:

1. Launch the Backup program.

2. Select the Drives window.

3. Select the local server hard drives you want to back up in the Drives windows of the Backup application. Typically you would select c:\ drive because it typically contains the SBS operating system, user data, and company data. Possibly you have additional drives such as D: or E: that also need to be backed up. Select those as well.

4. Click the Backup button.

5. Complete the Backup Information dialog box as shown in Figure 6.1.

**FIGURE 6.1**

*Backup Information.*

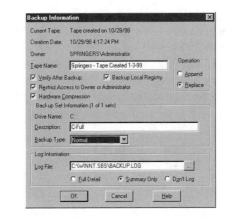

Complete the tape name with a reference to the backup date (for example, "Springers - Tape Created 1-3-99"). Select the Verify After Backup and Backup Local Registry options. You might consider selecting Restrict Access to Owner or Administrator to protect you if this tape were to become lost and fall into the wrong hands (This option would prevent a thief from restoring and using your important business data).

If the Hardware Compression option is available, I recommend that you select it. This statement assumes, of course, that your tape backup hardware actually supports compression (be sure to double-check that fact). You also need to name each backup set. A backup set is created for each drive that you back up. In the

Description box, I suggest you enter the drive letter plus a comment. For example, you might enter **C-Full**. The default Backup Type, Normal, is acceptable, but the Backup and Restore discussion via the SBS Console defines the other options for you (Copy, Differential, Incremental, Daily). Typically the default log file path is acceptable as well as the Summary Only logging option.

**Note**

The Full Detail logging option creates a huge log that quickly becomes overwhelming and unreadable.

6. Click OK after you have completed the Backup Information dialog box. The tape backup commences and the Backup Status dialog box is displayed, giving you up-to-the-minute information about the backup job (files skipped, verification status, and so on).

**Note**

The backup job can take anywhere from several minutes to a couple of hours depending on how much data you back up and the speed of your tape backup unit.

7. When the verification is performed, the Verify Status dialog box is presented. Click OK to acknowledge the Verify Status dialog box at the end of the backup process.

## Restoring Your Data

For every backup, you should consider performing a test restore. Practically speaking, you should perform a test restore at least once per week. The reasons to perform a test restore are many, including the fact that you don't want to learn how to restore from tape in a crisis with a small business owner looking over your shoulder. Performing a daily test restore should be your responsibility or that of someone on staff (much like cleaning the coffeemaker and dishes in the company kitchen). Test restores are best performed wherein a sample text file is restored to a temporary directory such as \TEMP.

To restore using the SBS Backup application, complete the following steps:

1. Launch the Backup application.
2. Select the Tapes window (see Figure 6.2).
3. Select the backup set that you want to use from the right windowpane. In this case, Set 3, from 1-3-99, is selected and expanded via a double mouse click. A separate window showing the contents of this backup set is launched, as seen in Figure 6.3.

**FIGURE 6.2**

*Tapes window in Backup.*

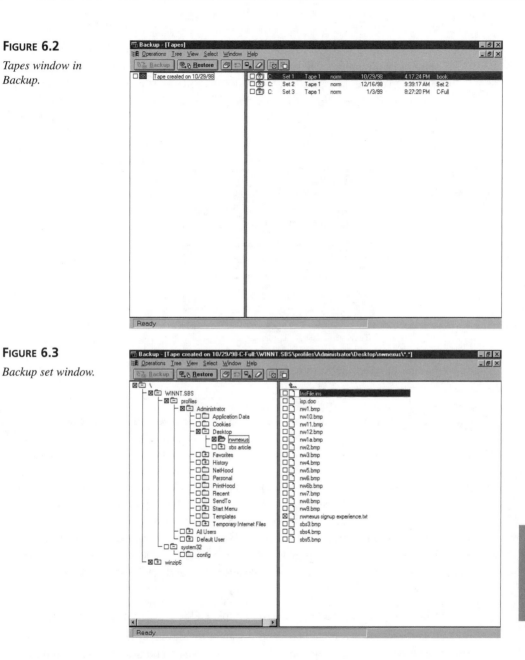

**FIGURE 6.3**

*Backup set window.*

6

4.  Select a text file to perform a test restore with. The file nwnexus signup experience.txt was selected in Figure 6.3.

5.  Click the Restore button.

6. When presented with the Restore Information dialog box, be sure to direct your output to a directory such as TEMP if you are merely performing a daily test restore. (You would typically avoid restoring a file to its original location during a test restoration scenario so that you don't overwrite the original file.) Restore to another location such as TEMP by completing the Alternative Path field, as seen in Figure 6.4.

**FIGURE 6.4**

*Restore Information.*

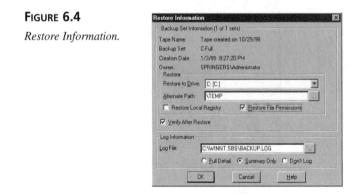

In this scenario, select the Restore File Permissions and Verify After Restore options.

| **Tip** | In fact, it is always a good idea to verify both your backup and restores. |

*Do not* select the Restore Local Registry option for this test restore. The Restore Local Registry checkbox is a blessing and a curse in the SBS backup application. If you're not careful, you can overwrite Registry modifications that you've made since the backup tape (that saved the local Registry values) was created. One Registry change that I frequently make in SBS relates to the OppLocks value under HKEY_LOCAL_MACHINE for the benefit of the Great Plains Dynamics application. Be careful how you treat the Registry backup option.

1. Click the OK button after you have completed the Restore Information dialog box.

2. The Restore Status dialog box appears and provides an up-to-the-minute status report of your restore operation. This test restore should take less than a minute because the text file that was selected was small. When the verification is performed, the Verify Status dialog box is presented.

3. Click OK in the Verify Status dialog box when the restore job is complete.

4. Exit Backup.

5. Launch Windows Explorer via the Start button on your desktop. Windows Explorer is found in the Programs program group.

6. In Windows Explorer, navigate to the TEMP subdirectory (this is where the text file was restored to in the test restore). See Figure 6.5.

**FIGURE 6.5**

*Restored text file.*

7. Find the text file you restored, and double-click it to open it in Notepad. Observe that the text file is complete (as compared to the original). Modify and print the text file. Close the text file.

8. You have now successfully completed your test restore. Congratulations.

## Task 6.1: Testing the Backup and Restore

Now is a great time to perform a test backup and restore. Keep it simple by backing up and restoring one file. There's no moment like the present to apply the lessons learned herein.

## E-mail Backup

The backup and restore you just performed with Backup did not back up your Microsoft Exchange e-mail. In fact, only your data was backed up. Your all-important e-mail was not backed up because the Exchange Directory and Information Store services were running, causing several Exchange files (.edb, .log, .dat) to remain open and not be backed up. Needless to say, losing your organization's e-mail due to an unsuccessful backup would be unacceptable, so be sure to complete the following steps with Backup to obtain a valid backup of your e-mail. Follow these steps to back up your Exchange e-mail:

1. Launch the Backup program.
2. Select the Microsoft Exchange - Springers window as seen in Figure 6.6.

**FIGURE 6.6**

*Microsoft Exchange - Springers window.*

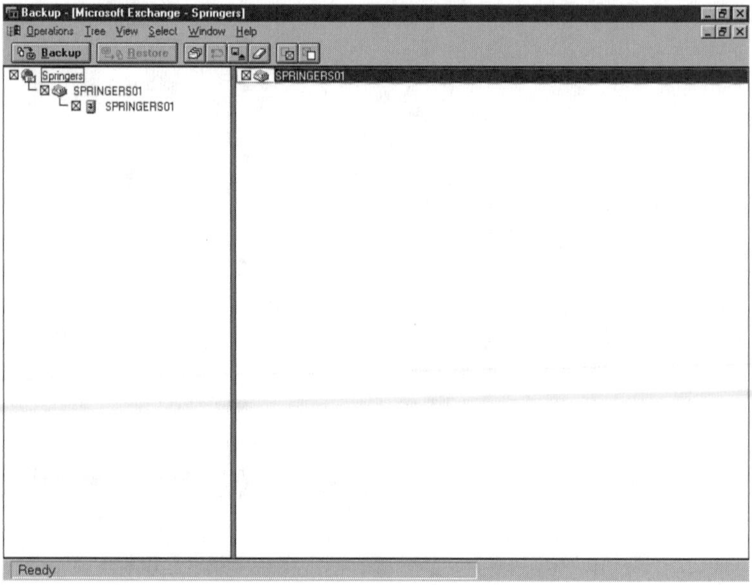

3. Select the top-left icon, representing your Microsoft Exchange organization, in the left windowpane. The other descending check boxes are automatically selected.
4. Select the Backup button.
5. Complete the Backup Information dialog box in a manner similar to that shown in Figure 6.7.

**Note**

The Backup Set Information portion of the Backup Information dialog box reports two backup sets. One set is the Exchange Directory, and the other is the Exchange Information Store. You need to back up both, for reasons I describe in the "Advanced Backup Issues" section, later today. Be sure to provide a description for both backup sets (use the vertical scrollbar to move between backup set descriptions).

**FIGURE 6.7**

*Backup Information for Exchange-based backup.*

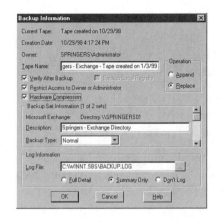

6. Click OK after you have completed the Backup Information dialog box. The back-up job commences.

7. After the backup job is complete, the Verify Status dialog box is displayed. Click OK to close this dialog box.

If you've followed all the steps over the past several pages, you have now performed a test backup and restore using Backup. You have also used Backup to make a backup of your e-mail.

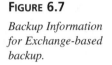

> **Tip**
>
> Be sure to make a complete backup of your data and e-mail each day. I would also recommend you perform a test restore with a sample text file each day (at least once a week).

> **Note**
>
> The Backup application in SBS does a very poor job of backing up SQL Server-based databases (.dat files). You need to use the Daily Maintenance Wizard in SQL Server to create a successful backup of your SQL Server databases. Databases backed up in SQL Server (which reside as a closed file on your server's hard disk) can then be successfully backed up by the Backup application.

**6**

## Suggested Backup Routine

Now you need a backup schedule that ensures you get the backups you need to protect your information. Start with a group of nine tapes. Place a blue dot on the outside of each tape (you'll see why in a moment). Four tapes are used for normal backups between Monday and Thursday. Four tapes are used for normal backups each Friday (Friday1, Friday2, Friday3, Friday4). The last tape is used for normal backups performed at month's end. Label each tape for its respective role (Monday and so on). So far, so good.

Now, at the end of the month, remove the end-of-month tape that contains a verified normal backup from the group and store off-site. (Of course you might want to have other tapes, such as the Friday tapes, rotated off-site as well.)

Purchase a new tape, place a red dot on it and label it Monday. Take the existing Monday tape (blue dot) and label it for the end-of-month-two normal backup. Repeat this scenario the next month, removing a used blue-dot tape from the mix.

So what's the bottom line? Threefold:

1. Each month you purchase a fresh tape that has a recent "born on" date from the manufacturer.

2. Each month you retire a tape from the original "blue dot" group so that after nine months, all of the tapes have red dots and are fresh.

3. By taking a daily or Friday tape and promoting it to the monthly role, ideally no daily or Friday tape suffers excessive usage before being replaced.

**Note**   Don't forget that excessive media usage is a common cause of restoration failure.

## Third-Party Backup Applications

The Backup application has limitations that I'll discuss in more detail in the next section, but it is free. However, when it comes to reliable backups of your data, I've found that free isn't always a bargain. In the process of installing and being responsible for many SBS sites, I've started to recommend third-party backup applications such as Computer Associate's ARCserve Storage Suite for Microsoft Small Business Server (www.cai.com) and Seagate's Backup Exec Small Business Server Suite for Windows NT (Version 7) (www.seagatesoftware.com).

I've used both products with great success, and both products are similar. Each offering modifies the SBS Console to enable you to access the tape backup application. In fact, you should *not* use the Start button to launch either the ARCserve or the Backup Exec application from its traditional Windows NT Server program group.

> **Caution**  Remember what you learned several days ago: do everything from the SBS Console. Running a third-party SBS tape backup program is no exception.

Most importantly, these third-party backup programs contain Microsoft Exchange and Microsoft SQL Server backup agents, ensuring that you successfully back up your data, e-mail, and SQL-based databases each time you run a complete backup job. These programs create an automatic backup schedule, so you don't have to think about it (call it simple, stupid). All told, the backup agents and automatic scheduling are worth the $500 that these programs cost!

> **Note**  On a couple of occasions I've worked with the development team from Seagate's Backup Exec division to help them better understand SBS. They were very honest in expressing mild bewilderment at SBS. These Backup Exec developers are more familiar with the enterprise-level, so I was impressed that the developers were touring real SBS sites to see how their product worked, what was misleading, and so on. As of this writing, Seagate is preparing to release a robust upgrade to its SBS Backup Exec suite to take advantage of SBS 4.5.
>
> You should read this into the lines above: the bewilderment expressed by the Seagate Backup Exec team has translated, on occasion, into "gotchas" for you and me in the real world. For example, you can't create a bona fide tape rotation (grandfather, father, child) via a media set from Backup Exec's SBS interface.

With either ARCserve or Backup Exec, when launched from the SBS Console, you are guided through several steps to create a backup job (see Figure 6.8). Basically, by being integrated into the SBS Console, these products are easily configured and maintained.

**6**

> **Note**  Figure 6.8 displays the Backup Exec Small Business Server Suite for Windows NT as it is installed on SBS 4.0/4.0a. As of this writing, Seagate had not released its upgraded Backup Exec Small Business Server Suite for SBS 4.5.

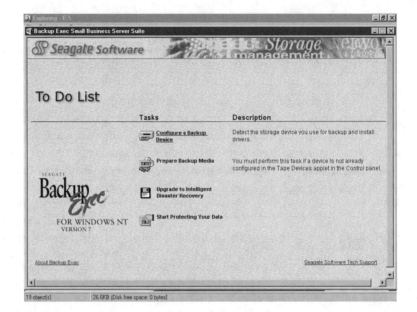

**FIGURE 6.8**

*Backup Exec Small Business Server Suite for Windows NT (Version 7).*

## Advanced Backup Issues

Out of the box, the Backup application does not handle SBS backups especially well. Disappointment is another word that comes to mind. Like you, I eagerly waited with high hopes that the drawbacks of Windows NT Server's native backup program had been dramatically improved when I saw the tape backup option on the SBS management console. But alas, it's the same old backup application that requires you to start jobs manually. You'll discover this when you drill down into the Backup button on the SBS management console.

## Scheduled Backups

One of the most requested features in the SBS community is the capability to schedule automatic after-hours backups (so your staff doesn't need to remember to start the backup when leaving for the evening). This isn't a problem with SBS's native Backup program if you follow these steps:

1. Make sure the Schedule service is running. Set this service to start automatically via the Services applet in Control Panel.

2. Create the following command file in Notepad to back up your SBS server's C: drive and your Microsoft Exchange e-mail. Save it at the SBS server as **c:\mybackup.cmd**):

```
net stop MSExchangeIS
net stop MSExchangeDS
c:\winnt.sbs\system32\ntbackup.exe backup c:
➥/v /d "My Backup Files" /b /hc:on /L "c:\backup.log"
```

```
net start MSExchangeDS
net start MSExchangeIS
```

3. Next, execute the following AT command to schedule the job for each workday evening (Monday through Friday) at 10 p.m.

```
c:\> AT 22:00 /every:M,T,W,Th,F c:\mybackup.cmd /interactive
```

The interactive switch enables you to interact with the backup routine at the SBS server if necessary (insert tape, and so on.).

**Note**

> The command file has the same limitations as executing a command at the command prompt: no single command line contained within your *.cmd file may exceed 256 characters or strange results can occur, files aren't backed up, or the process might stop without warning.
>
> Also, it is critical that you type in the commands in step 2 and 3 above exactly as displayed. Take your time. It's easy to make typos here.

If you own the Windows NT Server or Workstation resource kit, you can copy the winat.exe file from the utilities CD-ROM to a directory on the SBS server and then launch the file to give you a GUI-based AT scheduler that faithfully performs the commands listed previously. Windows 2000 Server, which I believe will be incorporated into a future release of SBS, will natively offer a GUI-based AT-like task scheduler that is much more robust than the winat.exe (shown in Figure 6.9) solution today.

**FIGURE 6.9**

*WinAt program.*

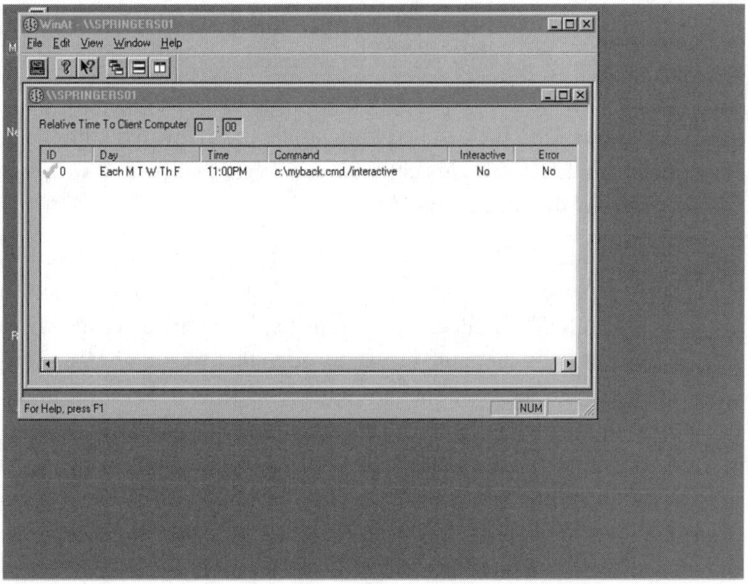

6

## Logging

Another advanced issue is the native SBS backup application: logging. I've had SBS clients correctly ask for logging so that they know their precious data is being backed up. The /L switch used previously creates an incredibly robust logging file that is total overkill for the small-business person. Literally every file that is backed up is logged, creating 30-page log files for each backup. In a normal five-day work week, that's over 150 pages! That doesn't play well in Peoria or at an SBS site. Figure 6.10 shows a detailed backup log.

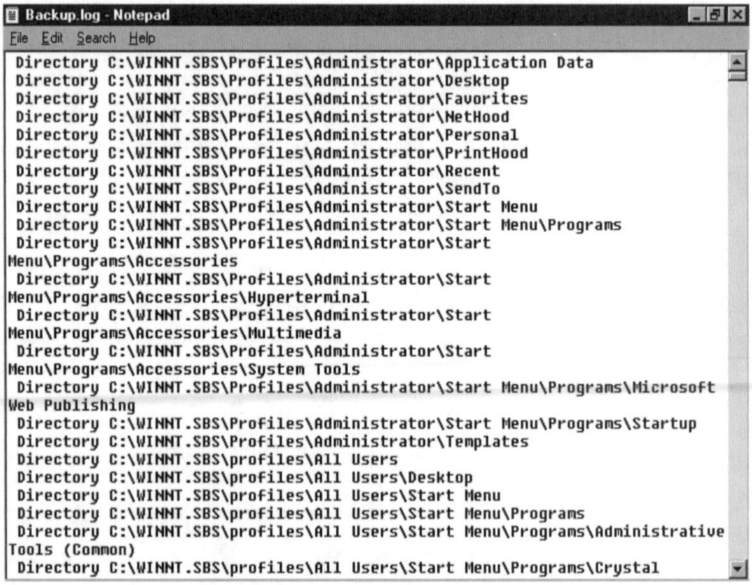

**FIGURE 6.10**

*Detailed backup logging (/L switch).*

If you don't use the detailed logging via the /L switch with the automated backup approach detailed in this column, you might be satisfied with the abbreviated logging offered by the SBS Event Viewer.

So are you stuck between two much logging detail as seen in Figure 6.10 or too little detail as seen in the application log in Figure 6.11? Fortunately, a happy medium exists that I call the "Goldilocks compromise." You remember the childhood story of Goldilocks and the three bears: porridge that was too hot, too cold, and just right? If you manually initiate your backups with the SBS Backup application, you are offered the "just right" logging option. This is the Summary Only logging option, shown in Figure 6.12, that is selected from the Backup dialog box. However, it is not available when you are attempting to automate your tape backups with the AT command.

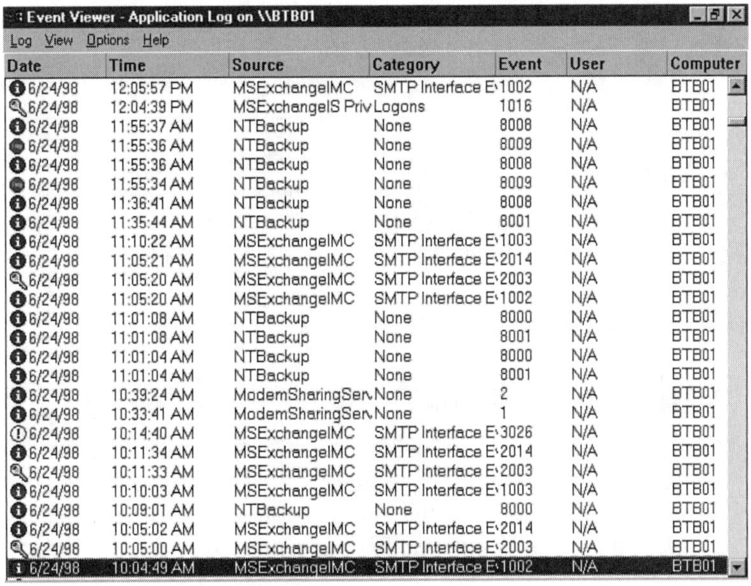

FIGURE **6.11**

*Application log.*

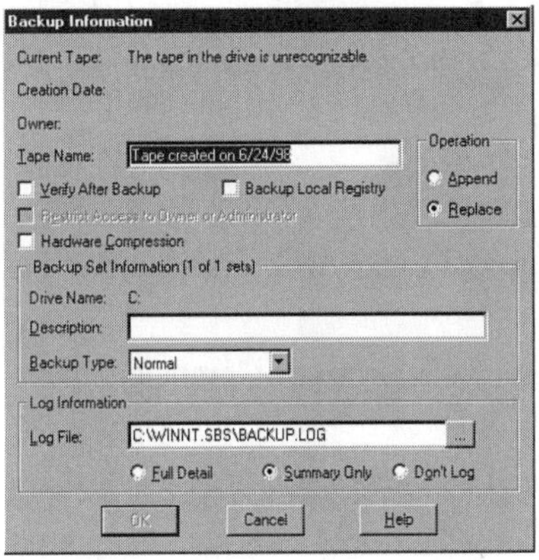

FIGURE **6.12**

*Summary Only logging option.*

6

## Don't Get Confused

When using the SBS Backup application, don't be confused by the opening screen.
When Backup opens, it displays the Microsoft Exchange backup option by default. I've
had SBS clients select a checkbox here believing that they were correctly backing up
their entire SBS server (the NetBIOS or SBS server name (for example, SPRINGERS01)
and the Microsoft Exchange server name (for example, SPRINGERS01) are the *same* by
default, easily leading to this confusion!).

Of course they were backing up only the Exchange e-mail, and you can bet they were surprised when they went to restore a file from the tape (it wasn't there!).

> **Note**
>
> This is an issue specific to SBS because Exchange is installed by default when the complete setup option is selected when you build your SBS server. I haven't performed an SBS installation where Exchange wasn't installed. To do so, you must select the custom SBS installation option when you build your SBS server machine (discussed on Day 3, "Installing Small Business Server").

# Folder and File Security: Sharing and NTFS

A primary reason for having a computer network is sharing information in an easy and secure manner. Hardly a day goes by where users won't ask you to assist them in gaining access (legitimately so) to information they need to do their jobs. You can satisfy this request by sharing files and folders.

Sharing files and folders is very easy and can be accomplished completely from the SBS Console. Follow these steps to share folders via share-level permissions (which are adequate for most SBS sites). I'll discuss NTFS folder and file-level permissions in a moment.

## To Share Folders

1. Make sure you are logged on to the SBS server machine as an Administrator or equivalent.

2. From the Start button, select the Manage Computers menu option to launch the SBS Console.

3. Select the Manage Shared Folders button from the Tasks sheet.

4. Select the Create or Share a Folder option. The Share a Folder Wizard starts. This enables you to apply share-level permissions to a folder.

5. Select the folder you want to share in Select a Folder window. In Figure 6.13, the winzip6 folder has been selected. Note you can create a folder called winzip6 by typing that name in the To Create a New Folder, Type a New Name Field (you'll be asked to confirm the folder creation). Click Next.

6. Provide a share name and description in the Specify the Shared Name for this Folder dialog box (seen in Figure 6.14). Note the default share name is the same as the folder name. As always, a shorter name is preferred to a longer name (it is easy to spell and type). And don't overlook the description box. Remember that it is important to complete every field in any SBS dialog box.

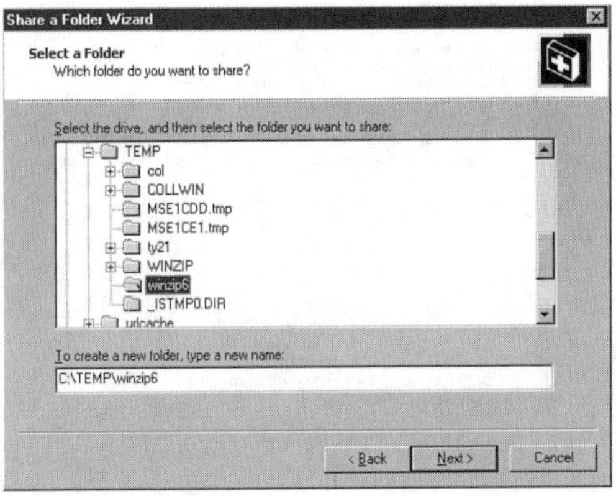

**FIGURE 6.13**

*Select a folder to share.*

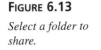

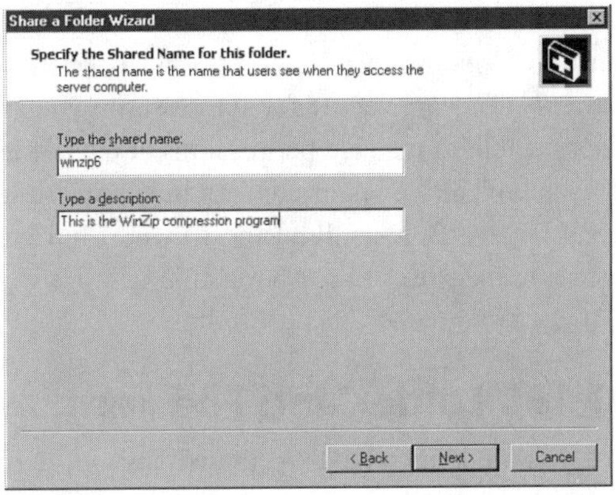

**FIGURE 6.14**

*Folder share name and description.*

7. Carefully select the users who may read, edit, or delete files in the folder you are sharing (for example, wz6) in the Select the Users who Can Access wz6 dialog box. In this example, only Barry Kech and Elvis Haskins should have read, edit, and delete rights. No one should have read-only permissions (see Figure 6.15). Be very careful about your use of the Apply These Permissions to All Subfolders checkbox. (I discuss this check box in the Advance Sharing Issues section later today.) Click Next.

8. Click Finish in the Share wz6 dialog box to complete creating the share. You have now shared a folder. Click OK when the shared folder creation is acknowledged with a small dialog box.

The Manage Shared Folders page also enables you to modify user access to a shared folder (such as when a project is over), unshare a folder, and move a folder to a new location with its share permissions intact. However, you cannot manage the permissions assigned to individual files from the Manage Shared Folders page or anywhere else in the SBS Console.

6

**FIGURE 6.15**

*User permissions.*

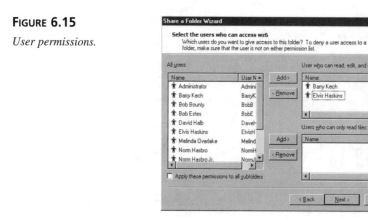

To manage file permissions, it is necessary to go under the hood and use a traditional Windows NT Server tool, Windows NT Explorer. It is also essential that you've formatted your partition as an NTFS partition. If for some reason you are working with a FAT partition, you will not be able to manage permissions at the file level. Managing user access at the file level is typically a larger concern in enterprise-level organizations (several hundred users and larger). But, small business owners have unique security needs, such as allowing access to their user folder but invoking strict security on their TurboTax data file (true story!).

## To Manage NTFS Folder and File Permissions

1. Make sure that you are logged on as Administrator.

2. From the Start button, select the Windows NT Explorer from the Programs menu.

3. Navigate to the folder or file on which you seek to modify the access permissions. In this example, select the Readme.txt file in the \msp folder (which is the readme file for Microsoft Proxy Server).

4. Right-click Readme.txt and select the Properties menu option on the secondary menu.

5. Select the Security tab sheet on the Readme.txt Properties dialog box.

6. Select the Permissions button. The File Permissions dialog box is displayed.

7. Give everyone the Read permission instead of the default Change permission by selecting Read from the Type of Access drop-down box. The File Permissions dialog box should look similar to Figure 6.16.

8. Click OK. You have now applied the Read (a.k.a. read-only) permission to the Readme.txt file in the \msp folder.

**FIGURE 6.16**

*File Permissions.*

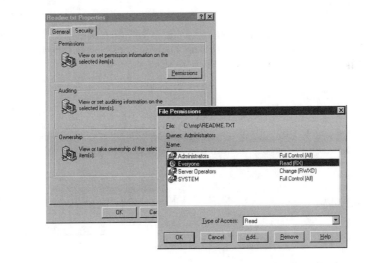

File-level permissions (especially the Special Access permissions) are a complex area beyond the scope of this book. If you are interested in learning more about File Permissions, I suggest you read the *Microsoft Windows NT Server 4.0 Resource Kit* from Microsoft Press (ISBN 1-57231-344-7). Quite frankly, this expensive reference book (around $150 bucks) is overkill for most SBS sites. Think like the millionaire next door and spend those hard earned dollars wisely.

## Task 6.2: Create and Share a Test Folder

Feeling rather randy and full of energy? Go ahead and create and share a test folder applying what you learned above. If you're feeling extra energetic, consider applying the security you deem desirable.

## Advanced Sharing Issues

Let's visit folder and file security in general. The share permissions that you set in the SBS Console are but one level of security known as share-level security. For most small businesses, this share-level security is sufficient. But be advised that more robust security implementations surround the use of NTFS-based security. NTFS security can be applied to folders and files that might or might not be shared. Let's take a moment to distinguish between share-level and NTFS security.

Share-level security can be applied to both FAT and NTFS-formatted partitions. At a minimum, it might be the only security you need. Typically, share-level security acts as a mask that sets the tone for other types of security.

6

**Power Tool Tip**

> If you have a Novell NetWare background, perhaps you know where I'm going with this discussion. I'm basically laying out the case for the Inherited Rights Mask (IRM). Read on.

This mask, the share-level permissions, acts as a filter that allows certain types or classes of permissions to flow or not flow through. For example, suppose you had a shared folder named foo (see Figure 6.17). Note that foo contains two additional folders and files.

**FIGURE 6.17**

*Share-level and folder- and file-level security.*

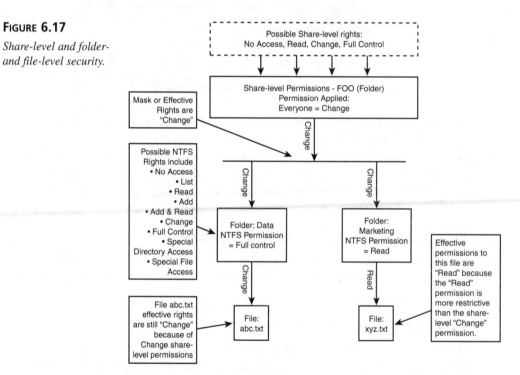

Via the SBS Console, you applied the Change permission to foo for everyone. This permission means that the users on your staff could only change the files stored in foo. Change includes the capability to

- View file and folder names
- Change folders (for example, rename)
- View data in files and folders
- Add files and folders to the shared directory

- Modify or change data in files
- Delete files and folders

The primary difference between Change and Full Control is ownership. The Change permission allows neither a change in the underlying folder ownership nor the capability to change permission on the folder. Only someone with Full Control can actually change permissions on the folder.

> **Note**
>
> When discussing SBS security, the terms *folders* and *subdirectories* are interchangeable.

Thus, the change permission at the share-level sets the mask from which all lower permissions are evaluated. For most SBS sites, this highest layer of security, share-level security, is sufficient. As previously mentioned, share-level permission is the only type of security you can manipulate via the SBS console.

Going to the next level of complexity, now assume you apply NTFS-level security settings to the folders and files contained in foo. You might do this because you have unusual security requirements. An example of this is the restaurant I once worked with that was especially concerned about the dissemination of its proprietary recipes.

If such is the case, return to Figure 6.17 and observe that the Change mask flows down from the top part of the figure where the share-level security was implemented. Then, NTFS-level security is applied to the folders Data (NTFS permission = Full Control) and Marketing (Read). So what's the bottom line in the example on Figure 6.17? The abc.txt file would have the Change right applied to it because the more restrictive Change share-level permission is acting as the mask that sets the tone for all other security rights. The file xyz.txt would have the Read permission set on it because the Read permission, applied via NTFS at the folder-level, would pass through the Change mask created at the upper share-level. Whew! I warned you some of this stuff was beyond the scope of this book.

**6**

> **Note**
>
> Any and all of the security scenarios I have discussed above can be applied to everyone, groups or individuals. For example, NormH, the president at Springer Spaniels Unlimited, has broad and sweeping Full Control rights to just about everything on the SBS network. Everyone else working at Springer Spaniels Unlimited can have varying degrees of share-level rights that differ from NormH's (see Figure 6.18). The point is that one person's security restriction isn't necessarily someone else's security restriction. This simple fact is easy to forget as you manage your SBS network.

**FIGURE 6.18**

*Different security.*

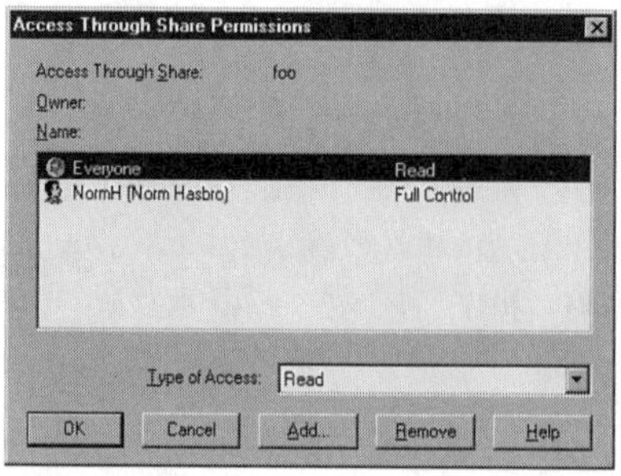

**Access Through Share Permissions**

Access Through Share: foo
Owner:
Name:

| | |
|---|---|
| Everyone | Read |
| NormH (Norm Hasbro) | Full Control |

Type of Access: Read

OK | Cancel | Add... | Remove | Help

Last but not least, the capability to have hidden shares exists within SBS, but you have to play a trick to make it happen. First you have to answer the question regarding why you would have a hidden share on your SBS network. Basically, it is another way to keep honest people honest. For example, you can have applied appropriate and restrictive share-level and NTFS folder- and file-level security to your folder titled PAYROLL. But if that folder weren't even visible when your SBS users navigated around your SBS network using Network Neighborhood, might you sleep better at night? You bet you would. Other popular share names that I've hidden include TERMINATIONS (is that a share name bound to make your staff nervous or what?).

**Power Tool Tip**

NetWare users should recognize this hidden trick in SBS as the hidden right.

## To Create a Hidden Share

1. Make sure that you are logged on as Administrator.

2. Follow the steps to share a folder via the SBS Console's Manage Shared Folders button (see the steps in the section "To Share Folders" earlier today).

3. When entering the share name, end the share name with the $ sign. For example, the PAYROLL share would now be called PAYROLL$. This would be entered in the Specify the Shared Name for this Folder screen in the Share A Folder Wizard. Click Next.

4. Complete the "To Share Folders" steps by selecting the users who can access the PAYROLL$ share, click Next, and then select Finish to complete creating the PAYROLL$ share.

> **Note**
>
> Creating a hidden share makes the share invisible when browsing via Network Neighborhood from a workstation. However, you can still map drives to that share and run applications. I discuss mapping to a hidden share in the section "Mapping Drives," later today.

## Transfer Directory

Beyond the default User Shared Folders and Company Shared Folders automatically created by SBS during the setup phase, you might strongly consider creating additional useful folders on your SBS server machine. One such folder is a TRANSFER directory where users collaborating on a work project might temporarily store files for use by others. Typically a TRANSFER folder allows everyone the Change or Full Control right. And don't forget to create TRANSFER on a hard disk partition with lots of room so you don't have disk space problems at an inconvenient moment (the system partition is probably a poor candidate for housing the TRANSFER directory with its 4GB limitation).

## Subfolders

One final thought on sharing. An easy-to-overlook check box, Replace Permissions on Subdirectories, is not selected by default when you are applying NTFS folder and file security (see Figure 6.19).

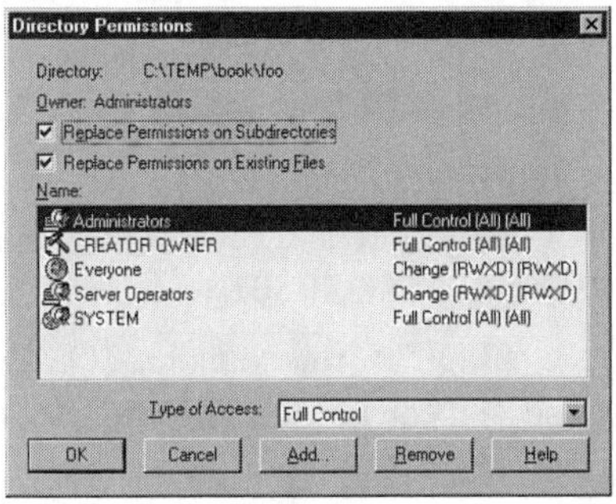

**FIGURE 6.19**

*Checking the Replace Permissions on Subdirectories option.*

In most cases, you would want this to be selected because you typically want the NTFS-related changes to apply to any folders (nested folders) beneath the folder you modify permissions on.

6

### Dangerous Defaults

**Caution**

> Although I've implied that share and NTFS permissions are too generous by default, let me reiterate that fact before moving to the Mapping Drives section. The default Sharing permission in SBS is Everyone = Full Control. The default NTFS permission on a folder and file is Everyone = Change. These are extremely generous and dangerous default security levels. Enough said.

# Mapping Drives

In order to create, modify, and otherwise use data on a server, you must first have access to folders on the server. There are three ways to gain this access to folders located on a server that involve creating a path or mapping a drive to the server.

## The Graphical Method

The first method is;drives;mapping;graphical method the easiest and—it has been my observation—the most preferred method. This method, also known as point-and-shoot, consists of browsing via the Network Neighborhood applet, finding the shared folder of interest, and mapping a drive.

### To Map a Network Drive via the Graphical Method

1. From the user's Windows 9x or Windows NT Workstation machine, log on to the SBS network.

2. Double-click Network Neighborhood and navigate to a desired shared folder on the SBS server. An example of this would be COMPANY (the share name for the Company Shared Folders) on SPRINGERS01.

3. Single-click the desired shared folder (for example, COMPANY) to highlight this folder or give it the focus so you can perform a command involving it.

4. Select the secondary menu (right-click) while COMPANY is selected. Select the Map Network Drive command.

5. Select a drive letter to identify this mapped drive to this shared folder. For example, you might select Drive F: as being mapped to COMPANY.

6. Select the Reconnect at Logon check box if you want this drive to be remapped each and every time you log on to the SBS network. You typically select the Reconnect at Logon check box.

7. Click OK. You have now mapped a network drive via the graphical method.

## The Dialog Box Method

This method requires that you know the folder's share name in advance of mapping it. Assuming that you do, complete these steps to map a shared drive via the dialog box method.

### To Map a Network Drive via the Dialog Box Method

1. From the user's Windows 9x or Windows NT Workstation machine, log on to the SBS network.

2. Select the secondary menu for Network Neighborhood by secondary clicking or right-clicking on the Network Neighborhood applet on the user's desktop.

3. Select the Map Network Drive command. The Map Network Drive dialog box, similar to Figure 6.20, is displayed.

**FIGURE 6.20**

*Map Network Drive.*

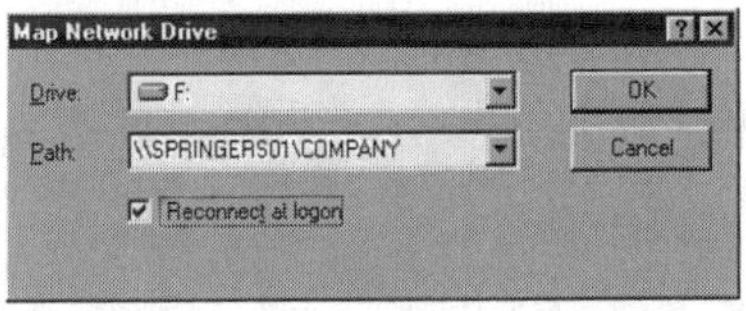

4. Select the drive letter and enter the path to the shared folder on the SBS server machine. For example, if you want to map drive F: to the COMPANY folder on SPRINGERS01 (the SBS server machine), select F: from the Drive drop-down menu and type **\\SPRINGERS01\COMPANY** in the Path field. By the way, this pathname is known as the Uniform Naming Convention (UNC) and is discussed in a moment.

5. Select the Reconnect at Logon check box if you want this drive to be remapped each and every time you log on to the SBS network. You typically select the Reconnect at Logon check box.

6. Click OK. You have now mapped a network drive via the graphical method.

## The Command Line Method

You can also map drives from the traditional command line (a.k.a. command prompt). If you follow these steps, use the NET USE command to map drives to the SBS server.

### To Map a Network Drive via the Command Line Method

1. From the user's Windows 9x or Windows NT Workstation machine, log on to the SBS network.

6

2. From the Start menu, select Programs and MS-DOS prompt. A command prompt window is displayed.

3. At the command prompt, type the following command if you want to map drive F: to \\SPRINGERS01\COMPANY on your SBS network: **NET USE F: \\SPRINGERS01\COMPANY**

4. Type **EXIT** to close the command prompt window and return to your desktop operating system.

**Note**

> The NET USE command must be executed each session to map your network drives. The NET USE command does not offer the option of Reconnect at Logon like the graphical or command line method does.

You have now learned three ways to map network drives to shared resources on your SBS server machine. I will now discuss advanced drive mapping issues.

### Task 6.3: Mapping a Drive

Try to map a drive from one of your SBS user's workstations to the SBS server using each of the drive-mapping methods shown above. Practice makes perfect.

## Advanced Mapping Drives Issues

In this section, I will discuss the Uniform Naming Convention (UNC) definition of drive mappings, compare SBS network drive mappings to NetWare drive mappings, show you how to map a drive without a drive letter, map a drive to a hidden share, and illustrate how to use mapped drives via user logon scripts.

### Defining the Uniform Naming Convention (UNC)

SBS uses the UNC approach to make network drives from the workstation to the server. The UNC can be broken down into two parts, as shown in Figure 6.21.

Part 1 of Figure 6.21 shows the traditional UNC drive mapping command. This command comprises the SBS server machine's NetBIOS name (SPRINGERS01) and the share name (COMPANY). Part 2 of Figure 6.21 displays the folders and files you would see when you explore or navigate the mapped drive. For example, you might see a folder named foo or a file named abc.txt.

**FIGURE 6.21**

*Analyzing UNC net-work drive mappings.*

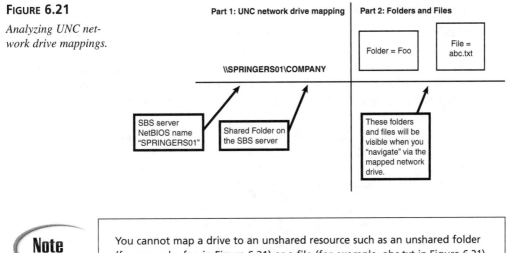

| Part 1: UNC network drive mapping | Part 2: Folders and Files |

Folder = Foo

File = abc.txt

\\SPRINGERS01\COMPANY

SBS server NetBIOS name "SPRINGERS01"

Shared Folder on the SBS server

These folders and files will be visible when you "navigate" via the mapped network drive.

**Note**    You cannot map a drive to an unshared resource such as an unshared folder (for example, foo in Figure 6.21) or a file (for example, abc.txt in Figure 6.21).

## SBS Versus NetWare Drive Mappings

The SBS and NetWare environments have common features, just different terms when it comes to mapping drives. Table 6.2 contrasts SBS and NetWare when mapping drives.

**TABLE 6.2**   SBS VERSUS NETWARE DRIVE MAPPINGS

| SBS Feature | NetWare Feature | Comments |
|---|---|---|
| \\SPRINGERS01\ COMPANY | F:=SPRINGERS01\ COMPANY: | Comparable network drive mappings |
| Share Name = COMPANY | Volume = COMPANY | SBS uses Share Name and NetWare uses Volume |
| NetBIOS Machine Name = SPRINGERS01 | Machine = SPRINGERS01 | Comparable use of machine names. |
| No directory mapping. Must explore or navigate to directory FOO | Directory mapping allowed: F:=SPRINGERS01\ COMPANY:FOO | Big difference between SBS and NetWare. |
| No search drives | Search drives allowed. S1 - S16. | Big difference between SBS and NetWare. |

6

## Avoiding Drive Letters

You can access resources on the SBS server machine by mapping without drive letters. This is best displayed by the Company folder shortcut, shown in Figure 6.22, that is placed on your desktop. If you look at the properties for the Company folder shortcut, you should observe that the path or map to the server contains no drive letter, just the basic UNC command. This approach is similar to how the Apple Macintosh accesses network resources: without drive letters. More importantly, using just the UNC path to access network resources is a great way to avoid using up all your drive letters (typically F through Z).

**FIGURE 6.22**

*Mapping without drive letter.*

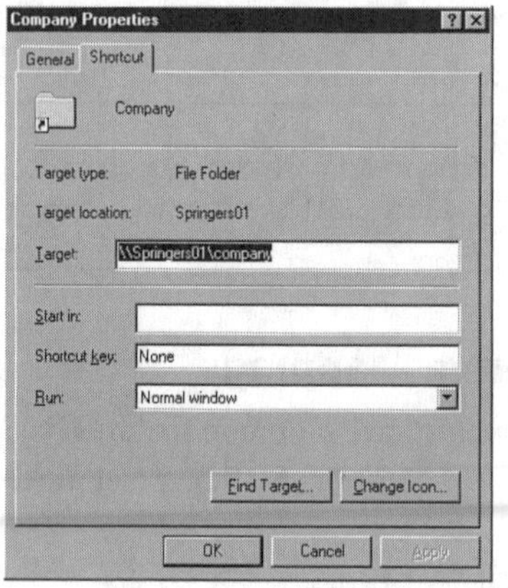

> **Note**
>
> Many applications expect drive letters and can't properly use just the UNC path to access information on the network. Be sure to check your applications for UNC fitness before using network mappings without drive letters. In my experience, older applications that expect drive letters include various Tax Code software applications such as BNA.

## Mapping to a Hidden Share

Earlier, I shared with you three ways to map a drive to the SBS server on your SBS network. The first method, the graphical method, does not work with the hidden share approach ($) discussed earlier in this chapter. Why? Because the hidden share point you created for your sensitive information (for example, PAYROLL$) does not appear when you explore via Network Neighborhood.

In fact, to map a drive to a hidden share, it is essential that you know the exact name of the hidden share you are trying to map to. Such intimate knowledge can indeed serve as another level of deterrence! To map a drive to a hidden share, you would enter the correct UNC path (for example, \\SPRINGERS01\PAYROLL$) using either the dialog box or command line mapping methods discussed above.

## Task 6.4: Creating a Hidden Share

Take a moment to create a hidden share on a folder on the SBS server machine. Go to an SBS user's workstation and, via Network Neighborhood, browse to the SBS server machine (for example, SPRINGERS01) and see if you can see the hidden share. You shouldn't if you've done it correctly.

## Mapping Via a Logon Script

Before ending the discussion on mapping drives, it is essential that you understand the drives I have mapped in this section are local to the workstation from which these drives were mapped. That is, if I mapped drive F: to \\SPRINGERS01\COMPANY and selected the Reconnect at Logon check box, this drive would be mapped each time I log on and each time you log on. Thus, the mapping resides with the workstation, not the user.

This is problematic for several reasons. First, it suggests a possible security lapse if someone logs on at your machine and is party to your drive mappings. Although share-level and NTFS security would likely prevent this party from truly doing damage, in many businesses I've worked with I don't want the wrong person to even see other mapped drives. For example, at the small law firm that I serve, the partners use drive M: for partner-related matters. The shared folder that drive M: points to is secure. However, the partners and I at this law firm prefer that the others not even know about drive M:. If you logged on to a partner's machine at this law firm, you would see drive M: mapped even though you couldn't manipulate any files in the partner area.

With safety and security in mind, another limitation regarding local workstation drive mappings to the network is that many organizations want anyone to be able to log on at any machine and complete their work with their unique drive mappings and no compromises to security. Different people often need different drive mappings because of the application's use (for example, perhaps only one or two people in your organization need to use QuickBooks). This is the "anyone can work on any machine at anytime" policy. It's a good organization strategy but somewhat difficult to implement in SBS. The key to implementing this approach is to take advantage of SBS's logon script.

**Power Tool Tip**

NetWare users should quickly see that SBS doesn't have true individual and system login scripts like NetWare. With SBS, you simply create a batch file and place it in the SmallBusiness folder inside the NETLOGON shared folder. There is no login script creation tool such as SYSCON to help you create these files.

When you add a user to the SBS network via the SBS console, a logon script is created for that user and placed in the SmallBusiness folder inside the NETLOGON shared directory (\winnt.sbs\system32\repl\import\scripts). This file is a batch file that is named after the user. For example, for NormH, the file would be called normh.bat and contains the following:

```
@echo off
REM
REM This file is the template used to create the
➥logon script for each user.
REM

REM
REM If this is running on dos, exit
REM

if "%windir%" == "" goto exit

if "%COMPUTERNAME%" == "" goto proc_test
if "%COMPUTERNAME%" == "SPRINGERS01" goto exit

:proc_test

REM
REM Use PROCESSOR_ARCHITECTURE to pick the right directory
REM

if "%PROCESSOR_ARCHITECTURE%" == "" set DIRECTORY=win95
if "%PROCESSOR_ARCHITECTURE%" == "x86" set DIRECTORY=i386
if "%DIRECTORY%" == "" goto exit


\\SPRINGERS01\Clients\Setup\%DIRECTORY%\startcli.exe
➥/s:SPRINGERS01 /u:NormH /l:c:\startcli.log


:exit
```

In order to implement drive mappings that stay with the user and not the workstation, I typically add my NET USE drive mapping statements just above the :exit term at the bottom of the logon file. In the case of NormH, his logon file (normh.bat) might appear as:

```
NET USE F: \\SPRINGERS01\COMPANY
:exit
```

Now, when NormH logs on at any workstation on his SBS network, he gets the drive mappings contained in his logon file.

To implement this approach successfully, you need to consider the following:

1. Don't use a combination of local workstation drive mappings to the SBS server machine and via the logon script. Such a combined approach is confusing and difficult to manage. Go with either logon script–based network drive mappings or local workstation–based network drive mappings. One or the other.

2. Note the user's logon file is overwritten every time you modify the user account via the SBS Console. This is problematic in SBS and means that you need to double-check and likely enter your user's network drive mappings after any user account changes.

3. Consider placing the common network drive mappings that everyone uses in the common logon file template. This file, located at c:\SmallBusiness\Template\ template.bat, is the base from which all user logon scripts are created. If you put the most common network drive mappings at the bottom of this file, you need to edit only individual logon files to insert user-specific network drive mappings.

## Error #71

If you every attempt to map a drive and use a resource on an SBS server and see Error #71 returned, first double-check that you haven't exceeded the allowed logons for your SBS network. For example, if you have a five-user license for your SBS network, it is possible you are logged on to the network as normal, even if you are the sixth user attempting a logon. However, if you are that user in excess of your SBS Client Access License count, when you attempt to map a drive or access a network resource, Error #71 is displayed on your workstation.

To fix this, either add more Client Access Licenses (CALs) to your SBS network or have another user log off from the SBS network.

## Mapping Drives to Other Workstations

Did you know that you can map a network drive to a shared resource on another SBS user's workstation? It is very simple to do. First, the SBS magic setup disk at the workstation level automatically turns on file and printer sharing, making the workstation eligible to share a folder for others to use. Assuming this has been accomplished, you would simply map a drive to the shared folder on the workstation, using the UNC drive mapping approach (any of the three methods discussed previously will work). For example, if the workstation was named CAREFEED01 and the shared folder was FOOD, the UNC command would be \\CAREFEED01\FOOD.

6

# 🥪 Lunch

Today's lunch speaker is a person from the real world of SBS computing. I say that because Dawn Bingaman is a system administrator who clearly fits the profile that Microsoft had in mind when it designed SBS. As a part-time systems administrator, Dawn could greatly benefit from SBS's easy "just add water" networking paradigm, but did she?

## The SBS Administration Challenge

*by Dawn Bingaman*

Decision in hand to migrate to SBS from our small NetWare 4.x network, I immediately immersed myself in the ins and outs of SBS. I quickly learned a few things about SBS that were contrary to my NetWare background. First, SBS is significantly different from a NetWare-based network. Nowhere is this more evident than the way in which SBS is managed. In NetWare, either you manage the NetWare server with NWAdmin, a GUI-based management tool that works from a client workstation, or you manage the NetWare server from a set of character-based screens at the server. With SBS, you get a Windows interface (GUI) at the server, which is impossible with NetWare. Other subtle differences include the ways in which drives are mapped and printers are managed.

But on a day-to-day administrator level, my early experience with SBS is that it is easier to manage compared to my previous NetWare environment. How so? The emphasis with SBS appears to be not so much the underlying network operating system (NOS) but the BackOffice applications that run more in the foreground. With NetWare, the NOS is foreground, front and center!

I have also found that an SBS network focuses more on the applications people need, such as Microsoft Exchange, rather than the underlying operating system. In fact, I've found my role changing. Whereas I used to spend my network-related time focusing on NetWare, I now spend my SBS time focused on BackOffice applications such as Microsoft Exchange (watch out SQL Server...here I come!).

Many things haven't changed from my NetWare network days. Users still fuss when they can't print. The workstations and even the server need to be rebooted occasionally. And applications such as our accounting system don't always perform flawlessly. But that's just a day in the life of a network administrator.

One thing I haven't discussed is the end users. At one level, the migration to SBS from NetWare was seamless. The users often don't know the difference, if you will, whether they were logged onto a NetWare network or an SBS network. For awhile, we ran both. Come to think about it, that's the way I like it as a systems administrator: a network that is in the background. That allows the user's foreground focus to remain the business applications they use each day.

I'd like to add a couple of comments. I started with NetWare as a PT systems administrator, but after less than a year I became a FT administrator. I am still a FT administrator, now I just have more time to devote to mastering the NOS and learning about BackOffice apps. On big NetWare, I was treading water just to keep up with the NOS.

The main difference I've noticed between SBS and NetWare 4.10 is security. Out of the box, NT/SBS is designed with usability in mind, not security. However, NT has the capability to be very secure. SBS sys admins for whom security is important will have to venture beyond the Manage Console screen and delve into the workings of NT 4.0 to achieve a secure network.

An example of the difference noted above is that in NetWare, the Admin account has access to user's home directories by default. In NT/SBS the Administrator must specifically be granted permissions to the user shares. Also in NT, there apparently is no concept of workgroup-based administration like there is in NetWare. In NT, a user who is made a user administrator can control *all* users in the domain. (Because SBS is a single domain, by default the "workgroup" admin gains access to the entire network.) My point in highlighting these two examples is that the network operating systems come at the same concept from different angles, not that one is better than the other.

SBS is a good platform for system administrators with a little or a lot of networking experience. Although an administrator in SBS never need venture beyond the management console to get the basic network up and running, more experienced admins will like the ability to get their hands dirty in the feature-rich environment of NT/SBS. I manage my network using both jumping off points.

> **Note**    Dawn Bingaman is the systems administrator at the Seattle Tennis Club. She started her network management career with Novell NetWare prior to jumping ship to SBS!

## PM **More SBS Dirty Dozen**

# Adding and Managing Users, Groups, and Computers

On any given day, you likely need to either add or delete a user or computer from your SBS network. Hey, people come and go from organizations all the time.

You might recall from Days 3, "Installing Small Business Server," and 4, "Setting Up the Workstation Client," that users and computers are added, deleted, and managed from the

SBS Console. In fact, the step-by-step process for adding users is shown during Day 4. For user-related management tasks, use the Manage Users console screen (see Figure 6.23). For computer-related management tasks, use the Manage Computers console screen (see Figure 6.24).

FIGURE 6.23

*Manage Users.*

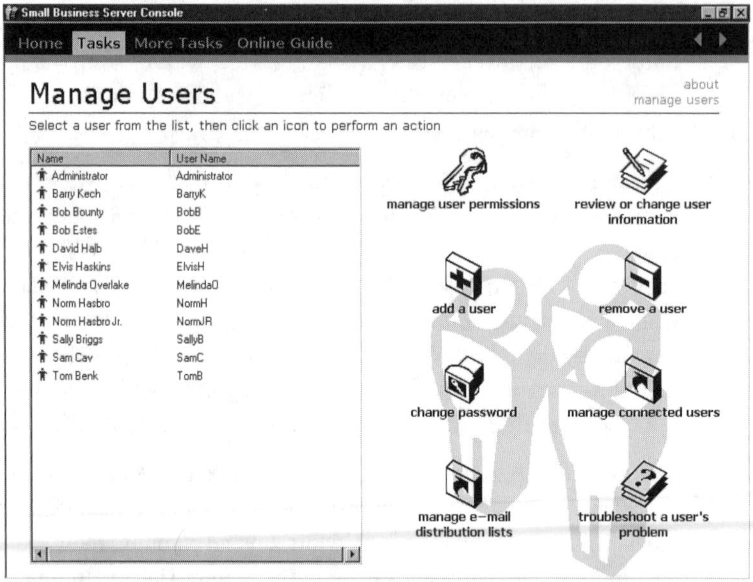

FIGURE 6.24

*Manage Computers.*

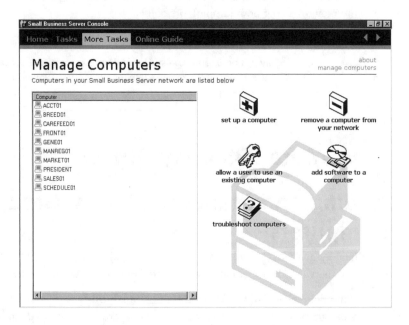

## Advanced User/Group/Computer Topics

The SBS Console provides basic user and computer management capabilities. However, the capability to manage groups is possible via the SBS Console. For those of you who have worked as network professionals, you know that management of permissions and rights via groups is a best practice in the world of network management.

### Creating Groups

It is typically easier to assign someone to a group with certain rights than to manage individual rights assignments (which can become confusing). For example, you might want to have a group called Project1 with certain rights to a project folder. As project team members come and go, you typically simply place the users in the Project1 group, not having to think especially hard about who has or needs what rights to work on the project. At the end of the project, simply remove the group and you've addressed any rights matters related to Project1. Managing network resources via groups is a time-tested approach.

In order to use groups on your SBS network, you need to drop beneath the hood on SBS and use a regular Windows NT Server tool known as User Manager for Domains.

### To Create a Group

1. Make sure you are logged on to your SBS server machine as Administrator or member of the Administrators group.

2. From the Start button on the desktop, select Programs, Administrative Tools (Common), and User Manager for Domains. User Manager for Domains appears similar to Figure 6.25.

**FIGURE 6.25**

*User Manager for Domains.*

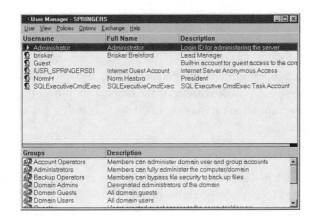

6

3. From the User menu in User Manager for Domains, select New Local Group.

**Note**  SBS supports only one domain, so there is no need to use Global Groups (one of the group options).

4. Type **Project1** in the Group Name filed in the New Local Group dialog box. Add the following to the Description field: **Springer's Project 1 Team**.

5. Add a member to this group by clicking the Add button. For this example, add **NormH**. Remove Administrator from this group if necessary. The New Local Group dialog box should appear similar to Figure 6.26.

**FIGURE 6.26**

*New Local Group.*

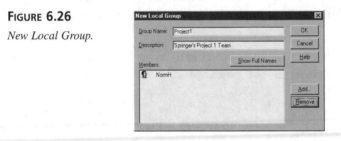

6. Click OK to create the local group Project1.

You would now add this group to share-level or NTFS-level permissions as needed instead of the individuals where appropriate.

## Disabling User Accounts

Another important network management tool that is lacking in the SBS Console is the capability to disable a user account. Typically, when an employee is terminated, you first disable the account prior to deleting the account. That way, just in case the employee legitimately returns, you can reactivate the account for proper use. In fact, I typically disable an account for up to two weeks before deleting it. It's just another best practice in network management.

### To Disable a User Account

1. Make sure you are logged on to your SBS server machine as an Administrator or member of the Administrators group.

2. From the Start button on the desktop, select Programs, Administrative Tools (Common), and then select User Manager for Domains.

3. Select the user account you intend to disable and select the Properties menu command from the User menu. You can also double-click the username to display the properties for the user.

4. Select the Account Disabled check box in the User Properties dialog box, similar to Figure 6.27

**FIGURE 6.27**

*Account Disabled.*

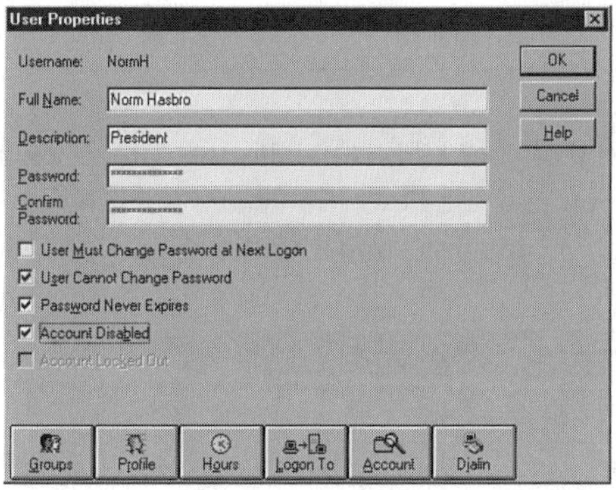

5. Click OK. The account is now disabled.

To reactive the account, simply uncheck the Account Disabled check box for the user account.

# UPS Power Levels

As part of your SBS network management stewardship, it is critical that you periodically monitor the power feed to the server machine. Recall from Day 2, "Planning for Small Business Server," that I planned for and purchased a backup battery known as an uninterruptible power supply (UPS).

One popular brand of UPS is the Smart UPS series from American Power Corporation (APC). Typically, a UPS shipped by APC includes a UPS monitoring application called PowerChute. PowerChute is far superior to the UPS application included with SBS (found in Control Panel). In fact, some people out in SBS land will bomb my e-mail box if I don't call a spade a spade: the UPS application in the Control Panel is the absolute worst. Don't ever use it.

PowerChute installs like any other application, but you must do this after you have completely installed SBS. That's because PowerChute requires that you attach a serial cable from the back of the UPS battery to one of the COM ports of your SBS server machines.

6

**Power Tool Tip**

Be prepared to purchase a multifunction I/O card to provide you with an additional physical COM port on your SBS server machine. Because Microsoft recommends that SBS be installed with two or more modems, I've had the great pleasure of looking behind the SBS server machine, ready to cable the UPS, only to discover that I have no free COM port available. Later, after installing a new multifunction I/O card on my server, I have the ability to attach the serial cable from the UPS to my SBS server machine.

To view the power level that your UPS is monitoring, simply launch the PowerChute application (assuming you're using PowerChute and it has been correctly installed). You can observe power level information similar to that displayed in Figure 6.28.

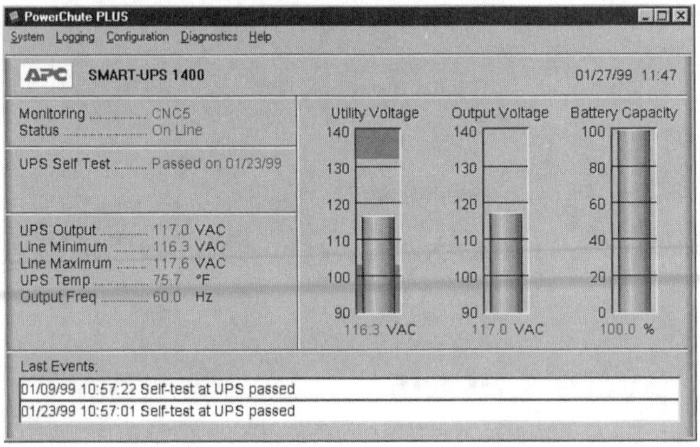

**FIGURE 6.28**

*PowerChute UPS Monitoring.*

| PowerChute PLUS |  |  |  | _ □ × |
| --- | --- | --- | --- | --- |
| System  Logging  Configuration  Diagnostics  Help | | | | |

**APC   SMART-UPS 1400**                                                 01/27/99  11:47

| | Utility Voltage | Output Voltage | Battery Capacity |
| --- | --- | --- | --- |
| Monitoring ............ CNC5 | | | |
| Status .................... On Line | 140 | 140 | 100 |
| | 130 | 130 | 80 |
| UPS Self Test ........ Passed on 01/23/99 | 120 | 120 | 60 |
| UPS Output ........... 117.0 VAC | 110 | 110 | 40 |
| Line Minimum ......... 116.3 VAC | | | |
| Line Maximum ........ 117.6 VAC | 100 | 100 | 20 |
| UPS Temp ............. 75.7 °F | 90 | 90 | 0 |
| Output Freq ........... 60.0 Hz | 116.3 VAC | 117.0 VAC | 100.0 % |

Last Events:

01/09/99 10:57:22 Self-test at UPS passed
01/23/99 10:57:01 Self-test at UPS passed

## Advanced UPS Matters

Beyond UPS monitoring, you might need to work with your utility company to determine whether your site is getting bad power. Bad power could be defined as unstable power, brownouts, and blackouts. Your site might be afflicted by power maladies that UPS monitoring can help identify, but not resolve.

Remember that a UPS is only effective if the power fluctuations are somewhat sporadic or cataclysmic. For example, if your site fully loses power often, a UPS will properly shut down your SBS server as expected, but you've still got bad power feeding your site. It's unlikely that you'd get much work finished under these circumstances.

# Logon/Logoff Status

It is relatively easy to determine who is logged on to the SBS network. This is done by selecting the Manage User Connections option from the Manage Users screen (accessed via the SBS Console). This is show in Figure 6.29.

**FIGURE 6.29**

*Manage Connected Users.*

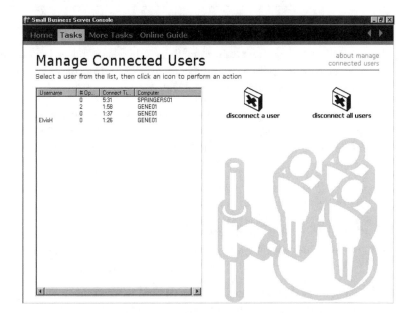

Being able to determine who is logged on to your SBS network quickly enables you to answer a user who asks "Am I logged on?" Why might a user ask such a question? Most likely, this question would be asked when a user is unable to accomplish something such as being able to access a file or print a document. Thus the need to know whether the user is logged on to the SBS network.

Likewise, it is very easy for users not to log on to your network, even though their intentions are good. I call it the CEO factor. On occasion, a CEO or other prominent businessperson accidentally escapes past the SBS network logon dialog box from his Windows 9.x workstation (often while distracted on telephone call). Soon thereafter, said CEO believes the SBS network is broken because he can't get his e-mail, print, or surf the Web. And it is I, the SBS consultant, who receives his call.

6

> **Tip**
>
> Did I mention how important this discussion is and how easy it is to resolve? So many times, in the heat of battle in SBS land, the user's question is Am I logged on? Read and reread this discussion to learn for yourself how easy it is to answer this question. Sorry to repeat myself, but it's important.

There is another way of telling whether a user is explicitly logged on to the SBS network. I call it the decentralized method. Whereas Manager User Connections displays connected users from a central location (the SBS Console), you can also determine the same by visiting each workstation and checking the SBS user's logon status.

For Windows NT Workstation, you can easily check the SBS user's logon status by pressing Ctrl+Alt+Delete to display the Windows NT Security dialog box. The top part of the Windows NT Security dialog box contains a Logon Information section. It is here the user's logon name, the domain name, and the logon date are displayed. Once they're displayed, you can click Cancel to close the Windows NT Security dialog box and return to your desktop.

### Task 6.5: Taking a Look Around

Strech your legs and walk around the floor of your office. See which users are logged on by applying the logon discovery approached discussed above.

For Windows 98 workstations, you can tell whether the user is logged on by looking at the second command on the Windows 98 menu bar (which is displayed when you click the Start button). This is the Log Off menu option. If it were to say Log Off NormH, you would be able to determine that indeed NormH is logged on to the SBS network (hence, he has something to log off from). However, if the Log Off command is not followed by a username, the user is indeed not logged on to the SBS network.

## Advanced Logon/Logoff Issues

A few advanced comments about Manage Connected Users are necessary. First, a name can be listed multiple times reflecting multiple connections to the SBS network. Such connections might be to different resources (share points, printers). Second, I've seen the Manage User Connections screen present logon connection used by the system for administrative share, network management, or other communication purposes (such as IPC$—Inter Processes Communication—connections). IPC connections are way beyond the scope of this book, but you can think of IPC connections as maintaining the computing session between user workstation and SBS server machine. Those logons typically show #Open Files, Connect Time, and Computer entries, but no logon name. It's very puzzling indeed to see so many connections sometimes for so few users logged on (in fact, Figure 6.29 shows only ElvisH logged on but many connections appear).

Along the same lines, the Manage User Connections often displays two connections per user. Such is the case in Figure 6.29 for the first two entries from SPRINGERGS01. The first entry for SPRINGERS01 that has no username is an IPC$ connection (again, don't worry about it, but please don't mess with it either!). The second connection for SPRINGERS01 is the actual user connection for the Administrator account. Note that the Administrator is also logged on from MKT1.

Another interesting item regarding Manage Connected Users is the case of the slowly appearing and quickly disappearing users. Often, a username appears in the Username category only to disappear quickly. Conversely, sometimes it takes forever for a connected user's name to appear.

To some extent, this is by design in SBS, according to Microsoft. Only users who have actively used their connections within the last few minutes are listed. For advanced users, you can find this discussion in article Q175376 on Microsoft TechNet. Thus, the Manage User Connections screen aggressively drops user connections from the list, but be aware the user might still be connected, just inactive. Also be aware that modern clients using 32-bit workstation clients (such as Windows NT Workstation, Windows 95 and Windows 98) automatically reconnects if a network connection has been dropped (such as a server reboot). This is a fact not easily reported by Manage User Connections.

Manage User Connections is not nearly as accurate as the `userlist` command on NetWare servers (such a command instantly and reliably presented a list of logged on users). However, two other ways enable you to see who is connected to your SBS network. These are the `net session` command and the netwatch.exe file contained in the Windows NT Server 4.0 Resource Kit.

To use the `net session` command to observe current logons:

1. From the machine running SBS, select the Start button at the lower left of your SBS machine's desktop.
2. Select the Programs option.
3. Select the Command Prompt menu option.
4. At the command line (C:>) type **net session**, and you will see a result similar to Figure 6.30.

Likewise, if you install and run the netwatch.exe file on your SBS machine from the Windows NT Server 4.0 Resource Kit, you should see user connections displayed similar to Figure 6.31. NetWatch conveniently displays not only who is logged on but what resources are being used in a graphical tree. This is very handy.

6

**FIGURE 6.30**

*net session.*

**FIGURE 6.30**

*net session.*

**FIGURE 6.31**

*NetWatch displaying user connections.*

To install the netwatch.exe file, simply copy the netwatch.exe file from the appropriate directory from the Windows NT Server 4.0 Resource Kit CD-ROM. Assuming you are using drive D: for the CD-ROM, you are running an Intel-based machine, and you want to copy this file to the temp directory (C:\temp) on your SBS machine; you could execute the following command at the C: prompt:

```
copy d:\i386\netdiag\netwatch.exe c:\temp
```

Then simply double-click netwatch.exe to launch the Net Watch application.

**Tip**

> You might also want to create a NetWatch shortcut and place it on your SBS machine desktop for easy access.

Neither the `net session` command nor NetWatch are subject to the slowly appearing and rapidly disappearing connected usernames that SBS's Manage User Connections screen shows. Thus these two approaches are more reliable when faced with answering the question of "Who is logged on to the SBS network?"

Finally, depending on your situation, you might elect to impose logon/logoff restrictions for users by time of day or specific workstations. These types of restrictions cannot be accomplished natively via the SBS Console. Rather, you need to go under the hood and launch User Manager for Domains in the Administrative Tools (Common) program group. In User Manager for Domains, simply select the properties for the user who needs logon restrictions . (Just double-click the username or select Properties via the User menu.) To restrict the hours a user can log on to the SBS network, select the Hours button in the User Properties dialog box. To restrict which workstation the user can log on from, select the Logon To button.

# End-User Support

Something you do every single day is support end users. End-user support is a truly a multifaceted area; issues can come at you from any angle. Here are some of the most common end-user support issues I've encountered on SBS networks, but of course the sky is the limit.

## Printing

"I can't print" is a frequent cry for help from the SBS user base. The Manage Printers screen from the Tasks sheet on the SBS Console is where you would manage this function. The Manage Printers screen is discussed at length in Day 5, "Managing the Small Business Server Management Console." From Manage Printers, you can perform most, if not all, of the printing management issues you are likely to encounter. This includes verifying that the server received the print job for processing (queuing) and canceling a print job.

But exceptions exist. For example, if you use a printer that is directly connected to the network, you likely use a printer management software application such as HP's JetAdmin software to manage the printer (in addition to Manager Printers in the SBS Console).

## Applications

"How do I do that?" is an applications refrain that SBS users sing. Even though you might not have application-specific expertise, SBS users associate you, the SBS guru, with anything and everything related to the SBS network. Perhaps that why I've found

6

myself supporting Westlaw's WESTMATE legal application at the law firm in the morning and MasterBuilder construction accounting software at the homebuilding company in the afternoon. Such is a day in the life of an SBS guru. More importantly, being an SBS guru requires that you think quickly on your feet and have the ability to learn new user applications very quickly. Hey, it's not like I'm certified in WESTMATE or MasterBuilder!

## E-Mail

Want to find yourself providing user support, as if you didn't have other things to do? Just do something to interrupt the e-mail service on an SBS network. A few words to the wise regarding e-mail service. If the user hasn't successfully logged on to the SBS network, it is entirely likely that the user's e-mail won't function. First, verify whether the user is logged on to the SBS network (see the "Logon/Logoff Status" section above). If the user is not logged on, simply have him log on. It is likely that e-mail service will be restored. Second, can you distinguish whether local e-mail on your internal SBS network is working and whether the Internet e-mail service is working? Often the internal e-mail system is working while the Internet e-mail isn't. It's an important distinction that you will want to make. Third, is only one user experiencing e-mail problems or are other users displaying similar problems? Here, the individual user might have somehow corrupted his Microsoft Outlook profile, resulting in an interruption in the specific individual's e-mail service.

## Special Requests

"Can you just do…" is typically the opening phrase of a special request from an SBS user. Such requests are really an affirmation that the SBS users want to do more with the SBS network. I think that's a good thing: SBS network acceptance! However, it is a time management challenge for SBS administrators and gurus alike everywhere to respond to such requests (perhaps you have other duties pulling at your limited time availability as well).

## End-User Training

One easy way to mitigate support requirements is to better train your SBS end users. The training might take the form of guide-by-the-side, where you mentor SBS end users one-on-one by assisting individual users who have a need to know something SBS-related. The other training method to consider is sage-on-the-stage. Here, you or a trainer you retain provide traditional classroom-style training for SBS end users on SBS network usage or applications such as Microsoft Outlook and Microsoft Office 2000. In fact, at my consulting firm, I built a training room to better serve our SBS clientele. It has been a big success.

## Advanced End-User Support Issues

If you can't beat 'em, join 'em. This strategy concerns using end users to support end users on your SBS network. Having end users as support resources takes two forms. First, you might be able to enlist one or two of your power users into mentoring the weaker SBS users. Second, you should strongly consider using local college interns for part-time SBS end-user support. Either approach can save you from the endless parade of SBS end-user support issues (and spend your time introducing enhanced SBS features, such as new Web pages).

**Note**

> Keep the context of my suggestions above in perspective. Although I do think power users can be your eyes and ears helping end users out on the floor of your office, I do suggest that you be very careful about letting power users on the actual SBS server machine. Use your best judgment.

You should also consider being a one-minute SBS manager. Here, the strategy is to introduce cool and neat features as you survey your SBS kingdom. One such one-minute goodie is creating a shortcut on the SBS end user's desktop. Often, desktop real estate goes unused while users navigate several layers deep in the menu system to launch applications. Consider creating a shortcut for the application and placing it on the SBS end user's desktop.

# Check System Health

You can do three things each day to quickly check the health of your SBS server machine: run Task Manager, check Event Viewer, and view the e-mail queue.

## Task Manager

Task Manager is my SBS buddy. It reports a wide range of current information about your SBS server. To launch Task Manager, simply right-click the task bar at the bottom of your screen on your SBS server machine. From the secondary menu, select Task Manager. Task Manager launches and offers you three tabbed sheets to select from: Applications, Processes, and Performance.

### Applications

Here, open applications are displayed. You can end the applications via the End Task button. More importantly, the Applications tab enables you to determine whether an application has crashed or stopped running. If an application has crashed, Not Responding is displayed in the Status column. At that time, you need to use the End Task button to crash the application.

6

## Processes

This technical tab displays processes currently running on the SBS server. To be brutally honest, it's likely you would view this screen if you were answering questions posed to you over the telephone by a Microsoft technical support engineer. Enough said.

## Performance

The Performance tab is my absolute favorite! Here, at a glance, I can tell what the CPU utilization (processor activity) is on my machine (see Figure 6.32). Typically, the CPU Usage value is in the single digits. But if that value remains above 80% for an extended period of time (say, several days), I'm on notice that I have performance issues on my SBS network and perhaps I should purchase a more powerful processor (or additional processors) for my SBS server machine.

**Power Tool Tip**

Be extremely careful in upgrading from a single processor to two or more processors on an SBS server machine. I haven't enjoyed great success doing this using the suggested uptome.exe application, but other SBS gurus have told me that they've had success using the up2smp.exe utility to accomplish the same (upgrading to multiple processors). Because reports conflict here, I highly recommend you study both before acting when adding processors to your SBS server machine. Plus you should perform the processor upgrade in a test scenario (on a test server) if possible. Good luck.

**FIGURE 6.32**

*Task Manger - Performance tab.*

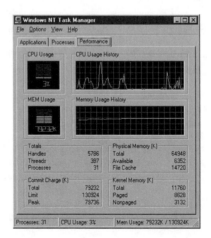

The other cool thing on the Performance screen is the memory usage information. The Memory Usage History histogram enables me not only to determine what amount of my

SBS server machine's RAM memory is being consumed, but if I observe a upward sloping trend line, I know I might have leaky applications (an application that is robbing memory).

**Power Tool Tip**

In fact, I try to record the Mem Usage value located at the lower-right of the Performance screen every several days. This value might appear similar to Mem Usage 87824K/130928K. If you reboot, the numerator (the top number) is smaller because the SBS server machines memory has been flushed and reset. Over time, moderate growth in the numerator value is acceptable. However, if I have a major problem with an application robbing memory, the numerator can grow rapidly to a very large number. In fact, I've seen badly behaved applications eat up all the memory to the point that the SBS server machine runs out of memory, causing it to stop functioning!

# Event Viewer

The Event Viewer application enables you to peek at the health of your system. You can observe three logs (system, security, and application), but only the system and application logs hold real meaning for most of us. The security logs requires that you implement auditing, a feature that is typically beyond the scope of the average SBS site.

A few general comments regarding Event Viewer are in order. First, blue is a great color. When viewing any of the Event Viewer logs, blue-dotted information entries are good. Typically, blue-dotted information entries reflect the starting of a service. The yellow-dotted information messages reflect, as a yellow traffic signal does, caution. Further investigation is necessary, but often yellow-dotted information messages are relatively harmless. The red Stop sign messages can be bad, reflecting a service that failed to start. But, when it comes to red Stop sign messages, Event Viewer is often a "wolf crier," in my opinion.

For example, the SBS tape backup program makes entries for NTBackup in the Application log when it backs up and verifies a tape. But, I bet you didn't know that it makes a red Stop sign entry for the end of its verify job, even though there isn't anything especially alarming about the end of a verify job to justify a Stop sign!

## System

The system log in Event Viewer shows operating system–related information. Here is where important network information is communicated to you, such as the network card failing.

**6**

> **Tip**
>
> The System log is where you can also tell when the SBS server machine was last restarted or rebooted. This is accomplished by looking for the most recent entry titled EventLog (it has a blue information dot associated with it). This is the moment the computer restarted, as far as SBS is concerned. The entries above EventLog apply to the current session, as shown in Figure 6.33.

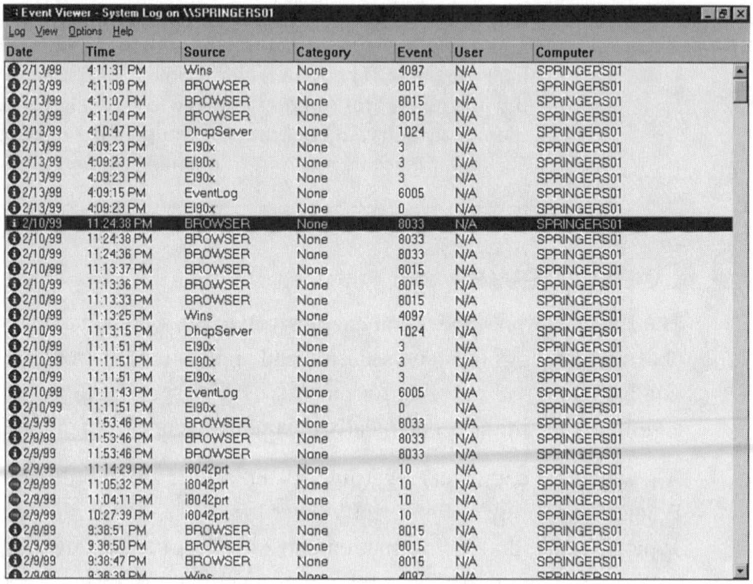

**FIGURE 6.33**

*Event Viewer - System Log.*

## Security

Unless you have turned on auditing (via User Manager for Domains), the security log in Event Viewer is blank. This is typically sufficient for most SBS sites.

## Application

The application log reports important information on various applications, including tape backup applications, the Microsoft Exchange e-mail application and the Microsoft SQL Server database application (as well as many other applications that write to the application log).

## E-mail Queuing

Via the Manage E-mail sheet in the SBS Console, you can check how e-mail is performing. Ideally, as seen in Figure 6.34, the Outgoing E-mail and Incoming E-mail are empty. This would typically show e-mail is being both sent and received in a timely manner without being trapped in the e-mail queue.

**FIGURE 6.34**

*The Manage E-mail sheet, showing outgoing and incoming e-mail.*

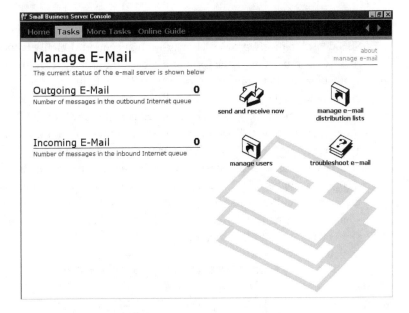

However, if a user were to complain that he hadn't received an important piece of e-mail from the Internet, quickly checking Manage E-mail would enable you, at a glance, to see whether e-mail is trapped in the outgoing or incoming queue. At that point, you would have the information to proceed with Internet connectivity or e-mail troubleshooting. These topics are discussed on Days 9, "Connecting to the Internet," and 16, "Using Microsoft Exchange." If the e-mail queues are empty and you can verify that the Internet connection is sound (click the Send and Receive Mail Now button to force an Internet session to send and receive e-mail), you must, sadly, inform your SBS user that no one has e-mailed him. Be sure to let him down gently, as absolutely no one likes to hear they received no mail at mail call.

## Task 6.6: Checkup

Time for another breath of fresh air. Take a few minutes to check the health of your SBS network using the system health approaches discussed above.

**Power Tool Tip**

For the hearty among us, you can observe even more details relating to the Microsoft Exchange Internet e-mail queues via the Queues sheet of the Internet Mail Service in the Microsoft Exchange Administrator. This tool is discussed on Day 16.

# Run Virus Detection

SBS doesn't natively provide virus protection support. I highly recommend that you purchase virus protection in the form of a robust, third-party server-based virus protection application such as Computer Associate's Cheyenne Inoculan for Windows NT. This server-based application provides real-time or ongoing virus protection for the server, traffic on the network, and Internet-related activity (downloaded files). Inoculan is a complex product that allows numerous setup configurations, including the capability for it to phone home over the Internet (a feature I discuss on Day 7, "Monthly and Annual SBS Duties"). One of the most valuable features in Inoculan is the real-time monitor that reports the number of files scanned and the number of viruses detached. This is shown in Figure 6.35, and I recommend you look at this screen each day to monitor the status of your network (but be advised Inoculan has several advanced virus monitoring and reporting features I won't discuss here).

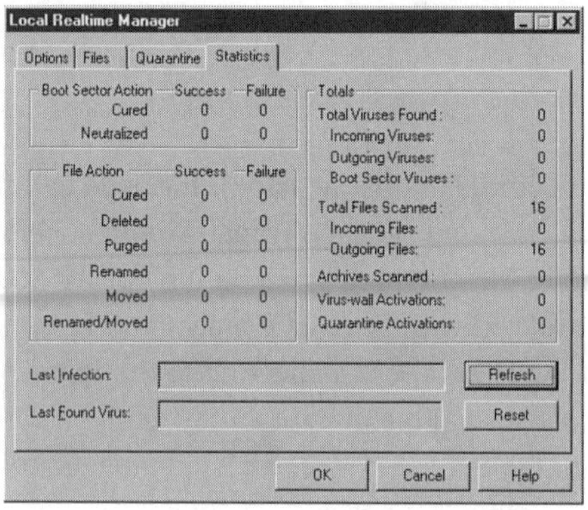

**FIGURE 6.35**

*Inoculan's Local Realtime Manager.*

> **Note**
>
> You can purchase Inoculan for $500 to $600.

There are two other less desirable ways to invoke virus protection on your SBS network. I've seen both used, but I've become disenchanted with either method because the virus protection is incomplete. These methods are the tape backup method and the workstation mapped drive method.

## Tape Backup Method

If you purchase Seagate's Backup Exec tape backup application discussed earlier in this chapter, you have the opportunity to perform a virus scan on files that are being backed up to tape. This approach is certainly cheaper than purchasing Inoculan, but the virus protection isn't real-time. It is performed at a fixed point in time, when the tape backup job runs. That means you have virus exposure the other 23 or so hours per day on your SBS network. Also, the tape backup method doesn't scan incoming e-mail attachments for viruses.

## Workstation Mapped Drive Method

Today, workstations purchased from leading computer manufacturers such as Dell arrive with bundled software applications already installed for your enjoyment. One of these applications is typically McAfee's VirusScan virus protection application, but this version of VirusScan works only on your workstation, not the network. However, there is one trick you can play to have it scan the data on your network. Map network drives (such as F:, G:, and so on) to the root of the SBS server machine hard disk (for example, C$). Then have VirusScan scan the drive you mapped (for example, Drive F) so that the data stored on the SBS server machine is scanned for viruses. This is shown in Figure 6.36.

**FIGURE 6.36**

*Virus scanning via mapped network drives.*

This method, of course, has the same weaknesses as the tape backup method: timeliness and Internet file-related scanning. I don't recommend this method, but it is better than nothing. In short, don't shortcut the protection of your data on the SBS network when it comes to virus protection.

## Advanced Virus Detection Issues

The area of virus protection is very important on your network, ranking right up there with tape backups. To better monitor virus protection issues and thus better protect your data, you should consider reading Dr. Solomon's Virus Report. This is a periodic newsletter that you can find more information on at www.drsolomon.com.

6

# Installing/Removing Applications

You can count on installing and removing applications on any given day. You can perform these tasks on either a workstation or the SBS server machine itself. I will first show you how applications are installed on the SBS server machine. I'll end the discussion in this section with tips for installing applications on the SBS user's workstation.

There are basically two ways to install programs on an SBS server machine: Add/Remove Software and InstallShield.

**Note**
On Day 15, "Implementing Microsoft Office 2000," I'll mention how Office 2000–specific applications autoinstall when needed. Very cool.

## Add/Remove Software

The first method, Add/Remove Software, is preferred as it will, more likely than not, register the application as being installed on the SBS server machine. Programs that are registered on the SBS server are shown in Figure 6.37 at the bottom part of the dialog box.

To install an application via Add/Remove Software

1. Make sure you are logged on to the SBS server machine as Administrator or a member of the Administrator's group.

2. From the Start button on the desktop, select Settings, Control Panel.

3. Select Add/Remove Programs from Control Panel.

4. The Add/Remove Programs Properties dialog box is displayed, as seen in Figure 6.37.

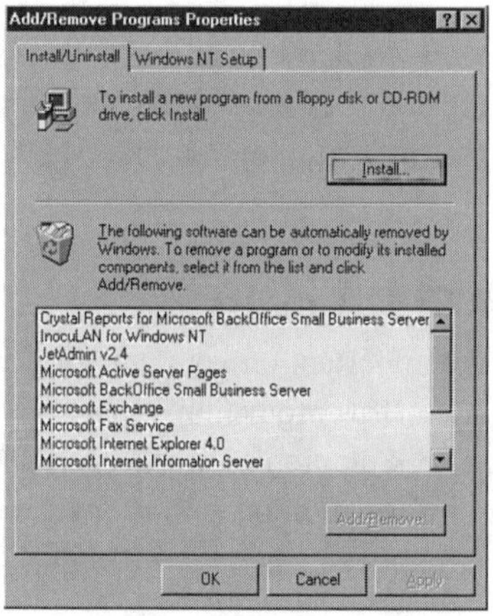

**FIGURE 6.37**

*Add/Remove Programs Properties.*

| Add/Remove Programs Properties | ? X |
|---|---|
| Install/Uninstall | Windows NT Setup |

5. Click the Install button to launch the Install Program from Floppy Disk or CD-ROM Wizard. Click Next.

6. Provide the path to the setup file for the application you are attempting to install in the Run Installation Program dialog box (as seen in Figure 6.38). Click Finish. The application installs.

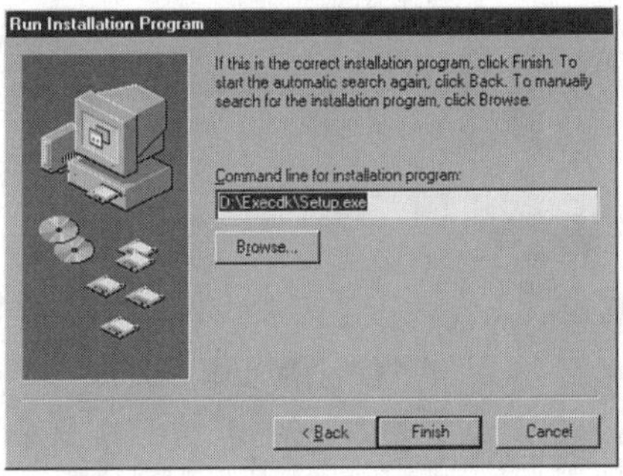

**FIGURE 6.38**

*Run Installation Program.*

7. Note when the application installation routine starts, it is often necessary to answer setup questions related to the application (such as agreeing to the software license). Answer these questions as needed. The application completes its installation.

8. Typically, after applications have been installed on the SBS server machine, it is necessary to reboot.

## InstallShield

This popular installation program is used by large and small software developers alike to assist you in application installations. InstallShield launches a setup wizard, similar to that seen in Figure 6.39, that enables you to answer several questions about how to set up the application (whether to install everything, where to install the application). While the application is installing, a set of progress bars report how far along the application installation is.

## Uninstall

Many programs, when registered on the Add/Remove Programs, can be uninstalled. Uninstalling a program is much more than erasing the folder from the hard disk and the icon from the menu on your desktop.

6

FIGURE 6.39

*InstallShield's setup wizard.*

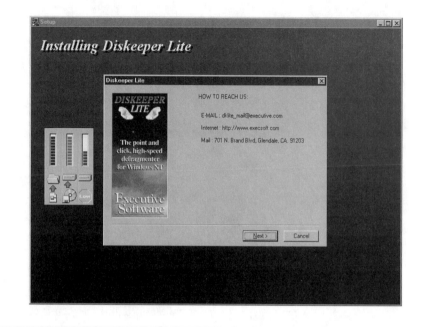

---

**Tip**

Indeed, simply erasing an icon and a folder likely results in an incomplete uninstall because applications today make important entries in the SBS Registry (a configuration database). These Registry entries aren't removed when you simply delete the application's folder and icon.

Properly uninstalling an application results in the removal of the application's folder, icons, Registry entries, and any special configuration files such as Dynamic Link Libraries (DLLs) that is installed on to your system.

**Power Tool Tip**

I usually retain the DLLs from a program, even though I am typically asked in the uninstall process if I want to remove such files. I've found little harm from retaining DLLs but, conversely, I've created havoc by removing DLLs that one application thought no other application was using.

To remove an application

1. Make sure you are logged on to the SBS server machine as Administrator or a member of the Administrator's group.

2. From the Start button on the desktop, launch the SBS Console via the Manage Console menu option.

3. Select Add/Remove Software from the More Tasks sheet. The Add/Remove Programs Properties dialog box is displayed.

4. Select the program you want to remove with a single click.

5. Click the Add/Remove button and respond to the dialog boxes presented to you to uninstall the application. Note that the types of dialog boxes and the questions presented to you vary by application.

You might also see that an application provides an Uninstall icon in its program group (typically accessed via Programs, in the Start menu). This is an alternative way to uninstall applications. Also note that installing and uninstalling applications on your SBS workstations is very similar.

# Reporting

Oh, did I forget to mention along the way that you should create an SBS network notebook to record information about your network, such as the setup sheets you created on Day 2? If I did, please take a moment to find a three-ring notebook and label it SBS Network.

Now that you've finished that, let's look at a few reports that you might like to look at each day and periodically place in your SBS Network notebook. Based on my experience, the reports SBS administrators most like to see are Internet usage and Fax activity. I have one bummer note to share: Some very valuable E-mail reports that were available in SBS 4.0/4.0a have been removed in SBS 4.5.

## Internet Reports

The SBS Console lets you see who the largest users of the Internet are and what the most popular Web sites are. To be brutally honest, these reports are typically run to see whether SBS users are visiting inappropriate sites. As you might know, many companies have policies that speak clearly towards Internet-related abuse, It is the Internet activity reports via the SBS Console that enable you to observe whether such abuse is occurring. Recall that I introduced Internet reporting on Day 5 when you toured the SBS Console, but I'll quickly review the reporting again.

To view Internet activity reports in SBS:

1. Make sure you are logged on to the SBS server machine as Administrator or a member of the Administrator's group.

2. Launch the SBS Console from the Start button from the desktop.

3. Select the More Tasks tab sheet.

6

4. Select the Manage Internet Access button.
5. Select Generate Internet Reports. You have the opportunity to select from several Internet reports. The most meaningful reports are the Top 10 Sites Hit, the Top 10 Users, and the Activity by Hour of the Day reports. Figure 6.40 shows the Top 10 Sites Hit (and indeed, the top site is an inappropriate site).

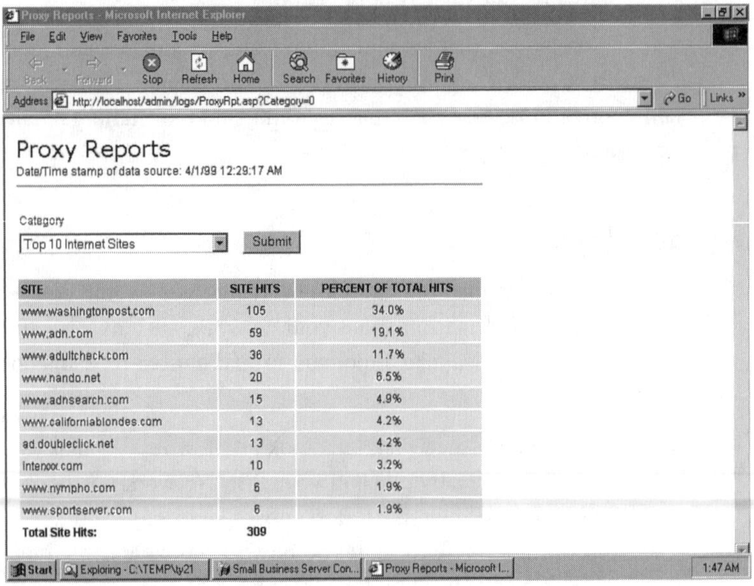
Proxy Reports - Microsoft Internet Explorer
File Edit View Favorites Tools Help
Back Forward Stop Refresh Home Search Favorites History Print
Address http://localhost/admin/logs/ProxyRpt.asp?Category=0
Go Links
Proxy Reports
Date/Time stamp of data source: 4/1/99 12:29:17 AM
Category
Top 10 Internet Sites
Submit
SITE SITE HITS PERCENT OF TOTAL HITS
www.washingtonpost.com 105 34.0%
www.adn.com 59 19.1%
www.adultcheck.com 36 11.7%
www.nando.net 20 6.5%
www.adnsearch.com 15 4.9%
www.californiablondes.com 13 4.2%
ad.doubleclick.net 13 4.2%
Interxxx.com 10 3.2%
www.nympho.com 6 1.9%
www.sportserver.com 6 1.9%
Total Site Hits: 309
Start
Exploring - C:\TEMP\ty21
Small Business Server Con...
Proxy Reports - Microsoft I...
1:47 AM

**FIGURE 6.40**

*Top 10 Sites Hit.*

## Fax Reports

Last but not least are the Fax reports. If your SBS site is using the fax capabilities of SBS, you will be interested in this set of reports. In particular, the Sent Faxes Report is the only place in SBS where you can confirm that you sent a fax and the other party received it. This report is one of the most important reports for small law firms using SBS. Being able to confirm a sent fax is mission critical for many lawyers (and others too!).

To view E-mail activity reports in SBS

1. Make sure you are logged on to the SBS server machine as an Administrator or a member of the Administrator's group.
2. Launch the SBS Console from the Start button from the desktop.
3. Select the Manage Faxes button on the More Tasks tab sheet.
4. Select Generate Fax Reports.
5. Several Fax reports are presented. Select the report that is of interest to you.

## Advanced Reporting

Leave it to a client to educate me on the appropriate and inappropriate use of the Internet by her staff. This supervisor correctly asked What if Internet abuse is occurring, but it isn't appearing on the Top 10 Sites report because it is the 11th or higher site measured by visits? How could she see who is going to these sites? All good questions.

Fortunately, I had paid my dues in another life with Proxy Server, and I just happened to know that Proxy Server, properly configured via the Internet Service Manager (found in the Microsoft Proxy Server program group), reports *everything*! By that I mean every hit on every site is recorded in detail (site visited, time visited, machine, and user that visited this site). These Proxy Server logs are located in c:\winnt.sbs\system32\wsplogs folder. Although the log files are raw text, a close look at the contents enables you to see amazing details (perhaps more than you ever wanted to know!). On a lighter note, reviewing these logs once with a client allowed us to discover that the night cleaning staff was very adept at Web browsing (to all the wrong places). This was proven by extensive log entries showing Web activity at 2 a.m.!

# Working Smarter Each Day

I'd like to close by encouraging you to consider the following SBS paradigm: working smarter each day. The best way to get value from your SBS network is to—as they say at IBM—think!

## The Web

One easy way to work better each day is to browse the Web for SBS topics. A list of SBS-friendly Web sites is included in Appendix A, "SBS Resources." I would also encourage you to use a popular engine such as Infoseek and search on the word SBS.

## Microsoft TechNet

Consider subscribing to Microsoft's monthly CD-ROM subscription service known as Microsoft TechNet. For approximately $300 per year, you will receive a set of CD-ROMs that provide invaluable SBS support information.

**6**

**Tip**

To search in Microsoft TechNet, click the binocular-looking icon on the toolbar and type the term SBS. The results of such a search are shown in Figure 6.41.

FIGURE 6.41

FIGURE **6.41**

*SBS search on Microsoft TechNet.*

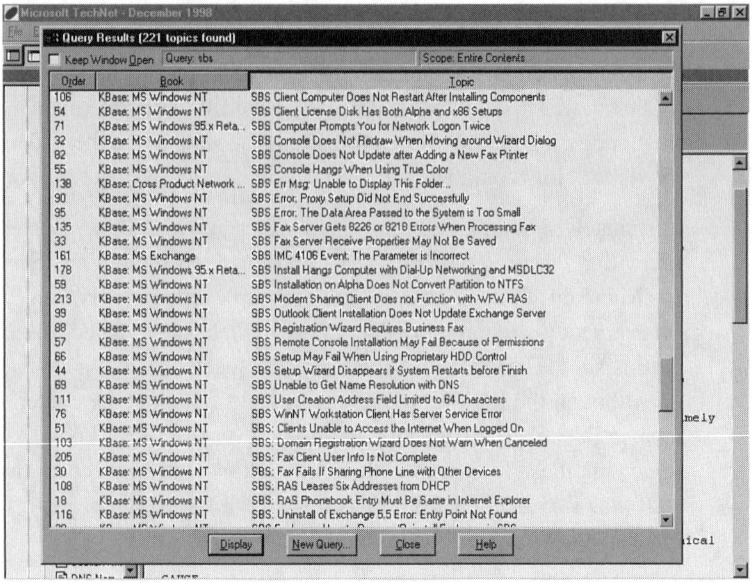

## Windows NT-isms

Consider exploring more of Windows NT Server as your time allows. For example, you might try to become more familiar with the programs contained in Administrative Tools (Common) such as Windows NT Diagnostics, and Performance Monitor (both of which I discuss tomorrow on Day 7.

## Research

Keep an eagle eye out for SBS articles in technical trade journals such as InfoWorld. I am also seeing in increase in SBS-related articles in business magazines such as INC. and Success. I've always felt an hour of research saves many hours of learning the hard way (the trial-and-error method).

# SBS Dirty Dozen Checklist

In Appendix C, "SBS Project Kit," you will find a check list for managing the SBS Dirty Dozen tasks discussed in this chapter. Enjoy!

# Summary

This chapter presents the 12 most important and frequent tasks you are likely to perform to keep both your SBS network and SBS users up and running, but feel free to ads to this list as your own unique experience dictates. I suspect for many of you, the above SBS Dirty Dozen will grow to the SBS Dirty Two Dozen. See you tomorrow on Day 7.

# DAY 7

# Monthly and Annual SBS Duties

 **AM**

Good morning. This lesson extends the daily and weekly view of Day 6, "Daily and Weekly SBS Administration (The Dirty Dozen)," to include SBS network monthly and annual tasks. Although they are not as extensive as the daily and weekly tasks you undoubtedly perform on your SBS network, monthly and annual SBS-related tasks are no less important. In fact, overlooking some of the monthly tasks such as defragmentation can result in declining performance, frustrated users, and a damaged server.

In the morning session, I'll discuss most of the monthly dozen tasks you should perform on your SBS network. These tasks are outlined in Table 7.1. In the afternoon session, I'll complete the monthly dozen task discussion and discuss important annual tasks that you must perform.

**TABLE 7.1** SBS MONTHLY DOZEN TASKS

| Task | Description |
|------|-------------|
| 1 | The Monthly Reboot |
| 2 | Disk Defragmentation |
| 3 | Service Packs, Upgrades, Hot Fixes |
| 4 | Hard Disk Space Management |
| 5 | Virus Protection - Verify Phone Home |
| 6 | Updating Your SBS Toolkit |
| 7 | Y2K Testing |
| 8 | Adding Hardware |
| 9 | Updating the Emergency Repair Disk |
| 10 | Research—Web, Periodicals, Books, Check BugNet (www.bugnet.com) |
| 11 | Performance Monitor Logging |
| 12 | Updating SBS Network Notebook |

# The Monthly Reboot

In my experience, every server needs an occasional reboot. For several reasons, I like to reboot the SBS machines under my stewardship once per month. First, all computers suffer from RAM leaks as services, processes, and applications are opened and closed. These memory leaks occur because whatever used the memory doesn't completely return it to the computer when finished.

Granted, for most services, processes, and applications, the memory leak is very small (sometimes none at all). But, as they say in my neighborhood, Queen Anne Hill has always has one bad kid. Such is life with your SBS network. You can count on one bad service, process, or application to be a RAM robber at some point. These are typically poorly developed applications that the software vendor fixes at a future date.

**Power Tool Tip**

Memory leaks are discussed extensively in two Microsoft Certified System Engineer courses: Windows NT Core Technologies and Windows NT Server Enterprise Technologies. In fact, in the Core Technologies course, you will complete a lab with bad applications that consume excessive resources including RAM.

Before rebooting, be sure to observe the following memory value via Task Manager (and record it in the Monthly SBS worksheet discussed later). This memory value is the Mem Usage value in the lower right corner of Task Manager's Performance tab sheet. It is shown in Figure 7.1 as 90416K/130880K.

**FIGURE 7.1**

*Mem Usage before reboot.*

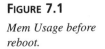

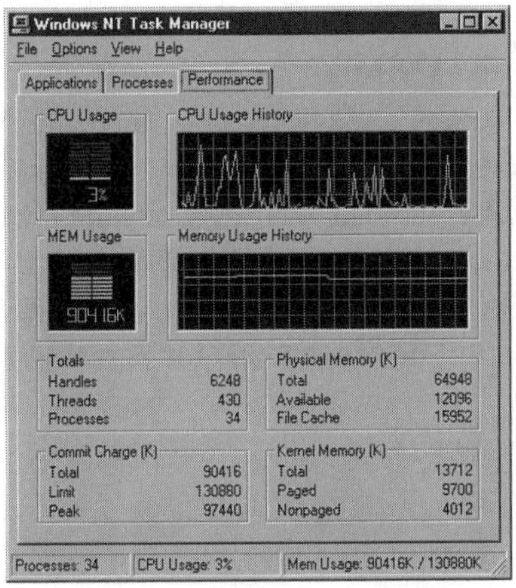

After performing a reboot on your SBS machine, once again observe the Mem Usage value in Task Manager. The numerator portion of the Mem Usage value should be significantly lower. That is because the reboot flushed the RAM (your SBS machine now has more RAM to work with).

The second reason I like to reboot an SBS machine each month? I need to know that any SBS machine I'm working with is basically healthy, at least to the extent that I'm not afraid to reboot it. Believe me, in other networking environments, such as the early days of LAN Manager or NetWare, I managed machines I was afraid to reboot! Today, with better machines and better operating systems such as SBS, that fear of rebooting doesn't cut it. Thus, the monthly reboot shows me the machine is in good working order.

Rebooting your SBS machine is, of course, very simple. Select Shutdown from the Start menu at the desktop of the SBS machine. Or, if you prefer, simultaneously hold down Ctrl+Alt+Delete, and the Windows NT Security dialog box appears. Select Shutdown and approve either Shutdown or Shutdown and Restart.

**Note**

The reboot time in SBS 4.5 is much faster than SBS 4.0/4.0a, if you haven't already noticed. That's because critical services such as Microsoft Exchange's System Attendant are now stopped early in the shutdown.

7

I have two final thoughts on rebooting. Make sure you've notified your SBS users that a reboot will occur so that they can log off properly and not leave any important files open (such as Great Plains accounting files). Better yet, consider coming in after hours to reboot the server when no one is around.

# Disk Defragmentation

Believe it or not, the hard disks in your SBS machine, as well as your SBS user's machines, are subject to fragmentation. Fragmentation occurs when information is written, in a fragmented way, to different locations. Here is what I mean. Suppose you had a large Microsoft Excel spreadsheet file titled BUDGET.XLS. It is possible this file could be written to numerous spots or locations on your hard disk to get it to fit when performing a file save. On the surface, this notion that one file is really stored across different locations on your hard disk isn't terribly bothersome, but when this happens with many files, including important operating system files, both you and I should be much more concerned.

Why concerned? Because these files, being stored in a somewhat discontiguous manner, have become fragmented. Such fragmentation results in poor performance on your machine because the hard disk must perform additional read/write activity to either retrieve or save the file. You see this phenomenon when you observe an incessantly grinding hard disk on your SBS machine during normal network activity (such as SBS users opening files to work on).

**Power Tool Tip**

Contrary to popular belief, the NTFS formatting scheme used on SBS machines is indeed subject to fragmentation. Rumors have abounded during the life of Windows NT Server, the underlying operating system in SBS, that NTFS partitions didn't suffer from fragmentation. That is wrong, as you'll see shortly in Figure 7.2.

So, if we agree that fragmentation is bad, how might you address this problem? Simply stated, on a monthly basis (more frequently on heavily used SBS systems), you should defragment the hard disk on your SBS machine. SBS doesn't natively provide defragmentation support. Rather SBS provides the command line utility CHKDSK (known as check disk). CHKDSK tests the integrity of your SBS machine's hard disks and marks bad spots as off-limits for future storage. If you've ever shut off an SBS machine before you were notified it was okay to do so, CHKDSK will run automatically at the next reboot. To see the different options for CHKDSK, simply type **CHKDSK /?** at the command prompt.

I still haven't answered the underlying question about defragmenting a hard disk. To defragment a hard disk, you need to deploy a third-party solution such as Executive Software's Diskeeper (a sample version is included on the CD-ROM found with this book). Basically, Diskeeper identifies how badly fragmented your hard disk is and then proceeds to defragment the hard disks (see Figure 7.2). The defragmentation process recombines files, resulting in free space that is contiguous or whole, not choppy. Bottom line? When the hard disks on your SBS machine are defragmented, you will notice better SBS machine performance, and thus higher network performance.

**FIGURE 7.2**

*Executive Software's Diskeeper and fragmented SBS hard drive.*

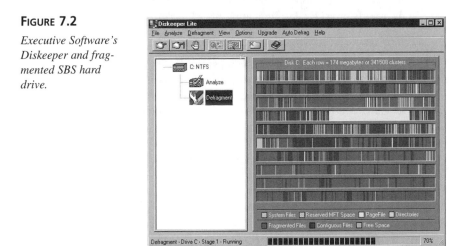

Because Diskeeper relies on colors to show the current status of your hard disk, it is difficult to see how badly the hard disk on a real SBS machine is fragmented. Believe me when I say that Figure 7.2 shows a badly fragmented hard disk.

## To Defragment an SBS Machine Hard Disk

1. Log on to your SBS machine as Administrator or as a member of the Administrators group.

2. Install a third-party defragmentation application such as Executive Software's Diskeeper.

3. Make sure you have a good tape backup of everything (data, Registry, applications, and so on) on the hard disks of your SBS machine. This is in case something goes terribly wrong during the defragmentation process. Tape backups are discussed on Day 6.

4. Launch the defragmentation application.

7

5. Select the hard drive that you want to analyze and defragment (the two steps used by Diskeeper). Each defragmentation utility has its own menu commands for performing defragmentation activity.

6. If asked by the defragmentation application, reboot your SBS machine after the defragmentation process concludes.

If the workstations that your SBS users employ use Windows 98, your life is a lot better when it comes to performing the monthly defragmentation for them. Like the SBS machine, the user's workstations aren't immune to fragmentation. And on a monthly basis, you should strongly consider defragmenting their hard disks as well.

> **Tip**
>
> If you've been especially negligent and haven't performed disk defragmentation in ages, it might take more than one pass for the disk defragmentation utility to optimize your hard disk space. That's reasonable. Use your judgment, but if the shoe fits, run the defragmentation utility twice.

## To Defragment a Windows 98 Machine

1. Select Disk Defragmenter from the System Tools program group by clicking the Start button on the Windows 98 desktop, and selecting Programs, then Accessories. The System Tools folder is visible.

2. When Disk Defragmenter is running, identify the drive you want to defragment (for example, drive C). Click OK.

3. Observe the disk defragmentation activity in the Disk Defragmenter dialog box (see Figure 7.3).

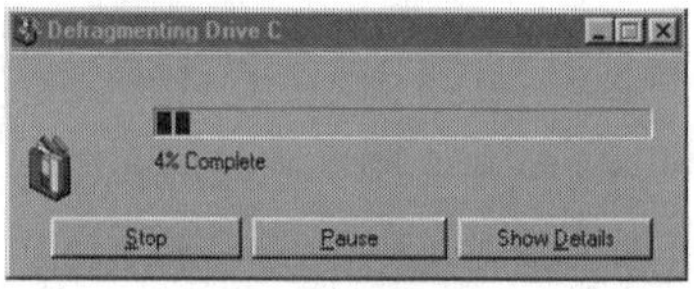

**FIGURE 7.3**

*Windows 98's Disk Defragmenter.*

# Service Packs, Patches, Upgrades, and Hot Fixes

Whatever name you use, be it service packs, patches, upgrades, or hot fixes, software manufacturers such as Microsoft periodically release enhancements to either fix problems or add features. These enhancements, known generically as service packs, upgrades, or hot fixes, can be released for the operating system (which is Windows NT Server 4.0 in SBS 4.5) or the applications (such as Microsoft Exchange Server or Microsoft Word).

One of the largest ongoing SBS administration challenges is keeping track of the service packs, upgrades, and hot fixes that are released for your SBS computer system. If you are an SBS consultant, this is just another day at the office. Clients running SBS look to you to know this information and use it to watch out for the clients' best interests.

If you are an SBS administrator working for a small business, the challenge is knowing what service packs, upgrades, and hot fixes have been released for your SBS network and applications. For starters, you could peruse www.microsoft.com each month. At Microsoft's Web site, click the support button to learn more about service packs, upgrades, and hot fixes. You should typically view information for each operating system you have (Windows NT Server 4.0, Windows 9x) and each application. Remember that applications include the BackOffice applications such as Microsoft Exchange and Microsoft SQL Server plus user applications such as Microsoft Word. For non-Microsoft applications, such as accounting software applications, visit the specific software manufacturer's site.

> **Caution**
> Even for the best of us, keeping up with new service packs, upgrades, and hot fixes is difficult. So while giving yourself a break, don't be negligent. Each month, make it part of your SBS administration duties to seek out service pack, upgrade, and hot fix information (or at least seek out someone who knows this information).

I have a few final thoughts regarding service packs, patches, upgrades, and hot fixes. First, assess whether you really need to apply it. Does your computer system actually benefit from the service pack, upgrade, or hot fix? If not, think twice about installing it.

Here is a case in point. One of my clients, an industrial storage facility, attempted to apply service pack 4 (SP4) to its Compaq server running Windows NT Server 4.0 with service pack 3 (SP3). Because Compaq servers provide their own hardware-layer drivers (HAL.DLL), applying a new service pack to a Compaq isn't as easy as it looks; you must also have the new Compaq hardware-layer drivers. Alas, he discovered that last point when SP4 was being installed and both the client and I learned that Compaq didn't (on that day) have SP4-compliant hardware-layer drivers. In fact, the client and I ultimately used a beta version of Compaq HAL.DLL file so that SP4 would complete its installation. If I had it to do over again, I for one would have questioned the wisdom of installing SP4 at all.

Second, one of the SBS challenges you will ultimately face is knowing which version of the service packs, upgrades, or hot fixes you have installed on your machine. Don't laugh! It's easy to forget sometime whether hot fix 45a was already applied. To assist

7

you with this dilemma, you will find HotFix Control on the CD-ROM included with this book. HotFix Control is an application that allows you to see which service packs, patches, and hot fixes have been applied to a system.

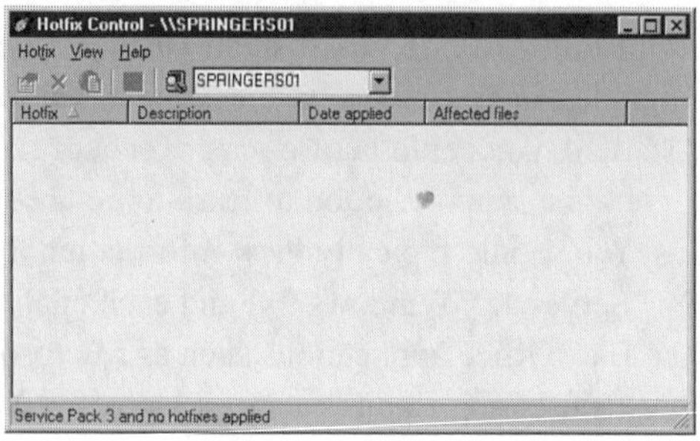

**Figure 7.4**

*HotFix Control.*

Third, understand that service packs, upgrades, and hot fixes are typically acquired one of two ways. You can either download the files from your software manufacturer's Web site or order the files on a CD-ROM (again, from your software manufacturer). My advice? If you have a high-speed connection to the Internet, simply download the files you need. However, if you have a modem-based connection, be sure to order the files on CD-ROM. Modem downloads of any significant size not only take forever but the download process is often unreliable (the modem drops the connection at midpoint or creates corrupted files).

And last, countless stories in the short history of network computing relate to inappropriately applied service packs. Just ask your networking guru buddy about Service Pack 2 circa Windows NT Server 4.0. It was the infamous service pack that, in many cases, broke more than it fixed. Perhaps you have your own story about a service pack, patch, or hot fix that was more problematic than you anticipated. The point is this: Don't always be the first on your block to apply the latest service pack, patch, or hot fix. You probably want to wait a few weeks while the larger computing community acts as your personal fleet of regression testers. In other words, let them pay too much and pass the savings on to you.

# Hard Disk Space Management

Each month, you should monitor the amount of hard disk storage space you have remaining on SBS machine. Tracking this information monthly assures that you won't be caught by surprise as applications take more and more space for data. One such example is an accounting application. Month in and month out, accounting transactions and the like cause the accounting software database to grow. Often, before you know it, you're out of hard disk space on the SBS machine, and that can clearly be problematic.

There are a few good reasons for not letting the hard disk space on your become in short supply:

- The 20% Rule—Long known by veteran network administrators, it is essential that your maintain at least 20% free space on your SBS machine hard disks. This free space allows file swapping and accounts for bad sectors on the hard disks. In my experience and that of others, falling below 20% free space can cause operating system instability.

- Printing—You might not have known that a print job, sent by an SBS user, first prints to the printer queue on the SBS machine's hard disks. In effect, you first print to the hard disks before the printer (whether you like it or not). The good news is that this approach allows print jobs to queue up and await actual printing. The bad news is that running out of hard disk space on your SBS machine means the network printing capabilities are kaput!

- New Applications—Monthly monitoring of your hard disk space allows you to plan for the installation of new applications on your SBS machine. Hardly a month goes by when one of your SBS users won't suggest some new application they have read about. You need to anticipate such requests when observing how much free disk space you have on your SBS machine. Don't underestimate the space you need; rare is the day that you truly have too much hard disk space. Of course, with the low prices of storage space today, adding another drive isn't really a problem for many small businesses.

Checking for the amount of free hard disk space on your SBS machine is very simple. Instead of the CHKDSK command from DOS days of old, I prefer the SBS Console method, followed by the GUI method. The SBS Console method has become much easier in SBS 4.5 compared to SBS 4.0/4.0a. Wanna see? Just complete Task 7.1.

## Task 7.1: Using the SBS Console Method

1. Launch the SBS Console to display the Home page (via the Home tab).
2. Look at the drive space information under Drives on the far left.
3. There you have it!

Ah, but I'm not going to let you off so easy. Now tell me another location in the SBS Console that displays useful hard disk space information. You have two minutes.

Done? The answer is the Manage Disks page from the More Tasks tab. Congratulations if you got it right. By the way, when you look at the hard disk space values under Manage Disks, you will be interested to know that CD-ROMs will read 0, or zero, free space because this medium is read-only.

▼TASK

7

Now I'll present the GUI method. Simply launch My Computer from the SBS machine desktop and look at a hard drive's properties. The GUI method steps are

1. Double-click the My Computer icon on the SBS machine desktop.

2. Select one of the local hard disks with a single click. This hard disk is now high-lighted or has the focus.

3. Right-click the hard disk you selected in Step 2.

4. Select Properties from the secondary menu.

5. Select the General tab sheet in the Properties dialog box. The results should be a screen similar to Figure 7.5.

6. Click OK when you have recorded the amount of free space to close the Properties dialog box.

**FIGURE 7.5**

*Determining hard disk free space.*

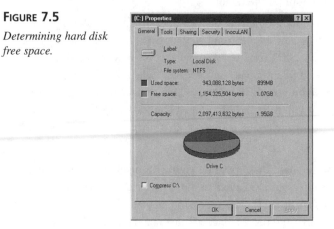

There are three approaches for increasing the amount of hard disk space on your SBS machine, should you find one month that you've fallen below the 20% free space thresh-old: the cheap way, the trade-off way, and the expensive way.

The cheap way is to use WinZip, a compression application long favored by network professionals to send large files as e-mail attachments. WinZip can also be used to com-press data files stored on your SBS machine that you are not frequently accessing. An example of this might be project-related files for a project that has been completed. A copy of WinZip is included on the CD-ROM that accompanies this book. To use WinZip, follow these instructions.

1. Install WinZip on your SBS machine.

2. Launch WinZip from the WinZip program group (found under Programs via the Start button).

3. Click the New button on the left side of the toolbar to create a new archive of compressed files.

4. Provide a filename for the archive in the File Name field. Such a filename might include the date (for example, PROJECT-A-2-16-99).

5. When the Add dialog box appears, navigate to the folder that contains the files you would like to archive, as seen in Figure 7.6. Click Add.

**FIGURE 7.6**

*Adding files to the WinZip archive.*

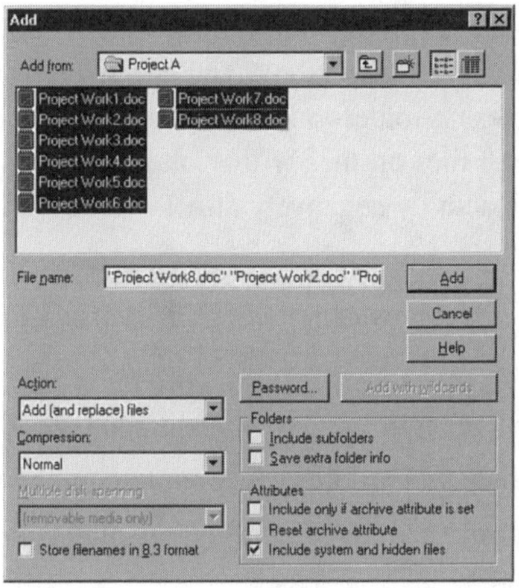

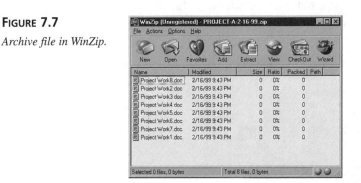

6. The files are automatically added to the archive and you are returned to the main WinZip screen, which shows the files added to the archive (See Figure 7.7).

**FIGURE 7.7**

*Archive file in WinZip.*

You have now created a WinZip file that has the .zip extension. Typically .zip files are only 10% the size of the original data that was compressed, but that number can vary depending on the type of file being compressed. Text files tend to compress better or more efficiently than files containing photos. That's saving disk space, my friend. Later,

7

when you need to access a file contained in a WinZip archive, simply double-click the .zip file containing the files you seek. WinZip automatically launches and allows you the opportunity to expand the files of interest.

For the trade-off method of gaining more space, simply use the compression capabilities provided by Windows NT Server. This approach is very simple to implement. If you revisit Figure 7.5 where you learned to determine the amount of free space on your hard disk, you will notice a check box in the lower-left corner of the General tab that allows you to Compress C:\ (or whatever drive letter you are looking at). Simply select the option by clicking on the Compress check box. You're finished, but at a steep price. Because you will be compressing folders and files you'll be actively using, the computer will have to decompress these files on-the-fly for you to use them. This decompression/compression activity negatively affect overall SBS sever machine performance.

You can compress selected folders instead of entire drives, as I implied earlier today. To compress a folder

1. Launch Windows Explorer from the Programs group (accessed via the Start button).

2. Select a folder via Windows Explorer you want to compress.

3. Right-click the folder you want to compress to display the secondary menu.

4. Select Properties on the secondary menu.

5. Select the General tab.

6. Select the Compress check box in the Attributes section, as seen in Figure 7.8.

7. Click OK. The compressed folder appears in a blue color when observed in Windows Explorer.

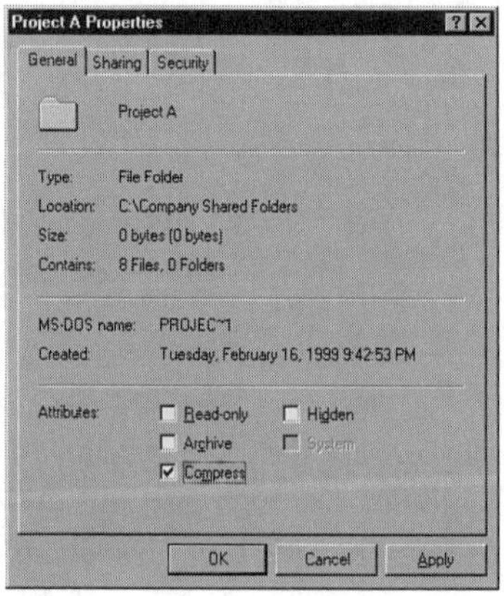

**FIGURE 7.8**

*Compressing a folder.*

**Note**    Compression provided by Windows NT Server, as discussed in the past two paragraphs, is available only on NTFS partitions.

The expensive method of increasing your hard disk space is simple: Add more hard disk space. This can take the form of another hard disk or an external array or collection of hard disks. The sky (and your budget) is the limit! But I serve up these dramatics half in jest. Hard disks are far cheaper today than just a year or two ago, so although some cost is associated with adding a hard disk to your SBS server machine, the cost is much lower than you might imagine if you haven't looked at hard disk prices lately.

### Task 7.2: Making Room

What other ways can you think of to recover hard disk space? Approaches that I've seen include moving the Windows NT Server paging file to another hard disk on systems with multiple hard disks, removing unused applications, or clearing out the \temp folder of unused and unneeded temporary files (*.tmp) files. Care to add to this list?

# Virus Protection: Verify Phone Home

Yesterday, on Day 6, I discussed the importance of comprehensive virus protection on a day-to-day basis, but there is more to it. Each month, or sooner if you prefer, you must ensure that your robust virus protection program has called home to download the latest virus protection files. These files, typically called *image files*, contain the latest update from the virus detection software manufacturer so that your system can detect the latest viruses. As you might know, new viruses are introduced almost daily around the world, so it's critical that you have an up-to-date list, which you can obtain by the phone-home function found in many software applications. For example, in Figure 7.9, you can see Inoculan's AutoDownload Manager. Via an Internet connection using a method called File Transfer Protocol (FTP), the AutoDownload Manager phones home and downloads the latest Inoculan image file. Very nice feature!

The AutoDownload Manager can also be configured to allow for a set schedule, as shown in Figure 7.10.

7

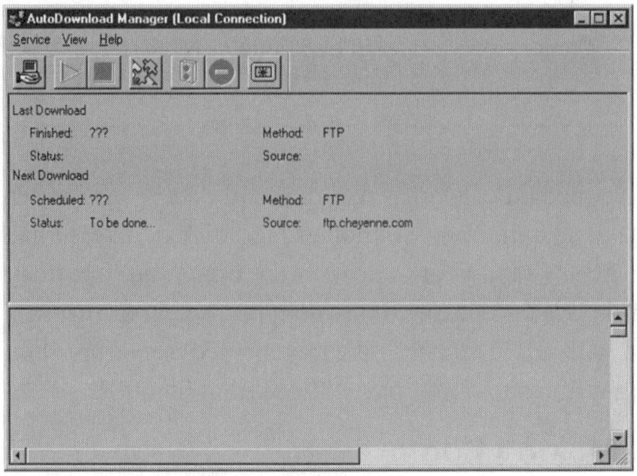

**FIGURE 7.9**

*AutoDownload Manager.*

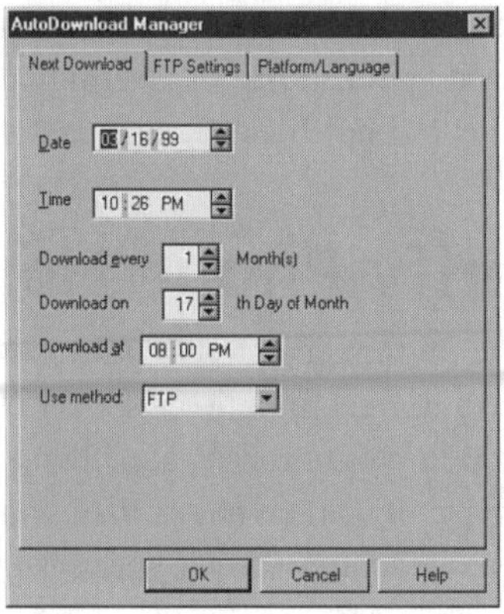

**FIGURE 7.10**

*Scheduling downloads.*

# Updating Your SBS Toolkit

If you're an SBS network administrator or consultant, you'll need to carry a toolkit, which can consist of physical tools to open a computer and add components as well as CD-ROMs containing valuable software.

The hardware toolkit is easy enough to obtain. For this, go to an online merchant such as PC Zone (www.zones.com) and order a computer hardware toolkit, ranging in price from $25 to $200. Often, the lower-priced toolkits will meet your needs just fine. You will want to have some of the basics, including

- T-10 and T-15 six-point drivers
- IC inserters
- 1/4" and 3/18" nutdriver
- Three-prong parts retriever

- Reversible and four 5/8" tweezers
- Screwdrivers: 5-1/4", 6", and 7-1/4" flat head.
- Screwdrivers: 0, 1, and 2 Phillips head.
- Wire cutter/stripper
- 5" needle-nose pliers
- Adjustable wrench

**Note**

> You should be able to purchase such a kit for under $50 with an imitation-leather case thrown in.

The software-side of your toolkit can take longer to build. In fact, I suggest you set a goal of adding one meaningful program each month to make your life better (and more effective) as an SBS administrator. Start with the CD-ROM contained with this book, and the next month add a subscription to Microsoft's TechNet monthly CD-ROM service. On the third month, you're on your own. But I can suggest you look at online stores such as PC Zones to find SBS toolkit goodies! You might also try shareware stores to find little known and low cost utilities.

**Tip**

> Another way to add to your SBS toolkit is to join a trade association such as the Network Professionals Association (NPA). Go to this organization's Web site at www.npa.org for more information. Upon joining, you'll receive a CD-ROM library of useful networking tools and utilities. This library is updated periodically. More importantly, go to the monthly NPA meetings in your area to receive many of the free CD-ROMs given away by software vendors. Not only that, but the give-and-take of fellow network professionals at these meetings is where you'll hear about great new utilities to add to your SBS toolkit. This is one of the best ways to build up your SBS toolkit!

# Y2K Testing

At least for the next several months, the looming date change associated with the start of the year 2000 must factor into your monthly SBS duties. This problem, known as the Year 2000 (Y2K) problem, occurs because computers and software cannot properly operate with the year field as two digits when the year goes from 1999 (99) to 2000 (00).

7

**Power Tool Tip**

Y2K testing will continue for any new application that is added for the next several years, even though the magical date of January 1, 2000 will have passed. Just because you will be living in the year 2000 doesn't mean you won't test new software applications and hardware for Y2K compliance.

For approximately $50, numerous Y2K applications can assess the Y2K fitness of your computer and popular software applications. Figure 7.11 shows one such program, Check 2000, manufactured by Greenwich Mean Time (www.gmt-2000.com).

**FIGURE 7.11**

*Check 2000 Y2K testing application.*

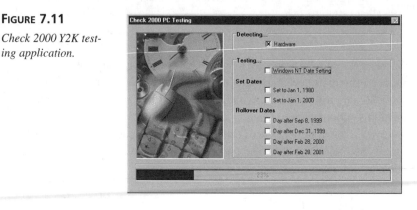

When you run the tests in Check 2000, your computer's BIOS is checked as well as the common software applications on your computer's hard disk.

**Note**

These low cost Y2K assessment programs do not check custom software applications for Y2K compliance.

**Note**

Microsoft has stated that SBS 4.5 is Y2K compliant.

Whew! It's been a long morning. Let's get some lunch! When we return, we'll complete the monthly dozen tasks and dig in to the annual half-dozen, if that's okay with you.

## Lunch

And on the seventh day, the chef rested! Today you're on your own. Might I suggest you consider a nearby eatery, so you can resume shortly, complete the afternoon session, and get out early!

## PM Continuing Monthly and Annual

Welcome back from lunch. I'll start the discussion with how to add hardware.

# Adding Hardware

Hardly a month passes that you won't add hardware somewhere on your SBS network. These additions can occur at the SBS machine itself (say a CD-ROM tower) or at an SBS user's workstation (say a PalmPilot docking station). It's simply part of your job as an SBS administrator.

At the SBS machine, you might add a CD-ROM tower—as I alluded to earlier today—so that your SBS users can access libraries of information in an instance. This is a common addition I make at small law firms as their collections of CD-ROM–based libraries grow. By deploying a CD-ROM tower, all these CD-ROMs are available in real-time for all the users. With respect to installing hardware, you typically want to follow the hardware manufacturers directions to a T. Often, you insert a driver disk into the SBS machine and run an install or setup program so that the proper hardware device driver is installed and SBS can both recognize and use the hardware device.

At the SBS user's workstation, a common hardware addition is the docking stations for hand-held personal information managers such as the PalmPilot 5. Typically, these external docking stations are connected to the communications port (COM) on the back of the SBS user's workstation. When requested, you need to install software that allows the docking station to communicate with the computer. One such program is called HotSync and it is provided with the PalmPilot docking station. HotSync installs via the Add/Remove Programs applet in Control Panel (discussed on Day 6). One twist on the installation is that you will need to attach the PalmPilot docking station to a 9-pin COM port on the back of your computer.

HotSync interacts with Outlook 2000, the all-around e-mail/contact/scheduling application included with SBS 4.5. With pushbutton ease, you can easily transfer e-mail, contacts, and scheduled appointments to and from the PalmPilot and Outlook 2000. This popular setup at many of my SBS sites is primarily used to make appointments and view

7

contacts while out of the office. The PalmPilot connection to Outlook 2000 is a winner and deserves your consideration if you're either a busy small-business person or busy SBSer.

# Updating the Emergency Repair Disk

Over the course of a month, you have likely made changes to the SBS network such as adding users, changing security, and so on. These changes modify the SBS Registry, a database where key configuration information is stored. Updating the Emergency Repair Disk (ERD) allows you both peace of mind and the ability to store key system configuration information on a disk—separate from the SBS machine.

You might recall that you created an ERD on Day 3, "Installing Small Business Server." At that time, creating the ERD was the last step on the To Do List in the SBS Console's checklist. Each month, you can return to the To Do List in the SBS Console to create your ERD or you can accomplish the same from the command line. The command-line method to create an ERD uses the following steps:

1. From the SBS machine's desktop, select the Start button.
2. From Programs, select the Command Prompt menu option.
3. At the command prompt, type **RDISK** and press Enter. The Repair Disk Utility application launches (see Figure 7.12).
4. If you want to update your existing ERD, place your ERD in the floppy disk drive and click Update Repair Info. Or you can place a new floppy disk in the floppy disk drive and click Create Repair Disk. (This is my preferred method because you use a fresh disk each month!)
5. Click Exit after the ERD creation/update process ends.

**FIGURE 7.12**

*Repair Disk Utility.*

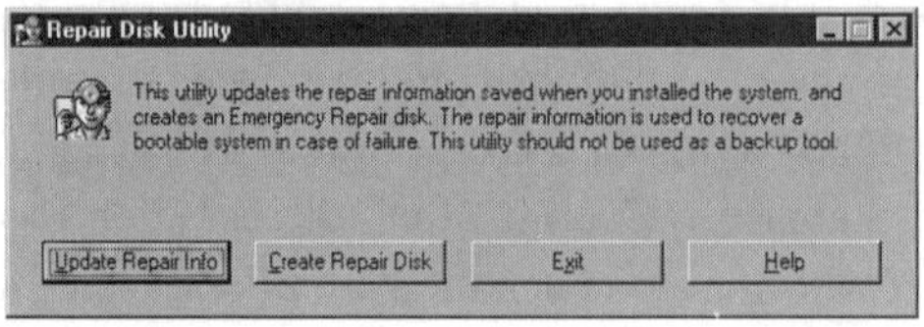

## Task 7.3: Running RDISK

Run the RDISK command with the /S switch. The command is

RDISK /S

and you enter it at the command line. Go ahead and do it now.

Do you care to guess what this command does? Hint: Check the timestamp for the files in the \winnt.sbs\repair directory. You will notice they were just updated (which is what the RDISK /S command does).

Be sure to store your ERD in a safe and secure place. One idea is a fireproof safe, although more than one SBSer has strong feelings opposed to that (I guess if the fire is too hot, you'll have melted floppies inside…ouch!). Another strategy is to store your ERD offsite at your home or a bank safety deposit box. Then there's Sharon at the land development company. She stores the ERD in her car! I guess she figures her car and place of employment won't either burn up or disappear at the same time. Whatever works!

# Research: the Web, Periodicals, and Books

An hour of research will save countless hours of misdirected effort when managing your SBS network. That said, take at least an hour each month to surf the Internet for SBS issues. Likewise, peruse popular computer magazines and other periodicals for computer network, SBS-specific, and end-user issues. And don't forget to pick up this book each month to review a section or two.

I can suggest at least three Internet sites of SBS interest. First, be sure to visit www.microsoft.com each month for the latest information on SBS. Second, I highly recommend that you visit BugNet at www.bugnet.com (see Figure 7.13). Here you can assess whether any recently found software bugs pertain to either your SBS network or any applications being used by your SBS users.

**Note** The full BugNet service requires a subscription fee, but the free stuff isn't bad either!

My final favorite Web surfing method is using one of the search engines such as Infoseek (www.infoseek.com) and searching on these keywords: *SBS*, *Small Business Server*, *computer*, *networks*. These terms, typically used all at once, will lead you to sites dedicated to SBS topics.

**Note** SBS-related sites come and go, so you should perform this type of keyword searching via search engines each month to stay current with SBS.

7

**FIGURE 7.13**

*BugNet.*

### Task 7.4: Share the Wealth

▼ TASK

I've noticed a severe shortage of periodicals dedicated to the SBS world. In your travels, if you discover such SBS periodicals, kindly e-mail me at harryb@nwlink.com, and I'll include your find in a future edition of this book.

Don't let the lack of SBS periodicals stop you. I'd encourage you to become an avid reader of weekly periodicals such as InfoWorld (www.infoworld.com) or PCWeek (www.pcweek.com).

# Performance Monitor Logging

This monthly task isn't the most exciting, and to exploit it fully, you'll likely need to retain an Microsoft Certified System Engineer (MCSE) to interpret the results. But the results can be invaluable when tracking the performance of your SBS network over time. Basically, you will use Performance Monitor to create a trend line of core computer system data. And as that trend line either improves or displays degrading performance, you'll have the ammunition you need to justify the purchase of a new server or better hub.

The Performance Monitor tool is located in the Administrative Tools (Common) program group (which you can access via Programs from the Start button on the SBS machine's desktop). Performance Monitor is an MBA-type's dream come true! This tool allows the capture and reporting, in a graphical format, of SBS computer system information.

Each month, using Performance Monitor, I recommend that you capture or log the following SBS computer system items (known as objects) in Table 7.2. These items represent common measurements that MCSEs need to look at over time to fully assess the health of your SBS network. Better yet, something I've always felt was going on with Performance Monitor logging was recently confirmed when I attended an SBS focus group on Microsoft's Redmond campus. There, participants shared that although Performance Monitor logging is a foundation for solving really complex problems, it's more likely to be used for showing long-term performance declines. This use of logging to display trends is typically used to get budget approval for a bigger and better toys like a new server.

**Power Tool Tip**

I've included descriptions of the objects so that you can better understand what is being measured. However, full discussion of this complex area is beyond the scope of this book. Refer to the Windows NT Workstation 4.0 Resource Kit for more information on Performance Monitor.

**TABLE 7.2**  PERFORMANCE MONITOR OBJECTS TO LOG

| Object | Description |
| --- | --- |
| Cache | Primary memory area that holds such items as recently used documents and file pages, data. Caching file pages, access time is dramatically improved. |
| Logical Disk | Logical views of disk space including disk partitions. |
| Memory | This allows you to analyze performance matters relating to real memory. Includes both primary (RAM) and virtual (paging file) memory. |
| Objects | Relates to system software objects. Objects have properties and are subject to access control restrictions imposed by SBS security. |
| Physical Disk | Secondary storage such as hard disks, Physical Disk measurements can be unreliable when you have a RAID array (a discussion that's beyond the scope of this book). |
| Process | A software object that is an active or running program. |
| Processor | Provides measures relating to the central processing unit (CPU). |
| Redirector | Assesses network connections between your computer and other computers. |
| Server Work Queues | Used to measure processor backlogs on your SBS machine. |
| System | Measures the activity on system hardware and software. |
| Thread | The basic unit of execution. Every running process will contain one or more threads. |

7

I suggest you log these counters in Performance Monitor for approximately 24 hours. To log the object in Table 7.2, perform the following steps:

1. Start Performance Monitor from the Administrative Tools (Common) program group.

2. From the View menu in Performance Monitor, select Log.

3. From the Edit menu, select Add To Log.

4. Add each of the objects listed in Table 7.2. Click Done to close the Add To Log dialog box.

5. From the Option menu, select Log. The Log Options dialog box will be displayed.

6. Provide a filename for file, such as Feb99Log.

7. Set the Periodic Update time to 900 seconds (15 minutes) in the Update Time portion of the Log Options dialog box.

8. Click the Start Log button. Performance Monitor logging will commence as displayed in Figure 7.14.

**FIGURE 7.14**

*Performance Monitor logging.*

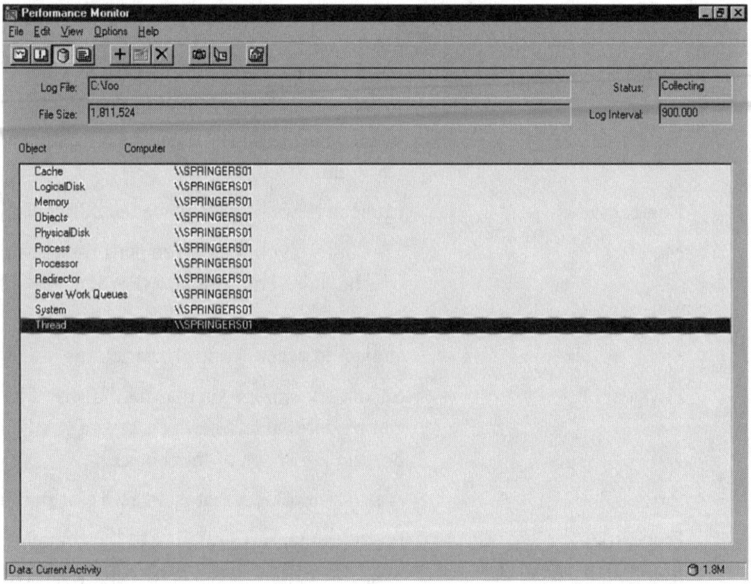

**Note** A few notes about logging. Make sure your hard disk has enough space to accommodate a 30MB log file, which is the size of a log file after 24 hours of logging using the above objects. Historic log files are great candidates for zipping via WinZip to save disk space (see step 4). And finally, please *do not* log off of your machine while logging is occurring. The mere act of logging off your SBS machine terminates the logging process!

# Updating SBS Network Notebook

Last but not least, you need to update your SBS network notebook to reflect your monthly findings. Such an update, although not especially meaningful when viewed as one month, is incredibly valuable when viewed over time, say several months. It is here that you can see what changes to your system have been made and what the effect of those changes was.

Each month, I suggest you complete the monthly worksheet in Table 7.3. Daily, weekly, monthly, and annual worksheets are included in Appendix C, "SBS Project Kit," for your benefit.

**TABLE 7.3** SBS MONTHLY MAINTENANCE WORKSHEET

| Task | Description | Completed (Y/N) |
| --- | --- | --- |
| The Monthly Reboot | Memory Usage Reading Before Reboot: Memory Usage Reading After Reboot: | |
| Disk Defragmentation | Degree of Disk Defragmentation: (Heavy) (Moderate) (Light) | |
| Service Packs, Upgrades, Hot Fixes | Were any service packs, upgrades, or hot fixes applied? | |
| Hard Disk Space Management | Drive C:\ Free Space Drive D:\ Free Space Drive E:\ Free Space Drive F:\ Free Space | |
| Virus Protection— Verify Phone Home | Verified Image File Update? | |

7

*continues*

**TABLE 7.3** CONTINUED

| Task | Description | Completed (Y/N) |
|------|-------------|-----------------|
| Updating Your SBS Toolkit | Added additional tools/ programs to your SBS Toolkit? | |
| Y2K Testing | Performed Y2K Tests? | |
| Adding Hardware | List any hardware added (type of hardware, machine):<br>1-<br>2-<br>3-<br>4-<br>5-<br>6- | |
| Updating the Emergency Repair Disk | Updated ERD? | |
| Research—Web, Periodicals, Books, Check BugNet (www.bugnet.com) | Studied/Researched SBS?<br>List Web sites visited:<br>1-<br>2-<br>3-<br>4-<br>5-<br>6- | |
| Performance Monitor Logging | Conducted 24 hours of Performance Monitor logging? | |
| Updating SBS network notebook | Updated SBS network notebook? | |

# Annual Tasks

I want to present a half-dozen annual tasks related to SBS for you to both consider and perform:

1. Getting Help from Consultants and Interns

2. Security Review

3. Hardware and Software Upgrades

4. Training

5. SBS Budget

6. SBS Mission Statement

Before getting into the technical discussion, allow me the opportunity to set to discussion framework for the half-dozen topics listed immediately above. As your planning horizon expands from daily to weekly to monthly to annually, the tasks you perform necessarily become broader and more general. If you're a businessperson, it's why a mission statement is more general than specific tactics in the world of strategic planning. My remaing conversation today necessarily echoes that perspective. Whereas the first part of Day 6, with its daily tasks, was very detail-oriented, the end of Day 7 (right now) is much broader in scope. Enjoy the discussion and put on the SBS planning hat.

# Getting Help from Consultants and Interns

In my experience with SBS, the average SBS site is stuck between a rock and a hard spot when it comes to getting competent SBS support and consultation cost effectively. Here is what I mean. Larger firms can afford to have MCSE-types on staff to administer, engineer, maintain, and otherwise optimize their networks. SBS sites can't afford the $60K per year computer gurus (heck…many small business owners *themselves* don't make $60K per year). Yet the needs of the SBS site aren't that different from the large sites: allowing people to do their jobs better with the aide of a computer network.

So most SBS sites need to maintain some form of consulting relationship with an outside guru. Armed with a book such as this one, it is hoped the on-site SBS administrator (usually a staff person at the business) can perform most of the duties to run the SBS network. That way, you can selectively use SBS consultants with bill rates well into the $100–150/hour range (depending on region) to complete the toughest SBS assignments. SBSers around the country report bill rates ranging from $50 an hour in smaller towns to over $200 an hour in the largest cities. The $100–150 range is the median. You will recall this exact topic was discussed by Jon Eastlake during lunch on Day 4, "Setting Up the Workstation Client."

One trick I've shared with many of the SBS sites that I work with is the use of low-cost college interns. Each quarter, a bright and eager intern arrives at many of my SBS sites to provide a presence in the ongoing administration and oversight of the SBS network. By being there, the intern can respond immediately to user requests about "How do I do this?" (the kind of question asked several times per day). Clearly, we rather expensive (and more-experienced) SBS consultants can't be sitting around every day to field those questions, but interns potentially can be.

7

# Security Review

Each year—if not every six months—it behooves you to review the security you have placed on folders on your SBS network. Perhaps something slipped by last year and, now identified, the security needs to be tightened and made more restrictive. More likely, you might want to make someone on your staff a member of the Administrators group. Why? Because over the course of a year, you're likely to see one or two staff members take a keen interest in the operations of your SBS network. If this person can be trusted, add them to the Administrators group and have the curiosity turn into competent SBS administration.

**Power Tool Tip**

> On Day 18, "Advanced Topics," I discuss the Security Configuration Editor (SCE) tool that is available for free in Service Pack 4 for Windows NT Server 4.0. This tool greatly assists in your security review. More importantly, once configured, it actually tests your security assumptions.

# Hardware and Software Upgrades

Each year, you will likely need to replace one or two workstations due to failure or obsolescence. In fact, many small businesses replace between 20% and 33% of their fleet of workstations each year so that they stay current (and more importantly, running efficiently). And as mentioned earlier today in the monthly discussion, you'll always be adding hardware to your server and workstation during the year. Count on it.

**Tip**

> Although I haven't seen it at my SBS sites, word has reached me that some sites lease hardware for financial reasons and to match the life of the asset (hardware) with the actual use. The point is, in certain situations, leasing allows you to acquire hardware for little money down and get rid of it before it becomes obsolete.

With respect to software upgrades, you can safely plan on major upgrades to SBS and your applications every 12–18 months. It's the nature of the computer business. Not only do you need to factor in the costs for both your hardware and software upgrades, but you also need to account for time it will take to implement these upgrades. And time not only includes the time to install software, but also the lost time as the staff learns to use the new upgrades. Yes, you guessed it. It's the software learning curve now playing at your SBS site!

# Training

Consider offering an annual reimbursement to your SBS users to get computer training each year. For the small business, perhaps $500 per year per staff member is sufficient. Larger companies often offer greater training dollars, but their needs tend to be greater. If you're worried that you might be training your competition, that is, your trained staffers will join another firm to make more money, consider having a training dollar repayment plan in place. At my firm, if anyone receives training and leaves within two years, a portion of the training dollars must be repaid. Such an arrangement is, of course, evidenced by an agreement.

Most importantly, because you're dealing with knowledge workers here when it comes to using the SBS network, anything you can do, such as computer training, to increase the user's knowledge will yield dividends in excess of your outlays.

# SBS Budget

Ah, the annual technology budget. This is actually a simple topic to address. In large companies, I've seen annual technology budgets of $3,000–5,000 per user per year! Smaller companies can get by with smaller technology budgets, thank goodness. At a minimum, I can't envision you budgeting less than $1,000 per user per year when you account for recovering the costs of your SBS user's workstations and spreading the costs of your server machine and SBS software. More likely, you're probably spending at least $1,500 per user per year if you're sufficiently training your staff, upgrading your software, and so on. Although that number seems large, remember that is $5 per day per person to give them the tools they need to do a better job for you!

Let me share a few budget specifics with you that I've encountered in the SBS world:

- Tape backup devices—Due to the mechanical nature of these devices, I've observed that tape backup devices can fail after only one year. A new tape backup device can cost in excess of $1,000, but I've had little trouble receiving purchase approval from an SBS site after they understand that hours of data are at stake!

- Training pays—Unfortunately, small-business owners often cut training from budgets. Perhaps it's because many small-business owners fit the mold of the "millionaire next door" and never complete college, thus they have an underlying anger toward education. More likely, the small-business owner has been burned by newly trained employees who leave for higher-paying jobs. First, you need to convince the reluctant budget gods at your SBS site that training returns more value in increased productivity than it extracts from the corporate coffers. Okay, so that

7

didn't work.More practically speaking, small-business owners might be more receptive to an arrangement wherein employees receiving training will reimburse the company if they depart within 24 months. My company has such an arrangement. If I leave within the next 24 months, the $10,000 I'm spending this year to obtain Cisco certified is due, on a prorated basis, to my (wonderful, kind, gracious) current employer. I hope the sweet-talking in the last sentence wasn't lost on you because that's also how you get your budget approved.

- MBA-style—Don't overlook the comments I made earlier about justifying your technology outlays via reports, such as the type you can create from the data you obtain from your Performance Monitor logs.

# SBS Annual Retreat

Did someone mention *retreat*? Once per year, treat your SBS stakeholders to some type of planning retreat not only to review the year just passed, but more importantly, to plan for the year ahead. You'd be surprised that a simple planning retreat might enable you to think of ways to better use SBS in your organization. For example, consider the following:

- The SBS faxing capabilities as a tool to increase your sales
- Small business electronic commerce via SBS
- Lowering your SBS costs by performing more SBS management yourself (armed with this book, of course)
- The future of SBS (thinking about SBS 5.0)

Who knows, you might even come out of your annual planning retreat with an SBS Mission Statement! Try this one on for size: "Making the world a better place, one small business at a time."

As of this writing, there are no national SBS conferences on the planning horizon. When I asked several marketing department employees from Microsoft at an SBS beta-training class in early 1999 about such offerings, I was told that Microsoft has none planned. Rather, Microsoft intends to interact with the SBS community via its monthly Direct Access offerings held at local Microsoft sales offices.

This leads to the next topic. You'll just have to take the bull by the horns and create your own SBS retreat, as alluded to in the first paragraph of this section. I'm attempting to do exactly that for my clients in the Pacific Northwest. Top spots I've set my eyes on are Summit at Snoqualmie ski resort or Rosario Resort in the San Juan Islands. Both are entirely acceptable getaways for both my SBS customers and yours truly to brainstorm about the SBS year ahead! I'd highly recommend you do the same. In fact, if you feel the need for a national SBS conference, drop me an e-mail at harryb@nwlink.com.

# Summary

This lesson provides you with the fundamentals needed to administer your SBS network on a monthly and annual basis. Combined with Day 6, you now have the knowledge to manage your SBS network from daily, weekly, monthly, and annual perspectives. Next up, a quick introduction to Microsoft Outlook, one of the most popular SBS end-user applications.

# WEEK 2

# Communicating with SBS

8

9

10

11

12

13

14

DAY **8**

# Implementing Outlook

You start the second week of your 21 days taking a distinctly different tack. The first week focused on planning, installing, and configuring the SBS network. It clearly had a server-centric focus. The second week starts with the most popular user application in SBS, Microsoft Outlook. Why? No sooner than you finish implementing your SBS network than users will want to take advantage of Outlook with its e-mail, scheduling, contact management, and general groupware functions. The morning session focuses on basic Outlook use; the afternoon session focuses on advanced Outlook use.

## AM The Role of Outlook

Leave it to an SBS client to teach me a thing or two along the SBS journey. On paper, during the SBS planning phase, it appeared as if the networked business application such as the accounting package would be the most popular feature of the SBS network. When planning, business applications are typically the primary reason for implementing the new SBS network. But leave it to users to decide for themselves what is the most popular SBS network application. And without question, that application, from literally day one of the SBS network's life, has been Outlook.

A short true story serves to make the point. It was a late winter afternoon, and I was across the desk from a prominent Northwest businessman. I had just completed installing the SBS network at his small company, but something was wrong. I could sense he wasn't completely pleased with the new SBS network. So I launched into a long (and tiresome) dissertation about the high performance levels of his new Dell PowerEdge 2300 server, 100MB-per-second dual-speed hub, DSL Internet connection, and so on. Still, he wore his disappointment out and openly. Ah, I thought. He must be disappointed with new construction/property management accounting software running on the SBS server (whew...that was installed by the other consultant!). Wrongo! The CEO felt the full pain of his $10,000 plus outlay for his SBS network because his Outlook application ran too slowly. For him, having to count seconds when he switched between Outlook's e-mail and calendar modules represented a failed SBS implementation, and, as you know, the client is always right!

Closer examination revealed that this individual maintained over 700 Outlook calendar entries and had a notoriously finicky machine. So we archived many of his historical calendar entries and moved much of his information into public folders (some I'll discuss with you later today). Bottom line: We solved his Outlook problem and changed his attitude, for the better, about his new SBS network.

This learning experience taught me an important lesson about Outlook. It's a mission critical application on an SBS network and in many cases, it's how you—the SBS consultant or administrator—are evaluated. So take Outlook's role very seriously on your SBS network. Your users do.

# Outlook Overview

Let's learn what Outlook is. For many SBS users, Outlook is simply e-mail. It is where e-mail is composed, sent, received, and read. End of story. Other SBS users not only take advantage of e-mail but also enjoy Outlook's other functions, all of which are listed in Table 8.1.

**TABLE 8.1**  DEFINING OUTLOOK

| Outlook Feature | Description |
| --- | --- |
| Mailbox | This contains the Inbox, Outbox, Sent Items, and other electronic mail folders you might create. |
| Calendar | This is the appointment schedule where you can enter appointments for yourself and others. |
| Contacts | This is the contact manager for tracking names, addresses, telephone and fax numbers, e-mail addresses, and basic contact information. |

| Outlook Feature | Description |
|---|---|
| Tasks | This is a To Do List where you can enter items that need to be accomplished. When accomplished, these items are typically marked as complete. |
| Journal | This tool allows you to enter journal entries that are time stamped for you, track the editing of popular data files by date and create quick-and-dirty project schedules. |
| Notes | These are basically electronic yellow sticky notes that allow you to capture quick thoughts on a time-stamped note. |

Much like SBS on the server-side, you could consider Outlook the SBS user's all-in-one solution (that is, "just add water"). Combined with a popular application suite such as Microsoft Office, Outlook rounds out the tools that the average SBS user needs. I've heard Outlook referred to as a Swiss Army Knife.

In my experience, these are the most popular Outlook functions, ranked in order: e-mail, calendar/scheduling, and contacts (see Figure 8.1). I'll review these three popular functions with you this morning.

**FIGURE 8.1**

*Microsoft Outlook - Opening Screen.*

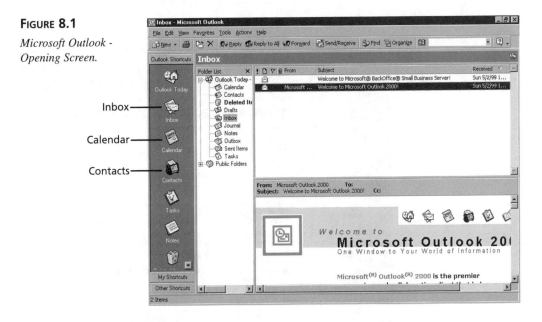

# E-Mail Basics

For many SBS users at any given moment, using Outlook is all about sending and receiving e-mail. I guarantee that this is something your users will want immediately when logged on to the SBS network. Electronic mail is, of course, a way to communicate with internal and external (via the Internet) parties. It is often used for communicating with business associates, friends, and family.

## Defining the Outlook Messaging Window

One of the things that you and your users will appreciate in Outlook is that each major window is, to the extent possible, consistent. For example, the upper-left toolbar button is typically where you add or compose something, be it an e-mail message or a calendar entry. The upper-right toolbar button is typically the question mark symbol for launching the Office Assistant and getting help. Such consistencies aren't lost on the SBS consultant. I've found that after teaching the e-mail capabilities of Outlook to a group of SBS users, the remaining Outlook features are progressively easier to teach.

Let's take a moment to meet the Outlook messaging or e-mail window. I'll highlight several key features shown in Figure 8.2.

**FIGURE 8.2**

*Microsoft Messaging window.*

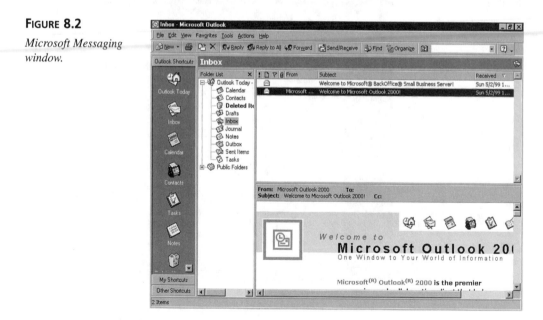

8

## New Mail Message

This upper-left button, when clicked, allows you to compose an e-mail message. You can also compose a new e-mail message via the File menu (Select File, New, Mail Message), the Compose menu (Compose, New Mail Message), or the Ctrl+N keystroke.

## Print

The Print button (shown as a printer icon), of course, allows you to print the highlighted e-mail messages. The print job is sent to your default printer because, via the Print button, you are not offered the opportunity to select other printers. You can also print an e-mail message via the File menu (File, Print) or Ctrl+P. .

## Delete

This is the one button every SBS user should avail themselves of as often as possible (it is the *X* icon on the toolbar). Selecting the Delete button removes the e-mail from the current folder (for example, Inbox) and places it in the Deleted Items folder. Depending on your Outlook settings, the Deleted Items folder can delete its contents each time you exit Outlook. Otherwise, it might be necessary for you to delete the items in the Deleted Items folder periodically (something I discuss more in the Deleting section later today).

> **Tip**
>
> If you're an SBS network administrator or consultant, I highly recommend that you teach your users to delete e-mail early and often. I can't tell you how many SBS users simply let old e-mail languish in their Inbox folder. And if you subscribe to the paradigm that information that is over 90 days old has expired, far too many of us carry around far too many e-mail messages. Too many e-mail messages in your Outlook Inbox negatively affect Outlook's performance and your SBS experience.
>
> And yes, this is a case of the pot calling the kettle black. My Outlook Inbox currently has 349 items, of which 35 are unread. Ouch!

You can also delete e-mail messages from the Edit menu (Edit, Delete) or with the Ctrl+D keystroke. Finally, it is possible to delete an e-mail message by highlighting it and pressing your Delete key on your keyboard.

## Reply

It's one thing to read your e-mail diligently, but you typically must reply to the sender with a response that communicates an answer, more information, or whatever. The Reply button replies only to the original sender, regardless of who else received the e-mail message.

> **Tip**
>
> Good e-mail etiquette suggests that you acknowledge, to the extent possible, the receipt of e-mail messages. This act of courtesy allows the sender to know that you received the message. This approach is what I call the sailboat racing method. In sailing, the crew always acknowledges the skipper's command so that everyone knows the command was heard and understood. I try to live by the same set of rules while on land using my e-mail system. Sometimes my replies are nothing more than "got it...will get back to you later with the information." Call it overcommunicating but it's what e-mail is all about.

You can also select the Reply command via the Compose menu or the Ctrl+R command.

## Reply to All

Similar to the Reply button, the Reply to All button sends your e-mail reply to the original message sender and everyone else in the loop (that is, everyone else who received the e-mail message). The Reply to All command can also be found under the Compose menu or invoked via the Ctrl+Shift+R keystrokes.

## Forward

You ever hear a good joke that you simply can't wait to share with someone else? Then you'll greatly appreciate the Forward button in Microsoft Outlook. *Forwarding* is the act of receiving an e-mail and then resending it to another recipient or party. The Forward command is also located under the Compose menu or via the Ctrl+F command.

> **Note**
>
> When you forward an e-mail in Outlook that contains an attachment, the attachment is also forwarded. Other e-mail programs do not behave this way and the attachment isn't forwarded.

## Address Book

The Address Book button displays the address book that contains potential e-mail recipients. The Address Book dialog box appears after the Address Book button is selected, allowing you to select the name or names of people to whom you would like to send an e-mail. The global address list is displayed by default. You can also enter new addresses in the Address Book dialog box.

## Organize

Selecting the Organize button displays a screen (similar to that seen in Figure 8.3) that provides you several ways to organize your Inbox. One way to consider organizing your

Inbox is to select the Using Views link and then select Messages with AutoPreview. This allows you to see the first three lines of any e-mail message (before actually opening that message).

**FIGURE 8.3**

*Organize.*

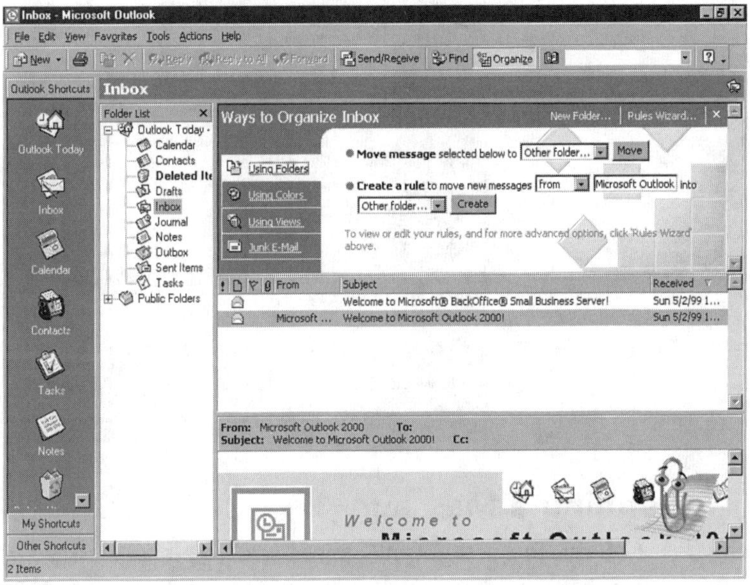

## Find Items

The Find Items button will someday, in some way, be your friend. It'll be at a time where you're desperately seeking that marketing lead sent to you by a professional associate, but you can't remember anything about it except the prospective client company had the name "Springers" in either the subject line or the message body. This command finds that missing e-mail message! The Find dialog box, shown in Figure 8.4, is displayed when you select the Find Items button.

## Microsoft Outlook Help

The Office Assistant, when selected, shows you the paper clip helper (nicknamed Clippit). This tool is both an online help system and a decision-tree type troubleshooting system. Quite frankly, this option is great for new users but is rarely used by more experienced Outlook users. It is also available in other Office 2000 applications, so you'll see that blinking paperclip again.

FIGURE **8.4**

*Find.*

## Sending a Message

One of your first acts in Outlook is to send an e-mail message. Funny how that is. No sooner than the SBS network is up and running, then the first thing the new SBS users do is try to send e-mail to each other. It's safe to say that, during those first few hours of the SBS network's life, that brand new accounting system plays second fiddle to those who want to fiddle with the e-mail capabilities of Outlook.

In this exercise, you'll send e-mail to several employees of Springer Spaniels Unlimited plus an Internet e-mail account.

### Task 8.1: Sending an E-Mail Message

1. Log on to the SBS network from your workstation as ElvisH. Launch the Outlook application.
2. Select the New Mail Message button. An untitled message appears, similar to that displayed in Figure 8.5.
3. Select the To button in the Untitled message window. This is found on the left side. The Select Names box appears, displaying the usernames for Springer Spaniels Unlimited. You will also note in Figure 8.6 that the e-mail distribution list, Springers, is also displayed.

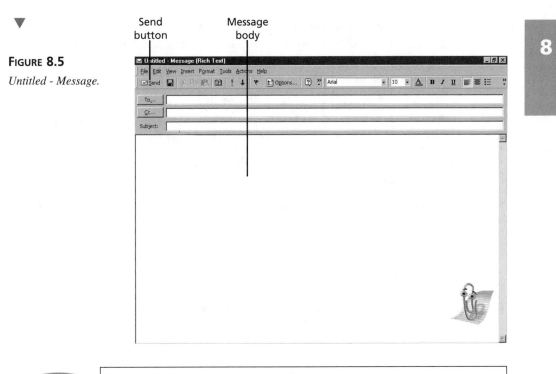

**Send button**     **Message body**

**FIGURE 8.5**
*Untitled - Message.*

**Note**

My preceding comments assume that you entered all the users for Springer Spaniels Unlimited when you completed the tasks on Days 4, "Setting Up the Workstation Client," and 6, "Daily and Weekly SBS Administration (The Dirty Dozen)."

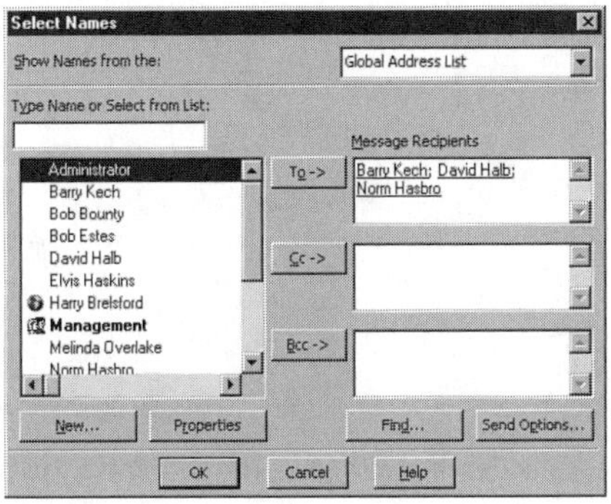

**FIGURE 8.6**
*Select Names dialog box.*

8

▼    4. Double-click the following names: Barry Kech, David Halb, and Norm Hasbro. The names appear on the right of the Select Names dialog box in the Message Recipients field. Click OK. You are returned to the Untitled - Message screen (this is the untitled message).

5. In the CC address field, type the following Internet address: **harryb@springers.nwnexus.com**.

6. In the Subject line, type **2000 Husky Year-End Party**.

7. In the body of the message, type the following:

   **Greetings...**

   **Anyone up for attending the Husky Year-End Party this year? Please let me know!**

   **Elvis**

   Your e-mail message should look similar to Figure 8.7.

**FIGURE 8.7**

*Complete e-mail message.*

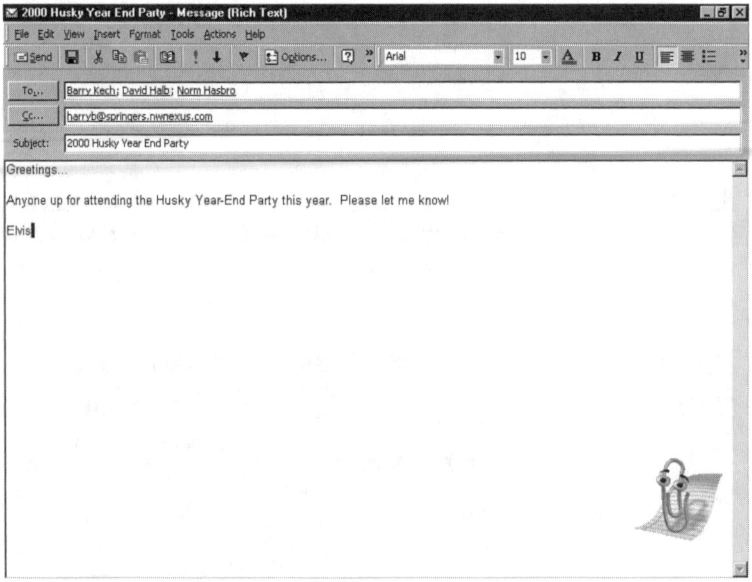

| | |
|---|---|
| ☒ 2000 Husky Year End Party - Message (Rich Text) | _ ☐ ☒ |

File  Edit  View  Insert  Format  Tools  Actions  Help

⊡Send  ☐  ✂ ▣ ▣  ☒  !  ↓  ▼  ⊞Options...  ⑦  »  Arial          ▼  10  ▼  ⒶＢ  Ｉ  Ｕ  ☰ ☰ ☰

| To... | Barry Kech; David Halb; Norm Hasbro |
|---|---|
| Cc... | harryb@springers.nwnexus.com |
| Subject: | 2000 Husky Year End Party |

Greetings...

Anyone up for attending the Husky Year-End Party this year.  Please let me know!

Elvis|

Tip

You can enter partial names in the To: field, and the names are automatically resolved. For example, if the name you want to enter is Barry Kech, you could simply enter **Bar** in the To: field, and the remainder of the name, *Barry Kech*, would automatically appear. This is great stuff!

▼

8. Click the Send button in the upper-left corner of the Untitled - Message window.

▲ 9. Congratulations! You've sent your first e-mail message in Outlook.

## Reading a Message Sent to You

In order to read an e-mail message, go ahead and send an e-mail to yourself (ElvisH - assuming you are still logged on as ElvisH) using the steps just presented. Feel free to give the e-mail any subject line and text message. Such a message might appear similar to the message in Figure 8.8.

**FIGURE 8.8**

*Sample e-mail message to ElvisH.*

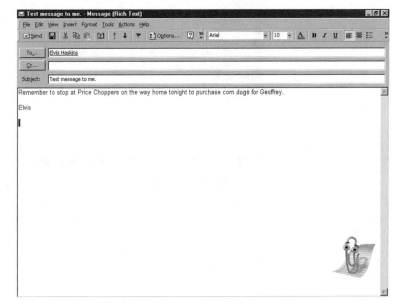

Send the message, and you should notice that it appears in your Inbox, similar to Figure 8.9. You can now read this e-mail message.

To read the e-mail that you sent yourself (ElvisH), double-click the message. The message appears in a separate window similar to that shown in Figure 8.10.

You can now print, reply to, delete, or close this e-mail message. If you close the message, you return to the main Outlook window (Inbox view), and the message appears again in your list of messages.

FIGURE 8.9

*Inbox with e-mail messages.*

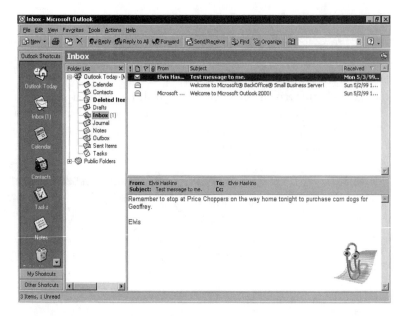

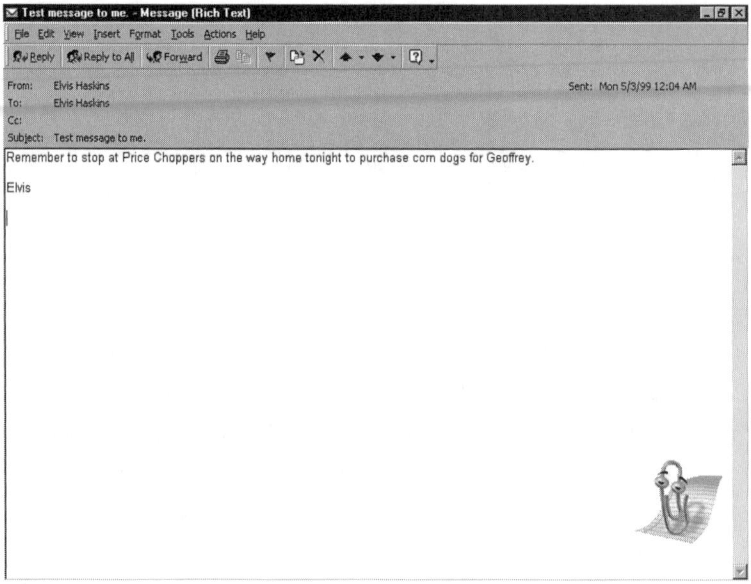

FIGURE 8.10

*Sample e-mail message opened.*

## Task 8.2: Replying to an E-mail Message

You now reply to the e-mail message that you sent to yourself.

1. Open the e-mail message that you sent to yourself (remember that you are Elvis).

2. Select the Reply button in the upper left corner of the Message window.

3. Type the following in the message body (note your cursor appears at the top of the message body):

   **Elvis-**

   **Great idea!**

   **Elvis**

   Your message should appear similar to Figure 8.11.

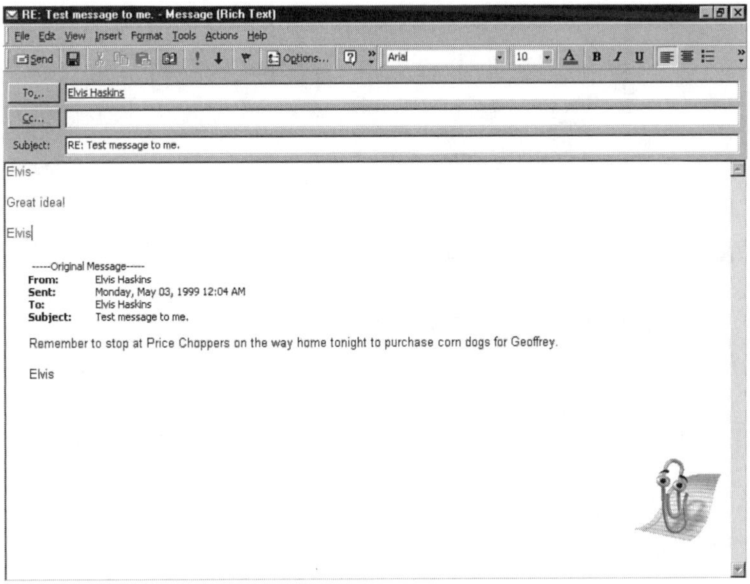

**FIGURE 8.11**

*Your reply.*

4. Click the Send button in the upper-left corner of the Message window. You have now replied to yourself.

**Note** | The Reply to All option is similar to the Reply option. As discussed earlier today, the Reply to All option would have sent your e-mail reply to everyone who received the original message, not only the sender.

## Task 8.3: Forwarding an E-mail Message

You now forward the reply e-mail that you just created in the Reply section earlier. By now, this reply message should have appeared in your Inbox. To forward a message, perform the following steps:

1. Select the e-mail message you intend to forward. I recommend you use the message you replied to in Task 8.2.

2. Click the Forward button.

3. In the To: field, type `harryb@springers.nwnexus.com`.

4. In the message body, type a message similar to

    **FYI -**

    **Thought you might enjoy!**

    **Elvis**

5. Click the Send button. You have forwarded a message.

## Deleting a Message

You now delete a message. Select the message of your choice in your Inbox. There should be at least two messages to select from (both from Elvis). Click the X or Delete button on the toolbar. You have now deleted an e-mail message.

## Attaching a File

One of the most popular uses for e-mail is to transfer files back and forth between workgroup members, friends, and family. The ability to send an attached file, known as an attachment, with your e-mail message has greatly improved business productivity at most of the SBS sites I've consulted. Now the owner, manager, or staff member can simply receive a file via e-mail. When that person completes his or her work with the file, he or she can resend the file via e-mail.

> **Tip**
>
> Be careful not to send extremely large files as attachments. The person who receives your e-mail with the attachment might not be able to open it (some e-mail servers restrict incoming attachment sizes). Worse yet, large attachments take forever to download when you have a modem connection to the Internet. Large file transfers are better handled via File Transfer Protocol (FTP), which is discussed on Day 10, "Internet Information Server/Index Server."

## Task 8.4: Attaching a File to an E-mail Message

In this exercise, you send an e-mail with an attachment to a fellow employee at Springer Spaniels Unlimited.

1. Log on to the SBS network from a workstation as ElvisH (password is Platinium1).

2. Launch Microsoft Outlook.

3. Compose a new e-mail message by selecting the New Mail Message icon or using the Compose menu.

4. Click the To: button to select someone from the list of Springer Spaniels Unlimited users.

5. Select Sally Briggs as the recipient of the message. To do this, double-click the name Sally Briggs in the left pane of the Select Names dialog box. Her name should automatically populate the To: Message Recipients field on the left side of the Select Names dialog box. Click OK.

6. In the Subject field of the e-mail, type **Sending You An Important File**.

7. In the body of the e-mail, type a short note such as **Here it is!**

8. To insert a file, use the Insert menu (Insert, File). You are presented with the Insert File dialog box.

9. Find and select c:\startcli.log as the file to insert. This file was created when you ran the SBS magic disk on Day 4. Click OK in the Insert File dialog box to insert this file.

10. You e-mail should appear similar to Figure 8.12. Click the Send button to send the e-mail to Sally Briggs.

*Your e-mail message
with a document
attached.*

▲          Congratulations. You have now sent an e-mail with an attachment.

## Printing a Message

To print an e-mail message, select the e-mail message and either click the Print icon or
select the Print menu option from the File menu. Your e-mail message is sent to the
printer.

But here's another take on printing e-mail messages. I'll never forget sitting in a board
meeting for a nonprofit organization during the Christmas season, seeking approval to
implement an SBS network. One of the more distinguished and older businesspeople on
the board—someone from the old school, if you will—started to speak about his use of
e-mail at his business. He found that the introduction of e-mail resulted in the purchase
of additional printers. What? Isn't e-mail supposed to reduce the use of paper in a business? Isn't it because of e-mail that we're becoming a paperless society? Wrong! The
businessperson continued his story. He prints out all his e-mail messages so he can write
on them by hand, take them home and file them, as does his staff. So the introduction of
Outlook with its e-mail capabilities in your organization can result in more, not less
printing. Don't be surprised; I told you.

## Saving Messages in Folders

You can save messages in folders similarly to the way that you save documents into folders on the SBS network. The difference between saving an e-mail in Outlook versus a file on the network is this: When you save an e-mail in Outlook, it is saved to an Outlook-based folder. When you save a file on the network, it is saved to a traditional file folder or subdirectory.

Thus, the folders you create in Outlook aren't folders in the traditional sense. These are not folders that you can see via Windows Explorer. Rather, Outlook folders are designed to help you organize your e-mail.

Because you're still logged on ElvisH, you'll create a folder to help him manage his e-mail. If you aren't logged on as ElvisH, do so now.

### Task 8.5: Creating a Folder

1. Select the New command from the File menu. The New command spawns another submenu. Select Folder from this submenu, as seen in Figure 8.13.

**FIGURE 8.13**

*Folder menu option.*

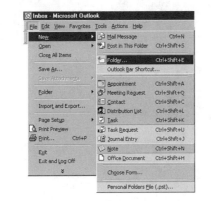

2. The Create New Folder dialog box is displayed. In the Name field, title the folder **Hot-Hot**. Allow the folder to contain Mail Items. Make the Hot-Hot folder a subfolder of Mailbox - Elvis Haskins, as displayed in Figure 8.14.

3. Click the OK button in the Create New Folder dialog box to create the Hot-Hot folder. ElvisH intends to use this folder to store very important e-mail that needs his attention.

4. If prompted by the Add Shortcut to Outlook Bar dialog box, click No.

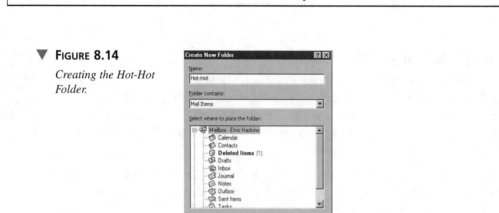

▼ **FIGURE 8.14**

*Creating the Hot-Hot Folder.*

Observe that the Hot-Hot folder now appears under Mailbox - ElvisH in the center pane, as seen in Figure 8.15.

**FIGURE 8.15**

*Hot-Hot Folder.*

| **Note** | Be careful what e-mail you save in folders. If the e-mail message isn't work-related, such as those silly e-mail messages you receive from friends and family, perhaps you should delete (not save) the e-mail. Deleting was discussed earlier in the section "Deleting a Message." I'd hate for you to save e-mail that might prove embarrassing to you later, as in litigation proceedings. |

# E-mail Security

One of the biggest concerns expressed regarding e-mail has been that of security. The e-mail security issue has several angles, including secure transmission over the Internet, secure transmission over the SBS network within your four walls, and the all-important question answered by small business CEOs and staff alike: "Can anyone else read my e-mail?"

I address the Internet security e-mail issue on Day 11, "Using Proxy Server." The SBS network security issue is easily answered. Because the Microsoft Exchange site is housed on your SBS server, it benefits from being on a protected server (both physically secure and password protected). Furthermore, the Microsoft Exchange Information Store (where e-mail is stored on the server) isn't readable by mere mortals.

That leaves the third and all-important question: "Can anyone else read my e-mail?" The answer to this is that it depends. Your Outlook e-mail is inherently secure on an SBS network because of the use of Mailboxes. To access a Mailbox, you must successfully log on to the network. If you aren't logged on to the network, you can't access your Mailbox-based e-mail in Outlook. In this case, the answer is no, your e-mail is secure (as long as someone else doesn't log on to the network using your username and password).

If you are the type of user who leaves his or her workstation logged on to the network while away (say at lunch, evenings, weekends), your e-mail isn't as secure as you think it is. Under this scenario, the answer is then yes, other people can read your e-mail. Think about it. If you keep your workstation logged on to the network and go to lunch, I can come along behind you, launch Outlook, and read your e-mail. Worse yet, I can send an e-mail on your behalf, giving everyone on the staff a 25% salary increase. I truly have the keys to the kingdom, don't I?

**Power Tool Tip**

> One SBSer I know uses screen saver passwords to attempt to restrict access to a workstation that is running. You can invoke a screen saver password via the Display applet in Control Panel (Screen Saver tab).

**Note**

> I also cover e-mail security from a networking standpoint toward the end of this chapter.

# Calendar Basics

Back to the prominent Northwest small business CEO. Hands down, his main use of Microsoft Outlook was the Calendar. Not only did he keep at least historic appointments in his calendar for both legal and memory recall reasons, he kept several years of future appointments in his Outlook calendar as well. All told, he kept over 7,000 appointments in Outlook. This gentleman was the most impressive user, especially for an SBS site, of Outlook that I've every witnessed.

I share that story with you to underscore this fact: The calendar in Outlook isn't a toy. In fact, it's reliable and ready for your most demanding uses. It works well with external handheld devices to help you track your appointments, such as the PalmPilot from 3Com. I discuss handheld devices at the end of this section.

## Defining the Outlook Calendar Window

Let's take a moment to discuss the Calendar window, as shown in Figure 8.16, which is displayed when you click the Calendar button found in the left window pane of Outlook program or via the Calendar object in the center pane. You can also select the Calendar windows via the Go menu (Go, Calendar).

**FIGURE 8.16**

*Outlook Calendar window.*

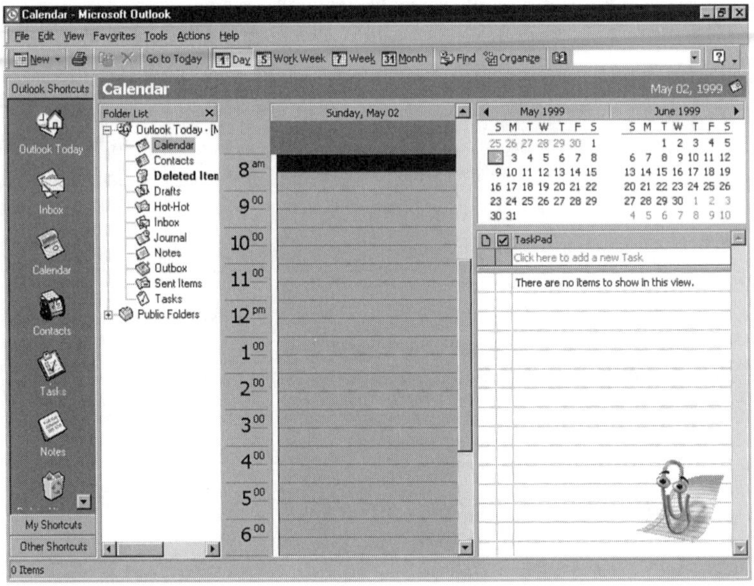

Some of the toolbar buttons in the Calendar window (such as Print, Find Items, and Microsoft Outlook Help) are the same as discussed earlier today. But the Calendar window offers several new toolbar buttons. I'll discuss these.

## New Appointment

This button allows you to create a new calendar appointment.

## Go to Today

Clicking this button immediately returns the Calendar view to the current date. The current date is based on the date being maintained by your computer (that is, the Windows 98 operating system time and date).

## Day

Clicking the Day button creates the default view seen in Figure 8.16.

## Work Week

This displays the five-day work week as seen in Figure 8.17.

**FIGURE 8.17**

*Work week view.*

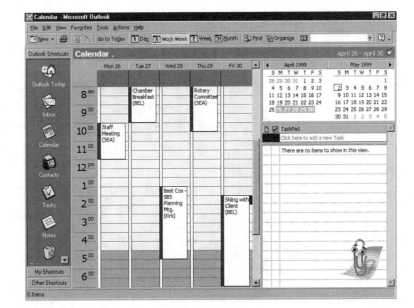

## Week

This displays a week-style view, as seen in Figure 8.18. This is one of my favorite views because I'm able to see appointments several days forward where each day has its own box.

**FIGURE 8.18**

*Week view.*

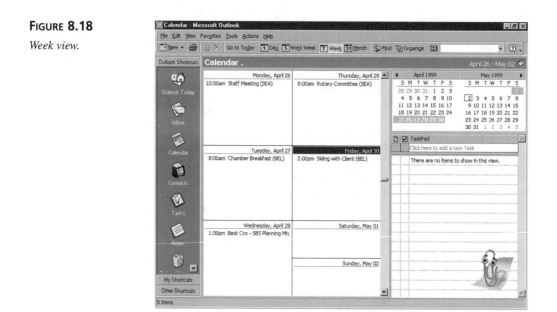

## Month

This displays a month-style view as seen in Figure 8.19.

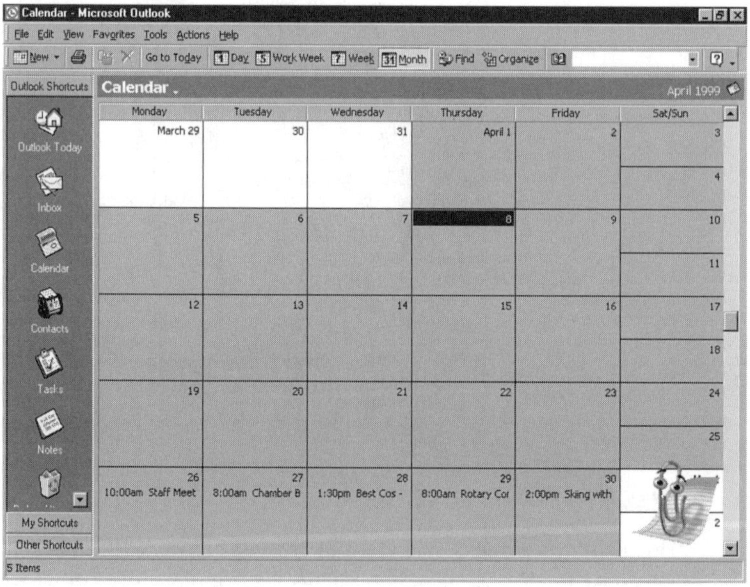

**FIGURE 8.19**

*Month view.*

## Task 8.6: Creating an Appointment

You now create an appointment for ElvisH on the Springer Spaniels Unlimited SBS network. Make sure you that you are logged on to a workstation as ElvisH.

1. Select a date on the small monthly view on the right side of your Outlook Calendar. Select a date that is several days hence.

2. Click the New Appointment button. The Untitled - Appointment dialog box appears.

3. Enter **Dog Show** in the Subject field.

4. Enter **San Francisco** in the Location field.

5. Select a start time of 9 AM and an end time of 4 PM using the time drop-down menus.

6. Allow the Reminder checkbox to remain selected. If you have Outlook open on your workstation, you will receive a reminder 15 minutes prior to the appointment. Allow the Show Time As field to remain as Busy (this would reflect a busy or occupied time if others looked at your schedule over the SBS network).

7. Underneath the Reminder checkbox is the appointment description area. Enter the following: **Take Sir Brisker to show**. The appointment dialog box should look similar to Figure 8.20.

**FIGURE 8.20**

*Complete appointment.*

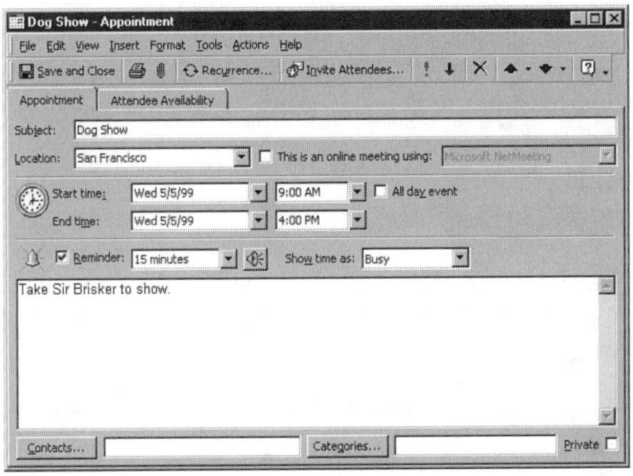

8. Click Save and Close in the upper-left corner of the appointment dialog box to book the appointment in Outlook.

> **Note**
>
> Recurring appointments can be scheduled with ease in Outlook 2000. These are typically staff meetings that occur each week at the same time. To create a recurring appointment, simply click the Recurrence button when you are creating a new appointment. The Appointment Recurrence dialog box appears, similar to Figure 8.21.

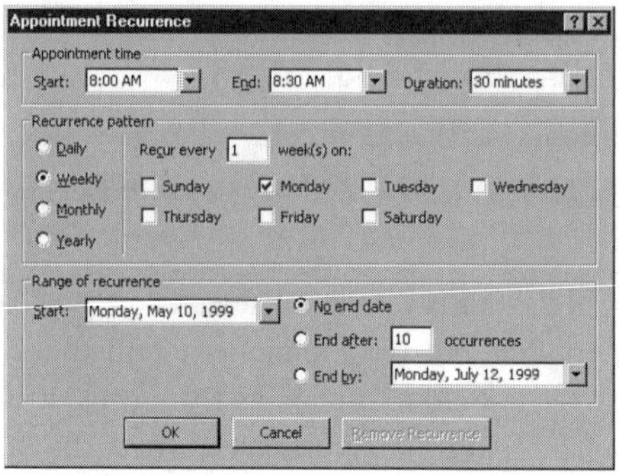

**FIGURE 8.21**

*Appointment
Recurrence.*

## Deleting an Appointment

Occasionally, you need to cancel an appointment. Any small-business person knows that. You can easily accommodate that real world behavior in Outlook. To delete an appointment, simply select the appointment with a single mouse click and select the Delete menu option from the Edit menu. You can also delete a selected appointment with the Ctrl+D keystroke or by right-clicking and selecting the Delete option from the secondary menu.

## Alternative Uses

There are many ways to use the Calendar in Outlook above and beyond simply maintaining your own personal schedule. Alternative ways that Calendar is used on real-world SBS networks include

- Scheduling rooms—Some small firms using SBS use Calendar to schedule conference rooms.
- Group calendars—The Calendar function can be used to schedule group meetings, company ski days, the annual golf tournament, and so on.
- Check-in/Check-out—Front desk receptionists in many companies on SBS networks use Calendar as an In/Out board to know of your whereabouts.
- Equipment scheduling—Scheduling the overhead projection unit or company car can be managed via Outlook's Calendar.

## Transferring the Calendar for Handheld Devices

One of the coolest—and I suspect most popular—Calendar option in the near future is the Outlook Calendar/handheld device connection. Here, SBS users can synchronize their Outlook Calendars with their PalmPilots and other similar handheld devices. This interaction allows you to download and upload scheduling, contact, and e-mail-based information between the two systems. I'll discuss this matter more later today.

## Printing the Calendar

You can, of course, print your calendars by selecting the Print button on the toolbar or the Print menu command from the File menu. But did you know that Outlook supports a variety of reports so that you can place your printouts in your day planner or similar book? I've found the report formats to be one of the better secrets in Outlook. In fact, only this last year, I finally stopped ordering the annual renewal of my day planner's calendar inserts. Rather, I now enter everything on my networked version of Outlook at work (something I was already doing so co-workers would know my whereabouts) and simply print out my calendar. The calendar printout fits right in my old full-sized day planner! As far as I'm concerned, I saved both time and money—time because I've eliminated one set of entries and money because I haven't purchased an expensive calendar renewal. I suggest you consider my approach or the handheld devices I discussed earlier to further extend the Outlook scheduling capabilities in your life.

**Power Tool Tip**

I highly recommend that you print out each Calendar type on a laser printer so that you can better learn the strengths and weaknesses of each. You can then better advise your SBS users on how to implement Outlook's Calendar capabilities.

# Contacts Basics

Of the three Outlook capabilities discussed today, this has been the lesser of the three on SBS networks that I've worked with. I suspect this is for four reasons:

- It takes too much effort to enter data. Few small-business people truly have the time to sit and enter their contacts, business cards, loose scraps of paper, and so on into Outlook.

> **Tip**
>
> As an SBS consultant, I always enter my own name, address, and telephone number into my client's Outlook Contacts so that they see Contacts being used and, of course, I'm first on their list for a call when SBS-related work is available.

- Outlook's Contacts aren't as powerful as third-party apps. Some of my SBS clients are indeed into contact management in a big way. These tend to be sales and marketing people. The problem I've encountered with "Contactmanics" is that they use more powerful, third-party standalone contact management applications such as GoldMine. Indeed GoldMine has some capabilities that are absent in Outlook, such as a stronger database management function, but you would expect that with a standalone, specialized application. My position is simple. Although the Contacts feature in Outlook might not surpass the GoldMines of the world, the integration with the schedule, e-mail, and other capabilities of Outlook outweigh any feature-by-feature shortcomings.

- People still use business cards. The old school still likes paper business cards as their contact management system, God bless them.

- Many SBS users simply don't know the power of Outlook and its Contacts capabilities. That's the underlying purpose of meeting today. Training and education make a heck of a difference in how your users take advantage of Contacts. For example, some SBSers are enamored with the automatic dialing feature (AutoDialer) in Contacts (a feature that speed dials the telephone number displayed on your screen).

## Defining the Outlook Contacts Window

Take a moment to learn about Outlook Contacts. It is in the Contacts window that you enter and manage your contacts. The default Contacts window is displayed in Figure 8.22, and you will note it is empty (its initial appearance before you enter a contact).

Several buttons on the Contacts toolbar differ from the other Outlook windows. I will discuss the New Contact and AutoDialer buttons.

### New Contact

Clicking the New Contact button presents the Contact dialog box. It is in the Contact dialog box that you enter a contact into Outlook.

**FIGURE 8.22**

*Outlook Contacts window.*

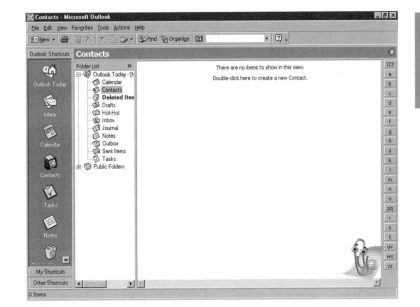

## AutoDialer

The AutoDialer (the telephone icon) is Outlook's attempt to provide a sales call management function. Clicking the AutoDialer button presents the New Call dialog box. It is here that you would select a contact and telephone number to call. If you have a telephone attached to your personal computer (perhaps via the telephone port on your modem), the contact number is dialed without any further user involvement. This function is similar to the cold calling/telephony dialer function found in third-party contact management applications such as GoldMine.

## Add a Contact

It's time to add a contact for Springer Spaniels Unlimited. Again, I assume that you are currently logged on as ElvisH.

1. Click the New Contact button on the left side of the upper toolbar. A dialog box titled "Untitled - Contact" appears.

2. Enter the following information from Table 8.2. Note this name, Jane Union, is taken from the SBS Stakeholders list on Day 2, "Planning for Small Business Server," (see Table 2.2) and an e-mail address and Web page site has been added for Jane.

**TABLE 8.2** SAMPLE CONTACT INFORMATION

| Contact Field | Information to Enter |
|---|---|
| Full Name | **Jane Union** |
| Job title | **Cabling Specialist** |
| Company | **Union Cabling** |
| Address | **Box 3333** <br> **Union, WA 98111** |
| This is the mailing address | Select this check box |
| Phone - Business | **222-333-4455** |
| Phone - Mobile | **222-444-3344** |
| Phone - Pager | **222-123-4567** |
| E-mail | **jane@unionjane.com** |
| Web page | `www.jane.union.com` |
| Description | **This is a cabling specialist for the Springer Spaniels Unlimited SBS network.** |

The contact information you've entered should appear similar to Figure 8.23.

**FIGURE 8.23**

*Jane Union contact information.*

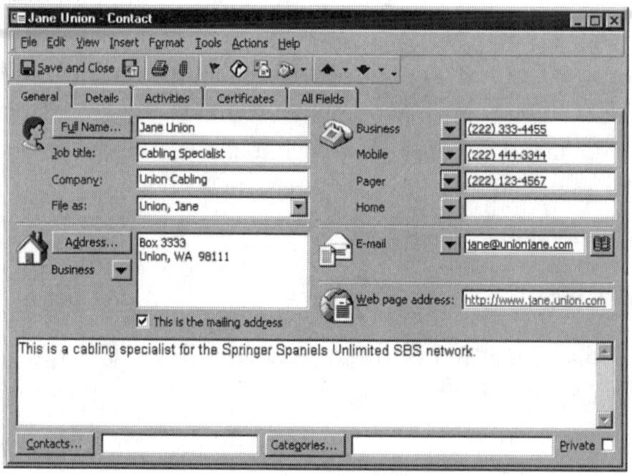

3. After entering the information from Table 8.1, click the Save and Close button.

4. Observe your entry in the Contacts window. Congratulations. You've entered your first contact, which should appear similar to Figure 8.24.

**FIGURE 8.24**

*Contacts - Jane Union.*

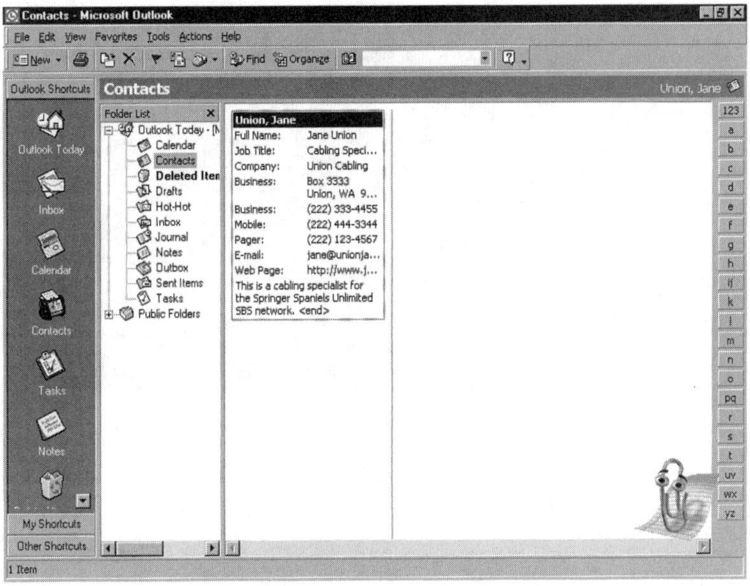

## Deleting a Contact

Occasionally, you need to delete contacts from Outlook. Perhaps you no longer conduct business with the individual or the individual is deceased. Whatever the reason, deleting a contact is very simple:

1. Highlight or select the contact that you want to delete.
2. Select the Delete menu option from the Edit menu.
3. The selected contact is deleted.

You can also delete a contact via the secondary menu when the contact is selected or by using the Ctrl+D keystroke.

## Printing a Contact

Printing a contact is similar to printing other items in Outlook. You can click the Print button on the toolbar or select Print from the File menu. When the print command is invoked, you see a Print dialog box similar to Figure 8.25.

**FIGURE 8.25**

*Print.*

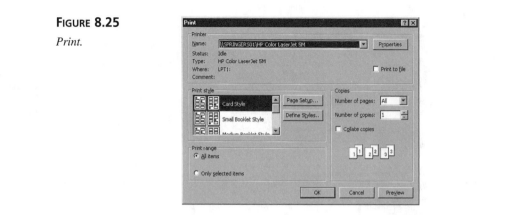

You will notice that you are presented with several printout styles, which include Card Style, Small Booklet Style, Medium Booklet Style, Memo Style, and Phone Directory Style. I encourage you to try each style to discover your favorites.

**Note**

> The setup for each of these print styles is very simple. Outlook assumes you are printing to blank paper; it handles the actual rendering. (You don't have to use special preprinted forms.)

## Additional Contact Considerations

Anyone using Contacts in Outlook, including yourself, will quickly expect the contact information to preserved as metainformation. That is, you want to enter the information into the system once, maintain it in a central location such as Contacts, but use it in multiple ways, such as merge lists for Microsoft Word. It is a very common expectation, one that is expressed at virtually every SBS site I worked at.

For example, the CEO of a landscaping company where I set up an SBS network expressed a desire to take the Contacts information and use it for marketing letters, faxes, and e-mail. No problem with Outlook Contacts.

## Lunch

Today's lunch speaker in Tami Caesar from the National Multiple Sclerosis (MS) Society. Tami has recently embraced Outlook after first trying Netscape Navigator.

## Navigator Versus Outlook

*by Tami Caesar*
*National Multiple Sclerosis (MS) Society, Washington Chapter*

Originally, our chapter office used the suggested e-mail solution that was recommended by our national office. This solution was Netscape Navigator. As a browser, no problem, but when it came to e-mail, Netscape Navigator's capabilities were a step below Outlook. Initially, we used Netscape Navigator before the SBS network was implemented at our office. So far so good, but when the SBS network was implemented and Outlook was installed at each workstation, users (including myself) began to discover that Outlook offered things that Netscape Navigator didn't. These discoveries included robust e-mail management, scheduling, and contact management capabilities.

So reflecting back on our Netscape Navigator era, I can honestly say we've been there and done that. The good news is that I and the other staff members probably appreciate Outlook more than we would have, having intimately learned the alternative. Thanks for the chance to share my story.

**Note**

Tami Caesar is operations director from the National Multiple Sclerosis (MS) Society, Washington Chapter. Tami oversees a 20-user SBS network in the Pacific Northwest.

## PM Advanced Outlook

Early on, SBS users embrace the use of e-mail as a core business tool. For that reason, many of the most common features of Outlook's e-mail capabilities were shown to you earlier today.

This afternoon, I will show you one feature relating to Internet e-mail and Outlook that you might not have been aware of: Internet e-mail distribution lists. Why? Because SBS users quickly favor Internet-based e-mail, often more than any other Outlook feature.

# Internet E-mail Distribution Lists

Assume that you still get together with the old ski team for Wednesday night skis. E-mail is a powerful tool for quickly getting the word out to the gang. You can, of course, enter each individual e-mail name, but did you know that, much like internal e-mail names (SBS users on your internal network), you can also create e-mail groups with Internet e-mail addresses? You can; this capability of Internet e-mail groups is a little-known feature of Outlook.

## Task 8.7: Creating the List

▼ TASK

To create an Internet e-mail group, complete the following steps.

1. Start Microsoft Outlook.

2. From the Tools menu, select Services.

3. Verify that Personal Address Book service is installed, as seen in Figure 8.26. If not, click the Add button to add this service.

**FIGURE 8.26**

*Personal Address Book service.*

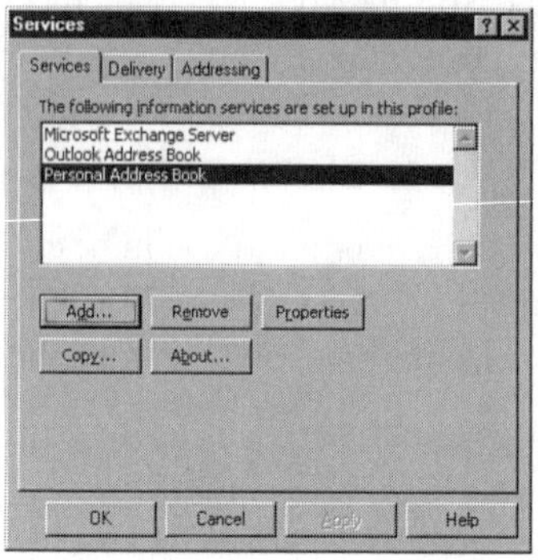

4. Exit and restart Outlook to complete the Personal Address Book service installation if it was just installed; otherwise, continue to step 5.

5. From the Tools menu in Outlook, select the Address Book menu option. This option can also be selected with the Ctrl+Shift+B keystroke. The Address Book dialog box appears similar to that seen in Figure 8.27

**FIGURE 8.27**

*Address Book.*

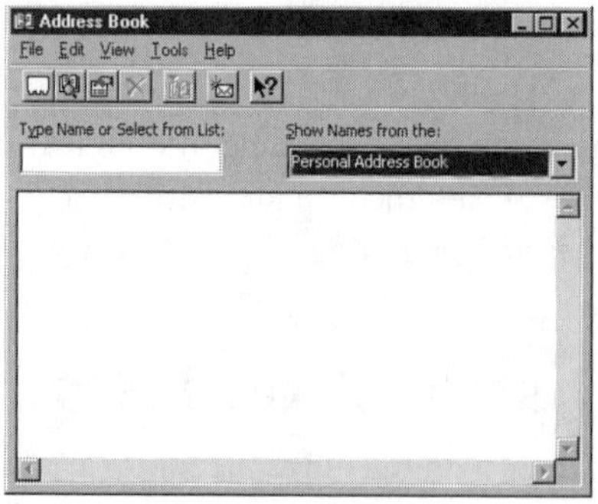

▼

▼ 6. Make sure the Show Names From The: drop-down menu shows Personal Address Book. Enter several names and Internet e-mail addresses into the Personal Address Book (feel free to make up a few names for the purposes of this task). You can enter new names via New Entry from the File menu. When the New Entry dialog box is displayed, select Personal Address List and Internet Mail Address.

Alternatively, you can have names in Contacts with Internet e-mail addresses as well. As you will see in a moment, e-mail distribution lists can be created with names listed in either a Personal Address Book or Contacts.

7. To create an e-mail group containing these names and Internet e-mail addresses, do the following. From the File menu, select New Entry.

8. From the New Entry dialog box, select New Distribution List. Under the Put This Entry section, at the In The radio button, select Contacts. This is shown in Figure 8.28. Click OK.

**FIGURE 8.28**

*Selecting the New Distribution List.*

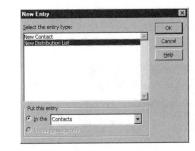

9. The Untitled - Distribution List dialog box appears. Select the Select Members button . You can select names from your Personal Address Book (names entered in step 6), Contacts, or the Global Address List. I've selected three names from the Personal Address List and one name from the Global Address List. After selecting names, your Untitled - Distribution List dialog box should appear similar to Figure 8.29.

10. Be sure to enter a group name in the Name field of the New Personal Distribution List Properties. As seen in Figure 8.29, I used the group name Skiing. Click Save and Close.

11. Notice that the e-mail group Skiing now appears in Contacts, as seen in Figure 8.30. What's important here is that you now have a e-mail group that contains a variety of e-mail recipients (Internet e-mail address, Contacts, and local e-mail names). This is a wonderful new feature in Outlook 2000.

**FIGURE 8.29**

*Untitled - Distribution List.*

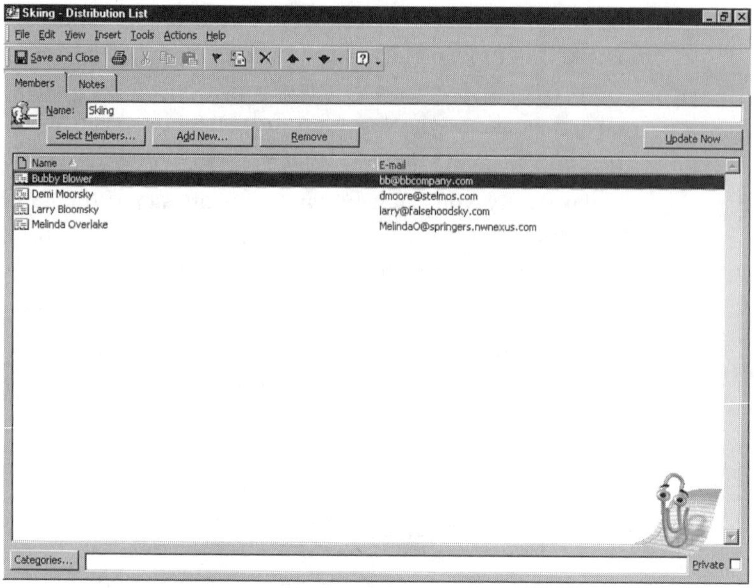

![Skiing - Distribution List window showing Members tab with Name: Skiing. Members listed: Bubby Blower (bb@bbcompany.com), Demi Moorsky (dmoore@stelmos.com), Larry Bloomsky (larry@falsehoodsky.com), Melinda Overlake (MelindaO@springers.nwnexus.com)]

**FIGURE 8.30**

*Skiing group in Address Book.*

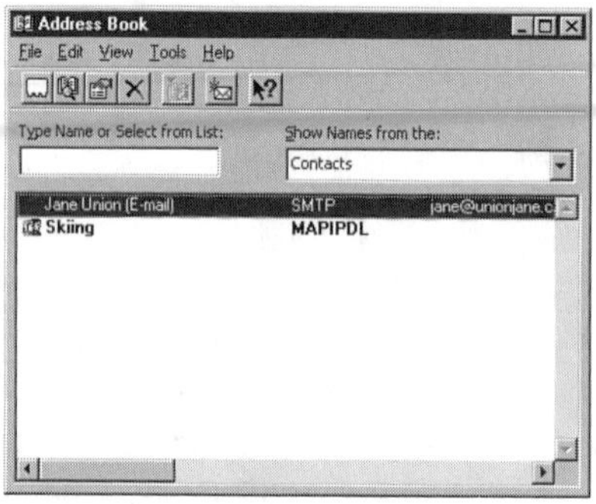

![Address Book window showing Contacts list with Jane Union (E-mail) SMTP jane@unionjane.c and Skiing MAPIPDL]

# Advanced Contacts Topics

As SBS users experiment more with Contacts, naturally their needs change for working with Contacts. Three such needs are discussed in this section including e-mailing a Contact, writing a letter to a Contact, and performing queries against your Contact list.

## Task 8.8: Sending E-mail to Contacts

One obvious need is to send e-mail to Contacts from the Contacts view. You accomplish this by following these steps:

1. Select Contacts in Microsoft Outlook.

2. Single-click a Contact name that you would like to send an e-mail to.

▼     3. Right-click while the Contact is highlighted. Select the New Message To Contact
         menu option.

      4. Compose the e-mail message as you normally would in Microsoft Outlook. The
         To: field is automatically filled in for you.

▲     5. Send the e-mail.

## Task 8.9: Writing a Letter to a Contact

Another advanced Contacts feature often requested is the capability to write a letter to a
Contact easily, using the basic Contact information as the address for your letter:

   1. Select the Contact in the list of Contacts that you want to send a letter to. I suggest
      you select Jane Union (a name that you entered earlier today).

   2. From the Actions menu, select New Letter to Contact menu option. (This option
      assumes that you have Microsoft Word installed on your workstation.)

   3. A Word session starts and the Letter Wizard launches, as seen in Figure 8.31.

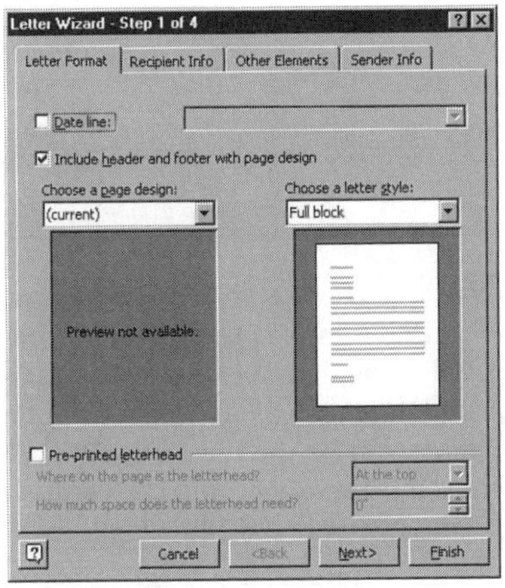

**FIGURE 8.31**

*Letter Wizard.*

   4. Select or deselect any items of interest in Step 1 of 4 in the Letter Wizard (see
      Figure 8.31). Click Next.

   5. Complete Step 2 of 4 in the Letter Wizard. This is the Recipient Info tab. Typically
      at this stage you simply confirm that the address information is correct. You can
      also select the greeting (for example, Dear Jane) for the letter. Click Next.

   6. Complete Step 3 of 4 in the Letter Wizard. This is the Other Elements tab. Click
      Next.

   7. Complete Step 4 of 4 in the Letter Wizard. This is the Sender Info tab. Click
▼     Finish.

▼  8. The letter looks similar to Figure 8.32. You would now complete the rest of your letter with your own information.

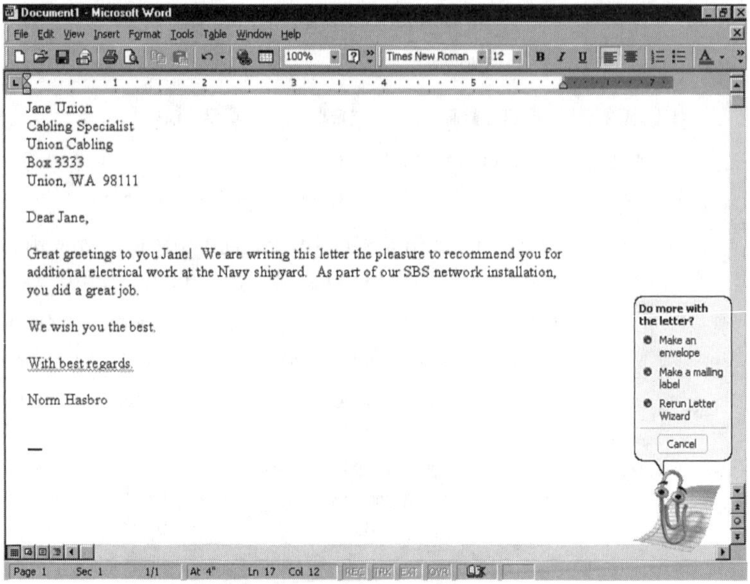

FIGURE **8.32**

*Letter addressed to a Contact.*

> **Tip**
>
> There is no easy way to perform a mail merge for a group of Outlook Contacts with Word. That's unfortunate because other personal information managers such as GoldMine do a very good job of this. To do a mail merge between Outlook and Word, you would export the Contacts via the Import and Export menu option under the File menu. The problem with that is the export is global for complete export. You can't selectively export all Contacts in a range of zip codes (for example). Bummer!

## Queries on Contacts

Remember the landscaping company that I've mentioned through the book? Of course you do. I hope you remember the story on Day 1, "Welcome to Small Business Server," where the landscaping company owner wanted to take advantage of SBS to increase his business. One of the ways in which he intended to do this was via the effective use of Contacts in Outlook. This effective use largely centered around the ability to query Outlook and mail to selected groups and so on.

There are two ways to apply queries against the Contact list in Outlook: Categories and Advanced Find.

## Task 8.10: Using Categories

You can display contacts by categories. Here, the idea is to define your Contacts by Category when creating them. To select a Category for a Contact, perform the following steps:

1. From Contacts in Microsoft Outlook, click the New Contact button on the Contacts toolbar (far left).

2. Complete the Contact information (name, telephone numbers, and e-mail). I suggest that you enter several contacts from the SBS Stakeholders list shown on Day 2 (see Table 2.2).

3. Select the Categories button at the bottom of the Contact dialog box.

4. Observe the list of categories in the Categories dialog box, as seen in Figure 8.33.

**FIGURE 8.33**

*Categories list.*

5. Select the categories that you want associated with this contact. Select a similar category (for example, Business) for at least two of the Contacts. Click OK. Save and close the Contact. Repeat this step as necessary.

6. To view Contacts by the categories you have selected, choose the Current View menu option under the View menu. Select By Category as you view.

7. You can now manipulate Contacts by different groups of Categories. Expand the Business category (assuming you placed several Contacts in the Business category). Such manipulations might include sending an e-mail to each Category member.

## Task 8.11: Using Advanced Find

Using the advanced find capability in Microsoft Outlook is closer to performing a real database query. Here is how you use the advanced find capability:

1. From Contacts in Microsoft Outlook, select Find from the Tools menu.
2. Select the Advanced Find link. The Advanced Find dialog box is displayed.
3. Select the Advanced tab. Enter field-specific search criteria in the Define More Criteria portion of the Advanced Find dialog box, similar to Figure 8.34. In this example, I have selected ZIP/Postal Code by clicking the Field button and select from Address fields. I then entered the zip code 98000. This should display David Jaeger when I run the query.

**FIGURE 8.34**

*Creating a Contacts query.*

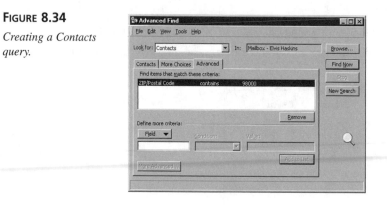

4. Be sure to save your query for future use, so you don't have to rebuild it again. To save your query, select Save Search from the File menu of the Advanced Find dialog box.
5. Click Find Now to perform your query or search.

You now see a list of Contacts that meet your criteria. In this example, David Jaeger is displayed. You might now use these listed contacts for sending e-mail and so on.

# Advanced Calendar Topics

The last discrete advanced area I want to cover is Calendar. Again, Calendar remains a wildly popular function in Outlook, and my SBS clients are using Calendar in ways that are somewhat unusual but highly effective. These areas include group appointments, automatic meeting planning, scheduling resources, and Public Folders.

## Making Group Appointments

No sooner than you get you own scheduling act together with Calendar than you will want to extend its capability to schedule group meetings with fellow SBS users. You can easily accomplish this by following the steps in Task 8.12.

### Task 8.12: Creating Group Appointments

1. In Calendar in Microsoft Outlook, create a new appointment by selecting the New Appointment button on the Outlook toolbar.

2. Create a new appointment (for example, Tour new training facility). Add an appointment location, time, and description.

3. Click the Invitee Attendees button on the Appointment toolbar as seen in Figure 8.35. The appointment is modified to include the To: line. (See Figure 8.36).

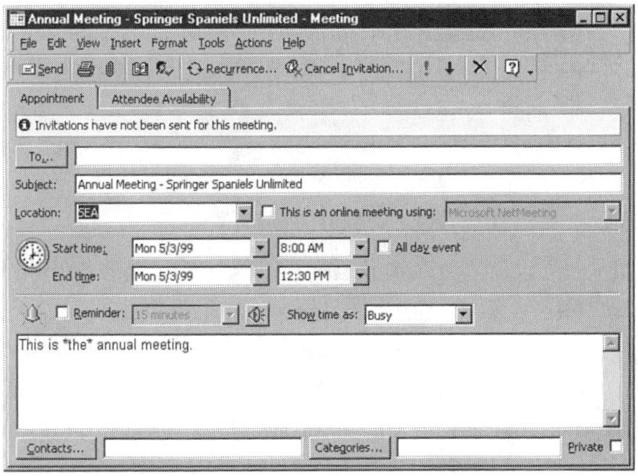

**FIGURE 8.35**

*Creating an appointment.*

4. In the To: field, add names of individuals you would like to invite to the meeting. You can use the names of internal SBS users (shown by clicking the To: button), or you can simply type an Internet username (for example, **NormH@springers.nwnexus.com**). Select three internal users: Barry Kech, Elvis Haskins, and Sally Briggs. Click the Send button.

5. You have now invited users to a meeting. The invitation that is received looks similar to Figure 8.36. Note the recipient can accept, decline, or tentatively elect to attend the meeting.

▼ FIGURE 8.36

*Meeting invitation.*

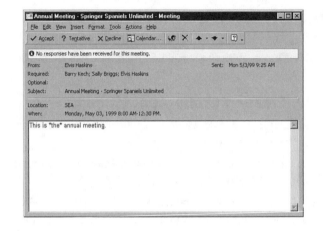

> **Tip**
>
> The key to using this approach is the ability to invite individuals via Internet-based e-mail. That's a practical way of scheduling meetings and doing business today.

## Automatic Meeting Planning

There is an algorithm in Outlook that reminds me of that darned linear programming class I took in college. You might or might not know that *linear programming* is oriented toward finding an optimal solution given constraints. This Outlook-based tool is called the *AutoPick*, which evaluates the calendars for SBS users and selects a time that is mutually agreeable or open on all calendars. Then, potential attendees are scheduled for this meeting. There are two caveats that must be noted when using AutoPick. First, all SBS users maintain up-to-date calendars. Second, this feature works only with SBS users on your network. That said, AutoPick is a great feature.

### Task 8.13: Using AutoPick

To use AutoPick, do the following steps:

1. Create an appointment in Calendar. Consider scheduling a retreat several months hence.
2. Complete the appointment information such as time, date, and description.
3. Select the Attendee Availability tab.
4. Add Attendees in the All Attendees column. Their calendar busy times should show up as filled lines. I suggest you select at least two employees of Springer Spaniels Unlimited (Barry Kech and Norm Hasbro). Simply enter their names in the attendee name field.

▼ 5. AutoPick automatically runs and reports, as seen in Figure 8.37, to select a mutually agreeable time.

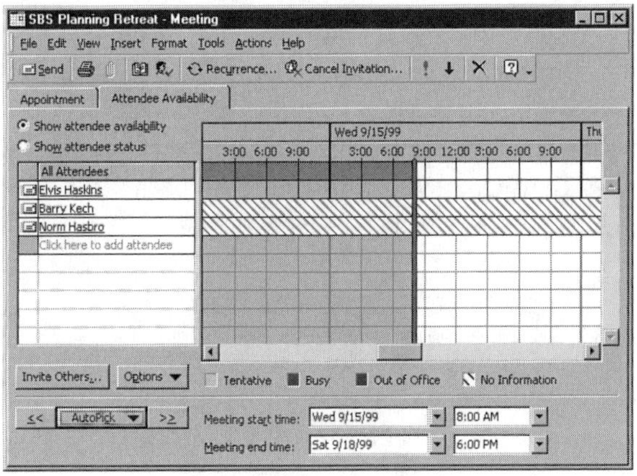

**FIGURE 8.37**

*Automatically scheduling a meeting.*

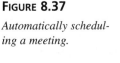

▲ You have now automatically scheduled a meeting in Microsoft Outlook.

## Scheduling Resources

Another popular use of Outlook is the scheduling of resources, such as the company car or conference room. You can easily accomplish this by creating a Calendar item in the Public Folders.

### Task 8.14: Booking a Conference Room

1. In Outlook, make sure the folder list is displayed in the center pane by clicking the Folder List button on your Microsoft Outlook toolbar.

2. Expand the Public Folders icon.

3. Expand the All Public Folders icon.

4. While All Public Folders is highlighted, launch the secondary menu via a right-click.

5. Select New Folder from the secondary menu.

6. Name the folder something meaningful such as "Conference Room A Calendar."

7. Verify that the All Public Folders object is highlighted (or has the focus). Make sure the Folder Contains field reflect Appointment Items (if not, drop down the menu to show Appointment Items). Click OK.

8. To modify the permission for this calendar item, right-click the new Calendar icon.

9. Select Properties from the secondary menu to display the Calendar Properties dialog box.

&#9660;    10. Select the Permissions tab.

       11. Select which SBS users may have permissions to review the calendar. Typically, you give reviewer rights for read only (for simply viewing the schedule). The editor right would allow you (or any SBS user with this right) to schedule the resource. That means, given the editor right, an SBS user may schedule Conference Room A for a meeting. More importantly, even as a reviewer, an SBS user may see whether the resource is available. This approach prevents double-bookings of resources. The suggested permissions have been set in Figure 8.38. Click OK to make the permissions-related changes.

**Figure 8.38**

*Calendar Properties - Permissions.*

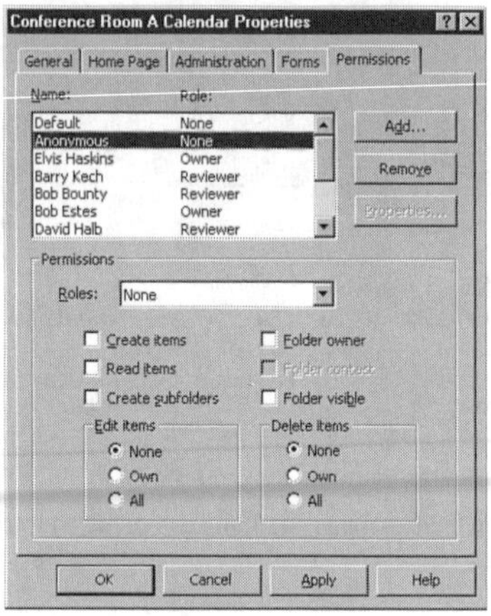

&#9650;   You have now created a shared calendar for scheduling a resource.

# Public Folders Again

You can use Public Folders in additional ways. I'll discuss two here: companywide calendars and companywide contacts. The underlying idea, all specifics aside, is to manage critical company information at a single location (centralized management). That way, your SBS users know what is occurring when, how to contact individuals, and so on.

## Companywide Calendar

Back to the small law firm I assist. One huge need, met by Outlook, was the use of Outlook's Calendar for scheduling law firm–wide appointments, litigation, and employee schedules. I specifically satisfied this need by the following approach:

- A Calendar, titled Law Firm, was placed in a Public Folder. To do this, I followed the same steps you used to create a resource calendar.

- All SBS users were given the edit right to the calendar. To do this, I followed the steps related to granting Calendar permissions that I presented earlier today.

- Entries booked into the Calendar adhered to a code system. Each entry was preceded by the SBS user's initials to reflect who the appointment related to. For example, "HMB - In Court (Johnson Matter)" as a calendar entry would reflect that a lawyer with the initials *HMB* was booked in court for the Johnson matter. A sample entry is shown in the Company Calendar for Springer Spaniels Unlimited in Figure 8.39.

**FIGURE 8.39**

*Entry in Company Calendar.*

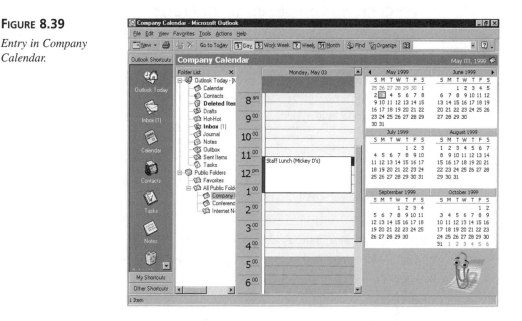

## Companywide Contacts

Similar to having a companywide Calendar, there is great merit in having a companywide Contact book. Why? Because of all matters, Contacts are probably the most suited to centralized management. Clients, stakeholders, associates, and prospects come and go. Not only that but last names, telephone numbers, and most of all, e-mail addresses, are tricky to type correctly.

By having companywide Contacts, you can centralize both the presentation and administration of key contacts. Typically, one of the SBS users, such as an administrative assistant, performs the administration of the Contacts.

> **Tip**
>
> Only one user should have the right to edit the companywide Contacts for many of the reasons stated earlier, such as correct spellings. Identify who that person in your organization might be. In a moment, I'll show you how to set permissions on the companywide Contacts to implement this approach.

## Task 8.15: Creating Companywide Contacts

The process of creating companywide Contacts is similar to that for the Calendars that you just created. The steps are these:

1. In Outlook, make sure the folder list is displayed in the center pane by clicking the Folder List button on your Outlook toolbar.

2. Expand the Public Folders icon.

3. Expand the All Public Folders icon.

4. While All Public Folders is highlighted, launch the secondary menu via a right-click.

5. Select New Folder from the secondary menu.

6. Name the folder "Company Contacts" or some other appropriate title.

7. Select Contact Items in the Folder contains field.

8. Make sure All Public Folders are highlighted in the Make this folder a subfolder of list.

9. Click OK.

10. Right-click the new Contacts item to set permissions.

11. From the secondary menu, select Properties.

12. Select the Permissions tab when the Contacts Properties dialog box is displayed. (The Default permission of Author is much too generous.)

13. Make the Default permission that of reviewer and give one user (by clicking the Add button) the rights of Editor. This individual will maintain the companywide Contacts (everyone else will review the Contacts). Your screen should appear similar to Figure 8.40.

14. Start entering and using the companywide Contacts!

▼ **Figure 8.40**

*Contacts permissions.*

▲

Having a current Contacts list that has correct spellings can offer your firm a significant competitive advantage. Why? Because as you approach the new century, the new phrase that pays is "You Are Your Database!" Thus, accurately maintained company metainformation, such as companywide Contacts, can significantly enhance your competitiveness.

# Faxes

One of the cooler tricks possible with SBS is to merge the e-mail capabilities of Outlook (and Microsoft Exchange in the background) with SBS's faxing capabilities. Although I discuss faxing in detail on Day 14, "Faxing," I want to extend that discussion to show how your SBS users can benefit by receiving their faxes over e-mail.

The mechanics are simple. Faxes are received digitally by the SBS server. The inbound faxes are routed to a single e-mail account (as discussed on Day 14) and then forwarded via e-mail to the ultimate recipient, an SBS user.

The fax arrives as an e-mail attachment embedded in an e-mail that shows up in the SBS user's Outlook Inbox. This is similar to receiving an attachment via e-mail. When opened, all the SBS user does is double-click the attachment and the fax appears on the users screen, similar to Figure 8.41.

What are the benefits of having your SBS users receive faxes via Outlook e-mail? Two come to mind. First, the ability to forward your fax to others without suffering degraded quality. By that I mean, have you every tried to refax a traditional fax? If you have, you know that each time you resend a fax, the quality declines. By forwarding the fax via e-mail, you maintain the same fax quality.

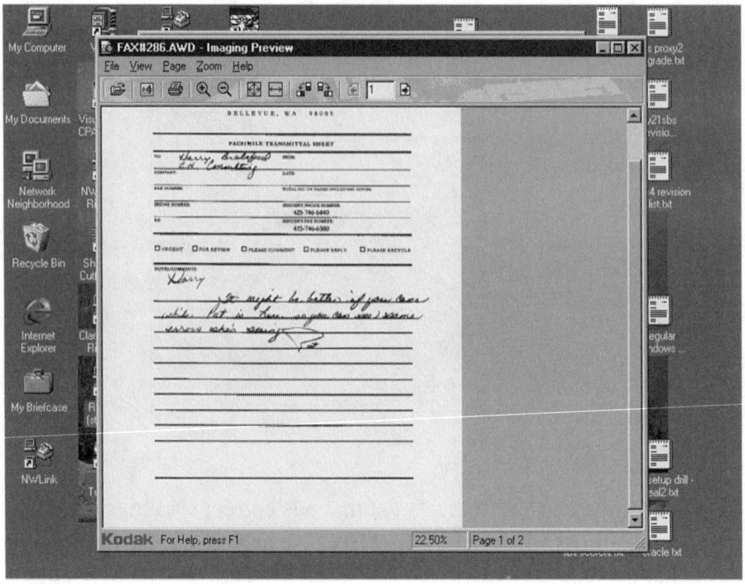

FIGURE 8.41

*Fax received via*
*Outlook e-mail.*

Second, my favorite reason for receiving faxes via Outlook e-mail is that I can dial in to the company network from home, get my faxes, and avoid a trip across the bridge across the lake back to the office. Those days of driving up to 90 minutes to go to the office and back simply to retrieve a paper-based fax are now gone! Thank God.

# Manual Configurations

Behold the day that you will need to configure Outlook on your network manually. The reasons are varied, ranging from a corrupt magic disk installation to an adventuresome user who has trashed his Outlook e-mail configuration. In reality, you should probably run the magic setup disk again, but here's a quick peek at how Outlook is configured to work with Microsoft Exchange on your SBS network.

The primary Outlook/Exchange configuration occurs via the Microsoft Exchange Server service at the Outlook client. (I am, of course, assuming that the SBS user has already been created on the SBS network and has a bona fide Microsoft Exchange e-mail account.) To modify the Microsoft Exchange Server service at the Outlook client, perform the following steps:

1. Launch Microsoft Outlook at the SBS user's workstation.
2. From the Tools menu, select Services. The Services dialog box is displayed, as seen in Figure 8.42.

**FIGURE 8.42**

*Outlook's Services
dialog box.*

3. Select the Properties button while the Microsoft Exchange Server service is selected. The Microsoft Exchange Server dialog box, similar to Figure 8.43, is displayed.

**FIGURE 8.43**

*Microsoft Exchange
Server dialog box.*

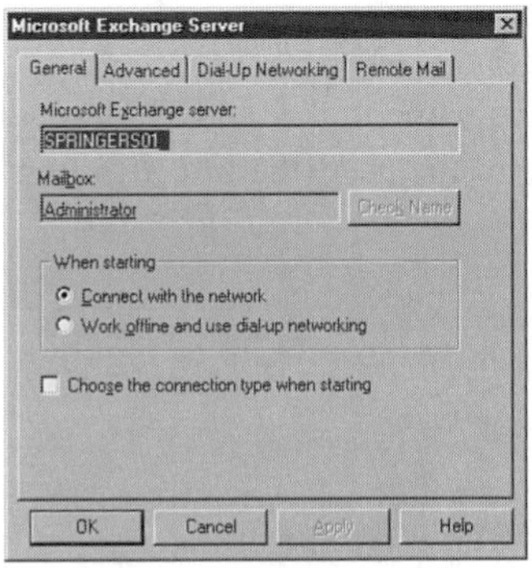

Four tabs are displayed in the Microsoft Exchange Server dialog box. I'll discuss the two that are the most applicable to an SBS network: General and Advanced.

## The General Tab

The General tab is where the basic connection between Outlook and Microsoft Exchange Server occurs. You will note that both an Exchange Server name (which is the same as the SBS server machine name by default) and an SBS username have been provided.

**Power Tool Tip**

If, for some reason, you need to fix the Exchange server and SBS user information on the tab, the server name must be spelled exactly and the SBS username can be spelled partially. If you put in only part of the SBS username, simply click Check Now for the name to be resolved.

The General tab was displayed in Figure 8.43.

## The Advanced Tab

The Advanced tab is your opportunity to add additional mail boxes for viewing. Here is the story. At my job, those of us on staff have freely granted editor rights to our Calendars (a technique discussed earlier today). That way, at a glance, fellow co-workers can tell where we are and schedule appointments for us. In our case, Elena (our department secretary) frequently checks our individual calendars, makes appointments, and so on.

So how does Elena do it? Very simply, by following these steps:

1. From the Tool menu in Microsoft Outlook, select Services.
2. When the Services dialog box is displayed, click the Microsoft Exchange Server service.
3. Click the Properties button.
4. Select the Advanced tab.
5. Click the Add button.
6. Type the additional SBS user's name in the Add Mailbox dialog box. You only need to type the partial name of the user (the full SBS user's name is resolved automatically). Click OK.
7. Observe the SBS user's name you added now appears in the Open these additional mailboxes section of the Advanced tab, similar to Figure 8.44. Click OK.
8. Click OK at the Services dialog box.

**FIGURE 8.44**

*Advanced tab.*

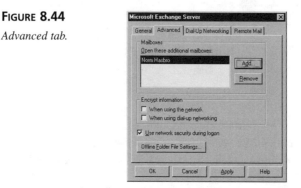

**Note**

You can add fellow SBS user's mailboxes to your Outlook application all day long if you like, but it doesn't mean anything if the user hasn't granted you some type of permission to at least review items in the mailbox such as the Calendar. These permissions were discussed earlier today in the context of shared Calendars.

# Working Offline

I'm sure that you have several SBS users who travel with their laptops, be it the nightly drive home, business trips, or even vacations. A frequently requested Outlook need is the ability to write e-mail, read old e-mail, and update calendars and contacts from a laptop while away from the office. Such a request is easy to fulfill.

## Task 8.16: Synching to a Laptop

**▼ TASK**

To provide offline capabilities for your laptop SBS users, perform the following steps:

1. Launch Outlook and make sure the folder list is displayed in the center pane. If not, simply select the Folder List button on the Outlook toolbar.

2. Select the Inbox icon in the Folder List.

3. Right-click to display the secondary menu for the Inbox icon.

4. Select Properties from the secondary menu.

5. Select the Synchronization tab from the Inbox Properties dialog box.

6. Select the When Offline or Online radio button in the This Folder Is Available area. This is shown in Figure 8.45.

**FIGURE 8.45**

*Synchronization tab.*

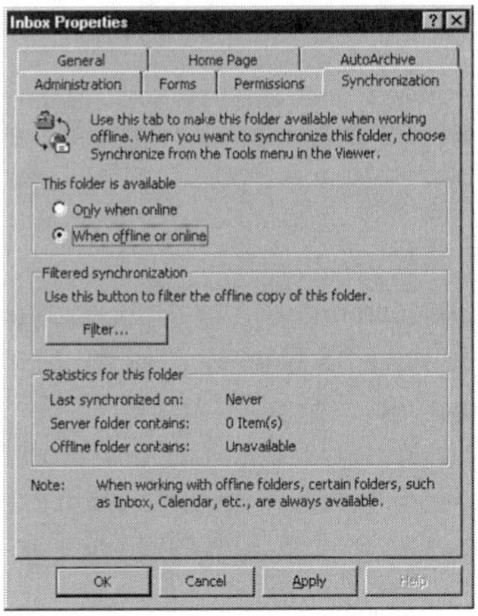

7. Click OK and Confirm (Yes) that you want to configure this.

Now, each time your user enters and exits Microsoft Outlook, a synchronization process occurs. The process can be lengthy, taking several minutes. When synchronization occurs, e-mail that was created offline are sent, new e-mail are received, calendar and contacts entries are sent and received, and so forth. This capability has proven very popular with

▲  SBS users who carry laptop computers.

# Security

And now, I'll provide a quick note on security. When SBS configures the workstation, the Outlook application is configured to use a mailbox for the user who is assigned to that workstation. That is good because it means if another SBS user tries to works at your workstation, that person can't see your Outlook mailbox.

For example, if I log on to your workstation and I launch Outlook, I receive an error message when I try to access your Outlook mailbox. This error message indicates your Outlook mailbox can't be opened. Why? Because I am not logged on as you. Your Outlook mailbox is protected by Windows NT Server-level security. Thus, your private and confidential e-mail remains private to you even if I am logged on.

However, if you somehow installed the Personal Folders capabilities under the Services dialog box (found under the Tools menu as discussed earlier), I'm on my way to reading your e-mail. Why? Because if you use Personal Folders for your Outlook activity (e-mail, contacts, calendar, and so on), you do not benefit from the Windows NT Server security model described earlier. In fact, if I merely walk up to your workstation, log on as myself or even bypass the SBS network logon dialog box by hitting the Esc key, I can easily read your e-mail simply by opening your Outlook application.

**Note**

> You should take seriously the weaknesses discussed earlier regarding Personal Folders. Few SBS users appreciate having their e-mail read without first providing permission to do so!

The solution to having multiple users on one workstation, each having the ability to read their own e-mail is very simple. In the SBS Console, via the Manage Computers sheet, simply add each user who will likely use the workstation via the Allow a User to Use an Existing Computer option. This creates a separate Outlook profile for each user. What's the bottom line? When different users log on to a single workstation, they'll see their own Outlook mailbox by default when they launch Outlook.

# Third-Party Devices

Lastly, I address the use of popular third-party handheld personal digital assistants (PDA) such as 3Com's PalmPilot. These PDAs can integrate with Microsoft Outlook so that you have an up-to-date calendar with you when you're out of the office. You can also integrate your e-mail and contacts.

The key to this integration is the synchronization process that must occur between the PDA and your Outlook mailbox. This process is shown in Figure 8.46.

**FIGURE 8.46**

*Outlook/PIM Synchronization.*

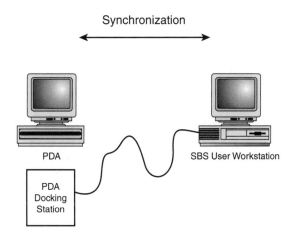

In the case of the PalmPilot, you simply dock it into its docking station while Outlook is open and running on the workstation (to which the docking station is attached). Then, launch an application that is included with the PalmPilot called HotSync. This application performs the transfer of information such as e-mail, contact, and calendar items to and from the PalmPilot and Outlook. It works very well (and easily!).

# Summary

With the end of Day 8 at hand, you now have the basic and advanced Outlook skills that you need to be successful with Outlook on your SBS network. I discussed several topics including basic features, such as sending e-mail, creating a contact, and setting an appointment. Additionally, I presented advanced features using e-mail, calendars, and contacts. I also covered advanced configurations, security, and use of third-party devices. Your next step in the world of SBS will connect your network to the Internet in Day 9. See you there!

# DAY 9

# Connecting to the Internet

Good morning. Today kicks off the first of several days dedicated to SBS and the Internet. Today finds us connecting to the Internet and using Internet Explorer (a Web browser). Following days including learning about these additional SBS Internet-related components:

- Internet Information Server—Enables businesses to publish and manage Web-related information (Day 10)
- Index Server—A search engine similar to Yahoo! that searches for information on your Web server (Day 10)
- Proxy Server—A secure firewall gateway (Day 11)
- Front Page—A Web page creation application (Day 12)

The format today follows the format I've followed throughout much of this book, but don't let the afternoon session preclude the attendance of an overly adventurous SBS newbie, just be advised. Oh, did I forget lunch? Today the guest speaker is…me. Yes, that's right. I plan to entertain you with SBS 4.5's new paradigm: improved Internet connectivity.

# AM Making the Internet Connection

First introduced in SBS 4.0, the capability to connect your SBS network with ease to the Internet has been greatly improved in SBS 4.5. Not only can you connect via the traditional modem but also via digital connections ranging from IDSN, DSL, and even WAN-like connections (router-based frame relay communications). Figure 9.1 shows the basic Internet connection for Springer Spaniels Unlimited. Here, the SPRINGERS network is connected to an ISP that is hosting the `springers.nwnexus.com` domain name. The Internet connection allows each user of the SPRINGERS network to send and receive e-mail and browse the Internet.

**FIGURE 9.1**

*SBS and the Internet.*

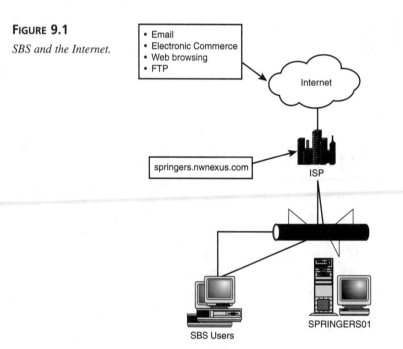

But before the details, I'll spend a moment on the Internet connection life cycle as I've observed it from the SBS trenches. I share this with you because it can assist you in managing the expectations of both you and your SBS stakeholders. The three phases to the SBS Internet connection life cycle are

- Ignorance or Early Adapter
- Modem
- High-speed

**Note**

By design, I've waited until today to connect your SBS network to the Internet. I first wanted you to spend a couple of days planning for your SBS network in Days 1, "Welcome to Small Business Server," and 2, "Planning for Small Business Server." Then, I wanted you to spend a couple of days building your SBS network in Days 3, "Installing Small Business Server," and 4, "Setting Up the Workstation Client." Next, I wanted you to spend a few days learning to manage your SBS network in Days 5, "Managing the Small Business Server Management Console," 6, "Daily and Weekly SBS Administration (The Dirty Dozen)," and 7, "Monthly and Annual SBS Duties" and learning a popular SBS user application, in Day 8, "Implementing Outlook," which in many ways will take advantage of your Internet connection. That gets us to Day 9, and you're now completely ready to introduce the Internet connection on your SBS network! Go forth with Godspeed.

9

## Ignorance or Early Adapter

During the earliest stages of an SBS network, the SBS community is divided between those who don't see the business benefit of an Internet connection (the paving contractors of the world) and those who want to sign up an ISP using the Connect to an ISP menu option from the initial To-Do List. The latter group, early adapters, usually has a compelling reason to sign up with an ISP as soon as possible. One such example is the printing shop that needs File Transfer Protocol (FTP) capabilities to transfer large Linotronic files. In my experience, the average SBS site is skewed toward the ignorance category rather than early adapter.

## Modem

Most SBS sites, in my experience, start with a simple dial-up modem connection to the Internet. This is typically done just to get the ball rolling, as it were. Experienced computer consultants shouldn't ignore or laugh at this phase; you should embrace it! That's because, if you listen to your SBS clients, they most likely communicate three things. First, they have a small budget for the Internet connection to start with (until it proves itself and larger monthly outlays are justified). Second, they or their boss might suggest that they can have a $20/month dial-up Internet connection at home via America Online (AOL). So doesn't it make sense that they can have a dial-up connection for at or close to the same fee at work? Although it's unlikely you will find $20/month dial-up service for your ISP, it is likely that a simple dial-up solution between your SBS network and your ISP will be significantly cheaper than the solutions I discuss later today.

The third message your SBS clients might be communicating is that they are somewhat fearful of the Internet, its potential power and abuses. By starting with a dial-up connection, the SBS client can, as I alluded to previously, get the ball rolling. Interestingly, these SBS clients tend to become my best Internet clients within 6–12 months. At that point, they are educated on Internet use and can now appreciate more speed (via the solutions later today) and will gladly pay for it (and your consulting time to hook it up). The moral? Today's SBS modem-based Internet connection is tomorrow's high-speed digital connection. This moral works almost every time without fail.

## High-speed

What three things are unavoidable for every SBS user? Give up? The answer is death, taxes, and a high-speed Internet connection. Sooner or later, the need for speed will afflict your SBS site. The reasons are varied and the following are all true: A younger, more computer-savvy person takes over the company from Dad, the sales force needs a faster Internet connection for more immediate e-mail and Web browsing, the popularity of the SBS network and the Internet grow so that a modem connection is inadequate. I'm sure you can name your own, but although most SBS sites might not opt for a high-speed Internet connection early on, like death and taxes, most SBS sites will have such a connection within 12 months. Trust me.

> **Note**
>
> The high-speed Internet connection life cycle stage I spoke of previously relates to the router and broadband connections discussed in a moment in the "Internet Connection Wizard" section.

## Internet Connection Wizard

The Internet Connection Wizard (ICW) can be launched from two places in SBS: the To-Do List and the Manage Internet Access selection on the More Tasks sheet (on SBS Console). The ICW is the preferred way to connect your SBS network to the Internet.

> **Power Tool Tip**
>
> Always try to connect to the Internet via the ICW before going under the hood and manually configuring SBS much like you would regular Windows NT Server. I think you'll be pleasantly surprised with the ICW improvements in SBS 4.5 over previous additions. Read on.

The ICW now supports three types of Internet connections: dial-up connections, router connections, and broadband connections.

## Dial-up Connections

The simplest and most common form of connection, a dial-up connection to the Internet, uses an analog or ISDN modem to call the ISP. This is seen in Figure 9.2, and it really is as straightforward as it appears. A connection is established at modem speed which is typically 28.8 Kbps or greater.

**Note**

Modems that purport to have speeds of 56 Kbps typically connect at speeds slightly less, such as 38.5 Kbps, due to telephone line connection quality. ISDN modems operate at speeds greater than twice those of analog modems, depending on the ISDN configuration (one or two ISDN channels).

9

**FIGURE 9.2**

*Modem connection.*

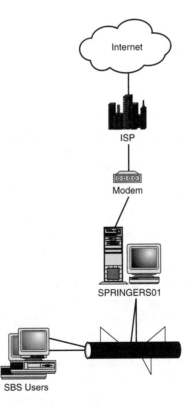

Pros to a simple modem connection, such as a single analog modem connected to an ISP, include the ease of connection configuration and maintenance and the relatively low cost to initiate and continue this type of connection.

Cons center around transmission speed. Not only do many people view an analog modem connection as a slow connection when deployed on a standalone PC, the situation is exacerbated when a single analog modem is servicing an entire SBS network!

## Router Connections

A *router* is a device that directs traffic from one network to another. In the case of SBS and the Internet, a properly deployed router sends SBS information to the Internet and vice versa. Routers are deployed in SBS environments in one of two ways: dial-on-demand or fulltime.

### Dial-on-Demand

This approach provides certain benefits to both the SBS site and the ISP. For the SBS site, dial-on-demand allows you to elect a lower service level and pay a correspondingly lower monthly fee to enjoy a robust Internet connection.

**Note**

This lower service level doesn't imply a slower speed, rather it means you don't have a fulltime connection to your ISP. So it's kinda the best of both worlds: high-speed and lower costs!

The ISP benefits from having an on again/off again relationship with your Internet connection account: Because your Internet session is somewhat intermittent (established only when you need it), you don't consume a connection (as far as the ISP is concerned) on a fulltime basis. This allows the ISP to oversubscribe its given capacity slightly. For example, if the ISP could support five router-based connections simultaneously, the ISP could support either five fulltime router-based SBS sites or perhaps ten dial-on-demand router-based SBS sites. The ISP benefits by leveraging its capital equipment over a larger SBS user base.

Dial-on-demand works by establishing a connection with the ISP whenever Internet-bound traffic warrants. Such Internet-bound traffic might well include a SBS user surfing the Web via Internet Explorer from her desktop or the Microsoft Exchange Internet Mail Service (ISM) making a routine connection to the mail servers at your ISP.

**Power Tool Tip**

Clearly, many SBS sites can satisfy their Internet connection needs with a dial-on-demand approach to their Internet connection. Most SBS sites, relatively small when compared to enterprise-level environments, are completely satisfied with dial-on-demand connections. If not, discover the need to upgrade to a fulltime connection after you've tried a dial-on-demand connection first. Why? Because trying the cheaper dial-on-demand approach is in keeping with the small business entrepreneur's graduated thinking approach when it comes to service-levels and costs.

Microsoft recommends that a dial-on-demand connection to the ISP be configured as a Dial-Up Networking (DUN) connection: A *dialer* is configured to initiate the call to the Internet. The dialing is very fast. Unlike analog modems that take 15 or more seconds to establish an Internet connection, I've seen dial-on-demand Internet connections attach within one to three seconds.

**Power Tool Tip**

You can also configure your SBS network dial-on-demand connection to the Internet as a traditional WAN-style Internet connection. You can actually have the router dial the ISP when it has activity directed to the Internet. Such Internet-bound activity forces the router to dial the ISP. After the Internet activity ceases and a reasonable timeout period occurs, the router disconnects from the ISP. These statements will make more sense in a moment when I discuss networking topologies.

**Power Tool Tip**

One final observation on regarding dial-on-demand. With the interest in accessing internal networks across the Internet—a technique known as *virtual private networking* (*VPN*)—it was only a matter of time before the SBS community would have to address the VPN issue.

I'll say this about the VPN solution in the context of creating your Internet connection. If you deploy your router connection, you'll need to use a trick to make sure an Internet connection exists between the SBS network and the ISP. This trick is to generate Internet-bound activity between the SBS network and the ISP on a frequent basis. This you accomplish by using a tool such as Ping Plotter (included on the CD-ROM that ships with this book) to ping an IP address of a host at the ISP on a regular basis. (Another tool that has been successfully used by SBS consultants is SocketWatch.) That way, when users attempt to attach to the SBS network via a VPN approach, it's likely you'll have an Internet connection between your SBS network and ISP in progress. Be aware that this trick can result in excessive connection hours, making the fulltime connection, discussed next, a more viable solution for VPN implementations.

9

## Fulltime

This is simple to understand. The router on the SBS network simply maintains a fulltime connection to the ISP via a leased or dedicated line. End of story.

## Router Topologies

I can think of three router topologies: gateway method, double NIC method, and hybrid method. But be aware that, depending on the WAN architect, there are a variety of router-based connectivity solutions being deployed all the time. That is, this list of three will undoubtedly grow as more connectivity scenarios are perfected.

**Gateway Method**    This method should be simple to understand. At each user's SBS workstation, you simply type the router's internal (local) IP address in the TCP/IP Property sheet's Gateway field. That way, when an SBS user attempts to access the Internet, such activity results in the Gateway field on the SBS user's workstation being consulted and the Internet traffic being sent through the router to the ISP. This method does not take advantage of the firewall protection afforded by Microsoft Proxy Server (discussed on Day 11, "Using Proxy Server"). The gateway method is shown in Figure 9.3.

**FIGURE 9.3**

*Gateway method.*

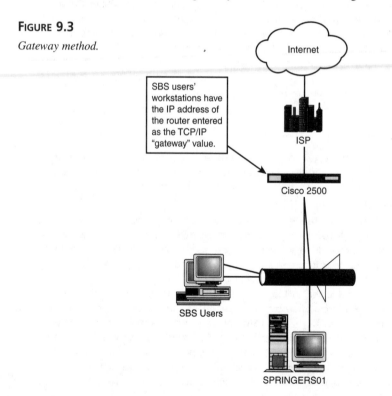

**Power Tool Tip**

I'm assuming each SBS user workstation has an internal SBS IP address of 10.0.0.x. If such is the case, you need to get out the manual that shipped with your router and both read up on and employ the router's network address translation (NAT) capability so that traffic can proceed to-and-fro between SBS user workstation and ISP.

If your SBS workstation has real Internet IP addresses, never mind what I just said.

**Double NIC Method**    This is the preferred method on an SBS network with a router. Here, the SBS server machine has two network interface cards (NICs). This approach, known in technical circles as the *multihomed approach*, results in one NIC having an internal IP address (10.0.0.x on SBS networks by default). The second NIC has a real Internet IP address and, via a crossover cable (a special network cable), connects directly to the router. The space between the two NICs is what allows Proxy Server to function as a firewall in addition to its local address table (this is explained on Day 11). The double NIC method is shown in Figure 9.4.

**FIGURE 9.4**

*Double NIC method.*

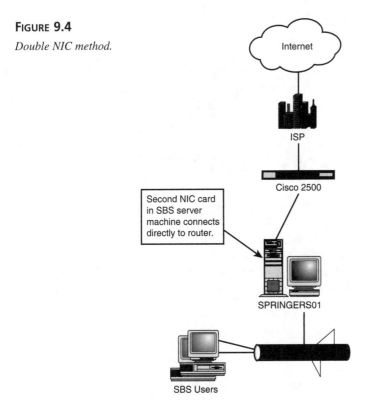

**Hybrid Method**    As I alluded to before, there are several ways to skin the
SBS/Internet router-based connection cat. One such hybrid I've seen essentially com-
bines the parts of the previous method. The SBS server had one network adapter, and all
the SBS user's traffic was routed through the SBS server, allowing Proxy Server to do its
thing: provide firewall protection. The router had the internal IP address of 10.0.0.1 (the
SBS server was 10.0.0.2 by default, as you would expect). This method is shown as
Figure 9.5.

**FIGURE 9.5**

*Hybrid method.*

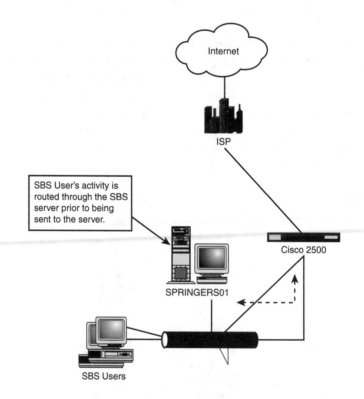

So what are the pros and cons of using the router connection approach for your SBS network? The pros are obvious: higher speed and the ability to expand your Internet connection by changing the service you have with your telco (either more or less bandwidth).
The cons are several. A router-based Internet solution requires basic design work to get it

right. You also need to coordinate different service providers, an art in its own right. These additional service providers include telcos, wiring contractors, and so on. Finally, routers are inherently more complex than simple analog modems. Routers must be programming initially and reprogrammed if changes or problems occur.

## Broadband Connections

This is a newer type of Internet connection solution and depends largely on whether your geographic area offers such services. Two broadband solutions that are available in some areas include asymmetric digital subscriber line (ADSL) or digital subscriber line (DSL) and dedicated digital line (DDL) cable modems. An ADSL/DSL solution requires that you are located within one mile of your telco's central office (CO). That's because the strength (or lack of) requires the host be relatively close to the CO. A DDL solution requires that your cable service provider offer such a service.

**Power Tool Tip**

Although these services are truly wonderful and often very cost effective, I want to emphasize my point about service limitations. Whereas my house is located three blocks from a US West CO (which I knew because it was that telco building on my neighborhood with no windows), a construction company client of mine, on a popular street with many businesses, was measured as being 2.5 miles from the nearest CO. That means they were disqualified from using a ADSL/DSL solution.

As seen in Figure 9.6, the broadband solution approximates the double NIC solution seen previously in the "Router Topologies" section.

Interestingly, these broadband solutions often offer faster download speeds than upload speeds. Why? Because Internet users typically download far more traffic than they upload!

The pros for using a broadband solution include having a high-speed Internet connection for a cost often dramatically lower than traditional router-based Internet connection solutions. The cons include the limited service availability: It is possible your location will not have either service available. Bummer!

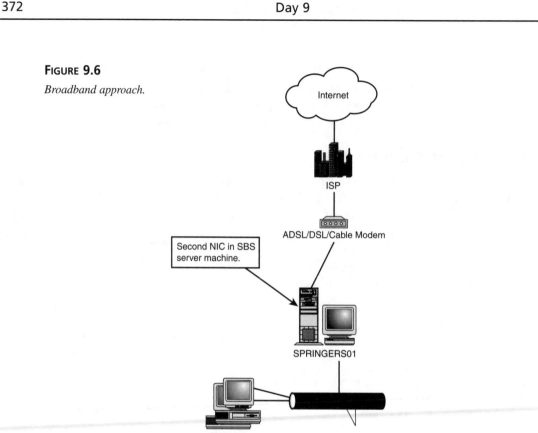

**FIGURE 9.6**

*Broadband approach.*

# Using the ICW

Now that you have spent the past few pages better understanding how SBS networks connect to the Internet, it is now time to do so. Basically, the ICW allows you to select from a list of local ISPs that are SBS friendly. This is done by calling the Microsoft Internet Referral Service via the ICW. The results of this process (known as Locate an ISP) are a list of local ISPs who can serve you.

**Caution**

Do yourself a favor and call the ISP you intend to use and ask a technical support representative whether it is SBS 4.5 friendly. In the olden days, when knights were bold, kings owned the gold, and SBS 4.0/4.0a ruled the land, trying to connect to ISPs with the ICW was a challenge on many occasions (and late nights).

Next, select an ISP and initiate the sign-up process. The ISP's sign-up server will need some basic information, which is shown in Table 9.1 for Springer Spaniels Unlimited.

**TABLE 9.1** INTERNET CONNECTION INFORMATION FOR SPRINGER SPANIELS UNLIMITED

| Item | Description | Where Used (Basic, Modem, Router, Broadband) |
|------|-------------|----------------------------------------------|
| ISP Phone Book Entry | This is the name of the dialer. | Modem |
| ISP Account Name | This is the logon Authentication account name for use when connecting with your ISP. | Modem |
| Mail Type | What type of mail do you receive? XX Exchange (SMTP) Server __ POP3 | Modem, Router, Broadband |
| Exchange SMTP Mail | Host name or IP address of ISP's SMTP server: `smtp.nwnexus.com` | Modem, Router, Broadband |
| Exchange SMTP Mail | How does your ISP receive a signal to send mail to your Exchange server: __ ETRN __ Custom Command File Location (_____) __ TURN with authentication __ No signal | Modem, Router |
| Exchange SMTP Mail | If a signal is sent to retrieve mail, how often should it be sent? _____ | Modem, Router |
| SBS Site Internet Domain Name | `springers.nwnexus.com` | Modem, Router, Broadband |

*continues*

9

**TABLE 9.1** CONTINUED

| Item | Description | Where Used (Basic, Modem, Router, Broadband) |
|------|-------------|----------------------------------------------|
| Web URL (address) | www.springers. nwnexus.com | Modem, Router, Broadband |
| Web posting URL if necessary) | ftp.springers. nwnexus.com | Modem, Router, Broadband |
| Web posting account name | cspringers | Modem, Router, Broadband |
| Web posting account password | brisker99 | Modem, Router, Broadband |
| Your router's IP address | 10.0.0.1 | Router |
| Primary DNS Server (provided by ISP) | 198.137.231.1 | Router, Modem (via Dialer) |
| Secondary DNS Server (provided by ISP) | 206.63.63.1 | Router, Modem (via Dialer) |
| Exchange SMTP Mail | DNS of ISP's mail server: N/A | Router, Broadband |
| Second NIC Card Settings | IP Address: 209.66.77.22 Subnet Mask: 255. 255.255.0 Default Gateway: 209.66.77.21 | Broadband |

**Note** This information is similar to that captured via the Information Form button on the Small Business Server Internet Connection Wizard shown in Figure 9.8. You will find a blank version of Table 9.1 in Appendix C for your use.

After you dial the ISP and provide this information, your account is created, and the ISP downloads a *.ins configuration file that configures Microsoft Exchange, Proxy Server, RAS, and so on. You will then configure your Internet connection hardware (modem, router, broadband). Got it? Great. Now do it. If this explanation wasn't clear, check for understanding with Figure 9.7 and then proceed to the following steps for using the ICW.

**Figure 9.7**

*How the ICW works.*

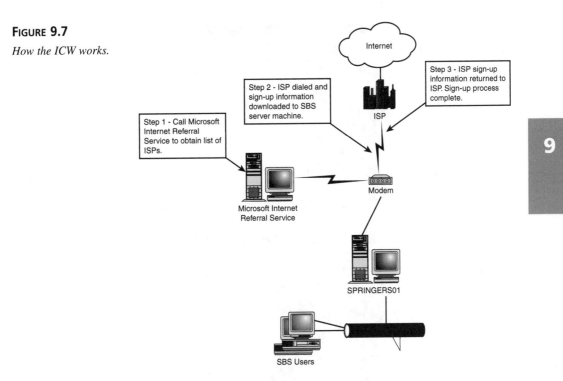

## Connecting to the Internet via the ICW

1. Make sure you logged on as an administrator or member or the Administrators group at the SBS server machine.

2. From the Start button on the desktop of the SBS Server, select SBS Console.

3. Select More Tasks.

4. Select Manage Internet Access.

5. Select Connect to the Internet. The Small Business Server Internet Connection Wizard launches, as seen in Figure 9.8.

6. Click Next. The Set Up Connection to Your ISP screen appears in the Small Business Server Connection Wizard.

7. You can now elect whether you will configure your Internet Connection via the online signup (Select an ISP for a New Internet Account) or manual configuration (Connect to the Internet) approach. This is shown in Figure 9.9. In the case of Springer Spaniels Unlimited, choose Select an ISP for a New Internet Account.

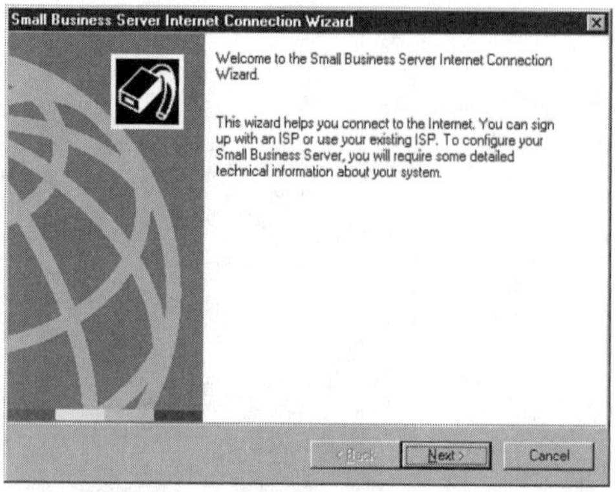

FIGURE **9.8**

*Small Business Server Internet Connection Wizard.*

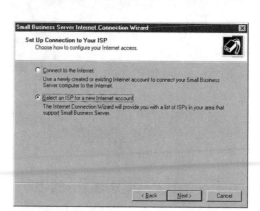

FIGURE **9.9**

*Set Up Connection to Your ISP.*

**Power Tool Tip**

The manual configuration option is a wonderful improvement in SBS 4.5 (compared to SBS 4.0). With SBS 4.0, it was difficult to configure your SBS server to use an existing ISP account. The manual configuration option radio button addresses this important issue and takes you immediately to the configure hardware stage, which I discuss in the following section, "Configuring Internet Hardware."

8. The Prepare to Sign Up Online screen appears. Make sure your modem is turned on and connected to the telco jack and press Finish.

9. The Internet Connection Wizard now starts. Click Next at the Begin Automatic Setup screen.

10. The Location Information screen appears. Confirm your area code, and type the first three digits of your phone number as requested.

11. The Microsoft Internet Referral Server is called, as seen in Figure 9.10. This is step 1 of 3 of the ICW process ("Selecting an Internet Service Provider").

**FIGURE 9.10**

*Calling the Microsoft Internet Referral Server.*

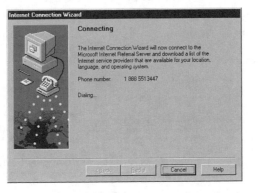

**Note**

If, for some reason, the call to the Microsoft Referral Server cannot be completed, you will see a Dialing Error dialog box similar to Figure 9.11. The Dialing Error dialog box allows you to change the way that the Microsoft Internet Referral Server is contacted.

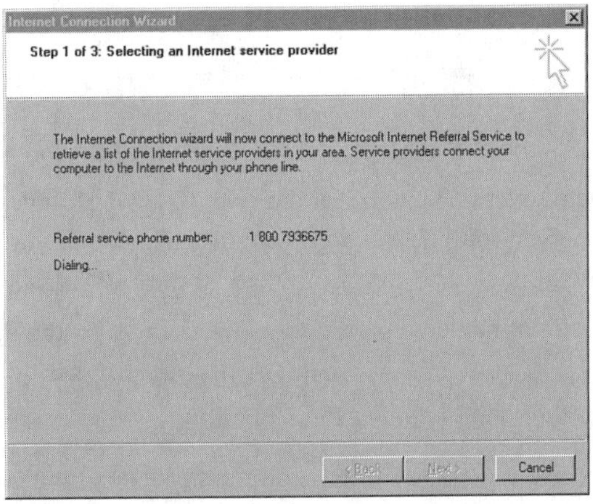

**FIGURE 9.11**

*Dialing Error.*

**Power Tool Tip**

One possible reason I've found that the call to the referral server might fail is that the dialing activity here does not use the general dialing properties (such as dialing 9 to hook an outside line). To fix specific problem (dialing 9), click the Dialing Properties button shown in Figure 9.11.

12. A list of ISPs that are SBS friendly (or compliant) is downloaded, as seen in Figure 9.12. Select the ISP that best meets your SBS Internet connection needs. If you want more information, select the More Info icon in the first column on the left; otherwise, select the Sign Me Up icon. For Springer Spaniels Unlimited, I've selected Northwest Nexus.

**FIGURE 9.12**

*ISP list.*

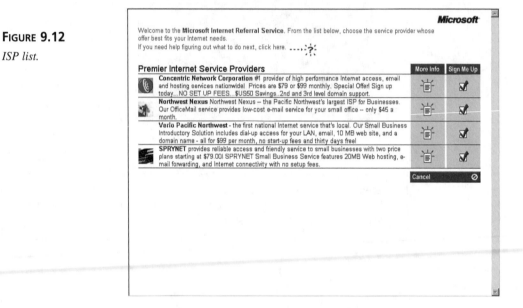

13. The ICW calls the ISP's signup server. Click Next to start the registration process.

14. You complete several steps to sign up with the ISP of your choice. This includes providing registration information including name, address, city, state, zip or postal code, country, phone, and fax. Complete all the ISP sign-up steps now.

15. Provide a domain name when requested as seen in Figure 9.14.

16. Complete any additional steps such as selecting a billing option, as seen in Figure 9.15. You will typically click a Finish button to complete the ISP sign-up process.

17. You will receive a message which communicates that the configuration process will take several minutes. Afterward, the telephone call terminates.

Congratulations! You've now successfully signed up on the Internet! SBS has been extensively configured via the ICW. These configurations include Exchange and Proxy Server. It's a very powerful process.

**FIGURE 9.13**

*Registration information.*

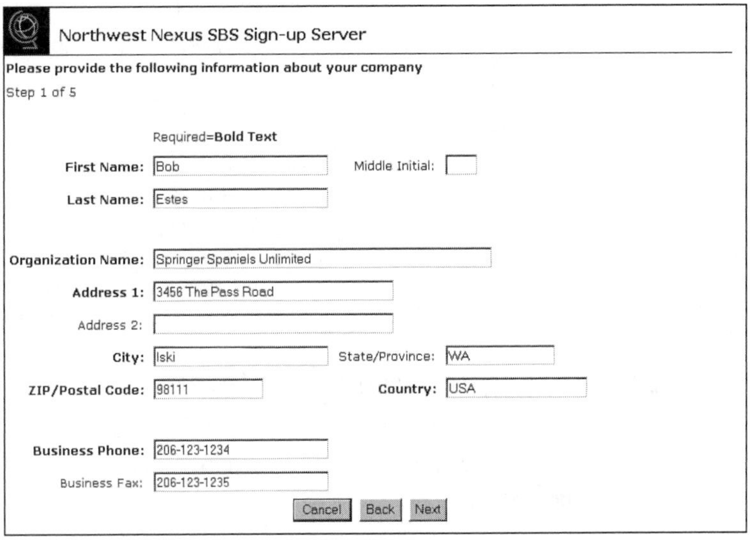

Northwest Nexus SBS Sign-up Server

Please provide the following information about your company

Step 1 of 5

Required=**Bold Text**

**First Name:** Bob        Middle Initial: [  ]

**Last Name:** Estes

**Organization Name:** Springer Spaniels Unlimited

**Address 1:** 3456 The Pass Road

Address 2: [  ]

**City:** Iski        **State/Province:** WA

**ZIP/Postal Code:** 98111        **Country:** USA

**Business Phone:** 206-123-1234

Business Fax: 206-123-1235

Cancel | Back | Next

**FIGURE 9.14**

*Select domain name.*

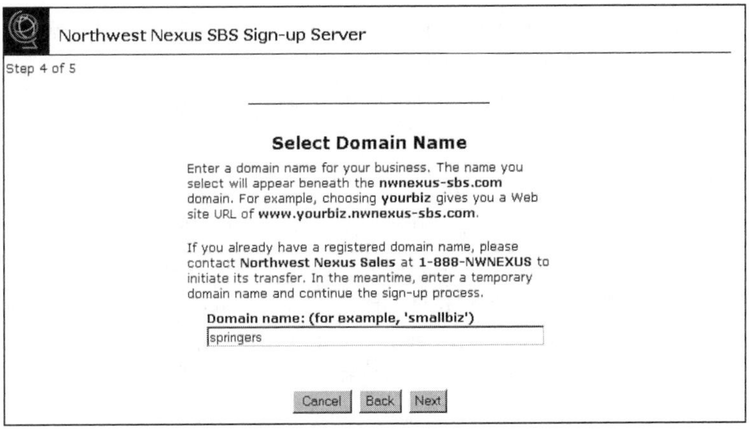

Northwest Nexus SBS Sign-up Server

Step 4 of 5

**Select Domain Name**

Enter a domain name for your business. The name you select will appear beneath the **nwnexus-sbs.com** domain. For example, choosing **yourbiz** gives you a Web site URL of **www.yourbiz.nwnexus-sbs.com**.

If you already have a registered domain name, please contact **Northwest Nexus Sales** at **1-888-NWNEXUS** to initiate its transfer. In the meantime, enter a temporary domain name and continue the sign-up process.

**Domain name: (for example, 'smallbiz')**

springers

Cancel | Back | Next

**FIGURE 9.15**

*Billing information.*

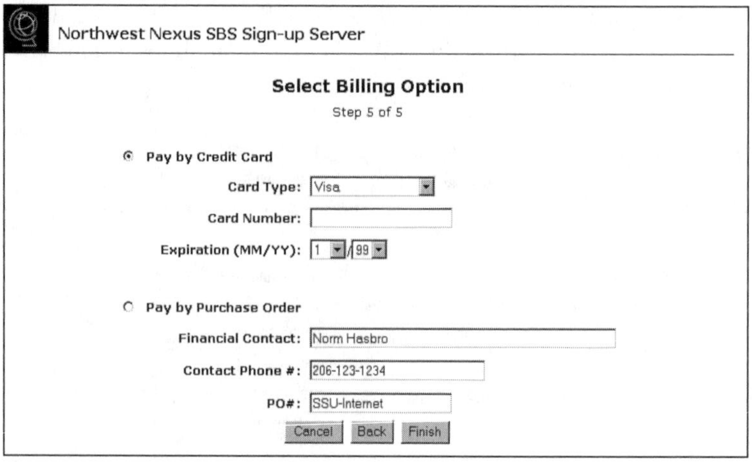

Northwest Nexus SBS Sign-up Server

**Select Billing Option**

Step 5 of 5

○ **Pay by Credit Card**

Card Type: Visa

Card Number:

Expiration (MM/YY): 1 / 99

○ **Pay by Purchase Order**

Financial Contact: Norm Hasbro

Contact Phone #: 206-123-1234

PO#: SSU-Internet

Cancel   Back   Finish

## Configuring Internet Hardware

After you complete the basic account creation with the ISP, you will next configure the Internet-related hardware used by your system. Again refer to Table 9.1 for information related to these steps.

To configure Internet hardware

1. Make sure you're logged on as an administrator or member of the Administrators group at the SBS server machine.

2. From the Start button on the desktop of the SBS Server, select SBS Console.

3. Select More Tasks.

4. Select Manage Internet Access.

5. Select Configure Internet Hardware. The Small Business Server Internet Connection Wizard launches (similar to that seen in Figure 9.8). Click Next.

6. The Configure Hardware screen appears as seen in Figure 9.16. I will explore each of the options: Modem (starting with step 7), Router (starting with step 16) and Full-time/Broadband Modem (starting with step 19).

7. Select Modem or Terminal Adapter and click Next.

**Note**

Selecting the Modem Form button displays a table that allows you to gather and organize the type of hardware information presented in Table 9.1.

**FIGURE 9.16**

*Configure Hardware.*

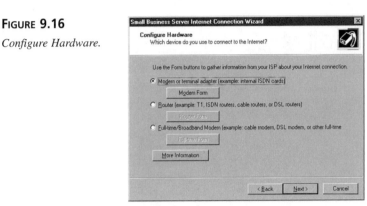

8. The Set Up Modem Connection to ISP screen appears. Figure 9.17 shows it completed for Springer Spaniels Unlimited. Click Next.

**FIGURE 9.17**

*Set Up Modem
Connection to ISP.*

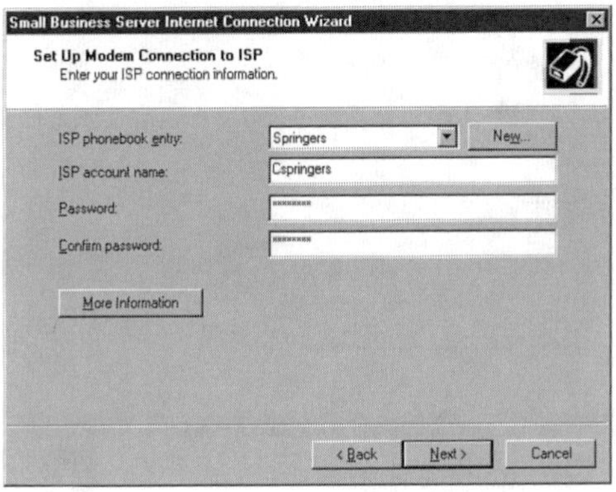

9. The Configure Internet Mail Settings screen appears, as shown in Figure 9.18. For Springer Spaniels Unlimited, select Use Exchange Server for Internet Mail. Note that this is the most common selection when setting up SBS. Click Next.

10. The Configure SMTP Mail Delivery screen appears. Figure 9.19 shows it completed for Springer Spaniels Unlimited. Click Next.

11. The Receive Exchange Mail screen appears. For Springer Spaniels Unlimited, select Send a Signal and select the ETRN command. This is shown in Figure 9.20. Click Next.

12. The Configure Internet Domain Name screen appears. Enter your Internet domain name similar to that seen in Figure 9.21. Select the I Want to Use the Web Publishing Wizard check box. Click Next.

**FIGURE 9.18**

*Configure Internet Mail Settings.*

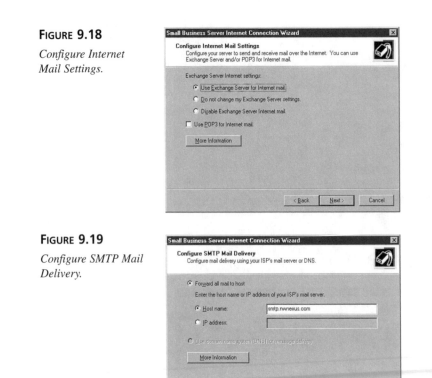

**FIGURE 9.19**

*Configure SMTP Mail Delivery.*

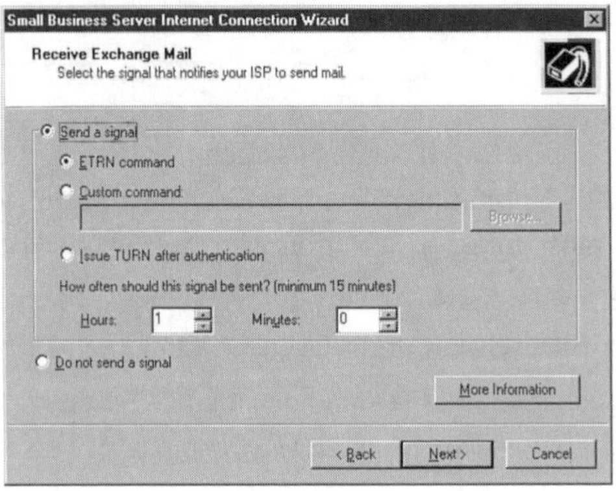

**FIGURE 9.20**

*Receive Exchange Mail.*

**FIGURE 9.21**

*Configure Internet
Domain Name.*

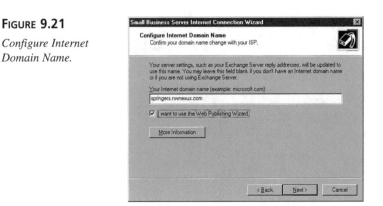

13. The Configure Web Site Information screen appears (see Figure 9.22). It has been completed for Springer Spaniels Unlimited based on the information contained in Table 9.1. Click Next.

**FIGURE 9.22**

*Configure Web Site
Information.*

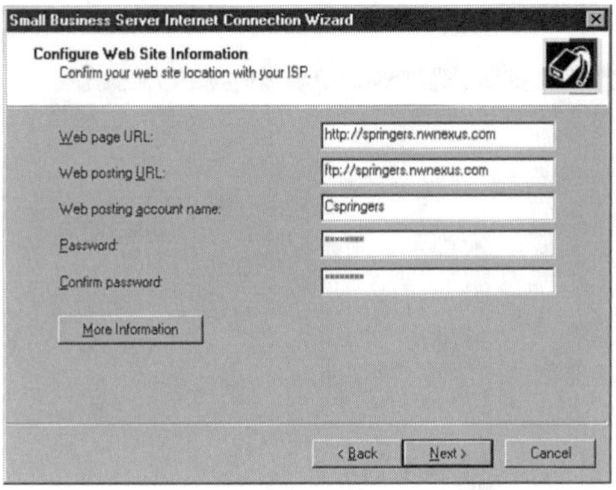

14. The Complete Firewall Settings screen appears and is seen in Figure 9.23. Click Next.

**Note**

This has been completed for Springer Spaniel Unlimited and will be fully explained on Day 11.

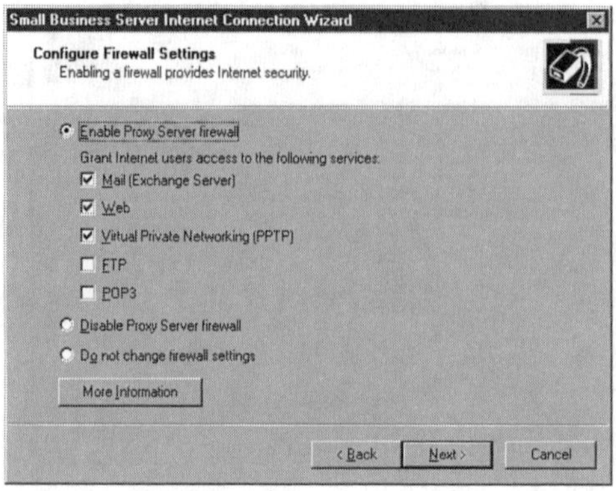

**FIGURE 9.23**

*Configure Firewall
Settings.*

15. Click Finish to complete the Internet hardware configuration.

16. If you selected the Router option on the Configure Hardware screen (Figure 9.16) and click Next, you will see the Set Up Router Connection to ISP screen (Figure 9.24). This has been completed for Springer Spaniels Unlimited. Click Next.

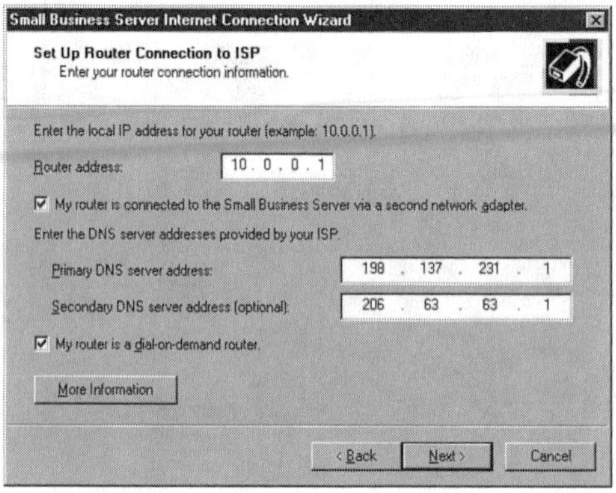

**FIGURE 9.24**

*Set Up Router
Connection to ISP.*

17. If you use a second NIC, you then select which NIC you want to use for the LAN and which NIC you want to use for the Internet (on a screen similar to Figure 9.25). If you use only one NIC, go to step 18.

18. You then provide e-mail, Exchange-related, domain naming, and Web site information similar to that seen in steps 12 through 15.

19. If you select the Full-time/Broadband Modem option on the Configure Hardware screen (Figure 9.16) and click Next, you see the Network Interface Card Configuration screen.

**FIGURE 9.25**

*Network Interface Card Configuration.*

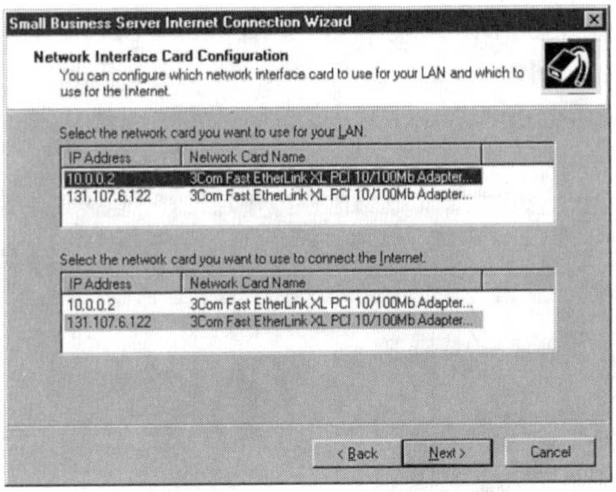

20. Provide the necessary IP address and DNS address information. Click Next. Note this information was gathered on Table 9.1.

21. You will then provide e-mail, Exchange-related, domain naming and Web site information similar to that seen in steps 12 through 15.

You have now completed your connection to the Internet using the SBS way! This includes both the Internet account setup and hardware setup.

# Using Internet Explorer

Before you break for lunch, here is an opportunity to either learn or revisit your skills in using Microsoft's Web browser of choice in SBS, Internet Explorer (IE) version 5.0.

**Note**

This is another key area of improvement between SBS 4.0 and SBS 4.5: the upgrade of IE 4.0 to IE 5.0. You might recall that I first introduced key IE 5.0 features on Day 1 of this book.

IE is, of course, a Web browser. A *Web browser* is the tool you use to surf or navigate the Web. To surf the Web, you simply type a valid Web site address in the Address field located near the top of IE and press the Enter key. Such an address might look like www.microsoft.com or www.mcp.com. After a connection to the Internet is established (using one of the approaches discussed previously), the home page for the Web address you selected will be displayed. There are, as you probably know, millions of Web addresses on the Internet (and plenty of search engines such as www.infoseek.com to help you find these addresses).

By default, IE launches the Microsoft Small Business Server Home Page when you double-click the Internet Explorer icon on the desktop of an SBS user's computer. This is known as the default home page and is shown in Figure 9.26.

**FIGURE 9.26**

*The Microsoft Small Business Server home page.*

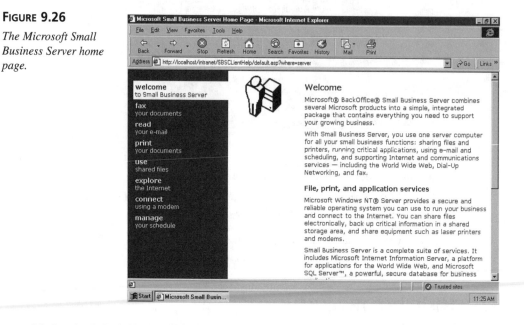

Notice the default home page for SBS users displays a variety of help topics in the left pane, ranging from a welcome notice to tips on how to manage your schedule.

If you are interested in learning the finer points about IE 5.0, consult *Sams Teach Yourself Internet Explorer 5 in 24 Hours* by Jill Freeze (ISBN 0-672-31328-6).

**Note**

Although I only introduced IE 5.0 here, don't underestimate the importance of IE 5.0 on an SBS network. With the world moving toward Web-based network computing, your SBS users will likely use IE 5.0 often during the day and keep the browser open at all times.

# Lunch

It's time for lunch. Go grab a quick bite to eat and when you return, I'll speak to you about how the Internet connectivity area is one of the key reasons for upgrading to SBS 4.5.

Welcome back. I want to spend a few moments painting a slightly different picture of SBS 4.5 and its value to the small business. Prior to SBS 4.5, you were basically locked into using a modem-based solution for your automatically configured Internet solution. If you were brave in the SBS 4.0 days, you might have ventured forward and manually configured the underlying Windows NT Server operating system and BackOffice applications to use a faster Internet connection. More likely, you paid an MCSE-type consultant to come in and do it for you, and I'll bet you were surprised when said consultant billed you for 8 hours in the $100–200-per-hour range. For some, hiring a consultant to implement a high speed Internet solution quickly surpassed the initial outlay for the SBS software itself.

But, suffice it to say, everything has changed in SBS 4.5 with respect to Internet connections. Plain and simple, Microsoft got it right with the Internet Connection Wizard in SBS 4.5. You are now offered seven ways to Egypt to configure your Internet connection, all from the ICW! It's a great improvement over the SBS 4.0 days. It's also a practical improvement because it saves small businesses real money as they seek to implement high-speed Internet connections. And you, as well as I, know that high-speed Internet connections are a reality for small businesses today.

I've already found that the ease in configuring the Internet connection is a compelling reason for firms to implement SBS 4.5. It's a major improvement between SBS 4.0 and SBS 4.5: something that's not lost on SBS consultants such as myself and small-business people seeking the biggest bang for their SBS bucks!

Speaking of bucks, implementing a robust Internet connection today under SBS 4.5 is the first step toward participating in the exploding world of electronic commerce (e-commerce). Consider it a first step, but before you can grasp and exploit e-commerce opportunities, you need a high-speed Internet connection. That's because you need to transfer files to and from your ISP. For example, you'll benefit from the fast upload speed when you post a new price list, graphics, or inventory list to your Web page (I'm assuming it's hosted at the ISP's site). You'll also benefit greatly when you download the files, loaded with purchase transaction data, from the ISP's database to your accounting system. That's a lot of fun when the dollars roll in.

Thanks for listening.

# ☾ PM Advanced Network Topology and Internet Configuration Issues

This morning I showed you how to take advantage of the various Internet connection configurations supported by the ICW. This afternoon I'll share a hodgepodge of tips and tricks related to SBS 4.5's Internet connectivity. You might even conclude the day a few minutes early, allowing you to beat the evening rush hour!

## Dealing with Broadband Networks

One network topology issue you're likely to encounter concerns broadband networks. Here I happen to have personal experience. On the West Coast, a regional telco (US West) offers ADSL/DSL service, known as MegaBit, to businesses as part of a broadband Internet connection solution. For a nominal fee (under $250 for setup and starting at $40 per month), you receive an ADSL/DSL service, a second NIC for your computer and a Cisco 675 router. The Cisco router, however, isn't really acting as a router: it's acting as a bridge. That means all Internet traffic destined for your site is passed through unfiltered (not a super-huge concern given you have Microsoft Proxy Server 2.0 to act as your firewall).

Because traffic passes through unfiltered in the ADSL/DSL broadband scenario, the SBS server in this case (located at the same Northwest property management firm I've mentioned throughout the book) received DHCP Server broadcast announcement packets directed to its second NIC (the one with the real Internet IP address). Again, this is relatively harmless except for one thing: These rogue DHCP Server broadcast announcement packets caused the SBS's DHCP Server service to shut off. Hours of work and lots of mind share later, I ultimately disabled SBS's DHCP Server service and assigned a 10.0.0.x static IP address to the SBS workstations on the property management firm's SBS network. It worked like a charm!

Likewise, Microsoft has an official position concerning competing DHCP Servers on the same SBS network. According to Microsoft, when using a router-based solution for your SBS Internet connection, it is critical that you disable the router's DHCP Server functionality, or else SBS's DHCP Server service will shut down. Sound familiar?

## Changing an Internet Domain Name

One matter sure to rear its head during your life as an SBS practitioner is changing an Internet domain name. This matter can become important to you because, using the ICW, many ISPs support only third-level Internet domain names (for example `springers.nwnexus.com`). But, in reality, most businesses desire a second-level domain name for marketing and appearance purposes (for example `springers.com`).

Here, using some of your Windows NT Server–centric knowledge can actually get you in trouble (you're probably tempted to change the domain name settings under the DNS tab of the TCP/IP Properties dialog box and monkey with the Microsoft Exchange ISM). Instead, you need to practice a little SBS Zen and think like the SBSer you're quickly becoming. That is, use the SBS Console to solve this problem.

> **Tip**
>
> Any time you obtain or change an Internet domain name, be sure you're working hand in hand with your ISP. Your failure to do so will, at a minimum, result in a disruption of service.

To change your Internet domain name in SBS:

1. Make sure you logged on as an administrator or member or the Administrators group at the SBS server machine.
2. From the Start button on the desktop of the SBS Server, select SBS Console.
3. Select More Tasks.
4. Select Manage Internet Access.
5. Select Change Internet Settings. The Small Business Server Connectivity Wizard launches. Click Next.
6. The Change Internet Settings dialog box appears. Select Change Internet Domain Name. This is seen in Figure 9.27. Click Next.

**FIGURE 9.27**

*Change Internet Settings.*

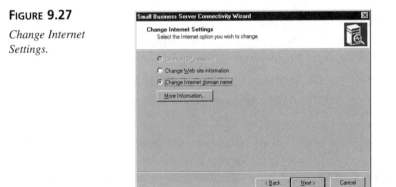

7. The Change Internet Domain Name dialog box is displayed as seen in Figure 9.28. I'd advise you to coordinate the Internet domain name change with your ISP. Select the My ISP Has Changed My Internet Domain Name check box. Click Next. In this example, the domain name `springers.nwnexus.com` is being changed to `springers.com`.

FIGURE 9.28

*Change Internet Domain Name.*

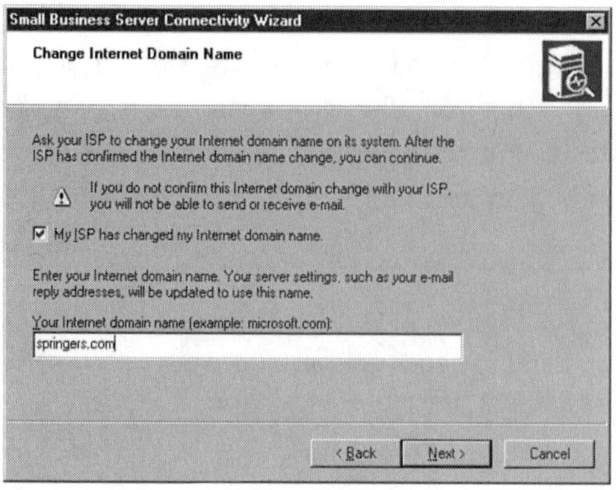

8. In the next dialog box, select Finish for the Internet domain name changes to be made. These changes include Registry changes, TCP/IP configuration changes, and Microsoft Exchange changes.

## ISP and INS Files

SBS uses two critical files to set up the Internet service. The msicw.isp file is used by the ICW to initially call the Microsoft Internet Referral Service server and download a list of SBS friendly ISPs. When you select an ISP, the ISP downloads its own ISP file which, running as a script, collects the following information from you:

- Accounting information (name, address, billing information)
- Creation of a third-level Internet domain name
- Storage space at the ISP configured to host your Web site (Microsoft's preferred solution that I discuss more on Days 10, "Internet Information Server/Index Server," and 12, "Publishing on the Internet/Intranet.")
- The DNS resource records (A host name and MX mail exchange) at the ISP
- The mail server at the ISP to queue and dequeue e-mail associated with your account

Next, when the ISP is called again (when you complete the sign-up information), an INS file is downloaded from the ISP to your SBS server machine. This INS file has all the information needed to seamlessly configure your SBS server machine to use the ISP. This configuration includes

- Creating a RAS configuration connection to call the ISP
- Configuring the ISM in Microsoft Exchange Server
- Modifying the Registry as needed

**Power Tool Tip**

This INS file that is downloaded from the ISP is sacred! It is stored as \winnt.sbs\connection wizard\sbscfg.ins and can be used to restore your correct ISP connection parameters if said parameters somehow become corrupt. Such a restore process requires that you type the following command from a command prompt while in the \winnt.sbs\connect wizard folder: **isignup sbscfg.ins**.

## Advanced IE Issues

At more SBS sites than I care to recall, there is always an SBS user (or two or three) who insists on maintaining his existing ISP services (typically AOL, MSN, or CompuServe). Often, these users have a local modem that they've used for years to call their ISP (and they're not interested in giving it up!). Because accommodating an SBS user's request is a virtue, I often permit these dual ISP service scenarios to exist. However, you must make one minor change at the SBS user's workstation to allow multiple ISP services to coexist in a manner similar to what I've described.

This change is simple, but it must be managed by the end user. First, you need to understand that, as part of the SBS client installation process, the Winsock Proxy (WSP) icon is added to the SBS user's workstation Control Panel. It is automatically selected to redirect Internet-related activity such as Web browsing to the Proxy Server running on the SBS server machine. This is normal and good.

But, when the SBS user wants to call AOL, MSN, or CompuServe, the user needs to deselect the WSP setting titled Enable WinSock Proxy Client manually, as shown in Figure 9.29, and reboot. At that time, Internet traffic is not redirected to the Proxy Server on the SBS server machine, and the SBS user can surf via AOL or her old ISP to her heart's content.

**FIGURE 9.29**

*WSP settings.*

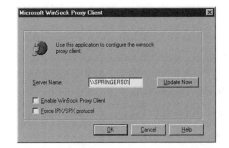

Likewise, when the AOL-type session is over, the same SBS user must reconfigure the WSP client by selecting the Enable WinSock Proxy Client check box in Figure 9.29.

> **Note**  Each time the WSP client is modified, a reboot of the SBS user's workstation must occur.

And then there was the online trading account matter at the downtown Seattle law firm. Here, the law firm managed its treasury cash via a Web-based session with its stock brokerage. Everything worked fine under Netscape and a simple local modem connection from Paula's workstation until I arrived and implemented a complete SBS network. Paula was now using the SBS IE client instead of Netscape, and she couldn't access her online stock brokerage account. A key point was that the on-line account used `https://`, not `http://`, which means, via the HTTP protocol, a secure session was established (which is what you would expect for an online trading account). A quick check at the SBS server machine revealed that Paula had sufficient rights to interact with the Internet, as far as Proxy Server was concerned. But, back at Paula's workstation, I noticed that SBS, as part of its client installation, doesn't allow secure or https:// activity to be directed from IE to Proxy Server. This is accessed via the Connection sheet in IE's Internet Explorer Properties dialog box.

In order to use a secure Web site (`https://`), you need to manually configure IE's Internet Properties:

1. From the SBS user's machine desktop, secondary-click Internet Explorer.
2. Select Properties from IE's secondary menu. Internet Explorer Properties is displayed.
3. Select the Connections sheet
4. Select the LAN Settings button. The Local Area Network (LAN) Settings dialog box is displayed.
5. Select the Use a Proxy Server check box in the Proxy Server portion of the Local Area Network (LAN) Settings dialog box.
6. Select the Advanced button.
7. Complete the Secure fields with the address of the proxy server (10.0.0.2 by default) and port (80) in a manner similar to that seen for the HTTP settings. This is shown in Figure 9.30.
8. Click OK successively (three times) until you are back at the SBS user's machine desktop.

FIGURE **9.30**

*Proxy Settings.*

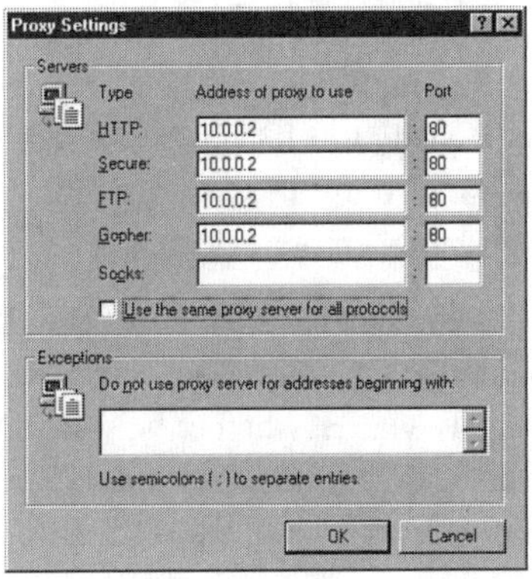

**Note**

By selecting the Use the Same Proxy Server for All Protocols check box on the Proxy Settings dialog box, you do not need to enter the address manually and port information for the Secure fields.

You have now configured IE to interact with secure Web sites such as stock brokerage firms. You do not need to reboot the SBS user's workstations and can simply double-click the Internet Explorer icon to use IE.

**Power Tool Tip**

You might have noticed that the Socks setting in Figure 9.30 was also not configured by default with SBS. You need to manually configure this setting if you have explicit Socks traffic via IE.

**Power Tool Tip**

Don't inadvertently modify IE's basic connection settings (no use of Proxy Server or modem connection); otherwise, you risk having the SBS Console fail at startup. For example, when I modified IE on the SBS server machine's desktop to use Proxy Server and a modem connection, I received an HTTP Error 403 that reported sternly "403.6 Forbidden: IP address rejected" when I launched the SBS Console. By the way, I eliminated this error message, IE-related Proxy Server and modem settings intact, by selecting the Bypass proxy server for local addresses check box on the Local Area Network (LAN) Settings dialog box.

Consider my advice and don't modify the IE 5.0 connection setting for the IE installation on the SBS server machine.

I end this day with the prominent Northwest developer I featured extensively on the Outlook day. This gentleman, a surprisingly savvy SBS user given his executive position, wanted to understand how he could easily use IE via Proxy Server on his laptop to connect to the Internet while at work but also use IS via a dial-up connection while on the road. Before I give you the answer, here is more evidence.

The core problem is this: In IE 4.0, you had to select between a LAN connection (where Proxy Server is located) and a modem connection. The Northwest developer was using this version. For him to connect easily via IE, whether he was in the office or not, he either had to have two copies of IE installed (one for Proxy Server, one for the modem) or use a switcher tool such as NetSwitcher (www.netswitcher.com).

IE 5.0, this matter has been addressed head on. On the Connections sheet on the Internet Explorer Properties dialog box (seen in Figure 9.31), you can configure your LAN settings via the LAN Settings button (for Proxy Server) but also select the Dial the Default Connection When Needed check box.

**FIGURE 9.31**

*Connections sheet.*

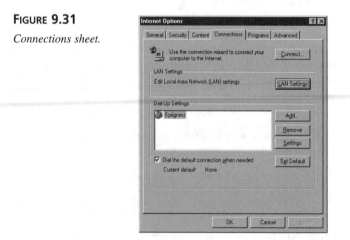

The bottom line? If IE can't connect via the LAN and Proxy Server, the dial-out connection you've configured will be tried. This is incredibly useful for your SBS laptop users.

# Summary

You've reached the end of Day 9, a key day for us because it focused on Internet connectivity. The improved Internet connectivity solutions in SBS 4.5 represents the greatest area of improvement for this SBS release, compared to its SBS 4.0 predecessor. Given that you have now connected to the Internet via SBS, you're ready to explore several Internet connectivity components over the next three days.

# DAY 10

# Internet Information Server/Index Server

Welcome to Day 10. Today you will learn not only about SBS's Microsoft Internet Information Server (IIS) and Microsoft Index Server but also about one or two ways that these products are being used at SBS sites. Today is a day for everyone to attend all day long because it's a relatively short day plus the morning and afternoon content don't easily divide between beginning and advanced discussions. In the morning session, I'll discuss IIS; the afternoon session is for Microsoft Index Server.

## AM Defining IIS

On the one hand, you can say "Wow! IIS sure has changed between SBS 4.0 and SBS 4.5." That is true, and I'll take a few pages to introduce IIS 4.0 to you. On the other hand, you can rightfully ask How does IIS really apply to my SBS site? I'll start with that matter: How does IIS apply to you, the SBS site?

## IIS and SBS Sites

Truth be told, IIS is used for only a few things at SBS sites:

- SBS Console hosting—Perhaps the best-known duty for IIS on an SBS server machine is to host the SBS Console. If, for some reason, IIS malfunctions (for example, the WWW service doesn't start), the SBS Console will not appear when selected.

- Intranet management—SBS has a default home page that is served by IIS to the SBS network. Don't believe me? Turn off the WWW service (found in the Services applet in Control Panel) and then try to launch the SBS Console or Internet Explorer (which automatically launches the default SBS home page). Without the WWW service running, both of these tasks fail. Turn on the WWW service, and everything will work.

> **Note**
>
> Services are a scary place to be if you don't know what you're doing. Services are, as they sound, applications that provide core services to the underlying Windows NT Server operating system in SBS. Make a mistake here and you're bound to pay. Be careful when interacting with services.

- Intranet creation—In your spare time as an SBS administrator, you might also be motivated to create your own intranet site. Use IIS to manage the directory that holds your intranet home page files. (You would use Front Page 98 to create the home page; Front Page 98 is discussed on Day 12, "Publishing on the Internet/Intranet.")

- IIS and Proxy service management—Out of the box, you should have little need to configure Proxy Server's Socks Proxy, Web Proxy, or WinSock Proxy services. If you do, you perform these configuration tasks via IIS.

- FTP site deployment and maintenance—FTP is an approach to transferring large amounts of data. SBS sites such as printing shops, which need to receive large files (50MB or greater in size) from clients, have embraced the FTP capabilities of IIS.

## IIS and the Enterprise

Contrast the previous points about IIS in an enterprise-level environment (over 1,000 users). First, you need to understand that IIS is a very popular application at the enterprise level. Electronic commerce is conducted here as Web sites are hosted locally. The enterprise is also the land of large intranets, so to somehow imply that IIS isn't robust and popular would easily offend my enterprise-level brethren. Indeed IIS is one of the most popular applications in Big BackOffice. It is one of the most underused applications in SBS. Feel free to draw your own conclusions.

## Microsoft's Position

Surprisingly, several public documents from Microsoft relating to IIS also downplay its importance as part of your SBS site. In fact, Microsoft recommends that you not use IIS to host a Web site on your local SBS server machine for a number of reasons: speed, connection reliability, and even security. Microsoft supports hosting your Web site at your ISP. Typically, ISPs make 5MB of disk space available to users for a nominal fee to store and serve Web pages to the public. The benefits of doing this are

- ISPs have fat Internet pipes—Whereas you can connect to your ISP from your Small Business Server with a modem, ISDN, or DSL line, the ISP is connected to the Internet with very large pipes (OC3, and so on). That means someone viewing your Web page hosted by your ISP benefits from the high connection speeds supported directly by the ISP.

- ISPs are very reliable—Compared to the small business, ISPs are far more reliable when it comes to ongoing service. In a windstorm, a small business can suffer intermittent power failures, but an ISP typically has huge backup batteries, generators, and so on to stay online.

- ISPs offer better security—Clearly, if your Web page is hosted at the ISP's site, surfers, hackers, and the like can't break into your local SBS system via their Web browsing activities (it is physically impossible). This last point allows small business owners to sleep just a little better at night.

> **Tip**
>
> I have heard from other SBS gurus who I trust greatly in this area, and the consensus is that you shouldn't even expose your SBS server machine to the Internet in such a prominent way as hosting your own WWW pages locally. Use the ISP!

## The Yvonne Test

One more take on IIS in SBS sets the stage for this discussion. Ask yourself, how does IIS pass the Yvonne test? The Yvonne test is a test I apply when evaluating how an organization will use SBS and be successful. Yvonne is a secretary in a small legal firm in the

Northwest. She is also the part-time SBS administrator. Her world is focused more on litigation and filing deadlines than on IIS and Index Server (as it should rightfully be). So, as you apply the Yvonne test, ask how would IIS, as part of SBS, make Yvonne's life substantially better? On a day-to-day basis, not greatly, but I don't want to leave you with that negative thought. As you'll see this afternoon, Microsoft Index Server passes the Yvonne test with flying colors!

## IIS Changes

Now, about the changes in IIS between SBS 4.0 and SBS 4.5. Primarily is IIS's appearance, as seen in Figure 10.1.

**FIGURE 10.1**

*IIS.*

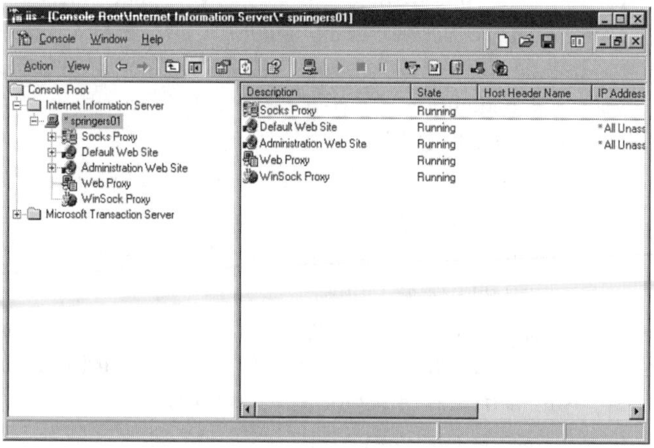

In SBS 4.5, IIS has been upgraded from IIS 3.0 to IIS 4.0, which includes many more features and functions (largely oriented toward enterprise-level sites). It runs inside of the Microsoft Management Console (MMC) which you can see in Figure 10.1. How can you tell this even though the MMC term isn't displayed on the screen? Go to the Help menu and observe the About Microsoft Management Console menu option.

**Power Tool Tip**

Want to prepare for the future? Then embrace the MMC today. It's Microsoft's new management tool that the company will increasingly incorporate into future releases of SBS and the underlying Windows NT Server operating system.

Another change is how IIS is presented in SBS 4.5. Earlier IIS had its own program group and was really viewed as an integral part of the Windows NT Server operating system. In SBS 4.5, IIS is now installed as part of the Option Pack, a topic that is discussed on Day 18, "Advanced Topics: Service Pack 4 and the Option Pack."

**Note**

> Just as interesting is noticing what is missing from IIS in SBS 4.5. By default, the FTP server service isn't installed when SBS 4.5 installs IIS. That's because SBS 4.5 performs a minimal, not a typical or a custom, installation of IIS, so the FTP server is left out in the cold. But fear not. I'll show you how to install the FTP server in SBS 4.5 later today (because this is one of the IIS services that has been embraced by SBS sites).

**10**

# IIS Specifics

Allow me to be a feature creature for just a bit so I can properly introduce you to IIS. In the next few paragraphs, I'll define the different services which provide IIS with its capabilities.

- World Wide Web Service—This is the core service for IIS and, in IIS 4.0, has taken a background role (even though it has a hand in everything the occurs). Technically speaking, the WWW service handles the publishing of Web pages, including directory identification, security, access capabilities, and so on. It is considered a Master Property in IIS and is managed from the site property sheet (which you'll see in a moment).

- Socks Proxy—This service allows UNIX and Macintosh client computers to access a rich variety of Internet services. This service is discussed on Day 11, "Using Proxy Server."

- Default Web Site—This is the default SBS Web site that is managed by the underlying WWW service.

- Administration Web Site—This is the IIS help system supported by the underlying WWW service.

- Web Proxy—This service supports the HTTP, HTTP-S (a.k.a. S-HHTP), FTP, and gopher protocols, providing wide-ranging access to the Internet/intranet for browsers and Internet applications. This service is discussed on Day 11.

- WinSock Proxy—This service enables a rich variety of Internet services for Windows-based client PCs. Technically, it supports such protocols as Telnet and RealAudio. This service will be discussed on Day 11.

# Using IIS with SBS

Practically speaking, IIS runs very well out of the box when you install SBS. For most SBS sites, you have little need to fiddle with IIS. But I'll share two practical real-world examples of how to use IIS on your SBS network: creating an intranet and creating an FTP site to transfer files with your external clients.

## Creating an Intranet

As you might know, SBS already ships with a canned intranet site known as the Default Web Site (see Figure 10.1). The SBS-related intranet home page content resides here (it is actually mapped to c:\inetpub\wwwroot). But you might desire to create your own intranet site separate from that provided at SBS's Default Web Site. Here is how you do that:

1. Log on to your SBS server machine as an administrator or member of the administrators group.

2. Launch the SBS Console from the Start button.

3. Select Tasks and then select Manage Shared Folders.

4. Select Create or share a folder. The Share a Folder Wizard will appear. Click Next.

5. In the To Create a New Folder, Type a New Name field at the bottom of the Select a Folder screen, type **c:\puppy** and click Next. Answer Yes if prompted to create the folder because it doesn't exist (this will be a small warning dialog box).

6. Accept the share name as "puppy" in the Specify the Shared Name for this Folder screen. Type the following description in the Type a Description field: **This is the Puppy Hall of Fame Web Site.** Click Next.

7. Accept the default access permissions on the Select the Users who can Access Puppy screen. Click Next.

8. Click Finish. Click OK when advised that the wizard successfully created puppy.

9. Close the SBS Console.

10. Launch the Internet Service Manager application from the Microsoft Internet Information Server program group. This is a difficult application to find, because it is nested four layers deep in the Start menu structure. First, click Start from the SBS desktop. Select Programs, Windows NT 4.0 Option Pack, Microsoft Internet Information Server, Internet Service Manager.

11. The new Microsoft Management Console (MMC) launches and displays two options underneath the Console Root in the left panel: Internet Information Server and Microsoft Transaction Server. Expand Internet Information Server.

12. You now see your site listed (which has the same name as your SBS server machine). As seen in Figure 10.2, this is springers01. Expand the site by clicking on the + sign next to the site name.

13. The expanded site displays allow of the IIS components in the left pane of the MMC, as seen in Figure 10.2.

**FIGURE 10.2**

*Springers01 IIS Site.*

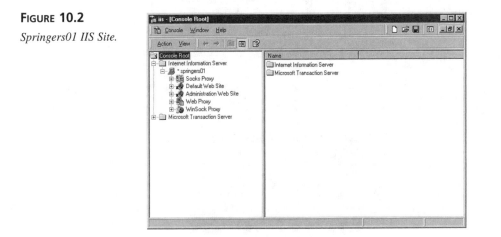

14. Right-click the site (for example, springers01), select New from the secondary menu, and select Web Site from the site menu that appears. The New Web Site Wizard runs, as shown in Figure 10.3. Type **Puppy Hall of Fame** in the Web Site Description field. Click Next.

**FIGURE 10.3**

*New Web Site Wizard.*

15. Accept the default conditions for IP address and TCP port on the next screen (see Figure 10.4). Click Next.

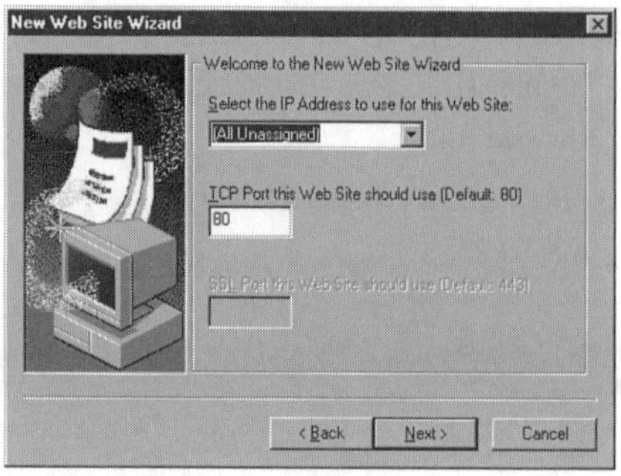

**FIGURE 10.4**

*IP Address and TCP Port.*

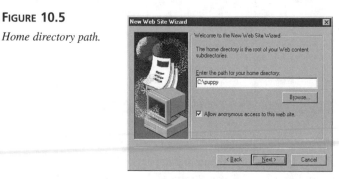

16. Click the Browse button and select the c:\puppy folder or type **c:\puppy** in the Enter the Path to Your Home Directory field (see Figure 10.5). Click Next.

**FIGURE 10.5**

*Home directory path.*

17. Accept the default permissions (Allow Read Access, Allow Script Access) as seen in Figure 10.6. Click Next.

**FIGURE 10.6**

*Access Permissions.*

18. Click Finish. You have now created the Puppy Hall of Fame Web site location. On Day 12, you'll create the Puppy Hall of Fame Web page.

19.  Close the MMC. Do not save the MMC setting when prompted (this message doesn't apply to the IIS tasks you just performed—it is a misleading message).

Note that the Puppy Hall of Fame Web site now appears in the left pane of the IIS MMC, as seen in Figure 10.7. You'll leave it alone for now until you create the Puppy Hall of Fame Web page on Day 12.

**FIGURE 10.7**

*Puppy Hall of Fame Web site.*

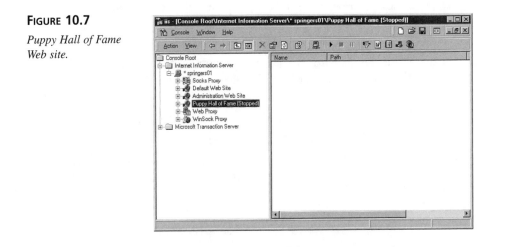

**10**

> **Note**
>
> Don't worry about the Stopped condition for the Puppy Hall of Fame Web site. You'll start it when you're ready to use it.

## Creating an FTP Site

Many small businesses need to transfer files between themselves and clients. In the printing and graphics businesses, these files are often very large, requiring an FTP server (which is best equipped for large file transfers). Using e-mail is impractical when it comes to transferring such large files.

> **Note**
>
> I assume you have either a full-time router-based or broadband connection from your SBS server machine to the Internet. This was discussed on Day 9, "Connecting to the Internet." Practically speaking, to have a functional FTP site, you must have a full-time Internet connection that allows your customers to access your FTP site to both send and receive files.

As I mentioned earlier, the FTP server service is not installed by default with SBS, so you must first install the FTP server service. Here's how you do it:

1. Log on to your SBS server machine as an administrator or member of the administrators group.

2. Launch the Windows NT 4.0 Option Pack Setup application from the Windows NT 4.0 Option Pack program group. This application is nested three layers deep in the Start menu structure. First, click Start from the SBS desktop. Select Programs, Windows NT 4.0 Option Pack, Windows NT 4.0 Option Pack Setup.

3. Note that Setup is initializing. If you see a setup message warning you about the risks of using the SMTP service with the Microsoft Exchange Internet Mail Service, click OK.

4. You see the Windows NT 4.0 Option Pack Setup Wizard. Click Next.

5. On the next screen, click the Add/Remove button.

6. You see the Select Components screen. Click or select the Internet Information Server (IIS) line item and click the Show Subcomponents button (seen in Figure 10.8). Click Next.

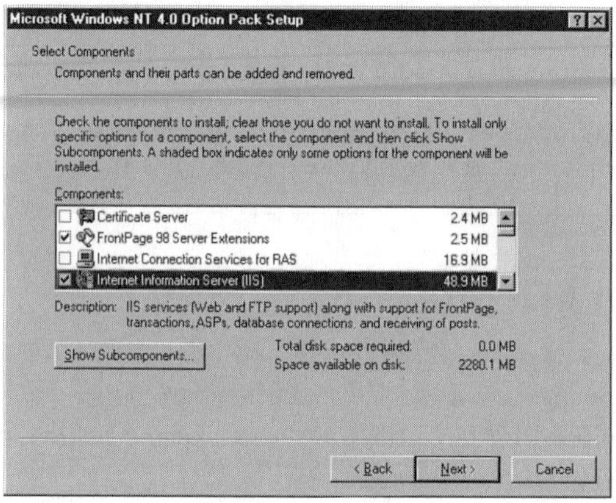

**FIGURE 10.8**

*Select Components.*

7. Select the File Transfer Protocol (FTP) Server check box, as seen in Figure 10.9. Click OK.

8. Click Next at the Select Components screen (which you were returned to).

9. Accept the default publishing directory for the FTP Service as seen in Figure 10.10. Click Next.

10. The Completing Installation screen appears, followed by a dialog box asking you to provide the iis4_03.cab file. You need to insert SBS setup CD-ROM Disc #2, provide the drive letter for your CD-ROM drive (for example, d:\), and click the Browse button.

**FIGURE 10.9**

*Select FTP Server.*

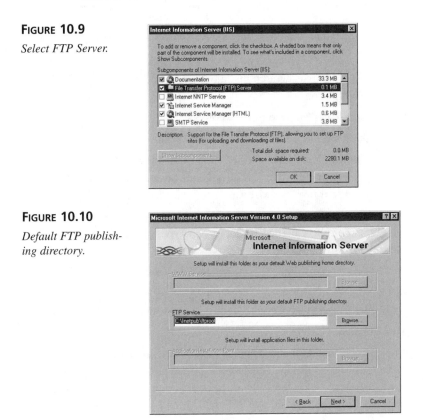

**FIGURE 10.10**

*Default FTP publishing directory.*

11. When the Locate File dialog box appears, iis4_03.cab is listed. Navigate to the following folder location: \ntoptpak\en\x86\winnt.srv. Click Open. Click OK when you return to the previous dialog box (asking you to browse the CD).

12. The FTP Server installation then completes. Press Finish to complete the setup.

**Note**

Don't forget to remove SBS Setup CD-ROM Disc #2 and place it with your other SBS Setup CD-ROMs. I hope that you store all your SBS source media in a safe location.

> You are not required to reboot your SBS server machine after installing the FTP Server service, but I'd recommend you do so to get a fresh start. Go ahead and get a cup of coffee while the machine reboots. You've earned it.

It's now time to create an FTP site that your clients can use over the Internet. Here's how you do it:

1. Assuming you are logged on as an administrator or equivalent, launch the SBS Console from the Start button.

2. Select Tasks and then select Manage Shared Folders.

3. Select Create or Share a Folder. The Share a Folder Wizard appears. Click Next.

4. In the To Create a New Folder, Type a New Name field at the bottom of the Select a Folder screen, type **c:\springersftp** and click Next. Answer Yes if prompted to create the folder because it doesn't exist (this will be a small warning dialog box).

5. Accept the share name as "springersftp" in the Specify the Shared Name for This Folder screen. Type the following description in the Type a Description field: **This is the SpringersFTP Site.** Click Next.

6. Accept the default access permissions on the Select the Users Who Can Access Springersftp screen. Click Next.

7. Click Finish. Click OK when advised the wizard successfully created springersftp.

8. Close the SBS Console.

9. Launch the Internet Service Manager application from the Microsoft Internet Information Server program group. This is a difficult application to find, because it is nested four layers deep in the Start menu structure. First, click Start from the SBS desktop. Select Programs, Windows NT 4.0 Option Pack, Microsoft Internet Information Server, Internet Service Manager.

10. The new Microsoft Management Console (MMC) launches and displays two options underneath the Console Root in the left panel: Internet Information Server and Microsoft Transaction Server. Expand Internet Information Server.

11. You now see your site listed (which has the same name as your SBS server machine). As seen in Figure 10.2, this is springers01. Expand the site by clicking on the + sign next to the site name.

12. Right-click the site (for example, springers01). Select New from the secondary menu. Select FTP Site from the site menu that appears. The New FTP Site Wizard runs.

13. Type **Springers** in the FTP Site Description field as displayed in Figure 10.11. Click Next.

**FIGURE 10.11**

*FTP Site Wizard.*

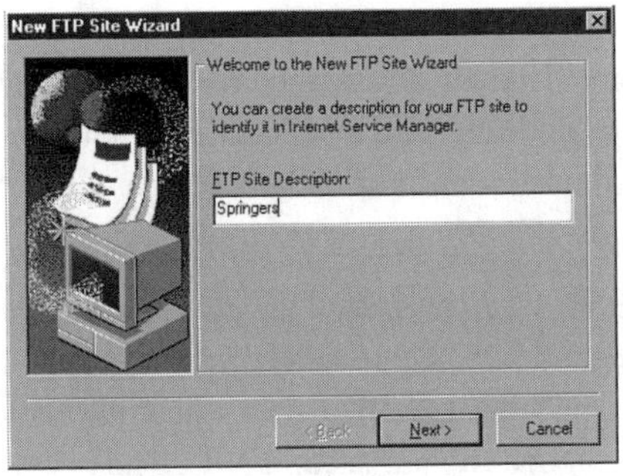

14. Accept the default TCP port on the next screen. For the IP address, type the address of your second network interface card (NIC) with the real Internet IP address (for example, 131.107.6.159). Click Next.

> **Note**
>
> Recall that SBS 4.5 uses private IP addresses by default for the internal network (10.0.0.x). You should interpret the IP addressed previously (131.107.6.15) as a real Internet address.

15. Enter the path for your home directory as **c:\springersftp** and click Next.

16. Allow both read and write access as seen in Figure 10.12.

**FIGURE 10.12**

*Read and Write Access.*

17. Click Finish. You have now successfully created the Springers FTP Site.

18. Next, right-click the Springers TP site in the left pane of the IIS MCC and select Properties.

19. Click Start to launch the Springers FTP site.

**10**

Your FTP site would be accessible to anonymous users, assuming that you have full-time Internet connection and a real IP address assigned to the second NIC on your computer. If these basic infrastructure conditions are met, your external users (for example, clients) would type a command in the address field of their Web browser similar to (feel free to do this) one of the following:

- The IP Address method—Assuming you haven't pointed your DNS Host record (A) record to your second NIC located physically in your SBS server machine, an external user would type **ftp://131.107.6.159** where the IP address is the real Internet IP address assigned to your second NIC. The result should appear similar to Figure 10.13 (note I created a simple text document, brisker.doc, in the Springerftp directory for you to see).

- The Host Name Method—Assuming your Host (A) name record points to your actual SBS server machine, you would type a command similar to **ftp://springers.com/springers** with the middle term (springers.com) being the actual Internet domain name.

**Note**

Don't let that advanced TCP/IP talk about Host (A) stuff get to you. The bottom line is very simple. When you register a domain name with the Internet gods, the (A) record points to your domain name. Upon domain name registration, this occurs automatically.

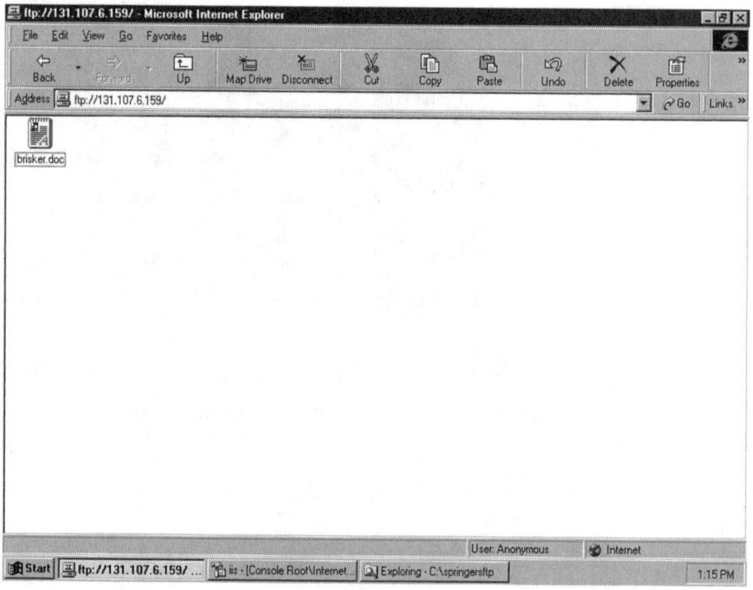

**FIGURE 10.13**

*Springers FTP Site.*

**Power Tool Tip**

> You might want to invoke specific security settings on your FTP site. Such discussion is beyond the scope of this book, but you are encouraged to consult one of the IIS-specific books listed in the next session.

## Next Steps

I've given you only a quick glance of IIS in SBS. I did so to be mindful of the small-business audience this book is intended for. But if you have the chutzpah to dig into IIS, I highly recommend that you consider these advanced texts from Macmillan: *Sams Teach Yourself MCSE Internet Information Server 4 in 14 Days* by Rob Scrimger (ISBN 0-672-31294-8) or *Special Edition Using Microsoft Internet Information Server 4* by Nelson Howell (ISBN 0-789-71263-6).

**10**

## Lunch

Whew! Another big day. How about lunch at a nearby restaurant, but hurry back so you can complete the following task.

### Task 10.1: Tuning the Site

I'd like you to performance-tune the Puppy Hall of Fame site for fewer than 10,000 hits per day. Hint #1: See the Performance tab on Puppy Hall of Fame Properties. Hint #2: See the Property tab in Hint #1, right-click the Puppy Hall of Fame Web site icon in IIS, and select Properties.

## ☽PM Microsoft Index Server

Welcome back from lunch. This afternoon you will explore one of the hidden jewels in SBS: Microsoft Index Server.

For all practical purposes, Microsoft Index Server is a keyword search engine that has great value in a small company when properly deployed. On the surface, it is very similar to other Internet search engines such as Yahoo! (www.yahoo.com), Infoseek (www.infoseek.com), or Dogpile (www.dogpile.com) that you might have used in the past.

One practical use of Microsoft Index Server on SBS networks has been to organize mass quantities of data. The example that you'll complete closely reflects what I've seen in the real SBS world. Here, you will go to the alt.animals.dog newsgroup and download the latest dog-related news into a single text file. You will then place this file in a folder on the SBS server machine and have the Index Server index it. You will then perform a keyword search on this data set.

The value of performing this function is at least twofold:

- Knowledge base—Over time, you can build a huge database or "corpus" on topics of interest. In the case of Springer Spaniels Unlimited, you will perform a keyword search seeking information related to dogs.

- Fuzzy logic—Microsoft Index Server organizes information in an unstructured format. This differs dramatically from the table approach used by SQL Server (discussed on Day 17, "SQL Server"). The use of keywords allows you to find your data using loose or fuzzy searches.

First, create a folder on the SBS server machine to house your data. Second, gather the data from the alt.animals.dog newsgroup. Finally, launch Microsoft Index Server, have it scan the directory, and perform a keyword search against the dog data.

## Task 10.2: Creating a Folder on the SBS Server Machine

1. Assuming you are logged on as an administrator or equivalent, launch the SBS Console from the Start button.

2. Select Tasks, Manage Shared Folders.

3. Select Create or share a folder. The Share a Folder Wizard appears. Click Next.

4. In the To Create a New Folder, Type a New Name field at the bottom of the Select a Folder screen, type **c:\company shared folders\research** and click Next. Answer Yes if prompted to create the folder because it doesn't exist (this will be a small warning dialog box).

5. Accept the share name as "research" in the Specify the Shared Name for this Folder screen. Type the following description in the Type a Description field: Springer-related Research. Click Next.

6. Accept the default access permissions on the Select the Users Who Can Access Springersftp screen. Click Next.

7. Click Finish. Click OK when advised the wizard successfully created c:\company shared folders\research.

8. Close the SBS Console.

## Task 10.3: Gathering Information from alt.animals.dog

1. Assuming you use Outlook as your newsreader to scan newsgroups on the Internet, download the contents of alt.animals.dog (see Figure 10.14). Note it might be necessary to perform this exercise from a SBS user's workstation that has Outlook installed.

FIGURE **10.14**

*alt.animals.dog.*

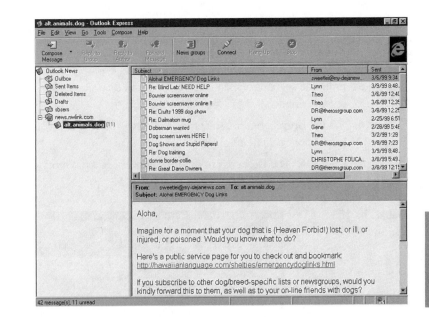

2. Now create a single text file that holds the contents of each posting in `alt.animals.dog`. From the Edit menu, select the Select All command. All the newsgroup postings will be highlighted.

3. From the Tools menu, select the Combine and Decode command. All the newsgroup postings are combined into a single window.

4. From the File menu, select Save As and save the combined newsgroup items as `dogs.txt` (a basic text file).

5. Place the `dogs.txt` file in the research folder you just created. You have now completed the information gathering exercise.

## Task 10.4: Using Microsoft Index Server

1. Log on to your SBS server machine as an administrator or member of the administrators group.

2. Launch the Index Server Manager application from the Microsoft Index Server program group. This is a difficult application to find, because it is nested four layers deep in the Start menu structure. First, click Start from the SBS desktop. Select Programs, Windows NT 4.0 Option Pack, Microsoft Index Server, Index Server Manager.

▼ TASK

10

▼   3. The Index Server MMC launches. Expand the Index Server on LocalMachine fold-
        er in the MMC's left pane.

    4. Right-click the Directories folder.

    5. From the secondary menu, select New and then Directory. The Add Directory dia-
        log box appears.

    6. Via the Browse button, select the Research folder you created previously (located
        in \Company Shared Folders).

    7. Click OK. The Research folder now appears as a directory in the right pane of the
▲       Index Server MMC, as seen in Figure 10.15.

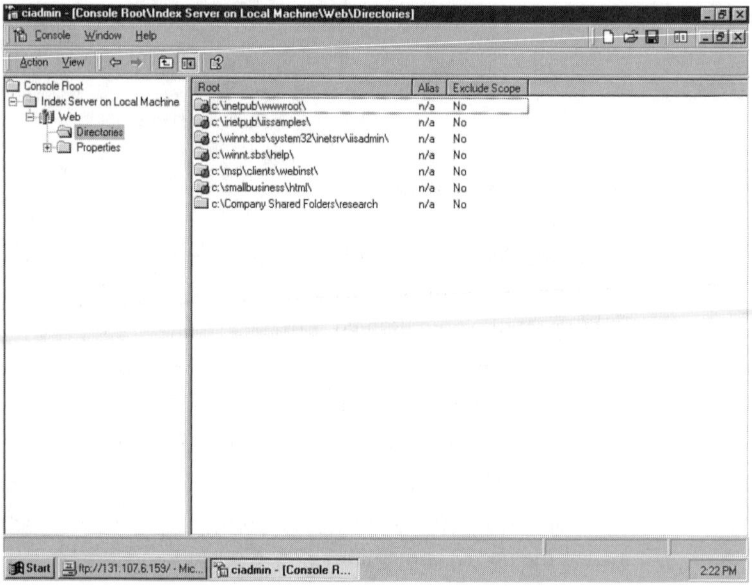

**FIGURE 10.15**

*Research folder.*

8. Right-click the Research folder in the right pane and select Rescan from the sec-
        ondary menu. This forces Index Server to gather keywords for your searching.

    9. Answer Yes when asked to perform a full scan. A full scan will be performed in the
        background. This can take several minutes.

## Task 10.5: Performing a Keyword Search

1. The moment has arrived to search your corpus of dog information. To search via
        keyword, use the Index Server Sample Query Form.

    2. Launch the Index Server Sample Query Form application from the Microsoft Index
        Server program group. First, click Start from the SBS desktop. Select Programs,

▼ Windows NT 4.0 Option Pack, Microsoft Index Server, Index Server Sample Query Form.

3. Type the word **dog** in the Enter Your Query Below field of the Index Server Sample Query Form.

4. Click Go.

5. The Microsoft Index Server returns four results or *hits*, as seen in Figure 10.16.
▲ The amount of hits displayed for you can very well vary.

**FIGURE 10.16**

*Hits on* dog.

10

You have now successfully created a corpus of important information, had it scanned by Microsoft Index Server, and successfully performed a keyword search via Microsoft Index Server. Congratulations!

**Note**

I suspect you can think of other creative ways to deploy Microsoft Index Server in your company. Don't forget that nearly every profession and industry has a newsgroup on the Internet that can be turned into a corpus similar to the example you just completed. Two ways in which I've seen Microsoft Index Server deployed include an instructor who created a class notes corpus for MCSE certification students to search on via keywords. Second, a public accounting firm created a corpus of every document ever created in the firm's history (at least since the modern PC arrived). This is dry stuff for you and me to read I'm sure, but the stuff made the CPAs' eyes twinkle. Good Luck!

## Summary

What a day. You've learned what Microsoft's Internet Information Server and Index Server is. More importantly, you've created the infrastructure for an intranet site and a FTP site. You also created a corpus of important information and performed a keyword search against it using Index Server.

Tomorrow, on Day 11, you will learn about and use Microsoft Proxy Server.

# DAY **11**

# Using Proxy Server

Today is one of the more important days of our 21 days together. The issue is Internet-related security. The solution is Microsoft Proxy Server 2.0, an application included with SBS that provides basic firewall protection from Internet intruders. More importantly, Proxy Server fits because the price is right (it is included with SBS for no additional charge). Even if purchased at its retail price of approximately $1,000, Proxy Server compares favorably to other firewall solutions costing over $5,000. Given virtually every small-business owner's paranoia about Internet intrusion on their networks, I've found the inclusion of Proxy Server in the SBS product to be a real deal closer. Proxy Server alleviates many Internet security concerns, giving SBS the nod of approval.

## AM **Proxy Server Basics**

If you did nothing more than perform a complete installation of SBS 4.5 and use the SBS Console to connect to the Internet, you would have basic firewall protection from Internet intruders (and I could end the chapter right here). For most small businesses, that is sufficient. In fact, it's possible that you will never need to perform any configuration tasks on Proxy Server explicitly. It's really that easy: just add water, so to speak.

You do need to know about a few Proxy Server basics so that you can call it a day and focus on other, more complex SBS areas of study. From an SBS administrator perspective, you need to understand these items:

- Proxy Server can be used to control Internet Access. This includes controlling which SBS users have access to the Internet and acts as a firewall to prevent unauthorized parties on the Internet from intruding on your network.
- Proxy Server is managed via the Internet Information Server (IIS) Microsoft Management Console (MMC).
- Microsoft Proxy comprises three services: Socks Proxy, Web Proxy, and WinSock Proxy.
- Proxy Server can also act as both a router and a gateway between different types of networks.

Regarding the three underlying services that comprise Proxy Server, let me quickly revisit each of the three definitions. You will recall you first learned about Socks Proxy, Web Proxy, and WinSock Proxy on Day 10, "Internet Information Server/Index Server."

- Socks Proxy—This service allows UNIX and Macintosh client computers to access a rich variety of Internet services.
- Web Proxy—This service supports the HTTP, HTTP-S, FTP, and Gopher protocols, providing wide-ranging access to the Internet/intranet for browsers and Internet applications.
- WinSock Proxy—This service enables a rich variety of Internet services for Windows-based client PCs. Technically, it supports such protocols as Telnet and RealAudio.

You've already seen Proxy Server if you attended Day 10 and saw the IIS MMC. Just in case, here is Proxy Server, *a la* the IIS MMC, in Figure 11.1 (the Proxy Server components have been highlighted).

**Power Tool Tip**

You stop and start Proxy Server services from the IIS MMC. Whenever major changes are made to Proxy Server services (when you're under the hood and not using the SBS Console), it is necessary to stop and start the affected Proxy Server service so the changes are invoked. A reboot of the SBS server machine accomplishes the same thing.

As an aside, Proxy Server is very sensitive to improper SBS shutdowns. I've had a fellow SBS guru tell me that he had to reinstall Proxy Server after an improper SBS shutdown. You might remember from Day 2, "Planning for Small Business Server," that Springer Spaniels Unlimited purchased an uninterruptible power supply (UPS) to help prevent improper shutdowns.

**Figure 11.1**

*Proxy Server.*

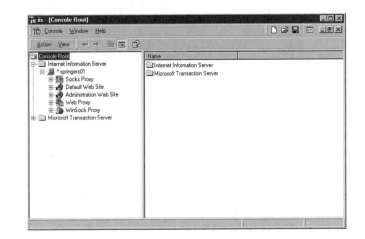

Hopefully, as the day-to-day SBS administrator, you won't have a great need to interact with Proxy Server (kudos again to Microsoft for making the Proxy Server implementation very user-friendly).

You will indeed make decisions regarding Proxy Server and how it is configured in one place, however: when you are configuring your Internet connection via the SBS Console and the Internet Connection Wizard. Several screens into the ICW process, you will be presented with the Configure Firewall Settings screen (I mentioned this on Day 9, "Connecting to the Internet"). This is shown in Figure 11.2.

**Figure 11.2**

*Configure Firewall Settings.*

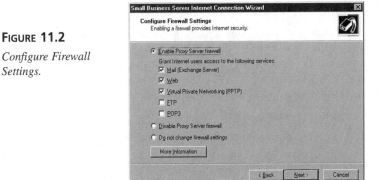

You will likely have compelling reasons to select the Enable Proxy Server firewall selection. If you do so, you allow outside (Internet-based) activity to "touch" your SBS server machine but not get past the firewall. Allowing an outside party to touch a computer that is connected to the Internet is unsettling because, if a machine can be touched, it can possibly be hacked. For your SBS Internet connectivity to function fully, it has to touch the Internet, right? So therein exists Proxy Server's firewall protection. Here are the configuration choices you can make when you enable Proxy Server's firewall protection:

- Mail (Exchange Server)—I recommend selecting this because it lets you transfer e-mail between Exchange Server on your SBS server machine and the mail server at your ISP.

- Web—I do not recommend that you make this selection unless you are hosting your own Web site on your SBS server machine. Remember that Microsoft actually recommends that you host your Web site with your ISP when using SBS.

- Virtual Private Networking (PPTP)—You should disable this selection unless you have implemented a VPN. Suffice it to say, you'll know if you need to select the option. This is an advanced area.

- FTP—If you have an FTP site that your customers want to copy files to, such as I discussed on Day 10, you need to make this selection.

- POP3—This advanced feature allows SBS users to log on remotely via the Internet so they can check their mailboxes. I recommend you not select this unless you really need it (and you'll know if you do).

Finally, you might need to restrict Internet access for your SBS users (be it they are misbehaving), you can invoke such restrictions via the SBS Console. This afternoon I revisit the naughty Internet reports first mentioned on Day 6, "Daily and Weekly SBS Administration (The Dirty Dozen)."

## Task 11.1: Modifying Internet Access Permissions

1. Log on to the SBS server machine as an Administrator or a member of the Administrators group.
2. From the Start button, select the SBS Console.
3. Select the More Tasks page.
4. Select the Manage Internet Access option.
5. Select the control access to the Internet option. The Internet Access Wizard starts.
6. You see the Welcome to the Internet Access Wizard screen. Click Next.
7. You see the Users Who Can Access the Internet screen. On the left, all SBS users are listed. On the right, SBS users who can access the Internet are listed. Use the Add or Remove buttons accordingly to add or remove an SBS user from the right pane (Users who can access the Internet).
8. Click Next.
9. Click Finish.

You have now successfully modified SBS user permissions pertaining to Internet access.

## Lunch

Lunch is so early today, let's call it Brunch. Here is a recipe for you to prepare Ham and Cheese Crustless Quiche.

### Ham and Cheese Crustless Quiche

6 eggs

1/2 C. flour

1 (3 oz.) pkg. cream cheese

1 C. (8 oz.) cottage cheese

4 T. butter

1 lb. (16 oz.) Monterey Jack cheese

1 C. cubed ham

1 t. baking powder

1 C. milk

1/8 t. salt

Cut cream cheese, butter and Monterey Jack cheese into small cubes. In large bowl, beat eggs. Add flour and baking powder; mix well. Add milk; beat until smooth. Add all remaining ingredients to egg mixture. Place in buttered 8×12" oblong baking dish. Bake in 350° oven for 45–50 minutes until set. Let stand at room temperature for 5–10 minutes. Cut into serving pieces.

11

## PM Working with Proxy Server

Hope you enjoyed your quiche! This afternoon, a collection of Proxy Server lessons learned, is not for the faint of heart! Let's get started.

# Two NICs

Truth be told, Proxy Server provides basic firewall services out of the box. To create a firewall scheme you can brag about to your sister at the U.S. Department of Defense, you really need to add a second network interface card (NIC) in your SBS server and create a second subnet or network. (Later today I also discuss a two server proxy firewall scenario, which is even better.) Depending on how you are connected to the Internet back on Day 9, it is entirely possible you've completed this step.

**Note**

> Indeed, I had trouble with two NICs in the same SBS server machine in the old SBS 4.0/4.0a days. There were several possible reasons for this. One reason was the original SBS (version 4.0) used Proxy Server 1.0, which was considered a weaker release than Proxy Server 2.0 that ships with SBS 4.5. Reason two is that—I've been told—the Windows Internet Naming Service (WINS) would upset the SBS server machine if two NICs were present and WINS interacted directly with DNS for name resolution.
>
> I've found no such problems with two NICs in SBS 4.5. The only anomaly has occurred during the setup of SBS 4.5: Only the first NIC is actually installed and used. If you want to add a second NIC at a future date, you'll need to do so manually.

The demilitarized zone (DMZ) or gap between the two NICs is where Proxy Server steps in. It is here that Proxy Server filters packets from one NIC to another (or one network to another). It's that simple. Don't forget, a modem is a form of a second NIC when it acts as the second network interface.

**Power Tool Tip**

> You can swiftly deplete the power of Proxy Server in a two-NIC scenario if you inadvertently select Enable IP Forwarding on the Routing tab of Microsoft TCP/IP Properties (shown in Figure 11.3). Remember that Microsoft TCP/IP Properties is selected from the Network property sheet (access via Network in Control Panel).
>
> If you select Enable IP Forwarding, you've eliminated the DMZ between the two NICs. Rogue traffic can travel back and forth between the two networks—the Internet and your SBS network—which is bad.

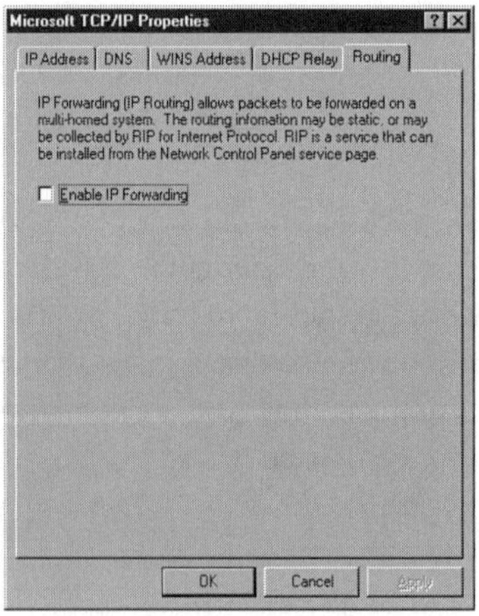

**FIGURE 11.3**

*Enable IP Forwarding—don't check this box.*

# The Naughty Reports

I wanted to quickly revisit something discussed on Day 6. The topic is Internet activity reporting. The SBS Console allows you to view Top 10–type Internet activity, but if you want to see exact details of Web sites visited, by whom and what time, review the Proxy Server logs in the c:\WINNT.SBS\System32\msplogs folder. These logs take advantage of Proxy Server's default settings that enable logging, as seen in Figure 11.4.

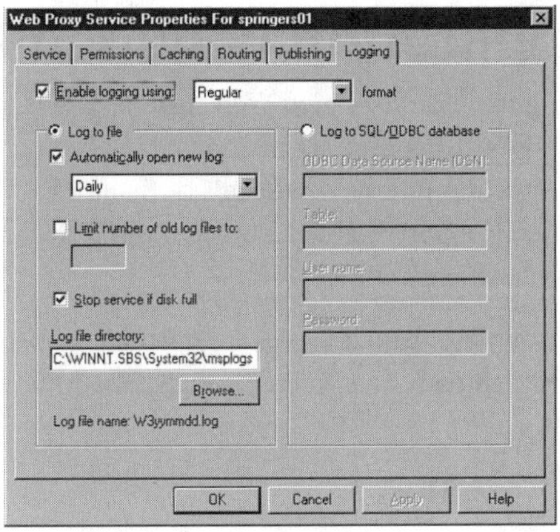

**FIGURE 11.4**

*Proxy Server logging.*

The Proxy Server logs (for example, W3990329.LOG) appear similar to the next few lines and report each and every site visited by whom and when (extremely powerful recording):

```
10.0.0.14, SPRINGERS\ElvisH, -, Y, 3/30/99, 23:16:37, 1, -, -,
www.washingtonpost.com, -, 80, 2413, 432, 1166, http, -, -,
http://www.washingtonpost.com/wp-srv/newsfront/images/back.gif,
 -, Inet, 200, 8388608

10.0.0.14, SPRINGERS\ElvisH, -, Y, 3/30/99, 23:16:42, 1, -, -,
www.washingtonpost.com, -, 80, 4657, 4586, 716, http, -, -,
http://www.washingtonpost.com/wp-srv/newsfront/images/navigation_
news.gif, -, Inet, 200, 8388608

10.0.0.14, SPRINGERS\ElvisH, -, Y, 3/30/99, 23:16:52, 1, -, -,
www.washingtonpost.com, -, 80, 45686, 47243, 1218, http, -, -,
http://www.washingtonpost.com/, -, Inet, 200, 1124335616

10.0.0.14, SPRINGERS\ElvisH, -, Y, 3/30/99, 23:16:53, 1, -, -,
www.washingtonpost.com, -, 80, 11086, 3344, 716, http, -, -,
http://www.washingtonpost.com/wp-srv/globalnav/images/
partners_homepg.gif,
 -, Inet, 200, 8388608
```

11

```
10.0.0.14, SPRINGERS\ElvisH, -, Y, 3/30/99, 23:16:54, 1, -, -,
www.washingtonpost.com, -, 80, 1192, 2582, 718, http, -, -,
http://www.washingtonpost.com/wp-srv/newsfront/images/
navigation_class.gif,
 -, Inet, 200, 8388608
```

Heck, just the threat of logging will probably deter any naughty surfing behavior on your SBS network, but just in case, there's always the Proxy Server logs.

# Third-Party Application Requirements

More than catching naughty and misguided Web surfers, you're more likely to interact with Proxy Server to support SBS user applications. Here's a case in point. I teach an evening MCSE course over the Internet on behalf of Seattle Pacific University. The virtual classroom software needs a port enabled if it's to be run over an SBS network protected by Proxy Server's firewall capabilities.

This virtual classroom software, called Embanet, must have port 510 enabled to allow a session to be established and packets to pass through. The following task explains how you do it.

### Task 11.2: Enabling A Port

1. Because this is the advanced group this afternoon, I'll assume you have the IIS MMC open.

2. Right-click Web Proxy in the left pane.

3. Select Properties from the secondary menu.

4. Select the Service tab on the Web Proxy Service Properties For dialog box.

5. Select the Security button under Shared Resources. Note *Shared Resources* implies the changes you make here apply to all Proxy Server services, not just the service you've selected.

6. The Security dialog box is displayed. Click Add.

7. The Packet Filter Properties dialog box is displayed. I've created a custom filter per Embanet's specifications to enable port 510 for TCP. The port setting is restricted to Embanet's IP address (206.186.54.102). This is shown in Figure 11.5.

8. Click OK.

9. Click OK at the Security dialog box.

10. Click OK at the Web Proxy Service Properties For dialog box.

11. You will need to stop and start the Web Proxy service for the change you've just made to take effect.

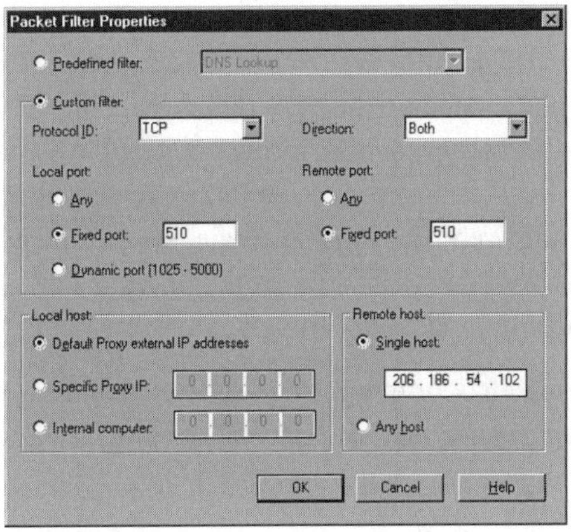

**FIGURE 11.5**

*Enabling port 510.*

Packet Filter Properties

- ○ Predefined filter: DNS Lookup
- ● Custom filter:
  - Protocol ID: TCP     Direction: Both
  - Local port:              Remote port:
    - ○ Any                ○ Any
    - ● Fixed port: 510    ● Fixed port: 510
    - ○ Dynamic port (1025 - 5000)
  - Local host:              Remote host:
    - ● Default Proxy external IP addresses    ● Single host
    - ○ Specific Proxy IP: 0.0.0.0    206.186.54.102
    - ○ Internal computer: 0.0.0.0    ○ Any host

[ OK ]  [ Cancel ]  [ Help ]

Although I've only given you an example of a package that I use frequently, I've performed the same exercise for Westlaw at the small Seattle law firm I often cite. It is increasingly likely you will have to make similar port configurations in Proxy Server to support user software in your respective industry.

> **Tip**
>
> Oh, did I forget to define ports for you? Oops! *Ports* are access points (a.k.a. sockets) when combined with an IP address. A port is a foundation item necessary for allowing a session between two hosts. Well-known port values are assigned by Request For Comment (RFC) 1700. For example, port 80 is HTTP, which is the Hypertext Transfer Protocol used by Web browsers. Port values above 1,023 are not assigned by 1,023 and are available for use by any two hosts to specify between themselves in creating a secure session. This is advanced stuff to be sure, and for more information I suggest you take the Support Microsoft Proxy Server 2.0 course (see www.microsoft.com/train_cert for details).

11

# Hyperactive Caching

The active caching capabilities are the main reason that some large enterprise-level sites purchase and deploy Proxy Server. Proxy Server features two types of caching: passive and active. The benefit to caching Web pages on the local SBS server machine is that these Web pages can be accessed at LAN speed, because they are being drawn from cache, not from the original site on the Internet. This beats the heck out of waiting for a modem download every time you want to access your favorite Web pages. Caching is conceptually similar to the History setting in Internet Explorer 5.0 (where the most recently accessed sites that you visited are cached on your local hard disk).

Passive caching is the most basic caching provided by Proxy Server. Here, Proxy Server steps in and looks at each Web browser request to see whether the request can be stored by a cached or stored home page on the SBS server machine. That's possible because, by default, SBS creates a 100MB cache for storing copies of Web pages. (You can see this under the Caching tab for Web Proxy Service Properties under Proxy Server 2.0's MMC interface.) By default, the Web pages managed via passive caching are updated every 24 hours. That's important for your cached pages that include news and sports scores. SBS 4.5 enables passive caching by default.

Active caching is a completely different story. Active caching overrides passive caching and, in a much more aggressive fashion, more frequently updates the cached Web pages. It does so by using an algorithm comprised of

- Web page popularity—More popular Web pages are updated more frequently.
- TTL—This time-to-live value is an expiration date. Pages are updated before they expire.
- Sever load—More aggressive active caching activity occurs when the SBS server machine's load is low, not when load activity is high.

**Note**       Active caching is disabled by default in SBS 4.5.

Now for the hyperactive caching story. For the longest time, at both the Seattle biotechnology firm and the Puget Sound homebuilder, I couldn't determine why the SBS server machine dialed the ISP so frequently. Later, based on my own experience and some research using Microsoft's TechNet CD, I learned that the active caching configuration in Proxy Server can cause frequently dialing to the ISP to refresh the cache of external Internet home pages cached on the SBS server machine. The active caching setting for Proxy Server is shown in Figure 11.6 and is accessed via the property sheet for Web Proxy.

After I turned off or at least tuned down active caching, the excessive modem dialing declined dramatically. The result was a much happier SBS client (because said client paid overage charges after exceeding a small number of ISP connection hours each month).

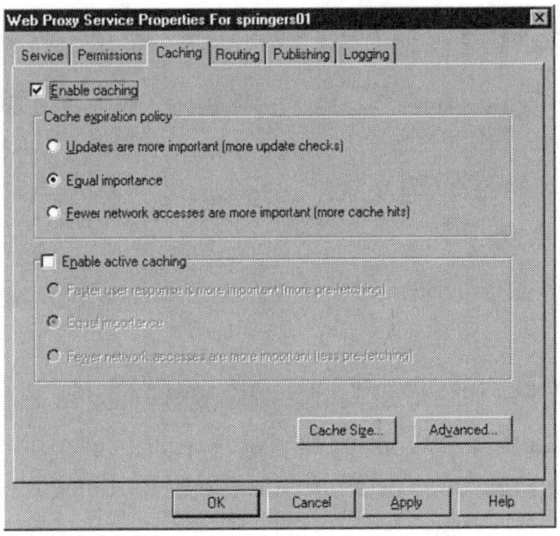

**Figure 11.6**

*Active caching.*

# Gateway and Router

Perhaps you've already drawn your own conclusion that Proxy Server acts as a router between two separate networks from the two-NIC discussion above. Such a conclusion is correct, but did you know that Proxy Server can also act as a gateway, spanning all seven layers of the Open Systems Interconnect (OSI) model? It's true because you can run an internal network that uses IPX/SPX as its network protocol and have those internal users communicate in a robust manner with the Internet (which of course uses TCP/IP as its network protocol).

Showing you how to have an IPX/SPX network communicate with the Internet, via Proxy Server, is beyond the scope of this book. But this process is well documented with the online documentation that accompanies Proxy Server 2.0. It's also another security measure for you to consider as darn near no one is going to get to your internal network when you are converting the underlying network protocol as part of your Proxy Server security scheme.

**Power Tool Tip**

If you want an IPX-based workstation to use Proxy Server, it's more complex than simply installing the WSP Client on the IPX-based workstation. The setup is more complex and is documented in the Proxy Server 2.0 documentation. Don't be lulled into complacency that it's the same quickie WSP Client install used with TCP/IP-based workstations. It's not.

# Dealing with Other Proxy Server Issues

Proxy Server is a lively topic among SBS gurus up on the SBS newsgroups, including the SBS newsgroup accessed at www.microsoft.com. Note I discuss numerous SBS resources, such as these, for you to take advantage of in Appendix A, "SBS Resources." Topics I've seen debated include

- Proxy Server 2.0's alleged memory leak problem and an associated hot fix from Microsoft
- Proxy Server services that won't start automatically on reboot (but will manually)
- The need to reinstall Proxy Server to resolve baffling problems such as user Internet access and reasons for changing the default cache size

All this and more on an SBS newsgroup near you!

# Browser Wars

Proxy Server is the Switzerland (neutral party) of the browser wars going on between Microsoft and Netscape. Proxy Server works equally well with Internet Explorer and Netscape Communicator. I'll offer a word of advice: when configuring Netscape Communicator for use with Proxy Server, I've had more success by pointing to the SBS server machine by its IP address (10.0.0.2) instead of its NetBIOS name (for example, SPRINGERS01).

# Advanced Internet Security

One concern for SBS sites needing the highest possible security is the fact that the SBS server machine is also the firewall device. In a real (that is, expensive) firewall solution, a separate device intercepts inbound traffic from the Internet before it ever touches an internal server, such as the SBS server machine. That's because of something I alluded to earlier in the chapter: You don't like Internet traffic directly touching your SBS server as a general rule. Technically speaking, it is a bad idea to expose the security accounts manager (SAM) directly to the Internet. So, let me display and show you a big-league firewall setup. First, observe Figure 11.7 and quickly observe that this implementation won't work with SBS because you have a trust relationship between domains. In fact, for this reason alone I also raise this discussion again on Day 21, "Upgrading to Big BackOffice."

**FIGURE 11.7**

*Big-league firewall scenario.*

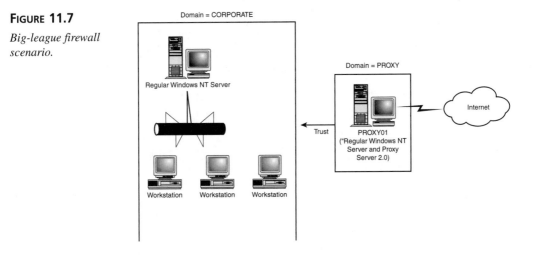

The key to understanding Figure 11.7 beyond the two domains is that a one-way trust relationship from the PROXY domain to the CORPORATE domain allows users in the CORPORATE domain to enjoy robust outbound access to the PROXY domain and beyond but not vice versa. So someone hacking in via the Internet can't access the SAM on the CORPORATE domain. This is important stuff that's beyond the scope of this book, but I did want to provide you this basic Internet security education.

# Summary

*Short but sweet* sums up this day with Proxy Server. That's by design because, outside of specific configuration requests and access control changes, it's unlikely you will have a great need to interact directly with Proxy Server on your SBS network. Have a good day.

11

# DAY **12**

# Publishing on the Internet/Intranet

Just a few years ago, desktop publishing and the output from laser printers had the eye of businesses seeking to improve their operations and market themselves better. Today, desktop publishing applications such as PageMaker have given way in popularity to Web page creation applications such as Microsoft FrontPage. And the good news is that Microsoft FrontPage 2000 is included as part of SBS 4.5.

Today, regardless of your skill level, plan to attend the entire day. The goal for today is to complete a Web page for Springer Spaniels Unlimited. Specifically, you will create the Puppy Hall of Fame home page.

## AM The WWW Standard

The World Wide Web has become the de facto Internet communication standard for conveying information. Other standards, such as Archie, Veronica, and Gopher, have come and gone during the short life of the Internet, but none have caught on like the World Wide Web. The Web allows you to present information in different media forms including text, art, photos, sound, animation, and video. Other standards rely primarily on either text or document files.

Today, the Web is the meeting place for just about everyone on the Internet and the place that businesses, whether large, medium or small, tout their services and wares. As an SBS site, you shouldn't be an exception. In fact, as I'll discuss later, Microsoft sees the greatest growth in Web-based commerce (a.k.a. electronic commerce) coming from small businesses that clearly fit the SBS profile.

## What Is a Web Page?

Although most people today know what a Web page is, let's take a moment to revisit Web basics. A Web page can be compared to a desktop-published document with its use of content, fonts, type styles, pictures, and art. But, unlike a desktop-published document, a Web page is a living document allowing the use of multimedia (sound, videos, and so on). And unless it's printed, a Web page is a virtual document, existing only on your screen via your browser application. Others have compared a Web page to a billboard on the information superhighway.

SBS provides you a completed Web page right away without any planning, creation, or modification tasks required of you. To see the default Web page in SBS, launch the Internet Explorer (IE) Web browser included with SBS. The default Web page in SBS is a Welcome notice, as seen in Figure 12.1.

**FIGURE 12.1**

*Welcome.*

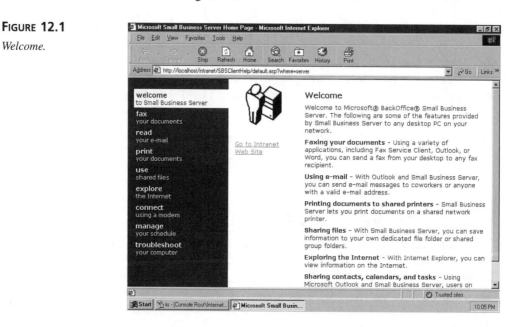

**Tip** By clicking the link Go to Intranet Web Site, you are presented with an overview of how to create an intranet site. This is good supplemental information to what is presented today.

From the Welcome default SBS home page, be advised that several valuable resource are right in front of your eyes. These include specific keystrokes, tips, and tricks for

- Faxing documents
- Reading e-mail
- Printing documents
- Accessing files
- Exploring the Internet
- Using a modem
- Time management via a schedule
- Troubleshooting

# Creating a Web Page

Creating a Web page involves several phases including planning, installing the Web page creation software (FrontPage 2000), creating the Web page, and deploying it. Each of these phases are discussed in the next several sections.

## Planning

Can't you just remember your high school and college athletic coaches saying "Proper preparation prevents poor performance"? Nowhere is this more true today than Web pages. Poor performance can be a combination of poor content, bad design, or truly poor performance as measured by transmission speeds and loading time.

My first words of advice to small businesses regarding Web page planning are Just get the ball rolling. First, consider storyboarding or hand-drawing your Web site on pieces of paper. Tape these paper pages to a wall; over several days observe the pages and see how they looks to you. Undoubtedly, you'll make changes to your paper pages as you think more about your site over several days.

**12**

**Power Tool Tip**

You might also consider using powerful planning tools such as Visio, a diagramming package mentioned on Day 2, "Planning for Small Business Server," for creating your as-built drawings. Visio also includes Web design templates, one of which is shown in Figure 12.2.

**FIGURE 12.2**

*Web site planning via Visio.*

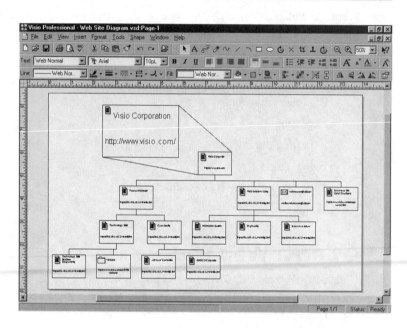

If you're not artistically inclined or especially creative, consider hiring an experienced Web page developer to create your site. The costs for such a strategy? Over $250,000 if you want to compete with the best Web sites; peanuts if you hire a high school kid to create a basic Web site for you.

As a final Web site planning thought, manage your expectations. With little doubt, you'll want to improve your Web site when you get it up and running. In fact, it's likely the improvements will never stop because initially you'll simply want to improve the quality and capabilities of your Web site. Later, you'll find yourself continually updating the content of your Web site to keep it fresh, meaningful (and thus valuable), and interesting. A Web site should be dynamic, not static, so manage your expectations accordingly.

Before you install Microsoft FrontPage 2000, a few caveats. Microsoft FrontPage ships with SBS for use on a single machine. It is not licensed for general or widespread use in your organization. Actually, for a small business, you can probably get by with having it on one machine, unless you're an advertising agency (wherein all your machines would probably need a Web creation application). Also, I found FrontPage to be slightly more challenging to learn than I remember the good old desktop publishing applications such as PageMaker to be. But maybe I'm just getting old. The point is, FrontPage has a learning curve, so allow yourself that. Plus, consider using the default templates in FrontPage to speed your development efforts. You'll use this approach in a moment.

## Installing Microsoft FrontPage 2000

FrontPage 2000 is located on Microsoft Small Business Server Disc 2. This is an upgrade from SBS 4.0, which provided FrontPage 97.

**Note** | If you purchased the SBS 4.5 version that includes Office 2000 Premium, you'll want to consider installing FrontPage 2000 as part of the Office 2000 Premium setup process. In this case, you would be installing FrontPage 2000 to each SBS user's workstation, not the SBS server machine.

Here are the steps for installing FrontPage 2000 on your SBS server machine:

1. Make sure you are logged on to the SBS server as an administrator or member of the Administrators group.

2. Insert Microsoft Small Business Server Disc 2 in your CD-ROM drive.

3. Run Setup.exe from the \FrontPg folder on Microsoft Small Business Server Disc 2.

4. The FrontPage 2000 installation wizard starts. At the Welcome screen, click Next.

5. You will see the name and organization name you used when installing SBS on the FrontPage Registration screen. Either change or accept these entries and click Next.

6. Click Yes on the Confirm FrontPage Registration screen if the information presented is correct.

7. Click Yes to accept the end-user license on the License screen.

8. Accept the default destination page of C:\Program Files\MicrosoftFrontPage by clicking Next on the Destination Path screen.

9. On the Setup Type screen, accept Typical unless you want to modify the FrontPage 2000–installed components (in which case you would select Custom). Note you have another opportunity to modify the destination path. Click Next. FrontPage 2000 is installed.

10. When asked via the Multihosted Servers screen, accept the Default Web Site and the Puppy Hall of Fame virtual servers on which you will install FrontPage Extensions. Recall that the Puppy Hall of Fame virtual server was created on Day 10, "Internet Information Server/Index Server." Click OK.

**12**

11. Accept the name Administrator in the Name field of the Administrator Setup for Puppy Hall of Fame screen. Click OK.

12. Click Finish to complete the installation of FrontPage 2000 on the Setup Complete screen.

Now that FrontPage 2000 is installed, you will want to create the Puppy Hall of Fame home page. This will be accomplished as Task 12.1.

## Task 12.1: Running FrontPage 2000

1. Make sure you are logged on to the SBS server as an administrator or member of the Administrators group.

2. From the Start button, select Programs and then Microsoft FrontPage. FrontPage 2000 starts.

3. From the File menu, select New, Page, Two-column Staggered Body. The Two-column Staggered Body page appears as seen in Figure 12.3. Click Next.

**FIGURE 12.3**

*Two-Column Staggered Body page.*

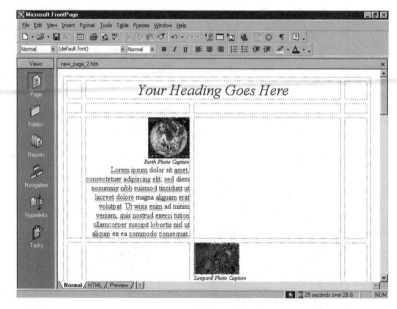

4. Save your page as default.htm to the \\springers01\puppy location.

5. Enter **Puppy Hall of Fame** as the title over the Your Heading Goes Here text.

6. In the left placement field below the Puppy Hall of Fame title you just created, type **Summer 1999**. In the right placement field, type **Springer Spaniels Unlimited**. Your page should look similar to Figure 12.4.

▼ FIGURE 12.4

*Puppy Hall of Fame in progress.*

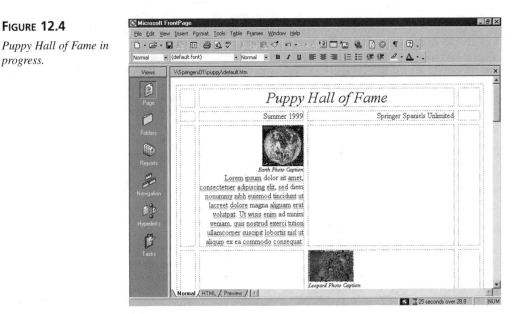

7. Delete the "Earth Photo Caption." Highlight the text beneath the earth photo and delete it. Type the following text:

   **World Conference and Puppy Hall of Fame Induction.**

   **Plan on attending the last major event for the springer spaniel community this century. In October 1999, Springer Spaniels Unlimited will host the annual World Conference and Puppy Hall of Fame Induction event. Details to be released soon.**

8. Highlight the "World Conference and Puppy Hall of Fame Induction" lead sentence. Make this selection bold and italic. Your page should look similar to Figure 12.5. Save your work.

9. In the text box next to the "World Conference..." text box, type **1999 Puppy Hall of Fame Nominations**. Highlight as bold and italic. Center the text.

10. Select the Insert menu on the Microsoft FrontPage menu bar. Select the Picture menu option. Select the From File option. Select the springers.jpg photo contained on the CD-ROM that accompanies this book. Beneath the photo, type **Sir Brisker and Sir Jaeger**. Center this text. Your Web page should look similar to Figure 12.6. You are almost finished with this assignment.

▼

**12**

▼ **FIGURE 12.5**

*Headline formatting.*

**FIGURE 12.6**

*Almost-completed Puppy Hall of Fame Web page.*

11. You can now add more information to the remaining text blocks on the Web page. Note that I have created information for an auction and an overseas breeders buying trip. I have also used some of the clip art provided with Microsoft Office 2000. To use this clip art, select Pictures from the Insert menu, and select Clip Art. You are shown a clip art gallery similar to Figure 12.7.

*Clip Art Gallery.*

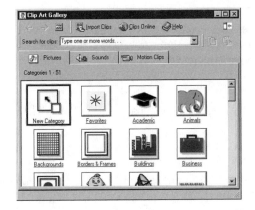

12. Save your work by selecting Save from the File menu.

13. From the File menu, select the Preview in Browser menu option. Internet Explorer 5.0 launches, allowing you to view your newly created Puppy Hall of Fame Web page. Click Preview in the Preview in Browser dialog box. Your Puppy Hall of Fame Web page is displayed, as shown in Figure 12.8.

**FIGURE 12.8**

*Completed Puppy Hall of Fame Web Page.*

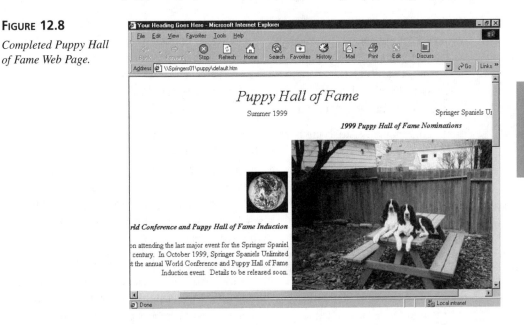

12

▼    14.  Close IE and FrontPage.

▼

| Note | Your SBS users can view the Puppy Hall of Fame home page on your SBS network by simply typing the following address in IE: \\springers01\puppy\default.htm. |
|------|------|

▲        Congratulations! You've created a home page for the Puppy Hall of Fame. Lunch is next.

 # Lunch

Today's guest speaker, Steve Bloom, is an Internet electronic commerce expert for Versus Law (www.versuslaw.com), an online legal research firm in Redmond, Washington. He'll spend a few minutes discussing electronic commerce for small businesses. Steve, take it away.

## Small Business E-Commerce
*by Steve Bloom*

Thanks Harry, and greetings everyone.

I'm here today to talk about some of the fundamental elements of an electronic commerce system. In ancient times, such as 1995, it was enough to have a Web page. Now, 20 Internet years later, Web pages have become Web applications. They support transactions, connect to databases, remember the names of people who visit them, and are highly scalable. What's called for is a platform for building your Web presence that supports these elements and allows management to focus on business strategy.

Long-term, mutually satisfying business relationships are built on the foundation of short, efficient transactions. When the customer is ready to purchase, capturing his credit card information must be as safe, convenient, and secure as possible. Should the transaction fail before completion, a mechanism must be in place for rolling back the entire purchase. Transaction Server, which ships with Internet Information Server, provides this rollback capability and requires only a few lines of code in your Web pages to do so. The details of every transaction should be written to a database.

Customization is critical to locking in your customers' loyalty. This is what your Web application must do by efficiently capturing transactional information in a database and presenting a customized greeting or entire page when a customer returns. As an example, Microsoft offers a customizable site at home.microsoft.com. Site Server, Commerce Edition from Microsoft provides a platform for building these kinds of personalized pages.

Also, your application must be scalable. You must configure it so that hundreds or even thousands of visitors can talk to your Web server at the same time. Internet Information Server is Microsoft's Web server implementation, and it exposes the functionality you'll need to tune your systems for the greatest scalability.

SQL server is an industrial strength database product. Together with IIS and transaction server, you have the beginning of an effective Web platform already available with Small Business Server. Although a Microsoft-enabled solution is cheaper than building everything from the ground up, you still have to compare the resources necessary to those of opening a new plant or physical storefront. Again, these aren't just HTML pages with some spinning globes. Careful capacity planning and expert project-management skills are essential to bringing a Web application to life.

Best wishes to you on the e-commerce highway of the Internet!

## PM Advanced Web Publishing Topics

This afternoon you'll explore a range of advanced Web publishing topics including transferring your Web page to an ISP, different type of Web pages, trends in Web page publishing, and next steps you can take to take better advantage of the Web from an SBS perspective.

# Uploading your Web Site

Just a quick matter before you leave early: uploading your Web site to your ISP. I'm assuming you're following Microsoft's recommendation to have your ISP host your Web site. This is easy to do.

**Note**

Remember that SBS really isn't designed to host your Web page for the world to come and visit. That is for a combination of reasons including network reliability, connection speed (bandwidth), advanced security, and hardware capacity.

**12**

You can upload your Web site via the SBS Console, as you would expect. Here is how you do it:

1. Make sure you are logged on to the SBS server as an administrator or member of the Administrators group.

2. From the Start button, select the SBS Console.

3. Select the More Task tab.

4. Select Publish on the Internet.

5. Select Update Your Web Site.

6. Follow the onscreen instructions to copy (or publish) the contents of the Puppy folder on SPRINGERS01 to your Web hosting space at your ISP.

There you have it. The act of publishing content to your Web site is really nothing more than an FTP program transferring files to a folder on a hard disk at your ISP.

**Power Tool Tip**

> In fact, you could use an FTP program, such as CuteFTP (downloadable from www.shareware.com) to copy of the contents of the Puppy folder on SPRINGERS01 to your Web hosting space at your ISP.

## Internet Hosting Costs

Now that I've opened the topic about ISP hosting, allow me the opportunity to discuss this matter. Typically, an ISP provides a modest amount of hard disk space at its site (on one of its servers connected to the Internet) to host your Web page. With a personal Internet account, I've seen the default amount of hard disk space average 5MB, enough for a personal Web page. With business accounts in my experience, ISPs charge for Web hosting and the hard disk space that you consume. I have seen ISPs charge business customers $50 a month for 10MB of space with rates that climb steadily upward when you use more space. Still, it's a relatively good deal for most small businesses given the benefits (mentioned earlier) of having your ISP host your Web page.

## FrontPage Extensions

One of the advanced terms you are likely to encounter while working with FrontPage 2000 on your SBS network is *FrontPage extensions*. So just what are FrontPage extensions? Simply stated, these are server-based applications that

- Allow users to collaborate simultaneously on the same Web site and Web Server. This is known as *multiserver authoring*.

- Allow users to write to the Web server using a PC or laptop computer from any location in the world over the Internet. This is known as *remote authoring*.

- Allow users to add forms on their Web pages. You can also dictate how the results of those forms are compiled.

- Allow users to include discussion threads on their Web pages.
- Allow users to take advantage of full text-search capability on a Web site. This is similar to Index Server, which was discussed on Day 10.
- Allow users to display hit recorders (number of visitor counters) on their Web pages.

In short, FrontPage extensions provide additional Web-related functions that aren't available otherwise.

# Active Server Pages

Another term that you are likely to encounter is *Active Server Pages* as you explore the Web and the Internet from your SBS platform. So what is Active Server Pages?

Active Server Pages is the SBS server-based execution environment that enables you to run ActiveX scripts and ActiveX Server Components on the SBS server machine. Organizations can create dynamic content and powerful Web applications by combining scripts and components. *Dynamic content* means Web pages customized for individual users in real time or dynamically, based on the user's actions or requests. This dynamic content can be created by skilled Webmasters using programming languages such as Visual Basic, JavaScript, Perl, REXX, or C++.

# CGI and ISAPI

Two more terms you'll encounter are *CGI* and *ISAPI*.

**12**

Common Gateway Interface (CGI) applications are popular on UNIX systems to create executable programs that run on the Web server. CGI programs are typically written in the C programming language but can also be written in interpreted languages such as Perl. Remote users can launch CGI applications on the server simply by requesting a URL containing the name of the CGI application. Arguments following the question mark in the URL are passed to the CGI application as environment strings. The output of a CGI application similar to a desktop application: HTTP headers and HTML are generated using the basic output functions of the language (for example, C programming's `printf` statement).

CGI applications are easy to write, but scale very poorly on Windows NT. That's because UNIX was designed to handle multiple processes (such as CGI applications) with little overhead. Windows NT, which is optimized for traditional business applications, commits more system resources when creating and destroying application instances. Thus CGI performance on a Windows NT Server is disappointing compared to a UNIX server.

So what is the answer to CGI from the Windows NT Server community? This answer is the Internet Server API (ISAPI) application, which was developed specifically for IIS as a high-performance Windows NT alternative to CGI. An ISAPI *extension* is a run-time dynamic-link library (DLL) that is usually loaded in the same SBS server memory space occupied by IIS. In English, ISAPI is what you use instead of CGI on Windows NT Server, the underlying operating system for SBS 4.5.

# Summary

Thanks for attending Day 12 and not only installing FrontPage 98 but also creating and viewing the Puppy Hall of Fame home page. See you tomorrow.

# WEEK 2

# DAY 13

# Dial-In/Dial-Out

A feature that quickly catches on with an SBS site is dial-in and dial-out. Perhaps the greatest need today is the ability to dial in from home and remote locations to check your e-mail, transfer files, and so on. Dial-out is important for those SBS sites that use dial-up service to connect to their Internet server providers (ISPs). Only a few of my SBS sites have true dial-out needs beyond connecting to their ISP. These needs including dialing the bank to conduct business, dialing the credit bureau to obtain a credit report, and dialing the drug testing laboratory to obtain employee's urinalysis drug test reports (true story).

Today is a day when everyone, both newbies and gurus, can attend the entire day. I'll segregate the basic/intermediate discussion from the advanced discussion with Power User Tips. In the morning session, I'll define remote communications, Remote Access Service (RAS), and the modem sharing service. In the afternoon session, I'm greatly looking forward to sharing with you a third-party dial-in solution that greatly outperforms RAS.

# ☀ AM Remote Access

Before getting into the details about RAS, modem sharing, and the like, allow me a moment to present you with the different types of dial-in communications scenarios available to an SBS network: remote access and remote control. Dial-out is essentially handled only one way, via modem pooling, which I'll discuss more in a moment.

## Remote Access Versus Remote Control

Remote access is the existing paradigm for dial-in communications on an SBS network. With remote access, you log on from your laptop or remote computer as a node on the network. You receive all network traffic such as messages, but you can also update or synchronize your Outlook client (so that later, when you work offline, you have the most current copy of your Inbox). RAS uses a remote access approach (as its name implies).

Remote control is much easier to implement and manage than remote access is. With remote control, you dial in to a machine on the network running a product such as pcAnywhere (or on larger, enterprise networks, Microsoft's Windows Terminal Server). With pcAnywhere, you take over the machine you've dialed in to, which means that only screens transfer over the telephone line back to your remote computer. This is typically faster than remote access, but the drawback is that remote applications, such as your local Outlook personal folders, aren't updated. (If you want to see your Outlook Inbox, you must dial in to the computer network and do so live.) Figure 13.1 displays the similarities and differences between remote access and remote control.

**FIGURE 13.1**

*Remote access versus remote control.*

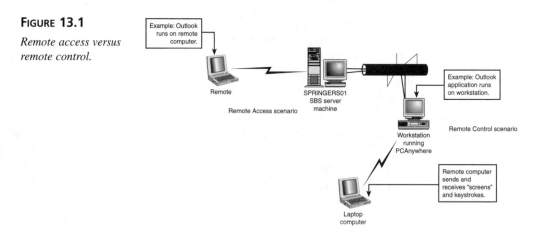

Both remote access and remote control have their respective advantages. For example, remote access is free because RAS ships with SBS. Remote access also allows you to compose messages offline, then dial in to the network to send, and receive your e-mail. This approach minimizes your connection charges. The benefits of remote control include its ease of implementation (you rarely have to worry about configuration trouble on the client side). I've also found the remote control solution to be more reliable. However, the remote control approach is generally more costly because you must purchase the remote control software (for example, pcAnywhere) and your online charges tend to be higher. (When your remote users typically compose their e-mail, they will be connected to the network, toll charges and all.)

**Power Tool Tip**

So you have a finicky CEO client, like I did, who has complained about the high cost of remote control. Again, with remote control, you must be online while running Outlook back at the workstation you've taken over. So, when you sit in London and connect to the SBS network in Seattle, the charges do accrue. But I've developed an approach that helps mitigate connection charges when sending e-mails.

In the case of the finicky CEO, I had the gentleman compose his e-mail messages offline in Microsoft Word and then simply copy and paste the text into the Outlook e-mail message he was sending via his remote control session. That way, he wrote five to ten messages long before he called in to establish his remote control session. I reduced the costs, and he was happier!

# Remote Access Service (RAS)

RAS is a service that SBS automatically installs during the server setup phase. Its role is to manage the communication function for modem and other communication (COM) port–based communications.

It is in RAS that you can take a modem that has been installed and make it a RAS device. When added to RAS, the modem can be designated as dial-out, receive calls, or both. You can also determine which network protocols (such as TCP/IP) are needed. For example, TCP/IP is used when you configure RAS to manage your dial-up Internet connection. Finally, RAS allows you to create a dialer for use by Dial-Up Networking (DUN). RAS is managed directly from Remote Access Service under the Service tab in Network properties (found via the Network applet in Control Panel). By clicking the Properties button on the Services tab when Remote Access Service is selected, you will see the Remote Access Setup dialog box, as seen in Figure 13.2.

13

**Power Tool Tip**

At the first sign of any RAS misbehavior, I strongly recommend you consider reapplying Service Pack 4 to your SBS 4.5 server machine. Early reports regarding SBS 4.5 indicate that reapplying SP4 will exorcise your SBS site of nasty RAS devils.

**FIGURE 13.2**

*Remote Access Setup.*

By clicking the Configure button in Remote Access Setup, you can configure whether the modem allows dial out, receives calls, or both via the Configure Port Usage dialog box. This is shown in Figure 13.3.

**FIGURE 13.3**

*Configure Port Usage.*

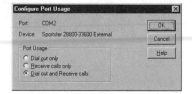

**Power Tool Tip**

I once tried to share a telephone line. The outbound part of the telephone line was RAS calling the ISP to check e-mail, allow Web browsing, and so on. The inbound portion of the telephone line was for the workstation running pcAnywhere. Long story short, I used a T-splitter at the telephone wall jack to facilitate this process. However, I forgot to set the RAS modem to dial-out only, so RAS answered the telephone before pcAnywhere could, causing (shall I say) SBS client frustration! To make matters worse, the telephone repairman, on-site for another matter, took matters into his own hands. He flipped a dip switch on the back of the external USR modem so, from a hardware perspective, the RAS modem wouldn't answer. The created another problem in that RAS now didn't work at all. The final solution? I flipped the USR dip switch back to its original position and used a software-based solution so that the RAS modem wouldn't answer the telephone. That is, I selected Dial Out Only on the Configure Port Usage dialog box (see Figure 13.3). Bottom line? RAS dialed out to the ISP as expected and pcAnywhere answered the telephone as expected over the same (albeit split) telephone line.

Two final thoughts on RAS and the Remote Access Setup dialog box. First, in its natural state as installed with SBS, RAS is ready to support your dial-in needs from day one with no further questions asked. It uses the TCP/IP protocol and automatically assigns TCP/IP addresses to remote computers that dial in. Case closed. Second, RAS is one of the few services that you actually configure via the Services tab on Network Properties. Recall that double-clicking Remote Access Service on the Services tab is what displays the Remote Access Setup. Other services are not configured this way; typically other services have a program group with an application that is launched to configure it.

## Task 13.1: Comparing RAS's Configuration to Other Services

**TASK**

▲

You've already double-clicked RAS in the Services tab on the Network Properties dialog box. Now try double-clicking Microsoft DHCP Server. What is the result? Answer: You should receive a Setup Message dialog box communicating "Cannot configure the software component."

Similar to other services, RAS does have an application for further configuration that is located in the Administrative Tools (Common) program group. This icon is titled Remote Access Admin, and when selected, it launches an application of the same name, as seen in Figure 13.4.

**FIGURE 13.4**

*Remote Access Admin.*

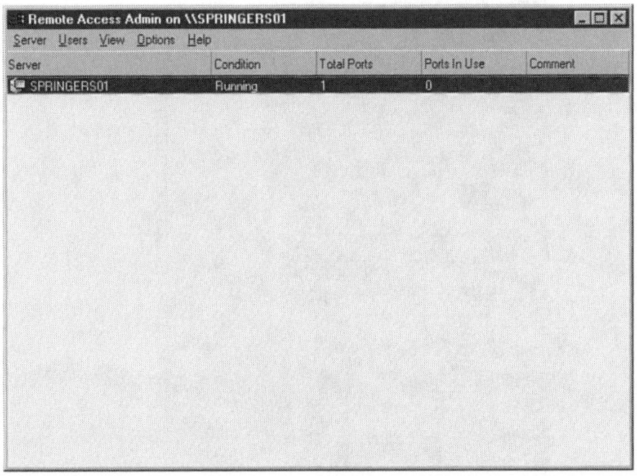

13

The Remote Access Admin application provides the following features:

- Current status of RAS-enabled devices (for example, modems)
- Capability to start, stop, and pause RAS
- Capability to grant dial-in privileges to remote users

One final tool of the trade when discussing RAS is the Dial-Up Monitor, an applet found in Control Panel (found via Settings from the Start menu). Dial-Up Monitor first allows you to verify that you are establishing a dial-out connection or your modem is busy with an inbound connection. In short, Dial-Up Monitor tells you the following:

- Modem condition and most recent response
- Connection speed (Line bps)
- Connection duration
- Basic transmission statistics (Bytes in, Bytes out)
- Basic error report
- Other settings, including capability to place Dial-Up Monitor as an icon on the task bar when it is running, make a sound and show status lights

Dial-Up Networking Monitor, seen in Figure 13.5, is one of the few places in SBS that you can actually disconnect a call (via the Hang Up button on the Status tab). Speaking of the Status tab, note that the information communicated by Dial-Up Monitor isn't limited to RAS-related calls. It is here that you can also observe Modem Sharing and Fax Server–related activity as well (from the modem's perspective).

**FIGURE 13.5**

*Dial-Up Monitor.*

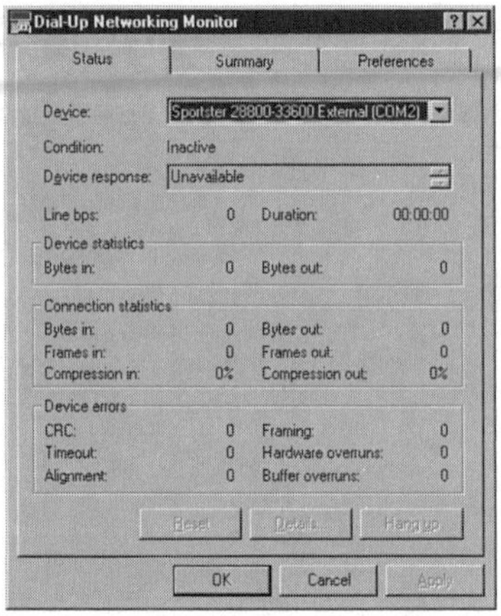

**Power Tool Tip**

> I've found Dial-Up Monitor to be so useful in conjunction with the SBS server that I've created a shortcut of it and placed it in the Startup folder so that it automatically launches on startup of the SBS server. Such a shortcut is created the same way other shortcuts are created with SBS: via the secondary menu when the icon is selected.

# Modem Sharing

The previous section, dedicated to RAS, was presented (more or less) from the paradigm of dial-in communications. But one of the more interesting features found in SBS is the capability to use Modem Sharing to facilitate dial-out communications. As mentioned earlier today, dial-out communications was a feature lacking in regular Windows NT Server and its implementation of RAS. This SBS dial-out capability is popular for connecting via modem to your ISP for e-mail and Web browsing, calling bulletin boards (BBS), and placing direct computer-based calls to other sites (credit bureaus, banks, drug testing labs, client sites, and so on). Modem sharing has two components: server and client.

## The Server Side

With SBS, modem sharing is installed on the server when you perform a complete SBS installation. Little additional configuration is necessary, unless you intend to install additional modems, change a modem, or so on. On the server-side, modem sharing is managed via the Modem Sharing applet in Control Panel (found via Settings from the Start menu).

Double-clicking the Modem Sharing icon launches the Modem Sharing Admin dialog box. Modem Sharing Admin allows you to

- Observe active modem sharing connections.
- Turn on Event Logging so that modem sharing–related information can be viewed by Event Viewer. I recommend you make this election on the General tab, as seen in Figure 13.6.

**FIGURE 13.6**

*Modem Sharing Admin.*

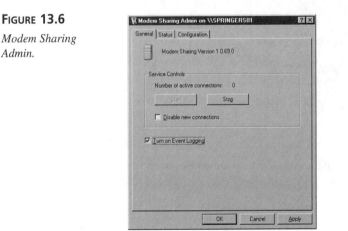

13

- Observe which user is using SBS's modem sharing capabilities, listed by user, system, port, and duration on the Status tab. This is a very useful screen.
- Commit or assign additional COM ports (communication ports) to be included in a modem pool. This commitment makes the port/modem eligible to participate in modem sharing.

## The Client Side

The second half of the modem sharing equation is at the SBS user's workstation. When the SBS workstation setup disk (that is, Magic Disk) is created, you might elect to install the modem sharing capability on the workstation. Assuming you have made that election, Microsoft Modem Sharing is installed with other SBS workstation applications. A program group called Microsoft Modem Sharing appears under Programs (accessed via the Start menu) at the SBS user's workstation.

After the Magic Disk has been run on the SBS workstation, you will need to undertake a few additional steps to use SBS's modem sharing.

To configure the workstation to use SBS's modem sharing

1. From the Start menu, select Program, Microsoft Modem Sharing. Run the Modem Sharing Setup application. The Modem Sharing Setup Wizard is launched as seen in Figure 13.7.

**FIGURE 13.7**

*Modem Sharing Setup Wizard.*

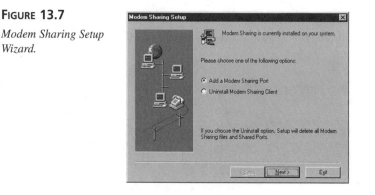

2. Select the Add a Modem Sharing Port radio button and click Next.
3. Enter the pool path that points the modem pool back on the SBS server in the Pool Path field on the Pool Path dialog box, as seen in Figure 13.8.

FIGURE **13.8**

*Pool Path.*

**Power Tool Tip**

You must enter the correct UNC path to the modem pool on the SBS server. Failure to do this will result in your SBS users receiving a bogus error message at their workstations that states "The modem is being used by another Dial-Up Networking connection or another program." Such is not the case; in reality, the UNC path to the modem pool is incorrect. For example, instead of a correct path such as \\SPRINGERS\MODEMS\, I've seen incorrectly entered UNC modem sharing paths such as \\SPRINGERS\COMPORTS. Make this mistake and you'll see the bogus error message I've shared with you here.

    4.  Click the Finish button.

Remember that, on the client-side (that is, the SBS user's workstation), the modem sharing capability is really using an approach I call the *redirector.* Communication activity destined for a COM port is actually trapped and redirected to a COM port (and thus, a modem) located on the SBS server. (The COM port is usually a local port that you can visually observe on the back of your computer.) Why do this at all? Because, by redirecting this type of activity (modem-related), you can use fewer modems, telephone lines, and so on at an SBS site.

To verify that everything is shipshape with respect to modem sharing at the SBS workstation, perform the following simple modem sharing verification test whether the workstation is of the Windows 9x (95/98) variety:

    1.  At the SBS workstation (Windows 9x), right-click My Computer.

    2.  Select Properties from the secondary menu. System Properties is displayed.

    3.  Select the Device Manager tab.

    4.  Scroll down and select and expand the Ports listing.

**13**

5. Observe the Modem Sharing Port line items under ports for one or more COM ports (assuming you've completed the COM port configuration). This is shown in Figure 13.9.

**FIGURE 13.9**

*Modem Sharing Port.*

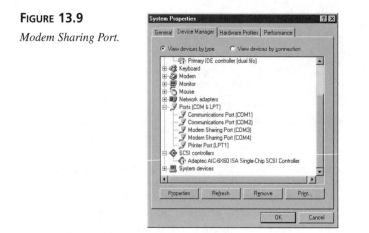

6. Double-click one of the Modem Sharing Port lines to display the Modem Sharing Port (COM3) Properties dialog box, as seen in Figure 13.10.

**FIGURE 13.10**

*Modem Sharing Port (COM3) Properties.*

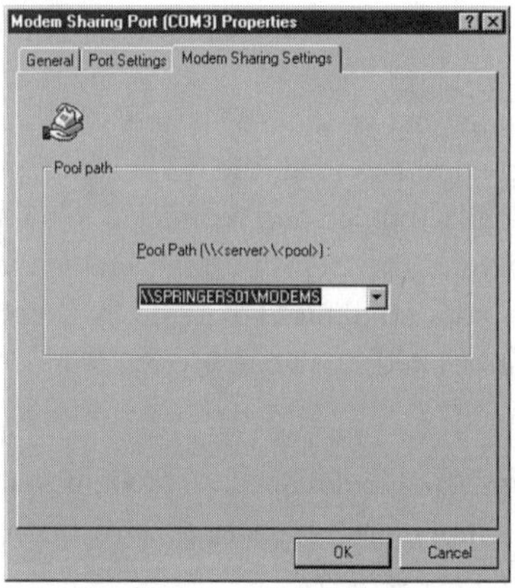

7. Select the Modem Sharing Settings tab and observe the Pool Path. If it is incorrect, change it in the Pool Path field and click OK.

# The Case Against Modem Sharing

I've spent the past few pages showing you how modem sharing works. Did you know, however, that if you connect your SBS server to your Internet service provider (ISP) via the Internet Connection Wizard and you have no need to dial out directly to BBSes, banks, and the like, you actually have little or no need for the dial-out modem sharing capabilities in SBS? Correctly connected to the Internet via the SBS Internet Connection Wizard, if you only use Microsoft Exchange–based e-mail and browse via Internet Explorer on the Web, you're not only not using modem sharing, but you don't need to. Here's why.

## Web Browsing

The basic SBS Internet configuration includes automatic setup and deployment of the Microsoft Proxy Auto Dial application to intercept Web-bound traffic. This is typically generated by SBS users browsing the Web with Internet Explorer. I discussed the Microsoft Proxy Auto Dial application, which dials out to your ISP when a connection to the Internet is desired, on Day 11, "Using Proxy Server." This application is seen in Figure 13.11.

**FIGURE 13.11**

*Microsoft Proxy Auto Dial.*

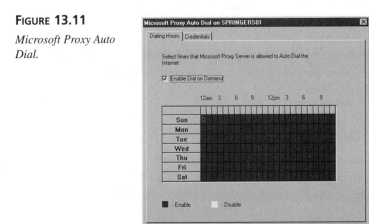

## Internet E-mail

If you use Microsoft Exchange for your Internet-based e-mail communications—which I assume you are because it is the default configuration on an SBS network—you again have no need for modem sharing because the sending and receiving of Exchange-based Internet e-mail is managing on a schedule via the Internet Mail Service (ISM). This ISM checks your ISP's mail server on a regular schedule (say, every 2 hours). Given a modem-based connection to your ISP, the ISM really uses just a local COM port to dial the modem on your SBS server. Why? Because Exchange's ISM is installed on the SBS server, thus no fancy modem sharing is needed; call it a local call if you will!

Let's take lunch and complete a task.

## 🥪 Lunch

Today's lunch is a task, so I hope you brought your own meal. Take the time you need to complete the following task.

### Task 13.2: Surfing for Solutions

I assume that, as you're nearing the end of the second week, you have connected to the Internet with your SBS network. Good. Then, to test for understanding from the morning session and better prepare you for the afternoon session, use an Internet search engine such as Infoseek (www.infoseek.com) to research the following dial-in/dial-out solutions:

- LapLink
- CloseUp
- ReachOut

Here's a hint: search on each term listed previously as a keyword in a search engine. Hopefully, by performing this research, you'll have a better grasp of the main topic matter presented today. Good luck!

## 🌙 PM Dialing In

This afternoon the mission is simple. First, I'll show you how to dial in, via RAS, to your SBS network. I'll show this from a Windows 9x workstation. Second, I'll show you my favorite way to connect to an SBS network, which is to use pcAnywhere.

# Dialing In to Your SBS Network via RAS

Of course, RAS provides the politically correct way to dial in to your SBS network . Given a Windows 9x workstation, here is how you do exactly that.

1. Start your Windows 9x machine. This machine is typically a laptop that you carry to a remote site to dial in to the SBS network. It can also be a home PC that you use after hours.

**Note**    I assume the modem connected to your workstation is also connected to a telephone line.

2. When presented with the Winlogon dialog box in Windows 9x (which asks you for a logon name, password, and domain), press the Esc key to bypass. This is a critical step to perform. You will automatically be taken to the Windows 9x desktop.

3. From the Start menu, select Programs, Accessories, Dial-Up Networking (with Windows 98, this is located in the communications folder). The Dial-Up Networking window appears.

4. If a dialer hasn't been previously created for you, double-click the Make New Connection icon. This launches the Make New Connection wizard, as seen in Figure 13.12.

**FIGURE 13.12**

*Make New Connection wizard.*

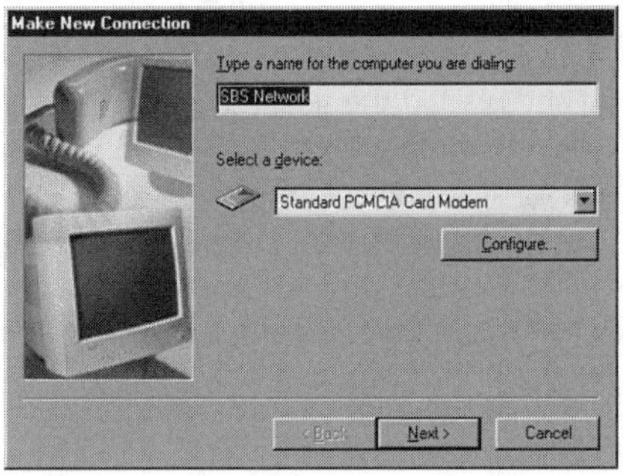

5. Name your dialer and select an installed modem on your local machine to use. Click Next.

6. Type the SBS server dial-in telephone number. This is the line that the RAS modem on your SBS server is connected to.

7. Click Finish to complete creating your dialer.

8. You're not finished yet! You're going to further modify the dialer you just created by right-clicking on the dialer (which now appears in the Dial-Up Networking window). Select Properties from the secondary menu.

9. Select the Server Types tab.

10. Remove checkmark from the NetBEUI and IPX/SPX Compatible protocol options. Verify that Type of;IPX/SPX Compatible protocol option Dial-Up Server is set to PPP.

**13**

11. Click the TCP/IP Settings button and verify that you will receive a Server-assigned IP address and name servers (two different radio buttons speak to these points). Click OK.

12. Click OK to close the dialer.

13. Double-click the dialer and enter your SBS network user name and password in the Connect To dialog box. Click Connect.

14. After your dialer dials your SBS server and you are logged on, you can use the network just as if you were on a workstation back at the office. You can map drives, check e-mail, save files, and so on.

That's it: 14 easy steps to setting up and using a dialer to connect, via RAS, with your SBS server.

**Power Tool Tip**

As shared by another SBS master, consider the following RAS optimization tip. Dial-up networking seems to work faster if you use only NetBEUI or if you use TCP/IP to create a LMHOSTS file by putting the domain in RAM with the #DOM call and placing the server IP address with the #PRE call in the LMHOSTS file on the remote client.

If the terms *#DOM* and *#PRE* aren't familiar to you, don't fret. Simply read the lmhosts.sam file located at \winnt.sbs\system32\drivers\etc\. This 4KB text file contains full definitions on these and other terms along with advice on using your own LMHOSTS file to optimize resolution on your SBS network. It's great stuff.

# Using pcAnywhere

Now for my favorite part of the day. For so many SBSers, RAS is too tempting to pass up: it's both free and politically correct. I typically know when I'm in the presence of an experienced SBSer, however, because in all likelihood, these SBS gurus are using some type of third-party solution for the SBS network dial-in communications. Various third-party dial-in solutions exist including CloseUp, ReachOut, LapLink, and pcAnywhere. Here I'll profile pcAnywhere, one of the leading remote control solutions. If you completed Tasks 13.1 and 13.2, you have surface, if not deeper, understanding of the remote control solutions listed just a moment ago.

First, let me answer the larger question. What drove me to seek out and deploy a third-party communications solution that costs additional money (that is, it isn't included for free such as RAS in the SBS bundle)? More importantly, why am I such a big fan of remote control (*a la* pcAnywhere) over RAS-based remote access? One reason: reliability. I've been burned by RAS in the form of written-down hours and lost productivity, but

I've been pleasantly surprised by the likes of pcAnywhere and its remote control paradigm. As I told Dawn, the SBS system administrator at a local athletic club, "Go learn for yourself." Get RASed and then try a remote control solution such as pcAnywhere.

You still don't believe me? Well, I have several stories, but I'll have you revisit the finicky CEO story earlier today (it's one of my best). Perhaps more interesting than war stories is how, when other SBS consultants stumble with RAS at client sites, I'm invited to take over the account and, remote control solution in hand (such as pcAnywhere), my new-found client notices a drop in consultant hours related to dial-in support. In short, I love these situations where I have the chance to arrive and be the knight in shining armor!

pcAnywhere is a remote control solution; only the screens are passed between the SBS network and the remote user's workstation. Back at the office, pcAnywhere typically runs on a dedicated workstation (which has a modem). pcAnywhere just sits and waits for a remote user to dial in and start working.

**Power Tool Tip**

Do not even think about running pcAnywhere on the SBS server itself. That is a bad idea for two reasons. First, I saw such a setup once and noticed that the SBS running pcAnywhere had a nasty habit of *blue-screening* or shutting down unexpectedly. Bad news. Second, I configure pcAnywhere to reboot at the end of any remote session (regardless of whether the session ends by accident or as planned). This reboot is for security reasons. I don't want an open session on my pcAnywhere machine that any high-school hacker could dial in on and take over! So the rule is run pcAnywhere on any standalone machine.

I won't use these pages to give you the systematic details on installing pcAnywhere on a PC at work and your remote computer. The manuals that accompany pcAnywhere do a fine job of that. Plus the setup of pcAnywhere is nothing more than a setup wizard. You might recall that setup wizards were discussed on Day 6, "Daily and Weekly SBS Administration (The Dirty Dozen)."

After pcAnywhere is set up on the PC at the office, you should create a modem-based host. Remember, this is the pcAnywhere workstation back at the office that simply waits until you, the remote user, dial in remotely with pcAnywhere and establish a session. The host you configure should have a few specific settings:

- Reboot on session termination.
- Launch pcAnywhere with Windows. This is so that pcAnywhere stops at the Winlogon dialog box; a user must enter SBS network credentials (logon name, password, domain) before proceeding.

**13**

- Screen resolution matches remote PC. This setting prevents a mismatch between remote PC and host.

After installing and launching pcAnywhere, create a Remote Control icon on your remote computer that is named after your SBS site (for example, Springer Spaniels Unlimited) and configure it with the following information:

- The telephone number of your pcAnywhere host machine back at the office.
- The local modem you intend to use for dialing.

Now, assuming the pcAnywhere host machine back at the office is ready, simply double-click the Remote Control icon (for example, Springers - SBS) and observe pcAnywhere in action (its own form of dialer launches, as seen in Figure 13.13).

**FIGURE 13.13**

*pcAnywhere placing a call.*

## Summary

In its proper context, the effective use of SBS's dial-in/dial-out capabilities clearly extends the reach of SBS way beyond the four walls of its base site. Today, SBS users are looking to extend the power of the network to their homes, hotel rooms, and even boats! SBS's native support for dial-in/dial-out will get you to that goal. The selective use of third-party communication tools (such as remote control software) can even help you get there faster and more reliably.

# DAY 14

# Faxing

You end the second week with faxing. This topic is appropriately placed because it is usually the last aspect of the SBS network configuration that my SBS clients suddenly discover. Whereas e-mail and Web browsing are the main priorities out of the gate for most SBS sites, faxing is usually something I can show when things settle down and I have the client's attention. After other SBS features, such as Outlook, are accepted and widely used, the time is ripe to introduce faxing. In the morning, basic SBS faxing is defined as well as configured. In the afternoon, you send and receive a fax as well as discuss fax reporting and other advanced fax topics.

## AM Defining SBS Faxing

One of the first hurdles to overcome when generating excitement for the faxing function is to educate both yourself and the SBS users as to what faxing really is. In this secular world of atoms, bricks, and mortar, people have long known faxing as the capability to feed a page into a desktop device and send the contents of the page to another fax machine at a distant location. The SBS faxing function, shown in detail in Figure 14.1, includes

- Sending and receiving faxes via the fax modem attached to the SBS server machine
- SBS's capability to save faxes to a folder titled FaxStore (see the FaxStore folder in Figure 14.1)
- SBS's capability to print faxes automatically to a network printer (see the Laser Printer in Figure 14.1)
- SBS's capability to e-mail the faxes to a designated recipient (see the SBS User Workstation in Figure 14.1)

**FIGURE 14.1**

*Basic SBS faxing function.*

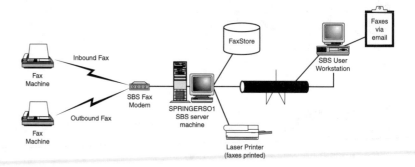

## Outbound Faxes

One of the first questions SBS users ask regarding faxing is "How do you get the document into the computer?" This question, when unanswered, poses such a mental block that I've seen small businesses not embrace the powerful SBS fax capabilities. Here is the answer to this fear of faxing question. First, in reality, you will continue to use your existing fax machine for odd-sized outgoing documents such as Dilbert comic strips that you're faxing to friends and family. You will likely continue to use the existing fax machine to transmit documents, such as letters, that need your signature (although later I'll show you how to scan your signature for your letters). And you'll probably use your fax machine to transmit handwritten notes. So there, I've now said it and clarified a major point of contention surrounding SBS faxing: you'll most likely continue to use your existing fax machine for very specific reasons.

But outbound faxing is in no way a total loser, either. Remember way back (in the first third of the book) when I discussed the landscaping company. The CEO of the landscaping company saw his greatest potential with outbound faxing, targeted to his landscaping customers. His idea was to send out spring planting notices. Here, the outbound faxing capability would be integrated with his Outlook Contacts, something that is easily done.

**Note**

> Some progressive SBS sites are using low-cost scanners to scan in odd-shaped documents for use in outbound faxing scenarios. More firms will most likely use this approach in the near future as scanners become cheaper and enjoy greater acceptance. I'll offer one word of caution with this approach. The scanned images that result when you scan odd-shaped documents are larger than you think. Even moderate scanning activity can result in over 100MB of scanned images. As you can see, you'll quickly eat up hard disk space that you might need.

A few key benefits to outbound faxing include

- Marketing announcements and flyers
- Form letters with a scanned signature
- Standard forms your customers might request
- Other documents appropriate for broadcasting

**Power Tool Tip**

> Understand that the capability to fax the same document to multiple parties via SBS faxing isn't true broadcasting. Fax broadcasting, in its pure form, is a service provided by a telco with lots and lots of extra fax lines (that is, burst capacity) with the ability to get your document out to tens or hundreds of parties within a few minutes. The telco uses a pool of lines to do this and charges you accordingly for such a wonderful service.
>
> SBS's outbound faxing capability is, shall I say, linear. Given a list of parties who are to receive the same document, the SBS server calls each party in succession and transmits the fax. Such a linear approach can indeed take hours to complete, as each fax call is made one at a time. But fear not, the good news is that this activity is automatic, meaning you do not have to attend to the process (allowing you to go home and slow-cook a great meal, go play golf, and so on).

## Inbound Faxes

SBS faxing really shines when inbound faxes are concerned. With inbound faxing, the SBS server machine answers the fax line when an inbound fax is arriving (the telephone line generates a ring like a normal telephone line). The fax is received by the SBS server and processed as an image file in one or all of three ways: printed, saved to the server's hard disk, or e-mailed to a single e-mail account.

**14**

SBS does not facilitate automatic routing or distribution of faxes to additional e-mail accounts like high-end standalone fax applications can do. Other faxing solutions include WinFax PRO (Symantec), Fax Sr. (Omtool), and RightFAX (RightFAX).

The benefits of having the SBS server machine receive a fax include

- The capability to forward a fax image to others via e-mail.

- The capability to store fax images on the SBS server for future use or as a permanent record.

- The capability to refax a document to another party without any loss of fax quality (with real fax machines, when you refax a document to someone else, you suffer a significant resolution loss).

- The capability to use your computer network laser printer as a plain-paper fax printer, thus eliminate the curly or heat transfer fax paper used by older fax machine (which a surprisingly high number of small businesses still use).

- The capability to view a fax on your computer display without printing it first. Under the SBS faxing model, when you receive junk faxes or faxes that simply aren't important, you can quickly glance at them with the SBS workstation fax viewer software (which I'll discuss in a moment) and then delete the fax, never sending it to a printer.

- The capability to read faxes remotely. When faxes received by the SBS server are either forwarded to me via e-mail or simply stored on the SBS server, I can dial in and read these faxes without having to cross the bridge and drive to the office just to retrieve my faxes. This feature alone has made a huge difference for me and my SBS clients, and we've all avoided a lot of unnecessary trips into the office to pick up faxes.

- The capability to scan graphics and signatures for use on your network. I'll show you how to do this later today.

- Using a third-party text-scanning application, such as OmniTool, to convert the faxed text into text that you can manipulate in your word processing application. (This is still an immature technology that doesn't always work correctly yet. You still have to proofread text that was converted.)

## More Fax Features

A few other cool features are included with the SBS Fax Server, many of which I'll discuss in more detail later today:

- Modem Pool Support—You can attach up to four modems to the SBS server for faxing purposes. Using the modem pool actually supports limited group faxing on outbound faxing. That is, if everyone prints to the same fax printer from the desktop, the faxes can all be sent at the same time, up to the four fax modem limit. This discussion is conceptually similar to printer pooling.

**Power Tool Tip**

> This modem pool capability, combined with a hunt line capability from your telco, allows you to offer never-a-busy-signal–level services for your customers trying to fax your firm. Essentially, all your customers send faxes to a single published fax line, say 206-123-1235 for Springer Spaniels Unlimited. If a customer attempts to send a fax, and the first fax modem is occupied, the telco's hunt capability provides the capability to have the second, third, or fourth modem receive the inbound fax call.
>
> Theoretically, all four fax modems, assuming you have that many, could receive faxes at the same time. And because a small business would almost never receive more than four faxes simultaneously, you could advertise your business as never having a busy fax line!
>
> I should also note that a fax modem pool also facilitates simultaneous inbound and outbound faxing operations, something many small businesses only have today if they have truly separate fax machines. It's a tip worth mentioning to the small business owner seeking more information on how to use multiple telephone lines and a fax modem pool.

- Cover Pages—The SBS Fax Server also includes a set of fax cover pages for your use. You can also create your own fax cover pages via Microsoft Word or the Microsoft Fax Viewer software. Be advised that the use of computerized faxing solution such as the SBS Fax Server eliminates the ability to use the popular Post-it Fax Notes. These tiny scraps of paper, with a sticky backing, are typically attached to the header of the first fax page when using a real physical fax machine. Because there you can't conveniently attach something physical such as a Post-it Note to a computer-generated fax, you need to be content with using SBS Fax Server–based cover pages when transmitting.
- Control—Via Manage User in the SBS Console, you can specify who may use the SBS faxing capabilities and who may not. Although not as critical of a need as preventing Internet usage abuse, I do have SBS sites—albeit, they tend to be old-fashioned companies—that want strict control over who can use the fax capability on the SBS network.

# SBS Fax Components

SBS's fax capabilities can be divided into server and client components. First I'll discuss the server side, where basic configuration issues are addressed. On the client side, I'll show what components are installed on an SBS user's workstation.

14

## The Server Side: Microsoft Fax Server

The actual faxing capability installed on the SBS server machine is known as Microsoft Fax Server. This server-side application is installed automatically when you install SBS using the complete installation feature (which I recommend). The following Fax Server components are installed including fax modem.

### Fax Modem

The modem that you installed with SBS on Day 3, "Installing Small Business Server," is automatically enabled as a fax modem. If you have at least one modem installed on the SBS server that is fax capable, you are ready to start using SBS's Fax Server (and can proceed to the next section).

To install an additional fax modem

1. Physically attach the modem to the SBS Server machine (in either an internal slot or to an external COM port). Do this while the SBS server machine is turned off.

2. Power on the SBS server machine and the modem (if it is an external modem).

3. Log on as Administrator to the SBS server machine.

4. Select Control Panel from the Setting menu option (found via the Start button).

5. Double-click the Modems icon.

6. Click the Add button. The Install New Modem Wizard starts, offering you the chance to have your new modem auto-detected or not.

7. If it's necessary either because you manually must select the modem or because the modem was misdetected, select the modem brand and model from the Install New Modem Wizard's manufacturers/models page.

8. After the modem is installed, you see a message communicating dial-up networking must be configured. Reply Yes.

9. The Remote Access Setup dialog box, similar to Figure 14.2, is displayed. Click the Add button to add your new modem to a list of RAS-capable devices. And don't forget my preference, mentioned during this book, for external modems. External modems require only that you turn the modem off and on to recycle them, not reboot the SBS server like an internal modem requires.

**FIGURE 14.2**

*Remote Access Setup dialog box.*

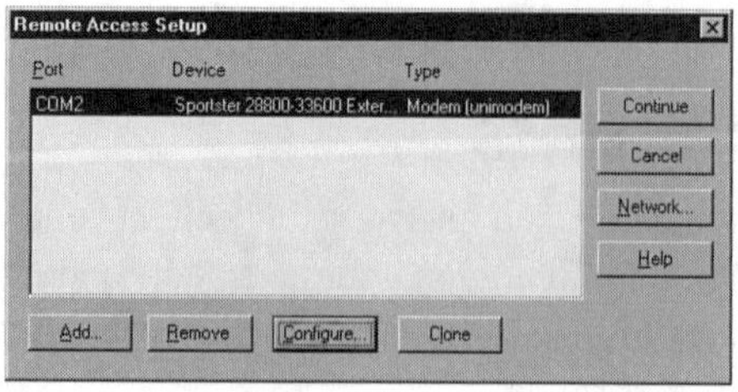

10. I also recommend that you click the Configure button while your newly installed modem is highlighted in the Remote Access Setup dialog box. This displays the Configure Port Usage dialog box and allows you to confirm that the modem is configured for both dialing out and receiving calls, as seen in Figure 14.3.

11. Click OK and restart the server for these changes to take effect.

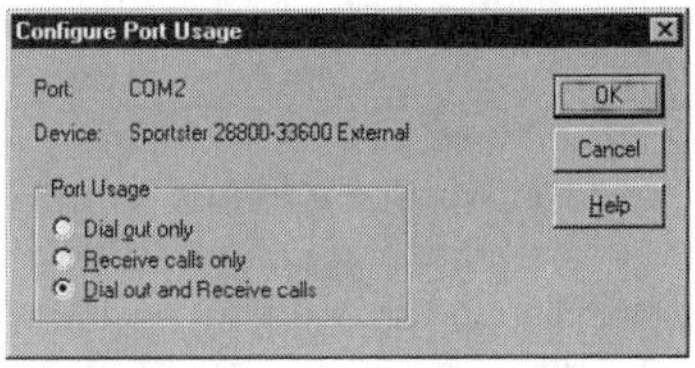

**FIGURE 14.3**

*Configure Port Usage.*

Next, you need to add the new modem to the existing fax printer. This is explained later today when I discuss the Send and Receive tabs of the Fax Server Properties dialog box). However, if for some reason you want to create a second fax printer with its own identity, launch the SBS Console, select Manage Faxes and complete the steps necessary via the Add or Remove Fax Printers menu option.

## Fax Server

The Fax Server icon is placed in Control Panel when you install Microsoft Fax Server (again, typically when you install SBS using the complete installation option). Double-clicking the Fax Server icon in Control Panel displays the Fax Server Properties dialog box as seen in Figure 14.4.

**FIGURE 14.4**

*Fax Server Properties - Dialing tab.*

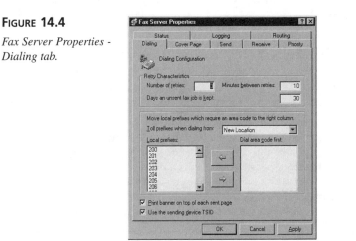

**14**

From the Fax Server Properties dialog box, you can configure or observe the following tabs: Dialing, Cover Page, Send, Receive, Priority, Status, Logging, and Routing.

**Dialing**   Here you set the basic dialing parameters for fax activity including number of retries, minutes between retries, and days an unsent fax job remains stored on the server. The local prefixes and area code options in the center of the Dialing tab allows you to attempt to associate local telephone dialing prefixes with a long distance call.

**Power Tool Tip**

> While attempting to associate prefixes with a long distance call, I've found it is better to handle this capability manually, instead of attempting to configure such activity via the Dialing tab. Here's why. Many local prefixes really aren't dialed as an 11-digit long distance call (1-area code-telephone number) but rather as a ten-digit local call (area code-telephone number). Such oddities are best handled by SBS end users when a fax is sent. See "Sending a Fax" later today.

Also note that, on the Dialing tab shown in Figure 14.4, selecting Print Banner on Top of Each Sent Page results in your fax telephone number being printed on each faxed page as a header. This is common and this check box is selected by default. In fact, I think it was some jailhouse lawyer or technical editor (same difference, eh?) who communicated that U.S. Federal law requires that you have your fax telephone number displayed as a header. Check with your lawyer just to be sure.

**Cover Page**   You can select from several default cover pages that are sent along with the fax. The Cover Page tab is shown in Figure 14.5 and one of the fax cover sheet templates is shown in Figure 14.6.

Note if you select the Client Must Use These Cover Pages check box, SBS users will be required to use one the of the cover pages when sending a fax.

**Power Tool Tip**

> You can create a cover page for your company and have that cover page be the only fax cover page which can be used on the SBS network. To do this, click the New button on the Cover Page tab to launch the Fax Cover Page Editor. Create the cover page, with graphics if desired, and save the file with the *.COV extension. This new cover page you've created can now be used as a fax cover page on the SBS network. Be sure to delete the other cover pages so that your SBS users must use your corporate fax cover sheet by default.

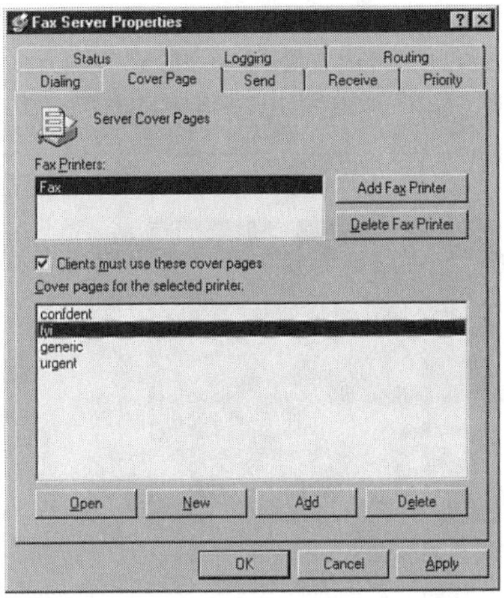

FIGURE **14.5**

*Cover pages.*

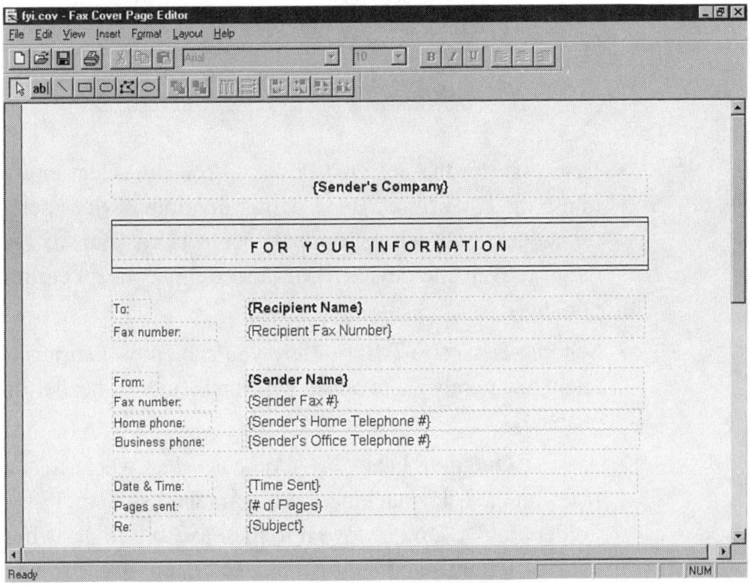

FIGURE **14.6**

*Cover page template (fyi).*

**Send** The Send tab is very important because it's where you configure the basic outgoing fax parameters for the SBS server. Several items must be presented and configured:

- Fax Printers—At least one fax printer must be displayed. By default, this is the case when Microsoft Fax Server is installed on an SBS server machine with a fax-capable modem. The default name of the fax printer is Fax.

14

**Note** Why is the fax device called a fax printer? As you will see later today, the fax metaphor is that of printing to the fax device. Standby.

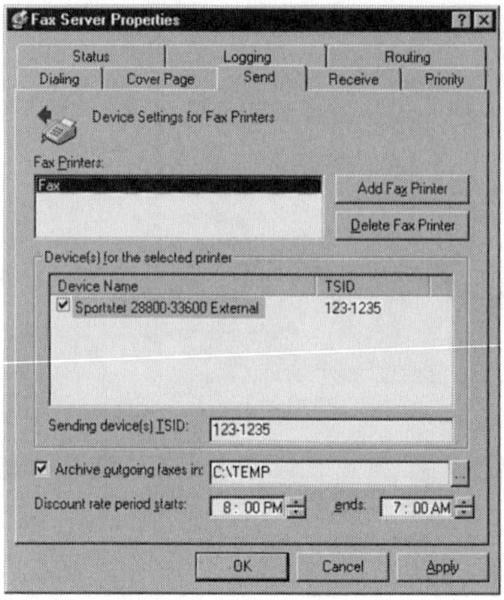

FIGURE **14.7**

*Send.*

- Device(s) for the Selected Printer—You can select multiple devices (fax modems) to use the Fax printer. By selecting multiple devices here, you effectively create a fax modem pool where if one device is busy, your fax request simply rolls over to the next available device. (I discussed this concept earlier today under modem pooling.)

- Sending Device(s) TSID—Here you can enter the transmitting station ID or fax telephone number that appears in the banner or header of each sent fax page (if so enabled).

- Archive Outgoing Faxes In—You can select where to save a copy of (archive) your faxes on the SBS machine. I'd recommend something such as the Company Shared Folders folder. Do not save it to the FaxStore folder where incoming faxes are held. (This will help avoid confusion as to which faxes are inbound and which were outbound.)

- Discount Rate Period Starts—For the financial controllers and bookkeepers among us, this setting will thrill you. Here you can define the lower long-distance rate time frame.

**Receive**    Even more important than the Send tab, in my opinion, is the Receive tab. Many of the settings (device, ID, rings) are similar to settings I've already discussed. The three settings of greatest interest are Print To, Save in Folder, and Send to Local Inbox:

- Print To—Here you select the printer on which the incoming fax is automatically printed. This is typically selected because most small businesses I've worked with need the comfort of seeing a printed fax. The good news about printing the faxes is threefold: it's the most understood way for the small business to receive a fax, odd-sized faxes such as incoming legal pages are automatically reduced to the printer's paper size (typically an incoming legal page is reduced to latter size), and small businesses especially enjoy receiving faxes from a laser printer, not on curly fax paper!

- Save in Folder—Incoming faxes are stored to the FaxStore folder (C:\Winnt.sbs\FaxStore) by default. This option is selected by default, and I suggest you allow it to remain selected. By saving faxes in the FaxStore folder, you can always go back and view them again (if somehow you've lost an important fax later) and make a permanent record of incoming faxes (perhaps for legal reasons).

- Send to Local Inbox—Here you can designate an individual to receive a copy of the incoming fax in her e-mail inbox automatically. Typically this person is an administrative assistant or secretary who then forwards, via e-mail, the fax to the ultimate receiving party. In the case of Springer Spaniels Unlimited, you will elect Melinda Overlake (MelindaO) to receive the incoming faxes via e-mail. You might recall that Melinda is the Front Desk Receptionist at Springer Spaniels Unlimited. This is shown in Figure 14.8.

**FIGURE 14.8**

*Receive.*

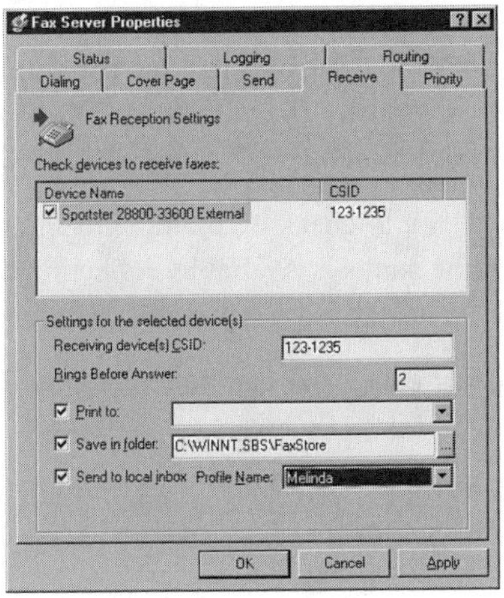

14

**Tip**

In order for Melinda's name to appear and be selected as seen in Figure 14.8, you must create a local e-mail profile for Melinda via the Mail and Fax icon in Control Panel. This must be done on the SBS server machine although Melinda will receive incoming faxes just fine when she is logged on at her workstation running her e-mail client (for example, Outlook). Chalk it up to another SBS configuration oddity. Note that I discussed creating e-mail profiles at length on Day 8, "Implementing Outlook," so I now refer you back to that day for those steps.

**Power Tool Tip**

So what happens if Melinda is sick one day and is unable to forward the faxes via e-mail? You should either have the faxes printed automatically or saved in the FaxStore folder in addition to this e-mail approach. That way, users have another way, perhaps not as convenient as e-mail, to receive their faxes. Kindly note that you will likely have to train users how to check for faxes in the FaxStore folder, where the filename is meaningless, and the time stamp (date/time received) is all-important.

Also, I'd recommend you select all three reception methods: print, save, and send (discussed previously) as an SBS site becomes familiar with the inbound fax capabilities of SBS Server. At a future date, you might elect to discontinue one or two of the fax reception methods.

**Priority**     The Priority tab applies to SBS sites that have multiple fax modem devices. You might elect which device has priority over the other. This is not a commonly used configuration feature, so it is best ignored.

**Status**     The Status tab allows you to check on the fax modem device status at a glance. Typically, the modem listed at the status is Available, reflecting that the modem is turned on and ready for activity. The Status tab isn't especially useful and is typically ignored.

**Logging**     Four types of logging categories can be elected via the Logging tab

- Inbound
- Initialization/Termination
- Outbound
- Unknown

For each logging activity, four types of logging levels can be chosen: none, minimum, medium, and maximum. The default condition is for all login categories to have maximum logging invoked. This default condition allows you to view the Fax-related reports, via the SBS Console, in a sincere and meaningful way. These reports are discussed at the end of today in the "Fax Reporting" section.

**Routing** The Routing tab allows you to configure the delivery of fax modifications. It is different than the inbound fax routing capability configured previously on the Receive tab. Select an e-mail profile, such as Melinda, to receive fax notifications (see Figure 14.9).

**FIGURE 14.9**

*Routing fax notifications to Melinda.*

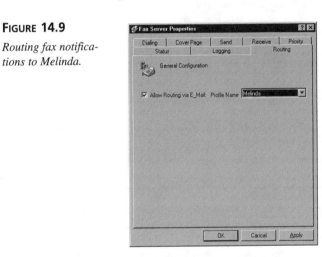

## The Client Side: SBS Faxing

On the client side, you handle the main configuration activity via the Fax Client icon in Control Panel on the SBS workstation. This icon is placed on the workstation when you select the Microsoft Fax client on setting up a new computer via Manage Computers in the SBS Console. The SBS server machine will also have an icon in Control Panel titled Fax Client.

### Fax Client

Double-clicking the Fax Client icon displays the Properties for Fax Client, as seen in Figure 14.10. Note on an SBS server machine, this same action displays a dialog box titled Properties for Fax Client.

14

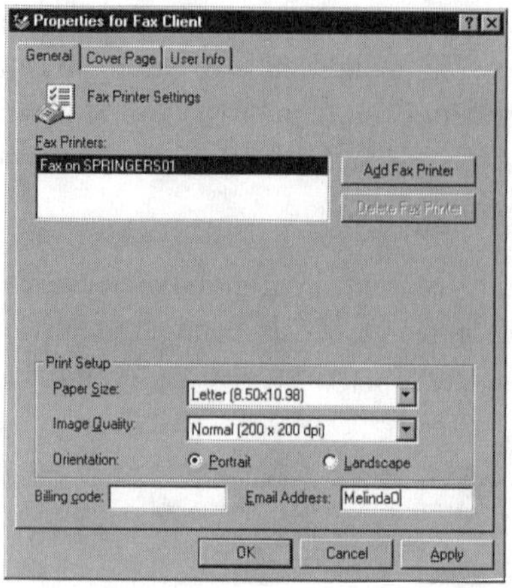

FIGURE 14.10

*Properties for Fax Client.*

There are three tabs: General, Cover Page, and User Info. I'll briefly discuss all three.

**General**  The General tab (shown in Figure 14.10) allows you to make general settings, such as the fax printer you will use. This tab is configured for you when you install the Microsoft Fax client on your workstation as part of the SBS workstation setup.

> **Tip**
>
> In order to receive information regarding the faxes you send from your workstation, be sure to put your e-mail address (for example, MelindaO) in the Email Address field. One such e-mail you will receive is reports on the delivery of faxes that you have sent. This is the closet thing I've found to a fax confirmation letter in SBS.

**Cover Page**  The Cover Page tab allows you to add or remove cover sheets you would like to have available when you send a fax.

**User Info**  The User Info tab allows you to provide user information that appears on fax cover pages, such as full name, mailbox, title, work phone, address, and so on. This information must be entered if you want it to appear because it is not carried over from the user setup information you entered for each user via Manager Users in the SBS Console.

## Lunch

Today's lunch is light, energy laden, and fast: deviled eggs!

### Deviled Eggs

Ingredients:

  6 hard-boiled eggs

  1 t. Worcestershire sauce

  1/2 t. salt

  3/4 t. yellow mustard

  2 t. lemon juice or vinegar

  1/8 t. ground pepper

  3 T mayonnaise

  dash paprika (to taste)

  dash parsley

Cut eggs in half. Remove yolks and press through sieve. Combine yolks with ingredients. Beat until smooth. Refill egg whites with concoction you've just created. Sprinkle with paprika. Garnish with parsley.

Hurry and eat so you can send and receive faxes on your SBS network!

## PM The SBS Fax Organization

So you've decided to become an SBS fax organization: you've decided to make the fax function part of your SBS network and everyday business world activity. You've possibly arrived at this decision, based on much of the discussion earlier today, by considering the following about SBS network faxing:

- Reduced hardware costs—Not only have you eliminated the need to purchase an expensive, modern fax machine, more importantly, you've eliminated the need to have each workstation equipped with its own fax modem and fax telephone line (I've seen it done). I've used the capability to eliminate multiple fax telephone lines in the past to help a firm justify the cost of an SBS conversion.

- Ease of use—Properly trained SBS users find that sending certain types of documents and receiving any document is easy with SBS network-based faxing. To read a typical fax, the user only needs to double-click to open the fax image. To send a fax, the user only needs to use the basic printing command.

14

- Monitoring and control—Again, depending on your unique situation, you might have an important need to control fax usage. That type of control is exceedingly difficult with a traditional fax machine, but with SBS, the network security model dictates who can use the fax service.

The next step to receiving and sending faxes is simple: just do it!

# Receiving a Fax

When constructed, the SBS server machine is ready to receive faxes. How do I know this? Call it the case of the disappearing faxes. There I was at a Northwest property management firm (yes, the same one mentioned in on Day 8), and I had just completed building and implementing the SBS server. Shortly thereafter, Pat called to report that some inbound faxes were missing. One site visit later and a quick peek at the FaxStore folder, and the missing faxes were found. Turns out the SBS fax was working perfectly; after I attached the modem to the telephone wall jack via a telephone cable, inbound faxes went directly to the FaxStore folder, by default, on the SBS server machine.

As discussed today, a fax can be received any and all of three ways when the fax modem on your SBS server commences its reception: print the fax, store the fax in the FaxStore folder, or e-mail the fax to an SBS user (who typically redistributes or forwards the fax to the receiving party).

## Viewing a Fax

When a fax is received, it appears similar to the fax that Norm Hasbro received in Figure 14.11. To view a fax in the FaxStore folder:

1. On the SBS user workstation with the Microsoft Fax client installed, log on to the SBS network as an SBS.

2. Launch the Fax Viewer application found in the Microsoft Fax Server Client program group (typically under Programs on the workstation's Start menu).

3. When Fax Viewer is running, select Open from the File menu.

4. Navigate in the Open dialog box until Network Neighborhood is displayed by clicking the Up arrow next to the Look in field. This typically requires four clicks on the Up arrow.

5. Double-click the Network Neighborhood icon displayed in the Open dialog box.

6. Double-click the SBS server (for example, SPINGERS01).

7. Double-click the FaxStore folder.

8. Double-click the fax (stored as a .TIF image) found in FaxStore. The fax image opens and looks similar to Figure 14.11.

FIGURE **14.11**

*Received fax.*

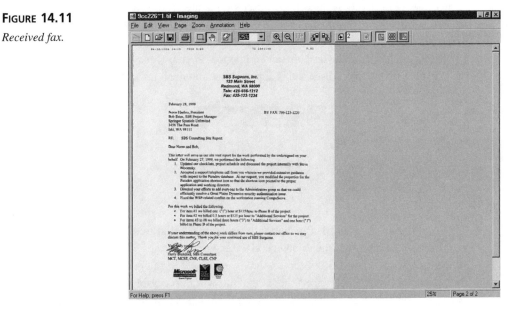

When the fax is opened, you can rotate, shrink, resave, and otherwise manipulate the fax via the Fax Viewer application. Here you could print faxes on different paper sizes.

> **Tip**
>
> I mentioned this once early, but I'll do so again. Odd-sized faxes are modified to fit the default paper in the printer that prints received faxes. For example, a legal document on legal-sized paper would be printed as a letter-sized document if the designated laser printer used letter-sized paper (8.5×11 inches) by default.

To open your fax when you receive it as an e-mail attachment in Outlook, simply double-click the fax attachment. The Fax Viewer automatically opens and displays the fax (that's because fax files are automatically associated with the Fax Viewer application).

14

## Unusual Receive Uses

I've used the capability to receive faxes as .TIF files in two unusual ways. First, by having each SBS user proffer his or her signature on a piece of paper, which I fax to the SBS server machine, I effectively scan each SBS user's signature. These signature image files, which look similar to Norm Hasbro's signature in Figure 14.12, are then stored in a central location, such as Company Shared Folders on the SBS servers. In the future, when composing and faxing a letter from the desktop, all you do to add your signature to your letter is insert the signature image file. I discuss this approach in a moment under "Sending a Fax."

**FIGURE 14.12**

*Scanned signature via SBS faxing.*

The second unusual use of fax reception is artwork. Similar to scanning a signature into a .TIF file as described earlier, you can also fax yourself maps, drawings, and photos. When received by the SBS fax server, the image is a .TIF image. The person receiving the fax can not only easily insert the image into word processing documents and Web pages but can also modify and manipulate it with popular drawing applications.

# Sending a Fax

Sending a fax from an SBS workstation is very simple. At its most basic level, sending a fax from an SBS workstation is nothing more than printing (via the Print command on the File menu in the application of your choice) the document you seek to fax somewhere. In other words, you simply print to the fax printer. That's it at the simplest level. You can also send faxes via the Send To command in Microsoft Office applications, to Contact in Outlook and via the Fax Send Utility (found in the Microsoft Fax Server Client program group via the Programs menu from the Start button on the SBS workstation).

Faxes can be sent to a variety of possible recipients including

- Ad hoc recipients. These are names you add each time you print to the fax device from an application.
- Outlook contacts.
- Exchange-based Personal Address Book members.

Here is a step-by-step example of how you send a fax. Here, Norm Hasbro is sending a memo to Roni Vipaul, the lender at Small Business Bank who has loaned the money necessary for Springer Spaniels Unlimited to implement the SBS network. Interestingly, you might recall from the list of SBS stakeholders on Day 2, "Planning for Small Business Server," that Roni's fax number is a vanity telephone number: 425-SBB-LEND. Note that SBS's faxing capability will not accommodate vanity telephone numbers; thus the number must converted to its digital form (425-722-5363).

To send a fax from a word processing program

1. At the SBS user's workstation, while working on the document you want to fax, select the Print command from the File menu. The Printing dialog box is displayed.

2. In the Name field, select Fax on SPRINGERS01 (or the name of your SBS server machine) as the printer. Click OK.

3. The Compose New Fax dialog box appears. Complete the To and Fax # fields, as seen in Figure 14.13. Click Next.

**FIGURE 14.13**

*Compose New Fax dialog box.*

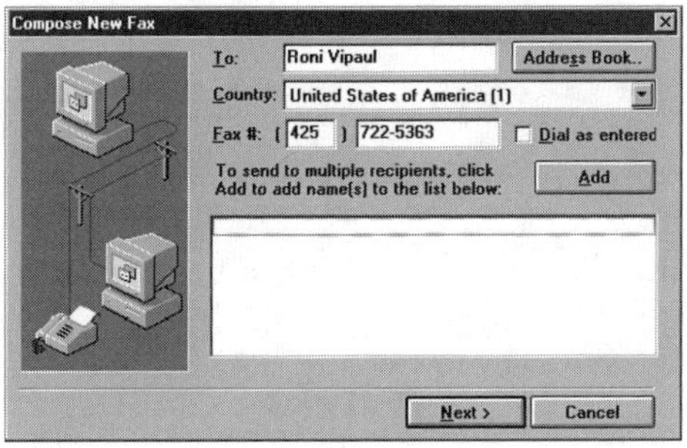

4. Select the Yes, Include a Cover Page check box on the second screen of the Compose New Fax wizard. Click Next.

5. Complete the Subject and Additional Note fields on the third screen of the Compose New Fax Wizard. Click Next.

6. The fourth screen of the Compose New Fax Wizard appears, allowing you to click Finish to send the fax. Click Finish.

Assuming no problems are encountered, the party for which the fax is intended receives it, which looks similar to Figures 14.14 and 14.15.

14

**FIGURE 14.14**

*Sent fax cover page.*

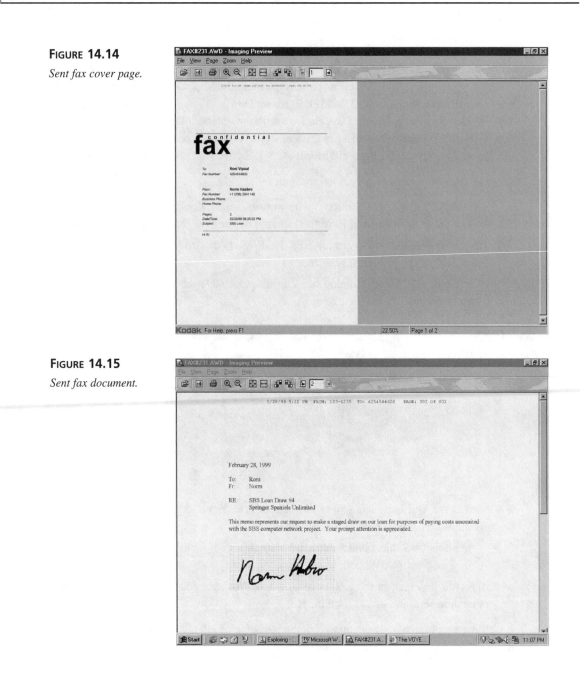

**FIGURE 14.15**

*Sent fax document.*

# Fax Reporting

Basic fax reports are viewed via Manage Faxes in the SBS Console. These reports were discussed on Day 5, "Managing the Small Business Server Management Console," and include

- Received Faxes Report

FIGURE **14.16**

*Received Faxes Report.*

FIGURE **14.16**

*Received Faxes Report.*

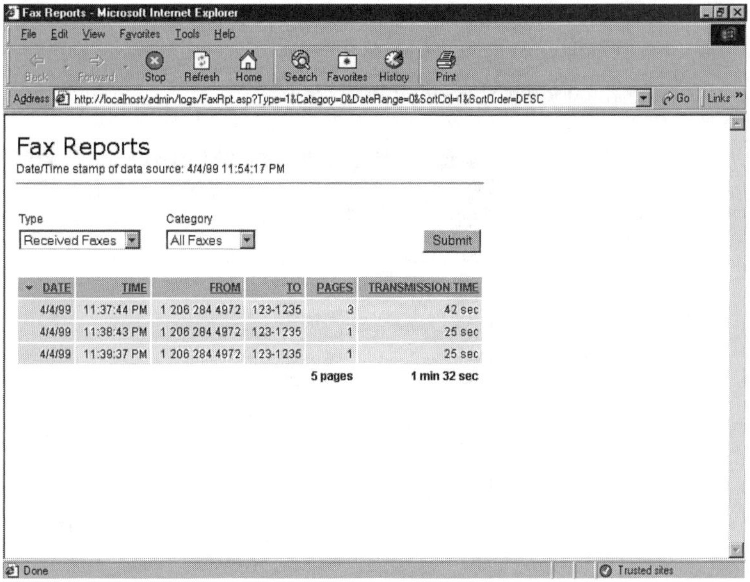

- Sent Faxes Report
- Sent Faxes - Top Numbers
- Received Faxes - Top Numbers

From the Manage Faxes screen, select the Generate Fax Reports option to view these reports.

Interestingly, as I've mentioned several times, the faxing function in SBS lacks the capability to create true fax confirmation letters, but there are two workarounds. First, you can simply print out the Sent Faxes Report.

Second, you can perform the following tasks on the SBS server machine and SBS user's workstation so that the fax sender receives an e-mail notification that the fax has been sent (which can suffice as a fax confirmation letter).

**14**

1. Make sure you are logged on as Administrator on your SBS server machine. Select Start, Settings, Control Panel.

2. Double-click Fax Server.

3. Click the Routing tab.

4. Click the Allow Routing via E-Mail check box.

5. Select the Administrator profile in the list box. The fax service requires this profile to send e-mail to your clients.

6. Click OK.

7. Reboot the SBS server machine.

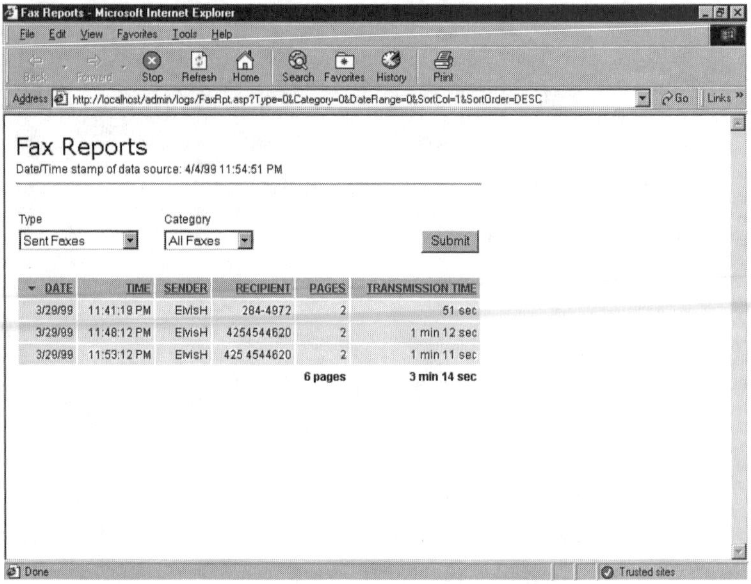

FIGURE 14.17

*Sent Faxes Report.*

At each SBS user's workstation that has the Microsoft Fax Client installed

1. Click Start, Settings, Control Panel.

2. Double-click Fax Client.

3. Fill in the E-Mail Address field on the General tab with the user's account name (for example, MelindaO). When MelindaO prints to the fax printer, the Microsoft Fax Service sends an e-mail message to the e-mail account MelindaO. This can suffice as a fax confirmation letter.

**FIGURE 14.18**

*Sent Faxes - Top Numbers.*

**FIGURE 14.19**

*Received Faxes - Top Numbers.*

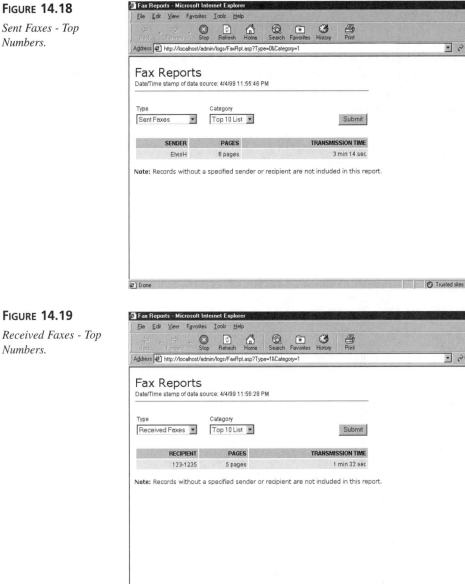

# Summary

For the right firms, the SBS faxing capabilities make the investment to install and maintain the SBS network all worthwhile. For others, faxing emerges later as a hidden gift that is often much appreciated. You spent this morning learning about and configuring SBS faxing. This afternoon, you took the practical steps of receiving and sending faxes. Onward to Day 15 and Office 2000!

# WEEK 3

# Extending SBS

15

16

17

18

19

20

21

# DAY 15

# Implementing Microsoft Office 2000

A word processor, a spreadsheet, and a database program—throw in a desktop publisher and a presentation application, and you have what sounds like a catchy title for an evening program on the Fox television network. Alas, it's actually Office 2000, and it's available for purchase with SBS 4.5 as a bundle. Whereas SBS 4.5 addresses the back office of your company, Office 2000 addresses the front office. Between the two, you have both offices covered.

In the morning session, I'll show you how to work with two Springer Spaniels Unlimited SBS project documents using Microsoft Word. At lunch, Ed Bott will share the new features in Office 2000. In the afternoon session, you will have a chance to work with Springer Spaniels Unlimited's Microsoft Excel–based working papers. You will also create a small project presentation in Microsoft PowerPoint.

Note that this chapter isn't meant to be a comprehensive or authoritative work on Office 2000. Holding such an expectation is only a recipe for disappointment. Rather, I intend to show you today, at a glance, how to incorporate Office 2000 into your Springer Spaniels Unlimited SBS networking project. If you have further interests in mastering Office 2000, I suggest you purchase these books from Macmillan Computer Publishing:

- *Sams Teach Yourself Microsoft Office 2000 Small Business Edition in 24 Hours* by Greg Perry (ISBN: 0-672-31568-8)
- *Sams Teach Yourself Microsoft Office 2000 in 21 Days* by Laurie Ulrich (ISBN: 0-672-31448-7)
- *Microsoft Office 2000 Small Business Edition 6-in-1* by Joe Habraken (ISBN: 0-789-71972-X)

## AM Microsoft Word Working Papers

On the CD-ROM included with this book, you'll find electronic versions of the working papers contained in Appendix C, "SBS Project Kit." As part of the Springer Spaniels Unlimited SBS experience, you will open and complete two of these working papers: Basic SBS Proposal and Early SBS Planing Questions. In the process, you will learn about Office 2000 from a practical or applied perspective.

The first topic is for SBS value-added providers (VAPs) and consultants. You will complete the SBS proposal contained in Appendix C as if you were bidding on an SBS project. You will next complete the SBS project planning questions.

You need to launch Microsoft Word 2000. I assume that you have loaded this program on the SBS user's workstations as part of the SBS installation. If you have not done so, please load Microsoft Office 2000 on an SBS user's workstation now.

To start Word, select the Microsoft Word program icon from the Program group (found via the Start button on your desktop). Word 2000 launches and looks similar to Figure 15.1. Then complete Task 15.1.

**FIGURE 15.1**

*Microsoft Word 2000.*

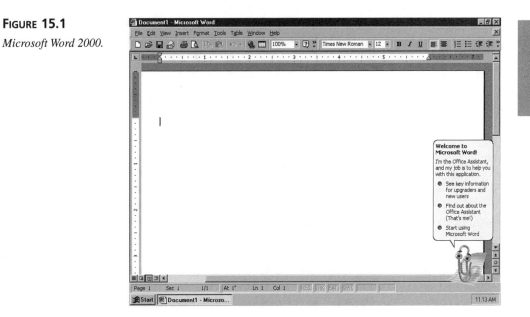

15

## Task 15.1: Completing the Basic SBS Proposal

▲ TASK

1. Place the CD-ROM that accompanies this book in the CD-ROM drive of your workstation.

2. From Microsoft Word 2000, select the Open command from the File menu. Open the Basic SBS Proposal document (Basic SBS Proposal.doc) on the CD-ROM. This document can be found in the Appendix C folder. Your screen should appear similar to Figure 15.2.

3. Note the Basic SBS Proposal is a template that you will complete. The areas that must be modified are highlighted in red. It is likely that you will want to make other additions and modifications to this proposal to suite your specific SBS bidding needs. In the next several steps, you'll complete this proposal for the benefit of Springer Spaniels Unlimited.

4. Highlight DATE and type today's date (for example, **July 15, 1999**).

5. Replace the first NAME highlight (in the address block) with the following information so that this proposal is directed to Norm Hasbro, President of Springer Spaniels Unlimited.

   **Mr. Norm Hasbro**

   **President**

   **Springer Spaniels Unlimited**

   **3456 The Pass Road**

▼ **Iski, WA 98111**

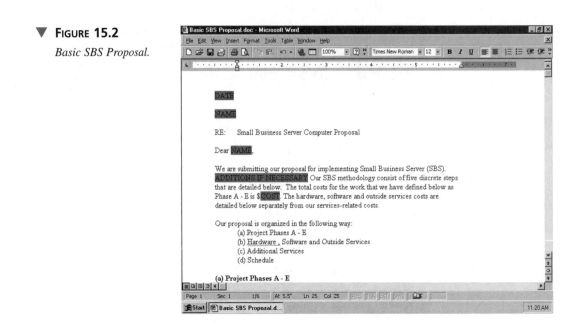

6. Replace the second NAME highlight with **Norm** (after the word *Dear*).

7. Replace the ADDITIONS IF NECESSARY highlight with the following text:

   **We have very much enjoyed learning about Springer Spaniels Unlimited over the past several months as part of our effort to assist you in implementing an SBS solution. Likewise, we're hopeful that you have benefited from learning more about us as well. It is in that spirit that we are presenting this SBS proposal.**

8. Replace the COST highlight with the value **$10,000**. This is the fee to be charged by the SBS consultant to Springer Spaniels Unlimited. Note that the total services budget, presented on Day 2, "Planning for Small Business Server," for the Springer Spaniels Unlimited project was $12,500. That larger figure ($12,500) included $2,500 for wiring and connecting to the Internet.

9. Scroll down and delete the ADDITIONS highlight under the Phase B does not include section. This highlight is a bullet point.

10. Now is a good time to save your work. Save your proposal to the My Documents folder on your workstation as "SSU SBS Proposal.doc".

▼

15

▼ 11. Delete the ADDITIONS highlight under the Phase C does not include section. This highlight is a bullet point.

12. Go to the end of the letter and type your name two lines below *Very truly yours*.

13. Save the document again.

14. You now have a completed SBS proposal for use on bidding SBS projects. Your completed work should look similar to Figure 15.3. Note that this completed document can be found in the Appendix C folder on the CD-ROM that accompanies this book (the filename is SSU SBS Proposal.doc).

**FIGURE 15.3**

*Completed Proposal.*

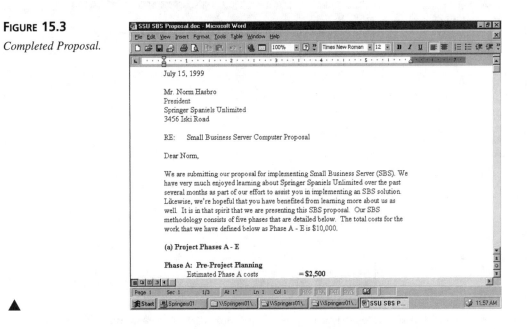

▲

Assuming the SBS project was approved and is underway, you would next complete the early SBS planning questions. This exercise is very simple.

## Task 15.2: Update the Early SBS Planning Questions Document

1. From Word, open the Early SBS Planning Questions.doc document on the CD-ROM in the Appendix C folder. The document should appear similar to Figure 15.4.

▼

2. You will complete the entire worksheet. Tab over to the Answer field for question 1 and type the following:

> **1. Cost - The SBS bundle is cost effective vs. purchasing each component individually. 2. Ease of use. The SBS network is easy to use and maintain. 3. Windows NT Server. Our software vendors are recommending Windows NT Server, the underlying operating system for SBS.**

3. Tab over to the answer field for question 2 and type **Six months**.

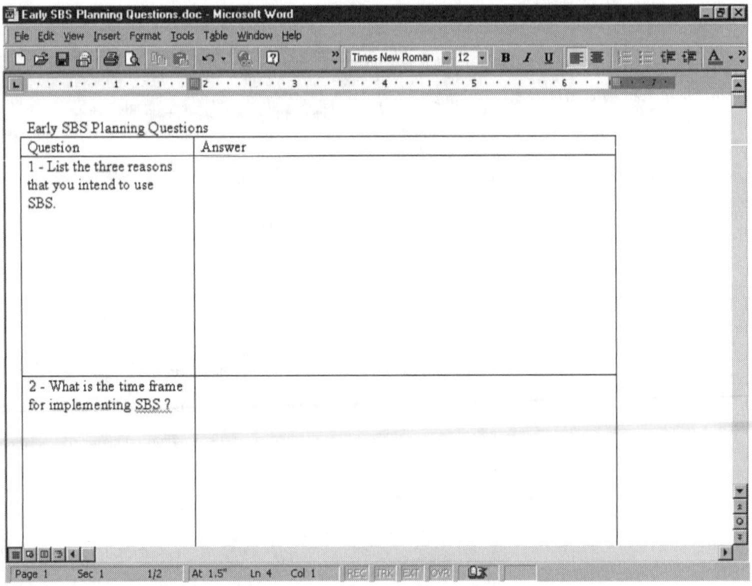

**FIGURE 15.4**

*Early SBS Planning Questions.*

4. Tab over to the answer field for question 3 and type **Lease financing, staff acceptance**.

5. Tab over to the answer field for question 4 and type **Yes - at ABC training center**.

6. Add the following as question 5: **5 - Identify the primary and secondary SBS administrators.**

7. Tab over to the answer field for question 5 and type **Primary: Bob Estes, Secondary: Melinda Overlake**.

8. Save the file to the My Documents folder on your workstation as "Completed Early SBS Planning Questions.doc". Note that this completed document can be found in the Appendix C folder on the CD-ROM that accompanies this book (the filename is Completed Early SBS Planning Questions.doc). Your finished work should look similar to Figure 15.5.

▼

**FIGURE 15.5**

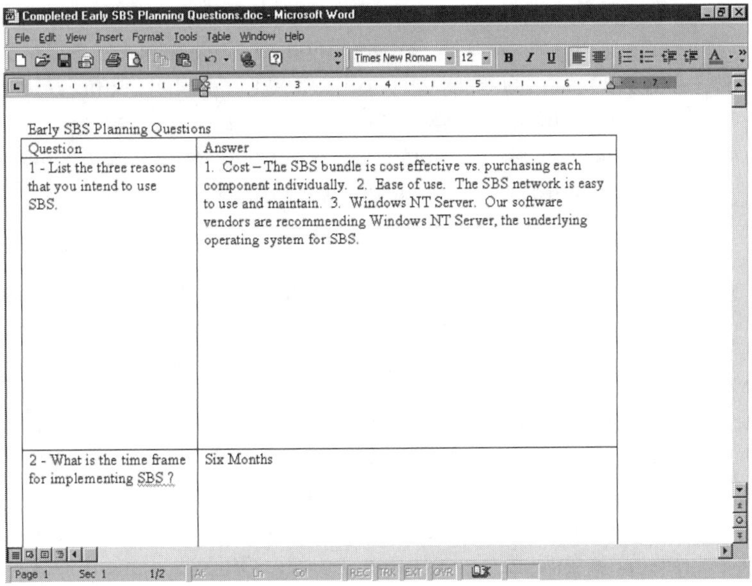

*Completed Early SBS
Planning Questions.*

With that exposure to Microsoft Word 2000, you'll now "listen" to a lunch speaker who
can enlighten you to the new features contained in Microsoft Office 2000.

# Lunch

The lunch speaker today is Ed Bott, senior contributing editor for *PC Computing* and fellow Macmillan author.

## What Is Office 2000?

*by Ed Bott*

Microsoft Office is the single best-selling application in the history of personal computing, with a user base that has grown to well over 70 million. The first version of Office
was little more than a glorified software bundle: a giant stack of floppy disks that included Word, Excel, and PowerPoint in a single package. Through the years, however, the
individual programs that compose Office have become more tightly integrated. The most
recent edition, Office 2000, includes huge chunks of shared code that guarantee a consistent look and feel for individual applications.

Compared with previous versions, Office 2000 includes an expanded lineup of applications, in a variety of different packages. The most basic collection, Office 2000 Standard
Edition, includes the core Office programs: Word 2000, Excel 2000, PowerPoint 2000,

and Outlook 2000, Microsoft's all-in-one e-mail client and personal information manager. For a slightly higher cost, you get the more expensive Professional edition, which adds Publisher 2000 (an easy-to-use desktop publishing program) and the database management application Access 2000. At the high end is Office 2000 Premium Edition, which includes all those programs plus Microsoft's award-winning Web-site management software FrontPage 2000 and a full-featured image-editing program, PhotoDraw 2000.

> **Note** PhotoDraw 2000 is not included in the Office 2000 version that is bundled with SBS 4.5.

The addition of FrontPage to the Office family isn't just an afterthought. Instead, it's part of a consistent strategy to make all the Office 2000 programs first-rate Web authoring tools. In previous versions, users had to force Word documents and Excel worksheets through cumbersome filters to convert them to Web format, usually with unsatisfying results. In Office 2000, you can save any Office document in HTML format with confidence that it will look the same in your browser as it does in the application that created it. Even more impressive is the fact that you can open and edit that document without losing any formatting or data. Office 2000 supports the concept of *Web folders*, too, which let users save and open documents on Web servers and corporate intranets as easily as they work with local hard drives.

## Usability Improvements

Every Office program is improved in some way over previous versions. Excel users, for example, will appreciate the easier interface for creating and editing PivotTables, whereas PowerPoint now lets you see an outline, a slide, and speaker notes in a new all-in-one Normal view.

Thanks to shared code, though, Office 2000 incorporates a wealth of subtle improvements to the user interface for every application, based on research conducted in Microsoft's usability labs. The payoff is especially noticeable for novice users—the most controversial enhancement "personalizes" menus and toolbars, hiding seldom-used icons and menu choices to simplify the interface. Power users who find this feature annoying can turn it off easily—in fact, the revised interface for customizing toolbars and menus is a power user's dream.

Usability research shows that novice users consistently have trouble finding files they previously saved, whereas power users have to click through tedious directory structures to locate files stored in different local and network locations. New common dialog boxes in Office 2000 make both tasks easier; thanks to the addition of the Places bar, a row of

**15**

five icons that let users quickly jump to the locations where documents are most frequently stored.

Other usability improvements include

- An Office-exclusive enhancement to the Windows Clipboard, which lets users collect up to 12 items and paste them into any document, all at once or one at a time.
- Greatly improved Help based on the Windows 98-style HTML interface, with surprisingly detailed content and superb search capabilities.
- Drop-down font lists in every program that let you see at a glance what each font will look like before you make any formatting changes.
- A new single document interface, which gives each open document, worksheet, or presentation its own taskbar button, making it easier for users to switch between open documents.
- A kinder, gentler Office Assistant. Yes, Clippit is still around, but the Office 2000 version is smaller and more manageable. Users who don't want advice from a cartoon character can silence the pesky paper clip with one click.

The most important reason to upgrade to Office, though, is literally invisible. Unlike previous versions, Office 2000 allows antivirus software to hook directly into the program to protect users from malicious macro viruses like Melissa and CIH. Recent updates to every popular antivirus program support this feature, giving Office 2000 users a level of protection that was impossible with previous Office versions.

# Easier to Manage

Administrators responsible for managing Office for departments or large organizations will find some major changes in Office 2000. The new setup program—based on the Windows Installer developed for Windows 2000—requires less effort than previous versions, and it also allows you to add new features more easily.

Using the Windows Installer gives administrators a big edge in managing setup on individual PCs:

- The Installer service keeps track of crucial system files and Registry settings. If a user inadvertently deletes a file or if the Registry becomes corrupted, the Windows Installer will automatically repair the damage the next time the program starts up.
- Unlike previous Office versions, which stashed user preferences and configuration settings in dozens of locations, Office 2000 keeps all configuration settings in the Windows Registry, making it much easier to back up and restore settings or move a user's profile to a new machine.
- To save disk space, administrators can specify that some features run from a network or a CD. You can also configure features or entire programs to be installed on

first use. Office adds a shortcut to the menu but doesn't actually copy files until the user tries to access that feature.

- Because the Office 2000 setup process is so streamlined, administrators can even use an administrative install to create a shared distribution point on a network. By mailing a shortcut to individual users, they can allow the users to upgrade at their own pace, with only a few clicks.

Multinational corporations and business that work in multilingual environments will find it much easier to configure Office 2000. Unlike previous versions, which required a different set of program files for each language, Office 2000 includes a single set of core files that work with all languages. To enable multiple languages, you install a minor update and use a simple utility to switch from, say, English to French or German.

Finally, offices that use Visual Basic for Applications (VBA) to tie Office programs together will notice two significant additions in Office 2000. For the first time, VBA support is available in every application, including Access, Outlook, and FrontPage. In addition, Office 2000 includes support for digital signatures, which let administrators control the ability of macros to run on individual systems. By digitally signing macros, developers can give users the confidence to load and run macros without having to worry about macro viruses or click past confusing dialog boxes.

**Note**

With two monthly columns and frequent cover stories on Microsoft Windows and other topics, Ed Bott is the senior contributing editor for *PC Computing* with a circulation of over 1,000,000 readers monthly. He's the author of several Que books—including *Special Edition Using Microsoft Office 2000, Using Microsoft Office 97 Third Edition, Using Windows 95*—and co-author of *Special Edition Using Windows 98* and *Platinum Edition Using Windows 98*; through these books, Ed has taught over 650,000 users. He is a two-time winner of the Computer Press Award, most recently for *PC Computing*'s annual *Windows SuperGuide*, a collection of tips, tricks, and advice for users of Windows 95, Windows 98, and Windows NT. For his work on both the sixth and seventh annual editions of the *Windows SuperGuide*, published in 1997 and 1998, Ed and article co-author Woody Leonhard earned the prestigious Jesse H. Neal Award, sometimes referred to as "the Pulitzer Prize of the business press."

# PM Excel and PowerPoint

This afternoon you will create an Excel spreadsheet that reports Springer Spaniels Unlimited financial information. You will also create a small presentation that provides a status report on the Springer Spaniels Unlimited SBS project.

# Microsoft Excel 2000

15

In my experience, Excel is a close second to Word in popularity of the applications contained in the Microsoft Office 2000 suite. Why? Everybody needs Word for their word processing needs. Nearly everyone needs Excel for their spreadsheet analysis needs.

You will create a spreadsheet containing financial information for use by Springer Spaniels Unlimited. A finished copy of this spreadsheet already exists on the CD-ROM that accompanies this book so that you can compare your results. Note that this spreadsheet will also be used on Day 20, "Advanced Server Management," when you modify the SBS Console.

I assume that you have Excel already installed on your workstation. If not, please install Excel at this time. Complete the following task to create the Excel spreadsheet-based executive information system (EIS) for Springer Spaniels Unlimited.

## Task 15.3: Creating an EIS for Springer Spaniels Unlimited

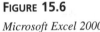

1. Launch Microsoft Excel 2000 from the Microsoft Excel program icon found in the Programs program group (from the Start button on your desktop). It should appear similar to Figure 15.6.

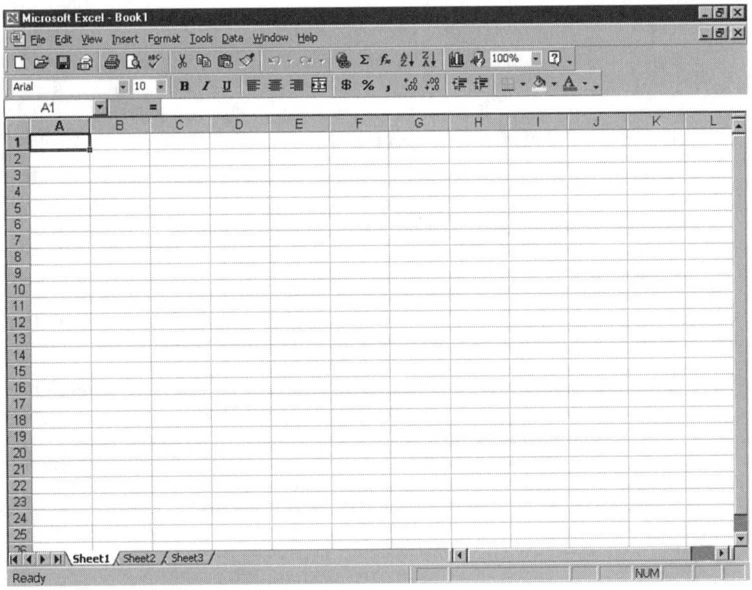

**FIGURE 15.6**

*Microsoft Excel 2000.*

2. Make the following entries contained in Table 15.1 on the spreadsheet.

▼ **TABLE 15.1**　EIS ENTRIES

| Cell | Entry | Formatting |
|------|-------|-----------|
| A1 | **Springer Spaniels Unlimited** | Arial, 14 pt., blue text color, bold |
| A2 | **Executive Information System** | Arial, 14 pt., blue text color, bold |
| A5 | **Sales** | Arial, 12 pt., black, bold |
| A6 | **Cost of Goods Sold** | Arial, 12 pt., black, bold |
| A7 | **Gross Margin** | Arial, 12 pt., black, bold |
| A9 | **Operating Expenses** | Arial, 12 pt., black, bold |
| A11 | **Net Profit** | Arial, 12 pt., black, bold |
| A13 | **Commentary** | Arial, 12 pt., black, bold, italic |
| A14 | **The past months have seen very high demand for** | Arial, 12 pt., black, italic |
| A15 | **dogs bred by Springer Spaniels Unlimited due in** | Arial, 12 pt., black, italic |
| A16 | **part to the success of Sir Brisker at regional dog** | Arial, 12 pt., black, italic |
| A17 | **shows. However, note that Sir Brisker will retire in** | Arial, 12 pt., black, italic |
| A18 | **December 1999, creating our own Y2K problem.** | Arial, 12 pt., black, italic |
| B4 | **Summer 1999** | Arial, 12 pt., black, bold |
| B5 | $10,000 (entered as **10000**) | Arial, 12 pt., black, bold, Currency with two decimal places |
| B6 | This is a formula: **=B5*0.44** | Arial, 12 pt., black, bold, Currency with two decimal places |
| B7 | This is a formula: **=B5-B6** | Arial, 12 pt., black, bold, Currency with two decimal places |
| B9 | $4,250 (entered as **4250**) | Arial, 12 pt., black, bold, Currency with two decimal places |
| B11 | This is a formula: **=B7-B9** | Arial, 12 pt., black, bold, Currency with two decimal places |

**Note**

You can modify the text via the Format Cells dialog box (see Figure 15.7). You'll find the Format Cells dialog box via the Cells menu selection under the Format menu. It is here that you can change the font color.

▼

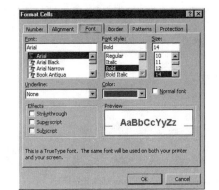

▼ **FIGURE 15.7**

*Format Cells.*

**15**

3. Save your spreadsheet as SSUEIS.XLS to the My Document folder on your work-station by selecting the Save command under the File menu. Your spreadsheet should look similar to Figure 15.8.

**FIGURE 15.8**

*Completed Springer Spaniels Unlimited EIS.*

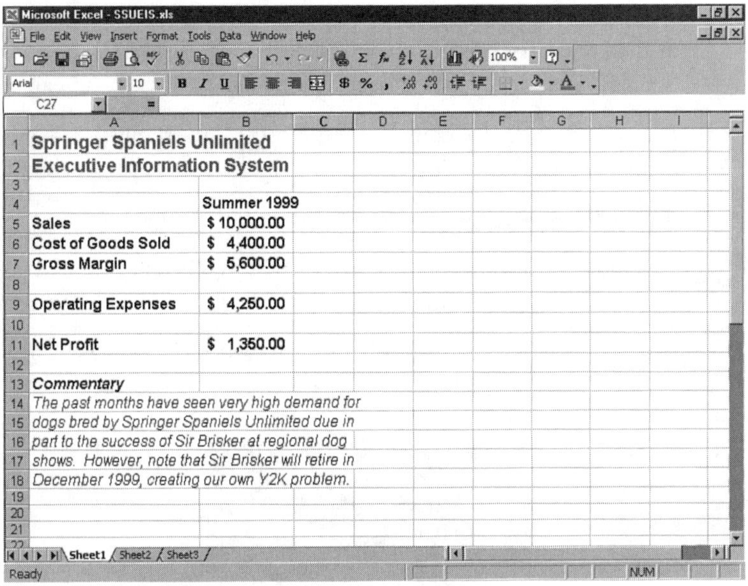

4. You will now need to save the file as an HTML file for use on Day 20 by selecting the Save As command and selecting Web Page (*.htm; *.html) in the Save as type field, as seen in Figure 15.9. Make this selection, name the file default.htm and click Save.

▼ **FIGURE 15.9**

*Save As Web Page.*

▲ You have now created the Springer Spaniels Unlimited EIS.

# Microsoft PowerPoint 2000

When implementing an SBS project, there is typically a need to communicate the status of the project to the stakeholders. Recall that a list of stakeholders for the Springer Spaniels Unlimited SBS project was created on Day 2 and can be found in Appendix C.

I assume that you have installed Microsoft PowerPoint 2000 on your workstation. If that is not the case, please install it now. You are now ready to complete Task 15.4.

## Task 15.4: Springer Spaniels Unlimited SBS Project Update

1. Launch Microsoft PowerPoint 2000 by selecting the Microsoft PowerPoint program item in the Programs program group (found via the Start button on your desktop).

2. When presented with the PowerPoint dialog box, select the AutoContent Wizard as seen in Figure 15.10. Click OK.

**FIGURE 15.10**

*Select AutoContent Wizard.*

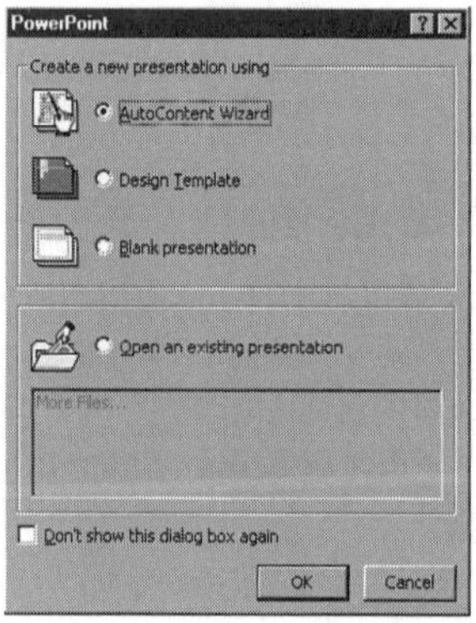

▼

▼ 3. The AutoContent Wizard appears. Click Next.

4. The AutoContent Wizard displays the Presentation Type screen. Select the Projects button and the Reporting Progress or Status selection, as seen in Figure 15.11. Click Next.

**15**

FIGURE **15.11**

*Reporting Progress or Status.*

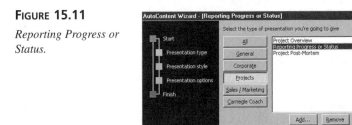

5. The AutoContent Wizard displays the Presentation Style screen. Select On-screen Presentation and click Next.

6. The AutoContent Wizard displays the Presentation Options screen. Enter **Springer Spaniels Unlimited SBS Project Update** in the Presentation title field. Enter **Springer Spaniels Unlimited - SBS** in the Footer field. These entries are shown in Figure 15.12. Click Next.

FIGURE **15.12**

*Entries for the Presentation Options screen.*

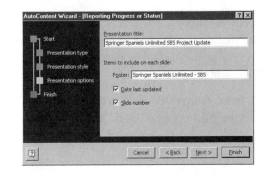

7. The AutoContent Wizard displays the Finish screen. Click Finish.

8. The presentation is automatically created with suggested talking points on each slide, shown in Figure 15.13.

▼ 9. Save the project update presentation. Save the file as "SSU Project Update" to the My Documents folder on your workstation by selecting Save from the File menu.

▼ FIGURE **15.13**

*Project Update presen-*
*tation.*

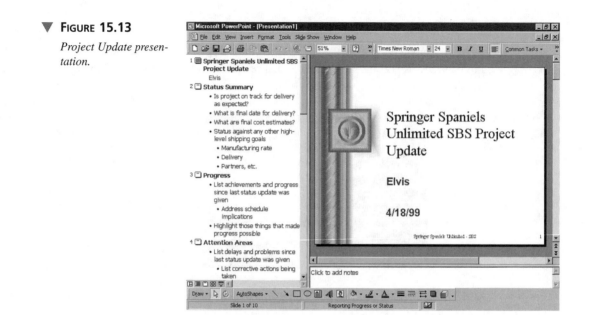

10. Modify the "canned" presentation created by the AutoContent Wizard to reflect the information you want to convey to the stakeholders. On slide 2 ("Progress"), remove the fourth bullet item ("Status against any other high-level shipping goals"). To remove the bullet item, highlight it with your mouse and press the Delete key on your keyboard.

11. Save the file again (it automatically saves to the name SSU Project Update.ppt because that was the filename you created in step 9) to update the presentation file for the change that you just made. You have now completed the creation of the Project Update presentation.

▲

You are now ready to make your presentation to the stakeholders associated with the Springer Spaniels Unlimited SBS project. Good luck.

## Summary

Today you learned how to use the three most popular applications contained in Microsoft Office 2000 (Word, Excel, and PowerPoint) to help you better deploy and manage the Springer Spaniels Unlimited SBS network. Again, today should only be viewed as a starting point for your use and ultimately path to mastery of Microsoft Office 2000.

# Using Microsoft Exchange

Needless to say, the first call you'll receive from your SBS users will be related to e-mail. Funny how that is. So many SBS sites purchase and implement SBS because of an important need to run business applications such as accounting software. But often e-mail assumes greater importance, often without the awareness of you, the SBS administrator, and your herd of SBS users. In fact, it's not until several months into the life of the SBS system that you realize most of your support calls are coming from e-mail issues, not other business application issues.

Microsoft Exchange is, of course, the server-based e-mail application that sends and receives SBS user e-mail. Contrast that with Microsoft Outlook, which runs on the SBS user's workstations. Microsoft Outlook is the client application used to compose, read, store, and otherwise manage individual user mailboxes.

One more thought about defining Exchange. Exchange is much more than an e-mail application. It is where SBS users store their calendars, contacts, and so on. Exchange is really known as a groupware application, which by definition is much more robust than plain old e-mail; Exchange is really a core communication application for the SBS site.

Exchange is huge! In fact, in the world of Big BackOffice, many people have niched their consulting practice to focus strictly on Microsoft Exchange (and made a good living at it). Many books are also dedicated to Exchange, including *Sams Teach Yourself Microsoft Exchange Server 5.5 in 21 Days* by Jason vanValkenburgh (ISBN: 0-672-31525-4). Perhaps after you get your SBS site up and running, you might consider reading one of these dedicated Exchange books to increase your knowledge of this powerful area.

In this chapter, I'll tell you what you need to interact with Exchange on your SBS network. Although I can't hope to teach you everything about Exchange in a few short pages, I can share with you the most popular Exchange issues that I've encountered at SBS sites. The morning session today is for the less experienced among us, but I encourage the gurus to attend the morning session as well. Likewise, the afternoon session is dedicated to the SBS gurus, hoping to sharpen their Exchange skills.

# AM Microsoft Exchange Basics

On the surface, Exchange is largely invisible to you, the SBS administrator. That's because it is automatically installed with SBS and the organization and site naming are handled for you. That said, you will likely interact with only two Exchange components: Microsoft Exchange Administrator and Microsoft Exchange Performance Optimizer.

You can access both of these applications via the Microsoft Exchange (Common) program group found via Programs (that shows when you click the Start button at the SBS desktop).

## Microsoft Exchange Administrator

The Microsoft Exchange Administrator is the primary management application for Exchange. It's one of those interfaces where, every time you drill down to perform some action, you are greeted with another layer of dialog boxes and tabs. It is a very rich application, as SBS gurus like to say. Through this chapter, I'll show you different aspects of the Microsoft Exchange Administrator, shown in Figure 16.1.

## Microsoft Exchange Performance Optimizer

The Microsoft Exchange Performance Optimizer is, in my experience, really used only for one reason at SBS sites: to move the Exchange information store (which is the central repository for everyone's e-mail, calendar, contact and other mailbox information) to another hard disk with enough storage space. It is common, over time, for the Exchange information store to grow (and grow and grow) to reflect the increased (and often intense) use of Exchange-based e-mail by your end users.

**FIGURE 16.1**

*Microsoft Exchange Administrator.*

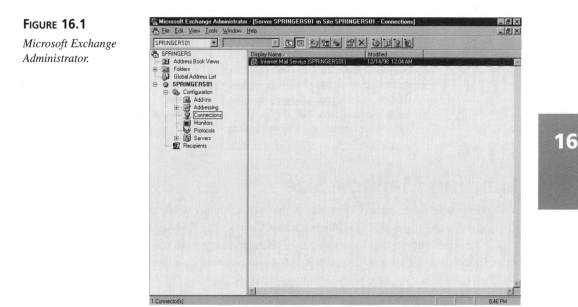

16

The cool thing about the Microsoft Exchange Performance Optimizer is that moving the Exchange information store is automatic. Really. Run the Microsoft Exchange Performance Optimizer and this application automatically picks the partition with the most space to move your Exchange information store to. The Microsoft Exchange Performance Optimizer is shown in Figure 16.2.

**FIGURE 16.2**

*Microsoft Exchange Performance Optimizer.*

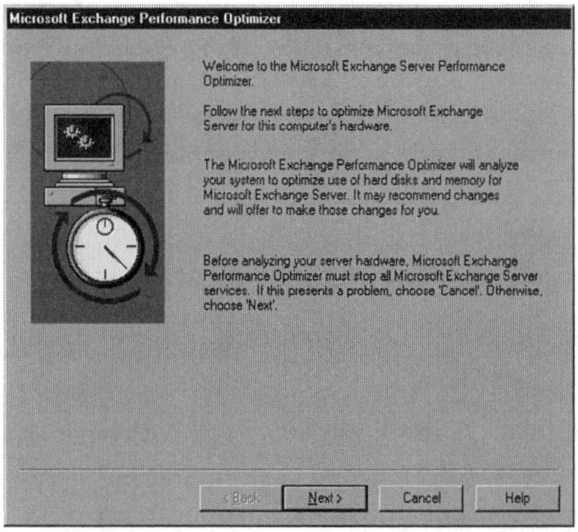

**Note**

> The Microsoft Exchange Performance Optimizer is really oriented toward improving Exchange's performance in large enterprises. So many of the questions presented on successive pages of the wizard shown in Figure 16.2 do not apply to SBS sites. Answer truthfully, and you'll be fine. Understand that this tool is typically used to move the Microsoft information store to a larger storage area. You can also use it to modify the RAM allocation (a.k.a. RAM footprint) for Microsoft Exchange Server.

# Limiting Mailbox Size

Many SBS users, myself included, are pack rats. I rarely delete an e-mail. Oh sure, perhaps I move my e-mails to folders such as Clients or Friends and Family to better organize them, but they still count as part of the size of my mailbox. Even your Contacts and Calendar count against the mailbox size equation. Now I've given you only the SBS user's side of the story, where mailbox-size limitations are typically viewed as a burden.

But SBS administrators must necessarily impose mailbox size limits in order to maintain order on their SBS networks. Why? Huge Exchange mailboxes take forever to load (which users ultimately complain about), and you can literally eat up your sever's hard disk space if no one ever deletes e-mail.

**Tip**

> Interestingly, the value that you set for the mailbox size limit will be reached, no matter what that size limit is. Call it the Law of Expanding E-mail, but if you set the limit for mailboxes to 50MB, guess what? Your SBS users will save e-mail messages until they hit the 50MB limit for their account. Likewise, if you set the mailbox limit to 100MB, users' mailboxes will grow to 100MB. Thank about the Law of Expanding E-mail when you decide what limit to impose on your SBS users' Exchange mailboxes.

Here is how you set the limit on your SBS users' mailboxes:

1. Make sure you are logged on to your SBS server as Administrator or member of the Administrators group.

2. From the Start menu, select Programs, Microsoft Exchange (Common), Microsoft Exchange Administrator.

3. Beneath the name of your organization (SPRINGERS01) in the left pane, select Configuration.

4. Expand Configuration and select Servers.

5. Expand Servers and select your Exchange server (SPRINGER01).

6. Expand your Exchange server and select Private Information Store.

7. While Private Information Store is selected, click the File menu on the Microsoft Exchange Administrator menu bar.

8. Select Properties. The Private Information Store Properties dialog box is shown (with the General tab as seen in Figure 16.3).

**16**

FIGURE **16.3**

*Private Information Store Properties.*

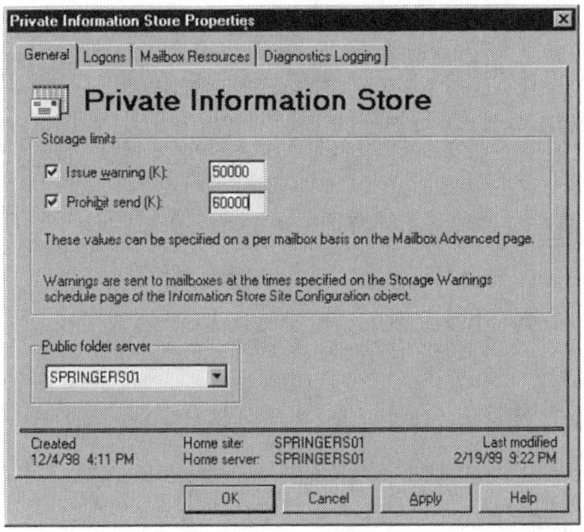

9. Set the Issue Warning (K) value to **50000** for 50 MB (my recommendation to you). It is here that SBS users receive a recurring and annoying message warning them that they have exceeded their mailbox limit.

10. Set the Prohibit Send (K) value to **60000** for 60 MB (again, my recommendation to you). When an SBS user hits this limit, no additional e-mail can be sent. This not only gets your SBS users' attention, but also forces them to clean house and delete old e-mail.

---

**Tip**

This is a global setting that applies to all SBS users' mailboxes.

---

**Tip**

File this discussion away in your brain for the future. The day will most certainly arrive when you will need to up the mailbox limit values. Trust me.

---

But of course life isn't as easy as the ten previous steps suggest for managing your SBS network's mailbox storage. For those days when people who directly influence your wellbeing demand that you increase their mailbox storage, I have what I call the president's workaround. Why "president's workaround"? Because the president most often influences my paycheck! Also, the president typically has the power, influence, and gumption to demand such changes as an increased mailbox size. In the spirit of the president's workaround, I will show you how to increase the individual mailbox size limitation for Norm Hasbro, the president of Springer Spaniels Unlimited.

## Task 16.1: The President's Workaround

1. Make sure you are logged on to your SBS server as Administrator or member of the Administrators group.

2. From the Start menu, select Programs, Microsoft Exchange (Common), Microsoft Exchange Administrator.

3. Beneath the name of your organization (SPRINGERS01) in the left pane, select Recipients.

4. With Recipients highlighted, select Norm Hasbro in the right pane of Microsoft Exchange Administrator.

5. Either double-click Norm Hasbro or select Properties from the File menu to display the Norm Hasbro Properties dialog box.

6. Select the Advanced tab.

7. Notice the Information store storage limits on the lower left side of the Advanced tab. Remove the check from the Use information store defaults item.

8. Select Issue Warning (K) and enter **100000** for 100MB.

9. Select Prohibit Send (K) and enter **125000** for 125MB. I like to set this to a significantly larger size when dealing with the company president (I want Norm to have lots of wiggle room before he can no longer send e-mail). The result of these configurations is shown in Figure 16.4.

10. Make a comment to yourself in the Administrative Note field if you want, and click OK to implement the new change.

**Note**

If you make the preceding changes to an individual's account using the President's workaround trick, be advised that said user will no longer participate in the global mailbox size limits that you set earlier. This is critical to understand because, at a later date, if you set all your SBS user's mailbox limits to an amount greater than that shown for Norm Hasbro (100 MB warning/125 MB prohibit send), Norm Hasbro wouldn't enjoy the benefit of having the larger mailbox size limitations that your other SBS users do.

What's the bottom line? If possible, manage from the global mailbox size limitations approach first and foremost!

**FIGURE 16.4**

*Advanced tab for
Norm Hasbro
Properties.*

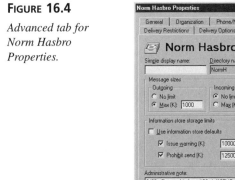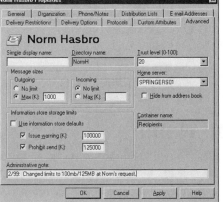

16

But I'm not finished with this topic yet. Just because one of your users doesn't affect your paycheck or isn't the company president doesn't mean you can't help her out as well when it comes to rigid mailbox size limits. I now introduce to you the "non-president workaround."

## Task 16.2: The Office Flunkie Workaround

▲ TASK

This workaround, office flunkie style, uses Personal Folders in the SBS user's Outlook client. After installing Personal Folders on Outlook at the SBS user's workstation, you simply cut-and-paste e-mails, contacts, and appointments from the SBS user's Exchange-based mailbox to her new Personal Folders. In fact, you can create the same folders (by name, such as Friends and Family) to store the newly transferred e-mails, for example. The bottom line is this: By transferring mailbox items such as e-mail to Personal Folders, the SBS user can retain important communications without having such retention count against her Exchange-based mailbox size limits. You learned how to install Outlook services, such as Personal Folders on Day 8, "Implementing Outlook."

**Tip**

I'd be less than honest if I didn't communicate that Personal Folders (which create .pst files) have been known to be fragile. So if you use Personal Folders, make sure that you have backups of them. Because Personal Folders are, by default, stored on the C: drive of your local workstation, you should somehow make a backup of this file to another part of your hard disk (via a simple file copy approach) or to a Zip drive.

Figure 16.5 depicts the Office Flunkie workaround.

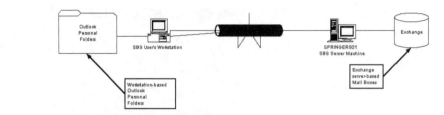

**FIGURE 16.5**

*Office Flunkie
workaround.*

# Internet E-mail Names

You can safely assume that you will be most interested in procuring and configuring an
Internet connection for the benefit of your SBS network as fast as you can. That is a
well-known fact, but depending on the type of connection you've implemented, you
might need to modify the Internet e-mail address for your user because the real Internet
domain name is different from the internal network names you used (in fact, such is
often the case).

If you need to change the Internet e-mail addresses for your SBS users, follow these
steps:

1. Launch the Microsoft Exchange Administrator from the Microsoft Exchange
   (Common) program group, as described earlier.

2. Expand the site SPRINGERS01.

3. Double-click Configuration.

4. In the right pane of the Microsoft Exchange Administrator, double-click Site
   Addressing to display the Site Addressing Properties dialog box.

5. Select the Site Addressing tab.

6. Select the SMTP line (the third line down) and click the Edit button.

7. Modify the address field to reflect the correct e-mail domain name (for example,
   `springers.nwnexus.com`). Click OK.

8. Observe the updated SMTP address, as seen in Figure 16.6. Note this new default
   Internet e-mail domain will be applied automatically to all future SBS user
   accounts added to your SBS network.

9. You are offered the chance to apply this Internet e-mail address change to all existing SBS user accounts. Click Yes when asked whether you would like to do so.
   This step prevents you from having to correct the Internet e-mail domain on all
   existing SBS user accounts.

FIGURE **16.6**

*New Internet e-mail domain.*

**Power Tool Tip**

A common and cool step to perform regarding Internet e-mail addresses is to offer your SBS users the ability to have multiple e-mail addresses. For example, with Norm Hasbro, you very well might have wanted to implement a second SMTP e-mail address for jobs@springers.nwnexus.com. That way, Norm Hasbro could run an ad for employees and have job candidates reply directly by e-mail to the jobs e-mail address. Norm would receive these for review.

# E-mail Reports

Sometimes you have to go one step backward for every two steps forward. If you agree that SBS 4.5 is at least two steps forward from its predecessor, that begs the question, what was the step backward? Unfortunately, it's in the area of e-mail reporting. SBS 4.0/4.0a had a rich set of e-mail reports (Server Summary, Top N Messages Receivers Report, Top N Message Senders Report, Daily Message Traffic) which were removed from SBS 4.5. However, you (or more likely, your SBS guru) can benefit from message tracking to troubleshoot Microsoft Exchange when it's having a bad-hair day.

Here are the steps to enable message tracking in Microsoft Exchange Server:

1. Launch the Microsoft Exchange Administrator from the Microsoft Exchange (Common) program group, as described earlier.

2. Expand the site SPRINGERS01.

3. Double-click Configuration.

4. In the right-hand pane of Microsoft Exchange Administrator, double-click Information Store Site Configuration.

5. Select Enable Message Tracking as shown on the General tab (see Figure 16.7). Click OK.

FIGURE 16.7

*Information Store Site Configuration—Enable Message Tracking.*

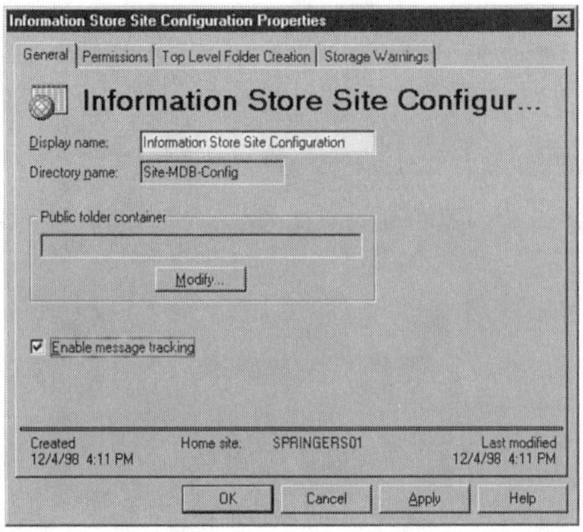

6. Double-click Connections in the left pane of Microsoft Exchange Administrator (found under Configuration).

7. Double-click the Internet Mail Service.

8. Check Enable Message Tracking on the Internet Mail tab.

9. Click OK.

10. You need to reboot the SBS server machine to stop and restart the Microsoft Exchange Internet Mail Service for the change in step 8 to take place.

**Note** You can also stop and restart the Microsoft Internet Mail Service via the Services applet in Control Panel (found via the Start button, Settings) if you so desire.

At this time, your SBS server machine now captures e-mail traffic information and makes it available in text logs contained in the \ExchSrvr\tracking.log folder.

## Immediate Send and Receive

If you have a dial-up connection to the Internet, the Exchange e-mail send and receive function is likely based on a scheduled dial-up, such as every four hours. Occasionally, this schedule is not acceptable when important e-mails must go out or important SBS users, such as the company president, are expecting an important e-mail. Fear not; an easy solution exists to this problem. Simply select the Send and Receive Mail Now option on the Manage Electronic Mail page in the SBS Console.

16

**FIGURE 16.8**

*Send and Receive Now.*

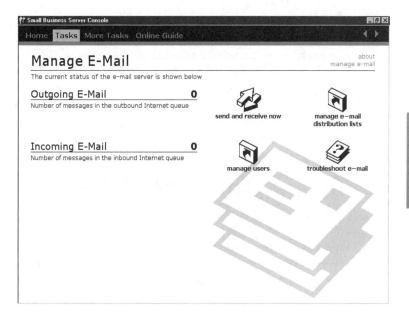

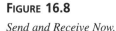 # Lunch

Today's lunch provides something quick and easy: Hot Ham and Cheese Sandwiches. Be sure to eat heartily as the afternoon topic will demand the energy that you have.

## Hot Ham and Cheese Sandwiches

6 buns (hamburger size)

6 slices ham (1/4" thick)

6 slices Swiss cheese (1/8" thick)

Mix together:

1/2 cup softened butter

1/4 cup prepared mustard (yellow)

1/4 cup chopped onions

1 T. poppy seeds

Open buns and spread mixture over both bun halves. Place ham and cheese on buns and close. Wrap in foil. Bake in 325° oven for approximately 15 minutes or until cheese melts and is warmed through.

# ☽PM Advanced Microsoft Exchange

Welcome back from lunch. The discussion now shifts to SBS guru land. This afternoon I will focus on configuring the Internet Mail Server using Outlook's Web client, moving SBS user's Exchange mailboxes to other servers, and backing up Exchange and non-Exchange e-mail options for your SBS users. I'll even show you how to maintain an account on the client's SBS network as its consultant but keep your e-mail name invisible (assuming you have your client's permission to do so).

# Configuring the Internet Mail Service

In its natural and unimpeded state, the SBS Internet Connection Wizard automatically configures the Microsoft Exchange Internet Mail Service for you to send and receive Internet e-mail. But unnatural things happen on all computer networks, SBS being no exception. Thus, it behooves both you and I to understand how the Internet Mail Service is configured. I will use the next few pages to do exactly that.

First, you must launch the Internet Mail Service (IMS) via the Microsoft Exchange Administrator (it is found under Connections as you saw this morning). The IMS has the following tabs (entries with an * contain SBS-related configuration):

- Delivery Restrictions—Allows you to accept or reject e-mail messages from specific individuals. This is a great way to thwart spammers and harassing senders.

- Advanced—Allows message and transfer time configurations.

- Diagnostics Logging—Allows you to configure specific types of IMS logging. This tab is typically accessed if you are on the telephone with Microsoft Support troubleshooting an Internet e-mail problem. Be careful about exploring too much here because you can inadvertently create huge log files without knowing it (until you see the disk space on your computer drop dramatically).

- Internet Mail*—Allows you to designate an administrator mailbox (the account that receive Internet e-mail error messages). You also enable message tracking here.

- Dial-up Connections*—Allows you to configure the dial-up e-mail connection to your ISP. Note this not the same as Dial-Up Networking (DUN) connection, which also must be configured to dial-up or call your ISP.

- General—Allows you to set the maximum message size that can pass through the Internet connection.

- Connected Sites—This is an advanced setting which allows you to configure directory replication between other connectors in the organization .

- Address Space*—Creates the path needed by the connector to send mail outside to the ISP.

- Connections*—Allows you to configure basic connector settings including message delivery (DNS, forwarding, transfer mode, and other settings). This is an important tab that you will want to ensure is set correctly.

**Power Tool Tip**

> If you use the DNS option under the Message Delivery section, it is critical that the domain name contained in the Domain name field of the DNS tab under Microsoft TCP/IP Properties (accessed via Protocols in the Network applet from Control Panel) has the exact name of your Internet e-mail domain.

**16**

- Queues—Allows you to see the same inbound and outbound queue information displayed via Manage Electronic Mail in SBS Console.

- Routing*—This allows you to reroute mail for one domain to another domain. This is a global setting and doesn't apply to individuals who would like to have their individual e-mails forward to another e-mail account (discussed later today).

- Security—This allows you to invoke Windows NT Server-level logon security .

The step-by-step approach to configuring the IMS is

1. Internet Mail tab configuration—Set the administrator mailbox to an account that receives IMS-related administrative alerts and notifications (shown in Figure 16.9).

**FIGURE 16.9**

*Internet Mail tab.*

[Screenshot: Internet Mail Service (SPRINGERS01) Properties dialog box showing tabs: General, Connected Sites, Address Space, Connections, Queues, Routing, Security, Delivery Restrictions, Advanced, Diagnostics Logging, Internet Mail, Dial-up Connections. Internet Mail Service (SPRING... Address Type: SMTP. Administrator's Mailbox: Administrator, with Change and Notifications buttons. Message Content Information: Send Attachments Using MIME with Plain text checked, HTML, UUENCODE, BinHex; Interoperability button. Character Set Translation: MIME: Western European (ISO-8859-1), Non-MIME: US ASCII. Specify message content by E-Mail Domain; Use fixed-width font checkbox; E-Mail Domain button. Enable message tracking checked. Buttons: OK, Cancel, Apply, Help.]

2. Dial-up Connections tab configuration—Select the desired retrieval schedule as seen in Figure 16.10. Select Mail Retrieval and configure for ETRN. (Don't worry about the definition, but it is given in the Internet Request For Comment 1985…yuk!)

3. As instructed to do so by your ISP (see Figure 16.11). ETRN is a retrieve mail/send mail approach that must be supported by your ISP to work properly.

   You must also complete the Logon Information dialog box (see Figure 16.12), accessed via the Logon Information button on the Dial-up Connections tab. You must complete this regardless of the fact you've provided the same ISP logon information for your Dial-up Networking (DUN) connection and most likely for the Microsoft Proxy Server Auto Dial Configuration (discussed on Day 11, "Internet Security: Proxy Server").

**Note**

The Dial-Up Connection tab might not open if the IMS isn't started (You can start the IMS via the Services applet in Control Panel.)

**FIGURE 16.10**

*Dial-up Connections tab.*

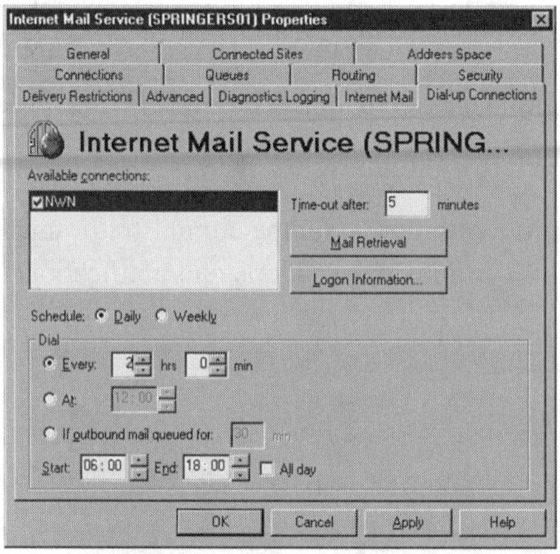

**FIGURE 16.11**

*Mail Retrieval.*

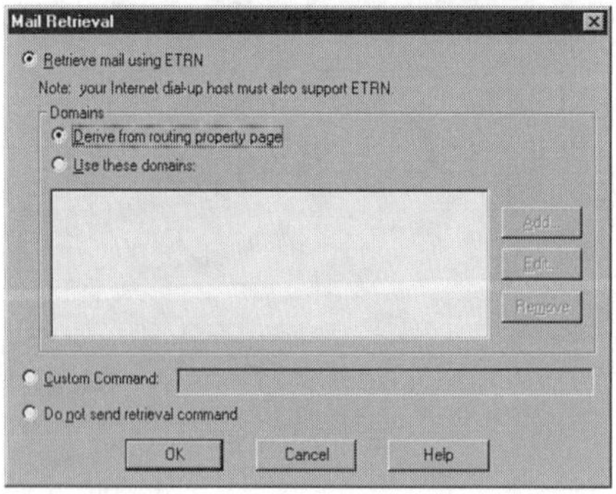

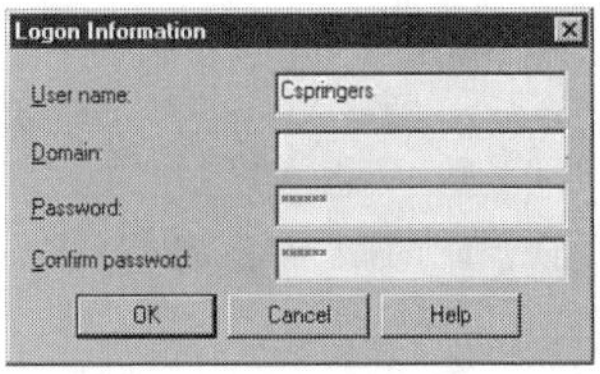

**FIGURE 16.12**

*Logon Information.*

**Logon Information**

User name: Cspringers
Domain:
Password: ******
Confirm password: ******

[ OK ]  [ Cancel ]  [ Help ]

**16**

4. Address Space tab—You must create a new Internet address space. In the E-mail Domain field, place a * character. In the Cost field, enter **1** (as shown in Figure 16.13).

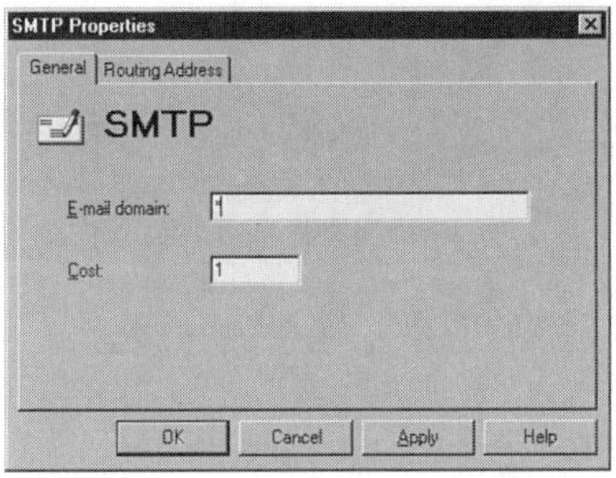

**FIGURE 16.13**

*Address space.*

**SMTP Properties**

General | Routing Address

**SMTP**

E-mail domain: 1
Cost: 1

[ OK ]  [ Cancel ]  [ Apply ]  [ Help ]

5. Connections tab—Configure the Message Delivery section based on instructions from your ISP (such configurations will vary). Be sure to select Dial Using if you are using a dial-up connection to your ISP for e-mail transfers. The Connections tab is shown in Figure 16.14.

**FIGURE 16.14**

*Connections tab.*

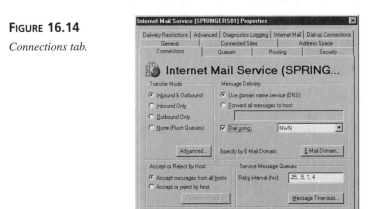

Internet Mail Service (SPRINGERS01) Properties

Delivery Restrictions | Advanced | Diagnostics Logging | Internet Mail | Dial-up Connections
General | Connected Sites | Address Space
Connections | Queues | Routing | Security

**Internet Mail Service (SPRING...**

Transfer Mode
- Inbound & Outbound
- Inbound Only
- Outbound Only
- None (Flush Queues)

[ Advanced... ]

Message Delivery
- Use domain name service (DNS)
- Forward all messages to host:

☑ Dial using: NWN

Specify by E-Mail Domain: [ E-Mail Domain... ]

Accept or Reject by Host
- Accept messages from all hosts
- Accept or reject by host

[ Specify Hosts... ]

Service Message Queues
Retry interval (hrs): 25,.5,1,4

[ Message Time-outs... ]

[ OK ]  [ Cancel ]  [ Apply ]  [ Help ]

6. Routing tab—Select the Do Not Reroute Incoming SMTP Mail to disable message routing (see Figure 16.15).

FIGURE **16.15**

*Routing tab.*

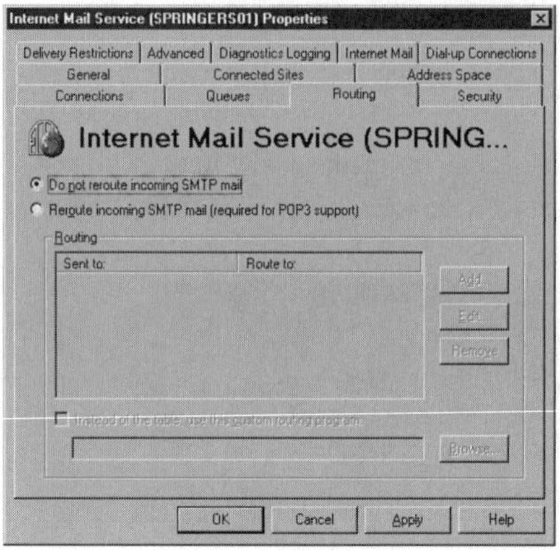

You now know what you need to know to configure the IMS.

# Outlook Web Client

A popular Exchange-related feature that you might consider implementing after you have everything up-and-running on the SBS network is the Outlook Web client. Here, given a full-time Internet connection between your SBS server running Microsoft Exchange and the Internet, your users can access their SBS Exchange-based e-mail from any Internet browser anywhere. Huh? Yes, it is true. My favorite use is to be at a client site, launch a Web browser at a borrowed workstation, and check my corporate e-mail. It's wonderful. The Outlook Web Client is shown in Figure 16.16.

Configuring the Outlook Web Client is beyond the scope of this chapter, but you might find the instructions via Exchange's Books Online. And at least one SBS guru has told me it's cranky (although that hasn't been my personal experience...yet!).

**Power Tool Tip**

> You will need to have Exchange's Active Server Page support installed (which is the default condition on SBS servers).

FIGURE 16.16

*Outlook's Web client.*

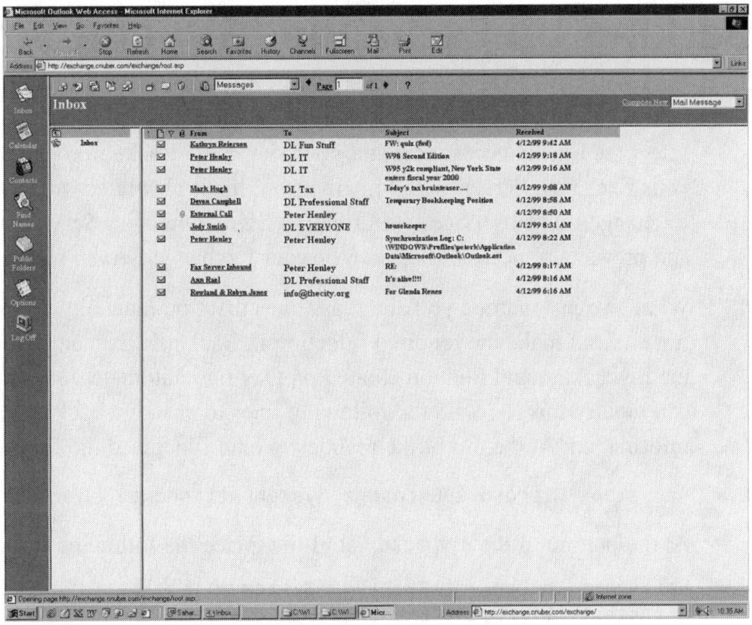

16

# Moving Exchange to a New Server

Here's the drill. Your SBS client has purchased a brand new server because you suggested it would improve performance and provide more storage. So far, so good. Now the greater challenge is moving the SBS user's mailbox without losing anything (not a single e-mail, contact, or appointment!).

Here is how you do it:

1. Make at least two SBS server machine backup tapes where you can verify that you have successfully backed up the Microsoft Exchange Information Store and Directory Services.

2. At the SBS user's workstation, export the Exchange Server–based mailbox to a .pst file on her local hard disk.

3. Complete your SBS server–related conversion to the new server machine. This would include many steps that I won't detail here, but you would install SBS on the new server machine, add the users and computers via the SBS Console, and so on.

4. From the SBS user's workstation, import the .pst file you created in step 2 into the Exchange Server–based mailbox for this user.

5. The user's mailbox containing e-mail, appointments, and contacts appears.

# Backing Up Exchange (GUI and Batch File)

Back on Day 6, "Daily and Weekly SBS Administration (The Dirty Dozen)," I discussed tape backups and restores . In passing, I made reference to the fact that you need to select the Exchange window and your site in the Backup program in order to back up your Exchange Server–based mailboxes. This is absolutely true; otherwise, the open Exchange-related services (Information Store, Directory Services) maintains open files and prevents a successful backup of your Exchange Server–related mailboxes. Bummer.

What I've just warned you about assumes that you manually configure your backup to run and can make the required selection in Backup's Exchange window. What if you use the mybackup.cmd file you created on Day 6 to automate your backup? Fear not, you can modify this file with the following lines to ensure a backup of your Exchange-related information. At the top of the mybackup.cmd file, place the following line:

```
net stop "Microsoft Exchange System Attendant"
```

At the bottom of the mybackup.cmd file, place the following lines:

```
net start "Microsoft Exchange System Attendant"
net start "Microsoft Exchange Directory"
net start "Microsoft Exchange Event Service"
net start "Microsoft Exchange Information Store"
net start "Microsoft Exchange Internet Mail Service"
net start "Microsoft Exchange Message Transfer Agent"
```

**Tip**

> Remember that third-party backup applications, such as Seagate's Backup Exec or Computer Associates's ARCserve, offer the best Microsoft Exchange backup solution.

# Non-Exchange E-mail Solutions

Did you know that you don't need to use Microsoft Exchange as your e-mail solution on your SBS network? Other possibilities exist, including using POP accounts offered by ISPs and free Web e-mail services such as Hotmail.

To use a POP e-mail account, where the ISP acts as your mail server (not Exchange), you would simply load the Internet E-Mail service in Outlook and configure it based on information provided by your ISP. Such information typically includes

- POP3 server configuration
- SMTP server configuration
- E-mail logon account name and password (which might be different from your dial-up account name and password)

The use of POP e-mail accounts in SBS environments is popular when the ISP has provided a bargain arrangement of several POP accounts for a low fee or when some SBS users desire to maintain a second, independent e-mail account not associated with the SBS network.

> **Note**
>
> Outlook aside, I've seen POP e-mail solutions implemented using the Outlook Express e-mail capability in Internet Explorer or the Netscape's e-mail application embedded in its Web browser.

**16**

Another popular option is the use of free Web-based e-mail accounts. From any Web browser, an SBS user can check an e-mail account not associated with the SBS network. With these accounts, you don't need to configure any POP or SMTP server information, thus it receives high marks for ease of use. But users are typically subject to lots of ads on the Web page (which effectively pays for the e-mail service). Perhaps the most popular free Web-based mail service is Hotmail, as shown in Figure 16.17.

**FIGURE 16.17**

*Hotmail.*

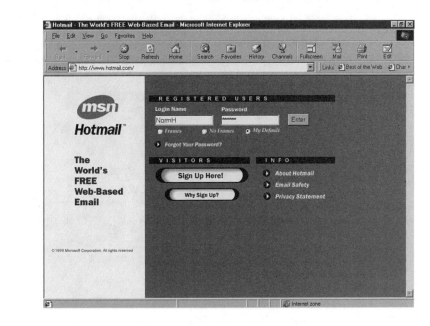

# Hidden Recipients

Possibly you maintain a user and e-mail account on a client's SBS networks for administrative purposes. I typically create an account called CN at each SBS site I consult so that I can log on and perform administrator-level duties. I create and maintain this account with the permission of my clients, but I often hide CN from being listed internally on Exchange-related user lists because it's not appropriate for the business staff to see my account, send me e-mail, and so on. More importantly, I shouldn't be party to their internal business e-mails, and if my CN account were visible, I might mistakenly be selected to receive confidential internal e-mails.

So, in this case, the solution is to make my CN account invisible to the Exchange e-mail users. This is easily done via the Microsoft Exchange Administrator by following these steps:

1. Expand the site name SPRINGERS01.
2. Double-click Recipients to show the SBS users in the left pane of Microsoft Exchange Administrator.
3. Double-click one of the SBS users to display that user's property sheet.
4. Select the Advanced tab.
5. Select the Hide from Address Book checkbox as seen in Figure 16.18.

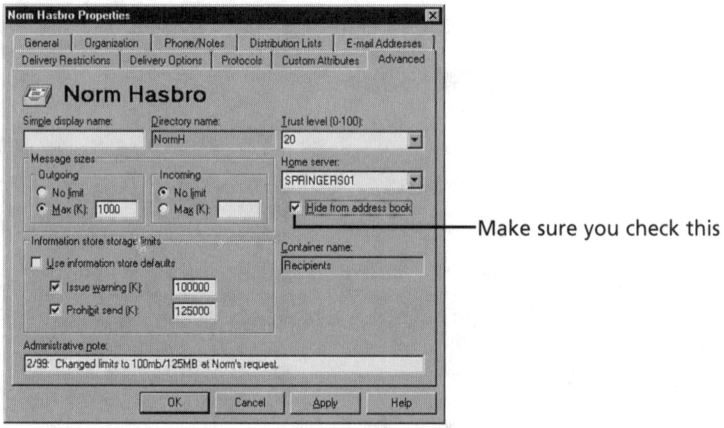

**FIGURE 16.18**

*Hiding a user name.*

—Make sure you check this

# Creating Internet E-mail Addresses via Exchange's Global Address List

You might recall that, on Day 8, I showed how to create groups of Internet e-mail addresses from the Outlook-side using personal address books. You can accomplish the same thing (better!) from the Microsoft Exchange Server side.

Why would you do this? Two reasons. First, from Day 8 you can appreciate the need for e-mailing a list of your buddies to go play golf, sail, or ski. You'd prefer to send this Internet e-mail to a distribution list instead of sending the same e-mail to individuals. Second, as I'll show you in a moment, you can forward your own e-mail to another e-mail system (for example, AOL) so that you can check your business e-mail when out of town or overseas by calling an AOL local access line (and not pay huge long distance charges, and so on).

To create Internet e-mail addresses in the Global Address List, do the following:

1. Log on to your SBS server machine as an Administrator or member of the Administrators group.

2. Launch the Microsoft Exchange Administrator from the Microsoft Exchange (Common) program group.

3. Select the Global Address List in the left pane. The e-mail account display names appear in the right pane.

4. Select New Custom Recipient from the File menu.

5. Approve any message to switch to the Recipients container by clicking OK.

6. When the new E-mail Address dialog box appears, select Internet Address.

7. The Internet Address Properties dialog box will be displayed. Type your external Internet e-mail address (for example, **harrybrelsford@aol.com**) in the E-mail address field. This is seen in Figure 16.19. Click OK.

**FIGURE 16.19**

*Internet Address Properties.*

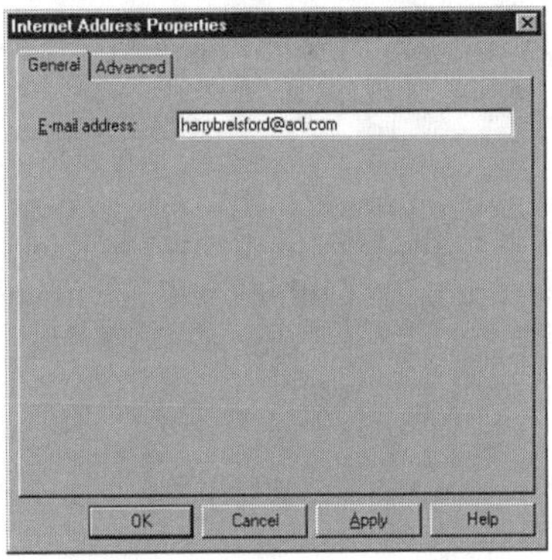

8. Complete the standard Properties sheet for this recipient (First, Initials, Last, Display, and Alias) as seen in Figure 16.20. Click OK.

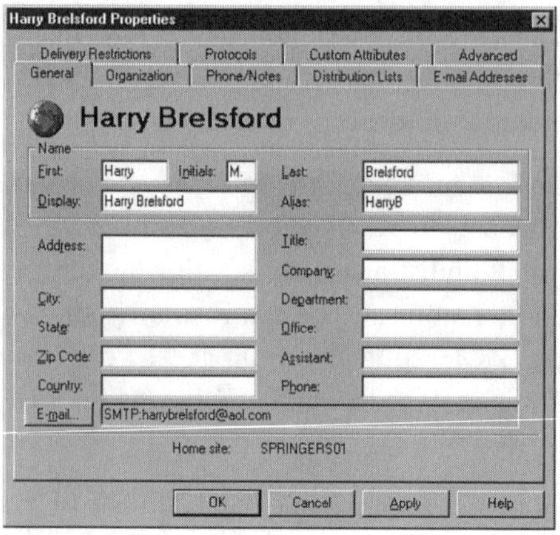

**FIGURE 16.20**

*E-Mail account properties.*

9. Observe how the Internet e-mail name you have entered now appears in the Global Address List just like any internal e-mail name does. This is very powerful because you can now create distribution lists that contain external Internet e-mail addresses.

To create a distribution list

1. Log on to your SBS server machine as an Administrator or member of the Administrators group.

2. Launch the Microsoft Exchange Administrator from the Microsoft Exchange (Common) program group.

3. Select the Global Address List in the left pane. The e-mail account display names appear in the right pane.

4. Select New Distribution List from the File menu.

5. Approve any message to switch to the Recipients container by clicking OK.

6. The Properties sheet for Distribution Lists is displayed. Complete the Property sheet to appear similar to Figure 16.21.

7. Click OK.

Not only does this list now appear in the Global Address List (see Figure 16.22), but more importantly, your SBS users running Outlook will see it when they select To and look under the Global Address List, when they compose e-mail.

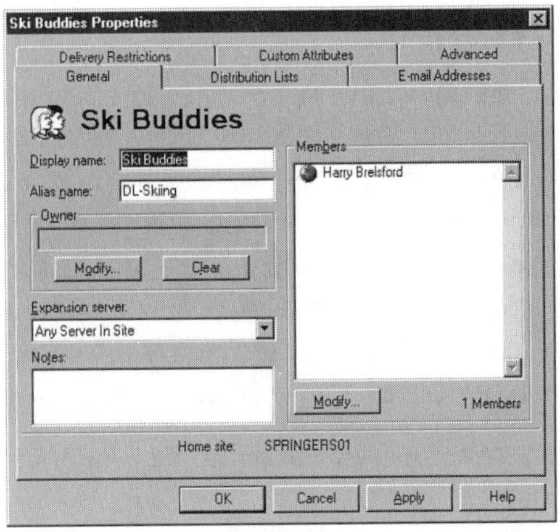

**FIGURE 16.21**

*Distribution list properties.*

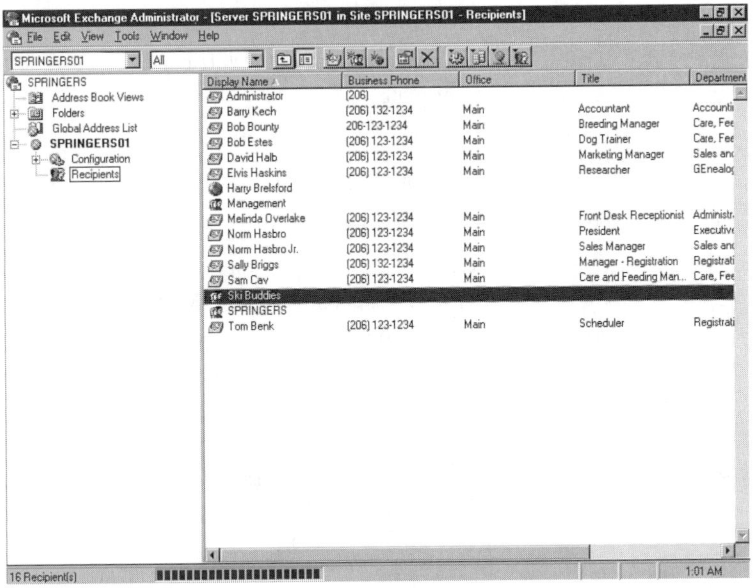

**FIGURE 16.22**

*Distribution list (Ski Buddies) in Global Address List.*

16

Best of all, what SBS users running Outlook were previously required to do manually (select individual Internet e-mail addresses from Contacts) can now be better handled via distribution lists containing external Internet e-mail addresses. Wow! This improvement in SBS 4.5 (and more specifically, Microsoft Exchange Server 5.5) provides a big answer for several of my existing SBS sites who had the underlying question about Internet e-mail account groups.

# Forwarding E-mail

Now that you've created an external Internet e-mail address in the previous example, you can resolve the final issue I've encountered at my SBS sites. Let me set the stage for you. I have a couple of SBS clients with wealthy owners who travel extensively. In the past, these people of means had only a CompuServe or AOL account because they could dial a local number to get their e-mail while traveling in the Middle East. When Microsoft introduced SBS, the question became how these people could receive their business e-mail from the SBS network on their CompuServe or AOL account. It's easy to do using an approach called *forwarding*. Here's how you do it:

1. Log on to your SBS server machine as an Administrator or member of the Administrators group.

2. Launch the Microsoft Exchange Administrator from the Microsoft Exchange (Common) program group.

3. Select the Global Address List in the left pane. The e-mail account display names appear in the right pane.

4. Select the Norm Hasbro e-mail account Display Name in the right pane.

5. Double-click this e-mail address to display its Properties.

6. Select the Delivery Options tab.

7. In the Alternate Recipient section, select the second radio button and select the external Internet e-mail account (via the Modify button) you created earlier. When you select the Modify button, your screen should look similar to Figure 16.23. (The external Internet e-mail account has a globe icon to the left of the name.) Click OK.

**FIGURE 16.23**

*Mailbox selection.*

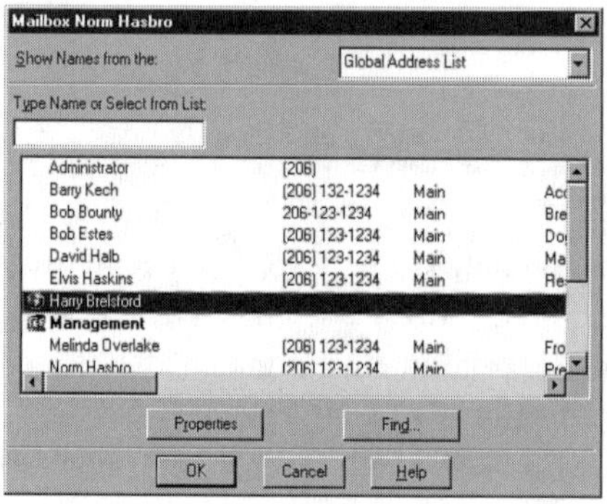

8. Select the Deliver Messages to Both Recipient and Alternate Recipient checkbox. The Alternate Recipient field should now look similar to Figure 16.24. Click OK.

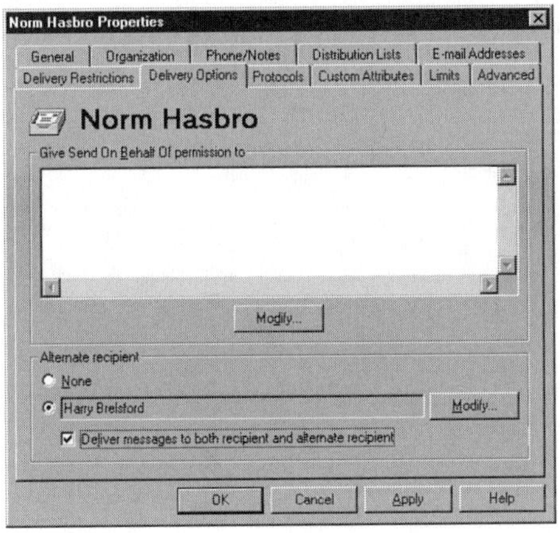

**FIGURE 16.24**

*Alternate Recipient.*

Now, whenever Norm Hasbro receives e-mail at `springers.nwnexus.com`, he will receive a duplicate copy of the e-mail at the external Internet e-mail account you just designated.

# Summary

Out of the box, Exchange is installed and configured for you as part of the SBS installation process. This chapter provided valuable tips and tricks for optimizing Exchange and implementing little-known Exchange features that aren't initially supported on your SBS network.

# DAY 17

# SQL Server

Talk about a career path. Not only can you find very good (and large) texts dedicated to the SQL Server database, but more than one Microsoft Certified Professional (MCP) has made a good living doing the SQL thing. Studying SQL Server introduces you to one of the largest bodies of knowledge contained within SBS 4.5. Given this overwhelming perspective, I've made the decision to keep the SQL Server discussion germane, practical, and relatively brief (and, as always, with a Springer Spaniels Unlimited view). If you so desire, Macmillan publishes other great books to dive deep into SQL Server, including

- *Sams Teach Yourself Microsoft SQL Server 7 in 21 Days* by Richard Waymire (ISBN: 0-672-31290-5).
- Que's *Special Edition Using Microsoft SQL Server 7.0* by Stephen Wynkoop (ISBN: 0-789-71523-6).

On the one hand, you can say SQL Server 7.0 is a very important part of SBS 4.5. Call it the "It's the data stupid" crowd. When you really think about it, the whole reason any of us technology professionals are here is because the underlying data drives business computing. Get it?

On the other hand, I can't deny that, in its natural state, SQL Server is one of the least used components in SBS 4.5. In fact, the MSSQLServer and SQLServerAgent services—I'll define these terms shortly—are set to manual and do not start when SBS 4.5 boots. In other words, while it is present, SQL Server isn't emphasized in SBS 4.5, and for good reason. It's highly unlikely you'll actually program inside of SQL Server (using the SQL programming language) as an SBS site. SQL Server is much more at home in development and enterprise environments.

Fear not, though. SQL Server has a very important role that I haven't even discussed yet. I actually discuss this role, to support third-party applications such as Great Plains Dynamics, at length on Day 19, "Installing Business Applications." To understand this role, today you'll learn the basics of SQL Server. Such an understanding will aid greatly in supporting applications that run on top of SQL Server.

To understand SQL Server at an appropriate level for an SBS site, you'll spend the morning session creating a simple table to manage some information for Springer Spaniels Unlimited via SQL Server. After lunch, the focus shifts to advanced SQL Server tidbits that you need to know about to better manage SQL Server. I do want to manage your expectations today. Today is not a day to master SQL Server; today is a day to meet SQL Server.

# AM Defining SQL Server

This morning starts with defining SQL Server and ends with having you create a table to track Springer Spaniel registrations.

At its heart, SQL Server is a database, but you likely knew that. Did you know, however, that it differs from other databases you might have worked with in the past in that SQL Server is a client/server database? Perhaps you've worked with other databases, such as dBASE, which are relational databases (similar to SQL Server), but don't exploit the power of the network's server (the SBS server machine on an SBS network). Figure 17.1 shows how SQL Server works as a client/server database and how other databases (such as dBASE) work.

## The Server Side

On the SBS server machine, the data resides not only in tables but also in the SQL Server engine. This SQL Server engine actually comprises three services:

- MSSQLServer—This is the SQL Server engine as you know it. This is the piece that processes the SQL statements (officially known as Transact-SQL). This service also allocates server resources such as memory, manages the tables (for example, prevents collisions between users), and ensures the integrity of the data (via various tests). In SBS 4.5, this service is set to manual, meaning that it does not start when the SBS server machine starts.

- MSDTC—This is the Microsoft Distributed Transaction Coordinator, which acts as a traffic cop, managing the sources of data that compose a transaction. In SBS 4.5, this service is set to automatic (meaning it starts when the SBS server machine is booted).

- SQLServerAgent—This is a new service in SQL Server 7.0, and it manages scheduling activities and sends alerts.

**FIGURE 17.1**

*SQL Server client/server versus other databases.*

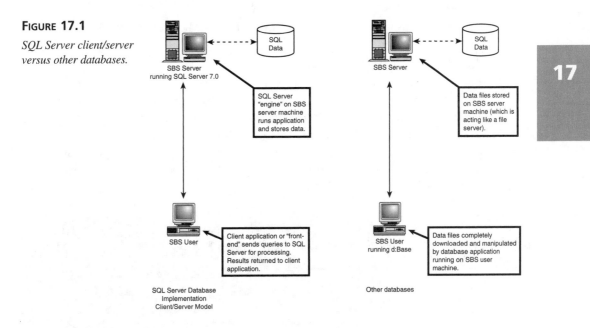

**17**

SQL Data

SBS Server running SQL Server 7.0

SQL Server "engine" on SBS server machine runs application and stores data.

SBS User

Client application or "front-end" sends queries to SQL Server for processing. Results returned to client application.

SQL Server Database Implementation Client/Server Model

SQL Data

SBS Server

Data files stored on SBS server machine (which is acting like a file server).

SBS User running d:Base

Data files completely downloaded and manipulated by database application running on SBS user machine.

Other databases

The following SQL Server system databases are automatically built when SBS 4.5 installs SQL Server 7.0:

- Master—This is the mother of all tables in SQL Server; lose it (with no back up) and you'll die. Simply stated, it controls SQL Server operations completely (including user databases, user accounts, environmental variables, system error message, and so on). It is critical that you back up this database on a regular basis.

- Model—This template provides basic information used when you create new databases for your own use. This is akin to the metainformation you entered when you installed SBS 4.5 (company name, address, fax telephone number) that reappears each time you add a users, via the SBS Console, to your SBS network. You might recall that I defined *metainformation* early in this book; it is information that is used globally by the computer system, not just in one place.

- Msdb—SQLServerAgent uses this for scheduling and job history.

- Tempdb—This is another very important database to the operation of SQL Server. It's a temporary storage area used by SQL Server for working storage. This is akin to the paging file used by Windows NT Server (the underlying operating system in SBS).

- Northwind—This a sample database. Consider using this as the prototype for developing your own company database. This is an addition in SQL Server 7.0 that wasn't present in prior versions of SQL Server. This was the sample database in Microsoft Access.

- Pubs—This is a second database used in most of Microsoft's SQL Server manuals.

## The Client Side

This is where you will spend your time with SQL Server. The client side, from a management perspective, is the SQL Server Enterprise Manager (which uses the Microsoft Management Console), various SQL Server administration tools and wizards, and the books online, to name a few. To introduce yourself to the full array of SQL Server management tools (which are technically considered client applications), simply display the contents of the Microsoft SQL Server 7.0 program group (found via the Start button, Programs) as seen in Figure 17.2.

**FIGURE 17.2**

*Microsoft SQL Server 7.0 program group.*

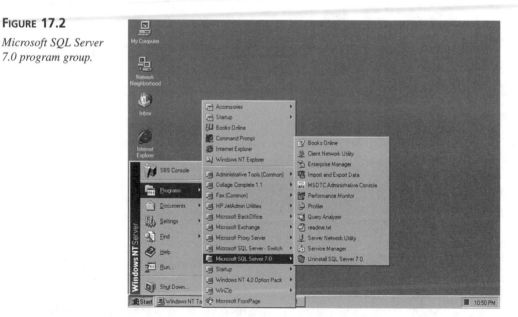

The client side also speaks to the wide range of applications that use SQL Server, including,

- Third-party applications, such as Great Plains Dynamics accounting software.

- Microsoft Access running on the SBS user's workstations.

- Microsoft Excel spreadsheets that link to databases housed on an SBS server machine running SQL Server.

- Microsoft Visual Basic–created applications that use SQL Server. These are typically homegrown applications written by either an employee at an SBS site or a consultant to use data stored and managed by SQL Server.

- Other applications. I've seen a wide range of applications, including Microsoft Excel, Word, and PowerPoint, that access a SQL Server database to extract and place data. Rumor has it the advanced pivot table feature in Microsoft Excel works very nicely with SQL Server–based data.

**17**

**Note**

Client-side applications typically connect to SQL Server (running on the SBS server machine) via the following database application program interfaces (API) or connectors:

- Open database connectivity (ODBC)—ODBC is the connector by which many front-ends running on the clients (a.k.a. client applications) connect to the SQL Server database. I'll show you ODBC in action shortly.

- Object linking and embedding (OLE)—OLE, in English, is what I like to think of as copy-and-paste kept alive. When you paste data from one source to another and you change the data back at the source, it's automatically updated at the destination you created. With respect to SQL Server, imagine a Microsoft Excel spreadsheet containing financial information from a SQL Server–based table. The financial information changes in the table and the Microsoft Excel spreadsheet is updated automatically....Plain and simple.

- ActiveX Data Objects (ADO)—This is a connector that, among other things, provides access to record-level access to VSAM, AS/400, and PDS data.

- Remote Data Objects (RDO)—RDO provides a framework for using code to create and manipulate components of a remote ODBC database system.

# Common Uses of SQL Server on SBS Networks

First and foremost, the greatest need I've seen for SQL Server 7.0 on SBS networks is support for third-party applications such as Great Plains Dynamics and other narrow, vertical-market applications in the legal, medical, and instrument-repair industries (to name just a few). In fact, so prevalent is this type of use of SQL Server 7.0 on an SBS network that I've dedicated an entire day to this topic: The thrust of Day 19 is to show two major business applications running on top of SQL Server 7.0.

Secondary uses for SQL Server 7.0 on an SBS network include creating your own databases and learning SQL Server 7.0 for MCSE certification purposes. (I'm just calling it like I see it.)

# SQL Server and Springer Spaniels Unlimited

No chapter on SQL Server, in any book, would be complete without having you create a database or a table or two, enter some data and then display the data you've entered. This book is no exception. But again, understand that this exercise is almost an exception to the rule on SBS networks; you're far more likely to work with third-party applications that sit on top of the SQL Server 7.0 engine.

That said, revisit your friends at Springer Spaniels Unlimited. Because no third-party software exists that explicitly tracks dogs, you'll create a database to accomplish this business purpose.

> **Tip**
>
> Whenever considering the creation of a database, be sure you understand the purpose for undertaking this project. Poorly considered database projects are like poorly written books: difficult to read and soon ignored.

Now get to work and create a database for Springer Spaniels Unlimited. Afterward, you will create a table and populate it with meaningful dog tracking information.

### Task 17.1: Creating the SSUDOG Database

To create the database for Springer Spaniels Unlimited, perform the following steps:

1. Log on to the SBS server machine as an administrator or member of the administrators group.

▼ 2. Click Start, Programs, Microsoft SQL Server 7.0 (program group) and select Enterprise Manager.

3. The SQL Server Enterprise Manager appears. Expand the following objects in the left pane: Microsoft SQL Servers, SQL Server Group, SPRINGERS01, as seen in Figure 17.3. (You will experience a slight pause when you expand SPRINGERS01 as the MSSQLServer service starts.)

**FIGURE 17.3**

*SQL Server Enterprise Manager.*

**17**

4. Click SPRINGERS01 to display the Getting Started Taskpad in the right pane. Select Set Up Your Database Solution, as seen in Figure 17.4.

**FIGURE 17.4**

*Set Up Your Database Solution.*

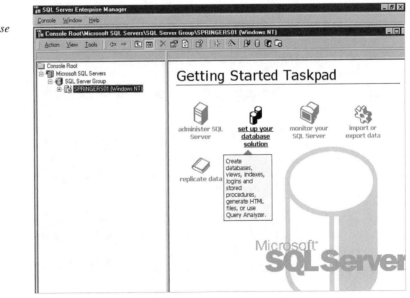

▼

▼          5. The Setup Your Database Solution screen appears. Select Create a Database, as
              seen in Figure 17.5.

**FIGURE 17.5**

*Create a Database.*

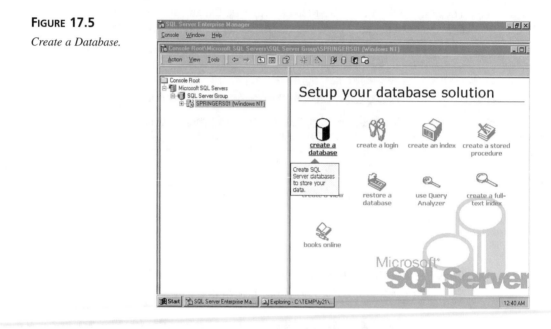

           6. The Create Database Wizard - SPRINGERS01 wizard starts. Click Next.
           7. The Name the Database and Specify its Location screen appears. Enter **SSUDOG**
              in the Database name field as seen in Figure 17.6. Click Next.

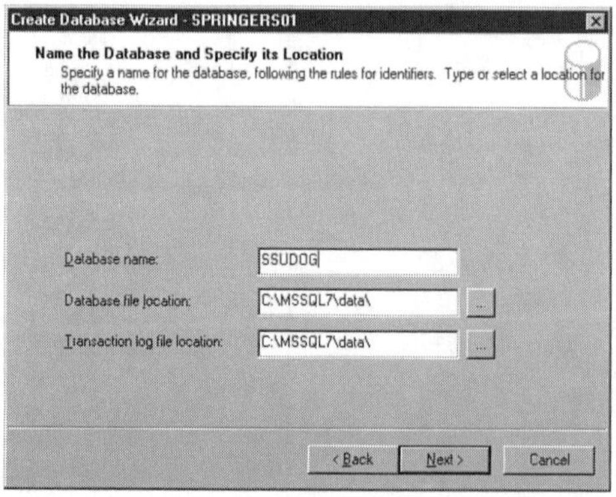

**FIGURE 17.6**

*Database name and
location.*

           8. The Name the Database Files screen appears. Accept the default file name of
▼             SSUDOG_Data and the initial size of 1MB. Click Next.

▼    9. Accept the defaults on the Define the Database File Growth screen. These defaults relate to how active the database will be, how large it will grow, and how fast it will grow. Click Next.

10. Accept the default file name of SSUDOG_Log on the Name the Transaction Log Files screen. Click Next.

11. Accept the defaults on the Define the Transaction Log File Growth screen. This screen is similar to the screen described in step 9. Click Next.

12. Click Finish on the Complete the Create Data Wizard screen after verifying all the settings you've selected (see Figure 17.7). Click OK when you see the notice that you successfully created the database.

**FIGURE 17.7**

*Finish - Completing the Create Database Wizard.*

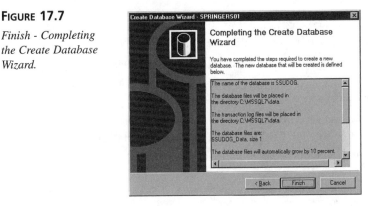

13. You are asked whether you want to create a maintenance plan for the database SSUDOG. Click Yes.

**Tip**

It is critical that you set up a daily maintenance plan for your key databases (the master database and any databases you create). On more than one occasion, I've had to rely on the SQL Server–based database backups when a traditional backup tape failed me. A SQL Server-based database backup places a bona fide copy of your database on another part of the SBS server machine's hard disk. It's unbelievably valuable!

14. The Database Maintenance Plan Wizard launches. Click Next.

▼ 15. Select master and SSUDOG on the Select Databases screen, as seen in Figure 17.8. Click Next.

▼ FIGURE **17.8**

*Select Databases.*

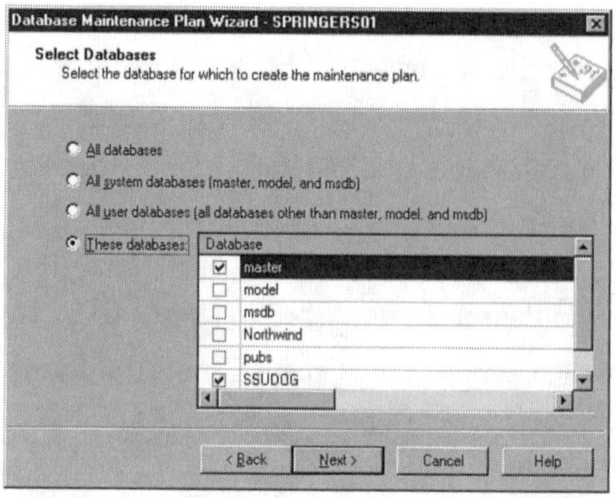

16. On the Update Data Optimization Information screen, select the Reorganize Data and Index Pages check box. Accept the schedule and click Next.

17. On the Database Integrity Check screen, select the Check Database Integrity check box and click Next.

18. On the Specify the Database Backup Plan screen, select the Back Up the Database as Part of the Maintenance Plan check box. Select the Change button and select Daily in the Occurs column. Click OK. The Specify the Database Backup Plan screen should look similar to Figure 17.9. Click Next.

FIGURE **17.9**

*Specify the Database Backup Plan.*

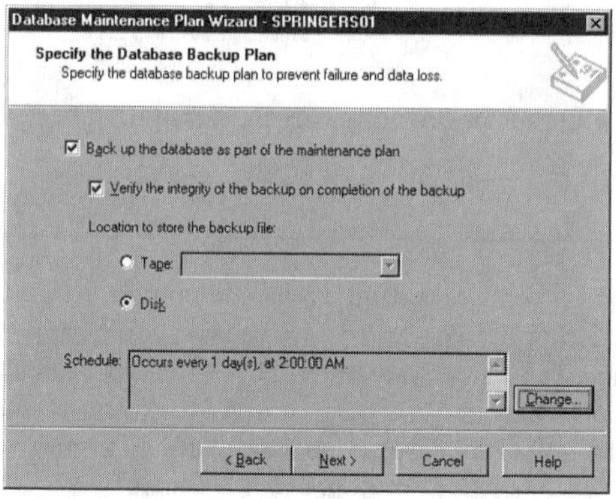

19. Accept the defaults on the Specify Backup Disk Directory. Click Next.

20. Click the Back Up the Transaction Log as Part of the Maintenance Plan check box on the Specify the Transaction Log Backup Plan screen. Click Next.

21. Accept the defaults on the Specify Transaction Log Backup Disk Directory screen. Click Next.

▼

▼    22. Select the Write Report to a Text File in Directory check box on the Reports to
         Generate screen. Accept the default report storage folder (c:\mssql7/log) and click
         Next.

     23. Accept the default settings on the Maintenance History screen and click Next.

     24. Click Finish on the Completing the Database Maintenance Wizard screen. After a
         few minutes, a dialog box advises you that the maintenance plan was created suc-
▲        cessfully. Click OK.

## Task 17.2: Creating the Tracking Table

You should always have a bona fide business purpose for creating a database and populating it with information. Springer Spaniels Unlimited is no exception. Here the underlying business purpose is clear: to use SQL Server to solve a problem. The problem is
that, with the sheer volume of springer spaniels that enter the world at Springer Spaniels
Unlimited, you must have a method for tracking their whereabouts and exact origin. The
simple table you'll create here, the Tracking table, achieves this important business goal.

Table 17.1 shows the data dictionary that you will use to create the database.

**TABLE 17.1**   SPRINGER SPANIELS UNLIMITED DATA DICTIONARY

| Item | Description |
| --- | --- |
| SSUDOG | Database name |
| Tracking | Table for tracking springer spaniels |
| DogName | Name of dog (column name, Datatype = char, Length = 30) |
| ShowName | Long name of dog for show purposes (column name, Datatype = char, Length = 50) |
| FatherDN | Father dog's name (column name, Datatype = char, Length = 30) |
| MotherDN | Mother dog's name (column name, Datatype = char, Length = 30) |
| DDOB | Dog's date of birth (column name, Datatype = datetime, Length = 8) |
| AKCNum | American Kennel Club (AKC) registration number (column name, Datatype = char, Length = 15) |

Now commence the task of creating your Tracking table:

     1. Expand SSUDOG and then right-click the Table icon in the left pane. Select New
        Table from the secondary menu.

     2. A Choose Name dialog box appears. Type **Tracking** in the Enter a Name for the
▼       Table field. Click OK.

**17**

▼  3. The New Table in SSUDOG on SPRINGERS01 screen appears. Create the table based on the information contained in Table 17.1. The result should look similar to Figure 17.10.

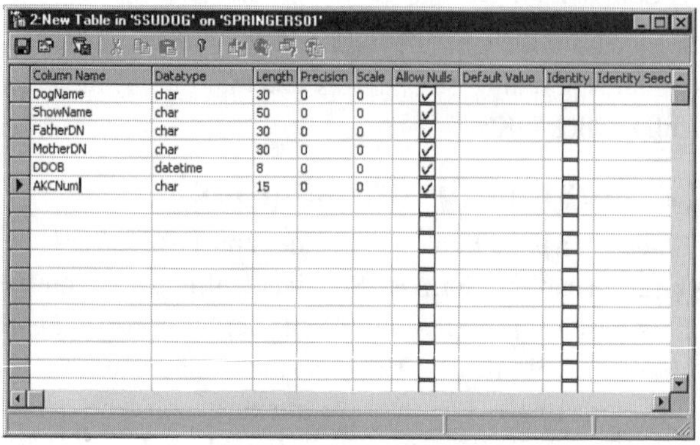

**FIGURE 17.10**

*Tracking table setup.*

| Column Name | Datatype | Length | Precision | Scale | Allow Nulls | Default Value | Identity | Identity Seed |
|---|---|---|---|---|---|---|---|---|
| DogName | char | 30 | 0 | 0 | ✓ | | | |
| ShowName | char | 50 | 0 | 0 | ✓ | | | |
| FatherDN | char | 30 | 0 | 0 | ✓ | | | |
| MotherDN | char | 30 | 0 | 0 | ✓ | | | |
| DDOB | datetime | 8 | 0 | 0 | ✓ | | | |
| AKCNum | char | 15 | 0 | 0 | ✓ | | | |

**Note**

Move your cursor from field to field just like in a spreadsheet. When your cursor is in the Datatype field, a down arrow appears. This is a drop-down menu containing the different types of data fields you'll be working with (for example, datetime).

4. Click the Save icon on the left side of the toolbar (disk icon) on the New Table in SSUDOG on SPRINGERS01 screen. Close the window via the X in the upper-
▲    right corner of the screen.

# Lunch

Time for lunch. Believe it or not, you've accomplished a fair amount of work this morning. Launching SQL Server and creating a database and table is something that many courses take three days to accomplish, not just a morning. After lunch, you will enter Springer Spaniels Unlimited–related data into the table and perform a query against the table.

## Task 17.3: Create Your Own Database

1. On a blank sheet of paper, draw a business process for your existing business. For example, if you are a small law firm, perhaps you could benefit from a SQL Server–based database that tracks files by docket number.

▼ 2. After you've identified the business process that you want to improve with SQL Server, use another sheet of blank paper to create the table. This table contains the information fields you'll need to create and use to accomplish your desired business goal.

3. Now, take a few minutes to go out to lunch. On your return, look over the planning that you did in steps 1 and 2 to see whether the outcomes (as displayed on your paper) are still valid. Make modifications as necessary. As a side note, you'd be amazed at what your short lunch break will do for your insight into your database design. So often, after returning from a break in the database design process, I'll have new insights and clarity into my business process planning that simply escaped me before. It's a healthy design approach.

4. Following the database and table creation steps shown this morning, it's time to transfer your creation from your planning papers to SQL Server. Good luck, and don't be afraid to perform this step. SQL Server can accommodate multiple databases and tables with ease. You will in no way damage the work you've already performed for Springer Spaniels Unlimited (because that information is contained
▲ in a separate database).

17

## ☽PM Using Your Springer Spaniels Database

Welcome back from lunch. You will now enter real business information into the Tracking table. Afterward, you will query the table to retrieve the data. Finally, I'll end the day with some advanced SQL Server topics.

## Task 17.4: Data Entry

It is now time to enter data into the Tracking table. In Table 17.2, I've provided the data needed for two springer spaniels. You will use this information to populate the database.

**TABLE 17.2**   SSUDOG DATA

| Item | Dog1 | Dog2 |
|------|------|------|
| DogName | Brisker | Jaeger |
| ShowName | Sir David Brisker | Sir Jaeger Matthew |
| FatherDN | Pepper | Pepper |
| MotherDN | Maria | Maria |
| DDOB | 8-15-93 | 8-15-93 |
| ▼ AKCNum | WA98119A | WA98119B |

▼ Assuming you are still in the SQL Server Enterprise Manager, perform the following steps:

1. Right-click Tracking in the right pane listing all of the SSUDOG table. From the secondary menu, select Open Table, Return All Rows as seen in Figure 17.11.

**FIGURE 17.11**

*Return All Rows from secondary menu.*

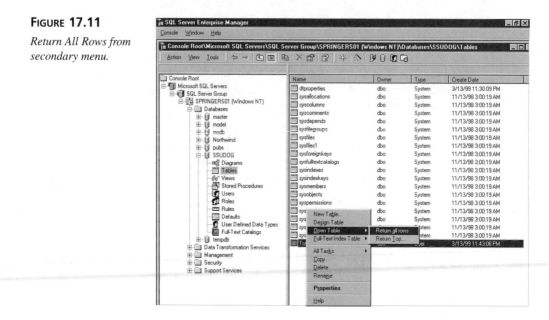

2. The Data in Table Tracking window appears. Enter the information from Table 17.2 into this window. Figure 17.12 shows the result. (You can move between fields with your Tab key.)

**FIGURE 17.12**

*Complete Tracking table.*

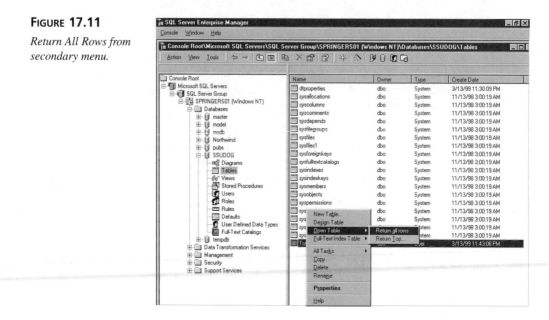

3. Close the Data in Table 'Tracking' window by clicking the X on the upper-left cor-

▲     ner of the window.

## Task 17.5: Query the Data

You will now query the SSUDOG database, much like a client application does. Why? Because in and of itself, a table populated with data is relatively worthless. For your relationship with SQL Server to have true value, you must use the information. That's an action verb as in *query*. Thus, after populating a table with information, you will query it to return the information in a synthesized or value-added form. And that's essentially the database food chain.

1. Launch the Query Analyzer application in the Microsoft SQL Server 7.0 program group (found via Start, Programs).

2. If asked, type the SQL Server name **SPRINGERS01** and accept sa with no password for logon purposes in the Connect to SQL Server dialog box. Click OK.

3. A Query window appears inside of SQL Server Query Analyzer. In the Query window, select SSUDOG from the DB drop-down menu (upper far right in Query window).

4. In the Query window, click the blank space in the center of the screen and type the following command: **select * from tracking**

5. Select Execute from the Query menu (you can also press F5 or click the green right arrow on the Query window toolbar). The contents of the Tracking table are returned to you, as seen in Figure 17.13.

**FIGURE 17.13**

*Successful query against Tracking.*

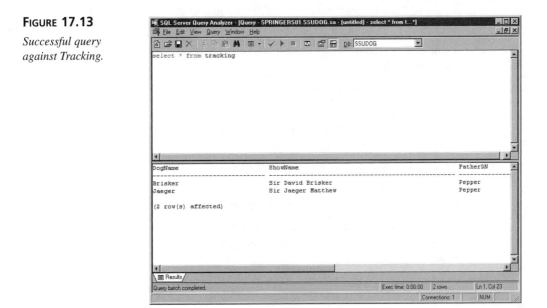

# Success!

Enjoy your success. You've had a busy morning performing the following SQL Server-related duties:

- You learned SQL Server basics.
- You created a SQL Server database title SSUDOG.
- You created a table titled Tracking in the SSUDOG database.
- You entered data for Springer Spaniels Unlimited in the Tracking table.
- You queried (that is, used) the data in the Tracking table by executing a simple SQL query.

I want to emphasize one final point before you call it a day: This short chapter on SQL Server is only a start, and you have a lot to learn about SQL Server 7.0 if you so desire.

# Advanced SQL: You've Only Just Begun

So you're interested in learning more about SQL Server. That's great! It's a huge area where you can always grow; it has no upper knowledge limit. Aside from the advanced SQL Server books mentioned earlier today, there are several key areas to master as you continue in your quest to learn and use SQL servers. These study topics are

- Learn SQL basics including these SQL commands: SELECT, UPDATE, INSERT, and DELETE.
- Learn the rules: how to define primary keys, secondary keys, and indexes; and how to normalize a database.
- Learn the power of stored procedures. Create a stored procedure of your own.
- Learn, inside and out, the tools that ship with SQL Server 7.0 including SQL Server Enterprise Manager, SQL Server Query Analyzer, and Books Online (to name my three favorite tools).
- Learn and master client-side connectivity, especially ODBC.
- Learn how third-party applications use SQL Server 7.0. Such third-party applications include Great Plains Dynamics, an application that I discuss on Day 19.
- Learn to connect Web pages to SQL Server 7.0. This is, of course, a very popular and in-demand skill set. It is the basis of many electronic commerce implementations.

# Summary

Today you worked with SQL Server 7.0, the powerful database included with SBS 4.5. I hope that the exercise in creating a database for Springer Spaniels Unlimited went a long way toward debunking the myth that databases are hard to use. If you followed the steps in the chapter, you not only created a database, but used it as well.

That said, I emphasized the following point several times: on an SBS network, your interaction with SQL Sever 7.0 will likely be limited to installed third-party applications that use SQL Server 7.0 as a database engine. This observation will be fully explored on Day 19 when you see how two business applications take advantage of SQL Server. The applications, Great Plains Dynamics and BenchTop, use SQL Server to store the business information created by the end user, manage the data and provide information, and report back to the end user. Basic database functions, eh?

If for some reason you decide to program SQL Server directly, such as you did in creating the SSUDOG database table for Springer Spaniels Unlimited, remember to keep your databases simple and friendly, very much like you did today. That's my $29.95 advice to you. Good day.

17

# DAY **18**

# Advanced Topics: Service Pack 4 and the Option Pack

As you turn the corner on your time spent learning SBS 4.5, I'll use today to discuss two advanced features included with SBS 4.5: Service Pack 4.0 and Option Pack. A service pack typically comprises bug fixes and additional features. The option pack provides additional applications that extend the capabilities of your SBS network.

## Go Forward

Before I get into all that discussion, here is the plan for today. Simply stated, today is an advanced day. By design, it occurs near the end of the 21 days. By now, you should have completed or at least experienced the following:

- Planned for an SBS 4.5 network
- Installed SBS 4.5 on a server machine

- Added SBS workstations to your SBS network
- Started to perform regular daily and monthly activities on your SBS network, such as tape backups
- Implemented some level of Internet connectivity for your SBS network
- Implemented an e-mail solution using both Microsoft Outlook 2000 and Microsoft Exchange Server
- Implemented modem sharing (if necessary)
- Implemented some form of dial-in solution either using RAS or a third-party communications software package
- Implemented faxing
- Started using Office 2000 on your SBS network
- Implemented Microsoft SQL Server (if necessary)

That's a long list of accomplishments in such a short period of time, but today clearly represents a turn in the remainder of our days together. Today's advanced topics precede successive days of additional advanced topics including installing applications on top of Microsoft SQL Server, advanced server management issues, and upgrading to Big BackOffice.

In large part, your SBS network is now completely set up. (Congratulations, by the way, if I forgot to recognize that milestone.) If you're new to the world of networks and SBS, I encourage you to skim this and the remaining days, but it can't hurt you, as your time allows, to delve into the depths of SBS. More importantly, scan the remaining days now with interest and return a few months later, after you have just a little more SBS experience. You'll be amazed at how the topics discussed from this point forward will take on new relevance for you and your SBS network. Hang in there!

Now for the other group—the SBS power users, gurus, MCSEs, and consultants. Whereas some of the early days might have been somewhat elementary, your time has now arrived. Indeed your SBS network should now be up and running. The time has now arrived to enhance, upgrade, and otherwise improve your SBS network. Today's topical areas of Service Pack 4.0 and the Option Pack are a start in that direction.

Without further ado, the morning session will cover Service Pack 4.0 and the afternoon session will cover the Option Pack.

## AM Service Pack 4.0

Microsoft and other software developers often release several service packs during the life of an operating system or application. These releases are welcome because each contains a range of bug fixes that makes the underlying operating system more usable and reliable. As I mentioned before, I don't deploy a Microsoft operating system until Service Pack 1 has been released (although I install the same operating system on a test machine well before the first service pack arrives). The most conservative among us often wait until the third or fourth service pack before deploying an operating system. This conservative group maintains that an operating system is only ready for prime time when it has aged to maturity, as measured by service pack releases. It's analogous to wine aficionados, waiting for their nectar of the gods to age. Such thinking makes perfect sense to me when you're running a regional hospital network (a true 7-days-a-week, 24-hours-a-day environment) with hundreds of users (and lives) at stake!

An interesting twist in modern times is the use of service packs to introduce new features. Such is the case in Service Pack 4.0, which contains not only bug fixes but also new features for the underlying Windows NT Server operating system. I'll have more on that in a moment.

First a few comments about Service Pack 4.0 (SP4) and SBS 4.5:

- Modified SP4 on SBS 4.5—What you see is *not* what you get. SBS 4.5's SP4 isn't the same SP4 that you can order from Microsoft on a CD-ROM or download over the Internet at www.microsoft.com. Indeed, the SP4 version contained in SBS 4.5 is a slipstreamed or modified version of SP4. To enjoy all the new features that SP4 offers, you must obtain a copy of the real SP4 from one of the two sources I just mentioned.

- Automatic installation—You don't have a choice as to whether you want to install SP4 on your SBS 4.5 network. As I said on Day 3, "Installing Small Business Server," when you installed SBS 4.5, SP4 is automatically installed as part of the SBS 4.5 build.

- SP4 Reinstallation—Whenever you remove and reinstall a major service in SBS 4.5 such as RAS, SQL Server, or Exchange to name a few, you must reinstall SP4 so that the underlying service you just reinstalled enjoys the bug fixes provided by SP4. This is a common step on any Microsoft network and adheres to the law that you also reinstall the latest service pack after making major changes to your system.

  Reinstalling SP4 on your SBS network is very easy. Simply insert SBS CD 1 in your CD-ROM drive on the SBS server machine. Next, run the sp4setup.exe file in the \bkoffice\i386 folder on SBS compact disc 1. Follow the onscreen instructions.

- SP4 is necessary—Many underlying SBS 4.5 components such as SQL Server 7.0 rely on SP4 to operate. How do I know this other than reading each product's requirement sheet? I know this from the School of Hard Knocks. In a larger Windows NT Server environment, a few others and I looked slightly foolish one

**18**

morning when we arrived with SQL Sever 7.0 and didn't have SP4 in hand. We were only a few minutes into the SQL Server 7.0 installation when we received an error message that the installation could not continue without SP4 installed. Three hours later, via a modem download, SP4 was installed followed by SQL Server 7.0. Fortunately for you, when using SBS 4.5 you won't hit a similar snag. That's because, as mentioned earlier, SP4 is automatically installed for you.

Those SBS 4.5–specific comments relating to SP4 aside, I'll look closer at what SP4 is: bug fixes and enhancements.

## Bug Fixes

The bug fixes contained in SP4 fall into five general categories:

- Year 2000 Fixes—This fix, in large part, makes SBS 4.5 Y2K-compliant. (Other SBS 4.5 features, such as Microsoft Proxy Server 2.0 also contributed to the "Y2K-OK" designation.)

- Internet Explorer 4.01 Service Pack 1—This part of SP4 is ignored because SBS 4.5 runs Internet Explorer version 5.0.

- Option Pack Fixes—Among the Option Pack fixes contained in SP4 are fixes for Certificate Server, Internet Information Server (IIS) 4.0, Message Queue for Windows NT, Microsoft Transaction Server SMTP, and NNTP. From that list, fixes that apply directly to the Option Pack edition installed with SBS 4.5 include the IIS and Microsoft Transaction Server fixes.

- The Bizarre and Minor—Fixes to the interface of the Chinese edition of Windows NT Server 4.0.

- Networking Updates—Here the list is extremely long and includes fixes for
  - Dynamic Host Configuration Protocol (DHCP)
  - Domain Name Server (DNS)
  - Windows Internet Naming Service (WINS)
  - Routing Information Protocol (RIP) Listener
  - Microsoft Routing and Remote Access Service (RRAS)
  - Point-to-Point Tunneling Protocol (PPTP)

For a complete list of specific SP4 fixes, and it's a long one, see the knowledge base article Q150734 ("List of Bugs Fixed in Windows NT Server 4.0 Service Pack 4") at http://support.microsoft.com/support.

**Power Tool Tip**

If you watched the setup process closely, you will note that SP4 installed itself immediately after the underlying Windows NT Server 4.0 operating system completed its setup. The reason is simple. As previously mentioned, some BackOffice applications such as SQL Server 7.0 require that SP4 be installed.

Also note, with both ears wide open, that Option Pack is very SP4-sensitive. If you ever install additional Option Pack components, such as Microsoft Certificate Server, you must reapply SP4. I discuss the Option Pack immediately after lunch.

## Enhancements

The full version of SP4 offers these enhancements:

- Security Configuration Editor—This tool, known in networking circles as SCE, is a valuable tool that provides security templates to assist in the management of your network security. No new security features are introduced, though. I discuss SCE later today.

- NetShow Server 3.0—NetShow is similar to CU-SeeMe in that it's a collection of services that provides multimedia conferencing (audio and video) across the Internet.

- Site Server Express 3.0—This tool enables you to create a map of your Web site so that you can manage your Web pages and observe their layouts.

- Miscellaneous SP4 Items—Another long list of items, discussed in detail in the readme file that accompanies SP4, includes the following:
  - Microsoft Active Accessibility (MSAA) support
  - DCOM/HTTP Tunneling
  - Euro Key Patch
  - Internet Group Management Protocol (IGMP) v2
  - Microsoft File and Print Service for NetWare (FPNW) support for Client 32
  - Profile Quotas (badly needed disk space limitations)
  - Remote Winsock (DNS/Port 53)
  - Remote Procedure Calls (RPC) Enhancements for Visual Basic (VB)
  - Routing Information Protocol (RIP) Listener

**18**

> These enhancements are not present in the slipstreamed or modified version of SP4 that is automatically installed with SBS 4.5 (more on that issue in a moment).

Before I discuss the full version of SP4, understand that the SP4 included with SBS 4.5 basically includes ordinary and necessary bug fixes that SBS 4.5 relies on. The enhancements are in the full version of SP4, which I discuss next.

## Obtaining the Full Version of SP4

To enjoy the full benefit of SP4, you need to download the full copy from www.microsoft.com or order the SP4 CD-ROM version directly from Microsoft.

**Power Tool Tip**

> I highly recommend that you do exactly as I suggest earlier: Get your hands on the full version of SP4. For the remainder of the morning session, I assume you have done exactly that and have the full version of SP4 in your possession.

That assumption in place, you will now spend the time between now and lunch installing one of the SP4 enhancements: Security Configuration Editor.

## Security Configuration Editor (SCE)

I try never to forget what makes a book such as this relevant. It is observing how you—the readers, end users, power users, and gurus of the SBS community—actually use the SBS product. For your sharing of those insights with me, both in person in my daytime consulting role and via e-mail when I have my author hat on, I am deeply grateful. Such sharing allows me to decipher what is germane to share with you and what is not. One application from SBS that is germane is SCE. I've actually used SCE on an SBS network (the landscaping company I've mentioned before), and if it's used, it's germane to me and hopefully to you.

SCE allows SBS system administrators to consolidate all system-related security settings into a single configuration file. You can then deploy these security settings in any number of Windows NT machines (which is a key point: this capability only applies to Windows NT machines).

You must acquire, via one of the methods I suggested earlier, the full version of SP4 to deploy SCE. The SP4 release with SBS 4.5 doesn't provide SCE. Assuming you've met that requirement, here's how you install, configure, and deploy SCE.

**Note**

Only attempt the following exercise on your test SBS server machine named SPRINGERS01. Do not perform the following exercises on a production SBS server machine until you have learned SCE on SPRINGER01. When you are comfortable with SCE, you can introduce it on your live SBS server machines.

## Task 18.1: Installing SCE

You are now ready to add SCE to your SBS server machine. Before completing the following steps, make sure that you have the full version of SP4 in hand. You are now ready to start:

1. Log on to your SBS server machine as an administrator or member of the administrators group.

2. Insert your SP4 (full version) CD-ROM disc into a CD-ROM drive on the SBS server machine.

3. On the SP4 CD-ROM, run mssce.exe from the \mssce\i386 directory. This will install the correct files and MMC snap-ins required by SCE.

4. The Microsoft Windows NT Security Configuration Manager dialog box asks whether you want to perform the full installation. Click Yes. Numerous files are copied and the SCE engine initializes.

5. Click OK when you see the message "Setup completed successfully."

## Task 18.2: Configuring SCE

When installed, SCE must be configured. You are now ready to perform that configuration by completing the following steps:

1. Log on to your SBS server machine as an administrator or member of the administrators group.

2. From the Run command, accessed via the Start button, type **MMC** and click OK. The Microsoft Management Console (MMC) version 1.1 launches.

3. From the Console menu, select Add/Remove Snap-in. The Add/Remove Snap-in dialog box appears.

4. Click the Add button on the Standalone tab sheet.

18

▼     5. The Add Standalone Snap-in dialog box appears. Select Security Configuration
         Manager (which should be listed at or near the bottom of the Snap-in column).
         This is shown in Figure 18.1. Click the Add button and then the Close button.

**FIGURE 18.1**

*Add Standalone
Snap-in.*

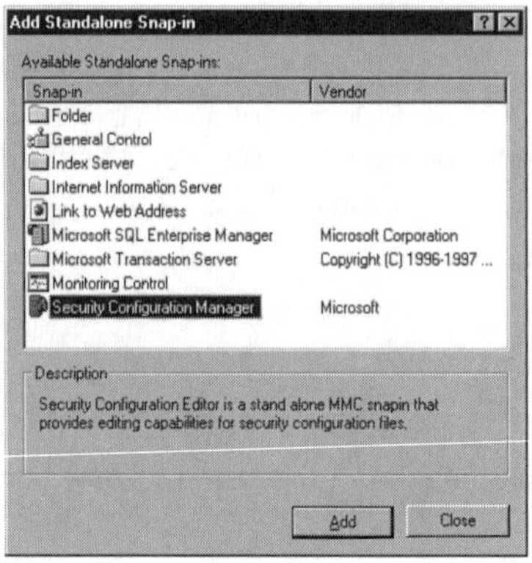

Add Standalone Snap-in                                    ? X

Available Standalone Snap-ins:

| Snap-in | Vendor |
|---|---|
| Folder | |
| General Control | |
| Index Server | |
| Internet Information Server | |
| Link to Web Address | |
| Microsoft SQL Enterprise Manager | Microsoft Corporation |
| Microsoft Transaction Server | Copyright (C) 1996-1997 ... |
| Monitoring Control | |
| Security Configuration Manager | Microsoft |

Description

Security Configuration Editor is a stand alone MMC snapin that
provides editing capabilities for security configuration files.

                                    Add        Close

      6. The Security Configuration Manager snap-in appears on the Standalone tab sheet
         of the Add/Remove Snap-in dialog box. Click OK.

**Power Tool Tip**

Working with the MMC is excellent training for using the forthcoming
Windows 2000 Server operating system. The MMC will be a key underpinning of interface for Windows 2000 Server.

      7. You are returned to the MMC console view. Expand the Security Configuration
         Manager in the left pane in a manner similar to Figure 18.2.

      8. Expand the basicdc4 object in the left pane (nested under Configurations). The
         object basicdc4 is the basic (default) Windows NT Domain Controller 4.0 settings.

      9. Highlight and expand Local Policies. Select Security Options under the Local
         Policies object.

     10. In the right pane, double-click the Message Text for Users Attempting to Log On
         item.

     11. The Message Text for Users Attempting to Log On dialog box appears. Type
         **Welcome to Springer Spaniels Unlimited SBS 4.5 Network** in the Change
         Configuration Setting to field and click OK. The SCE MMC should look similar to
▼        Figure 18.3.

FIGURE **18.2**

*SCE MMC.*

FIGURE **18.3**

*User text in SCE MMC.*

**18**

12. You now save the customized configuration file settings by right-clicking on the
    basicdc4 object and selecting Save from the secondary menu.

## Task 18.3: Deploying SCE

Now that SCE is installed and configured, you are ready to deploy it. Although *dep ing* is just another word for *using*, it's essential you follow these steps to successfull, deploy SCE:

1. Assuming you still have the SCE MMC open and are logged on as an administrator or member of the administrators group, proceed to step 2.

2. Click the object in the left pane titled Database: None. In a moment, the object is populated with the default database c:\winnt.sbs\security\database\secedit.sdb.

3. Right-click the Database object and select Import Configuration from the secondary menu.

4. The Select Configuration to Import dialog box appears. Select the file named basicdc4.inf and click OK. (This is the file that you modified earlier in the Configuring SCE section.)

5. The Security Configuration Manager dialog box appears asking whether you would like to save changes to the basicdc4.inf file. Answer Yes.

6. Right-click the Database object. Select Configure System Now from the secondary menu.

7. The Configure System dialog box appears. Accept c:\temp\secedit.log as the entry in the Error log file path. Click OK.

8. The Configuring System Security process runs, shown in Figure 18.4. This configuration process might take several minutes.

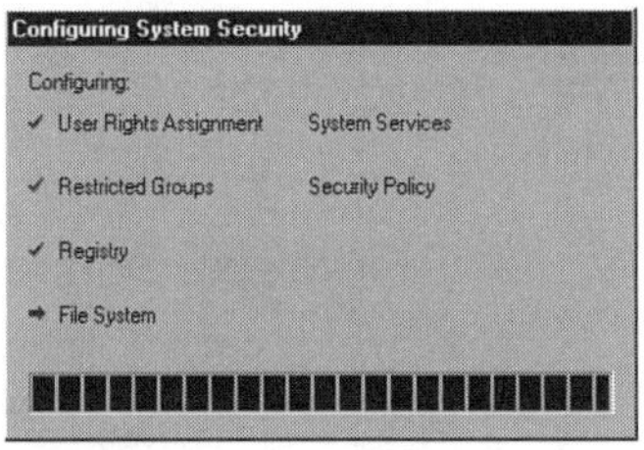

FIGURE **18.4**

*Configuring System Security process.*

9. Close the SCE MMC. Select No to save console settings.

## Task 18.4: Testing SCE Settings

You now test the SCE settings you've applied to SPRINGER01. To do this, perform the following steps:

1. Log off from the SPRINGERS01 server machine.

2. When you see the Winlogon dialog box message, press Ctrl+Alt+Del.

3. You should see a text message that says, "Welcome to Springer Spaniels Unlimited SBS 4.5 Network." Click OK.

 4. The Logon Information dialog box appears. Log on as usual.

Congratulations! You've successfully installed, configured, deployed, and tested SCE. Here are two final thoughts. Work with SCE only on your SPRINGERS network until you learn more about its capabilities. Second, I've provided you with only a surface view of SCE. You have a lot more to learn about SCE. Additional SCE resources are available via Microsoft TechNet.

# Lunch

Time for lunch. Today's special features a guest speaker, Jim Kiniry from Compaq Corporation. Jim will speak about the Option Pack (something you will work with this afternoon).

## Welcome to the Big Leagues!
*by Jim Kiniry*
*Compaq Corporation*

I know you thought you could avoid some of the complexities of computing by using SBS, but to avoid such complexities is also to hide from many of the powerful applications that Microsoft provides its faithful. To see these big league goodies, look no further than Service Pack 4 and the Option Pack.

I work in a testing environment at the enterprise level of computing. Because of that, I'm always interested in what Microsoft is offering to improve its networking components. So I was greatly pleased when Microsoft released the Option Pack as a set of tools and applications to extend the hand of BackOffice. You will be pleased that it is included in SBS 4.5.

The Option Pack is analogous to the power packs that are often sold to enhance the desktop operating systems. For example, with Windows 98, you can purchase the Plus Pack to further extend your desktop. It comes with additional programs, games, wallpaper, and screen savers. The Option Pack does the same thing for systems engineers working with BackOffice.

In our test lab, we have installed several of the Option Pack components: IIS 4.0, Certificate Server 1.0, Index Server 2.0, and Microsoft Management Console 1.0 on our Production Server. This server is our corporate intranet connection for Compaq Redmond. On this server using IIS 4.0, we maintain two distinct Web areas: an unsecured area and a

18

secured area. The unsecured area contains general information, such as driving directions from the airport to our office, and other unclassified information. In our secured area, we maintain a database with our latest test results and confidential information, such as soon-to-be-released computer code names and specifications. With Certificate Server, we can control access to our secured Web areas by issuing browser certificates and requiring them when accessing our secured Web areas. Using Index Server 2.0 gives us the ability to search both secured and unsecured Web areas by using different keyword catalogs.

Lastly, the Option Pack is one way to take an early peek at some technologies that Microsoft will release in the forthcoming Windows 2000 Server network operating system. One example of this early view would be Microsoft Management Console 1.0, something you saw running on Days 10, "Internet Information Server/Index Server," and 11, "Using Proxy Server." We use the MMC as a Central Management point where we can control the other Option Pack components we have installed on our Production Server.

**Note**

> Jim Kiniry, Jr. has achieved the MCSE and MCP+Internet certifications. He is a systems software engineer for Compaq Computer Corporation, Server Division, in Redmond, Washington. At Compaq Redmond he is currently testing Windows 2000 on Compaq servers. He is also a board member consultant and NT SIG co-chair for the BackOffice Professionals Association (www.BOPA.org).

## PM The Option Pack

Welcome back from lunch. This afternoon I will define the Option Pack, which ships with SBS. You will learn how to use one Option Pack component, Transaction Server.

Similar to SP4, the Option Pack that ships with SBS 4.5 is a modified version from the real Option Pack. The SBS 4.5 Option Pack contains the following components:

- Microsoft Internet Information Server 4.0
- Transaction Server 2.0
- Index Server 2.0
- Microsoft Script Debugger
- Microsoft Management Console (MMC) v1.1

The full Option Pack contains additional components including

- Microsoft Certificate Server
- Microsoft ActiveX Data Objects

- Microsoft Remote Data Service
- Microsoft Content Analyzer
- Microsoft Usage Import and Report Writer
- Microsoft Posting Acceptor
- Microsoft Message Queue Server
- Microsoft Connection Manager Administration Kit Wizard
- Microsoft Connection Point Services
- Microsoft Internet Authentication Services
- Microsoft NNTP Service
- Microsoft SMTP Service

**Note**

> For detailed explanations of each of the full Option Pack components, select Release Notes from the Windows NT 4.0 Option Pack program group.

**Power Tool Tip**

> You cannot install these additional Option Pack features. If you attempt to do so, via the Microsoft BackOffice 4.5 Setup application (found in the Microsoft BackOffice program group under Programs from the Start button), you will receive an error message no additional components are available to set up. It's an SBS thing.
>
> If you want any other Option Pack components, you will need to purchase the full Option Pack from Microsoft. See www.microsoft.com for details.

# Microsoft Transaction Server (MTS)

MTS is another arrow in the quiver of Web and e-commerce solutions in the Microsoft family. MTS is a development environment that facilitates creating Internet/intranet applications that provide a development framework for building and testing distributed applications.

So why would you spend a few minutes with Transaction Server? Is it likely that you would ever use such a tool? The answer is *yes*, for one simple reason. Remember the first heading at the start of today: "Go Forward"? This heading underscores what this advanced session is all about: looking toward tomorrow and how SBS will be used. This forward thinking is consistent with the direction for small business computing that Microsoft telegraphed to the media at an e-commerce seminar in early March 1999 (in San Francisco). There, several Microsoft executives, including Bill Gates, announced several strategic initiatives that speak toward implementing e-commerce solutions for small businesses. SBS and add-ons, such as Transaction Server, will play a huge role in the deployment. For that reason, you should join me for a few minutes to learn about Transaction Server. The time you invest today in learning about Transaction Server and putting Internet applications on your radar screen will yield great benefit tomorrow. That said, let's take a tour of Transaction Server.

**Note**

> MTS is automatically installed on your SBS server machine when you perform a complete SBS 4.5 installation. Thus, there is no need to show you how to install MTS.

## Task 18.5: Using MTS

Now it's actually time to see MTS in action. To do this, you will use a sample program, also known as object, to generate activity. This sample program is the Bank client application.

1. Make sure you are logged on as an administrator or member of the administrators group.

2. Launch the Transaction Server Explorer from the Microsoft Transaction Server program group (which is nested inside the Windows NT 4.0 Option Pack program group). The MTS MMC launches.

3. From My Computer on your desktop, run tclient.exe from the C:\Program Files\MTS\Samples to launch the Bank client application. This is a representative application for what you might see at an electronic commerce site.

4. Enter an amount in the Amount field (for example, 175) of the Bank client application and click OK. The Bank client application is displayed in Figure 18.5.

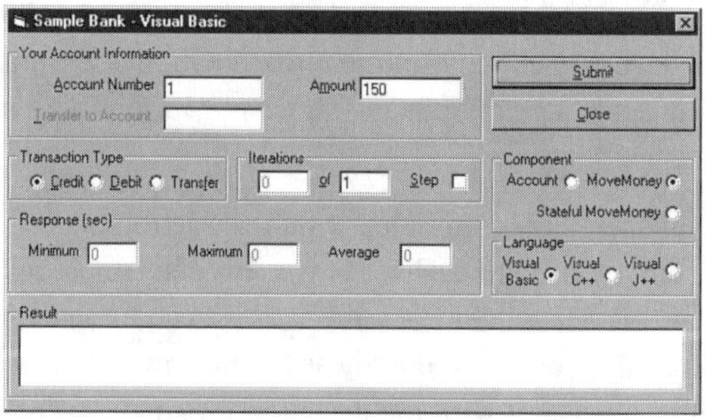

**FIGURE 18.5**

*Bank client.*

5. Switch back to the MTS MMC and expand Microsoft Transaction Server, Computers, My Computer. Select the Transaction Statistics object. The Transaction Statistics appear in the right pane. These statistics reflect activity being monitored by MTS. This is shown in Figure 18.6.

**FIGURE 18.6**

*Transaction Statistics.*

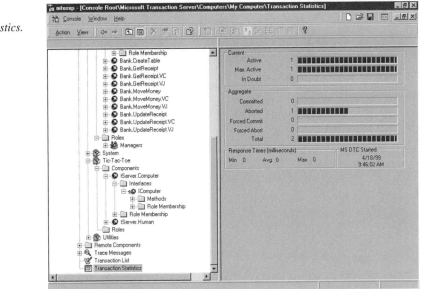

You have now been introduced to MTS. So what have you learned about MTS, in English? First, it's really a server-side development tool used primary by developers. Second, this world is quickly coming to an SBS network near you by the fact that MTS is used for managing business rules objects. One such object, in the world of e-commerce, would be the sample banking application shown in Figure 18.5 that creates a financial transaction. What's the bottom line? Look for this application and other Internet-related tools to play an bigger role in the SBS community as more small businesses embrace e-commerce.

# Summary

Today was a milestone. It was a crossover day wherein you recognized that your SBS network is basically complete and set up. That recognition allowed the exploration of advanced SBS features such as SP4 and Option Pack. Although these two tools might not be for everybody, the road to SBS stardom requires that you honor SP4 and Option Pack in a sincere and respectful way. See you tomorrow!

# DAY 19

# Installing Business Applications

More often than not, the real purpose behind planning for, purchasing, deploying, and maintaining SBS is to support important business applications. For many sites, it's the bottom line and thus the reason for this important chapter: to show you how to install one real-world business application on an SBS network and give you a glimpse of other business applications being used on SBS servers.

The applications I'm speaking of aren't Office 2000, which was introduced and discussed on Day 15, "Implementing Microsoft Office 2000." These are bona fide business applications that typically require raw server power to perform (that is, these applications don't run locally on the C: drive of an SBS workstation). These are business applications that often take advantage of SQL Server, which was discussed on Day 17, "SQL Server." In fact, this afternoon, when I show you BenchTop, I'll speak to how SQL Server, the underlying database engine for BenchTop, was one of the primary decision-making drivers for purchasing SBS. But more on that later.

Three final thoughts before you start the morning session and install Great Plains Dynamics, an accounting package that uses SQL Server:

1. Business applications—In my experience, business applications installed on SBS fall into three distinct classes:

   - Accounting applications—These include accounting applications such as Great Plains Dynamics, MasterBuilder, and Timberline.

   - Narrow vertical market applications—Everyindustry—be it legal, medical, or instrument calibration—has its own narrow vertical market application. This afternoon you review one such application, BenchTop.

   - Custom databases and applications—Many businesses running SBS employ custom databases, often using SQL Server. Same story applies to applications. These applications range from Visual Basic applications to sophisticated macros running underneath Word Perfect 8.0.

2. SBS time management—Managing business applications is where, for better or worse, you'll spend a great deal of your SBS-related time, now that (I assume) your SBS server and workstations are up and running. After the initial flurry to plan and deploy your SBS network, the network should necessarily take a back seat to the more important work at hand of running business applications that allow you and your users to get more work finished.

   This point about application deployment and management wasn't lost on me when I created the outline for this book. As you approach the end of your 21 days doing the SBS thing, I assume that you are SBS network functional, so what better time than Day 19 to discus how to deploy and run business applications on your SBS server.

3. AM/PM agenda—This morning you'll observe how a business application is installed on an SBS server. This business application, Great Plains Dynamics, is appropriate to look at because it uses SQL Server as its engine to manage its data. By observing how one such application is installed, you'll better understand, I hope, not only how to install a powerful business application on an SBS server but also how such applications interact with SQL Server. In the afternoon, I'll show you two applications that are running on a real SBS server.

# AM Installing Great Plains Dynamics

First, you should understand that prior to installing a powerful business application such as Great Plains Dynamics, many hours in advance would have gone into the planning. Such planning is widely considered a good use of time to ensure a successful application installation. In the case of an accounting application, the specific planning typically involves such as important issues as what chart of accounts to use and what accounting reports you'll need. In fact, the planning and upstream work necessary to implement a business application is very similar to the SBS planning you undertook on Days 1, "Welcome to Small Business Server," and 2, "Planning for Small Business Server," for the Springer Spaniels Unlimited SBS network.

Second, the actual software is installed. Because Great Plains Dynamics is one of the best-selling business accounting software applications, those of you who are SBS consultants might see it at more than one of your SBS sites. For those of you who are good old-fashioned SBS administrators at a single company, Great Plains will likely be on your short list of possible accounting applications when you consider an accounting system conversion. In fact, the installation of Great Plains Dynamics on SBS 4.5 is conceptually similar to installing other popular accounting applications such as MAS 90 or Solomon. The goal here is to understand how an application is installed on an SBS server.

Let's get going, and of course you'll be using Springer Spaniels Unlimited as your beloved sample company.

**Note**

The underlying assumptions to installing powerful business applications such as Great Plains Dynamics are twofold: First, the SBS server machine is up, running, and stable; and, second, you've installed SQL Server, and it is fully functional.

Before you actually run the setup programs from the application's CD-ROM, you must verify that the underlying database engine, SQL Server, is configured correctly for Great Plains Dynamics. Part of this configuration occurred when you installed SBS 4.5 and selected the character set (ISO) and sort order (Dictionary, case insensitive) for SQL Server 7.0. You might recall that those two settings are global settings in SQL Server 7.0 that are one-time elections at setup; these settings can't be changed at a future date. The good news is that applications such as Great Plains Dynamics typically accept the default SQL Server setup settings, and thank goodness they do! Otherwise, if such wasn't the case, you'd quickly discover that you'd need to have multiple, unique editions of SQL Server running to support your array of important business applications. Ouch!

Prior to launching the Great Plains Dynamics setup routine, you also need to check the explicit SQL Server environmental settings found via SQL Server's Enterprise Manager.

## Task 19.1: Setting SQL Server Configuration Settings

1. Launch Enterprise Manager from the Microsoft SQL Server 7.0 program group (found via the Start button, Programs group).

**19**

**TASK**

▼ 2. Expand the left pane's objects to display the actual SQL Server (for example, SPRINGERS01). This is seen in Figure 19.1.

**FIGURE 19.1**

*SQL Server Enterprise Manager.*

3. Right-click the server object (for example, SPRINGERS01) to display the secondary menu. Select Properties from the secondary menu.

4. The SQL Server Properties - SPRINGERS01 dialog box is displayed, as seen in Figure 19.2. Based on configuration information supplied by your vendor, you will configure such options as default sort id, locks, memory, open objects, and user connections.

**FIGURE 19.2**

*SQL Server Properties - SPRINGERS01.*

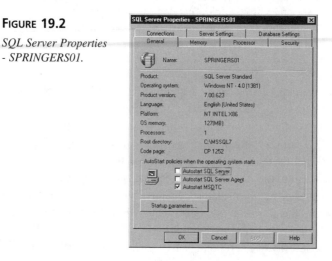

> **Tip**
>
> Allow me to reemphasize a point. Typically, the only reason you would be inside Enterprise Manager and, more specifically, the SQL Server Properties dialog box is that you've been invited by the vendor of your business software application. *Do not* explore these SQL Server settings on your own; rather make the necessary changes under explicit guidance and get out!

▼

5. Stop and restart the specific SQL Server machine (SPRINGERS01) so that the changes you've made will take effect. Do so by selecting Stop and Start from the secondary menu for the specific SQL Server (SPRINGERS01).

6. One final SQL-related configuration matter is to create an ODBC configuration from Control Panel for Great Plains Dynamics to talk to SQL Server. If you find this is necessary for your business software application, I can assure you that your documentation will provide explicit instructions on how to do this. One view of the ODBC creation process is shown in Figure 19.3. Enough said. Time to install Great Plains Dynamics.

**FIGURE 19.3**

*ODBC Configuration.*

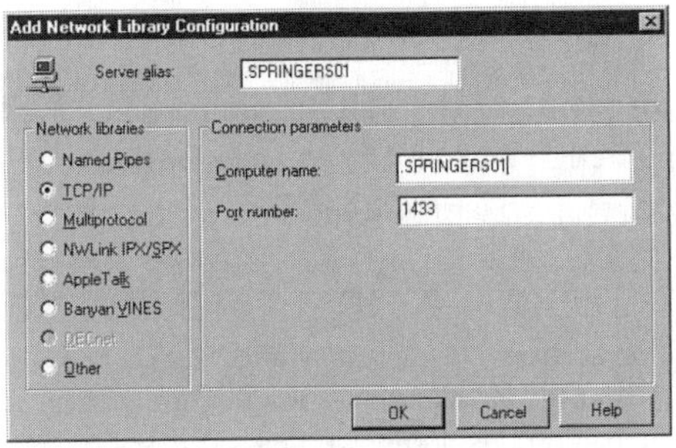

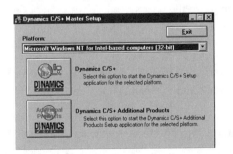

## Task 19.2: Installing an Application on an SBS Server Machine

1. As you do with many software applications, you'll likely place the application CD in your CD-ROM drive. Great Plains Dynamics is no exception. Place the CD in the drive. An Autorun file launches the setup screen seen in Figure 19.4.

**FIGURE 19.4**

*Dynamics C/S+ Master Setup.*

19

**Power Tool Tip**

Did you see in Figure 19.4 that Microsoft Windows NT for Intel-based Computers (32-bit) was selected instead of an SBS-specific selection? That's because very few vendors have specific SBS-compliant business applications.

▼

Rather, many vendors who have regular Windows NT Server applications got lucky in the sense that these applications run without modification on SBS server machines.

So, when confronted with an application setup screen such as that seen in Figure 19.4 without an SBS-specific selection, be sure to select the option for Windows NT Server. In most cases, that selection is correct, and the application installs and functions normally.

Not only does Appendix A, "SBS Resources," list many SBS research-related resources, but it also lists software applications that are considered to be either SBS-specific or SBS-compliant (will run on an SBS server machine).

2. After selecting the platform to install for, simply click the large Dynamics C/S+ button on the middle-left part of the setup screen seen in Figure 19.4. A familiar InstallShield-type setup wizard will launch.

**Note**

You will recall from Day 6, "Daily and Weekly SBS Administration (The Dirty Dozen)," that InstallShield is a common application setup wizard used by many application developers. In fact, it's likely that the business applications you will install on a server will use InstallShield. The good news is that when you've worked with this setup wizard, installing any application will seem easy and comfortable for you.

3. You will answer questions on successive setup wizard screens, clicking Next after each response to move to the next screen. In the case of Great Plains Dynamics, these screens include

- Welcome
- Select Setup Type (including Typical, Full, Minimal, Custom)
- Select New or Existing Dynamics Settings
- Select Country
- Select Database Type (in this case, the selection was MS SQL Server)
- Select Application Path (this is the application installation path: C:\Great Plains Dynamics CS+\)
- Select Help Path (this is the path where the on-line help system will be placed)
- Select Program Folder (this is the program group name)

▼
- Start Copying Files (this is shown in Figure 19.5)

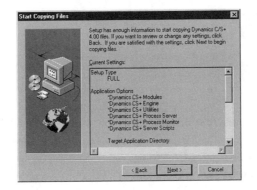

▼ **FIGURE 19.5**

*Start Copying Files.*

**Power Tool Tip**

At the construction company I support, the application installation path for a construction accounting package brought up an important issue about paths. The construction accounting package assumed that the Windows NT Server operating system was in the C:\WINNT directory. As you know, SBS installs the underlying Windows NT Server operating system to C:\winnt.sbs. This unusual path was just enough to upset the construction accounting package. Thus, I had to take this site backward (if you will) to Big BackOffice, which has Windows NT Server installed to the C:\WINNT directory, making the construction accounting package happy. Long story short, if the construction accounting software package couldn't be installed on a Windows NT Server machine that pointed toward the C:\WINNT directory, it wouldn't run.

**19**

4. Critical setup files necessary for installing Great Plains Dynamics are now copied to the server machine. This includes setup scripts, help files, and so on. You are alerted when this copying has been completed. When you acknowledge this fact, the real Great Plains Dynamics installation process commences. This process can take hours, not necessarily to enrich Great Plains Dynamics consultants who bill by the hour, but to create all the SQL Server databases, tables, and stored procedures necessary to run this powerful business application. This startup process commences with the logon dialog box in Figure 19.6. (This logon dialog box is making use of the ODBC driver you created at the beginning of this exercise.)

5. Between a couple and several hours later, the setup process is complete. You will have provided several serial numbers to unlock the application, provided accounting setup information (for example, account segment information), and answered additional configuration questions.

6. As a result, the server side of Great Plains Dynamics is successfully installed on your SBS server machine. You then install the Great Plains Dynamics client components on your SBS user's workstations.

▼

▼ FIGURE 19.6

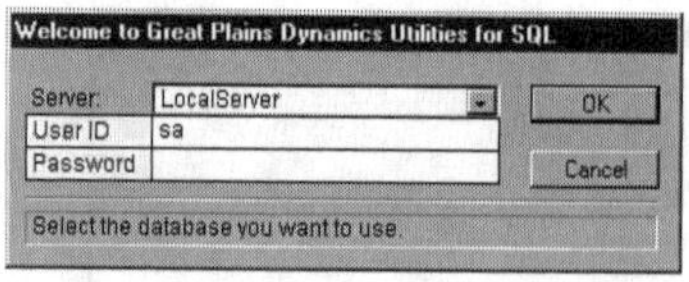

*Logon.*

7. To install the Great Plains Dynamics components on the SBS user's workstation, you simply copy the files displayed in Table 19.1 over to the C:\dynamics directory you would create on the SBS user's workstation. These files are found in the C:\Great Plains Dynamics CS+ folder on the SBS server machine. (I am assuming the SBS user's workstation is running the Windows 98 or Windows 95 operating system.)

**TABLE 19.1** GREAT PLAINS DYNAMICS CLIENT FILES

| Module | Filename |
|--------|----------|
| Dynamics Engine | WTR32.DLL |
| | CTPWIN32.DLL |
| | DEX.INI |
| | DELSLI.ISU |
| | DEXFIELD.TLB |
| | DEXVBA.DLL |
| | STREAM.DLL |
| | MFC40.DLL |
| | BIDI32.DLL |
| | CONTAIN.EXE |
| | XDLL32.DLL |
| | DEX.DIC |
| | DYNAMICS.EXE |
| | DEX.TLB |
| | DEXRFLD.TLB |
| | DEXVBA.TLB |
| | TNTLIB.DLL |
| | MSVCRT40.DLL |
| | WELCOME.WAV |
| | DYNAMICS.SET |
| Dynamics Modules | AUZERR.CNK |
| | AUZERR.DAT |
| | AUZERR.IDX |
| | UKERR.CNK |
| | UKERR.DAT |
| | UKERR.IDX |
| | DYNAMICS.DAT |
| | CAERR.CNK |

| ▼ Module | Filename |
|---|---|
| Dynamics Modules | CAERR.DAT |
| | CAERR.IDX |
| | README.HLP |
| | DYNAMICS.BMP |
| | DYNAMICS.DIC |
| | DYNAMICS.IDX |
| Dynamics Utilities | DYNUTILS.SET |
| | DYNUTILS.DIC |
| Help, Tutorial, and Sample Reports | DEX.HLP |
| | DYNAMICS.HLP |
| | DYNTUT.HLP |
| | IMPORT.HLP |
| | MOD.HLP |
| | OLFD.HLP |
| | RW.HLP |
| | TOCLESN.HLP |
| | DEX.CNT |
| | DYNAMICS.CNT |
| | IMPORT.CNT |
| | MOD.CNT |
| | RW.CNT |
| | TOCMAN.PDF |
| | TOCRPRT.PDF |
| | BRLESN.HLP |
| | INLESN.HLP |
| | MCLESN.HLP |
| | GLLESN.HLP |
| | IVLESN.HLP |
| | MCPMLESN.HLP |

**19**

8. The last step on the SBS user's workstation would be to create a shortcut for the C:\Dynamics\dynamics.exe application.

You have now successfully created the base installation of Great Plains Dynamics on an SBS network. Note that you would want to enlist the help of a qualified Great Plains Dynamics consultant before actually attempting to install Great Plains Dynamics on your SBS network. Great Plains frequently releases upgrades and fixes that might alter part of the process described previously. You get the point. In fact, for more information on Great Plains Dynamics, I recommend that you visit its Web site at www.gps.com.

Before I wrap up the Great Plains Dynamics discussion and you head to lunch, allow me to demonstrate an accounting transaction. As seen in Figure 19.7, a $100 journal entry is being made. This transaction is typical of the type of accounting transactions that you might make in Great Plains Dynamics.

**FIGURE 19.7**

*Great Plains Dynamics journal entry.*

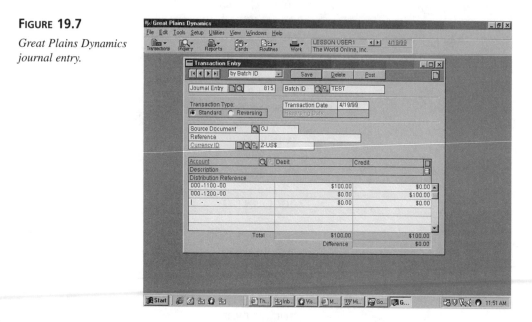

A few final comments before lunch regarding installing business applications. First, you would likely install a business application such as Great Plains Dynamics with the assistance of a Great Plains Dynamics consultant. I've never seen an SBS site do it any other way. The same could be said for other, very powerful SQL Server–based business applications: You will probably receive help from an application consultant during the setup. You might also be interested in knowing that many Great Plains Dynamics consultants are also active CPAs who can dispense bona fide accounting advice as part of their Great Plain Dynamics implementation.

Second, installinga business application such as Great Plains Dynamics is not only the first real test of your SBS network's reliability and performance, it's also where you perhaps cross over from being just an SBS administrator or consultant to all-around computer person. By that I mean when you install such a powerful business application, you're likely to be called on to support and enhance said application. That would include, in the case of Great Plains Dynamics, writing accounting reports via the FRx Report Writer.

> **Note**
>
> Even if your SBS site can't fully appreciate or exploit a powerful SQL Server[nd]based application today, it will soon. Implementing applications such as Great Plains Dynamics allows SBS sites to prepare for launching such goodies as bona fide electronic commerce solutions. You get the point: Now that you're at the application layer, your life with the SBS network has only just begun!

## Lunch

While you wait for the pizzas to be delivered, complete an exercise.

### Task 19.1: Updating the SBS Resources List

1.  To complete this task, sit at a workstation with Internet access and refer to Appendix A.

2.  I'd like you to peruse the list of SBS resources I've listed, especially the applications that are specifically tailored to SBS. Do any of those application appeal to you? Could one or two of those applications help you run your business better?

3.  If so, connect to the Internet, and via Internet Explorer 5, surf over to the Web site maintained by the application vendor and gather more information.

You might also search for the term *SBS* on the Internet search engine of your choice (for example, `www.dogpile.com`) to see whether other software application vendors are now providing SBS-specific offerings since this book was published. (I hope so!)

## PM **Installing More Applications**

Now I offer you a real treat. To me, and perhaps you, there's nothing like seeing proof of concept. Call it SBS, Missouri-style! That is, "Show Me." What I'll do for you now is probably no more than a feature tour of two business applications that are running on a true SBS network. There's no imaginary company and no dummy data here. Let's get started.

# Xtek Corporation

My "victim" is the oft-mentioned Xtek Corporation in Redmond, Washington. If you've followed along throughout this book, you'll recall that Xtek has been a source of many of my SBS workarounds, tips, and tricks. Today, Xtek is the source of my business application tour.

## BenchTop

The prevailing reason why Xtek purchased SBS was to take advantage of the SQL Server component. That's because a desirable enterprise database management package

**19**

(BenchTop, that is) for the instrument calibration business, Xtek's line of work, relies on SQL Server as its underlying engine.

> **Note**
>
> At the risk of repeating myself, I want to emphasize that many businesses purchase SBS for the right reasons. These reasons are fairly straightforward. Industry software such as BenchTop in hand, the potential SBS customer then looks for the solution that will run its industry software. Here SBS wins every time if the industry software somehow needs SBS (for example, for SQL Server). This is the old-fashioned way of purchasing: defining your needs, finding the right software, and then finding the operating system and hardware that will run your software.

Much like Great Plains Dynamics, the setup of BenchTop uses a setup wizard. When a series of setup questions are answered, the underlying SQL Server databases, tables, indexes, and stored procedures are created. So far, so good. You can see the result of the setup process in Figure 19.8, where BenchTop has created a database called Metrology. Plain and simple, that's how BenchTop interacts with SQL Server. Call it a done deal on the server side of BenchTop.

**FIGURE 19.8**

*Metrology database.*

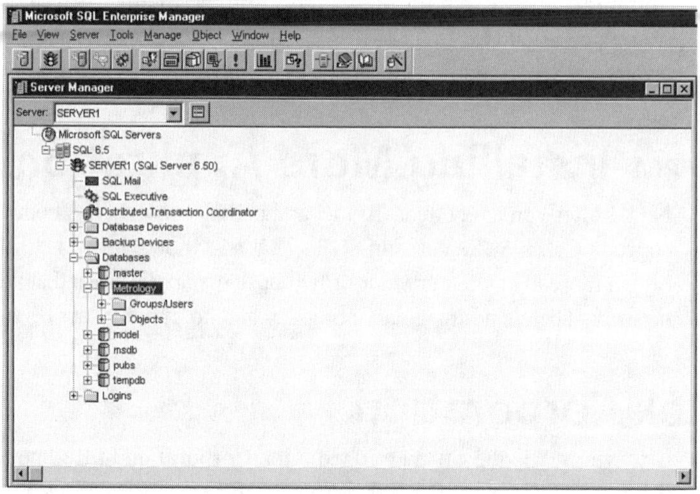

Then the focus, rightfully so, shifts to the SBS user's workstations. This is where the action really is. As seen in Figure 19.9, the client side of the BenchTop equation is a robust application that offers numerous user selections.

As you can see in Figure 19.9, BenchTop offers a selection of user components in the left pane that allows a calibration lab like Xtek to manage its repair jobs and overall enterprise from *a* to *z*. Not only can you schedule and track the work, but you can record quality observations at the instrument being repaired or calibrated. Perhaps most importantly, you can bill the client for your work. You get the picture.

**FIGURE 19.9**

*Client-side BenchTop.*

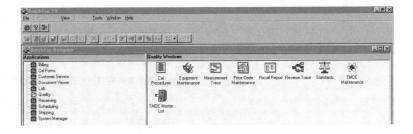

One such module, Quality, is highlighted in Figure 19.9. The Quality options appear in the right pane. In Figure 19.10, I display one of the Quality options, the Price Maintenance selection.

**FIGURE 19.10**

*BenchTop Price Maintenance.*

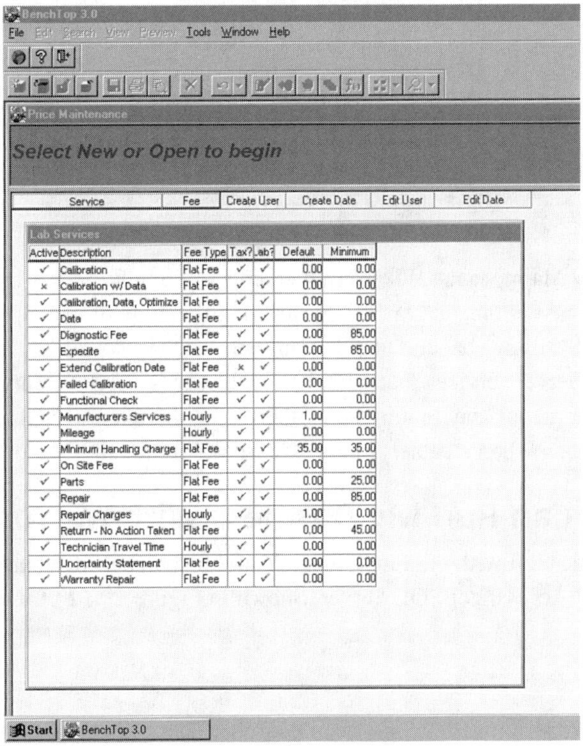

**19**

Needless to say, the goal of BenchTop, as you might well have inferred from the offerings in the left pane of Figure 19.9, is to provide a comprehensive database solution for a
very specific market. Needless to say (again), such narrow vertical market software solutions exist for your industry, whatever that is.

## BenchTop Maintenance

Before leaving BenchTop, let's look at one last critical function: native SQL Server backups. Using the daily maintenance Wizard, you can make periodic backups within SQL
Server whereby backup files are created similar to that seen in Figure 19.11.

**FIGURE 19.11**

*Metrology backups.*

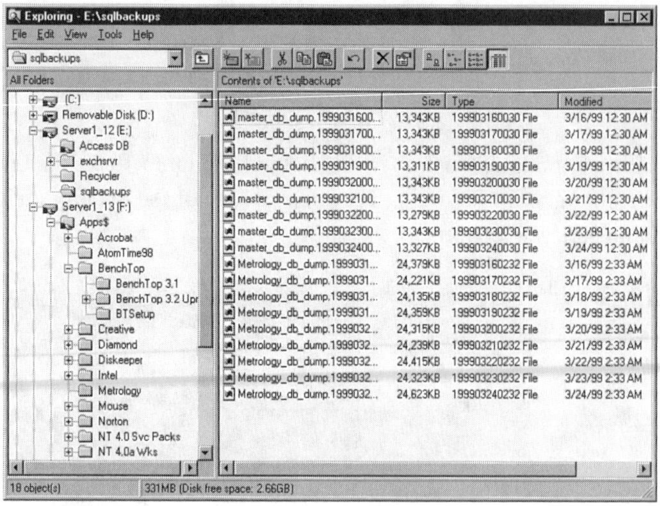

The Daily Maintenance Wizard implements these SQL Server-based database backups.
This I discussed this on Day 17. Performing this type of backup is critical if you are
using SBS's native backup application (because it lacks a SQL Server agent to shut down
the SQL Server services that would allow a successful SQL Server). Without going into
it here, let me just say that in November 1998, the internal SQL Server backup saved
Xtek's bacon when a cataclysmic database failure (a.k.a. fatal database failure) occurred.

## Yes! I Can Run My Business with Microsoft Office

This application with the funny name is an off-the-shelf database solution that uses
Microsoft Access, not SQL Server. Shown in Figure 19.12, it uses a series of templates

and underlying relationships when you install it over Microsoft Access. You then proceed to customize it for your company name and enter your data. Yes! I Can Run My Business with Microsoft Office is from HALLoGRAM Publishing (www.hallogram.com).

Xtek runs this application on its SBS network to address some underlying issues that BenchTop doesn't satisfy. One such issue is sales and marketing. Another involves some specific accounting matters. Interestingly, Norm Goobie selected this Access-based solution for his financial accounting solution over Great Plains Dynamics after an extensive review of both products. Norm reported that the significant cost differential between the two products was no small factor in his decision. An example of Yes!...'s accounting solution is shown in Figure 19.13.

**Figure 19.12**

*Yes!....*

**Figure 19.13**

*Yes!... General Ledger.*

**19**

# Summary

Today was a very practical day. You saw three business applications running on SBS. Don't lose sight (again) of the fact that business applications are often the real or underlying reason that SBS is purchased and deployed. If you're an SBS consultant, such wisdom allows you to better understand your role and why you're really at an SBS site. Whoever you are, please honor the serious nature of deploying a bona fide business application on an SBS network. Typically, you need to retain the services of a qualified consultant for the specific business application you hope to implement. Enough said, and good day.

# DAY 20

# Advanced Server Management

Communicating via metaphors is a very powerful communication approach. I often use metaphors from the medical profession to convey my thoughts, insights, and SBS expertise to my SBS clients and users. Perhaps you do something similar.

That being said, let me say this about advanced SBS management: Preventative care is far preferred to emergency room visits. Why? Because preventative care is clearly cheaper for everyone involved in an SBS scenario. The SBS client benefits from saving money directly. For example, by spending an extra $300 annually for a Microsoft TechNet CD-ROM library subscription, the same SBS client can typically cut consulting fees dramatically. That's because its people can use TechNet to research SBS challenges.

And preventative care helps you, the SBS consultant. If the SBS sites in your consulting portfolio are subject to many emergency calls, clearly you cannot stay booked as a consultant, make appointments you can reasonably keep, and so on. Why? Because your pager will always be going off, pulling you out of a meeting or appointment. That is very unprofitable for you, the SBS consultant.

Today is the last day that I'll discuss SBS 4.5 explicitly from an SBS perspective. That doesn't mean you'll want to miss Day 21, "Upgrading to Big BackOffice," but today is significant in that you recognize the end of your SBS 4.5–specific journey. That said, this morning I'll discuss some general and SBS-specific actions you can undertake to better manage your SBS network. After lunch, you'll look at SBS 4.5–specific management tools including the highly respected VAP tools and different ways to use the SBS Console.

 ## AM  Advanced SBS Management Part I

This morning, the discussion will be divided into three areas: hardware, software, and support.

# Hardware

No offense, but there are some simple stupid things you can do either up front or during the life of your SBS network that will help reliability greatly. These include configuring your server's hard disks for the greatest protection of your data. This is above and beyond the requisite need for a reliable and proven tape backup system. Three hard disk management strategies will be presented to you: disk mirroring, disk duplexing, and redundant arrays of inexpensive disks (RAID).

## Disk Mirroring

As the name implies, your server's hard disks are mirrored. By that I mean, a mirror reflection of the first hard disk exists on the additional hard disk on your system. That way, if anything unfortunate happens to the first hard disk, SBS maintains and uses an identical copy of the hard disk to keep on running. Mirroring is displayed in Figure 20.1.

**FIGURE 20.1**

*Mirroring.*

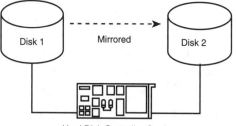

Assuming you've had a failure, you will be able to replace the failed "member" hard disk of the mirror set with a good hard disk. You will then reestablish the mirror.

**Power Tool Tip**

> Although I won't go into the explicit keystrokes for both editing your BOOT.INI file to update the ARC path (which is how SBS points to hard disks in your system) and breaking and recreating a mirror set, I can say this. If you're in a situation where you are using mirroring and one of the hard disks fails, don't panic. You will stay up and running. Take your time to go into the conference room and "white-board" your recovery strategy. You will also want to consult one of the support resources discussed later and in Appendix A, "SBS Resources," as part of your recovery plan.

Mirroring two hard disks is simple if you follow these general steps:

1. Install a second hard disk of equal or greater size in your SBS server machine. Because you will be using the same hard disk controller card, be sure to flip to switches on the second hard disk to make it a slave hard disk (your first hard disk will be the master). Be sure to replace the cover on your SBS server machine after installing the second hard disk.

2. Boot your SBS server machine. Log on as an administrator or member of the Administrators group.

3. Launch the Disk Administrator application from the Administrative Tools (Common) program group (found via the Start button, Programs).

4. The second drive will appear as unformatted free space. Click this unformatted free space and select Format from the Disk Administrator's Tools menu.

5. Select NTFS as the format type and click OK.

6. When the formatting is complete, select the drive space (for example, Drive C:_) that you want to have mirrored with a single mouse click.

7. Holding down the Ctrl key, select the newly formatted drive space from steps 4 and 5.

8. Select Establish Mirror from Disk Administrator's Fault Tolerance menu. Click OK when prompted.

9. Your drives will now be mirrored. This can take some time to accomplish as the information from the original drive (for example, Drive C:) is copied to the mirrored drive.

**20**

## Disk Duplexing

This is similar to disk mirroring. Disk duplexing is disk mirroring with one small twist: Each hard disk has its own controller card. That way, if the point of failure occurred at the controller card, the addition of a second controller card in your server ensures that you'll stay up and running. Disk duplexing is seen in Figure 20.2.

FIGURE **20.2**

*Disk Duplexing.*

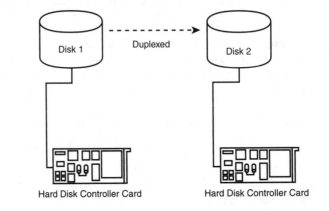

One often overlooked benefit to disk duplexing is the performance gain that this approach has over mirroring. By having multiple controller cards, you benefit from better performance; you have two channels or paths between your hard disks and the computer itself instead of one with mirroring (which uses a single controller card).

**Power Tool Tip**

There is no way to explicitly tell whether your hard disks are mirrored or duplexed from inside of SBS. Go ahead and give it a try. Even dropping beneath the hood and running Disk Administrator only tells you that you have mirrored hard disk but not whether each hard disk has its own controller card.

So, how can you tell whether your hard disks are duplexed (which is important information to know)? Three ways. First, on starting up your computer, if you are using SCSI controller cards, the devices attached to each SCSI card will be displayed as you boot the machine (during the character-based BIOS startup phase before Windows NT Server runs). The second way is simply to open your SBS server machine and see whether each hard disk has its own controller card. Finally, you can hire an SBS consultant to tell you.

When you have implemented a disk duplexing solution, you will want to mirror the two drives following the disk mirroring steps (using Disk Administrator) that I presented in the "Disk Mirroring" section.

## RAID

This is the best of all worlds in the eyes of many. RAID uses a set of disks (the minimum number is three) to distribute both data and data protection (known as *parity*) over the disks. This results in great protection and higher performance than either disk mirroring or duplexing.

How? The protection comes from the data distribution approach I just mentioned. The increased performance comes from what I like to call "dancing read/write heads." Hard disks have read/write heads that touch the magnetic disks as part of the data. If you have more disks working in a coherent fashion, you have what is technically called *concurrent read/write activity*. Cool! Let me temper your unbounded excitement, though. The greatest performance gain happens on the read side of the equation because on the write side of the equation, the parity calculations must be performed (that is, the reconstruction information must be written to the parity calculation zones, which increase the overhead or load on the SBS server machine). RAID is displayed in Figure 20.3.

**FIGURE 20.3**

*RAID.*

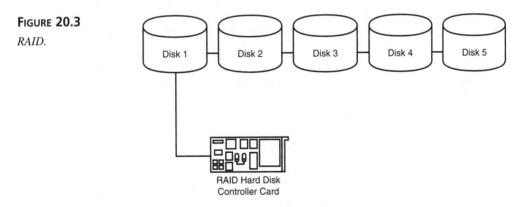

RAID Hard Disk
Controller Card

20

Oh, did I forget to mention costs? After a certain crossover point, RAID is actually more cost-effective than disk mirroring or duplexing. Here's how. First, understand that disk mirroring or duplexing yields only a 50% disk space utilization factor. For example, if you purchased and mirrored two 10GB hard disks, you would have purchased 20GB of hard disk space total to yield 10GB of truly usable storage space. That's a 50% disk space utilization factor.

Now, assuming you've implemented a RAID solution in a similar scenario, here's how the numbers work out. First, assume you have a five-disk RAID array with each drive being 4GB in size (totaling 20GB of hard disk space). Next, the disk space consumed for the parity protection area is the reverse fraction of the number of disk you have in the array. Here is what I mean:

Number of disks in array: 5 (expressed fractionally as 5/1)

Reverse fraction for parity protection area: 1/5 (20%)

Then, you would calculate the usable hard disk space by

Total Hard Disk Space–(Reverse fraction for parity protection area × Total Hard Disk Space)

20GB–(.20 × 20GB) = 16MG usable hard disk space

Notice that, given the same amount of total disk space (20GB), a RAID array results in 60% more usable space (16GB for RAID versus 10GB for mirroring/duplexing).

So far so good, but now the bad news. At lower storage levels, the costs of purchasing the extra disks and special RAID controller card easily exceed the mirroring/duplexing solution. Thus, a cost crossover point exists between a RAID solution and a mirroring/duplexing solution. That crossover point is, of course, a moving target with rapidly falling hard disk prices, but it's important you understand the framework for this discussion, as presented over the past several paragraphs. That way, if you decide you'd like to implement one of the hard disk solutions discussed herein, you'll understand what approach is best for your SBS site (and budget!).

# Software

I want to spend a moment looking at optimizing your SBS installation from a software perspective. You can undertake certain actions on the software side of the SBS management equation to optimize the performance of your SBS server machine. I'll show you one such approach you can take.

Remember yesterday when you installed Great Plains Dynamics on top of SQL Server? That means SQL Server will now run when you run Great Plains Dynamics (that makes sense so far). But let me show you that running additional services also uses RAM on your server, whether you like it or not. I will present this in a before-and-after fashion.

Simply stated, when the SQL Server engine (MSSQLServer service) is running, Task Manager reports the following memory being consumed: 107MB RAM (approximately) as seen in Figure 20.4.

**FIGURE 20.4**

*Memory use with MSSQLServer running.*

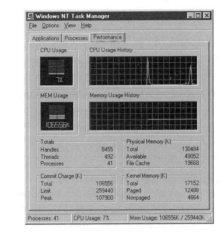

Then, turn off the MSSQLServer service in Control Panel and observe again the memory being consumed, as seen in Figure 20.5.

**FIGURE 20.5**

*Memory use with MSSQLServer stopped.*

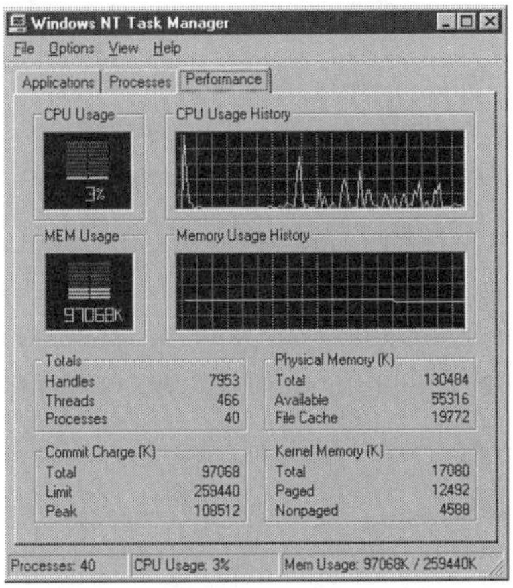

20

What's the bottom line? It's an improvement in the amount of RAM available for use by the SBS server machine (the consumed memory drops to approximately 97MB RAM).

> **Note**
>
> Fortunately, the MSSQLServer service is turned off by default in SBS 4.5. Kudos to the SBS development team at Microsoft for their understanding of server optimization, either intentionally or accidentally.

This was only one example of optimizing your SBS server from a software perspective. You'll best be able to decide which services can be turned off to return RAM to the server and so on. Be very careful as you discover this. SBS uses many more services than regular Windows NT Server. I'd play with turning on and off third-party software application services first. One prime candidate is the services associated with third-party tape backup programs (when the programs aren't being used).

**Power Tool Tip**

> As of this writing, the Backup Exec Suite (v.7.x) tape backup service known as the Backup Exec Engine (beengine.exe) has been a very poor SBS network citizen. It appears to have a bad memory leak that slowly but surely consumes important RAM on the SBS server machine. The solution for now is simply stop and start this service to flush and return the RAM where it best belongs for use by the SBS server machine.

# Support

I briefly want to touch on the support issue here before directing your full attention to Appendix A. Clearly, taking advantage of support resources will, time and time again, allow you to better manage your SBS network. Few dispute that.

But let me back up for a minute. The real question that matters is how are real people using support options to manage their SBS networks better? Let's take Dawn at the athletic club, a regular cast member in this book. Dawn has quickly embraced TechNet, the aforementioned monthly CD-ROM library subscription service offered by Microsoft.

Let's take two views at the support issue before sending you to Appendix A.

First, a general search of TechNet using the term *SBS* reveals 287 hits that address SBS. That means technical articles, guides, and manuals on the TechNet CD that discuss SBS have been identified and listed as you can see in Figure 20.6. In the next example, I provide the steps for searching via TechNet (in this first example, I merely show you the results of the search).

FIGURE 20.6

*Hits on* SBS *term in TechNet.*

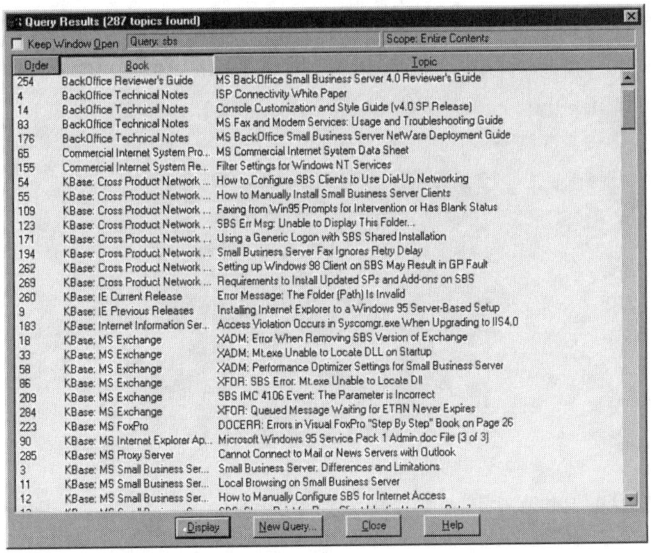

> **Note**
>
> The number of SBS hits on TechNet grows each month because the overall knowledge base about SBS, of course, continues to grow. Dawn, mentioned earlier, will regularly search terms such as *SBS* to see what new SBS-related information has been added to each month's TechNet release.

Another interesting way to use TechNet for SBS support is to try to search on specific errors. In fact, the standing agreement I have with Dawn and several other SBS clients is that they first endeavor to research their specific SBS problem prior to calling me. Many times, Dawn and the others find the answer on their own without having to call me, the SBS consultant. I don't have to turn on the consulting time clock unnecessarily (in fact, more clients have commented, in this respect, how fast a subscription to TechNet pays itself off!). I guess you could say I'm an SBS mentor as well as a consultant.

One specific error message in SBS, the SSUP1 error, occurs when your network adapter card isn't attached to an active network hub, but does it occur in other ways? Let's search TechNet on the term *SSUP1*.

1. Assuming you have installed TechNet on your computer, click Start, Programs, Microsoft TechNet, and the Microsoft TechNet application. TechNet will start.

2. On the TechNet toolbar, select the binoculars icon, which is the Query tool. Alternatively, select Query from the Tools menu. The Query dialog box appears.

**20**

3. Type **SSUP1** in the Query field of the Query dialog box.

4. In the Scope of Search area, select the Entire Contents radio button.

5. Click the Run Query button, as seen in Figure 20.7.

**FIGURE 20.7**

*SSUP1 query.*

6. The query returns one hit that addresses the SSUP1 issue, as seen in Figure 20.8.

**FIGURE 20.8**

*Query results.*

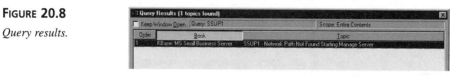

7. Click the Display button and the SSUP1 Knowledge Base article is displayed, as seen in Figure 20.9.

**FIGURE 20.9**

*SSUP1 article.*

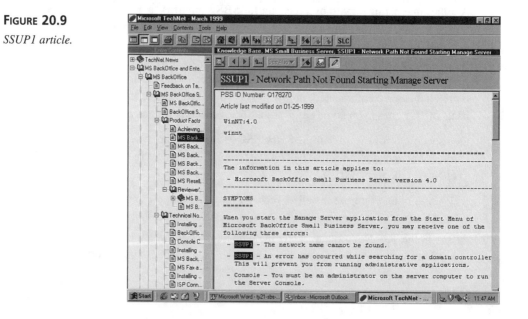

Your next step for taking advantage of SBS support and research resources is to visit Appendix A. Consider it part of your advanced SBS management strategy. Time for lunch!

#  Lunch

Time to recharge! Here's just the stuff: killer baked onion soup.

## Baked Onion Soup

5 C beef broth

4 thick slices of French bread

3 T butter

3 large onions, thinly sliced

1 T flour

4 T grated Parmesan cheese

4 T grated Swiss cheese

1/2 t salt

freshly ground black pepper (seasoned to taste)

In a heavy pan, melt butter, add sliced onion and cook slowly, stirring occasionally until golden. Sprinkle in the flour. Season with salt and pepper. Add the broth, stirring constantly. Bring to a boil, lower heat and let soup simmer partially covered for 30 minutes. Toast slices of bread oven until browned and then place in individual bowls. Preheat oven broiler. Sprinkle bread with Parmesan Cheese. Pour the soup over the bread and top with Swiss Cheese. Brown the cheese under the broiler and serve immediately. Eat and return for the afternoon session!

## PM Advanced SBS Management, Part II

20

Welcome back from lunch. This afternoon you'll take SBS management matters to a higher level by learning the new Administration Tools: Server Status Tool and Remote Administration. I'll then extend this discussion to include customizing the SBS Console, remotely using the traditional Windows NT Server tools, and modifying the Setup Computer wizard to allow you to install third-party applications. I'll also slip in a few comments about the next version of SBS, known as SBS 5.0, so you can start planning for tomorrow, today.

# Server Status Tools

In the eyes of many SBSers, perhaps the greatest improvement between SBS 4.0/4.0a and SBS 4.5 isn't necessarily the upgraded BackOffice applications such as Exchange and SQL Server. It's the paradigm shift toward *value-added providers* (*VAPs*), which is another funny term for resellers and consultants. In the early days of SBS, Microsoft believed it would be truly a "just add water" networking solution, but history has proven that virtually every SBS site, to some degree, has a relationship with an SBS VAP.

That realization has been built into SBS 4.5 with the new and wonderful Administration Tools. Select Administration Tools from the Tasks sheet in the SBS console, and observe that these tools include the Server Status tool, using remote administration approaches, and NetMeeting.

**Power Tool Tip**

> The Administration Tools provide SBS 4.5 with some of the management functions seen with big league networking management and monitoring tools such as Computer Associates's Unicenter. Status reports, remote monitoring, and so on have been used at the enterprise for some time; it's nice to see such capabilities introduced in SBS 4.5.

## Defining Server Status Tool

The server status tool, designed with the VAP in mind, sends critical system health information to the VAP. That is, the VAP, sitting in her office across town, can receive important SBS site information from her portfolio of SBS clients. This information can be sent via e-mail or fax.

**Tip**

> This reporting tool should lead to increased and legitimate billing opportunities for SBS consultants. By receiving these SBS system health reports proactively, you can offer additional servers to your SBS clients, troubleshoot problems earlier rather than later, and make legitimate suggestions to improve the health of your client's SBS systems.

Before SBS system health issues become major problems, the server status tool will notify you with important reports. It's all in keeping with today's preventative care paradigm, something that has been greatly expanded under SBS 4.5, including the new Server Status Tool.

The Server Status Tool offers these log files as part of its service:

- Hard disk space log—This reports the hard disk space on the SBS server machine.
- Service status log—This contains startup and status information on each Windows NT Server service.
- IIS log—Displays IIS-related activity.
- Proxy Server logs—Displays SBS site Internet usage, URL requests, destination hosts, and so on.

**Note**

The reports listed earlier are the type of reports that were discussed on Day 6, "Daily and Weekly SBS Administration (The Dirty Dozen)," in the "Reporting" section.

## Server Status Tool Setup

You'll need to configure the Server Status Tool before you can use it. This configuration is accomplished via the SBS Console using the following steps:

1. Make sure you are logged on to your SBS server machine as an administrator or member of the Administrators group.

2. From the Start button on the desktop, select SBS Console.

3. Select the Tasks sheet.

4. Select Administrative Tools.

5. Select Configure Server Status Tool. A help topic titled Configure Server Status Reports appears.

6. Read the help topic and select the first option, Server Status Configuration.

7. The Server Status Configuration dialog box appears as seen in Figure 20.10. On the Send Options tab (shown first by default), select the Send Status via Email or Fax radio button and enter **[SMTP: david@sbsrus.com]**. In the Subject Field, change <user company name> to **Springer Spaniels Unlimited**. Change <date> to **On-Going**. For the purposes of these steps, I assume you entered an SMTP (Internet) e-mail address.

20

**FIGURE 20.10**

*Server Status
Configuration.*

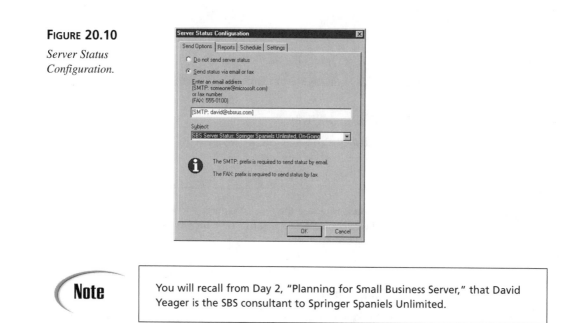

**Note**

You will recall from Day 2, "Planning for Small Business Server," that David Yeager is the SBS consultant to Springer Spaniels Unlimited.

8. Select the Reports tab and select the reports that interest you. These are shown in Figure 20.11. In the case of Springer Spaniels Unlimited, all reports are selected.

**FIGURE 20.11**

*Reports.*

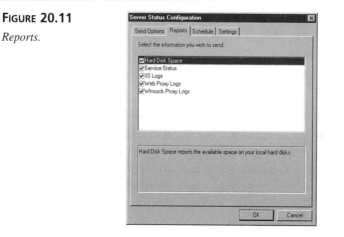

9. Select the Schedule tab and change the Every value, under Schedule Task Daily, to 5 days for Springer Spaniels Unlimited. It's unlikely the SBS consultant would want to receive daily reports. The Schedule tab is shown in Figure 20.12.

**FIGURE 20.12**

*Schedule.*

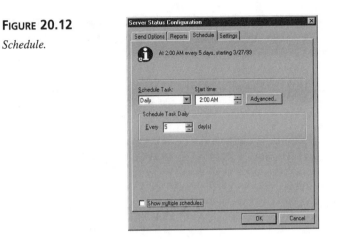

If you select the Advanced button, you can select the starting and ending dates for when the reports will be generated and delivered. This is very handy.

**Power Tool Tip**

I recommend you explore the functions of the Show Multiple Schedules check box. This allows you to select different times that the reports can be sent. For example, perhaps the SBS server machine at your SBS site runs fine every morning but performance degrades after lunch (for example, users report Outlook is running very slow). Then, via the Show multiple schedules, you could create reports that are sent in the early morning, late morning, and early afternoon. Such reporting would likely provide the evidence you would need to lead you to a solution.

10. The Settings tab lets you configure miscellaneous settings, including whether sending should occur if the SBS server machine is running on batteries.

11. Click OK on the Server Status Configuration dialog box. The first time you configure the Server Status Configuration dialog box, such as you did in the last several steps, you'll be presented with a Set Account Information dialog box to enter a service logon account. Use the default account, administrator, and enter the password (**password**). Click OK.

12. You have one final step to complete. You must now allow the Server Status Tool task—found under the newly added Scheduled Tasks folder—to log on correctly when it's time to run. To do this, double-click My Computer from the desktop of the SBS server machine.

13. Double-click the Schedule Tasks folder and notice that the Server Status Tool task is listed, as seen in Figure 20.13.

**20**

**FIGURE 20.13**

*Server Status Tool task in Scheduled Tasks.*

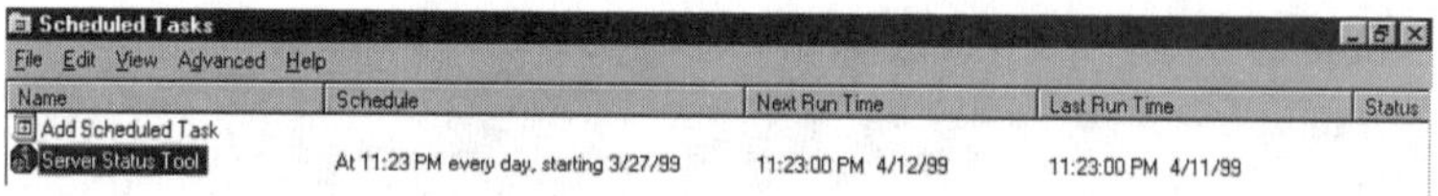

| 🗐 Scheduled Tasks | | | | _ ☐ ✕ |
|---|---|---|---|---|
| File  Edit  View  Advanced  Help | | | | |
| Name | Schedule | Next Run Time | Last Run Time | Status |
| 🗐 Add Scheduled Task | | | | |
| 🕐 Server Status Tool | At 11:23 PM every day, starting 3/27/99 | 11:23:00 PM 4/12/99 | 11:23:00 PM 4/11/99 | |

14. Double-click the Server Status Tool task to display the task properties. Notice that the Run as field contains the Administrator username. On the Task sheet, click the Set Password button.

15. The Set Password dialog box appear. Enter the Administrator password (which in the case of Springer Spaniels Unlimited is **password**). Click OK.

16. Click OK on the Server Status Tool task properties.

Now you have configured the Server Status Tool to send important SBS-related information to the SBS consultant for Springer Spaniels Unlimited every five days.

**Power Tool Tip**

You can customize the Server Status Tool to provide reports and logs on third-party applications. Personally, I would customize the Server Status Tool to provide Performance Monitor and Event Viewer (System, Security, and Application) logs on a regular basis. You will recall that I discussed Performance Monitor logging on Day 7, "Monthly and Annual SBS Duties," and Event Viewer (and its logs) on Day 6.

To customize the Server Status Tool, use the Small Business Server Customization Tool, which is available by taking Microsoft class 1399A, "Implementing Microsoft BackOffice Small Business Server 4.5" (it's in the Student folder on the CD-ROM that comes with the class book) or by purchasing the Small Business Server Resource Kit (it's on the CD-ROM).

## Remote Administration

Meanwhile, back at the Administration Tools sheet in the SBS Console, you will notice two options for remote administration: Configure Remote Administration and Share Console Remotely. You can accomplish this by configuring and using NetMeeting. Officially, NetMeeting supports the following activities:

- Chatting and talking between parties
- Video conferencing between parties
- Application and document sharing between parties
- Collaboration between parties, via shared applications
- Transferring files between parties
- A whiteboard to draw, share ideas, and so on.

## Configure Remote Administration

This is where you configure NetMeeting, an application that facilitates remote administration of an SBS server machine. Here are the steps to perform this configuration:

1. Assuming you are logged on as an administrator, select Configure Remote Administration from Administration Tools (via the Tasks sheet in the SBS Console).

2. A Help sheet for Configure NetMeeting for Remote Administration appears. Read it.

3. Select Task #1 - Start NetMeeting on the Help sheet.

4. You see the Microsoft NetMeeting wizard that defines what NetMeeting is. Click Next.

5. You are advised on the next screen that NetMeeting sharing must be enabled if you plan to share applications. For now, click Next.

**Note**

In a couple of steps, this sharing capability will be turned on so that you can use the SBS Console remotely via NetMeeting.

6. The next wizard screen allows you to elect whether you want your name listed in a directory server. This allows other people to call you using NetMeeting. You can also call other parties. For now, uncheck the Log on to a Directory Server When NetMeeting Starts check box. Click Next.

7. You next enter user information for Bob Estes, the de facto Springer Spaniels Unlimited SBS administrator. Your screen should look similar to Figure 20.14. Click Next.

**FIGURE 20.14**

*NetMeeting User Information for Bob Estes.*

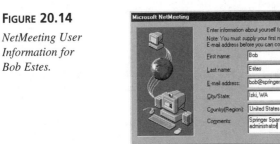

20

8. You will classify your content rating on the next screen. Select the For Business Use (Suitable for All Ages) radio button. Click Next.

9. The next screen asks you to specify the connection speed that NetMeeting will use. Select the Local Area Network radio button.

10. The last screen appears. Click the Finish button. If you don't have an audio card on your computer, you are warned that the audio features of NetMeeting will be disabled. You might recall from Day 2 that the server in use by Springer Spaniels Unlimited does not have an audio card.

11. NetMeeting automatically starts and looks similar to Figure 20.15.

**FIGURE 20.15**

*NetMeeting.*

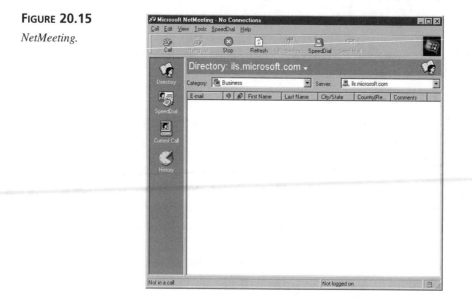

12. From the Tools menu in NetMeeting, select Enable Sharing and answer Yes to the dialog box that affirms this selection.

**Note**

You must reboot your machine to complete the installation of NetMeeting and enable sharing, even though you are not specifically asked to do so.

## Share Console Remotely

This allows you to set up a NetMeeting call to control and perform SBS administration tasks remotely. Here's how you do it:

1. Assuming you are logged on as an Administrator, select Share Console Remotely from Administration Tools (via the Tasks sheet in the SBS Console).

2. A Share the Console Remotely help sheet appears. Click the NetMeeting selection under Task #1 on the help sheet to launch NetMeeting.

3. Connect the client computer (typically the remote computer) to the server running NetMeeting. This might occur via an RAS modem session with Dial-Up Networking or via a direct Internet connection (typically known as Virtual Private Networking) where the NetMeeting server has a real IP address that can be called.

4. On the client computer, start its copy of NetMeeting. NetMeeting must be installed and running on both computers to establish a session.

**Power Tool Tip**

> This is very similar to setting up a session between two or more CU-SeeMe nodes, if you've ever had the pleasure of doing that.

5. On the client computer, place a call to the NetMeeting server by selecting New Call from the Call menu. You need to type the IP address of the NetMeeting server (for example, **131.107.6.200**).

6. On the NetMeeting server (or the other side) you need to accept the call.

7. On the NetMeeting server, select Share Application from the Tools menu in NetMeeting. Select Console.

**Note**

> The SBS Console must already be running in order for you to share it.

20

8. On the NetMeeting server, select Start Collaborating from the Tools menu in NetMeeting. You can now use the SBS Console on the SBS server machine from the remote machine. This is something VAPs will enjoy; it's something SBS customers will enjoy (the better service that VAPs will be able to provide).

**Note**

This approach for remote administration using NetMeeting replaces that remote SBS Console approach used in SBS 4.0/4.0a (where you installed a remote SBS console from the REMOTECSL folder on SBS 4.0/4.0a CD Disc 1).

# Customizing the SBS Console

You can also customize the SBS Console: You can add tasks or buttons to the Home, Tasks, or More Tasks pages. This is accomplished in one of two ways: the Small Business Server Customization Tool (mentioned earlier and available via Course 1399a or the SBS Resource Kit) or the hard way (via the Registry and a little programming).

Using the Small Business Server Customization Tool, you complete a dialog box titled Extending the Small Business Server Console. Here you select which SBS Console page to add your task. I highly recommend you consider attending Microsoft course 1399a and paying close attention to Module 5, "Building Custom Administration Solutions," to master the specific steps required to customize the SBS Console. To customize the SBS Console using the Small Business Server Customization Tool, see Task 20.1.

The hard way is, of course, more difficult. You make modifications directly to the Registry. This process is covered extensively in a white paper titled "Console Customization and Style Guide" available from Microsoft's Web site at www.microsoft.com/directaccess or from one of the other SBS-related Web sites mentioned in Appendix A.

You must understand that directly customizing the SBS Console affects the functionality of your SBS site. You need to be aware that

- You shouldn't modify the existing SBS Console tasks in any way. Not only might you break the task, but any such modifications to existing tasks you make will be forever lost in future SBS upgrades.

- You can add second-level and third-level pages, similar to the way you can drill down into the SBS Console with existing tasks.

- A task you add might not run an executable application file (.exe). Tasks are typically added to launch an HTML-based Web page. In fact, I present that challenge to you in a moment with Task 20.1, when you will attempt to place the Springer Spaniels EIS financial summary you created on Day 15, "Implementing Microsoft Office 2000" (the file is on the CD-ROM included with this book).

- Any task you create automatically assumes the next available position on the SBS Console page you are assigning it to. You may not provide task button X and Y screen coordinates.

- You can also modify the Online Guide to add your own help topics. This is a powerful capability that you shouldn't overlook.

## Task 20.1: Using the Small Business Server Customization Tool

Because you're near the end of the 21 days, I have the highest confidence that you can complete this advanced task. Simply stated, I want you to add a task to the Home page of the SBS Console that, when selected, displays the Springer Spaniels Unlimited EIS HTML-based file (this was the financial information chart you created in Microsoft Excel on Day 15).

Follow these steps:

1. Log on to your SBS server machine as an administrator or member of the administrator's group.

2. Copy the SSUEIS.HTM file from the CD-ROM that accompanies this book into the C:\Small Business\HTML folder on the SBS server machine.

3. Launch the Small Business Server Customization Tool, which is shown in Figure 20.16. (You will have to acquire this tool from one the sources I have previously mentioned.)

**FIGURE 20.16**

*Small Business Server Customization Tool.*

| Small Business Server Customization Tool |  |
|---|---|
| **Menu** | **Instructions** |
| Instructions | **Using this tool:** |
| Customize SBS Console | Click on an item to the left to extend either the Small Business Server Console or the Server Status Tool. |
| Configure Server Status Tool | SBS Console Customization. Add your own custom link to the Small Business Server Console Home Page. |
|  | Configure Server Status Tool settings. Configure additional server status reports to be added to the Small Business Server Server Status Tool. |
|  | **Warning:** |
|  | This tool will overwrite existing SBS Console custom entries and Server Status Tool reports that may have been input manually or added via a 3rd party tool. This will not affect any of the preconfigured SBS Console tasks or Server Status Tool reports. |
| Help   Close |  |

The Small Business Server Customization Tool enables you to easily extend the SBS Console and the Server Status Tool.

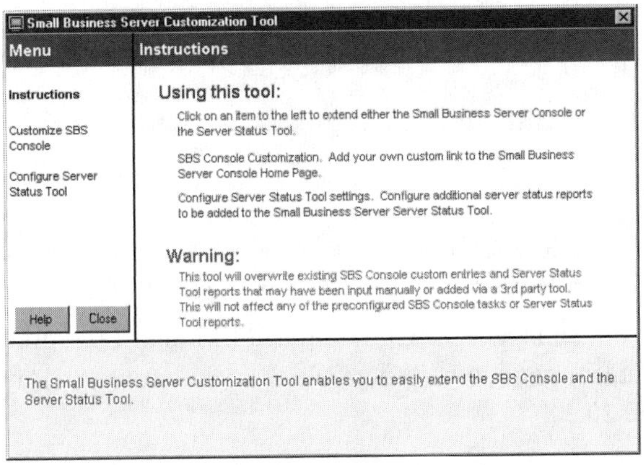

4. Select the Customize SBS Console option. The Extending the Small Business Server Console page is displayed.

5. Complete the Extending the Small Business Server Console page similar to that seen in Figure 20.17. The Console Page is Home Page, Task Name is Springer Spaniels Unlimited EIS, URL is ssueis.htm, and Target Location is In Frame.

**20**

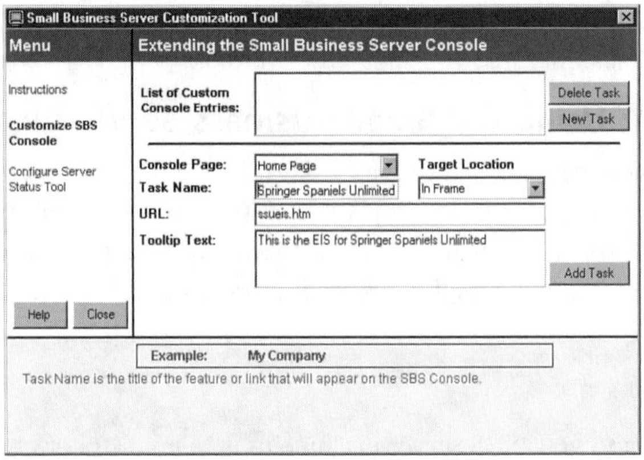

▼ FIGURE **20.17**

*Completed Task.*

6. Click Add Task. The information you entered in step 5 now appears in the List of Custom Console Entries.

7. The Registry Editor dialog box, shown in Figure 20.18, appears, communicating that the information in sbsinput.reg has been successfully entered into the Registry. Click OK.

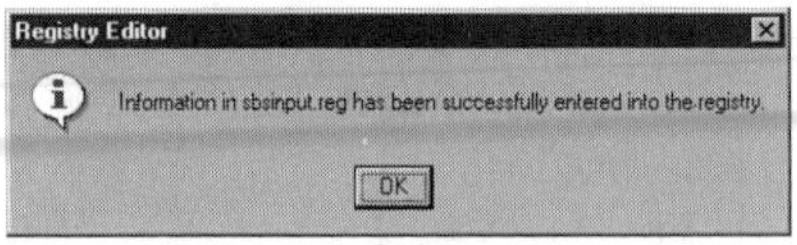

FIGURE **20.18**

*Registry Editor dialog box.*

8. Click Close.

9. Launch the SBS Console. Notice that the Springer Spaniels Unlimited EIS link appears on the Home page, as seen in Figure 20.19.

10. Click the Springer Spaniels Unlimited EIS link. The Springer Spaniels Unlimited Executive Information System file that you created on Day 15 appears, as seen in Figure 20.20.

▼ **FIGURE 20.19**

*Customized SBS Console.*

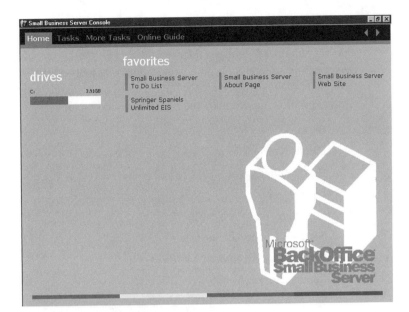

**FIGURE 20.20**

*Springer Spaniels Unlimited Executive Information System.*

That's it! You've successfully modified the SBS Console. Congratulations on completing Task 20.1.

20

# Traditional NT Server Tools

Another remote possibility is the use of the under-the-hood traditional Windows NT Server administration tools on a workstation. You will recall these tools, discussed throughout the book (specifically Days 6 and 7), are found in the Administrative Tools (Common) program group on the SBS Server and include

- Backup
- DHCP Manager
- Disk Administrator
- Event Viewer
- Migration Tool for NetWare
- Network Client Administrator
- Performance Monitor
- Remote Access Admin
- Server Manager
- System Policy Editor
- User Manager for Domains
- Windows NT Diagnostics
- WINS Manager

As you will see in a minute, you cannot run all these tools remotely.

No tricks are really involved with installing the Windows NT Server administration tools on a workstation. Here is how you do it:

1. At the workstation, log on to the SBS domain (SPRINGERS) as an administrator or member of the administrators group.

2. Insert Microsoft BackOffice Small Business Server Disc 1 in the CD-ROM drive of the workstation. If for some reason the workstation doesn't have a CD-ROM drive, you could always insert Disc 1 in the SBS server machine's CD-ROM drive and share it so it's accessible from the workstation.

3. Select the Start button on the workstation's desktop. Select Run and type the following path, assuming the CD-ROM drive is drive D and depending on the type of workstation you have.

   Windows NT Workstation 4.0:

   **d:\clients\srvtools\winnt\setup**

   Windows 98 or Windows 95:

   **d:\clients\srvtools\win95\setup**

4. Click OK in the Run dialog box. You see a notice that reads "Installing Client-based Network Administration Tools."

5. When requested, press any key to continue.

6. You will need to create shortcuts for the following programs located in c:\winnt.sbs\:

> poledit.exe (System Policy Editor)
>
> rasadmin.exe (Remote Access Admin)
>
> rplmgr.exe (Remote Boot Manager)
>
> srvmgr.exe (Server Manager)
>
> usrmgr.exe (User Manager)
>
> winsadmin.exe (WINS Manager)

You can do this by right-clicking the Start button and selecting Open All Users, Program, Administration Tools (Common). You would then right-click within the Administration Tools (Common) windows and select New, Shortcut. The Create Shortcut wizard appears and guides you through steps to create a shortcut for each application above.

7. The Administrative Tools (Common) program group should look similar to Figure 20.21.

**FIGURE 20.21**

*Administrative Tools (Common) program group.*

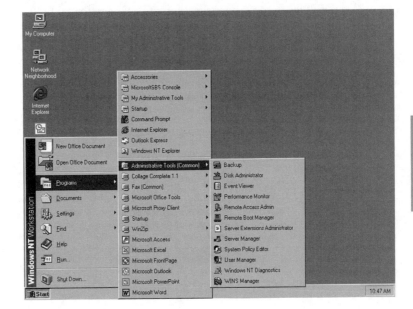

20

Tip

Remember that best network administration practices suggest that you try to do as much network administration, including the changing of server settings, from a workstation. You typically want to try to have your server locked securely away in a room or closet and use the remote approaches discussed over the past several pages to administer your network. That way, you aren't placing undue heavy loads on the actual sever machine (by using its keyboard, mouse, and so on). In the end, the users enjoy a higher performing and more reliable server when you, to the extent possible, use remote administration tools to manage your computer network.

# Extending the Set Up Computer Wizard

With SBS 4.5, you can install third-party applications with the Set Up Computer Wizard (SCW). You will recall that you can access SCW via the Manage Computer sheet in SBS Console. The benefit is that, via the magic disk during the setup of the workstation or if you simply want to add software to the workstation at a later date, you can do so via the SBS Console in an automated way. That is, you don't have to install the application manually at each and every workstation.

Here are matters to consider and complete before extending the SCW to accommodate third-party application installations:

1. Will the third-party application function with the SCW? Here's my rule of thumb. If the installation is straightforward, using the InstallShield approach discussed on Day 6, the chances are great this SCW approach will work. However, if the software doesn't install hands-free, such as the FRx Report Writer software for Great Plains Dynamics, you should not consider this SCW approach . If the software is shrink-wrapped and off-the-shelf, in my experience it installs automatically better than lesser-known software or sophisticated software packages resold by VAPs (such as high-end accounting packages).

Power Tool Tip

If you've worked with Microsoft's System Management Server (SMS), perhaps you're thinking what I'm thinking. This discussion sounds very familiar, eh? Modifying and using the SCW in SBS is akin to packages in SMS. I thought you'd like me to highlight this point.

Officially, SBS requires that the following conditions be met in order for a third-party application to be properly installed via the SCW.

- It must install automatically or unattended.
- There must be no required restart as part of the third-party application installation process.
- It can be installed in any order or out of order. The SCW can't accommodate third-party application installation scenarios that depend on a certain order. That is, the third-party application you're installing can't explicitly rely on an application being installed immediately before it.

2. You need to create an installation file (.inf) for the application being installed.

3. You need to modify the SCW's initialization file (scw.ini) to accommodate the installation of this third-party application.

4. You need to modify the SCW client optional component information file (clioc.inf) to accommodate the third-party application you are attempting to install.

You will walk through steps 2 through 4 over the next few pages. You will install the Ping Plotter program that is included on the CD-ROM included with this book (in the \pingplotter folder).

To set up this example, copy all the files (for example, pngplot_2.exe) from the \pingplotter folder on the CD-ROM that accompanied this book to the \ClientApps\newapps folder on your SBS server machine. (You will have to create the subfolder newapps.)

## Application Information (.inf) File Creation

To install the Ping Plotter application properly, you need to create an application information file (.inf) via Notepad or some other text editor. Here are the steps to do this:

1. Log on to the SBS server machine as an administrator or member of the administrators group.

2. Start Notepad from the Accessories program group (found via Start, Programs). Notepad starts with an Untitled document.

3. Save the Untitled document as PingPlotter.inf in the \ClientApps\newapps folder.

4. Add the following information to the PingPlotter.inf file:

```
; PingPlotter.inf
;
[Version]
Signature = "$Windows NT$
;
[Optional Components]
PingPlotter
;
```

**20**

```
[PingPlotter]
InstallCmd = \\%SBSServer%\clients\newsapps\pngplt_2.exe /s
;
; note the "/s" term above is necessary to
; make PingPlotter automatically install.
;
DiskSpaceEstimate = 3
;
; UnInstallCmd =
;
```

5. Save the PingPlotter.inf file.

6. Copy the PingPlotter.inf file to the \SmallBusiness\Template folder on the Small Business Server machine.

## SCW Initialization File Modification

This next step is very important, so I'll take the time necessary to explain it to you fully. Here the scw.ini file will be modified so that the application, Ping Plotter, appears on the application installation list when you run the SCW from the SBS Console. In other words, you want the Ping Plotter application to show up on the list of applications that can be installed when setting up a computer on the SBS network.

Here are the steps to modify scw.ini:

1. Log on to the SBS server machine as an administrator or member of the administrators group.

2. Using either Windows NT Explorer or My Computer, navigate to the \SmallBusiness folder and make a copy of the scw.ini file (name the copy scw2.old)

3. Double-click the scw.ini file. It opens and appears similar to Figure 20.22.

4. Notice the entry SCW_NumberOfApps=15 located in Figure 20.22 (near the top of your scw.ini file). Increment this value by one (in this case to equal 16). This is an important step that communicates the number of available applications for the SCW to install. (This number might vary on your machine.)

5. Next, add the Ping Plotter application information to the [SCW_OptionalApplications] section. Here you must be very care to follow each step correctly. First, scroll to the end of the [SCW_OptionalApplications] section and highlight the full application entry at the bottom. In Figure 20.23, the highlighted text is for the MS_OFFICE_PUBLISHER entry.

**FIGURE 20.22**

*Scw.ini file.*

```
scw.ini - Notepad
File  Edit  Search  Help

; This file contains information that the Setup Computer Wizard needs
; to do its' job.


; This section lists the paths to the individual setup programs for the
; optional applications and the name of each application.

[SCW_OptionalApplications]

SCW_NumberOfApps=15

; Entries are as follows:

;     Note: White space is NOT allowed in the SCW_AppName entry.

;     SCW_AppName<n>=<the name of the n'th application>

;     SCW_AppDisplayString<n>=<the string to be displayed in the application listbox
;                              for the n'th application>

;     Note: The SCW_AppSelectedByDefault entry specifies whether the n'th application
;           is selected for installation by default.

;     SCW_AppSelectedByDefault<n>=<YES | NO>

;     Note: The SCW_AppRequiresUnattendedTextFile entry specifies whether the n'th
;           application requires a special file for unattended mode installation.

;     SCW_AppRequiresUnattendedTextFile=<YES | NO>

;     Note: The SCW_AppTemplatePath entry specifies the path, relative to the "SmallBusiness"
;           directory, to the template for the special file that the n'th application
;           requires for unattended mode installation.

;     SCW_AppTemplatePath<n>=<the path to the template for the file that the n'th
```

**FIGURE 20.23**

*Highlighted SCW application entry.*

```
scw.ini - Notepad
File  Edit  Search  Help

SCW_AppTemplatePath13=
SCW_AppTemplateSourceName13=
SCW_AppTemplateDestName13=
SCW_AppSetupInfPath13=Template
SCW_AppSetupInfSourceName13=offsba.inf
SCW_AppSetupInfDestName13=
SCW_AppArchitectureList13=win95,i386
SCW_AppParent13=12
SCW_AppMSIFeatures13=SmallBusinessApplication,SBBPrimary,SBBPrimary2
SCW_AppOfficeCD13=2

SCW_AppName14=MS_OFFICE_PUBLISHER
SCW_AppDisplayString14=Microsoft Publisher
SCW_AppSelectedByDefault14=YES
SCW_AppRequiresUnattendedTextFile14=NO
SCW_AppTemplatePath14=
SCW_AppTemplateSourceName14=
SCW_AppTemplateDestName14=
SCW_AppSetupInfPath14=Template
SCW_AppSetupInfSourceName14=offpub.inf
SCW_AppSetupInfDestName14=
SCW_AppArchitectureList14=win95,i386
SCW_AppParent14=12
SCW_AppMSIFeatures14=PubPrimary
SCW_AppOfficeCD14=2



; This section specifies information related to the Operating System(s)
; that may beinstalled to the client computer.

; Note that the paths specified here are relative to the SAM Clients share.

[SCW_ClientOS]
```

**20**

6. While the text is highlighted, select Copy from the Edit menu of Notepad.

7. Move the cursor to a position two lines below the entry you just highlighted and copied and select Paste from the Edit menu.

8. Modify the entry you just pasted with the following information:

```
SCW_AppName15=PINGPLOTTER
SCW_AppDisplayString15=PingPlotter
SCW_AppSelectedByDefault15=YES
SCW_AppRequiresUnattendedTextFile15=NO
SCW_AppTemplatePath15=
SCW_AppTemplateSourceName15=
SCW_AppTemplateDestName15=
SCW_AppSetupInfPath15=Template
SCW_AppSetupInfSourceName15=pingplotter.inf
SCW_AppSetupInfDestName15=
SCW_AppArchitectureList15=win95,i386
```

Essentially, I've incremented every occurrence of *14* to the value *15* and made changes to the name, display string, and .inf source name entries. I also deleted the last three lines that were copied from the entry above. (These are not needed to install Ping Plotter.)

9. Save the file scw.ini that you have now modified and close Notepad.

**Power Tool Tip**

> The SBS 4.0/4.0a to SBS 4.5 upgrade process renames the existing scw.ini file to scw.old. Custom entries you've made such as the one earlier would need to be re-created. I suspect this behavior will also apply to any SBS upgrades from 4.5 to future versions. You've been advised.

## Modifying CLIOC.INF

Finally, you must modify the client optional component information file by adding the Ping Plotter installation information to it. SCW looks to clioc.inf for critical installation information. You will find clioc.inf in the \SmallBusiness\Template folder on your SBS server machine. Here are the steps for modifying the clioc.inf file:

1. Log on to the SBS server machine as an administrator or member of the administrators group.

2. Using either Windows NT Explorer or My Computer, navigate to the \SmallBusiness\Template folder and make a copy of the scw.ini file (name the copy cliof2.old)

3. Double-click the cliof.inf file. It opens and appears similar to Figure 20.24.

**FIGURE 20.24**

*Clioc.inf file.*

4. You are going to modify both the [Components.w95] and [Components.x86] sections at the top of the cliof.inf file (as seen in Figure 20.24) with the two entries.

   In the [Components.w95] section, add the following sentence directly above the last line (which reads client =

   ..\..\setup\Win95\ocsam.dll,OcEntry,client.inf):

   PingPlotter = '','',PingPlotter.inf

   In the [Components.x86] section, add the following line immediately above the last line (which reads client =

   ..\..\setup\i386\ocsam.dll,OcEntry,ntclient.inf):

   PingPlotter = "","",PingPlotter.inf

5. The result of these additions should look similar to Figure 20.25. Save the file clioc.inf that you have now modified and close Notepad.

That's it for the modifications. Now enjoy your efforts by having Ping Plotter install, via the SCW, on one of the machine on the SBS network. In this case, I'm going to install Ping Plotter, via the SCW, on Elvis's GENE01 workstation (a Windows NT Workstation 4.0 machine). Here is how you would do that:

1. Log on to the SBS server machine as an administrator or member of the administrators group.

**20**

2. Launch the SBS Console from the Start menu.

3. Select the More Tasks tab.

4. Select Manage Computers.

5. Select Add Software to a Computer.

6. The Set Up Computer Wizard appears. Click Next.

7. Select Elvis Haskins on the Select a User screen. Click Next.

8. Select GENE01 on the Computer Name screen. Click Next.

9. Select Ping Plotter at the bottom of the applications list on the Applications screen, as seen in Figure 20.26. Click Next.

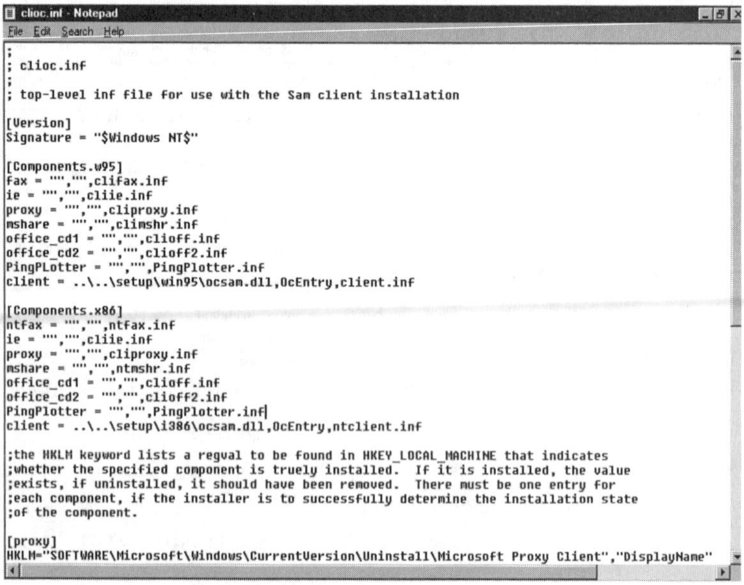

**FIGURE 20.25**

*Modified clioc.inf file.*

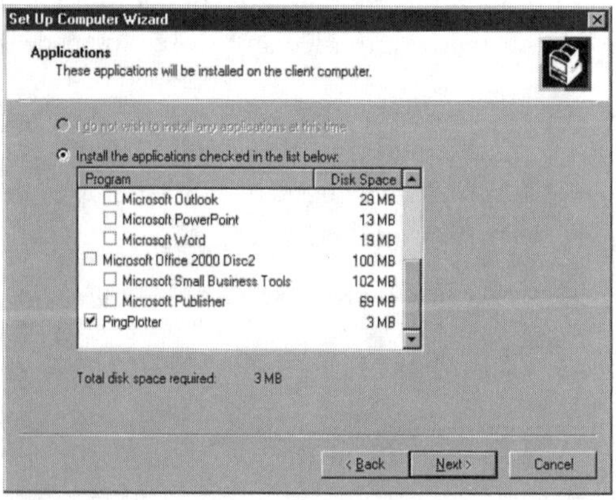

**FIGURE 20.26**

*Select Ping Plotter.*

10. Click Next on the Create the Setup File screen. The wizard creates the setup files.

11. Click Finish on the Complete the Set Up Computer Wizard.

12. Now, go to Elvis's workstation (GENE01) and log on as Elvis (user name is ElvisH, password is Platinium1).

13. The Microsoft Small Business Client Setup wizard initializes and the Welcome menu appears. Click Next.

14. The Select Components screen will appear. Ping Plotter will already be selected. Click Next.

15. Ping Plotter is installed and the Completing the Client Installation Wizard screen appears. Click Finish.

16. Launch Ping Plotter from the Ping Plotter program group. Observe Ping Plotter in Figure 20.27.

**FIGURE 20.27**

*Ping Plotter running on GENE01.*

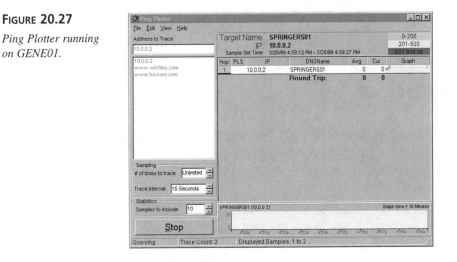

# Advanced Error Reporting

20

To be brutally honest, one of the most interesting SBS Console features I discovered in the SBS 4.5 release came very late in the writing of this book. As I worked with SB 4.5 day-in and day-out, I started to conclude I had seen most of it—in some way, shape, or form—but such was not the case. One day, while having trouble with my Internet connection, I looked at the SBS Console, and there, on the Home page, an error notice seen in Figure 20.28, was displayed. I found this error reporting to be both a pleasant surprise and valuable.

**FIGURE 20.28**

*SBS Console error
reporting.*

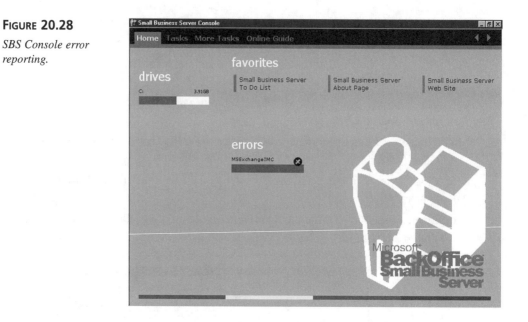

# The Future of SBS

Believe it or not, the highly skilled but nameless SBS developers at Microsoft are already hard at work on developing SBS 5.0, even thought SBS 4.5 was recently released! That begs the question, "What is the future of SBS?" First, no one, not even the Microsoft developers, really know. Second, I can only speculate, but consider the following about future releases of SBS:

- Look for significant functionality that enables small businesses to participate in online electronic commerce. Not only is this prediction consistent with Microsoft's early 1999 statement that small business e-commerce was a priority, if SBS doesn't support e-commerce in a meaningful way, obviously other software vendors will.

- Single disk or diskless client installations. Look for improvements in how client workstations are added to SBS networks.

- Bug fixes. Upgrades are often released to fix known bugs.

- Windows 2000 support for both the client (Professional) and server versions. The underlying operating system used by SBS will likely shift to Windows 2000 Server in the SBS 5.0 release.

- Underlying application upgrades. Look for Exchange, Proxy Server, IIS, and perhaps even Microsoft Office to be upgraded (again) in the SBS 5.0 release.

- Greater VAP support. Look for an increased emphasis on helping SBS consultants server their SBS customers better. Look for better exploitation of NetMeeting.

**Tip**

As an SBS consultant, keep in mind that many shortcomings in the existing version of SBS, such as the inability to manage domain groups from the SBS Console, will most likely be addressed in future releases of SBS. Thus, as part of your consulting strategy, it often behooves you to communicate with your SBS customers to, in many cases, wait for the next SBS release to fix specific SBS maladies.

# Summary

You're now truly at the end of working directly with SBS 4.5 as you know it. Whew! It's been a busy three weeks, but don't leave yet. Tomorrow, on Day 21, I share with you how to upgrade to Big BackOffice. That is something many of you will need to consider as your firms grow happy, healthy, and wealthy.

**20**

# DAY 21

# Upgrading to Big BackOffice

You reach the end of the journey today, so how appropriate it is to start the next journey: deploying and using Big BackOffice. I don't view this discussion in any way as a mistake or the result of poor planning. Rather, I view it as a positive, natural outcome for a thriving SBS network.

Here is what I mean. All businesses want to grow bigger, right? Often, this growth is accompanied by the need to move to new and larger office space and hire more staff. It's a problem most businesses would like to have, believe me. So can't you say the same about a network? Good network design decisions, such as implementing SBS, made while a business is young are still good decisions. Businesses come and go, and most of all, they grow. So when you're confronted with a business that has outgrown its SBS network, take solace in knowing that Microsoft, in designing SBS 4.5, has elegantly accommodated your new networking needs. This afternoon, I'll discuss at length the process for upgrading from SBS 4.5 to Big BackOffice (a.k.a. full BackOffice).

Before I start the morning session, where I'll compare and contrast SBS 4.5 with Big BackOffice, I want to make one final point regarding network growth. Firms that grow rapidly can make the best decision today by starting out with SBS 4.5. That's because they can benefit from SBS 4.5's all-in-one approach now while the energy and emphasis should be on growing the business. Later, when the business has grown, said hot shot business can benefit from the distributed nature of Big BackOffice (where individual components such as Microsoft Exchange Server) typically run on their own server machines. Most importantly, going with SBS 4.5 today allows for a smooth upgrade to Big BackOffice with little pain (and lots of gain!). The seamless upgrade process from SBS 4.5 to Big BackOffice is the key underpinning of this chapter.

Kindly note that today is a day in which everyone, newbie to guru, can benefit. Plan to attend the entire day.

## AM Comparing SBS 4.5 with Big BackOffice

As alluded to earlier, the morning is dedicated to definitions. Here, the goal is for you to understand why you might consider Big BackOffice beyond the practical reasons such as SBS's 50-user limit.

**Note**

> This discussion necessarily focuses on the server-side components of both SBS 4.5 and Big BackOffice. That's because Big BackOffice doesn't implicitly have client-side components. However, clients or workstations on Big BackOffice networks can and often do use many of the same client-side applications used by SBS 4.5, including Outlook 2000 and Internet Explorer 5.0.

# Compare and Contrast

It is possible, based on the Table of Contents and the Index, that you are perusing this chapter in advance of purchasing both this book and SBS 4.5. You might be doing so because you want to see whether both this book and SBS are for you. Call it *try-before-you-buy*, which I applaud.

Or perhaps you manage a thriving SBS network today, with an eye to the future. I hope that your motivation for thinking so strategically is based on some of the planning issues that surfaced on Day 7, "Monthly and Annual SBS Duties."

Whatever the reason that you're attending this morning, may I offer the following compare-and-contrast for analyzing SBS 4.5 with Big BackOffice?

# Defining SBS 4.5

Call it proper pedagogy, but allow me this opportunity to list again the components that comprise SBS 4.5, because nearly 21 days have past since I last did. This list is critical as you read the next section and understand the similarities and differences between SBS 4.5 and Big BackOffice.

SBS 4.5 includes the following components:

- Microsoft Windows NT Server 4.0 with Service Pack 4.0
- Microsoft Window NT Server Option Pack (including Internet Information Server 4.0, Transaction Server 2.0, Index Server 2.0, and Microsoft Script Debugger 1.0)
- Microsoft Exchange Server 5.5 with Service Pack 2
- Microsoft Outlook 2000
- Fax Server 4.5
- Microsoft Proxy Server 2.0
- Modem Sharing Service 4.5
- SBS Console
- Internet Explorer 5
- SQL Server 7.0
- Microsoft FrontPage 98
- Office 2000 (optional)

# Defining Big BackOffice

This is Microsoft BackOffice 4.5 as much of the world knows it. Typically seen in medium-sized and larger companies, Big BackOffice offers several advantages over SBS 4.5, including load balancing and distributed processing. I'll discuss this more in a moment.

Microsoft BackOffice 4.5 (a.k.a. Big BackOffice) includes the following components:

- Microsoft Windows NT Server 4.0 with Service Pack 4. This is the full version without a modified Registry. More than 50 users are supported (up to 40,000 in theory; a few thousand practically). Full domain participation and trust relationships are supported. License Manager, found in the Administrative Tools (Common) program group, is fully functional.
- Microsoft Windows NT Option Pack, including Microsoft Internet Information Server 4.0, Microsoft Transaction Server, and Microsoft Message Queue Server.
- Microsoft SQL Server 7.0. This full version of SQL Server allows databases that are larger than 10 GB in size.

**21**

- Microsoft Exchange Server 5.5 with Service Pack 2. This full version of Microsoft Exchange support multiple Exchange sites and servers.
- Microsoft Systems Management Server 2.0. This is a comprehensive network management tool that allows management and inventorying of Windows-based workstations, distribution of software, remote diagnostics, management, and troubleshooting.
- Microsoft SNA Server 4.0a with Service Pack 2.0. This application supports connectivity to IBM-based mainframes, and mid-range and AS/400 computing environments.
- Microsoft BackOffice Intranet Starter Kit. Sample Web pages let you quickly create your intranet.
- Microsoft Management Console (MMC) 1.1. This allows a consistent interface for managing BackOffice functions.
- Microsoft Proxy Server 2.0.
- Microsoft Site Server 3.0 with Service Pack 2.
- Microsoft Internet Explorer 5.0
- Microsoft FrontPage 2000 (single user).
- Microsoft Visual InterDev 6.0 (single user).
- Microsoft Outlook 2000 (for use by licensed client systems).
- Seagate Crystal Info 6.0 (five users).

## Making a Decision

You must ultimately make a technology decision within the constraints we all face of imperfect knowledge, a budget, and a deadline. In other words, if you had perfect knowledge, an unlimited budget, and no deadline, you could easily make the best technology decision every time.

Think back a moment to Management Information Systems 101. There, you probably tolerated a droning professor who carried on about needs analysis: determine what your needs are and then purchase the technology solution that best meets those needs. Well, life is a circle, and you're back were you started. Deciding between SBS 4.5 and Big BackOffice ultimately comes down to defining your needs. Consider these three needs analysis areas when deciding between SBS 4.5 and Big BackOffice.

### Practicality

This category is perhaps the easiest to address and understand. Here, you are either concerned about the 50-user logon limit of SBS or you aren't. The SQL Server 10GB database size limit is problematic, or it isn't.

Perhaps you fall into this category. You have only 15 users, but you don't fit the profile of an SBS 4.5 site. I've seen such a case: a small software developer. Although SBS 4.5 would have been an entirely acceptable networking decision for running the business side of this small software development firm, it was impractical from the developer side. Here, the software development firm had an important need to exist in a Windows NT Server environment most similar to that of its clients. That way, its products would be developed under real-world conditions, such as Big BackOffice.

**Note**

An amazing footnote to this particular small site that elected to go with big BackOffice is that it also had to maintain an array of workstations ranging from Windows For Workgroups 3.11 to Windows NT Workstation 4.0 so, again, the firm could replicate its client's environments.

## Performance

In a world of networks defined by limits (hardware, software, budget, expertise), both you are motivated to squeeze the highest performance out of your systems. In short, you have to play the hand you're dealt. Several performance-based strategies exist.

**Loading Balancing**    Several servers in the organization, each running a different BackOffice application, might make the most sense. This is a rudimentary form of load balancing. More sophisticated forms of load balancing include the implementation of server clustering.

**Geography**    SBS 4.5 is not well suited for (err…let's say it's incapable of) supporting remote offices and branches in a wide area network. Big BackOffice scales much better for satisfying this need.

**Reliability**    Let's face it. You're running critical applications and functions on your network. Perhaps you're a small hospital that demands the highest network uptime possible. In all likelihood, you'll look first to Big BackOffice and aforementioned solutions such as server clustering to meet your most mission critical needs.

**The MCSE Factor**    There's the aspiring MCSE candidate who'll interject his or her own biases into the SBS 4.5 versus Big BackOffice debate. An MCSE-type needs Big BackOffice to create an adequate test bed for exam preparation purposes. This is not always the best reason to select Big BackOffice over SBS 4.5, but I've seen it done! And, I'd be remiss if I didn't renew my observations early in this book that many MCSEs, with the underlying Big BackOffice mindset, really struggle when implementing SBS 4.5.

21

## Future

So you're in strategic planning mode and engaging in some forward thinking. You must not only assess whether SBS 4.5 will meet your needs based on user counts and database size restrictions, but also consider how external environmental factors will affect your organization. Here's what I mean. Suppose you intend to stay fewer than 50 users forever. On that basis, SBS 4.5 would theoretically meet your needs. Suppose, however, you're planning to move your entire product line from a retail store to an online store. That is, in the near future, you'll sell everything over the Internet. In that case, I encourage you to ask some really tough questions of SBS 4.5.

In the e-commerce picture I've painted, one such tough question might concern the issue of Web hosting. Suppose you become an e-commerce site instead of a physical site in the truest sense of the word. (Remember from Day 12, "Publishing on the Internet/Intranet," that Microsoft actually discourages Web hosting on your SBS 4.5 server machine.) Then stir in your newly acquired knowledge about third-party applications running on top of SQL Server (such as Great Plains Dynamics on Day 19, "Installing Business Applications"), and you have a recipe for an e-commerce deployment. More importantly, you have a recipe for possible failure if you use SBS 4.5. To be brutally honest, a real-world e-commerce site, while abiding by SBS's rules (for example, fewer than 50 users) can easily overwhelm the lone SBS 4.5 server machine. Ouch! Clearly, in the e-commerce scenario I've now painstakingly presented, Big BackOffice demands your serious purchase consideration.

## Reality Check

Don't lose sight of your better judgement as you look the Big BackOffice decision in the eye. Consider the following additions to your upgrade decision making framework:

- Duration—Remember that technology decisions are typically made for the next 36 months: A technology decision you make today will mostly likely have a three-year useful life. The decisions you make won't be forever; thus, SBS 4.5 now and Big BackOffice three years from now might be the best decision you can make.

- Chain of events—Remember that for every action, there is a reaction. Many times, when firms consider migrating from SBS 4.5 to Big BackOffice, the decision isn't simply to purchase the Big BackOffice media (a few CD-ROMs ordered from a reseller), it's also new server hardware, yadda yadda yadda. That's why a simple decision to upgrade to Big BackOffice can quickly become one expensive decision, all things considered.

- Piecemeal—A topic I'll discuss this afternoon deserves mention now: upgrading or adding individual BackOffice components. Perhaps you plan to purchase Great Plains Dynamics and run it on top of SQL Server as part of SBS, but you have legitimate and lingering concerns that other SBS applications such as Exchange will be crowded out in the default single server SBS server machine scenario. So you purchase real Windows NT Server 4.0 and SQL Server 7.0 versions to run on a separate member server. This is called a multiple server scenario using different versions of Microsoft BackOffice: SBS and Big BackOffice. You might also call it the best of both worlds: using the SBS machine as your primary domain controller (PDC) and a member server as your application server.

Now go to lunch.

## Lunch

Whew! It has been a long SBS journey over the past three weeks, so, this lunch hour, kick your feet up and enjoy a drink. Just don't operate on your SBS network after this lunch.

### Margaritas

> 1 1/2 oz. triple sec
>
> 1 1/2 oz. tequila
>
> juice from 1/2 lime
>
> coarse salt
>
> crushed ice

Rub rim of glass with lime rind. Dip into coarse salt. Blend tequila, triple sec, and lime with crushed ice. Serve.

---

**Caution**  Wait until tomorrow to work further on your network after this lunch, but enjoy the afternoon nevertheless.

---

## PM Upgrading to Big BackOffice

**21**

Welcome back from lunch. You'll jump right into the upgrade matter. I left you deciding whether you wanted to go from SBS 4.5 to Big BackOffice. I'll assume you've decided to do so.

# Paperwork

There are several facts of life when under any upgrade scenario:

- You must purchase full Windows NT Server when you purchase any Big BackOffice application. This can be the upgrade version of Windows NT Server, which will save you money. This purchase is necessary to facilitate the use of License Manager, a tool that is disabled in SBS 4.5 but necessary for managing Big BackOffice.

- You must purchase the appropriate amount of client access licenses (CALs) for any and all Big BackOffice components you purchase. Your SBS 4.5 CALs do not apply to an upgrade scenario to Big BackOffice.

- In other words, you must purchase a like number of Windows NT Server CALs to match the number of existing SBS CALs. You must also purchase a like number of Big BackOffice CALs to equal the number of SBS CALs.

- You must have at least 25 SBS CALs when you purchase the regular Windows NT Server or individual Big BackOffice application.

- You can purchase the upgrade version of the Big BackOffice application you seek to implement. This saves you money as you qualify for cheaper upgrade pricing.

> **Note**
>
> I highly recommend you check with Microsoft at www.microsoft.com regarding updates to its licensing policies. These policies change occasionally to reflect new market realities such as increased competition from Novell NetWare. Thus, before performing an upgrade from SBS 4.5 to Big BackOffice, take few minutes to research the licensing issues associated with such a decision.

# By the Drink

The most common upgrade scenario that I've witnessed is to upgrade individual Big BackOffice components. You would upgrade three Big BackOffice components on an individual basis. These are discussed by order of importance, based on my experience.

## Windows NT Server

You'll commonly do this for a couple of reasons. First, such a strategy of having regular Windows NT Server as your underlying operating system allows you to have trust relationships between multiple domains. A domain is Windows NT Server's way of organizing a network into administrative units or boundaries. More often than not, domains reflect either the geographic, functional department, or political reality of an organization. For example, a large corporation might have domains titled USA, Europe, and Asia. I've also seen domains titled Executive, Marketing, and Accounting (three domain names reflecting functional departments). You can read about domains in advanced Windows NT Server books including *Sams Teach Yourself Windows NT Server 4 in 21 Days* by Peter Davis (ISBN: 0-672-31555-6).

Second, you might purchase regular Windows NT Server in order to have a backup domain controller (BDC) or member server on your network. As mentioned in passing earlier today, member servers often run specific applications such as databases or accounting systems, but I'll revisit what a domain controller does. I originally discussed domain controllers early on Day 1, "Welcome to Small Business Server," at which time you learned that the SBS server machine by default must be the primary domain controller (PDC). The PDC controls the basic operations of the SBS network by maintaining the master list of users and associated security settings in the Security Accounts Manager (SAM). The PDC is also where the logon authentication function occurs; it's where you're approved to use the network. On larger networks, it's common to have a backup domain controller (BDC) to help out with logon duties and take some of the administrative load off the PDC. Usually I'll place a BDC at a remote office site so logon traffic doesn't need to travel over a slow WAN link (ouch!).

Member servers are simply good old Windows NT Server machines that don't participate in logon-related duties but perform a valuable function by running large database applications or account applications as I mentioned earlier. A member server relies on a domain controller for its security information.

Upgrading to regular Windows NT Server is very easy. When this upgrade is performed, the usernames and associated security settings that you have entered into the system are retained, thus you don't have to re-input your users. I'm assuming you will perform an upgrade installation with regular Windows NT Server to the same directory containing SBS (for example, C:\winnt.sbs). If you install regular Windows NT Server to a new directory, your existing user names and associated security settings would be lost.

> **Note**
>
> You need to reapply the latest service pack (that is, Service Pack 4) after upgrading from SBS to regular Windows NT Server.

**21**

To upgrade to regular Windows NT Server:

1. Log on to your SBS server machine as an administrator or member of the Administrators group.

2. Insert your Windows NT Server 4.0 CD-ROM in the CD-ROM drive of the SBS server machine.

3. Run **winnt32.exe /b** from the I386 folder. The /b switch allows for a floppy-less installation (so you don't have to use the three Windows NT Server setup disks). The Run dialog box is best place to run this command (found via the Start button on your desktop).

4. The Windows NT 4.0 Upgrade/Installation dialog box appears, as seen in Figure 21.1. Confirm the location of the Windows NT 4.0 files and click Continue.

**FIGURE 21.1**

*Windows NT 4.00 Upgrade/Installation.*

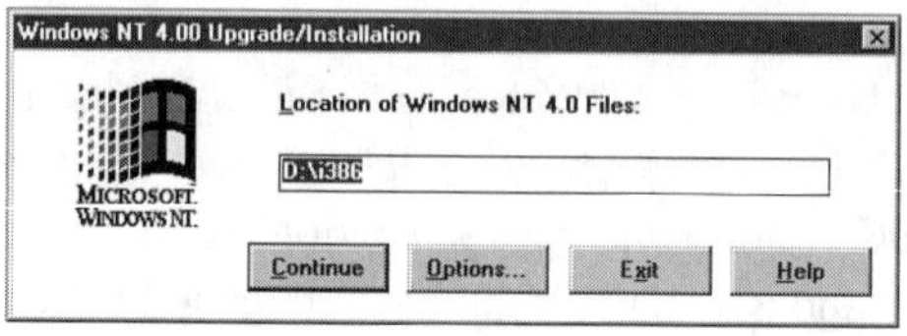

5. The Windows NT Server 4.0 setup files are copied to a temporary directory on your SBS server machine hard disk, as seen in Figure 21.2.

**FIGURE 21.2**

*Copying Windows NT Server setup files.*

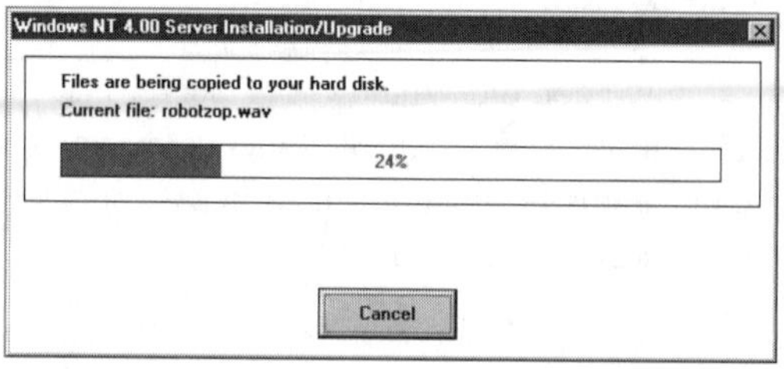

6. You are then prompted to restart your computer as seen in Figure 23.3. Click Restart Computer.

**FIGURE 21.3**

*Restart Computer.*

7. The Windows NT Server character-based setup phase commences. This is same as the Windows NT Server character-based setup phase discussed on Day 3, "Installing Small Business Server," for setting up SBS 4.5. When prompted, acknowledge that this installation is an upgrade and be sure to install Windows NT Server in the same folder as your existing Windows NT Server installing under SBS 4.5. (for example, C:\Winnt.sbs).

8. After the Windows NT Server character-based setup phase concludes, the machine reboots. The GUI-based setup phase commences. You answer questions regarding the time zone exactly as you did on Day 3. The machine reboots at the end of this phase.

9. You have now completed your upgrade to the regular version of Windows NT Server. Congratulations.

## Proxy Server

One of the most popular upgrades I've witnessed is the purchase and deployment of Proxy Server 2.0 (an additional full standalone copy of Proxy Server 2.0, not the copy that ships with SBS 4.5). Why? The firewall scenario implemented by SBS is a quick and dirty firewall that in most cases is sufficient for small businesses, but let me just say it doesn't conform to Department of Defense security guidelines. That's because Proxy Server should run on its own machine, in a separate domain with a one-way trust relationship pointing back to main domain. Such a scenario is shown in Figure 21.4.

**FIGURE 21.4**

*Bona fide Proxy Server implementation.*

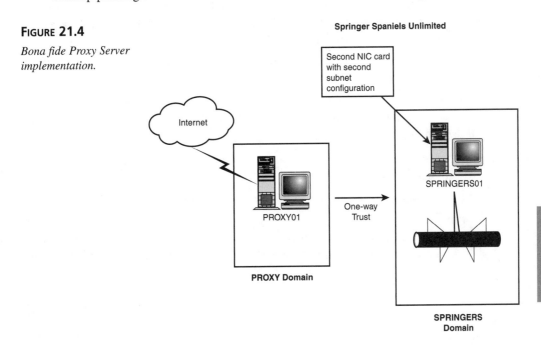

**21**

SBS sites needing the very highest levels of protection from external Internet-based intruders warrant this type of solution. When the added comfort from additional firewall security demands it, the additional costs aren't bothersome. Otherwise, if you're simply a small business running SBS 4.5 and you really have modest Internet security needs, the default Proxy Server 2.0 implementation (on the SBS server machine itself) is likely adequate.

**Note** You don't need to purchase a full, standalone copy of Proxy Server 2.0 if you plan to install it only on the SBS server machine. This was already accomplished on Day 3 when you built the SBS server machine. A second copy of Proxy Server 2.0 would be used to implement a solution shown in Figure 21.4.

## SQL Server 7.0

Upgrades to the full version of SQL Server 7.0 occur primarily to install SQL Server 7.0 on a standalone machine. This has certainly been my experience when SBS sites are running big-league industry-specific software applications such as BenchTop (discussed on Day 19). Typically, SQL Server 7.0, combined with an industry applications such as BenchTop, puts an amazing drain an SBS server machine, justifying the use of a member server to handle this specific set of chores.

Microsoft's official position is that you would consider an upgrade to the full version of SQL Server 7.0 when you approach the 10GB-per-database limit. That's a heck of a lot of space when measuring only the table and logs in a database. Thus, performance concerns, not space concerns, will most likely drive you to run SQL Server 7.0 on a member server.

When you upgrade to the full version of SQL Server 7.0, your existing SQL Server users, databases, tables, and information are preserved. To upgrade to the full version of SQL Server 7.0, follow these steps:

1. Log on to your SBS server machine as an administrator or member of the Administrators group.

2. Insert your SQL Server 7.0 CD-ROM in the CD-ROM drive of the SBS server machine.

3. Run setup.bat from the root directory of the SQL Server CD-ROM (for example, D:\setup.bat). The Microsoft SQL Server 7.0 setup wizard launches, as seen in Figure 21.5. Accept Local Install (the default selection). Click Next.

**FIGURE 21.5**

*Microsoft SQL Server
7.0 setup wizard.*

4. Type the 10-digit CD Key. Click OK.

5. You are asked to confirm the 10-digit CD Key you just entered. Click OK.

6. You are asked whether you want to upgrade the Small Business Server Edition to the Standard Edition of Microsoft SQL Server 7.0, as seen in Figure 21.6. Click Yes.

**FIGURE 21.6**

*Upgrade from SBS to
Standard Version.*

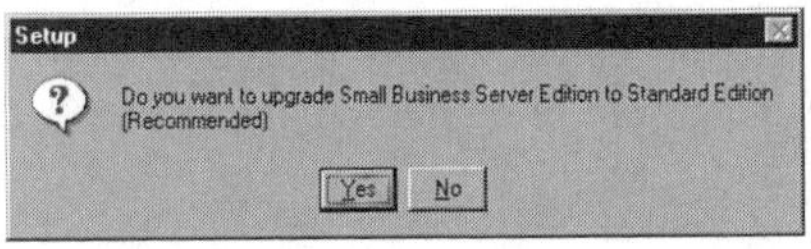

7. The Microsoft SQL Server 7.0 upgrade process runs automatically. When it's completed, you see the Setup Complete dialog box shown in Figure 21.7. Click Finish.

**FIGURE 21.7**

*Setup Complete.*

Congratulations. You have now upgraded to the full version of Microsoft SQL Server 7.0.

**21**

## Exchange

The three primary reasons to upgrade to the full version of Exchange are user limit, geography, and performance:

- User limit—Do you have more than 50 users operating Exchange concurrently? If so, an upgrade to the full version of Exchange might be warranted.

- Geography—Do you have a new branch office? If so, the full version of Exchange is much better equipped to handle multiple sites. For example, the full version of Exchange allows separate Exchange servers to operate as one site. That means your users, regardless of their office, can take advantage of the same Distribution Lists (DLs), which are a popular function in Exchange environments.

- Performance—Exchange is a beast. It's common to see a small business seek out performance enhancing options such as putting Microsoft Exchange on a bona fide member server, as that business's interest in Internet e-mail, public folders, scheduling, and contacts grows.

When you upgrade to the full version of Microsoft Exchange Server 5.5, you retain your information store containing user names, e-mail, and public folders. And that's a good thing. Could you imagine performing this upgrade and losing everything? That would be a disaster.

To upgrade to the full version of Microsoft Exchange Server 5.5

1. Log on to your SBS server machine as an administrator or member of the Administrators group.

2. Insert your Microsoft Exchange Server 5.5 CD-ROM in the CD-ROM drive of the SBS server machine.

3. Run the launch.exe file found in the root of the Microsoft Exchange Server CD-ROM disc (for example, D:\launch.exe). You see the setup screen displayed in Figure 21.8.

4. Select the Setup Server and Components option.

5. The Choose To Install screen, seen in Figure 21.9, is displayed. Select Microsoft Exchange Server 5.5.

6. The Microsoft Exchange Server Setup screen appears, as seen in Figure 21.10. Select the Add/Remove button.

7. The Microsoft Exchange Server Setup - Complete/Custom dialog box is displayed as seen in Figure 21.11. Select all available options (especially the Books Online option, which is excellent!). Click Continue.

FIGURE 21.8

*Microsoft Exchange Server 5.5 setup.*

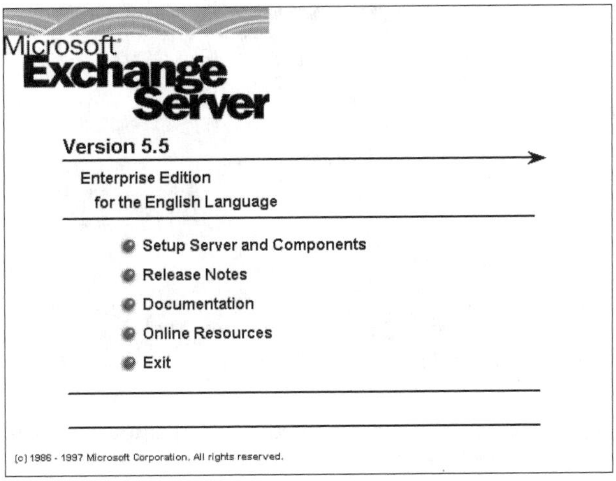

Microsoft®
**Exchange Server**

**Version 5.5**

Enterprise Edition
for the English Language

- Setup Server and Components
- Release Notes
- Documentation
- Online Resources
- Exit

(c) 1986 - 1997 Microsoft Corporation. All rights reserved.

FIGURE 21.9

*Choose To Install.*

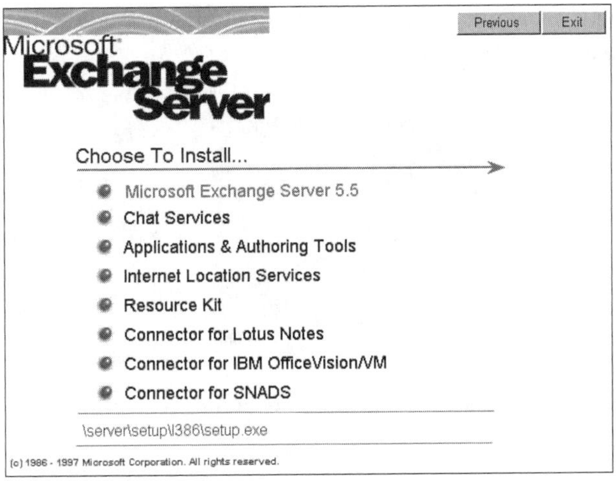

Microsoft®
**Exchange Server**

Choose To Install...

- Microsoft Exchange Server 5.5
- Chat Services
- Applications & Authoring Tools
- Internet Location Services
- Resource Kit
- Connector for Lotus Notes
- Connector for IBM OfficeVision/VM
- Connector for SNADS

\server\setup\I386\setup.exe

(c) 1986 - 1997 Microsoft Corporation. All rights reserved.

Previous | Exit

FIGURE 21.10

*Microsoft Exchange Server Setup.*

Microsoft Exchange Server Setup

Welcome to the Microsoft Exchange Server Setup program.

This program allows you to make changes to your current installation of Microsoft Exchange Server. Please select one of the following options:

Add/Remove... — Add new components or remove installed components from your current installation.

Reinstall — Repeat last installation, restoring missing files and settings.

Remove All — Remove all previously installed components.

Exit Setup

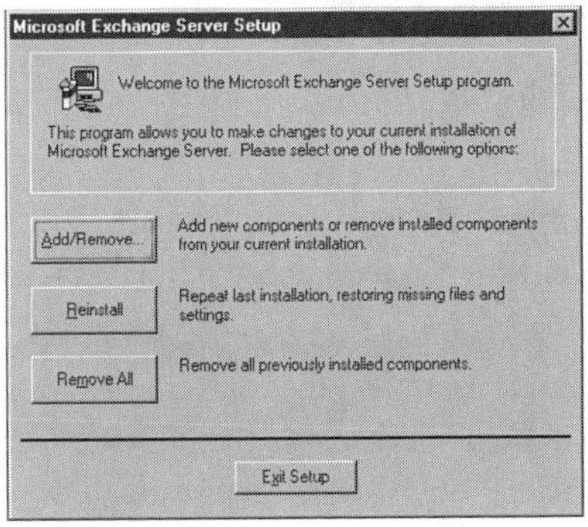

**21**

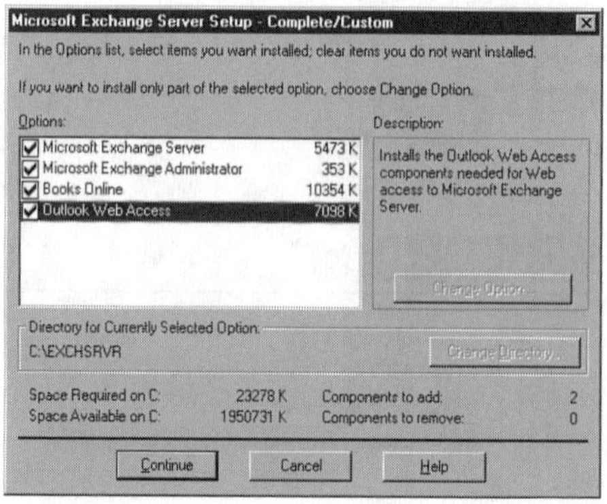

**FIGURE 21.11**

*Microsoft Exchange Server Setup - Complete/Custom.*

8. You receive a notice that the Internet Information Server services will be stopped temporarily. Click OK.

9. Microsoft Exchange Server 5.5 is automatically installed. When it's completed, you see the setup dialog box shown in Figure 21.12 that indicates the installation is complete. Click OK.

**FIGURE 21.12**

*Installation is complete.*

You have now successfully installed the complete version of Microsoft Exchange Server 5.5.

# Seven-Course Approach

You can also consider the full upgrade to Big BackOffice. There are several issues to consider with this strategy:

- Licensing—Believe it or not, the most complex part of the upgrade is maintaining your license compliance. Refer to the Paperwork section earlier for guidance.

- SBS functionality—The two features unique to SBS 4.5 that Big BackOffice doesn't natively provide—modem sharing and the fax server—are still usable after a full upgrade! That's a special treat because, via the upgrade from SBS 4.5 to Big BackOffice, you'll ultimately enjoy more features than those who only purchase and install Big BackOffice. (The modem sharing and fax server features remain fixed for modems total, exactly like SBS 4.5.)

- Performing the upgrade—The actual upgrade is very easy. Simply commence the setup process by launching the setup.exe file on the first CD-ROM of Microsoft BackOffice Server 4.5. The Setup Wizard walks you through the remainder of the process.

# It's a One-Way Trip

Be advised that the upgrade from SBS 4.5 to Big BackOffice is a one-way trip. It is easy to upgrade from an SBS site to Microsoft BackOffice Server 4.5, but it isn't possible to downgrade from Big BackOffice to SBS 4.5. Hey, in this era of downsizing, it's a legitimate question. If you actually need to go from Big BackOffice to SBS 4.5, you need to FDISK or reformat the hard disk on your server and install SBS 4.5. If you were ever going to do that, make sure you have at least two verified backups of your Big BackOffice installation and data.

# Summary

The upgrade from SBS 4.5 to Big BackOffice is easy, and it has been a tremendous advantage to me in the marketing of SBS 4.5 to have this upgrade path available. That's because firms on the cusp of SBS 4.5 are fully aware that a relatively cost-effective and easy exit strategy (upgrade to Big BackOffice) exists. The most difficult thing you'll encounter in the upgrade process is understanding the licensing ramifications. Not bad!

With that, we reach the end of our 21 days together discovering the magic of SBS. You're now a bona fide SBS user. I wish you the very SBeSt (get it?). Bye for now.

21

# PART IV

# Appendixes

A

B

C

D

E

# APPENDIX A

# SBS Resources

This appendix comprises numerous SBS resources that not only allow you to get the most from your existing SBS network but also allow you to stay current with SBS developments. The six resource categories are the Web, newsletters, newsgroups, E-mail distribution lists, periodicals, and general resources.

## Web

### www.smallbizserver.com

This Web site is dedicated to SBS and is the strongest, non-Microsoft SBS site I've found. Not only are solutions posted to common SBS problems, but there are helpful links to other SBS-related resources. You should bookmark this as an SBS favorite.

### www.microsoft.com/directaccess

This site, host by Microsoft, is updated frequently with SBS-related information. This site includes a small business sales center page with numerous SBS resources, including a regular column that frequently discusses SBS.

| |
|---|
| This page is primarily intended for resellers and consultants, but normal SBSers can benefit by frequently visiting this site. |

### www.winntmag.com

This site, dedicated primarily to Windows NT Server, offers a surprisingly healthy dose of SBS-related information. There is a regular column written for small businesses that often discusses SBS.

### www.zdnet.com/smallbusiness

This site, hosted by Ziff-Davis, discusses an array of small business issues from management to SBS. It's worthy because of its broad scope.

### www.worldowindows.com

This general Windows NT Server Web site has a special section on SBS. It also features individual BackOffice components that compose SBS. I find its third-party independent view to be refreshing.

### www.mcp.com

This is the Web site for Macmillan Computer Publishing, the publisher of this book. Not only can you monitor updates to this book, but you can find other SBS and Windows NT Server–related resources here.

# Newsletters

There are no easily found newsletters dedicated to SBS. *Windows NT Magazine* at one time published a monthly SBS newsletter, but that was discontinued in late 1998. The best small business newsletter that discusses SBS that I have found is *Small Business Advisor* from ZDNet (www.zdnet.com/smallbusiness).

# Newsgroups

I know of two active SBS-related newsgroups.

## Microsoft's SBS Newsgroup

This is a very active newsgroup that is monitored by Microsoft Most Valuable Players (MVPs) who are available to answer your questions. Simply point your newsgroup reader to microsoft.public.backoffice.smallbiz, and join in.

## www.smallbizserver.com

This Web site, mentioned above, has a Web board that offers an SBS newsgroup and chat room.

# E-Mail Distribution Lists

The very best SBS e-mail distribution list is managed by Grey Lancaster. To subscribe to the SBS list, send an e-mail addressed to sbs-request@dmvc.k12.sc.us. In the body of your message type the word **subscribe**. To leave, follow the same instructions but put **leave** in the body of the message. To send messages to members of the list server, address them to sbs@dmvc.k12.sc.us.

# Periodicals

In the absence of a specific SBS magazine, I've found SBS articles in the following magazines over the past two years:

- *Microsoft Certified Professional Magazine*
- *Business Week*
- *Windows NT Magazine*
- *PC World*
- *Windows Magazine*
- *InfoWorld*
- *Success*
- *Inc.*
- *Fast Company*
- *Fortune*

# General Resources

There are a variety of SBS resources at your fingertips whether you know it or not. These range from friends to broad Internet searches.

## Vendors

Don't overlook searching vendor Web sites such as Dell (www.dell.com) or Compaq (www.compaq.com). Both sites contain SBS-specific information.

## Resellers/VARs/Consultants

Check your local telephone book for yellow page listings for resellers, VARs, or consultants who specifically support SBS. Look for the term *SBS* in their ads.

## User Groups

Consider joining a general Windows NT Server or Microsoft BackOffice user group. One such group, the BackOffice Professionals Association (BOPA), can be reached at `www.bopa.org`.

## Search Engines

One way that I stay current is to search Infoseek (`www.infoseek.com`), Yahoo (`www.yahoo.com`), or Dogpile (`www.dogpile.com`) for SBS information. Just search on the term *SBS*.

## Users

Don't forget that your SBS users are one of your greatest resources for learning. It's a lesson I'm constantly reminded of.

## Peers

Like medical professionals, maintain those peer relationships so that you can periodically check in with your buddies when you need SBS-related help. Such a peer relationship might be a fellow SBS administrator at another company.

## Microsoft TechNet

I've mentioned this resource, a monthly CD-ROM library mailing from Microsoft, several times in the book. For $300 a year, you can subscribe to TechNet. This subscription is a monthly mailing that includes the TechNet knowledge base CD-ROM (full of guides, manuals, and product support articles), drivers (full of updated drivers from Microsoft), and service packs (the latest service packs from Microsoft). You can purchase TechNet from your reseller or from Microsoft (`www.microsoft.com`).

# APPENDIX B

# HCL

The SBS 4.5 HCL is a subset of the full Windows NT server 4.0 HCL. Microsoft has tested these components (network adapter cards, modems, and multiport adapter boards) to work with SBS. You should note with interest that SBS 4.5 supports much more hardware and does a better job of it than SBS 4.0/4.0a did.

**Note**

The HCL changes on a regular basis to reflect updated hardware offerings, device drivers, and discontinued products (modems and adapters). You should check the HCL on a regular basis if you're an SBS consultant. If you're an SBS administrator at an SBS site, realistically you need to check the HCL only when you want to add new hardware to your SBS server machine. The updated HCL is maintained at www.microsoft.com/backofficesmallbiz.

# Network Adapter Cards

Network adapter cards are required for network use. Cards that you use with server computers are listed in this section. Cards that you use with client computers must appear on the Hardware Compatibility List for the specific operating system, such as the Windows 95 or Windows NT Workstation Hardware Compatibility Lists.

At the time this book went to press, the following network adapter cards were tested and approved for use with Small Business Server:

- 3Com 3C509 EtherLink III Parallel Tasking Adapter—ISA (Coax, TP and Combo)
- 3Com 3C905 Fast EtherLink XL Adapter
- COMPAQ NetFlex-3/P
- DEC DE434 PCI Ethernet Adapter
- DEC DE500 Fast Ethernet Adapter
- Hewlett-Packard J3171A 10/100TX PCI Ethernet Adapter
- Intel EtherExpress PRO/10 ISA
- Intel EtherExpress PRO/10+ ISA
- Intel EtherExpress PRO/10 PCI LAN Adapter
- Intel EtherExpress PRO/100B PCI LAN Adapter
- Novell/Eagle Technology NE3200

The following network adapter cards are from the Windows NT Server Hardware Compatibility list. I expect these cards to be automatically detected during Small Business Server 4.5 setup and to work satisfactorily:

- 3Com 3C503 EtherLink II (Coax & TP)
- 3Com 3C503/16 EtherLink II/16 (Coax & TP)
- 3Com 3C507 EtherLink 16 (Coax & TP)
- 3Com 3C509B EtherLink III Parallel Tasking Adapter—ISA (Coax, TP and Combo)
- 3Com 3C523 EtherLink/MC (Coax & TP)
- 3Com 3C527 EtherLink/MC 32 Bus Mastering Adapter
- 3Com 3C529 EtherLink III Parallel Tasking Adapter—MCA (Coax & TP)
- 3Com 3C579 EtherLink III Parallel Tasking Adapter—EISA (Coax & TP)
- 3Com 3C590 EtherLink III PCI Bus-Master Adapter
- 3Com 3C592 EtherLink III EISA Bus-Master Adapter

B

- 3Com 3C597 EtherLink III EISA Bus-Master Adapter
- 3Com 3C770 FDDILink-F for Optical, UTP & STP
- Accton EN166X MPXII Ethernet Adapter
- Advanced Micro Devices PCnet Family Adapters
- Advanced Micro Devices PCnet-ISA+ Ethernet Adapter
- Advanced Micro Devices PCnet-32 VL Ethernet Adapter
- Advanced Micro Devices PCnet-PCI Ethernet Adapter
- Allied Telesyn AT1720 Series Ethernet Adapter
- Allied Telesyn AT2450 Ethernet Adapter
- Allied Telesyn AT2560 Series PCI/100 Ethernet Adapter
- Cabletron F30XX FDDI Adapter
- Cabletron F70XX FDDI Adapter
- Cogent eMASTER+ 960 PCI Ethernet Adapter
- COMPAQ 32-Bit Netflex Controller
- COMPAQ Ethernet 16TP Controller
- COMPAQ Integrated NetFlex-3
- COMPAQ Integrated Netelligent
- COMPAQ Netelligent 10/100 TX PCI UTP Adapter
- COMPAQ Netelligent 10 T PCI UTP Adapter
- COMPAQ NetFlex-2 ENET-TR Controller
- COMPAQ NetFlex-2 TR Controller
- COMPAQ NetFlex-2 DualPort TR Controller
- COMPAQ NetFlex-2 DualPort ENET Controller
- COMPAQ NetFlex-3/E
- COPS LTI ISA
- DayStar Digital LocalTalk Adapter
- DEC DE100 EtherWORKS LC
- DEC DE101 EtherWORKS LC/TP
- DEC DE200 EtherWORKS Turbo
- DEC DE201 EtherWORKS Turbo/TP
- DEC DE202 EtherWORKS Turbo TP/BNC
- DEC DE422 EtherWORKS EISA TP/BNC

- DEC DE435 PCI Ethernet Adapter
- DEC DE450-CA EtherWORKS Turbo PCI
- DEC DC21040 PCI Ethernet Controller
- DEC FDDIcontroller/EISA(incl. CDDI)
- DEC FDDIcontroller/PCI(incl. CDDI)
- Fujitsu ICL EtherTeam ISA Ethernet Network Adapter
- Fujitsu ICL EtherTeam PCI Ethernet Network Adapter
- Hewlett-Packard HP J2577A 10/100VG EISA LAN Adapter
- Hewlett-Packard HP 27246A MC LAN Adapter/16 TP
- IBM 100/10 PCI Ethernet Adapter
- IBM Auto LANStreamer™ MC 32 Adapter
- IBM Ethernet Quad PeerMaster Adapter
- IBM EtherStreamer MC 32 Adapter
- IBM ISA Ethernet Adapter
- IBM LAN Adapter/A for Ethernet
- IBM LANStreamer MC 32 Adapter
- ICL EtherTeam32 EISA Adapter
- Intel 82595 Ethernet Adapter
- Intel EtherExpress™ 16 MCA
- Intel EtherExpress 16 PCLA8110
- Intel EtherExpress 16C PCLA8100
- Intel EtherExpress 16TP PCLA8120
- Intel EtherExpress FlashC PCLA8105
- Intel EtherExpress Flash32 EISA LAN Adapter
- Linksys Ether16 LAN Card
- Linksys EtherPCI LAN Card
- Microdyne NE100 PCI Adapter
- NCR WaveLAN/MC
- Network Peripherals NP-EISA/S FDDI
- Network Peripherals NP-MCA/S FDDI
- Network Peripherals NuCard PCI FDDI
- Novell/Eagle Technology NE1000

- Novell/Eagle Technology NE2000
- Olicom Ethernet PCI/II 10/100, OC-2325
- Olicom Ethernet PCI/II 10 Adapter, OC-2185
- Racal InterLan ES3210
- Realtek RTL8029 PCI Ethernet Adapter
- RNS 2200 PCI FDDI LAN Controller
- Standard Microsystems 8013EBT EtherCard™ PLUS16
- Standard Microsystems 8013EP EtherCard PLUS Elite16
- Standard Microsystems 8013EP/A EtherCard PLUS Elite/A
- Standard Microsystems 8013EPC EtherCard PLUS Elite16
- Standard Microsystems 8013EW EtherCard PLUS EliteCombo
- Standard Microsystems 8013EWC EtherCard PLUS EliteCombo
- Standard Microsystems 8013W EtherCard PLUS Elite16T
- Standard Microsystems 8013WB EtherCard PLUS
- Standard Microsystems 8013WC EtherCard PLUS Elite16T
- Standard Microsystems 8013WP/A EtherCard PLUS Elite10T/A
- Standard Microsystems 8232 EtherCard Elite 32 Ultra
- Standard Microsystems 8432BT EtherPower PCI LAN Adapter
- Standard Microsystems 8432T EtherPower PCI LAN Adapter
- Standard Microsystems 8434 EtherPower2 PCI Adapter
- Standard Microsystems 9332DST EtherPower 10/100 PCI LAN Adapter
- SVEC FD0421P EtherPlug-ISA Adapter
- SVEC FDO455P EtherBoard-PCI Adapter
- SysKonnect SK-52xx MCA-bus FDDI Adapter
- SysKonnect SK-53xx EISA-bus FDDI Adapter
- SysKonnect SK-NET FDDI PCI Adapter
- SysKonnect SK-NET Flash (Coax and TP)
- SysKonnect SK-NET G32+ EISA Ethernet Adapter
- Tulip Computer NCC-16 PNP Adapter
- Ungermann-Bass NIUpc
- Ungermann-Bass NIUpc/EOTP
- Ungermann-Bass NIUps/EOTP

B

# Modems

A fax modem is required for Small Business Server installation. Several Small Business Server components (Fax Service, Remote Access Service, Proxy Server, and the Internet Connection Wizard) rely on the existence of a *class 1* fax modem.

In order to use the same modem for both incoming faxes or dial-up networking calls, you must use a modem from the following list:

- Diamond SupraSonic 336V+
- Diamond Supra FAX Modem 288 external
- Hayes Accura External 288 V.FC+FAX (Model 5205AM)
- Hayes Optima External 288 V.34/V.FC+fax+Voice*
- US Robotics Courier v.Everything external
- US Robotics Courier v.Everything internal
- US Robotics Sportster 33600 external
- US Robotics Sportster 33600 internal

# Multiport Serial Adapter Boards

The following multiport serial adapter boards have been tested with the Small Business Server Modem Sharing Service:

- Digiboard 8em (ISA 8 ports)
- Digiboard 16em (ISA 16 ports)
- Digiboard 8em (PCI 8 ports)
- Digiboard 16em (PCI 16 ports)
- Digiboard AccelePort 4r—ISA (4 ports)
- Digiboard AccelePort 8r—ISA (8 ports)
- Digiboard AccelePort 4r—PCI (4 ports)
- Digiboard AccelePort 8r—PCI (8 ports)
- Digiboard C/X (ISA 16 ports)
- Digiboard PC/8e (ISA 8 ports)
- Digiboard EPC/X (EISA 16 ports)

# APPENDIX C

# SBS Project Kit

The goals for Appendix C are both to give you some working papers for use with your own SBS project and to direct your attention to the Appendix C folder on the CD-ROM that accompanies this book for even more valuable resources.

First comes the hard copy presented in the following pages. I've printed the most important working papers that you can freely use for your own SBS project planning efforts. The working papers include the following:

- Early SBS Planning Questions
- SBS Stakeholders
- Hardware/Software/Service Provider List
- Existing User List
- SBS Server Setup Sheet
- SBS Workstation Setup Sheet
- Basic SBS Proposal
- SBS Checklist
- Project Budget versus Actual Variance Reporting
- Organizational Chart

- Sample Site Visit Letter
- Daily/Weekly and Monthly/Annual Checklists

Second comes the Appendix C folder on the CD-ROM that accompanies this book and contains additional resources that I've referenced during the course of this book. These additional resources include the following files:

- SSUEIS.XLS
- Default.htm
- SSU Project Update.ppt
- Completed Early SBS Planning Questions.doc
- SSU SBS Proposal.doc

All told, Appendix C, composed of both the printouts below and the materials on the CD-ROM, is your comprehensive SBS project kit for completing the 21-day journey herein and the real-world SBS projects in which you're likely to participate. Whatever the reasoning, use these SBS working papers often to ensure the greatest likelihood of success.

# Early SBS Planning Questions

| Question | Answer |
|---|---|
| 1. List the three reasons that you intend to use SBS. | |
| 2. What is the time frame for implementing SBS? | |
| 3. What roadblocks or problems can you identify today that might make the SBS project more difficult to complete? | |
| 4. How have you arranged for training for the new SBS network? | |

# SBS Stakeholders

| Name | Role | Contact Information |
|------|------|---------------------|
|      |      |                     |
|      |      |                     |
|      |      |                     |
|      |      |                     |

# Hardware/Software/Service Provider List

| Item | Description | Cost |
|------|-------------|------|
| Hardware |         |      |
| Software |         |      |
| Services |         |      |

C

# Existing User List

| |
|---|
| First: |
| Last: |
| User Name: |
| Password: |
| Job Title: |
| Department: |

| |
|---|
| First: |
| Last: |
| User Name: |
| Password: |
| Job Title: |
| Department: |

| |
|---|
| First: |
| Last: |
| User Name: |
| Password: |
| Job Title: |
| Department: |

| |
|---|
| First: |
| Last: |
| User Name: |
| Password: |
| Job Title: |
| Department: |

| |
|---|
| First: |
| Last: |
| User Name: |
| Password: |
| Job Title: |
| Department: |

# SBS Server Setup Sheet

| Item | Description | Completed |
|---|---|---|
| Server Name | | |
| Domain Name | | |
| Initial SBS Registration Name | | |
| Organization | | |
| Area Code | | |
| Dial Outside Number | | |
| Tone Dialing | | |
| Address | | |
| City | | |
| State/Province | | |
| Zip | | |
| Country | | |
| Business Telephone | | |
| Business Fax | | |
| Initial Administrator Password | | |
| Hard disk partitions | | |
| Time Zone | | |
| User Accounts | | |
| Printers | | |
| Registry | | |
| Folders | | |
| Shares | | |
| Misc. | | |

C

# SBS Workstation Setup Sheet

| Setup Field | Input/Value/Description | Where Used |
|---|---|---|
| User's Full Name (First, Last) | | Add a User (User Account Wizard) |
| User's Account Name (20-character limit) | | Add a User |
| Description for User | | Add a User |
| Password | | Add a User |
| Title (Job Title) | | Add a User |
| Company | | Add a User |
| Department | | Add a User |
| Office | | Add a User |
| Assistant | | Add a User |
| Phone | | Add a User |
| Address | | Add a User |
| City | | Add a User |
| State | | Add a User |
| ZIP Code | | Add a User |
| Country | | Add a User |
| Business telephone | | Add a User |
| Business 2 telephone | | Add a User |
| Fax telephone | | Add a User |
| Assistant telephone | | Add a User |
| Home telephone | | Add a User |
| Home 2 telephone | | Add a User |
| Mobile telephone | | Add a User |
| Pager telephone | | Add a User |
| E-Mail Distribution List (the default entry is the same name as the SBS network Domain name: for example, SPRINGERS) | | Add a User |
| Shared Folders: (R)ead, (E)dit, (D)elete Permissions | | Add a User |

*continues*

*continued*

| Setup Field | Input/Value/Description | Where Used |
|---|---|---|
| Shared Folders: (R)ead Permission | | Add a User |
| Shared Printer | | Add a User |
| Shared Fax Printer | | Add a User |
| Access the Internet? (Y/N) | | Add a User |
| Use a modem to access the server computer? (Y/N) | | Add a User |
| Administrative Privileges (Y/N) | | Add a User |
| Workstation NetBIOS name | | Set Up A Computer ("Set Up Computer Wizard") |
| Operating System: Windows 95 or Windows NT 4.0 Workstation (for Windows 98, select Windows 95) | | Set Up A Computer |
| SBS Programs to Install None, Complete *or:* ☐ Microsoft Fax Client ☐ Microsoft Internet Explorer ☐ Microsoft Modem Sharing Client ☐ Microsoft Outlook E-mail Client ☐ Microsoft Proxy Client ☐ Microsoft Office 2000 (optional) | | Set Up A Computer |
| Verify available workstation hard disk space based on SBS Programs to install listed immediately above (for example, 98 MB required) | | Set Up A Computer |
| Network Protocols | | Misc. |
| IP Address (Static or Dynamic) | | Misc. |
| Mapped Drives | | Misc. |
| Workstation Shares (shares on workstation) | | Misc. |
| Additional Applications to install (for example, Great Plains Dynamics accounting): | | Misc. |
| Special configuration issues | | Misc. |
| Comments | | Misc. |
| Tested Logon (Y/N) | | Misc. |
| Repairs/Reconfiguration Needed | | Misc. |

C

# Basic SBS Proposal

*DATE*

*NAME*

RE: Small Business Server Computer Proposal

Dear *NAME*,

We are submitting our proposal for implementing Small Business Server (SBS). We have very much enjoyed learning about **CLIENT NAME** over the past several months as part of our effort to assist you in implementing an SBS solution. Likewise, we're hopeful that you have benefited from learning more about us as well. It is in that spirit that we are presenting this SBS proposal. Our SBS methodology consists of five phases that are detailed below. The total costs for the work that we have defined below as Phase A - E is $*COST*.

# Project Phases A - E

## Phase A: Pre-Project Planning

**Estimated Phase A costs = $2,500**

**Timeline:** These hours are typically billed over 5 to 10 business days.

This work includes meeting with the client to review our engagement letter; making a final assessment of your needs; reviewing our project checklist; confirming the placement of the workstations and server; discussing infrastructure matters such as wiring, hardware, software orders, service orders (Telco, Internet service), and so on. The key client contact is identified, and issues such as building access are resolved. Our SBS workstation specialist will perform a walkthrough of the site with the key client contact. Finally, installation issues (such as machine names, domain names, user names, drive mappings, and so on) are resolved.

## Phase B: Server Build

**Phase B costs = $3,000**

**Timeline:** This work is typically performed over several business days commencing at the end of Phase A.

This includes setup of the server and installation and optimization of SBS so that, at the end of this phase, Springer Spaniels Unlimited has a functional file server that performs the following functions/roles: file server, print server, internal e-mail, and tape backups (including the installation of third party backup applications such as Backup Exec). The network printer(s) is/are installed at this phase as well as the user names and machine names are added to the SBS server console. User security is implemented. An emergency repair disk is created.

**Phase B does not include the following:**

- Installation of external Internet e-mail, remote access, or faxing services at the stage. This is accomplished in Phase D over a period of a few weeks.
- Migration of data from the existing server.
- Installation or configuration of additional servers.
- *ADDITIONS*

   **Important:** We will attempt to install Microsoft Small Business Server and a third-party tape backup application up to two times as part of the work defined in Phase B. Any additional installation attempts beyond two attempts will be billed as "Additional Services" at $125 per hour with your prior approval.

# Phase C: Workstation Build

**Phase C costs = $2,000**

**Timeline:** This work is typically performed over a 7 to 10-day period commencing at the end of Phase B.

This work includes the physical installation and SBS client setup of each workstation (client operating system, printers, modem sharing client, proxy client, faxing client, Microsoft Outlook, Microsoft Internet Explorer, and so on). The SBS workstation specialist dedicates up to one hour per user for answering user questions, providing basic SBS functionality training on a one-on-one basis, and so on. Additional time spent beyond this one hour assisting users during Phase C is charged as "Additional Services" at $80 per hour.

**Phase C does not include the following:**

- Installation/troubleshooting of user specific applications (for example, TimeSlips).
- Migration of user data.
- *ADDITIONS*

   **Important:** We will make up to two attempts to install the SBS client components on a workstation. Additional SBS client component installation attempts will be billed as "Additional Services."

## Phase D: Weekly Follow-ups

**Phase D costs = $2,500**

**Timeline:** Up to one day per week for five weeks following Phase C.

Each week, starting with the first week after Phase C is completed, we visit to install a new feature of SBS and provide ongoing support and user training. This work includes up to one full day per weekly visit. We suggest the following schedule:

- **Week One:** Internet E-mail via Microsoft Exchange (including modem pool turn up). Basic Outlook functionality. Proxy Server (firewall) will be configured.
- **Week Two:** Remote Access. You will note that we strongly recommend pcAnywhere. We no longer support Microsoft's inbound RAS capabilities. If we are asked to implement and support the inbound capabilities of RAS, we will bill this time as "Additional Services" at $80/hour.
- **Week Three:** Faxing, Inbound and Outbound.
- **Week Four:** Advanced Outlook Training for Users and Implementation of Advanced Outlook Features such as shared calendars, shared contacts, public folders, and so on.
- **Week Five:** To be determined WWW Page, Troubleshooting, and Internet Development. We typically hand off network administration duties to in-house staff at this point.

Note that these weekly visits typically include the ordinary and necessary resolution/troubleshooting of end user problems, network problems, and so on. We also encourage users to ask questions during each weekly visit so that they can better make use of the new SBS network.

## Phase E: End Of Project

**Phase E costs = $0**

This is a milestone wherein we typically recognize the discrete end of the SBS project and answer your final questions. This meeting typically takes the form of an end of project lunch.

We greatly look forward to working with you on your SBS computer project. We do not consider this proposal complete until we have had the chance to discuss the specific phases above with you and answer your questions.

With best regards.

Very truly yours,

# SBS Checklist

| SBS Methodology Customer Name: | | | |
|---|---|---|---|
| **Phases/Tasks** | **Date** | **Done** | **Comments** |
| **Phase A: Pre-Project Planning** | | | Worked performed over 10-business days |
| **I.) First Meeting** | | | |
| Review Meeting Agenda | | ☐ | |
| Review order of events—rough timeline | | ☐ | |
| Mention possible delays (HW/SW failures, 3rd party relations, and so on) | | ☐ | |
| Stress the importance of training and continuous learning. | | ☐ | |
| Check Infrastructure-existing equipment and cabling | | ☐ | |
| Hub | | ☐ | |
| Cabling | | ☐ | |
| Wall jacks | | ☐ | |
| Proposal written, delivered and discussed | | ☐ | |
| Network layout discussed and described | | ☐ | |
| TNG-SBS Checklist / Methodology discussed and revised as needed | | ☐ | |
| Write and deliver confirmation letters recounting meeting, telephone conversations | | ☐ | |
| Review engagement letter | | ☐ | |
| **Discrete Outcomes** | | | |
| Written Agenda | | ☐ | |
| Written Proposal | | ☐ | |
| Written Confirmation Letters detailing meeting content, telephone conversations | | ☐ | |
| Written SBS Checklist | | ☐ | |
| Written Project Schedule and Calendar | | ☐ | |

*continues*

*continued*

| Phases/Tasks | Date | Done | Comments |
|---|---|---|---|
| **Next Steps** | | | |
| Acceptance of proposal | | ☐ | |
| Receive signed engagement letter | | ☐ | |
| **II.) Second Meeting:** **Plan for Deployment** | | | |
| Specifically identify a point of contact for the project. | | ☐ | |
| Review estimated timeline | | ☐ | |
| Make yourself available by pager and voice and e-mail | | ☐ | |
| Offer written and/or verbal updates periodically | | ☐ | |
| Have the client order all services and equipment: | | ☐ | |
| Data Service ordered | | ☐ | |
| Make sure domain name move is underway if necessary | | ☐ | |
| All hardware ordered | | ☐ | |
| Order router from ISP if necessary | | ☐ | |
| All software ordered | | ☐ | |
| Confirm the correct number of SBS licenses are available | | ☐ | |
| Infrastructure (Ethernet jacks) ordered | | ☐ | |
| **Discrete Outcomes** | | | |
| Written Confirmation Letters detailing meeting content, telephone conversations | | ☐ | |
| Revised Project Schedule | | ☐ | |
| **Next Steps** | | | |
| Pre-Implementation Walkthrough | | ☐ | |

*continues*

*continued*

| Phases/Tasks | Date | Done | Comments |
|---|---|---|---|
| **III.) Pre-Implementation Walkthrough:** | | | |
| Building access | | ☐ | |
| All computer access (people off their machines for client installation) | | ☐ | |
| Assess training needs | | ☐ | |
| Outlook | | ☐ | |
| Win 95 | | ☐ | |
| Installation plan - Location Map, and so on | | ☐ | |
| Server | | ☐ | |
| Where will it sit? | | ☐ | |
| Who should be in the administrator's group? | | ☐ | |
| Clients | | ☐ | |
| Get a list of names of users with correct spelling | | ☐ | |
| Printers | | ☐ | |
| Routers & hubs | | ☐ | |
| Special circumstances | | ☐ | |
| **Discrete Outcomes** | | | |
| List of user names with correct spelling | | ☐ | |
| Location Map - Installation Map | | ☐ | |
| **Next Steps** | | | |
| Phase B: Server Installation | | ☐ | |

*continues*

**C**

*continued*

| Phases/Tasks | Date | Done | Comments |
|---|---|---|---|
| **Phase B: Server Installation** | | | Work performed over two or three business days |
| Physically unpack and construct server. | | ☐ | |
| Install SBS - Floppy, CD-ROM diskette installation | | ☐ | |
| Complete server installation information sheet (partitions, drive mappings, Dynamics modifications, passwords, and so on) | | ☐ | Dynamics: OppLocks, Btrieve, Create Subdirectory |
| Add SBS Licenses | | ☐ | |
| Add any server-based printers to the network | | ☐ | |
| Add users to network via SBS console | | ☐ | |
| Add workstations to network via SBS console | | ☐ | |
| Implement and verify Microsoft Exchange is working internally | | ☐ | |
| Begin a system log on the server | | ☐ | |
| Take note of any unusual circumstances | | ☐ | |
| Provide training on password security. | | ☐ | |
| Test tape backup/restore | | ☐ | |
| Implement tape backup policy | | ☐ | |
| Verify virus protection is working | | ☐ | |
| **Discrete Outcomes** | | | |
| Phase B Summary Report | | ☐ | |
| **Next Steps** | | | |
| Phase C: Workstation Installation | | ☐ | |

*continues*

*continued*

| Phases/Tasks | Date | Done | Comments |
|---|---|---|---|
| **Phase C: Workstation Installation** | | | Work performed over 5 to 10 business days |
| Physically unpack and construct workstations | ☐ | | |
| Complete installation of client operating system (win95/98) | ☐ | | |
| Create installation disk for each workstation | ☐ | | |
| Install SBS client components on each workstation | ☐ | | |
| Perform basic SBS client component tests, answer limited user questions, and so on | ☐ | | |
| Enable and demonstrate Network file sharing from client PCs | ☐ | | |
| Enable and demonstrate Network printing from client PCs | ☐ | | |
| Enable and demonstrate basic internal e-mail via Outlook | ☐ | | |
| Set a date to return to fully configure Outlook (calendar, contact list) | ☐ | | |
| Propose a date for Outlook training. | ☐ | | |
| **Discrete Outcomes** | | | |
| Phase C Summary Report | ☐ | | |
| Client completes mid-point Quality Survey (issued by Eileen Garcia) | ☐ | | |
| **Next Steps** | | | |
| Phase D: Weekly Visits | ☐ | | |

*continues*

C

*continued*

| Phases/Tasks | Date | Done | Comments |
|---|---|---|---|
| **Phase D: Weekly Visits** | | | Work performed over four to six weeks |
| **Week One: Outlook and Microsoft Exchange external Internet Connection** <br> Minimum criteria for proceeding with this phase: | | ☐ | |
|    Server installed and configured | | ☐ | |
|    Clients installed and configured | | ☐ | |
| Data transport service available from phone company(dialup, ISDN, T-1, etc...) | | ☐ | |
| ISP service available and ready to go with domain name in place | | ☐ | |
| Implement externally connectivity | | ☐ | |
| Configure Proxy and Exchange to use Outlook externally | | ☐ | |
| Configure and use Outlook externally and with Public Folders (contact lists, calendars) | | ☐ | |
| Verify external email and web browsing | | ☐ | |
| **Add'l Weeks** | | | |
| **Week Two: Remote Users** <br>    Implement pcAnywhere or RAS-based solution | | ☐ | |
|    Test remote user solution | | ☐ | |
|    Configure user machines for remote connectivity | | ☐ | |
|    Train users on remote connectivity | | ☐ | |

*continues*

*continued*

| | | | |
|---|---|---|---|
| **Week Three: Faxing** | | | |
| Implement inbound/outbound faxing services at server per client specifications | | ☐ | |
| Implement inbound/outbound faxing client configuration at user workstations | | ☐ | |
| **Week Four: Internet Development:** | | | |
| Install IIS 4.0 | | ☐ | |
| .asp pages | | ☐ | |
| internal web applications | | ☐ | |
| Encrypted e-mail? | | ☐ | |
| **Week Five: Network Administration Wrap Up/Punch List** | | | |
| Test backups | | ☐ | |
| Check security | | ☐ | |
| Apply OS fixes & upgrades | | ☐ | |
| Resolve configuration issues: printers, modems, SBS clients, etc… | | ☐ | |
| **Week Six and forward: Other work as agreed** | | | |
| **Discrete Outcomes** | | | |
| Weekly Activity/Summary Report | | ☐ | |
| Daily Site Visit Reports | | ☐ | |
| **Next Steps** | | | |
| Phase E: Project Completion | | ☐ | |

C

*continues*

*continued*

| Phases/Tasks | Date | Done | Comments |
|---|---|---|---|
| **Phase E: Project Completion** | | | No billable time associated with this phase. |
| Client/Consultant lunch, and so on to celebrate and review project | | ☐ | |
| **Discrete Outcomes** | | | |
| Client completes mid-point Quality Survey (issued by Eileen Garcia) | | ☐ | |
| **Next Steps** | | | |
| Additional work performed on an as-needed and by request basis. | | ☐ | |

## Reporting Percentage Completion Analysis from the *Project Budget versus Actual Variance Table*

| Percentage Completion Analysis | |
|---|---|
| Enter % Project Complete | 0.9 |
| Original Budget Hours Should Be: | 81.9 |
| Current Budget Hours Should Be: | 81.9 |
| Actual Hours Should Be: | 51.5 |
| Original Budget Costs Should Be: | 7240.5 |
| Current Budget Costs Should Be: | 7240.5 |
| Actual Costs Should Be: | 4738.75 |

# Project Budget versus Actual Variance Reporting

**PHASE A - Hours**

*Client* Springer Spaniels Unlimited

| Worker Bee | Original Budget | Current Budget | Actual Budget |
|---|---|---|---|
| Harry ($125/hour) | 2 | 2 | 2 |
| Steve ($80/hour) | 5 | 5 | 7.5 |
| Total | 7 | 7 | 9.5 |

**PHASE A - Costs**

| | Original Budget | Current Budget | Actual Budget |
|---|---|---|---|
| | 250 | 250 | 250 |
| | 400 | 400 | 600 |
| | 650 | 650 | 850 |

**PHASE B - Hours**

| Worker Bee | Original Budget | Current Budget | Actual Budget |
|---|---|---|---|
| Harry ($125/hour) | 10 | 10 | 3.75 |
| Steve ($80/hour) | 0 | 0 | 8.25 |
| Total | 10 | 10 | 12 |

**PHASE B - Costs**

| | Original Budget | Current Budget | Actual Budget |
|---|---|---|---|
| | 1250 | 1250 | 468.75 |
| | 0 | 0 | 660 |
| | 1250 | 1250 | 1128.75 |

**PHASE C - Hours**

| Worker Bee | Original Budget | Current Budget | Actual Budget |
|---|---|---|---|
| Harry ($125/hour) | 0 | 0 | 2 |
| Steve ($80/hour) | 45 | 45 | 22 |
| Total | 45 | 45 | 24 |

**PHASE C - Costs**

| | Original Budget | Current Budget | Actual Budget |
|---|---|---|---|
| | 0 | 0 | 250 |
| | 3600 | 3600 | 1760 |
| | 3600 | 3600 | 2010 |

**PHASE D - Hours**

| Worker Bee | Original Budget | Current Budget | Actual Budget |
|---|---|---|---|
| Harry ($125/hour) | 5 | 5 | 6 |
| Steve ($80/hour) | 24 | 24 | 0 |
| Total | 29 | 29 | 6 |

**PHASE D - Costs**

| | Original Budget | Current Budget | Actual Budget |
|---|---|---|---|
| | 625 | 625 | 750 |
| | 1920 | 1920 | 0 |
| | 2545 | 2545 | 750 |

**PROJECT GRAND TOTAL– HOURS (TO-DATE)**

| Worker Bee | Original Budget | Current Budget | Actual Budget |
|---|---|---|---|
| Harry ($125/hour) | 17 | 17 | 13.75 |
| Steve ($80/hour) | 74 | 74 | 37.75 |
| Total | 91 | 91 | 51.5 |

**PROJECT GRAND TOTAL– COSTS (TO-DATE)**

| | Original Budget | Current Budget | Actual Budget |
|---|---|---|---|
| | 2125 | 2125 | 1718.75 |
| | 5920 | 5920 | 3020 |
| | 8045 | 8045 | 4738.75 |

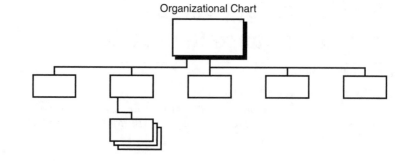

**Figure C.1**

*Organizational Chart*

# Existing Infrastructure

| Item | Condition/Notes |
|------|-----------------|
| Cabling | |
| Hubs | |
| Wall Jacks | |

# Sample Site Visit Letter

August 14, 1998

***CLIENT***

RE: Work Performed August 10, 1998

Dear *NAME*,

This letter will serve as our site visit report for the work performed by the undersigned on your behalf.

On August 10, we performed the following:

1. Updated our checklists and project schedule and discussed the project internally with Steve and Vernon.

2. Accepted a support telephone call from you wherein we provided extensive guidance with respect to the Paradox database. At our request, you modified the properties for the Paradox application shortcut icon so that the shortcut icon pointed to the proper application and working directory.

3. Directed your efforts to add everyone to the Administrators group so that we could efficiently resolve a Great Plains Dynamics security authentication issue.

For this work, we billed the following:

- For item #1 we billed one ("1") hour at $125/hour to Phase B of the project.
- For item #2 we billed 0.5 hours at $125 per hour to "Additional Services" for the project.
- For items #3 we billed three hours ("3") to "Additional Services" and one hour ("1") billed to Phase B of the project.

If your understanding of the above work differs from ours, please contact our office so that we can discuss this matter. Thank you for your continued use of *CONSULTING FIRM NAME*.

With best regards.

Very truly yours,

C

# Daily and Weekly SBS Administration (The Dirty Dozen) Checklist

| Task | Frequency | Completed (Date/Who) | Description (Starting Value/Ending Value, and so on) |
|---|---|---|---|
| Tape Backup and Restore | Daily | ☐ | |
| Sharing Files and Folders | Weekly | ☐ | |
| Mapping Drives | Weekly | ☐ | |
| Adding and Managing Users, Groups, Computers | Daily/ Weekly | ☐ | |
| UPS Power Levels | Daily | ☐ | |
| Logon/Logoff Status | Daily | ☐ | |
| End-user Support | Daily | ☐ | |
| Check System Health | Daily | ☐ | |
| Run Virus Detection | Daily | ☐ | |
| Installing/ Removing Applications | Weekly | ☐ | |
| Reporting | Daily | ☐ | |
| Working Smarter Each Day | Daily | ☐ | |

# Monthly and Annual SBS Tasks Checklist

| Task | Frequency | Completed (Date/Who) | Description (Starting Value/Ending Value, and so on) |
|------|-----------|---------------------|------------------------------------------------------|
| The Monthly Reboot | Monthly | ☐ | |
| Disk Defragmentation | Monthly | ☐ | |
| Service Packs, Upgrades, Hot Fixes | Monthly | ☐ | |
| Hard Disk Space Management | Monthly | ☐ | |
| Virus Protection –Verify Phone Home | Monthly | ☐ | |
| Updating Your SBS Toolkit | Monthly | ☐ | |
| Y2K Testing | Monthly | ☐ | |
| Getting Help from Consultants and Interns | Annually/ Ongoing | ☐ | |
| Security Review | Annually/ Ongoing | ☐ | |
| Hardware and Software Upgrades | Annually/ Ongoing | ☐ | |
| Training | Annually/ Ongoing | ☐ | |
| SBS Budget | Annually | ☐ | |
| SBS Mission Statement | Annually | ☐ | |

C

# APPENDIX **D**

# Migrating from SBS 4.0/4.0a to 4.5

While the book focuses on a fresh installation of SBS 4.5 for Springer Spaniels Unlimited, the fact remains that many readers are upgrading from SBS 4.0 or SBS 4.0a to SBS 4.5. The upgrade process is actually very easy. In essence, you refresh the existing SBS installation with SBS 4.5.

To perform the upgrade, follow these steps.

1. Log on to your SBS server machine as an administrator or member of the Administrators group.

2. Verify that you have at least two bona fide tape backups of your existing SBS server machine. This is an important step.

3. Place SBS 4.5 CD-ROM Disc 1 in the CD-ROM drive of your existing SBS server machine. The SBS 4.5 opening screen appears. (See Figure D.1.)

**FIGURE D.1**

*SBS 4.5 Opening
Screen.*

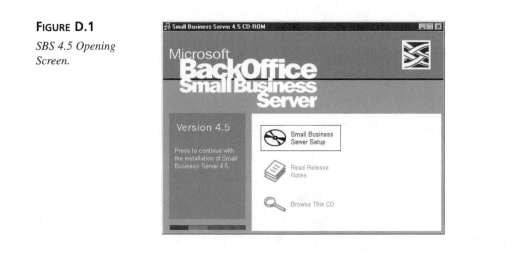

4. If you receive a warning regarding 40-bit encryption, select Yes that you want to continue.

5. After reading the upgrade notice, including the warning about having a complete backup, select Yes to continue the upgrade. This notice is shown in Figure D.2.

**FIGURE D.2**

*Upgrade Notice.*

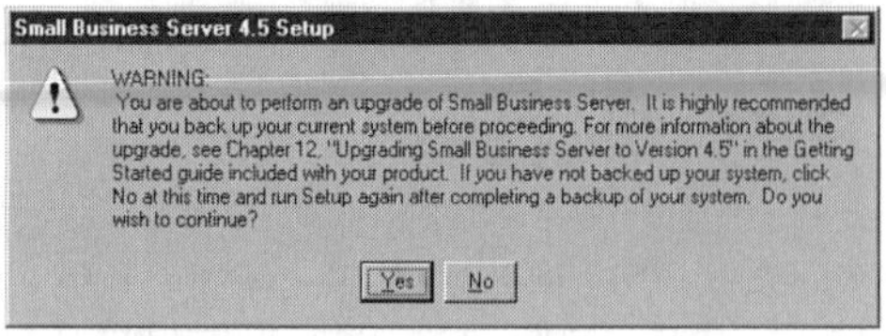

6. The Welcome to Microsoft BackOffice Small Business Server 4.5 Setup Wizard appears as seen in Figure D.3. Click Next to continue.

**FIGURE D.3**

*Setup Wizard.*

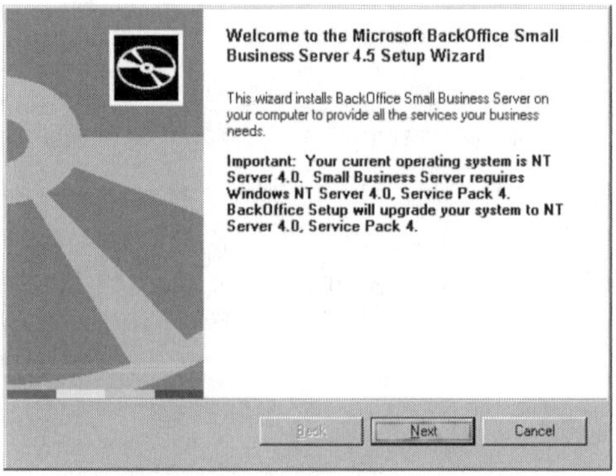

7. Agree to the license agreement, shown in Figure D.4. Click Next.

FIGURE **D.4**

*License agreement.*

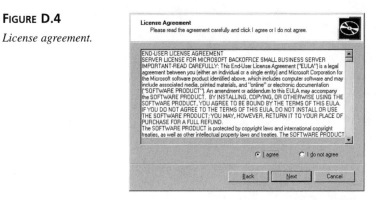

8. Complete the Identification dialog box as shown in Figure D.5. You need to enter your CD key.

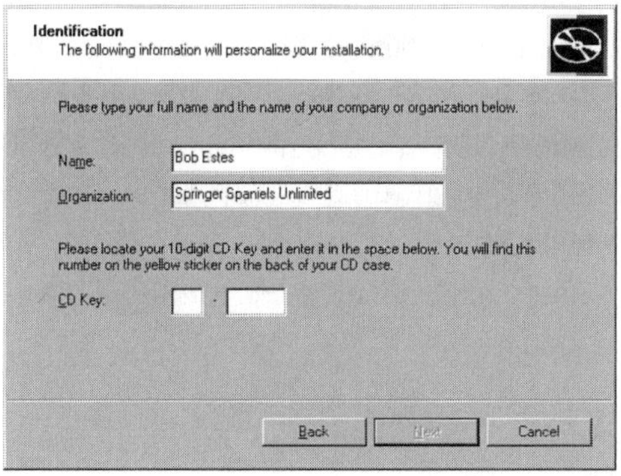

FIGURE **D.5**

*Identification.*

**D**

9. At the Autologon Password dialog box, enter the Administrator's password in the Password dialog box, as seen in Figure D.6. Click Next.

10. Setup copies installation files to your hard disk. You receive notice of this via the dialog box in Figure D.7.

11. You see a setup dialog box asking for your approval to restart the system. Click Yes. The computer reboots.

12. After an autologon, Service Pack 4 is automatically installed and the machine restarts.

13. The SBS BackOffice applications install next, in a manner similar to that discussed on Day 3, "Installing Small Business Server." You will be asked to insert SBS CD-ROM Discs #2 and #3.

**FIGURE D.6**

*Autologon Password.*

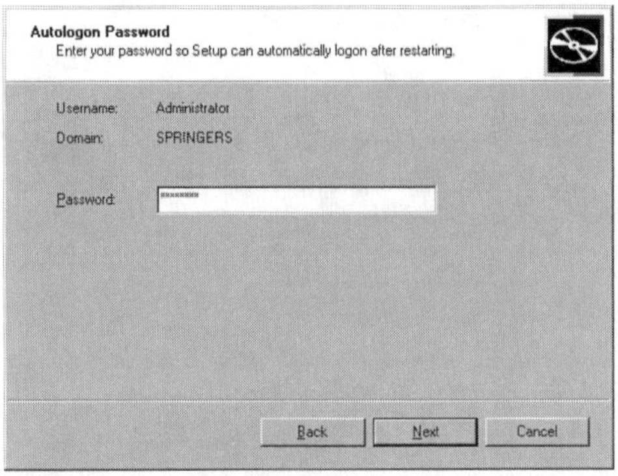

**FIGURE D.7**

*Files copied.*

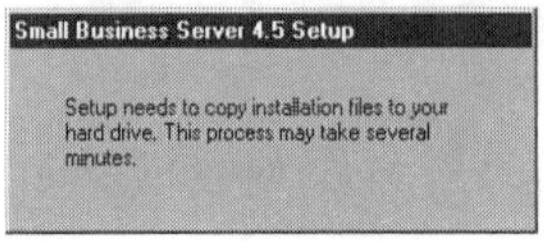

14. If applicable, Office 2000 is installed next. This step assumes you have purchased the SBS 4.5 version that contains Office 2000. If this is the case, you are asked to insert the two Office 2000 CD-ROMs.

15. You need to install the SBS client components at each workstation via the SBS client setup disk (a.k.a. magic disk) in order for the upgrade from SBS 4.0 to SBS 4.5 to be complete.

That's it! It's actually quite simple to upgrade from SBS 4.0/4.0a to SBS 4.5.

# APPENDIX E

# Springer Spaniels Unlimited User Information

# Springer Spaniels Unlimited

## SBS Workstation Setup Sheet

| Setup Field | Input/Value/Description | Where Used |
|---|---|---|
| User's Full Name (First, Last) | Norm Hasbro | Add a User |
| User's Account Name (20-character limit) | NormH | Add a User |
| Description for User | Founder and President | Add a User |
| Password | Purple3 | Add a User |
| Title (Job Title) | President | Add a User |
| Company | Springer Spaniels Unlimited | Add a User |
| Department | Executive | Add a User |
| Office | Main | Add a User |
| Assistant | N/A | Add a User |
| Phone | 206-123-1234 | Add a User |
| Address | 3456 The Pass Road | Add a User |
| City | Iski | Add a User |
| State | WA | Add a User |
| ZIP Code | 98111 | Add a User |
| Country | USA | Add a User |
| Business telephone | 206-123-1234 | Add a User |
| Business 2 telephone | N/A | Add a User |
| Fax telephone | 206-123-1235 | Add a User |
| Assistant telephone | N/A | Add a User |
| Home telephone | 206-111-1235 | Add a User |
| Home 2 telephone | N/A | Add a User |
| Mobile telephone | 206-999-1236 | Add a User |
| Pager telephone | N/A | Add a User |

| Setup Field | Input/Value/Description | Where Used |
| --- | --- | --- |
| E-Mail Distribution List (the default entry is the same name as the SBS network Domain name: e.g. SPRINGERS) | SPRINGERS | Add a User |
| Shared Folders: (R)ead, (E)dit, (D)elete Permissions | company, FaxStore, NormH | Add a User |
| Shared Folders – (R)ead Permission | (all users folders) | Add a User |
| Shared Printer | HP5MCOLOR | Add a User |
| Shared Fax Printer | Fax | Add a User |
| Access the Internet? (Y/N) | Y | Add a User |
| Use a modem to access the server computer? (Y/N) | Y | Add a User |
| Administrative Privileges (Y/N) | N | Add a User |
| Workstation NetBIOS name | PRESIDENT | Set Up A Computer ("Set Up Computer Wizard") |
| Operating System: Windows 95, Windows 98 or Windows NT 4.0 Workstation | Windows 95 | Set Up A Computer |
| SBS Programs to Install None, Complete –or– _ Micorsoft Fax Client _ Microsoft Internet Explorer _ Microsoft Modem Sharing Client _ Microsoft Outlook E-mail Client | Complete | Set Up A Computer |

E

| Setup Field | Input/Value/Description | Where Used |
|---|---|---|
| _ Microsoft Proxy Client<br>_ Microsoft Office 97<br>(optional) | | |
| Verify available<br>workstation hard disk<br>space based on SBS<br>Programs to install<br>listed immediately above<br>(e.g. 98 MB required) | Yes | Set Up A Computer |
| Network Protocols | TCP/IP | Misc. |
| IP Address<br>(Static or Dynamic) | Dynamic | Misc. |
| Mapped Drives | S: SPRINGERS01\NORMH<br>T: SPRINGERS01\USERS<br>U: SPRINGERS01\COMPANY<br>V: SPRINGERS01\ACCOUNTING<br>W: SPRINGERS01\OLD<br>X: SPRINGERS01\APPLICATIONS | Misc. |
| Workstation Shares<br>(shares on workstation) | N/A | Misc. |
| Additional Applications<br>to install (e.g. Great<br>Plains Dynamics<br>accounting): | Great Plains<br>Dynamics client<br>FRX Report Writer | Misc. |
| Special configuration issues | Double-check security.<br>This is the President's<br>PC. | Misc. |
| Comments | Complete this machine<br>last after all other<br>workstations. | Misc. |
| Tested Logon (Y/N) | N | Misc. |
| Repairs/Reconfiguration<br>Needed | | Misc. |

# Springer Spaniels Unlimited

## SBS Workstation Setup Sheet

| Setup Field | Input/Value/Description | Where Used |
|---|---|---|
| User's Full Name (First, Last) | Barry Kech | Add a User |
| User's Account Name (20-character limit) | BarryK | Add a User |
| Description for User | Accountant | Add a User |
| Password | 2redRed | Add a User |
| Title (Job Title) | Accountant | Add a User |
| Company | Springer Spaniels Unlimited | Add a User |
| Department | Accounting | Add a User |
| Office | Main | Add a User |
| Assistant | N/A | Add a User |
| Phone | 206-123-1234 | Add a User |
| Address | 3456 The Pass Road | Add a User |
| City | Iski | Add a User |
| State | WA | Add a User |
| ZIP Code | 98111 | Add a User |
| Country | USA | Add a User |
| Business telephone | 206-123-1234 | Add a User |
| Business 2 telephone | N/A | Add a User |
| Fax telephone | 206-123-1235 | Add a User |
| Assistant telephone | N/A | Add a User |
| Home telephone | N/A | Add a User |
| Home 2 telephone | N/A | Add a User |
| Mobile telephone | N/A | Add a User |
| Pager telephone | N/A | Add a User |

E

| Setup Field | Input/Value/Description | Where Used |
|---|---|---|
| E-Mail Distribution List (the default entry is the same name as the SBS network Domain name: e.g. SPRINGERS) | SPRINGERS | Add a User |
| Shared Folders – (R)ead, (E)dit, (D)elete Permissions | company, FaxStore | Add a User |
| Shared Folders – (R)ead Permission | (all users folders) | Add a User |
| Shared Printer | HP5MCOLOR | Add a User |
| Shared Fax Printer | Fax | Add a User |
| Access the Internet? (Y/N) | Y | Add a User |
| Use a modem to access the server computer? (Y/N) | Y | Add a User |
| Administrative Privileges (Y/N) | N | Add a User |
| Workstation NetBIOS name | ACCT01 | Set Up A Computer ("Set Up Computer Wizard") |
| Operating System: Windows 95, Windows 98 or Windows NT 4.0 Workstation | Windows 98 | Set Up A Computer |
| SBS Programs to Install None, Complete –or– _ Micorsoft Fax Client _ Microsoft Internet Explorer _ Microsoft Modem Sharing Client _ Microsoft Outlook E-mail Client _ Microsoft Proxy Client _ Microsoft Office 97 (optional) | Complete | Set Up A Computer |

| Setup Field | Input/Value/Description | Where Used |
|---|---|---|
| Verify available workstation hard disk space based on SBS Programs to install listed immediately above (e.g. 98 MB required) | Yes | Set Up A Computer |
| Network Protocols | TCP/IP | Misc. |
| IP Address (Static or Dynamic) | Dynamic | Misc. |
| Mapped Drives | S: SPRINGERS01\BarryK | Misc. |
| | T: SPRINGERS01\USERS | |
| | U: SPRINGERS01\COMPANY | |
| | V: SPRINGERS01\ACCOUNTING | |
| | W: SPRINGERS01\OLD | |
| | X: SPRINGERS01\APPLICATIONS | |
| Workstation Shares (shares on workstation) | N/A | Misc. |
| Additional Applications to install (e.g. Great Plains Dynamics accounting): | Great Plains Dynamics client FRX Report Writer | Misc. |
| Special configuration issues | | Misc. |
| Comments | | Misc. |
| Tested Logon (Y/N) | | Misc. |
| Repairs/Reconfiguration Needed | | Misc. |

E

# Springer Spaniels Unlimited

## SBS Workstation Setup Sheet

| Setup Field | Input/Value/Description | Where Used |
|---|---|---|
| User's Full Name (First, Last) | Melinda Overlake | Add a User |
| User's Account Name (20-character limit) | MelindaO | Add a User |
| Description for User | Front Desk Receptionist | Add a User |
| Password | Blue33 | Add a User |
| Title (Job Title) | Front Desk Receptionist | Add a User |
| Company | Springer Spaniels Unlimited | Add a User |
| Department | Administration | Add a User |
| Office | Main | Add a User |
| Assistant | N/A | Add a User |
| Phone | 206-123-1234 | Add a User |
| Address | 3456 The Pass Road | Add a User |
| City | Iski | Add a User |
| State | WA | Add a User |
| ZIP Code | 98111 | Add a User |
| Country | USA | Add a User |
| Business telephone | 206-123-1234 | Add a User |
| Business 2 telephone | N/A | Add a User |
| Fax telephone | 206-123-1235 | Add a User |
| Assistant telephone | N/A | Add a User |
| Home telephone | N/A | Add a User |
| Home 2 telephone | N/A | Add a User |
| Mobile telephone | N/A | Add a User |
| Pager telephone | N/A | Add a User |

| Setup Field | Input/Value/Description | Where Used |
|---|---|---|
| E-Mail Distribution List (the default entry is the same name as the SBS network Domain name: e.g. SPRINGERS) | SPRINGERS | Add a User |
| Shared Folders – (R)ead, (E)dit, (D)elete Permissions | company, FaxStore | Add a User |
| Shared Folders – (R)ead Permission | (all users folders) | Add a User |
| Shared Printer | HP5MCOLOR | Add a User |
| Shared Fax Printer | Fax | Add a User |
| Access the Internet? (Y/N) | Y | Add a User |
| Use a modem to access the server computer? (Y/N) | Y | Add a User |
| Administrative Privileges (Y/N) | N | Add a User |
| Workstation NetBIOS name | FRONT01 | Set Up A Computer ("Set Up Computer Wizard") |
| Operating System: Windows 95, Windows 98 or Windows NT 4.0 Workstation | Windows 95 | Set Up A Computer |
| SBS Programs to Install None, Complete –or- _ Micorsoft Fax Client _ Microsoft Internet Explorer _ Microsoft Modem Sharing Client _ Microsoft Outlook E-mail Client _ Microsoft Proxy Client _ Microsoft Office 97 (optional) | Complete | Set Up A Computer |

E

| Setup Field | Input/Value/Description | Where Used |
|---|---|---|
| Verify available workstation hard disk space based on SBS Programs to install listed immediately above (e.g. 98 MB required) | Yes | Set Up A Computer |
| Network Protocols | TCP/IP | Misc. |
| IP Address (Static or Dynamic) | Dynamic | Misc. |
| Mapped Drives | S: SPRINGERS01MelindaO<br>T: SPRINGERS01\USERS<br>U: SPRINGERS01\COMPANY | Misc. |
| Workstation Shares (shares on workstation) | N/A | Misc. |
| Additional Applications to install (e.g. Great Plains Dynamics accounting): | N/A | Misc. |
| Special configuration issues | | Misc. |
| Comments | | Misc. |
| Tested Logon (Y/N) | | Misc. |
| Repairs/Reconfiguration Needed | | Misc. |

# Springer Spaniels Unlimited

## SBS Workstation Setup Sheet

| Setup Field | Input/Value/Description | Where Used |
|---|---|---|
| User's Full Name (First, Last) | Sally Briggs | Add a User |
| User's Account Name (20-character limit) | SallyB | Add a User |
| Description for User | Manager – Registration | Add a User |
| Password | Golden1 | Add a User |
| Title (Job Title) | Manager - Registration | Add a User |
| Company | Springer Spaniels Unlimited | Add a User |
| Department | Registration and Scheduling | Add a User |
| Office | Main | Add a User |
| Assistant | N/A | Add a User |
| Phone | 206-123-1234 | Add a User |
| Address | 3456 The Pass Road | Add a User |
| City | Iski | Add a User |
| State | WA | Add a User |
| ZIP Code | 98111 | Add a User |
| Country | USA | Add a User |
| Business telephone | 206-123-1234 | Add a User |
| Business 2 telephone | N/A | Add a User |
| Fax telephone | 206-123-1235 | Add a User |
| Assistant telephone | N/A | Add a User |
| Home telephone | N/A | Add a User |
| Home 2 telephone | N/A | Add a User |
| Mobile telephone | N/A | Add a User |

E

| Setup Field | Input/Value/Description | Where Used |
|---|---|---|
| Pager telephone | N/A | Add a User |
| E-Mail Distribution List (the default entry is the same name as the SBS network Domain name: e.g. SPRINGERS) | SPRINGERS | Add a User |
| Shared Folders – (R)ead, (E)dit, (D)elete Permissions | company, FaxStore | Add a User |
| Shared Folders – (R)ead Permission | (all users folders) | Add a User |
| Shared Printer | HP5MCOLOR | Add a User |
| Shared Fax Printer | Fax | Add a User |
| Access the Internet? (Y/N) | Y | Add a User |
| Use a modem to access the server computer? (Y/N) | Y | Add a User |
| Administrative Privileges (Y/N) | N | Add a User |
| Workstation NetBIOS name | MANREG01 | Set Up A Computer ("Set Up Computer Wizard") |
| Operating System: Windows 95, Windows 98 or Windows NT 4.0 Workstation | Windows 95 | Set Up A Computer |
| SBS Programs to Install None, Complete –or– _ Micorsoft Fax Client _ Microsoft Internet Explorer _ Microsoft Modem Sharing Client _ Microsoft Outlook E-mail Client _ Microsoft Proxy Client _ Microsoft Office 97 (optional) | Complete | Set Up A Computer |

| Setup Field | Input/Value/Description | Where Used |
|---|---|---|
| Verify available workstation hard disk space based on SBS Programs to install listed immediately above (e.g. 98 MB required) | Yes | Set Up A Computer |
| Network Protocols | TCP/IP | Misc. |
| IP Address (Static or Dynamic) | Dynamic | Misc. |
| Mapped Drives | S: SPRINGERS01SallyB<br>T: SPRINGERS01\USERS<br>U: SPRINGERS01\COMPANY | Misc. |
| Workstation Shares (shares on workstation) | N/A | Misc. |
| Additional Applications to install (e.g. Great Plains Dynamics accounting): | N/A | Misc. |
| Special configuration issues | | Misc. |
| Comments | | Misc. |
| Tested Logon (Y/N) | | Misc. |
| Repairs/Reconfiguration Needed | | Misc. |

E

# Springer Spaniels Unlimited

## SBS Workstation Setup Sheet

| Setup Field | Input/Value/Description | Where Used |
| --- | --- | --- |
| User's Full Name (First, Last) | Bob Bounty | Add a User |
| User's Account Name (20-character limit) | BobB | Add a User |
| Description for User | Breeding Manager | Add a User |
| Password | BROWNish4 | Add a User |
| Title (Job Title) | Breeding Manager | Add a User |
| Company | Springer Spaniels Unlimited | Add a User |
| Department | Care, Feeding and Breeding | Add a User |
| Office | Main | Add a User |
| Assistant | N/A | Add a User |
| Phone | 206-123-1234 | Add a User |
| Address | 3456 The Pass Road | Add a User |
| City | Iski | Add a User |
| State | WA | Add a User |
| ZIP Code | 98111 | Add a User |
| Country | USA | Add a User |
| Business telephone | 206-123-1234 | Add a User |
| Business 2 telephone | N/A | Add a User |
| Fax telephone | 206-123-1235 | Add a User |
| Assistant telephone | N/A | Add a User |
| Home telephone | N/A | Add a User |
| Home 2 telephone | N/A | Add a User |
| Mobile telephone | N/A | Add a User |
| Pager telephone | N/A | Add a User |

| *Setup Field* | *Input/Value/Description* | *Where Used* |
|---|---|---|
| E-Mail Distribution List (the default entry is the same name as the SBS network Domain name: e.g. SPRINGERS) | SPRINGERS | Add a User |
| Shared Folders – (R)ead, (E)dit, (D)elete Permissions | company, FaxStore | Add a User |
| Shared Folders – (R)ead Permission | (all users folders) | Add a User |
| Shared Printer | HP5MCOLOR | Add a User |
| Shared Fax Printer | Fax | Add a User |
| Access the Internet? (Y/N) | Y | Add a User |
| Use a modem to access the server computer? (Y/N) | Y | Add a User |
| Administrative Privileges (Y/N) | N | Add a User |
| Workstation NetBIOS name | BREED01 | Set Up A Computer ("Set Up Computer Wizard") |
| Operating System: Windows 95, Windows 98 or Windows NT 4.0 Workstation | Windows 95 | Set Up A Computer |
| SBS Programs to Install None, Complete –or– _ Micorsoft Fax Client _ Microsoft Internet Explorer _ Microsoft Modem Sharing Client _ Microsoft Outlook E-mail Client _ Microsoft Proxy Client _ Microsoft Office 97 (optional) | Complete | Set Up A Computer |

E

| Setup Field | Input/Value/Description | Where Used |
|---|---|---|
| Verify available workstation hard disk space based on SBS Programs to install listed immediately above (e.g. 98 MB required) | Yes | Set Up A Computer |
| Network Protocols | TCP/IP | Misc. |
| IP Address (Static or Dynamic) | Dynamic | Misc. |
| Mapped Drives | S: SPRINGERS01\BobB<br>T: SPRINGERS01\USERS<br>U: SPRINGERS01\COMPANY | Misc. |
| Workstation Shares (shares on workstation) | N/A | Misc. |
| Additional Applications to install (e.g. Great Plains Dynamics accounting): | N/A | Misc. |
| Special configuration issues | | Misc. |
| Comments | | Misc. |
| Tested Logon (Y/N) | | Misc. |
| Repairs/Reconfiguration Needed | | Misc. |

# Springer Spaniels Unlimited

## SBS Workstation Setup Sheet

| Setup Field | Input/Value/Description | Where Used |
|---|---|---|
| User's Full Name (First, Last) | Sam Cav | Add a User |
| User's Account Name (20-character limit) | SamC | Add a User |
| Description for User | Care and Feeding Manager | Add a User |
| Password | Silver999 | Add a User |
| Title (Job Title) | Care and Feeding Manager | Add a User |
| Company | Springer Spaniels Unlimited | Add a User |
| Department | Care, Feeding, and Breeding | Add a User |
| Office | Main | Add a User |
| Assistant | N/A | Add a User |
| Phone | 206-123-1234 | Add a User |
| Address | 3456 The Pass Road | Add a User |
| City | Iski | Add a User |
| State | WA | Add a User |
| ZIP Code | 98111 | Add a User |
| Country | USA | Add a User |
| Business telephone | 206-123-1234 | Add a User |
| Business 2 telephone | N/A | Add a User |
| Fax telephone | 206-123-1235 | Add a User |
| Assistant telephone | N/A | Add a User |
| Home telephone | N/A | Add a User |
| Home 2 telephone | N/A | Add a User |
| Mobile telephone | N/A | Add a User |
| Pager telephone | N/A | Add a User |

E

| Setup Field | Input/Value/Description | Where Used |
|---|---|---|
| E-Mail Distribution List (the default entry is the same name as the SBS network Domain name: e.g. SPRINGERS) | SPRINGERS | Add a User |
| Shared Folders – (R)ead, (E)dit, (D)elete Permissions | company, FaxStore | Add a User |
| Shared Folders – (R)ead Permission | (all users folders) | Add a User |
| Shared Printer | HP5MCOLOR | Add a User |
| Shared Fax Printer | Fax | Add a User |
| Access the Internet? (Y/N) | Y | Add a User |
| Use a modem to access the server computer? (Y/N) | Y | Add a User |
| Administrative Privileges (Y/N) | N | Add a User |
| Workstation NetBIOS name | CAREFEED01 | Set Up A Computer ("Set Up Computer Wizard") |
| Operating System: Windows 95, Windows 98 or Windows NT 4.0 Workstation | Windows 95 | Set Up A Computer |
| SBS Programs to Install None, Complete –or– _ Micorsoft Fax Client _ Microsoft Internet Explorer _ Microsoft Modem Sharing Client _ Microsoft Outlook E-mail Client _ Microsoft Proxy Client _ Microsoft Office 97 (optional) | Complete | Set Up A Computer |

| Setup Field | Input/Value/Description | Where Used |
|---|---|---|
| Verify available workstation hard disk space based on SBS Programs to install listed immediately above (e.g. 98 MB required) | Yes | Set Up A Computer |
| Network Protocols | TCP/IP | Misc. |
| IP Address (Static or Dynamic) | Dynamic | Misc. |
| Mapped Drives | S: SPRINGERS01\SamC<br>T: SPRINGERS01\USERS<br>U: SPRINGERS01\COMPANY | Misc. |
| Workstation Shares (shares on workstation) | N/A | Misc. |
| Additional Applications to install (e.g. Great Plains Dynamics accounting): | N/A | Misc. |
| Special configuration issues | | Misc. |
| Comments | | Misc. |
| Tested Logon (Y/N) | | Misc. |
| Repairs/Reconfiguration Needed | | Misc. |

E

# Springer Spaniels Unlimited

## SBS Workstation Setup Sheet

| Setup Field | Input/Value/Description | Where Used |
|---|---|---|
| User's Full Name (First, Last) | Tom Benk | Add a User |
| User's Account Name (20-character limit) | TomB | Add a User |
| Description for User | Scheduler | Add a User |
| Password | White101 | Add a User |
| Title (Job Title) | Scheduler | Add a User |
| Company | Springer Spaniels Unlimited | Add a User |
| Department | Registration and Scheduling | Add a User |
| Office | Main | Add a User |
| Assistant | N/A | Add a User |
| Phone | 206-123-1234 | Add a User |
| Address | 3456 The Pass Road | Add a User |
| City | Iski | Add a User |
| State | WA | Add a User |
| ZIP Code | 98111 | Add a User |
| Country | USA | Add a User |
| Business telephone | 206-123-1234 | Add a User |
| Business 2 telephone | N/A | Add a User |
| Fax telephone | 206-123-1235 | Add a User |
| Assistant telephone | N/A | Add a User |
| Home telephone | N/A | Add a User |
| Home 2 telephone | N/A | Add a User |
| Mobile telephone | N/A | Add a User |
| Pager telephone | N/A | Add a User |

| *Setup Field* | *Input/Value/Description* | *Where Used* |
|---|---|---|
| E-Mail Distribution List (the default entry is the same name as the SBS network Domain name: e.g. SPRINGERS) | SPRINGERS | Add a User |
| Shared Folders – (R)ead, (E)dit, (D)elete Permissions | company, FaxStore | Add a User |
| Shared Folders – (R)ead Permission | (all users folders) | Add a User |
| Shared Printer | HP5MCOLOR | Add a User |
| Shared Fax Printer | Fax | Add a User |
| Access the Internet? (Y/N) | Y | Add a User |
| Use a modem to access the server computer? (Y/N) | Y | Add a User |
| Administrative Privileges (Y/N) | N | Add a User |
| Workstation NetBIOS name | SCHEDULE01 | Set Up A Computer ("Set Up Computer Wizard") |
| Operating System: Windows 95, Windows 98 or Windows NT 4.0 Workstation | Windows 95 | Set Up A Computer |
| SBS Programs to Install None, Complete –or– _ Micorsoft Fax Client _ Microsoft Internet Explorer _ Microsoft Modem Sharing Client _ Microsoft Outlook E-mail Client _ Microsoft Proxy Client _ Microsoft Office 97 (optional) | Complete | Set Up A Computer |

E

| Setup Field | Input/Value/Description | Where Used |
|---|---|---|
| Verify available workstation hard disk space based on SBS Programs to install listed immediately above (e.g. 98 MB required) | Yes | Set Up A Computer |
| Network Protocols | TCP/IP | Misc. |
| IP Address (Static or Dynamic) | Dynamic | Misc. |
| Mapped Drives | S: SPRINGERS01\TomB<br>T: SPRINGERS01\USERS<br>U: SPRINGERS01\COMPANY | Misc. |
| Workstation Shares (shares on workstation) | N/A | Misc. |
| Additional Applications to install (e.g. Great Plains Dynamics accounting): | N/A | Misc. |
| Special configuration issues | | Misc. |
| Comments | | Misc. |
| Tested Logon (Y/N) | | Misc. |
| Repairs/Reconfiguration Needed | | Misc. |

# Springer Spaniels Unlimited

## SBS Workstation Setup Sheet

| Setup Field | Input/Value/Description | Where Used |
| --- | --- | --- |
| User's Full Name (First, Last) | Norm Hasbro Jr. | Add a User |
| User's Account Name (20-character limit) | NormJR | Add a User |
| Description for User | Sales Manager | Add a User |
| Password | Yellow55 | Add a User |
| Title (Job Title) | Sales Manager | Add a User |
| Company | Springer Spaniels Unlimited | Add a User |
| Department | Sales and Marketing | Add a User |
| Office | Main | Add a User |
| Assistant | N/A | Add a User |
| Phone | 206-123-1234 | Add a User |
| Address | 3456 The Pass Road | Add a User |
| City | Iski | Add a User |
| State | WA | Add a User |
| ZIP Code | 98111 | Add a User |
| Country | USA | Add a User |
| Business telephone | 206-123-1234 | Add a User |
| Business 2 telephone | N/A | Add a User |
| Fax telephone | 206-123-1235 | Add a User |
| Assistant telephone | N/A | Add a User |
| Home telephone | N/A | Add a User |
| Home 2 telephone | N/A | Add a User |
| Mobile telephone | N/A | Add a User |
| Pager telephone | N/A | Add a User |

E

| Setup Field | Input/Value/Description | Where Used |
|---|---|---|
| E-Mail Distribution List (the default entry is the same name as the SBS network Domain name: e.g. SPRINGERS) | SPRINGERS | Add a User |
| Shared Folders – (R)ead, (E)dit, (D)elete Permissions | company, FaxStore | Add a User |
| Shared Folders – (R)ead Permission | (all users folders) | Add a User |
| Shared Printer | HP5MCOLOR | Add a User |
| Shared Fax Printer | Fax | Add a User |
| Access the Internet? (Y/N) | Y | Add a User |
| Use a modem to access the server computer? (Y/N) | Y | Add a User |
| Administrative Privileges (Y/N) | N | Add a User |
| Workstation NetBIOS name | SALES01 | Set Up A Computer ("Set Up Computer Wizard") |
| Operating System: Windows 95, Windows 98 or Windows NT 4.0 Workstation | Windows 95 | Set Up A Computer |
| SBS Programs to Install None, Complete –or- _ Micorsoft Fax Client _ Microsoft Internet Explorer _ Microsoft Modem Sharing Client _ Microsoft Outlook E-mail Client _ Microsoft Proxy Client _ Microsoft Office 97 (optional) | Complete | Set Up A Computer |

| Setup Field | Input/Value/Description | Where Used |
|---|---|---|
| Verify available workstation hard disk space based on SBS Programs to install listed immediately above (e.g. 98 MB required) | Yes | Set Up A Computer |
| Network Protocols | TCP/IP | Misc. |
| IP Address (Static or Dynamic) | Dynamic | Misc. |
| Mapped Drives | S: SPRINGERS01\NormJR<br>T: SPRINGERS01\USERS<br>U: SPRINGERS01\COMPANY | Misc. |
| Workstation Shares (shares on workstation) | N/A | Misc. |
| Additional Applications to install (e.g. Great Plains Dynamics accounting): | N/A | Misc. |
| Special configuration issues | | Misc. |
| Comments | | Misc. |
| Tested Logon (Y/N) | | Misc. |
| Repairs/Reconfiguration Needed | | Misc. |

E

# Springer Spaniels Unlimited

## SBS Workstation Setup Sheet

| Setup Field | Input/Value/Description | Where Used |
| --- | --- | --- |
| User's Full Name (First, Last) | David Halb | Add a User |
| User's Account Name (20-character limit) | DaveH | Add a User |
| Description for User | Marketing Manager | Add a User |
| Password | greeN25 | Add a User |
| Title (Job Title) | Marketing Manager | Add a User |
| Company | Springer Spaniels Unlimited | Add a User |
| Department | Marketing | Add a User |
| Office | Main | Add a User |
| Assistant | N/A | Add a User |
| Phone | 206-123-1234 | Add a User |
| Address | 3456 The Pass Road | Add a User |
| City | Iski | Add a User |
| State | WA | Add a User |
| ZIP Code | 98111 | Add a User |
| Country | USA | Add a User |
| Business telephone | 206-123-1234 | Add a User |
| Business 2 telephone | N/A | Add a User |
| Fax telephone | 206-123-1235 | Add a User |
| Assistant telephone | N/A | Add a User |
| Home telephone | N/A | Add a User |
| Home 2 telephone | N/A | Add a User |
| Mobile telephone | N/A | Add a User |
| Pager telephone | N/A | Add a User |

| Setup Field | Input/Value/Description | Where Used |
|---|---|---|
| E-Mail Distribution List (the default entry is the same name as the SBS network Domain name: e.g. SPRINGERS) | SPRINGERS | Add a User |
| Shared Folders – (R)ead, (E)dit, (D)elete Permissions | company, FaxStore | Add a User |
| Shared Folders – (R)ead Permission | (all users folders) | Add a User |
| Shared Printer | HP5MCOLOR | Add a User |
| Shared Fax Printer | Fax | Add a User |
| Access the Internet? (Y/N) | Y | Add a User |
| Use a modem to access the server computer? (Y/N) | Y | Add a User |
| Administrative Privileges (Y/N) | N | Add a User |
| Workstation NetBIOS name | MARKET01 | Set Up A Computer ("Set Up Computer Wizard") |
| Operating System: Windows 95, Windows 98 or Windows NT 4.0 Workstation | Windows 98 | Set Up A Computer |
| SBS Programs to Install None, Complete –or– _ Micorsoft Fax Client _ Microsoft Internet Explorer _ Microsoft Modem Sharing Client _ Microsoft Outlook E-mail Client _ Microsoft Proxy Client _ Microsoft Office 97 (optional) | Complete | Set Up A Computer |

E

| Setup Field | Input/Value/Description | Where Used |
|---|---|---|
| Verify available workstation hard disk space based on SBS Programs to install listed immediately above (e.g. 98 MB required) | Yes | Set Up A Computer |
| Network Protocols | TCP/IP | Misc. |
| IP Address (Static or Dynamic) | Dynamic | Misc. |
| Mapped Drives | S: SPRINGERS01\DaveH T: SPRINGERS01\USERS U: SPRINGERS01\COMPANY | Misc. |
| Workstation Shares (shares on workstation) | N/A | Misc. |
| Additional Applications to install (e.g. Great Plains Dynamics accounting): | N/A | Misc. |
| Special configuration issues | This is a laptop. | Misc. |
| Comments | | Misc. |
| Tested Logon (Y/N) | | Misc. |
| Repairs/Reconfiguration Needed | | Misc. |

# Springer Spaniels Unlimited

## SBS Workstation Setup Sheet

| Setup Field | Input/Value/Description | Where Used |
|---|---|---|
| User's Full Name (First, Last) | Elvis Haskins | Add a User |
| User's Account Name (20-character limit) | Elvis | Add a User |
| Description for User | Researcher | Add a User |
| Password | Platinium1 | Add a User |
| Title (Job Title) | Researcher | Add a User |
| Company | Springer Spaniels Unlimited | Add a User |
| Department | Genealogy | Add a User |
| Office | Main | Add a User |
| Assistant | N/A | Add a User |
| Phone | 206-123-1234 | Add a User |
| Address | 3456 The Pass Road | Add a User |
| City | Iski | Add a User |
| State | WA | Add a User |
| ZIP Code | 98111 | Add a User |
| Country | USA | Add a User |
| Business telephone | 206-123-1234 | Add a User |
| Business 2 telephone | N/A | Add a User |
| Fax telephone | 206-123-1235 | Add a User |
| Assistant telephone | N/A | Add a User |
| Home telephone | N/A | Add a User |
| Home 2 telephone | N/A | Add a User |
| Mobile telephone | N/A | Add a User |
| Pager telephone | N/A | Add a User |

E

| Setup Field | Input/Value/Description | Where Used |
|---|---|---|
| E-Mail Distribution List (the default entry is the same name as the SBS network Domain name: e.g. SPRINGERS) | SPRINGERS | Add a User |
| Shared Folders – (R)ead, (E)dit, (D)elete Permissions | company, FaxStore | Add a User |
| Shared Folders – (R)ead Permission | (all users folders) | Add a User |
| Shared Printer | HP5MCOLOR | Add a User |
| Shared Fax Printer | Fax | Add a User |
| Access the Internet? (Y/N) | Y | Add a User |
| Use a modem to access the server computer? (Y/N) | Y | Add a User |
| Administrative Privileges (Y/N) | N | Add a User |
| Workstation NetBIOS name | GENE01 | Set Up A Computer ("Set Up Computer Wizard") |
| Operating System: Windows 95, Windows 98 or Windows NT 4.0 Workstation | Windows NT Workstation 4.0 | Set Up A Computer |
| SBS Programs to Install None, Complete –or– _ Micorsoft Fax Client _ Microsoft Internet Explorer _ Microsoft Modem Sharing Client _ Microsoft Outlook E-mail Client _ Microsoft Proxy Client _ Microsoft Office 97 (optional) | Complete | Set Up A Computer |

| Setup Field | Input/Value/Description | Where Used |
|---|---|---|
| Verify available workstation hard disk space based on SBS Programs to install listed immediately above (e.g. 98 MB required) | Yes | Set Up A Computer |
| Network Protocols | TCP/IP | Misc. |
| IP Address (Static or Dynamic) | Dynamic | Misc. |
| Mapped Drives | S: SPRINGERS01\Elvis<br>T: SPRINGERS01\USERS<br>U: SPRINGERS01\COMPANY | Misc. |
| Workstation Shares (shares on workstation) | N/A | Misc. |
| Additional Applications to install (e.g. Great Plains Dynamics accounting): | N/A | Misc. |
| Special configuration issues | | Misc. |
| Comments | | Misc. |
| Tested Logon (Y/N) | | Misc. |
| Repairs/Reconfiguration Needed | | Misc. |

E

# Springer Spaniels Unlimited

## SBS Workstation Setup Sheet

| Setup Field | Input/Value/Description | Where Used |
|---|---|---|
| User's Full Name (First, Last) | Bob Estes | Add a User |
| User's Account Name (20-character limit) | BobE | Add a User |
| Description for User | Dog Trainer | Add a User |
| Password | dogcatcher1 | Add a User |
| Title (Job Title) | Dog Trainer | Add a User |
| Company | Springer Spaniels Unlimited | Add a User |
| Department | Care, Feeding and Breeding | Add a User |
| Office | Main | Add a User |
| Assistant | N/A | Add a User |
| Phone | 206-123-1234 | Add a User |
| Address | 3456 The Pass Road | Add a User |
| City | Iski | Add a User |
| State | WA | Add a User |
| ZIP Code | 98111 | Add a User |
| Country | USA | Add a User |
| Business telephone | 206-123-1234 | Add a User |
| Business 2 telephone | N/A | Add a User |
| Fax telephone | 206-123-1235 | Add a User |
| Assistant telephone | N/A | Add a User |
| Home telephone | N/A | Add a User |
| Home 2 telephone | N/A | Add a User |
| Mobile telephone | N/A | Add a User |
| Pager telephone | N/A | Add a User |

| Setup Field | Input/Value/Description | Where Used |
|---|---|---|
| E-Mail Distribution List (the default entry is the same name as the SBS network Domain name: e.g. SPRINGERS) | SPRINGERS | Add a User |
| Shared Folders – (R)ead, (E)dit, (D)elete Permissions | company, FaxStore | Add a User |
| Shared Folders – (R)ead Permission | (all users folders) | Add a User |
| Shared Printer | HP5MCOLOR | Add a User |
| Shared Fax Printer | Fax | Add a User |
| Access the Internet? (Y/N) | Y | Add a User |
| Use a modem to access the server computer? (Y/N) | Y | Add a User |
| Administrative Privileges (Y/N) | N | Add a User |
| Workstation NetBIOS name | SPRINGERS01 | Set Up A Computer ("Set Up Computer Wizard") |
| Operating System: Windows 95, Windows 98 or Windows NT 4.0 Workstation | Windows NT Server 4.0 | Set Up A Computer |
| SBS Programs to Install None, Complete –or– _ Micorsoft Fax Client _ Microsoft Internet Explorer _ Microsoft Modem Sharing Client _ Microsoft Outlook E-mail Client _ Microsoft Proxy Client _ Microsoft Office 97 (optional) | Complete | Set Up A Computer |

E

| Setup Field | Input/Value/Description | Where Used |
|---|---|---|
| Verify available workstation hard disk space based on SBS Programs to install listed immediately above (e.g. 98 MB required) | Yes | Set Up A Computer |
| Network Protocols | TCP/IP | Misc. |
| IP Address (Static or Dynamic) | Dynamic | Misc. |
| Mapped Drives | N/A – this is the SBS Server | Misc. |
| Workstation Shares (shares on workstation) | N/A | Misc. |
| Additional Applications to install (e.g. Great Plains Dynamics accounting): | N/A | Misc. |
| Special configuration issues | This is the SBS Server machine. | Misc. |
| Comments | | Misc. |
| Tested Logon (Y/N) | | Misc. |
| Repairs/Reconfiguration Needed | | Misc. |

# INDEX

# X - Y - Z

# SAMS
# Teach Yourself
## in 21 Days

**Sams Teach Yourself in 21 Days** *teaches you all the skills you need to master the basics and then moves on to the more advanced features and concepts. This series is designed for the way you learn. Go chapter by chapter through the step-by-step lessons or just choose those lessons that interest you the most.*

## Microsoft Office 2000

*Laurie Ulrich*
ISBN: 0-672-31448-7
$29.99 US/ $42.95 CAN

## Other Sams Teach Yourself in 21 Days Titles

### MCSE Internet Information Server 4 in 14 Days
*Rob Scrimger*
ISBN: 0-672-31294-8
$35.00 US

### VBScript in 21 Days
*Keith Brophy*
ISBN: 1-575-21120-3
$39.99 US/$57.95 CAN

### Internet Programming with Visual Basic
*Peter Aitken*
ISBN: 0-672-31459-2
$29.99 US/$42.95 CAN

### C++ in 21 Days
*Jesse Liberty*
ISBN: 0-672-31515-7
$29.99 US/$42.95 CAN

## STY Windows NT Server 4 in 21 Days

*Peter Davis*
ISBN: 0-672-31555-6
$29.99 US/$42.95 CAN

## STY Microsoft Exchange Server 5.5 in 21 Days

*Jason vanValkenburgh*
ISBN: 0-672-31525-4
$29.99 US/$42.95 CAN

*www.samspublishing.com*

All prices are subject to change.

# Other Related Titles

Sams Teach Yourself
Office 2000 Small
Business Edition in
24 Hours
*Greg Perry*
ISBN: 0-672-31568-8
$19.99 US/$28.95 CAN

Sams Teach Yourself
Outlook 2000 in
24 Hours
*Herb Tyson*
ISBN: 0-672-31449-5
$19.99 US/ $28.95

Sams Teach Yourself
Internet Explorer 5 in
24 Hours
*Jill Freeze*
ISBN: 0-672-31328-6
$19.99 US/ $28.95 CAN

Sams Teach Yourself
FrontPage 2000 in
24 Hours
*Rogers Cadenhead*
ISBN: 0-672-31500-9
$19.99 US/ $28.95 CAN

Microsoft BackOffice
Unleashed, 2nd Edition
*Joe Greene, et al.*
ISBN: 0-672-31085-6
$75.00 US/ $105.95 CAN

Sams Teach Yourself
SQL in 24 Hours
*Ryan Stephens*
ISBN: 0-672-31245-x
$24.99 US/ $35.95 CAN

Sams Teach Yourself
TCP/IP in 24 Hours
*Joe Casad & Bob
Willsey*
ISBN: 0-672-31248-4
$19.99 US/ $28.95 CAN

Microsoft Exchange
server 5.5 Unleashed
*Greg Todd*
ISBN: 0-672-31283-2
$49.99 US/ $71.95 CAN

Sams Teach Yourself
Windows Registry in 24
Hours
*Gerald Honeycutt, Jr.*
ISBN: 0-672-31552-1
$19.99 US/ $28.95 CAN

Roger Jennings'
Database Workshop:
Microsoft Transaction
Server 2.0
*Stephen Gray*
ISBN: 0-672-31130-5
$39.99 US/ $57.95 CAN

Sams Teach Yourself
Windows Networking in
24 Hours
*Peter Kuo*
ISBN: 0-672-31475-4
$19.99 US/ $28.95 CAN

Microsoft FrontPage
2000 Unleashed
*William Stanek*
ISBN: 0-672-31675-7
$49.99 US/$71.95 CAN

Peter Norton's Complete
Guide to Windows 98
*Peter Norton*
ISBN: 0-672-31230-1
$29.99 US/$42.95 CAN

*www.samspublishing.com*

All prices are subject to change.

# Get **FREE** books and more...when you register this book online for our Personal Bookshelf Program

*http://register.samspublishing.com/*

 Register online and you can sign up for our *FREE Personal Bookshelf Program...*unlimited access to the electronic version of more than 200 complete computer books—immediately! That means you'll have 100,000 pages of valuable information onscreen, at your fingertips!

 Plus, you can access product support, including complimentary downloads, technical support files, book-focused links, companion Web sites, author sites, and more!

 And you'll be automatically registered to receive a *FREE subscription to a weekly email newsletter* to help you stay current with news, announcements, sample book chapters, and special events, including sweepstakes, contests, and various product giveaways!

 We value your comments! Best of all, the entire registration process takes only a few minutes to complete, so go online and get the greatest value going—absolutely FREE!

## Don't Miss Out On This Great Opportunity!

Sams is a brand of Macmillan Computer Publishing USA.

For more information, please visit *www.mcp.com*

# DISCLAIMER AND INSTALL

If you have AUTOPLAY turned on, your computer will automatically run the CD-ROM interface. If AUTOPLAY is turned off, follow these directions:

1. Insert the CD-ROM into your CD-ROM drive.
2. From the Windows desktop, double-click the My Computer icon.
3. Double-click the icon representing your CD-ROM drive.
4. Double-click the icon titled START.EXE to run the interface.